GERMANY:

A NATION IN ITS TIME

HOLANDIA

GER MANIA

FRISIA

SAXON

VVESTFALIA

TVRINGIA

HASSIA

VASTVM REGN

LOTHA RING

BVRGVNDIE PARS

SVICERIA

GALLIAE PARS

ALPES

Hamburg molt
Loben-burg
Stade Luneburg bontzbet Albis fl.
Bremen werden zelle Sobwed SVI GA Gifforn
Emde Suer Gron Am afie fiue Ems fl. dehionhorst weser fl. alias Milesbuf querberg BRVN Hanofer Bruntuiga
Amsterdam kampe Swolis deuerde hermore Minden Hildesbei harnel Lotter
Trauer orum deuenter ofenbug plumberg humterd Gorsler halker stat Pir varia
Gwerth Monasteriu numegen wesalia padelborn wartburg Enibrok grotting northufen gwsta
Clene Geldrig leenus fl. dertmud Seest werla Cassel molbusen goten Erdfo
venloe Remund Sweden milthusen weslaha festar sildea
Aquisgranum gulch Colonia wester Sil Tresen melbin hursbg kotersbg fuch ylmenousal
Maters Leodmum borma Seren Marburg laxnsteim weffen gaulers fulda Tussen
haltsber eiffel confluentia pure grub grtha Inusfat eisfeld koburg
Treueris bergenstel Magu nna oppenheum worma Spir FRAnCO Schonfurt Bam berg NI A
Mo fia fl. Metis la fl. buten wilen wunshem Rotenburg Hetp
Tullui nanemu dufe Arge nnat Otten wilt helbrun Dinrkt buhel noilin grii VVIRT
Vo ge fius colmar dork Kirtinge Reddinge Elmge weisenhorn Stade Augusta VLma
Sotia flu baslea suffen SV E mangen uberlinge VIA lenfirch Regni hefer Ander
untasta Mons Solodorn Berna lucerna Constantia lindou Oifue
Rodanus A.
Mons S Gothard
Curia

GERMANY

A NATION IN ITS TIME

BEFORE, DURING, AND
AFTER NATIONALISM,
1500–2000

HELMUT WALSER SMITH

LIVERIGHT PUBLISHING CORPORATION

A DIVISION OF *W. W. Norton & Company*

INDEPENDENT PUBLISHERS SINCE 1923

Copyright © 2020 by Helmut Walser Smith

For information about permission to reproduce selections from this book, write to
Permissions, Liveright Publishing Corporation, a division of
W. W. Norton & Company, Inc., 500 Fifth Avenue, New York, NY 10110

For information about special discounts for bulk purchases, please contact
W. W. Norton Special Sales at specialsales@wwnorton.com or 800-233-4830

Manufacturing by LSC Communications Harrisonburg
Book design by Barbara M. Bachman
Production manager: Anna Oler

Library of Congress Cataloging-in-Publication Data

Names: Smith, Helmut Walser, 1962– author.
Title: Germany, a nation in its time : before, during, and after Nationalism, 1500–2000 /
Helmut Walser Smith.
Other titles: Before, during, and after Nationalism, 1500–2000
Description: First edition. | New York : Liveright Publishing Corporation, a division of
W.W. Norton & Company, [2020] | Includes bibliographical references and index.
Identifiers: LCCN 2019050560 | ISBN 9780871404664 (hardcover) |
ISBN 9781631491788 (epub)
Subjects: LCSH: Nationalism—Germany. | Germany—History.
Classification: LCC DD76 .S645 2020 | DDC 943—dc23
LC record available at https://lccn.loc.gov/2019050560

Liveright Publishing Corporation, 500 Fifth Avenue, New York, N.Y. 10110
www.wwnorton.com

W. W. Norton & Company Ltd., 15 Carlisle Street, London W1D 3BS

1 2 3 4 5 6 7 8 9 0

For Luca

CONTENTS

—

LIST OF MAPS

—

INTRODUCTION

—

THIS BOOK IS ABOUT NATION AND NATIONALISM IN GERMANY from 1500 to 2000. Its primary argument is that across five centuries, there were radically different ways of knowing, representing, and experiencing the German nation. It contends that nations, like many other historical phenomena, are neither timeless verities nor arbitrary historical inventions. Rather, they are real or true in different ways in different periods. Put simply, there was no transhistorical concept of the German nation. There was only a nation in its time. German nationalism mapped onto these changing constellations, but it was not the thing itself. There was a Germany before, during, and after nationalism.

This argument implies that the conception of the German nation—not the ideology of German nationalism—is the larger story, with the longer history. In chronological terms, German nationalism had a later beginning; it has gone through an extremely devastating middle phase; and, as is defined here, it may yet have an end. Crystallizing in an unambiguous form for the first time after the French Revolution, German nationalism was an explicitly political ideology that conceived of self and country as one, argued that allegiances to the nation should supersede other loyalties, and bound the male citizen in an unspoken, almost contractual obligation to sacrifice, die, and kill for his country. In the twentieth century, in its radical form, it brought about national cohesion through the persecution, and even expulsion and murder, of others.[1]

Against the grain of a significant interpretive tradition, this book asserts that German nationalists did not engender or invent the German nation.[2] Rather, they transformed its very meaning. The transformation came late in the nation's time line. From our starting point of 1500 (when German humanists first defined Germany as a nation, pictured it in two-dimensional space, and created a significant number of artifacts that showed it existing among other nations), to our end point of 2000 (when history, at least for now, begins to cede to current affairs), nationalism appeared well beyond the halfway mark of the long and changing history of how Germans imagined and experienced their nation. Encompassing the century between the later part of the Napoleonic Wars and the outbreak of the First World War, the age of nationalism, as this period will be called, was characterized by a social and cultural deepening of the nation on one hand, and nationalism as a powerful set of political ideas defining the nation on the other. Yet even in Imperial Germany on the eve of World War I, nationalism, as we will see, was a crucial but in many ways not yet dominant ideology. Nationalism became the dominant ideology of the age later still, in what we will call the nationalist age, when it provided a compelling if ultimately flawed justification for the sacrifice of life that Germany had required of its citizens during World War I. In its radical variant, nationalism in this period demanded the sacrifice of groups within the nation in order to achieve what to us seems a dystopia of ethnic homogeneity. During World War II, that dystopia ended in the death spaces implied in the Nazi idea of living space. In plain words: it ended with genocide. German nationalism, in this way of seeing it, was not the dark culmination point of a long and destructive history of Germany. Rather, it was a crucial, ultimately devastating, but also historical chapter in that history.

The second argument of the book is about the balance between war and peace in the *"longue durée"* of the German past. Shelves of books have been written on the military history of the German nation. Yet for long stretches of history, Germans conceived of their country as essentially pacific, and their neighbors have often concurred, sometimes in the form of a complaint. "Martial spirit and love of fatherland hardly exist for contemporary Germans," a dismayed Madame de Staël wrote in 1810. But when her brilliant book, *De l'Allemagne*, finally appeared after the defeat of Napoleon at the Battle of Nations in Leipzig in October 1813, her insight seemed out of step with events, and it is hardly necessary to recount that no small part of Germany's subsequent history occurred in the shadow of militarism, military destruction, and violence. Today we know a very different Germany—one concerned with social stability and economic growth rather than military might and territorial expansion; one that no longer requires its male citizens to serve in the army; and one in which death, to cite the historian Michael Howard, is "no longer part of the social contract."[3]

Yet peace does not leave us only with blank pages, as Hegel once said of happiness. Rather, in both an absolute and a relative sense, peace has been as important to the long historical arc of the German nation as war. Consider the measure that political scientists use to gauge bellicosity: the so-called conflict catalogue.[4] It charts major and minor conflicts of the last half millennium and estimates their lethality and duration. If one takes 1000 deaths as the threshold for war, filtering out smaller skirmishes, the German lands experienced roughly twice as many years of peace as of war between 1500 and 1914. Overall lethality (even when calculated against estimated population levels) remained low for decades in certain periods, like the eighty years after the Peasants' War of 1525, the late eighteenth century (after the Seven Years War), and for almost a hundred years after the conclusion of the Congress of Vienna in 1815. Skeptics will no doubt point out that Prussia, a martial state, unified Germany in 1871, and this fact inevitably skews the whole history. Yet this approach commits the error of the "small-Prussian school," which narrowed German history into an appendage of Prussian history, and forgot that for many decades, Prussia, as has been shown recently, was a weaker and less bellicose power than is often imagined.[5] The message of the conflict catalogue comes still more forcefully to the fore when Germany is considered in comparison with other European nations. It reveals, for example, that in the eighteenth and nineteenth centuries, Great Britain and France were the great martial powers; that in central Europe, Austria was a more menacing military might than Prussia; and that the German lands, often thought to be in a vulnerable central position, actually enjoyed more years of peace than many of the neighboring countries.[6]

The third argument of the book is about realism and tragedy. It is perhaps the most abstract of the three arguments, but it nevertheless might open a conceptual door to new ways of thinking about nations. It derives from a line of inquiry pursued by Erich Auerbach, a German-Jewish literary scholar who, between 1942 and 1945, wrote a remarkable work, *Mimesis: The Representation of Reality in Western Literature*, while in exile in Istanbul. In *Mimesis*, Auerbach argued that social realistic ways of seeing are achieved when the age-old, Aristotelian separation of literary styles, according to which only the high- and noble-born are fitting subjects of tragedy, is broken down and the everyday, the common, the low, become the object of "serious, problematic, and even tragical representation."[7] Auerbach's test—when a subject or group is capable of eliciting genuinely tragical representation—may also, it is argued in the pages that follow, be seen as a defining moment of compassion implied in national belonging.

The test forces us to think outside the conventional German nationalist narrative and to bring different literary and artistic works—sometimes in the canon, sometimes not—into focus, as well as directing our attention to other, often more ordinary kinds of cultural artifacts of nationhood. One could, for example, construe the hundreds of postwar German communities that commemorated destroyed or damaged synagogues as a turn toward the tragic element of their own hometown landscapes, and as evincing compassion for a group the Germans had persecuted.

It should be stated, as Walter Benjamin once did, that the catastrophes of the twentieth century left only "a ruin, a fragment," and offered only unfinished insights into the abyss.[8] Yet ruins and fragments can also be the foundation for new growth. In what follows, the focus rests on the possibilities that the past has created for a genuinely new understanding of what the German nation is. For while the argument that the postwar period reveals a "broader repudiation of nationalism," as one historian writes, rings true, the repudiation was always only partial so long as the fate of Jews and countless other victims of the genocide were not capable (as Auerbach might have put it) of being depicted with tragic seriousness as part of Germany's own history.[9] This is not a claim about a genre or about a specific literary or artistic form. It is an argument about how a nation summons compassion.

II

In lectures delivered in 1941 in a German prison camp near Lübeck, the great French historian Fernand Braudel likened history that arcs across large swaths of time to "a very long journey."[10] For such a journey, he might have added, it is helpful to have a map hinting at what to expect, telling how rugged the terrain will be, and what to find where.

This book has five parts, and each part, except the first, begins with a preface that seeks to outline how the world has changed and to put forward the arguments that follow. The first part, "The Nation Before National-ism," depicts the discovery and description of Germany for the first time and chronicles the changing representations of Germany up until the Thirty Years War, while Part II, "The Copernican Turn," narrates the great shift in the very understanding of what constitutes a nation, ana-lyzing this pivot in three dimensions. It addresses the advent of modern, state-based patriotism in a period when Germany was likely to devolve into separate German-speaking fatherlands; examines new forms of seeing and describing the nation as evidenced in travel journals; and investigates how unambiguous German nationalism crystallized in the context of military defeat.

The third part is called "The Age of Nationalism," a term borrowed from Immanuel Kant's famous and often cited question, first posed in 1784, of whether we live in an enlightened age—an idea he negated while conceding that, instead, "we live in an age of enlightenment."[11] Following and altering Kant's formulation, "The Age of Nationalism," covering the years 1815 to 1914, describes Germans seeing, shaping, and representing the nation in new ways, asking what it is, who belongs to it, where its bor-ders are, what its symbols mean, and what the nation might yet become. As with Kant's use of the term "enlightenment" for the age he lived in, nation-alism's preponderance is still not assumed. As historians of the subject realize, many people remained indifferent to nationalism's allures, and it divided as much as it unified the nation. Nevertheless, the German nation, which formed as a state in 1871, shaped possibilities, defined identities, and suffused the landscape with objects that made the nation seem, as it were, objective. While war was certainly important to the formation of the German nation in this period, it bears pointing out that a remarkable peace reigned for most of this era.

Part IV, "The Nationalist Age," is about the period 1914–1945, when two wars cast their shadow over peace, nationalism became the dominant ideology of the age, and radical nationalism came to power, as it did in 1933. In the Third Reich, this form of nationalism brought forth new, albeit destructive, forms of inclusion and exclusion, ultimately shaping Germany into a genocidal nation. Finally, Part V, "After Nationalism," addresses the attempt, mainly in the Federal Republic, to cultivate a compassionate, empathetic realism about belonging. The history concludes with an epilogue, in which the rise of a new nationalism in our own time is set into a larger context.

Some of what readers will find in the pages that follow will be unfamiliar. Other parts of the book belong to a known story. Before embarking on the journey, to use Braudel's term, it is perhaps helpful to recall our own *situ*. Despite globalization, we live in a world where precisely mapped countries occupy more than 95 percent of the inhabited surface of the earth, and roughly 97 percent of the world's people will die in the nation of their birth.[12] In 1500, when this book begins, porous empires, indistinct dynastic territories, and small city-states blanketed the land. Nearly three hundred years later, in the middle of our story, this was still true. Political and ethnic units were rarely congruent, and nationality counted for so little that states, when putting together statistics, did not even count it. Indeed, two of Germany's most famous poets, Goethe and Schiller, could still ask, "Germany, but where does it lie?" And in the first line of a jointly written distich reply: "I do not know how to find the country."[13]

This book seeks to answer their question. In its quest, it pays particular attention to descriptive geographies, travel journals, maps, and other kinds of spatial evidence, even plotting points using Geographic Information Systems (GIS) in order to see that nations, unlike the distant mountains that seem to float in late Ming paintings, actually have epistemological and experiential ground. In the end, though, it answers the question of Germany, and where it lies, by appeal to temporal frames, and sees Germany as a nation in its time.

THE NATION
BEFORE
NATIONALISM

CHAPTER 1

SEEING GERMANY FOR THE FIRST TIME

c. 1500

Our Germany, as if painted on a small panel.

—CONRADUS CELTIS, HUMANIST

As the fifteenth century drew to a close, Germany was still imperfectly known. Descriptions of the silhouettes of its cities, the bends of its rivers, the slopes and heights of its mountains, the location and density of its forests, and even the character of the people were rare, sparse in detail, and wanting in exactness. No charts drew the German lands to scale and no drawings showed its borders. And no one had described Germany as a space with a recognizable shape.

Perhaps a two-dimensional, scaled sense of space was as yet as unimportant as knowing the year of one's birth, was not important.[1] But the advent of print had already begun to transform the possibilities of word and image, giving wings to both, while discoveries across the Atlantic and along the jagged coasts of Africa set off a new curiosity about the world. As a result, an aesthetics of realistic description began to emerge and an epistemological shift from an itinerary-based to a mapped sense of space took hold. As Germans looked out, not in, this revolution in the imagination enabled them to see their country for the first time.

II

Although medieval Europe was not an entirely mapless world, precious few maps of landed areas of significant size have survived. They include

Matthew Paris's depiction of the British Isles in his *Chronica Majora*, made around 1250, and the so-called Portolan charts, which, from the late thirteenth century on, outlined the coasts of the Mediterranean, the Black Sea, and the European shores of the Atlantic. By the fourteenth century, some regional maps of Italy, derived from the Portolan charts, plotted large expanses of land in two dimensions, while the famous Gough map of the British Isles, conventionally dated around 1360, showed roads, represented distances in leagues, and displayed hundreds of towns with iconic churches or castles. By the early fifteenth century, mapmakers had created a number of territorial maps of Italian regions, including the areas around Padua, Parma, and Verona.[2] Across the Alps, by contrast, significant land areas remained uncharted.

Instead of mathematically modeling land areas in two dimensions, medieval maps north of the Alps bent space as if following itineraries. Even then, the only two-dimensional representations of the German lands that exist from the High Middle Ages are excerpts of world maps, of which the Ebstorf *mappa mundi*, from about 1300, is the best-known example.[3] A giant circular, eastern-oriented map, measuring more than 3.5 meters across, the Ebstorf world map shows some 500 buildings representing towns, churches, castles, and monasteries; the map also reveals more than 100 bodies of water, a great many islands and mountains, 45 human or humanlike creatures, and about 60 animals. Unlike modern world maps, which depict the earth in a moment of time, the Ebstorf map fused past and present, religious and worldly, into a comprehensive history of God, man, and nature.[4]

Historians of medieval cartography insist that we understand the Ebstorf *mappa mundi* on its own terms—as mapped sacral history—and that we not judge it as a scaled representation of the geographical world. Yet for the German lands, the Ebstorf map represents actual facts of place as the anonymous mapmaker knew or read about them.[5] It locates roughly 100 German cities and monasteries, at least 80 for the first time on a known map, identifying them by name and sometimes by an iconographic tower or castle.[6] For example, Lüneburg, the city nearest to the Ebstorf monastery, is represented by three towers, a flag, and an identifying moon (*luna*); Braunschweig, the next proximate city, is marked by a lion, for in its cathedral lay buried Henry the Lion and his lady Matilda; Cologne, then the largest city in the German lands, is displayed with the most formidable fortress; and Aachen, the resting place of Charlemagne, is identified by its hot springs, already famous in Roman times. Trier, Worms, Speyer, Erfurt, and Vienna are also prominently displayed, as are a number of monasteries, including Ebstorf, the abbeys of Corvey and Nienburg, and the three Carolingian cloisters on an exaggerated but recognizable island of Reichenau. Following Roman administrative designations, the map names regions, such as Upper Germania, Poland, Franconia, Westphalia, Frisia, Swabia, and Saxony, but offers little sense of their shape. Borders are also not delineated—save for commentaries scrawled on the map telling us "the Rhine divides Gallicans and Germans" or placing the designation "Poland" just to the east of the Oder River or "Teutonia" to the east of the Vosges. It also does not attempt to gauge the extent and breadth of mountains, though a sliver of Alps separates Salzburg, Augsburg, and Zurich from Bressanone, Trent, and Milan, and serves as the origins of the Rhine.

The Ebstorf map has a precision of its own, but mathematically calculated distance and direction do not govern it. Space is not projected onto a grid and areas are not represented to scale; rather, the route, or itinerary, determines what matters.[7] Two hundred years later, around 1500, trav-

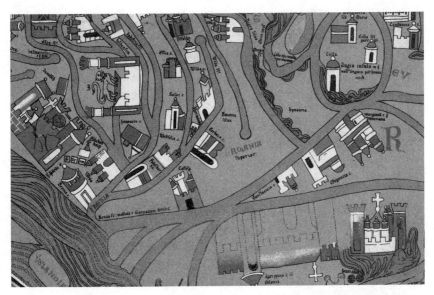

The German lands in the Ebstorf *mappa mundi*, circa 1300.

elers still used itineraries, not maps, to plan trips and in order to orient themselves. Often rolled up in small copper canisters, they listed places in sequence and were written, not drawn. The fifteenth-century Bruges itinerary is a prominent example. A compendium of trade routes, the itinerary lists cities and towns that merchants would travel through as they trekked from Bruges to Lübeck, or from Mainz to Cracow, or from Cologne to Rome, or along any of the other many routes that crisscrossed Europe.[8]

We can discern something of the experience of moving through space if we take the largest group of surviving itineraries—those that document journeys to the Holy Land—and follow noblemen and clerics traveling south across the Alps and to Venice, where German pilgrims found lodging in a "German house" before boarding galleys transporting them to Palestine.[9] Perhaps unsurprising, pilgrims mostly described sites of well-known miracles and places replete with religious relics.[10] As experiencing the sacred counted for more than knowing one's country, spatial markers remained sparse. Itineraries listed towns, recorded the distance separating them, and noted only the special status of imperial cities. Most towns received neither adjectives nor descriptive phrases, and in only a few cases would the scribe tell to whom or to what territory a town even belonged.[11] Borders were likewise registered without consistency or precision. In general, pilgrims, or rather the erudite men who kept their journals, represented borders not as lines but as zones of transition, marked by language use and spaced between cities and towns. Trent was "half-German, half-Welsch" and Verona "fully Welsch," wrote the scribe of William the Brave of Thuringia in 1461.[12] Germany, where German was spoken, shaded one side, Italy, where Italian was heard, the other. The knight Arnold von Harff captured this descriptive sense when he characterized the itineraries of pilgrims as travel reports "from city to city, from village to village, from language to language."[13]

III

Before the Ottoman Turks conquered Constantinople in May 1453, there were no two-dimensional, nonitinerary descriptions or images of Germany. With the "loss" of what was then probably the largest city in Christendom, this began to change. Employing a continental descriptor that had fallen into disuse in the Middle Ages, the papal legate Aeneas Silvius Piccolomini wrote to Pope Nicholas V on June 12, 1453, "We have been defeated and thrown down in Europe." He repeated this sentence almost verbatim at the Frankfurt Reichstag of 1454, when he appealed to "you, Germans" (*Vos, Germani*) to help fight the Turks, as "never before was so much Christian blood spilt" and "our religion so desperately shaken."[14]

The so-called Frankfurt Oration foreshadowed an extremely influential and widespread epistolary treatise, Piccolomini's *Germania* of 1457–1458, which in its first printed edition of 1496 was called *An Account of the Rites, Site, Mores, and General Condition of Germany*.[15] Rebuffing complaints about the abuses of the Roman Catholic Church, Piccolomini demonstrated that the Germans had become wealthy and civilized, and had Christianity and the Roman church to thank for it. Depicting Germany as an expansive country extending beyond the Danube and the Rhine, "which once made up *Germania*'s borders," Piccolomini extolled a country adorned with "tilled fields, vineyards, gardens, flower beds, fruit plants in the countryside and in towns," and which boasted "treasure-filled buildings, attractive manors, castles on hilltops, walled communities, and luminous cities."[16] Pulling from over two decades of experience traveling and holding various clerical offices in German lands, Piccolomini pronounced German cities "the cleanest and the most pleasurable to look at" in all of Europe.[17] He described some cities with respect to their characteristic details, such as Cologne, "whose magnificent churches and houses, large number of inhabitants, rich treasures, leaden roofs, grand palaces, and protective towers one marveled at"; or Strasbourg, "which resembled Venice, for it is traversed by many canals"; or Frankfurt am Main, "which although it has many wooden houses, is ornamented with a number of stone palaces, in which even kings would be accommodated with dignity."[18] For lesser places, Piccolomini often employed the clichés of urban panegyrics, describing cities and towns as splendid, ornate, illustrious, noble, magnificent, or, simply, not to be overlooked. He commended Germany's monasteries, "where hospitality is in a magnificent way shown to all sorts of people," and he admired its universities, "where many famous men have taught, and in our day there are no fewer who are famous."[19] Praising German customs and habits of work and devotion, Piccolomini argued that through Christianity the Germans had become a most culti-

AENEAS SILVIUS PICCOLOMINI'S SOJOURNS
and the CITIES *and* TOWNS DESCRIBED
in his GERMANIA *of* 1457-8

LEGEND
• Documented visits
▲ Described in his "Germania"
■ Documented visits and described in his "Germania"

vated people—much more civilized than the roughly hewn tribes in animal skins the ancient authors had described and praised. In Piccolomini's Germany, the peaceful nature of the Germans shines through, for despite their skill in warfare, they are, as he noted, in concord with their neighbors. Finally, Piccolomini's *Germania* struck one note of criticism. In the context of this laudation, the papal legate chastised the Germans for their all-too-congenital inability to follow a single leader, obeying him "only as far as you wish, and wishing to as little as possible."[20]

Historians often overlook Piccolomini's contribution to the idea of a German nation. A seasoned envoy, bishop, and eventually Pope Pius II, Piccolomini was, after all, an Italian, not a German. Writing in Latin and serving the interests of Rome, Piccolomini hoped to raise the funds necessary to fight the Ottoman Turks by no more than the dint of flattery. Yet his *Germania* represented the first time in the postclassical era that an author

Henricus Martellus, map of Central Europe, 1490s.

actually explicated Germany as a space and described the cities within it—and the description neither followed nor served as an itinerary. Moreover, it was around this time that Piccolomini's humanist friend Nicolaus Cusanus, plotted, or arranged to have plotted, the coordinates of central European cities.[21]

One of the most influential philosophers of the late medieval era, Cusanus had responded to the fall of Constantinople not with a cry for war but with a plea for peace. Perhaps he had a map made as well. Yet the original "Cusanus map," if there was one, has been lost, and we can only guess what it must have looked like by inspecting copies made in the 1490s, long after Cusanus's death in 1464. But whether based on coordinates or an actual map, the later copies display a great deal of precision, especially in what we now call eastern (but was then often called northern) Europe. In an elegant copy made in the 1490s by the German cartographer Henricus Martellus, cities are marked by icons and labeled by names; mountains, lakes, and rivers are pleasingly detailed; and regional landscapes like Silesia and Polonia flow into one another. Oriented to our north rather than to Jerusalem and the east, scaled and two-dimensional, this is the first seemingly accurate map of central Europe.

IV

If Piccolomini and Cusanus heralded the change from an itinerary-based to a two-dimensional, area-centered, mapped conception of space, three further developments hastened the transition. The first involved the rediscovery in Constantinople of the *Geography* of Claudius Ptolemy, the Greek mathematician and astronomer best known for his erroneous geocentric model of the solar system, and Jacobo d'Angelo's translation of the manuscript into Latin in 1406. Compiled in Alexandria in the second century CE, the *Geography* provided thousands of coordinates locating the cities, rivers, mountains, and coastlines of the three known continents.[22] Charting together the known and unknown world in bounded, uniform space allowed mapmakers to imagine the space of the earth as a grid marked by longitude and latitude and subdivided into degrees and minutes.

The new maps lit curiosity and spurred discovery. It was, after all, Ptolemaic charts that enabled Columbus to present his arguments about the possibility of circumnavigating the earth to Spain's Queen Isabella. Ptolemy also introduced a definition of geography as a "representation in picture of the whole known world" and opposed it to chorography, "dealing with the smaller conceivable localities, such as harbors, farms, villages, river courses, and such like."[23] He described new ways of projecting the three-dimensional globe onto a two-dimensional map, and he showed an image of the world in a singular moment of time. If medieval *mappae mundi* like the Ebstorf world map depicted the history of salvation in a single two-dimensional representation, Ptolemaic maps split the present from the past while separating space from a religious narration of time.

The second development hastening the transition to a mapped conception of the world was described by the moral philosopher and political economist Adam Smith as belonging to "the two greatest and most important events recorded in the history of mankind"—namely, Columbus's setting ashore on what he took to be the East Indies in 1492, and Vasco da Gama's sailing around the Cape of Good Hope and into the Indian Ocean in 1497.[24] The discoveries brought forth a genuine *"furor geographicus,"* which only intensified in the ensuing decades.[25] By the time Ferdinand Magellan's one remaining ship returned from the first circumnavigation of the earth in 1522, people began to understand that the ocean separating the new worlds from Asia was vast, and that the oceans connected rather than ringed the earth. By the 1530s, as explorers discovered Baja California and sailed down the St. Lawrence River, some humanists also realized that the earth's waters were navigable, the new lands continent-sized, and those new continents inhabited.[26] The discoveries reshaped spatial templates and placed Europe in a new frame. The existence of New World cities—mentioned neither in biblical texts nor by classical authors—shocked European observers. When Hernán Cortés destroyed Tenochtitlán in 1521, the city, now known as Mexico City, was likely three times larger than any German city.[27]

The third development, the invention of print in the 1450s, was arguably the most important, for it turned books, only recently liberated from the scriptoria of monasteries and the libraries of Europe's few universities, into "flying carpets of knowledge."[28] This was a far-reaching and irreversible revolution.[29] Printing brought a new permanence to language, arresting linguistic drift and slowing the decay and dissipation of new insights. Words became divorced from authors and took on a life of their own. Placed on a page, they could more easily be analyzed and dissected, refuted and improved. New techniques—like backward scanning and cross-referencing passages and particular points—reshaped and intensified the public discussion concerning the truth of statements. The printing press also brought ideas to wider audiences, not only in the cities but also in towns and even villages, where literate men reading books aloud slowly replaced the storyteller.[30] Moreover, not only texts but also images could be reproduced, creating what William M. Ivins Jr., the longtime curator of the Department of Prints at New York's Metropolitan Museum of Art, called "exactly repeatable pictorial statements."[31] Unlike scribal copies, replicas of images could be made without significant degradation; scholars could compare and correct them; and improvement in one area did not imply loss in another.

The transition—from a largely oral, sound-based, mnemonic world to a primarily visual culture—had profound consequences in almost all domains, even reshaping senses of time and space. Prior to the wide availability of the printed word, many people could not say what year of the Lord it was, most had no idea when they were born, and a religious rather than a numerical calendar paced their work and life.[32] But as printed calendars, books of hours, itineraries, and histories made dated material widely available, abstract numerical time came to coexist and even supplant Christian modes of temporal reckoning. More people began to mark time by centuries, decades, and calendar years; by months and days; and, with the proliferation of counterpoise clocks on church towers, by hours.[33]

Likewise, a slow but significant shift in spatial mentalities occurred. If itineraries continued to be published and print accelerated their distribution, maps also gained in popularity. Scholars estimate that there were only a few thousand maps in circulation between 1400 and 1472. After print, that number rose to an estimated 56,000 between 1472 and 1500, and by the end of the sixteenth century, perhaps even into the millions.[34] Maps promoted geographical knowledge, aided in the study of history, and served as mnemonic supports. When displayed in houses, they announced the owner's humanistic interests, cosmopolitanism, and patriotism. They were also useful for planning journeys, and they showed people how to think in spaces rather than lines, areas rather than transverses, and how to situate themselves in territories, countries, and continents.[35] Between 1470 and 1600, roughly two-thirds of all printed maps depicted Europe and places in it, while the rest portrayed other continents, the New World, the Holy Land (still the most mapped small place), and the oceans.[36] They imparted new knowledge about the curvature of coastlines, the shapes of nations, and the relative placement of cities, waters, and mountains. As maps placed "certain glasses before our eyes," as one sixteenth-century mapmaker put it, Germany, Europe, and the world came more precisely into view.[37]

V

Of course, the name of Germany long predates sixteenth-century maps of it. Between roughly the first century BCE and the sixth century CE, Romans referred to the lands north of the Danube and east of the Rhine as Germania, and it has since remained the standard Latin designation.[38] In the Germanic languages, however, the etymological trail is more complex. Prior to the eleventh century, "Germany" (*Diutschlant*) and the "German lands" (*diutschiu lant*) were rarely used as geographical adjectives and virtually unknown as proper nouns.[39] We encounter them in the Song of

Anno, an eleventh-century hymn to Cologne, "the most beautiful town ever built in German land."[40] Weaving the history of salvation with the history of the city and adding the deeds of Archbishop Anno II at the end, the song mainly tells of battles fought with the Romans.[41] In other documents, German lands refer to the vast if vague space where the German tongue was spoken. By the thirteenth century, it was common for minstrels like Walther von der Vogelweide and Reinbot von Durne to sing of the territory, the *"tiutsche Lant,"* whose immense span they knew and where princes paid for the melodious sound of their flattering poetry.[42]

The political resonance of the geographical term was a later development still. While the term "Germany" was certainly a part of the political vocabulary of the High Middle Ages, the term appears with less frequency than might be expected. The "Golden Bull," the involved constitutionlike text that established durable rules for imperial election in 1356, mentioned the term "German" or "Germany" only four times: twice in reference to the spiritual domain of the Archbishop of Mainz and twice to describe the lands where German was the vernacular.[43] By the middle of the fifteenth century, the pairing of "German" with "Empire" became more frequent, though it was not until the 1480s—when discussion of imperial reform intensified—that diplomats and statesmen regularly referred to the governing body as "the Holy Roman Empire and the Esteemed German Nation," or "the Roman Empire of the German Nation," and with the recess of the Imperial Diet of Cologne in 1512, the "Holy Roman Empire of the German Nation."[44] Thereafter, in the course of the sixteenth century, "Germany" was often heard in political parlance. In its nominative form, according to the *German Dictionary* of the Brothers Grimm, it denoted the area where German-speaking people lived.[45]

Germany, as the new title implied, was the geographical core of a medieval empire still closer to the spirit of kinship—"to be the man of another man"—than to the character of a sovereign state.[46] In the former, what mattered most was a lord's house and lineage, not the expansiveness of his land. Borders remained, in one scholar's words, "porous and indistinct, and sovereignties faded imperceptibly into one another." In sovereign states, by contrast, "sovereignty is fully, flatly, and evenly operative over each square centimeter of a legally demarcated territory."[47] The Empire, sewing together centers and peripheries, strong jurisdiction and weak, lands taxed and exempted, and territories of different levels of status, power, and autonomy, was a vast and complex set of legal, military, and ritual arrangements in which little was fixed. There was no permanent capital and the *Reichstage* (Imperial Diets, formal gatherings of the estates) were held sometimes in one city and other times in another. Even the Emperor's court was itinerant. Predicated on presence and visibility, his power reached as far as he could travel.

VI

As the recorded sojourns of Emperor Maximilian I reveal, his empire was a riverine realm, centered in the south and west, in which retreat to the safeguards of the high elevations remained a strategic necessity. Far from controlling the peripheries of the Empire, the Emperor never even saw

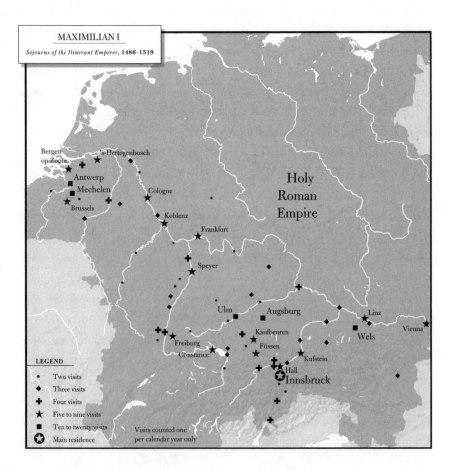

MAXIMILIAN I

Sojourns of the Itinerant Emperor, **1486–1519**

Holy Roman Empire

Bergen op Zoom
's-Hertogenbosch
Antwerp
Mechelen
Cologne
Brussels
Koblenz
Frankfurt
Speyer
Ulm
Augsburg
Linz
Kaufbeuren
Wels
Vienna
Freiburg
Füssen
Constance
Kufstein
Hall
Innsbruck

LEGEND

- • Two visits
- ◆ Three visits
- ✚ Four visits
- ★ Five to nine visits
- ■ Ten to twenty visits
- ✪ Main residence

Visits counted one per calendar year only

them. Especially the north and east remained out of his reach and beyond his grasp.

Within the area conventionally considered Germany, there were some four thousand towns, most of them small, with populations barely reaching beyond 2000 people.[48] There were also cities, like Prague, Cologne, Nuremberg, Augsburg, Strasbourg, Lübeck, and Vienna, all of which boasted populations over 25,000.[49] If they seemed modest when compared with European centers like Paris, Naples, Milan, Venice, and Grenada, to say nothing of such world cities as Beijing, Hangzhou, Kyoto, Vijayanagara, Delhi, Cairo, and Constantinople, some were centers of considerable social and intellectual fermentation.[50] It was, for example, in Germany's modest commercial cities—first in Mainz and Strasbourg, then in Nuremberg, Augsburg, and Basel—that the new technology of print flourished.[51] "The power of Germany certainly resides more in her cities than in her princes," the perspicacious Machiavelli wrote—they "are the real nerve centers of the Empire."[52] And the no less perceptive Jean Bodin, the French theorist of sovereignty, counted one city, Nuremberg, as "the greatest, most famous, and best ordered of all the imperial cities."[53]

VII

Teeming with interest in the published word and the printed image, Nuremberg was home to Anton Koberger, the most ambitious and successful publisher in Germany, as well as to Albrecht Dürer, the son of a goldsmith, who served his apprenticeship as a painter there before fleeing the plague in 1494 for Tuscany, where he applied the lessons of scientific perspective to the new style of painting. In Nuremberg, the cartographer Martin Behaim crafted the oldest globe still existing today from the maps of Ptolemy and the new knowledge from Portuguese explorers about the shape of the African coast.[54] The "eyes and ears of Germany," as Martin Luther later called it, Nuremberg connected Paris and Strasbourg with Prague and Cracow.[55] In many cities, its merchants enjoyed special rights and privileges and freedom from onerous tolls. It also became a hub for the creation of instruments that measured time and space, like Peter Henlein's pocket clocks, among the first small watches one could carry, and Johannes Schöner's globe of 1515, long thought to be the first map to show *"Amer-*

ika."[56] It was in the circles of the Nuremberg humanists that the Cusanus image of central Europe resurfaced, slightly altered, in a work that placed Germany in the context of the world.

That work, Hartmann Schedel's *Liber Chronicarum*, published in 1493, connected the late medieval imagination to new ways of conceptualizing space. Produced in "royal format" (47 x 32.5 centimeters), with 326 folio pages in its Latin edition and 297 in its German edition, the *Nuremberg Chronicle*, as it is still referred to in the English-speaking world, was adorned with 1809 woodcuts, making it the most profusely illustrated work in the early age of print, and one that expressed the pride, power, and wealth of the Nuremberg elite.[57]

Less the author than the conductor of the work, Schedel brought together an ensemble of extraordinary local talent, including the young Albrecht Dürer, Hieronymus Münzer (a doctor, traveler, and accomplished mapmaker), Georg Alt (who translated the Latin text into German), Michael Wohlgemut (from whom Dürer learned the art of making woodcuts), and Wilhelm Pleydenwurff, Wohlgemut's nephew and a brilliant carver, illustrator, and painter in his own right. It was an immense and expensive production. Yet despite its cost (the monetary equivalent of five and a half oxen, in one estimate), the *Nuremberg Chronicle* became an overnight success, selling some 1400 copies in Latin, and 700 in German.[58]

Like many medieval chronicles, Schedel's work narrates time along the seven days of creation, with each day standing for an era of history.[59] Within this scheme, Schedel told stories of biblical figures, saints and martyrs, the heretics who threatened the unity of the Christendom, and the churchmen who restored consonance. He also criticized excesses of outward piety, as occurred in Corpus Christi processions, and derided the proclivity of church dignitaries to cloak themselves in luxury. When it came to the critics of the church, Schedel was no less caustic, deriding men such as John Wycliffe, Jan Hus, or the Drummer of Niklashausen, who preached against clerical luxury and taught that wood and water belong to everyman.[60] Finally, the *Nuremberg Chronicle* also contains infamous—but at the time common—anti-Jewish woodcuts depicting how a Jew punctured an image of the crucifix and blood squirted out, as well as the alleged ritual murder of Simon of Trent in 1475, a scandal that caused scores of further accusations and ultimately led to the expulsion of innumerable Jews from a number of south German cities, including Nuremberg.[61] Blank pages conclude the book, reminding that the Day of Judgment had yet to come.

The depictions of cities in woodcuts proved particularly arresting, and they often seemed to literally jump off the page. Twenty-five illustrations took up half or two-thirds of a double spread, and in one case, Nuremberg, the whole of two pages. Many were based on actual observation or on sketches drawn from the observations of others. Commemorating and celebrating as much as documenting and describing, twenty-two of them constituted the first "naturalistic" pictures of cites in the German lands.[62] Michael Wohlgemut's portrait of Nuremberg, for example, provides a careful account of the city's south walls, ramparts, and towers, and delivers precise renditions of the St. Lorenz and the St. Sebald churches.[63] Yet Wohlgemut also artificially compacted the composition, centered it on the castle, and wrapped the city in imposing double-rowed walls, making the physical city and human community seem fused together.[64]

It was not the only drawing thus wrought. Throughout the *Nuremberg Chronicle*, empirical sketches of buildings jostle with stock towers and houses, making its images less like outdoor sketches than studio-made compilations. As with the depiction of Nuremberg, artists magnified major public buildings on purpose, simplified urban messiness, and mixed the real

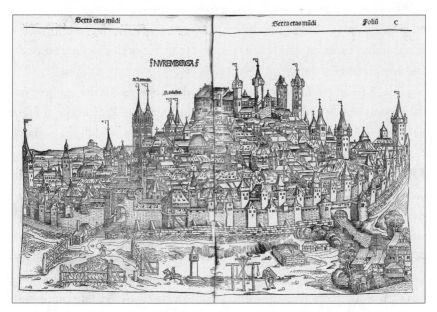

Woodcut of Nuremberg in the *Nuremberg Chronicle*, 1493.

with the ideal, the empirical with the conventional. Often, civic buildings cluster heavily in the image. In the depiction of Ulm, for example, the Herd-bruckertor (the main gate, torn down in 1827) is drawn way out of proportion, dominating even the Minster. In the image of Regensburg, patrician towers range nearly as high as the unfinished cathedral. And in the woodcut of Munich, the medieval gothic Isar Gate, likewise exceedingly large, takes up much of the middle of the image. Other woodcuts suffer from ill-executed perspectives and empirical mistakes. Pictured from the south across the Inn River, the Bavarian city of Passau, for example, is foreshortened and only the text tells the reader that the Danube also flows through the city. Finally, some images bear little relation to reality: Augsburg is recognizable only by the Perlacher Tower and Magdeburg only by the Elbe River.

One observes a constant shuttle between the ideal and the real. Much like Renaissance portraits of people, which tried to balance outward resemblance and interior character, the *Chronicle*'s depiction of cities strove less for verisimilitude than for a lifelike sense of place true to the city.[65] The artists rendered cities from the perspective of travelers either coming up to them from a road or looking onto them from a nearby hill. They showed imposing walled citadels beckoning with downed drawbridges, and they depicted traders and commoners being let into the city, even as the sense of being welcome was sometimes juxtaposed with symbols suggesting alarm or warning, such as a gallows cautioning that a city had its own jurisdictional authority, or imperial crests proclaiming "free cities" with territories and armies of their own.

The *Nuremberg Chronicle* also printed two maps. In the chapter on the second era, Schedel reproduced the world map of Ptolemy on a folding page, showing the earth divided into three parts, which the sons of Noah had split among themselves after the great flood, with Sem taking Asia, Cham Africa, and Japhet Europe, a thin, twiggy peninsula of the far larger continent to the east. The second map takes Germany as its subject. Hastily drawn and cut in wood by Hieronymus Münzer, the map was largely based on a much finer copper engraving of the 1490s, which was in turn derived from the since vanished map, or coordinates, of Nicolaus Cusanus.[66] Münzer added infelicities and changed the title, turning Cusanus's carefully plotted central Europe into what the medical doctor and cartographer called a map of Germany. The placement of the map is also

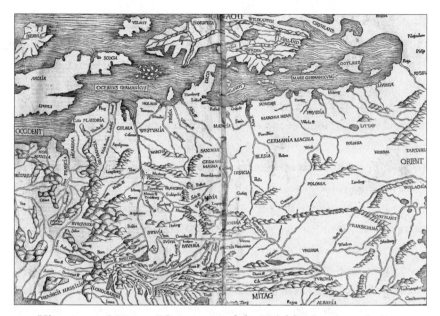

Hieronymus Münzer, "Germany and the Neighboring Areas in East and West," *Nuremberg Chronicle*, 1493.

revealing. Münzer put it at the end of a geographical afterword appended to the narrative of the seven eras, almost as if the religious scheme could not contain the new conception of nation. Schedel did not conceive of it in his original plan, and Münzer had to inform him in a letter that "at the end he had also added a general map of Germany and the neighboring areas in east and west so that the length and breadth of Germany, placed in front of the eyes, comes clearly to the fore."[67]

VIII

In the original *Historia von D. Johann Fausten*, published anonymously in 1587, the protagonist is a calendar maker and astronomer who has lost his battle with curiosity and science and made a fateful bargain with the devil. The devil offers him many things, including the chance to glimpse heaven and hell and travel to the stars, which Faust readily takes. On his skyward flight, Faust sees the cities, countries, and continents, *"Asiam, Aphricam und Europam,"* and the waters of the earth.[68] Having seen the globe as it really is (the New World had yet to secure continental status), he returns home, and on a flying steed travels first to the countries and then to the cities of Germany and Europe. His itinerary begins in Trier, after which follow Paris, Mainz, Naples, Venice, Padua, Rome, Milan, Florence, Lyon, and Cologne. The crisscross and puzzling route cannot easily be explained by the geographical ignorance common to the age. Seemingly irrational, the route instead follows the succession of European cities as they appear in Schedel's *Chronicle*.[69] The late-sixteenth-century anonymous author of the first *Faust* not only leafed through the *Chronicle*, admiring the woodcuts, but also copied the text, so that Schedel's descriptions of cities reappear, often verbatim, in the fateful chronicle of the Faust tragedy—a tragedy that first turned on curiosity as man's most fatal flaw.

In the Faustian Nuremberg of 1500, we find the first genuinely accurate, scaled map of Germany. It was made by one Erhard Etzlaub, of whom we know little, save that he was born in Erfurt in 1460, likely never enjoyed a formal or complete university education, and was listed for the first time in the Nuremberg register of citizens in 1484.[70] From a contemporary, we know "that [Etzlaub's] clocks are in demand in Rome," and that "he has an exceptional knowledge of geography and astronomy."[71]

Etzlaub's handheld sundials, compasses, clocks, calendars, almanacs, and maps tell of late medieval confluences of time and space. Illustrated with both biblical and contemporary scenes, and translated into Czech and Latin, Etzlaub's almanacs inform of the passing of the days, weeks, and months, and the positions of the moon and the stars. His handheld "compasses," the most innovative of his creations, combined sundials with a magnetic needle and featured a scale that allowed travelers to use the instrument at different latitudes. On the two that have survived there is also a wood-block, south-oriented map on the cover depicting Europe and Africa to the equator and identifying 132 place-names with surprising latitudinal accuracy.[72] Beyond his mechanical innovations, Etzlaub also made a regional map of Nuremberg's hinterlands. Engraved in 1492, it counts as one of more than one hundred regional maps scholars have discovered from the late Middle Ages, most of them made in Italy, England, and the Netherlands.[73]

Etzlaub's enduring achievement however would be the *Rom-Weg* or "Rome-Way Map" of 1500—a "very beautiful map of Germany, and in the German language, from which one can discern the distances of the cities

Erhard Etzlaub, "Rome-Way Map," 1500.

and the course of the rivers more exactly even than from the maps of Ptolemy," as a contemporary admirer put it.[74]

Following the sun, the map points upward to the south. This was not the usual orientation of medieval maps, which for religious reasons oriented toward the Holy Land, and placed east at the top. But nor was it the orientation chosen by Ptolemy, who, writing from Egyptian Alexandria, suggested a northern orientation "in order that there not be . . . any obscuration of the inhabited earth."[75] But as the Portuguese discovered the vast length of the West African coast in the second half of the fifteenth century, it made sense to make maps pointing south rather than north, giving place of pride to the newly charted territories. This is one possible reason for the southern orientation.[76] A simpler reason is that Etzlaub intended the maps to be used together with his "compasts," whose bearings pointed to the south, with midday at the apogee.[77]

A second, striking feature of the map is its latitudinal accuracy.[78] Using data from copied and printed itineraries, Etzlaub calculated the relative positions of towns and cities and measured distances between them, so that most German cities err by less than ten minutes of degree latitude. From the accurately mapped core area, a German civilization of cities and towns seems to pulse outward, an image reinforced in Etzlaub's map by geographical exaggerations taken from Ptolemy, the most obvious examples of which are the overly drawn western bend of Scotland and the sharper angle of the Italian peninsula. As one moves farther and farther from the center, other inaccuracies, not all of which can be ascribed to Ptolemy, also become evident. Berlin, for example, is marked on a map for the first time, though the Spree River flows not west into the Havel River, as it should, but meanders north into the Pomeranian Sea.

In the uncolored maps, countries like France and Germany appear no more significant than regions like Friesland and Flanders. Nations are not given visual priority over traditional landscapes; indeed, the two are rendered in the same way. The colored maps, however, present a very different image. In a separately printed register, Etlzaub instructed how the paints should be applied: "The seas are in blue, and the islands in red oxide of lead. Also Italy in which lie Naples and Rome are in vegetable or light green, France red, the Netherlands light yellow, Scotland green. . . ."[79] "Countries and language groups," as Etzlaub calls them, are depicted as bordering each other, with Germany in the middle.[80]

The title of the map, etched in block letters across a slim sliver of space at the top, is "This is the Rome-route mile by mile indicated by points from one city to the other through the lands of Germany."[81] The map's first purpose, then, was to aid pilgrims on their journey to the Eternal City in the centenary year of 1500. Perhaps too the map animated those who could only contemplate the journey, as cloistered monks and nuns were forced to do. Beginning mainly on or beyond the peripheries of Germany, Etzlaub's routes funnel across the Alpine passes before converging on Bologna in order to head south to Rome, where pilgrim tourists might stay in one of the city's some two hundred hostelries.[82] Etzlaub also included a scale in the margin, informing travelers how many hours of daylight to expect on the longest day. The scale ranges from eighteen hours in Denmark to fifteen hours in Naples and is graded by increments of fifteen minutes according to lines of latitude. In a time when nightfall meant almost complete darkness, save for torches, candles, moon, and stars, this was crucial information to pilgrims seeking all-too-scarce shelters en route.

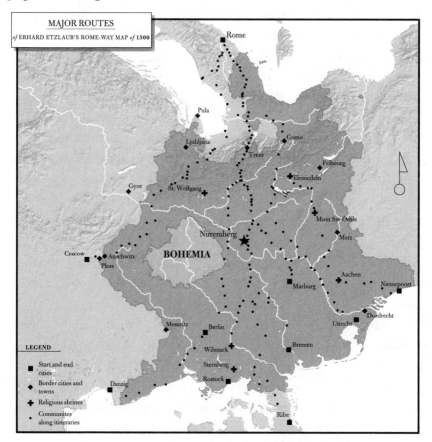

MAJOR ROUTES
of ERHARD ETZLAUB'S ROME-WAY MAP of 1500

Rome

Pula

Ljubljana   Como
                    Trent
                             Fribourg
                        Einsiedeln
Gyor   St. Wolfgang

                                Mont Ste-Odile
                                            Metz
            Nuremberg

Cracow   Auschwitz   BOHEMIA
      Pless
                                        Aachen
                                Marburg   Nieuwpoort

                                            Dordrecht
        Meseritz   Utrecht
                Berlin
LEGEND   Bremen
                        Wilsnack
■ Start and end   Sternberg
   cities
◆ Border cities and   Rostock
   towns   Danzig
✚ Religious shrines
• Communites   Ribe
   along itineraries

Etzlaub's maps also reflected worldly dimensions. This was especially evident in a second map, engraved in 1501 and cumbersomely entitled "These are the country roads through the Roman Empire from one kingdom to another, which touch Germany. . . ."[83] The map shows the Roman Empire (indistinguishable from the Germany of the Rome-Way Map) stitched together by roads and waterways and connected to the wider world via routes to Cracow, Ofen (Buda), Rome, Venice, Genoa, Aigues-Mortes (a commune near Marseilles), Paris, and Calais (and from there by water to Canterbury).[84] It was "the first large format travel map of Germany," in one scholar's words, and it held its ground well into the middle of the seventeenth century.[85]

IX

Around the time Etzlaub crafted his map, a remarkable manuscript surfaced, after having disappeared sometime in the millennia after its first-century composition. Throughout the Middle Ages, no one had even heard of *De Origine et Situ Germanorum*, subsequently famous as Tacitus's *Germania*, until Francesco Poggio Bracciolini, ruthless archival scourer for ancient texts, mentioned it in a letter in the 1420s, and it was not until Bracciolini later arranged to have it brought back across the Alps that the manuscript began to circulate again.[86] Locked for hundreds of years in the vaults of the Benedictine Abbey of Hersfeld, the tale of its travels, first to Italy, then back to Germany, is a richly complicated historical yarn. Possibly, Bracciolini exaggerated his importance to the story. What we know is that the early Italian humanist, Aeneas Silvius Piccolomini, who had described Germany's cities and towns, was also the first modern commentator to draw from it, and he traced a direct line from Tacitus's ancient Germanic tribes to the Germans of his day.[87]

According to Tacitus, the Roman senator and historian, the ancient Germanic tribes populated a vast, primeval wood north of the Danube and east of the Rhine. Freedom-loving and loyal, rough and reliable, passionate and decent, they embodied masculine virility and primitive virtue, valued courage and honor, prized simplicity and freedom, and with their "wild, flashing eyes, reddish hair, and large frames" prayed to Wodan, the god of war.[88] To the supposedly urban, decadent, individualistic, effete Romans of the first century, the intended audience of Tacitus's *Germania,* these Germans would certainly present a formidable foe.

Tacitus had also proffered a powerful fiction, with which not all Roman ethnographers of his day concurred. He described the German tribes as "indigenous"—original to the area, unmixed, a unified people closed to the outside world. Historians now agree that dozens of tribes, having little in common save for intermittent conflicts with Roman legions, inhabited the region. Much as the term "Indian" described from the outside the indigenous peoples of North America, the Latin term *"Germani"* simplistically bundled together diverse and often warring groups in a geographical area. The term did not correspond to an internal "Germanic" sense of commonality, nor was it how indigenous peoples called themselves.[89]

The *Germania* was not published north of the Alps until 1476, when it was largely ignored, and then again in 1500, when an edition edited and supplemented by Conradus Celtis lit up the humanistic imagination.[90]

The new editor literally put Tacitus on the map. A wanderer, a passionate scholar, a fiery orator, and an organizer of fellow humanists, Celtis belonged to the first generation of thinkers who extolled the virtues of Germany and conceptualized the country in spatial terms. Endowed with a prodigious imagination, he expounded his ideas in a poem of 283 hexameters that he appended to his Tacitus edition. Part textual commentary, part description of what Celtis had studied on maps and seen in his travels, the *"Germania Generalis,"* as the poem was called, wove together observations about the supposedly timeless characteristics of the Germans with a cartographic understanding of what learned men of the time called their *situ.*[91] Germans, Celtis wrote, populated a country that the Baltic Sea and the Ocean enclosed in the north, the Rhine bordered in the west, the Vistula limited in the east, the Danube and the Alps confined in the south, and the Carpathians restricted in the southeast.[92] This last boundary, unusual for the time, especially reflected the influence of a map. The 1482 edition of Ptolemy's *Geography,* published in the Danubian city of Ulm, contains a regional map of ancient Germania showing the Rhine and Vistula running as straight rivers down from the Ocean and the Baltic Sea, with the vertically arrayed western Carpathians providing a natural frontier where the Vistula tapers off.

Historians often portray Celtis as an early German nationalist with a chauvinistic streak.[93] This analysis misses his deep immersion in the religious and cosmological assumptions of the era and underplays how different his views were compared with those of later nationalists. This can be seen with particular clarity in another of Celtis's elegies to Germany: the *Quatuor Libri Amorum*, or *Four Books of Love*, published in 1501 and containing fifty-seven poems. It is about a wandering poet, unmistakably Celtis himself, who circles Germania, walking from Cracow to Regensburg and then to Mainz and Lübeck. Each of Germany's corners has a matching time of day, a season of the year, a phase in a man's life, one of the four temperaments (sanguine, choleric, phlegmatic, melancholic), one of the four signs of the zodiac (Aries, Cancer, Libra, Capricorn), one of the four elements (air, fire, water, earth), one of the four winds, one of the four colors, and one water. Far from extolling chauvinism in an ordinary sense, the four books map Platonic correspondences between the places of national geography and the movement of the stars. Celtis also insisted that love, not hate, binds the four corners of Germany together. To this end, he called for a *Germania Illustrata* that would collate what Tacitus knew and the modern humanists saw.[94] With a detailed portrait of the primeval German woods and a nuanced description of Nuremberg, it began brilliantly. But Celtis was a restless, Icarus-like scholar, and like an early flying machine, the project soon fell from the air, leaving other scholars to pick up the pieces.

X

One of those scholars was Johannes Cochlaeus, lay rector of the Latin School in Nuremberg. In 1512, he became the first German to write a prose description of Germany as a two-dimensional space.[95] Inspired by the maps of Etzlaub and Celtis's call to create a *Germania Illustrata*, and drawing in equal measure on Tacitus and Piccolomini, Cochlaeus appended his *Brevis Germaniae Descriptio* to a new edition of Pomponius Mela's first-century AD *Description of the World*. Intended for use in school, stringent and unadorned, the work exuded modest pride. While shying from a comparison of Germany to "the countries under a milder sky," Cochlaeus nevertheless asserted that Germany could claim great discoveries, like the catapult and the printing press, and great technical accomplishments, such as the spires of Strasbourg and Vienna.[96] Cochlaeus also took satisfaction in Germany's deep history, which he mainly drew from Tacitus, and its flourishing religious culture. Cologne, where Cochlaeus studied, "shines with as many holy men in Germany as nowhere else," he wrote, while Trier enshrined the bones of St. Matthias and Augsburg the relics of St. Ulrich.[97] The most fulsome praise was reserved for his hometown. Protected by thick walls and surrounded by deeply dug ditches, Nuremberg, according to Cochlaeus, boasted wise men in its government, pious men and women in its monasteries, and merchants who traveled all over the continent. It also made generous provisions for the poor, weaponless armies who gathered before its gates.[98]

Cochlaeus's description of Germany remained, in fact, centered on cities and towns. He mentioned nearly three hundred, and could have included more, except that many place-names sounded too coarse to be smoothed into the more elegant language of Latin.[99] While he focused on urban Germany, Cochlaeus also wrote about the nation as such. He referred to Germania as a distinct name, instead of using various appellations such as Teutonia or Alemannia, and notably employed the singular in the place of the plural form Etzlaub still used.[100] He did not, however, mark borders with precise lines. Rather, where Germany tapered off into another country, languages often became the marker. Cochlaeus, for example, wrote of the Silesians that "their language is to a large extent German, but beyond the Oder [River], Polish is also spoken."[101] "For this reason," he asserts, "the border of Germany to the east is there."[102] To the south, Trent constitutes the border, "because there the inhabitants speak the language of the Italians and also of the Germans."[103] To the west, Metz is "partly inhabited by Germans, partly by French, is subject to the Empire, the common border of France and Germany," while "most ascribe Trier more to France than to Germany, although German is the local language."[104]

Language was the principal but not the only marker of borders. When Danzig, a largely German-speaking Hanseatic city, fell under the lordship of Poland in the Second Peace of Torun in 1466, Cochlaeus conceded the political shift by acknowledging that it was "torn from them [the Teutonic Order] by the Poles" even as he left open the question of whether it was nevertheless situated in Germany.[105] Likewise, the Bohemians "are on all sides surrounded by Germans but do not speak German," and nevertheless are a people situated in Germany. Significantly, he criticized not their language but their religion, seeing them as "soiled by the evil of [the Huss-ite] heresy."[106] That there were peoples who lived in Germany but were not German-speaking was, for Cochlaeus, no contradiction, just as he observed that the people of Siebenbürgen speak German but clearly live in Hungary (now northern Romania), and Cracow, while it has a significant German-speaking population, is unmistakably situated in Poland.

XI

Similarly, Strasbourg was to Cochlaeus as much a German city as Nurem-berg. Situated on four rivers and at the borders of French and German civ-ilization, the city bustled beneath its luminously gothic cathedral, whose off-center spire pierced the sky. Cochlaeus had listed the church as one of Germany's technical marvels, and more than two centuries later the young

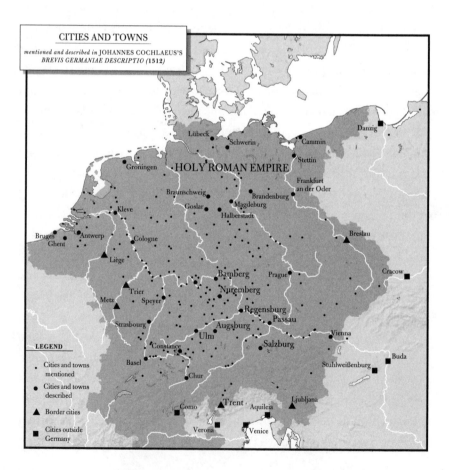

CITIES AND TOWNS

mentioned and described in JOHANNES COCHLAEUS'S *BREVIS GERMANIAE DESCRIPTIO (1512)*

LEGEND

· Cities and towns mentioned

● Cities and towns described

▲ Border cities

■ Cities outside Germany

Goethe would think of the cathedral as the finest flower of "German architecture, our architecture."[107] Like Nuremberg, Strasbourg also boasted a high caliber of humanist talent. Gutenberg had lived here before moving to Mainz, and so too did Sebastian Brant, the author of *The Ship of Fools* (a best-selling persiflage of human foibles published in 1494), perhaps the first work of literature to make poetic reference to the New World.[108] Another resident of the city was Jacob Wimpfeling, the humanist author of the *Epitoma Germanorum,* an attempt to "put together at least an outline of the great history of Germany," in light of the fact, as its author argued, that "every day the histories of Rome, Venice, England, Hungary, Bohemia and France are read."[109] Wimpfeling came to Strasbourg from nearby Schlettstadt, which, like the village of St. Dié in the Vosges Mountains, counted as one of the many small-town havens for the humanists of the Upper Rhine.

It was in St. Dié that the cartographer Martin Waldseemüller engraved three crucial maps. The first, made in 1507, depicted for the first time the entire world with a new "fourth part," along with a suggestion for how to name it. "I do not see why anyone should rightly forbid naming it Amerige, land of Americus, as it were, after its discoverer Americus, a man of acute genius, or America," wrote Waldseemüller (or more likely his wordsmith, the philologist Matthias Ringmann) in the *Cosmographiae Introductio* that accompanied the map.[110] Waldseemüller called "America" an island but named it as if it were a continent, and he closely followed the accounts of the explorer Amerigo Vespucci, whose "Four Voyages" Waldseemüller and his collaborators in St. Dié had received in manuscript from the Duke of Lorraine.[111] The second map, Waldseemüller's *"Carta Itineraria Europae"* of 1511, uses Etzlaub's southern orientation and point system for distances between cities; it counts as the first highly accurate printed map of Europe—even if some areas, notably eastern Europe and Spain, are not portrayed with the same precision as Germany and France, while others, like northern England and all of Scandinavia, are missing entirely.[112] The third map was the *"Germania"* contained in Waldseemüller's so-called Strasbourg Ptolemy edition of 1513, the first collection of the ancient geographer's maps in which newly surveyed and charted maps, the *tabulae modernae,* were juxtaposed to those based on ancient coordinates, the *tabulae antiquae.*[113] The new map of Germania was, in fact, a "unique symbiosis" of the mapmaking tradition of Ptolemy, as passed down through the maps

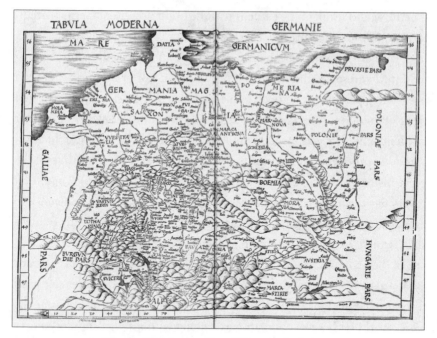

Martin Waldseemüller, *"Germania,"* 1513.

of Cusanus and Etzlaub, even if Waldseemüller sacrificed Etzlaub's dots between cities and eliminated the southern orientation.[114] Cusanus depicted central Europe; Etzlaub drew the German land in order that pilgrims might find their way to Rome and travelers to cities; but Waldseemüller rendered for its own sake a mathematically scaled two-dimensional map of Germany, a country of cities and towns stretching from the Meuse to the Vistula rivers, and from the Alps to the Mare Germanicum.

Yet even in Waldseemüller's *"Germania"* map, Germany was a nation among nations, surrounded by the countries of Gaul, Burgundy, Hungary, Poland, and Prussia. That Burgundy was a country of its own, and that Prussia was as distinct from Germany as Hungary, suggests that the modern map of Germany and Europe might have turned out differently, and that nations could also die away. But this is to get ahead of our story. The corpus of Waldseemüller's maps confirms that seeing Germany for the first time was an act of discovery, not chauvinism. It involved curiosity and imagination, science and art, looking up to God and out to the world.

CHAPTER 2

———

"GERMANY . . . AS IF IN A MIRROR"

c. 1500–1580

*No man can live without his fellow man and
no land without its neighbors*

—BEATUS RHENANUS

O N OCTOBER 31, 1517, MARTIN LUTHER SENT A LETTER TO ALBRECHT of Brandenburg, the Archbishop of Mainz. In this letter, which contained the famous 95 theses, Luther railed against indulgences, purchasable single-sheet documents that supposedly remitted sins. Whether Luther also nailed the theses to the door of the Court Church at Wittenberg remains a subject of historical debate.[1] What we are certain of is that Luther's criticisms centered fundamentally on the idea that God's grace is granted and received through faith alone, not good works or the intercession of priests. The idea had the potential to undermine Christianity as then practiced, and in June 1520, Pope Leo X threatened to excommunicate Luther if he did not recognize the doctrinal authority of the church. Already in his midthirties and at the height of his intellectual power, the Wittenberg monk responded with an open *Letter to the Christian Nobility of the German Nation*, which sold out its four thousand printed copies in only five days, and heralded the beginning of a historic explosion of religious pamphlets, polemics, prayer books, and scripture.[2]

In the *Letter*, Luther addressed the nation, or, more precisely, the Emperor and those noblemen who, as dignitaries of the Holy Roman Empire, provided tribute to Rome. In what must have been shocking rhetoric, he denounced the hierarchical structure of the church, condemned the authority of the pope, and challenged the interpretive monopoly of the Roman Catholic Church with respect to the word of God. In a subsequent pamphlet, *The Babylonian Captivity of the Church*, written in October 1520, Luther staked out essential positions, arguing that scripture authorized only baptism, the Eucharist, and penance as sacraments; he also attacked transubstantiation, the sleight of hand that allowed magician-priests, in his view, to turn the wafer into the body and the wine into the blood of Christ. These were scholastic tricks, Luther insisted. All believers, not just the priests, should drink the wine as well as eat the bread, and they should accept the real presence of Christ on the plain words of scripture.

Some humanists who sympathized with Luther preached caution. One was Desiderius Erasmus, who, in his letter to Luther of May 30, 1519, admonished the Wittenberg reformer to "continue what you are doing," but suggested it is "wiser to cry out against those who abuse the popes' authority than against the popes themselves."[3] The most revered of any humanist north of the Alps, Erasmus of Rotterdam was the first to earn his living by writing. He penned innumerable works and corresponded with hundreds of fellow men of letters and scores of rulers; some three thousand letters, most of them in Latin, have survived.[4] Elevating the epistle to an art form, Erasmus had become the nestor of a Christian humanism centered on biblical sources, with philology, ancient languages, and good literature paths to a truer faith. Strongly influenced by a practical, good-works-oriented piety, Erasmus at first defended Luther, arguing that reason could bring divergent positions together. He had grounds for his optimism. Coronated in Aachen in October 1520, the new emperor, Charles V, was a friend of the humanists, and Erasmus expected that under the young ruler, "the Christian world will enjoy a very long spell of prosperity."[5]

In Wittenberg a different turn of events transpired, however. On December 10, 1520, Luther set fire to *Exsurge Domine*, the papal bull threatening to expel him from the community of Christians, and on January 3 of the following year, the excommunication fell. Secular authorities were left to enforce it. To this end, Charles V convened the Diet of Worms and demanded that Luther renounce his writings. "Here I stand, I cannot do otherwise," a later printed version quotes Luther as saying.[6]

To generations of historians, religious crisis and conflict have seemed the inevitable consequence. Yet it bears recalling that it would take nearly a century for full-scale religious war to darken the German lands, and that, for all the sound and fury of the sixteenth-century Reformation, the world of classical learning retained considerable force, often flourishing in less polemical spaces. In this period, German humanists—whether Protestant or Catholic or without fixed denominational allegiances—persisted in thinking it was possible to know "our country," as Erasmus called Germany, by observing, measuring, classifying, describing, and rendering it.[7] Drawing on a new sensibility for the beauty of nature and for the diversity of peoples, they studied common manners and customs, engaged in critical history, and added detail to their descriptions of territories, cities, and towns. They also improved the accuracy of their maps. With increasingly sophisticated observation and measurement as well as growing artistic acumen, humanists plotted where Germany was, elucidated who lived there, and painted what it looked like. As they deepened their knowledge of their nation, they also beheld a greater vision, which, especially in the second half of the sixteenth century, they sometimes embedded as a coded message in their work. Religious faiths could coexist, next to one another, the message revealed, as nations did on maps. Whether as Lutherans, Calvinists, or Catholics, or as somewhere in between, northern humanists used depictions of nations to advance a plea for the necessity of Christian comity—whether it was extended to Jews as well remained an open question.

II

The deepening sense of a German nation began with closer attention to the German people. *Omnium Gentium Mores, Legges et Ritus* (*The Customs of All Peoples*), published in 1520, counts as one of the first modern surveys of peoples throughout the world and it contains the first serious study of the habits and customs of "the fourth estate of the Germans."[8] Written by a monk of the Teutonic Order named Johannes Boemus, it drew on the fifteenth-century revival of classical literature, especially Lorenzo Valla's translation of Herodotus into Latin. Boemus assumed Herodotus's understanding of peoples—that they are products of common language, religion, manners, and custom—and followed the ancient author's curiosity about things like dress, diet, and dwelling.[9] Animated by a vision that looked out rather than in, he imagined his book as a contribution to the understanding of cultural diversity in a wider, if still largely pre-Columbian world.

Boemus likened his account to a travel guide, as "if I faithfully conducted you by hand," and structured his European material from east to west, placing his treatment of Germany in the middle.[10] Boemus began his depiction of the Germans by repeating the now familiar refrain that Germany had long ago expanded beyond the borders the ancients assigned to it. He drew from this fact the conclusion that the Germans were shot through with foreign elements. Some were not very civilized, like the Prussians, "a most ferocious and idolatrous people," while others had contributed to progress, so that, as he wrote, Germany's "most beautiful and brilliant cities, castles, and villages are not even exceeded by those of France, Spain or Italy."[11]

As Boemus believed that nations, like so many children of God, have their own destined place, national or regional differences did not trouble him. Instead, he reserved his criticism for abuses within the vertical order of the estates. He scolded the German clergy because "most of them live very idly, bestowing little time in obtaining learning, but spending all their afternoons in playing and drinking," while also scorning unruly knights, who "subjugated the rural people to servitude and inflicted on them indescribable misery."[12] Conversely, he extolled the virtuous town, praising the urban citizen's sense of justice, devotion, and charity, and criticizing only such surface matters as fashion, where the Italians and French were to his mind too much imitated. As regards the peasantry, Boemus was more equivocal. He offered descriptions filled with greater sympathy and detail than any German author preceding him. Yet he believed them "in all times a very turbulent, toilsome and beastly people"—a condition not of their own but of their landlord's making.[13]

Uniquely, Boemus paid attention to the everyday life of townspeople and peasants, especially in his native Franconia. He recounted festivities on saints' days, fasting practices during Lent, and the celebration of carnival, or *Fastnacht*, in which a general madness possesses the people and causes them to "mask their faces, and deceive about their sex and age, the men wearing women's apparel and the women men's."[14] He also gave us the first reports of German Christmas ("parents will advise their children . . . that if they set their shoes under the table over night, what they desire they will find sent to them in the morning from the most generous bishop Saint Nicholas"). And he provided the first description of the German banquet of St. Martin's Day, when even poor people "eat swine and veal, and with no sparing of wine."[15]

When Boemus was writing, the peasantry had long been in a state of decline and even rebellion. In 1476, the Drummer of Niklashausen had led a revolt of some forty thousand poor people in the countryside around Würzburg.[16] Likewise, in 1493 and continuing through the second decade of the sixteenth century, peasants in Alsace and along the Upper Rhine staged a series of failed but alarming insurrections—part of the so-called *Bundschuh*, or Bound Shoe, movement. And in 1514, peasants, adopting the name "Poor Conrad," rebelled against the wealthy Duke Ulrich of Württemberg. These uprisings, however, proved but a prelude, because in 1525 a major popular revolt erupted.

The Peasants' War, the largest uprising in European history prior to the French Revolution, started with agrarian revolts in the southern Black Forest and in the Lake Constance area and spread to Allgäu and the Upper Rhine, assuming both a religious and political character. In February 1525, in the Upper Swabian city of Memmingen, rebels formulated the famous "Twelve Articles," which crystallized grievances and insisted on the community's right to elect its own pastor. Excluded by station or wealth from participation in governance, the common man, the rebels believed, ought to be free of bondage and have a say in how he runs his own life. As the rebellion broadened into the Palatinate and Thuringia, and south into Tyrol, it garnered more and more support, especially among the poor in towns and cities. By early April, according to the estimates of modern historians, as many as 300,000 people stood ready to take up arms against their oppressors.[17]

But the peasants were no match for well-armed, battle-tested soldiers, and when this became clear, Luther sided against the peasants. "Let everyone who can, smite, slay and stab, secretly or openly, remembering that nothing can be more poisonous, hurtful or devilish than a rebel," he wrote.[18] Having already published the German translation (from Erasmus's Greek text) of the New Testament, Luther was by now a commanding figure, writing pamphlets and sermons printed in thousands of copies.[19] Against "God's law," as advocated by the peasants, Luther insisted on the dual swords of state and church. With pikes and muskets, regular soldiers in the pay of the imperial estates predictably annihilated the poorly weaponed, deeply divided, and badly trained peasant armies, with contemporary accounts estimating that "more than 100,000 peasants" lost their lives.[20] Adjusting for population increase, it was as if today's German government were to kill nearly a half million of its poorest citizens.

III

The violence of the Peasants' War caused a number of humanists to retreat to a life of quiet scholarship. One was Beatus Rhenanus, the biographer of Erasmus and the editor of his works. Born in the town of Schlettstadt in Alsace, educated in Basel and Paris, Rhenanus spent the late 1520s transforming the study of Germany's history. His *Rerum Germanicarum libri tres* (*Three Books on German History*), published in 1531, was reliable, critical of sources, attentive to change over time, and suspicious of myths. Although left untranslated for nearly five hundred years, and forgotten about by generations of historians, this was, in fact, the first history of Germany by a genuine historian.

Like Boemus's ethnography, Rhenanus's history deepened the concept of the nation. He described his historical method as a kind of source criticism, always asking of documents, "at what time that which you are reading was written, by whom and about what" and then, in order to avoid mistakes, comparing "the new texts with the old or vice versa."[21] He subjected the early patriots to withering criticism, reproaching especially Conradus Celtis, who inquired only into origins, not into change over time, and who failed to separate the history of the Empire from the history of the Germans. The dispute turned on the interpretation of the *Germania* of Tacitus. Since 1500, German patriots assumed that Tacitus had revealed innate German national characteristics and then juxtaposed these characteristics—strength, virility, and love of freedom—with the supposedly effete and urban Italians. Rhenanus countered that more than a millennium of movement, tribal dispersion, migration, and war all meant that one could not simply transpose the locations of tribes from Tacitus onto a current map.[22] Seemingly straightforward, this critical insight opened up the question of what had happened to the Germans between the time of

Tacitus and the time of Charlemagne. It also challenged fellow humanists to write about the history of the Germans as if they were a people defined by movement and mixing, and not, as Tacitus had thought, simply indigenous to the area.

The problem led Rhenanus to rethink the relation between history and time. In place of the seven ages of the world, as outlined by Augustine, or the four empires in the dream of Daniel, of which the Roman Empire was to be the last, Rhenanus introduced a three-tiered (ancient—medieval—modern) temporality, and in doing so was the first German scholar to employ the term "medieval," referring to the period when monks corrupted manuscripts, "sewing legendary matters onto true things."[23] History, Rhenanus argued, was not a scheme in which temporal horizons, as in the *mappa mundi*, are fused, or the past prefigures the present. History, he posited, simply told what happened and how. Causality was a phenomenon of this world, not the next; and anachronism, projecting the present onto the past, was not a way to understand former ages—it was simply flawed historical thinking. Rhenanus's new concept of time also led to criticism of ancient authors, like Caesar, "not free of mistakes," and of recent German patriots. One of their many falsehoods was their assertion that the German warrior Arminius had defeated the Roman legionnaire at Augsburg, thus showing German tribes on the offensive.[24] The error, Rhenanus demonstrated, rested on a fallacious reading of sources; the real battle took place in the Teutoburg Wood of Westphalia, and it was a defensive battle.[25]

In the first of the *Three Books*, Rhenanus explicated the Germanic tribes, describing where they lived and to where they migrated. In essence, he wrote a history of routes, not roots. But he did not sentimentalize the ancient Germans either. He considered them barbarians, destroyers, not builders of civilization. In the second book, Rhenanus concentrated more on manners and customs, debunking myths, especially the fanciful stories of the foundations of towns in the south and west. In the third book, he praised the achievements of urban Germany, lavishing especial attention on Basel, where he had worked closely with Erasmus, and on his native Schlettstadt. When combined, the three books told a story of how language had soldered Germany together from disparate, even foreign parts, and how the country gradually attained civilization. And as if to emphasize that his was not a work of vulgar patriotism, he concluded

Three Books on German History with a description, partly in Greek, of
Paris, where he received his education.²⁶ "All this is Erasmian," wrote
Paul Joachimsen, a remarkable early-twentieth-century German-Jewish
scholar of the Reformation. "This is how Erasmus would have seen German history."²⁷

<h1 style="text-align:center">IV</h1>

The Rhine was the river of Erasmus as surely as Saxony was the land of
Luther. From Rotterdam to Basel, a chain of Rhenish cities marked the
stations of Erasmus's life and the departure point for his sojourns to Cambridge across the Channel and Padua over the Alps. The Rhine also harbored guarded experiments in religious openness, whether expressed in
the peaceful civility of Basel throughout most of the 1520s; the open-to-the
world Strasbourg of Martin Bucer, a moderate reformer, in the 1530s; or
the tolerant Cologne of Archbishop Hermann von Wied in the 1540s. In
this sense, the river was also a starting point for describing "our Germany,"
as Erasmus put it in a letter to the Hebraist Johannes Reuchlin, who, in
1510, defended Jewish books against imperial efforts to confiscate them
on the grounds that they impeded the conversion of Jews to Christianity.²⁸

Yet Erasmus's letter to Reuchlin also betrayed anti-Jewish sentiment. Like many humanists, Erasmus conceived of Judaism as inimical
to a Christianity that emphasized the New Testament over the Old, and
good works over ritual and law. He also had little empathy for the plight
of the Jews. In city after city, territory after territory, Jews had already
been expelled from Germany's urban communities or, as in Frankfurt am
Main, packed into ghettos with their rights curtailed. In the course of the
expulsions, thousands of Jews migrated to the countryside, where for the
next three hundred years they settled in rural Hesse and Franconia and
in a quilt of southwestern German territories. Whether caused by mounting debt to Jewish lenders, or a spate of late medieval ritual-murder and
host-desecration accusations, the expulsions changed the map of urban
Germany for centuries to come.²⁹ Cities and towns negotiated for the
privilege *"de non tolerandis Iudaeis,"* the imperial freedom to not tolerate
Jews. More than a few communities built churches where synagogues once
stood.³⁰ And many cities in which Christians and Jews once lived in the

Hans Holbein the Younger, *Erasmus of Rotterdam*, 1523.

same streets, as was the case in Nuremberg, now saw little or no Jewish presence. Sometimes, the expulsions lasted for a hundred years or less. But in most cases, Jews were forbidden to settle in the communities that expelled them for two or even three centuries. Especially in southern and central Germany, the home of German humanism, a swath of cities and territories barred Jews until the nineteenth century.

The career of the humanist Sebastian Münster reflected both the new interest in describing Germany and the vexed relation of learned Christians to Jews. Born in 1488 in Ingelheim, a short distance down the Rhine from Mainz, he became by the mid-sixteenth century Germany's most influential scholar of geography. For most of his lifetime, however, Münster was better known as the translator and editor of innumerable works in Hebrew, including the Jewish histories of Josippon written at the end of the first millennium, the twelfth-century philosophical works of Moses Maimonides, and numerous contemporary works of Hebrew grammar. Indeed, few Christians entered the Jewish house of learning as empathetically as Münster, who studied the epitaphs on Jewish graves, went to holy services in synagogues in order to hear the Torah read aloud, and corresponded with Jewish scholars. Among the first scholars to render part of the New Testament into Hebrew, Münster was also the first Christian to compose a Hebrew-language dialogue with Jews.[31] Not everyone applauded. According to the posthumously published student notes that comprise his *Table Talk*, Luther denounced Münster's "Judaizing tendencies," hurled obloquy at Münster's publication of portions of the Bible in Hebrew and Latin, and denounced Münster for not combating the "enemies of Christ" with sufficient vigor.[32]

If Münster dedicated the greater part of his best years to bringing Jewish learning into the Christian fold, his early geographical work was also cutting-edge, as is evident from a surviving notebook from his student years. Full of calendars, mathematical formulations, and descriptions of European nations, it contains entries on astronomy, Ptolemy's *Geography*, and a transcription of a chronology from the beginning of history until 1524 (when Johannes Stöffler, his Tübingen professor, calculated the world would end). It also includes a collection of maps, forty-four in all, twenty-seven copied from the second edition of the *Ulm Ptolemy* and fourteen from Martin Waldseemüller, including the world map of 1507 with "America" on it, and the *"Carta Itineraria Europae"* of 1511, the first stand-alone map of Europe.[33]

The notebook foreshadowed his cartographical work. So too did Münster's first published map, a complicated circular rendition of Germany printed on a single sheet in 1525; it was filled with dials allowing the user to estimate sunrises and sunsets, the date of Easter for years to come, and much else, suggesting Münster's interest in Platonic correspondences between heaven and earth, and the place of his country, Germany, within this scheme. Indeed, the map precipitated the precise calculations that became a hallmark of his cartographical work.

Yet, as Münster came to understand in the course of his travels, one man alone could not observe all the detailed features of German topography.[34] Münster needed trusted collaborators, and to aid them, he sketched a regional map of the area around Heidelberg, where he then taught. Modest in appearance, the map was the first to use sighting lines to form mathematically precise triangles, from which Münster could calculate the angles defining the relative positions of towns and estimate the distances to them. More accurate maps were only a start. Münster hoped that his collaboration with the leading humanist scholars of his day would reveal the "hidden beauties" of "our common German fatherland" and create a work "in which one will see all of Germany with its peoples, cities, and customs as if in a mirror."[35]

Parallel to his work in Hebrew, Münster spent nearly twenty years gathering evidence, taking measurements, collecting manuscripts, and entreating his fellow humanists to contribute histories, topographic views, and maps from their regions. He wrote a prodigious number of letters, "four to six a day" as he complained in 1549, seeking "support for our plan to describe Germany's territories, cities, towns, villages, distinguished castles and monasteries, its mountains, forests, rivers, lakes, and its products, as well as the characteristics and customs of the people, the noteworthy events that have happened, and the antiquities which are still found in many places."[36] The letters he sent throughout southern Germany received responses from almost everyone, allowing him to render that region of Germany in great detail.[37] Reports on other areas, especially in northern Germany, came in slowly and piecemeal. Even major cities, like Cologne, Aachen, and Utrecht, proved resistant. But in time, Münster gathered the maps and descriptions of the "whole German nation to Pomerania and Prussia."[38] He did not stop there. Diligent and ambitious, he also sent entreaties to humanists in Denmark, Poland, France, and England, drawing in the wider republic of learning. The difference made by the contributions of others can be seen by comparing the meager results of the first edition of the *Cosmographia*, published in 1544, with the striking successes of the third revised edition of 1550, "much swelled up," as Münster noted.[39]

The revised *Cosmographia* went through at least ten more posthumous revisions by 1628 and sold roughly fifty thousand copies in German and another ten thousand in Latin. It was also translated into French, Italian,

Czech, and, in excerpts, English.[40] The sales numbers paled in comparison to the full array of Luther's writings, but not, for example, to Luther's famous translation of the New Testament, which sold one hundred thousand copies in the great reformer's lifetime.[41] Packed in leather bales or in wooden barrels, the revised edition of the *Cosmographia* wended its way along post routes and down rivers to an influential minority of city dwellers—mainly men in the German lands and elsewhere in Europe—who gifted it to friends and family, treasured it as a conspicuous luxury that announced their learnedness, and perhaps even read it.[42] Jean Bodin, the French theorist of sovereignty, owned one, even if he thought it more a "*Germanographia*" than a description of the world.[43] Montaigne, statesman, skeptic, and prodigious essayist, also owned a copy, and regretted that he neglected to bring it on his travels through Switzerland, Germany, and Italy in 1580 and 1581.[44]

The *Cosmographia* was an imposing achievement. With 120 contributors in all, some Lutheran, others Calvinist, and Catholics as well, it placed Germany in the middle of the known world.[45] As readers leafed through the German sections (nearly half of the work) of the *Cosmographia*, they encountered a new spatial sensibility, ordered not according to sacred time schemes, as was the case with the *Nuremberg Chronicle*, but as if observing the layers of a map.

The new spatial sensibility represented what might be called the third deepening—after Boemus's ethnography, and Rhenanus's history. It was particularly focused on cities, and indeed the cityscapes of the *Cosmographia* were striking. In the first edition of 1544, they were still impoverished and confused, with the same woodcut serving, for example, for Basel, Koblenz, Nuremberg, and Kempten, and another for Chur, St. Gallen, Nördlingen, Eichstätt, and Hagenau. By 1550, however, humanist collaborators throughout Germany had sent hand-drawn cityscapes to Münster, who turned them over to form cutters in preparation for wood-block printing.[46] Unlike copperplate views, which required a rolling press, woodcut pictures could be placed along with text in the same form, allowing image and word to be printed simultaneously.[47] The number of "naturalistic" views in Münster's *Cosmographia* was double that in the *Nuremberg Chronicle* and far outstripped contemporary competitors.[48]

Whether from a slightly elevated hill or from a bird's perspective, city after city now appeared as the naked eye might see them. Often a lettered key accompanied the cityscape, allowing the reader to identify individual buildings, gates, and even streets. Sketched by a local humanist, the woodcut depicting Erfurt, for example, stretches out with an almost geometric sense of space, even if some of the church towers remain stereotypical.[49] The view of Augsburg, conventional save for the Perlacher Tower in the *Nuremberg Chronicle*, is seen as if from a surveyor's elevated eye, showing walls and towers, churches, municipal buildings, and houses of the patriciate while leaving minor residences and streets blank.[50] Some localities, such as Lindau on Lake Constance, received especially elegant depictions, rendering the modest imperial city a "Swabian Venice."[51]

Münster combined these naturalistic city views with comprehensive textual descriptions that deepened the reader's appreciation of urban life. The descriptions were hardly neutral. Praising the industriousness of city merchants and the wisdom of city councils, Münster particularly extolled the learning of Germany's humanists, some of whom, at least in the 1550 edition, are depicted in woodcuts. They include Erasmus, who had passed away in 1536 and is described in detail, and Luther, who is less lauded.[52] By contrast, nobles held little fascination for Münster.

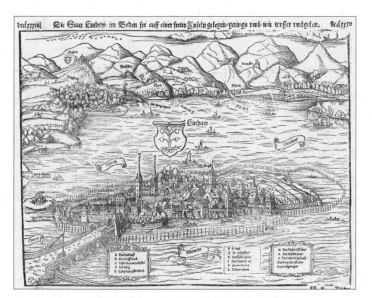

Sebastian Münster's view of Lindau,
from the third edition of his *Cosmographia*, 1550.

They ate well, dressed fancifully, proclaimed the rule of the sword over the law of the land, and oppressed the fourth estate. Like Boemus, whom he abundantly plagiarized, Münster betrayed marked sympathy for the peasants—not the mythical Germans drawn from a passionate reading of Tacitus or the idealized "*Volk*" of later centuries, but actual peasants. This too was new. Influenced by the discovery of indigenous peoples in the Americas, and nascent ethnographies, humanists began to see the vast numbers who lived outside city walls with less dismissive eyes. In the Antwerp of the 1560s, Pieter Bruegel the Elder began painting peasants as individual subjects, depicting their work and tribulations, if still with religious and moral motifs.[53] Yet even in Holland, the fourth estate was not seen as the quintessence of the nation. That was an invention of a later century, as was the notion that a ruler should bother to count how many peasants a country contained.

Münster also wrote about the history of Jews in Germany, and in particular about their persecution. The *Cosmographia* contained matter-of-fact descriptions of the murder of the Jews in Speyer, Worms, and Mainz during the First Crusade in 1096; stories of the devastation of the Jewish community in Nördlingen in 1290; and accounts of the Armleder massacres in upper Alsace in 1337. It also delineates the characteristic architecture of vanished Jewish communities—of the Jewish towers in Meißen and in Strasbourg, the empty *Judenplatz* in Würzburg, and the "murder alley" in which the townsmen of the Bohemian city of Eger killed the local Jews.[54] Münster also paid tribute to Jewish scholars, like the medieval grammarian and commentator David Kimhi, while publicly lauding Johannes Reuchlin.[55]

Münster's *Cosmographia* was far from a perfect work. It remained trapped in the cosmos of Ptolemy at a time when the theories of Copernicus were not only known but also published—in fairness, however, scholars hedged their bets well into the next century, and none of Münster's other sixteenth-century cosmographical competitors made the conceptual leap either.[56] The *Cosmographia* also propagated an inadequate knowledge about the New World, rendering indigenous peoples as cannibals, already by midcentury a hoary stereotype; and it trafficked in the sensationalism of monsters, which filled the folio margins of Münster's descriptions of faraway lands and deep seas.[57] But if Münster remained unsure about the wider world, it helps to recall his more modest aim. "My first intent," he informed his readers, "has been the description of the German nation with its regions and cities."[58]

V

The description was of a nation one could see—"the entire land of Germany . . . reflected as if in a mirror," as Münster put it.[59] In the mid-sixteenth century, sight was conceived as an almost mechanical act of reproduction: "the picture of the thing seen being formed on the concave surface of the retina," as one near contemporary, Johannes Kepler, later described the process.[60] Whether as a mirror or as a pictorial reproduction, the humanist image of Germany possessed numerous frames: Etzlaub's seven kingdoms and language areas, each with its special color and in the middle the white of Germany, for example; or the outer limits of a drawn circle in the cartographer Tilemann Stella's unfinished map of the "current nation at the current time," as a contemporary characterized the map in 1566.[61] These frames were not borders in a conventional modern sense. Rather than demarcate territory, they showed how the nation of Germany was situated among nations.

A sense of pride—in the rivers and mountains, in the dense forests and bountiful fields, and in the famous places and luminous cities—exuded from these images of the German nation: perhaps chauvinism, as well, especially toward Italy. Responding to Italian accusations that Germans were "barbaric donkeys," as Poggio Bracciolini once called them, German humanists like Conradus Celtis and Jacob Wimpfeling decried Italian arrogance, laxity, and amorality.[62] No doubt fueled by a sense of inferiority, this new chauvinism mainly characterized the second generation of German humanists, whose literary production fell in the period between 1490 and 1519, and whose poets circled in the orbit of the court of Maximilian I.[63] Avid readers of Tacitus, they affixed to the Germans a catalogue of virtues, including strength, bravery, loyalty, and steadfastness, which contrasted with the supposed vices of the Italians.

Yet with the exception of German attitudes to Italy, national stereotypes derived less from prejudice, as we might think of the term, than from classical sources. Recalibrated in the course of pilgrimages and crusades, reworked in medieval encyclopedias, and revised again at the universities of the late Middle Ages, national stereotypes assumed new life in the age of discovery. Far from reflecting mere chauvinism, they informed modern travel literature and provided shorthand for describing and recognizing peoples at a time when nations, however imprecisely defined, had become a legitimate way of conceptualizing the geographic world. Sometimes fleeting, sometimes enduring images proliferated, epitomizing the proud Spaniards, the rebellious Germans, the courageous Saxons, the elegantly gaited French, the wrathful Brits, or the allegedly libidinous Scots.[64] Print hardened these typecasts further. In one of the most successful epithet lexicons of the sixteenth century, Germans were described as ferocious, bellicose, truthful, and querulous, while the French were these things too but, unlike the Germans, also passionate lovers.[65] In the early modern period, stereotypes were sometimes displayed with rows and columns on a grid and illustrated by images of people in national dress.[66]

A similar argument may be made about national language. Piety and cross-cultural encounter, far more than chauvinism, shaped learned attitudes. Luther, for example, knew that God had revealed himself to man in Hebrew and Greek, and that Latin was the language in which Christianity converted the pagan peoples of Europe.[67] German, he nevertheless maintained, was a truth-telling language that brought those who spoke it as their mother tongue closer to God, not the nation.[68] Piety also motivated the first attempts to standardize the language in order to make it more understandable. In an age when silent reading remained the exception, and reading aloud in the company of others the norm, the grammarian Valentin Ickelshamer started with phonetics, the sound of the language, and attempted to bring the spoken and written language of German together. "Reading has never been as useful as now," he argued in *The Right Way to Learn to Read Quickly*, published in 1527, since "any man can learn to read God's word."[69] None of this was about nation making. Ickelsamer, as the historian Arno Borst wrote, "only looked up."[70]

Others looked out. In his *Grammatica Germanicae Linguae* of 1578, Johannes Clajus, the first author to laud Luther for his contribution to language unification, hoped to teach German, however inconsistent a language it may have seemed, to those who spoke another language.[71] In the sixteenth and seventeenth centuries, grammars were written for some sixty-three languages, few in the vernacular they intended to codify, mainly to help people learn to read and to comprehend foreign languages.[72] Discovery and the encounter of peoples, not language chauvinism, fueled this global proliferation of grammatical works. Grammars for Asian and American languages followed quickly the composition of the first European grammars, creating, as the French linguist Daniel Baggioni has argued, the "first sociolinguistic revolution," in the course of which many languages, German among them, were first set and stabilized.[73]

Finally, no one religious denomination enjoyed a special relationship to the nation. Mapmakers did not divide Germany, or even parts of it, into Protestant and Catholic spheres. In the sixteenth century, only one known map of an imperial territory even showed religious divisions, and it delineated not Protestant and Catholic influence, but Hussite strongholds. Printed in Nuremberg in 1518 and copied and amended by Münster in 1545, this was Mikuláš Klaudyán's map of Bohemia. Its Hussite towns were marked by a chalice and set off from Catholic towns, signaled in turn by the crossed keys of St. Peter.[74] The continuing fluidity of religious borders was not, as one might surmise, responsible for this lack of cartographical interest in religious division. In his descriptions of cities and towns, many of which had already adopted new creeds or retained the old faith, Münster omitted mention of whether a place was Catholic or Protestant, and instead described castles, churches, monasteries, municipal buildings, famous men, and remarkable inventions. Münster had himself converted to Luther's teachings sometime in the 1520s, but, like Erasmus and Rhenanus, he was horrified when rustics were "butchered like animals" during the Peasants' War of 1525, and when, four years later, the sculptures and paintings of Basel's churches and monasteries were smashed, trampled, and set to flame in a storm of iconoclasm.[75] In fact, Münster disdained inter-Christian controversy and professed ignorance of the whole contentious field.[76] Pacific in disposition, he tired of the "almost numberless books for and against" the Reformation.[77] He also had a sharp commercial sense, taking great care that the *Cosmographia* not offend one or the other religious party.

VI

By the 1540s Germany was nevertheless a nation, to use Münster's term, increasingly divided along religious lines. Emperor Charles V, whose European territories stretched from Germany to Spain, and from the Netherlands to Transylvania, had failed to suppress the Protestant revolt. Instead, the Reformation had engulfed almost all of northern Germany and most of the cities in the south; it had also penetrated deep into the hereditary lands of the Habsburgs.[78] At the same time, Jewish expulsions from German cities, carried out between 1420 and 1540, largely came to a close, with very few cities spared. When Luther published his subsequently infamous *The Jews and Their Lies* in 1543—in which he urged Christians "to set fire to the [Jews'] synagogues or schools and to cover over with dirt whatever will not burn"—he condoned an already widely accepted practice.[79]

In this context, a trio of crucial events—religious, military, and biographical—shaped how subsequent history unfolded. The first was the Council of Trent, summoned in December 1545, which would convene multiple times in the next eighteen years. The council affirmed the church's interpretive monopoly over scripture, the authority of tradition, the full range of the sacraments, and the veneration of the saints; it even justified a reformed version of indulgences. Yet the prelates at Trent also acknowledged corruption and developed strategies to win back the faithful, inaugurating a far-reaching Catholic Reformation.

The second event was Charles V's declaration of war against the Schmalkaldic League, an alliance of Protestant princes and cities who vowed to protect one another if the Emperor attacked them. The attack occurred in 1547, and the league, deprived of French help, was defeated at the Battle of Mühlberg, even though fighting continued thereafter. A numerical mismatch, Mühlberg augured the supremacy of a large territorial state, Austria, as against a league of small principalities and city-states capable of amassing serious concentrations of force. While not evident at the time, the battle also sounded an early death knell for independent city-states north of the Alps, and, as such, a defeat for northern humanism generally. The third significant event of the decade was the death of Luther in 1546.

By the time of Luther's passing, the divisions wrought by the sixteenth-century religious conflicts had hardened, and the initiative for reform passed to John Calvin and his followers. Centered in Geneva, the Calvinists emphasized God's ubiquitous power and man's utter depravity—salvation resulted from God's grace alone. A creed far removed from the Erasmian stress on faith and works, it nevertheless held considerable appeal to the urban patriciate throughout northern Europe. The Catholic Church likewise furthered religious reforms, although it also increasingly repressed dissent. In its first printed and public index of forbidden books, issued in 1559, it condemned not only the books and pamphlets of Luther, Calvin, and other leading reformers, but also all the works of Beatus Rhenanus, Sebastian Münster, and Erasmus. It even listed as forbidden Aeneus Silvius Piccolomini's "Commentary on the Councils of Basel," written before he became Pope Pius II.[80]

A more violent period of religious strife, especially concentrated in western Europe, ensued. In France, heightened violence between reformed Huguenots and orthodox Catholics reached a crescendo with the St. Bartholomew's Day Massacre of late August 1572. Fearful of Huguenot power and influence, King Charles IX ordered the murder of leading Protestant noblemen and encouraged Catholic mobs in Paris and other cities to strike down thousands of Huguenot men, women, and children. In the British Isles, religious wars, now in the realm of monarchical politics, cost Mary Queen of Scots her throne and her head. And in the Netherlands, Philip II's policy of repression, carried out against the Calvinists with astonishing brutality by Fernando Álvarez de Toledo, 3rd Duke of Alba, led to a popular revolt, the first to create a politically independent new nation: the Dutch Republic.

Germany, by contrast, witnessed a religious détente. The historic Peace of Augsburg quieted enmity while acknowledging the religious division between Lutherans and Catholics as a matter of imperial law. Signed at the nadir of Catholic influence in 1555, the Peace of Augsburg advanced the principle *cuius regio, eius religio* ("whose realm, his religion"). Implied in the text of the peace but not stated, this principle allowed the territorial ruler to choose the religious denomination of his subjects, and gave dissidents a grace period for "leaving their homes with their wives and children in order to settle in another."[81] In doing so, it created a patchwork geography of "toleration for rulers, coercion or exile for subjects" that powerfully shaped the religious and mental landscape of Germany for the next half millennium.[82] Crucially, the peace did not recognize Calvinism but only the "Old Religion" and the "Augsburg Confession" (the statement of faith penned by Philipp Melanchthon in 1530 for Lutherans in the Empire). It also mandated the coexistence of religious communities if they were already established in Germany's imperial cities. As the larger map of the sixteenth-century nation came to resemble a quilt, each patch a religiously distinct state, the daily negotiations of coexistence across creeds still characterized many of Germany's cities and towns.[83]

VII

Following Sebastian Münster's "first intent . . . the description of the German nation," humanists in the second half of the sixteenth century rendered individual territories within Germany with greater precision and artistry. In some cases, territorial mapping and description predated Münster's *Cosmographia*. Heinrich Zell's map of 1542, the first cartographic rendering of ducal Prussia, derived, for example, from earlier if now lost maps of Prussia drawn by the Polish astronomer Nicolaus Copernicus.[84] In other cases, Münster's *Cosmographia* spurred new interest in German territories, with the quality of regional mapping often far exceeding Münster's, as it did, for example, in Mark Jordan's map of Holstein or Martin Helwig's map of Silesia. Rulers who had until midcentury taken only a slight interest in mapping now began to commission precise surveys of their territories. One of the most significant of these commissions, in terms of its artistic and scientific achievements, was a large map of Bavaria that a man named Philipp Apian made for Duke Albrecht V in 1563.[85]

Apian depicted all of Bavaria on forty sheets, which together comprised a surface of thirty square meters.[86] Unfortunately, the maps did not survive the wear of time, and copies made in the late eighteenth century went up in flames during World War II.[87] Apian had, however, also made a smaller version, the twenty-four plates of the *Bairische Landtafeln* (*Bavarian Panels*), printed in 1568. Intended to aid in statecraft, delight rulers, and show off the territory, the maps were not only among the most beautiful of the sixteenth century, they also counted as belonging to the most accurate.[88] Setting out with his brother and an assistant,

Apian surveyed, in the course of "six almost seven summer times," Bavaria's cities, waters, mountains, and forests.[89] He rendered major cities as seemingly realistic views, with the two domes of Munich's Frauenkirche as recognizable as the thirteenth-century stone bridge that spans the Danube in Regensburg.[90] Especially remarkable was the portrayal of nature. Apian depicted mountains, still illustrated as gopher mounds in Münster's maps, with discernible accuracy: the "Watzmann" and the smaller "Watzmann's Wife," for example, as two connected angular peaks. Apian also lavished considerable attention on Bavaria's lakes and rivers, often exaggerating them in size to emphasize their prominence while keeping their outlines true. He similarly gave large woods their due while hinting at mid-sixteenth-century deforestation by depicting the cutting of wood and the burning of brush. But while Apian registered the effects of man on the land, including the rendition of a number of battles, his map conveyed an overwhelming sense of Bavaria's bountiful nature. Apian drew, for example, plentiful deer in the Perlacher Heath, mountain goats atop the Benediktenwand, beer hops north of Neuburg, and fishermen on

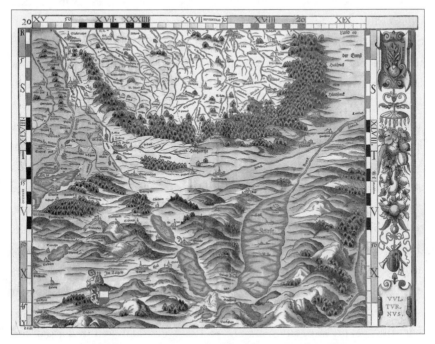

Philipp Apian, *Bavarian Panels*, 1568, plate XX.

Ammersee, and he adorned the maps' margins with colorful cornucopias of fruit, berries, and flowers.

The abundance Apian painted onto his maps masked the mounting pressure for religious conformity that would take a toll on his life and work. Committed to the ideas of the Reformation, Apian refused, in 1569, to sign an oath affirming the Council of Trent, whereupon Duke Albrecht forced him to quit his post at the Catholic University of Ingolstadt. Apian eventually settled at the University of Tübingen, where pressure to sign the Lutheran Book of Concord compelled him to resign again, in 1583. His forced resignations recall the religious and political strife under which humanism increasingly labored. Indeed, he belonged to a series of late-sixteenth-century mapmakers—among them Martin Helwig in Silesia, Theodor de Bry (famous for his images of the New World), and Matthias Quad—for whom religious flight and exile constituted the experiential ground for their geographical work.[91] Along the Lower Rhine, where mapmaking was on the verge of a cartographical revolution, that strife was sharper still.

Gerhard Mercator, "the Ptolemy of our century," as a fellow mapmaker called him, was, for example, nearly executed for "*Lutherey*" in 1544.[92] Skeptical about outward rites and rigid dogmas, preferring instead to contemplate concordances between the earth and the wider cosmos, Mercator had in fact resisted the public confessions of faith demanded of him in Catholic Louvain, and instead pursued his life's work in Duisburg, where a remarkable coterie of humanists enjoyed the protection of William V, the Erasmus-inspired ruler of the Duchy of Cleves.[93] It was in Duisburg that Mercator created his subsequently celebrated world map of 1569, which still influences our sense of the shape of the planet to this day. A conformal projection, it allowed rhumb lines, which sailors used to chart their course, to be drawn straight at the price of enlarging the lands of higher latitude. The famous projection, which in later renderings shows Greenland almost as large as China, was meant as a practical tool—not a Eurocentric statement, as is often alleged.[94] In his own time, Mercator was in any case better known for his finely detailed maps of France, Belgium, and Germany—scientifically precise, equal-area maps that were engraved in copper and beautifully lettered in the slanted script favored by the humanists, now known as italic.[95]

VIII

Mercator's prominence in the mapmaking world reflected the wider shift in economic centers from the Italian city-states, notably Venice and Florence, to the great hubs of commerce in the Low Countries, primarily Amsterdam and Antwerp. Mapmaking followed the path of commercial concentrations. The first centers of gravity of original printed maps were in Rome, Florence, and Venice; then Ulm, Nuremberg, Strasbourg, and Basel; and thereafter, in the latter half of the sixteenth century, the Lower Rhine, the Scheldt, and the Dutch seaboard. Roughly 80 percent of all new maps made in Europe between 1472 and 1600 were produced in this transverse stretching from Italy, through Germany, to the Low Countries.[96] Credible estimates for the number of printed maps in circulation in the core countries of Europe posit one map for every 720 persons in 1500, and one for every 4 persons a century later, with most maps, roughly two-thirds of the total, portraying the countries and regions of the continent.[97] These maps reshaped people's sense of space as surely as the proliferation of texts altered the practice of reading. Indeed, they created a cartographic revolution commensurate with the better-known transformation in print.

New forms of presenting maps also appeared. One was the atlas, first compiled by Abraham Ortelius, a mapmaker working in Antwerp, then still part of the Holy Roman Empire. Just as Hartmann Schedel had choreographed immense local talent to produce the *Nuremberg Chronicle* in 1493, Ortelius assembled cartography's best and brightest in 1570.[98] They comprised astronomers, clergymen, medical doctors, mathematicians, artists, and seafarers. Religious creed, by contrast, played virtually no role. Ortelius brought together Catholic mapmakers from Italy, Calvinists from the Netherlands, and Lutherans like Apian and Mercator from Germany. Not a few were on the run. Some, like the Lutheran Cornelius Adgerus and the Catholic Gerhard Stempel, fled Flanders for the Rhineland; others, like Johannes Florius, escaped to East Frisia, and still others, like the Dutch cartographer, Jodocus Hondius, fled to England.[99] Ortelius's cartographers faced problems not just in Flanders, however. Olaus Magnus, the first to map the northern countries, fled Sweden soon after the introduction of the Reformation, and settled initially in Danzig, then in Venice, and later in Rome. Likewise, the Calvinist faith of Georg Gadner made it impossible for him to remain at his post at the Catholic University of Ingolstadt.[100] Ortelius himself may have even belonged to a tightly knit sect known as the Familists, a small group who emphasized an unmediated relationship to God, affected disinterest in external rites and conflicts between religious groups, and welcomed almost all into their fold.[101]

The atlas Ortelius organized was in any case a great success. Entitled *Theatrum Orbis Terrarum*, or *Theater of the World*, it appeared in twenty-four editions in Ortelius's lifetime, and ten thereafter, with the number of map sheets expanding from 53 in the original edition of 1570 to 164 by 1612. It was also translated from Latin into German, Dutch, English, Spanish, and Italian.[102] Mercator thought especially highly of it, because "it can be bought at small cost, kept in a small space and even carried about wherever we please."[103] If Mercator underestimated the cost of the atlas—a month of a printer's wages for an unbound, uncolored copy, two months when bound and illuminated—it was nevertheless the case that the *Theatrum* could be viewed in the houses of well-off townsmen, making "one little room," as John Donne wrote of love, "an everywhere."[104] That Ortelius rendered this "everywhere" as a theater or stage no doubt struck contemporaries as apt, with the metaphor "all the world's a stage" familiar to us through Jaques's soliloquy in Shakespeare's *As You Like it*. Much as a play brings alive its dramatic personages, Ortelius's atlas portrayed the countries of the world within the covers of a single volume so as to arouse our sympathies for them.[105] And just as Shakespeare placed the stress on "and all the men and women merely players," Ortelius hoped that readers would "pass over the collective insanities of nations" and adopt a higher, less world-bound perspective, in which the "boundaries of mortals" appear "ridiculous."[106]

Ortelius's atlas was not alone in disseminating a hidden plea for peace. With pronounced Familist sympathies and in close cooperation with Ortelius, two Cologne engravers, Georg Braun and Franz Hogenberg, set out to complement the *Theatrum* with their own *Civitates Orbis Terrarum* (*Cities of the World*). Braun, a Catholic prelate much criticized for his religiously conciliatory positions, took over the organizational and editorial work. Hogenberg, the Protestant engraver who had made many of Ortel-

Abraham Ortelius, "Germania," from *Theatrum Orbis Terrarum*, 1570.

ius's plates for the *Theatrum*, assumed the artistic lead. Involving a concert of surveyors, artists, engravers, and printers from all corners of Europe, Braun and Hogenberg and their Catholic, Lutheran, and Calvinist contributors would eventually fill six volumes with exquisitely rendered, copper-engraved images of cities and towns.[107]

Starting with the 1572 edition, with no further volumes planned, volume one, as it became subsequently known, featured Europe's major cities from London to Seville, and centered on German and Dutch communities, which made up roughly half the total. Like Münster's *Cosmographia*, the *Civitates Orbis Terrarum* looked outward—to America, India, and Africa—and considered the ancient cities in these continents as part of a wider ecumene. When the success of the original volume was assured, Braun and Hogenberg began to collect more engravings. What began as a Germany-centered work broadened out so that by volume six the *Civitates Orbis Terrarum* had become a genuinely European project. Altogether, the number of cities rendered realistically—independent of formulas, stock images, and hackneyed arrangements—had increased dramatically. While

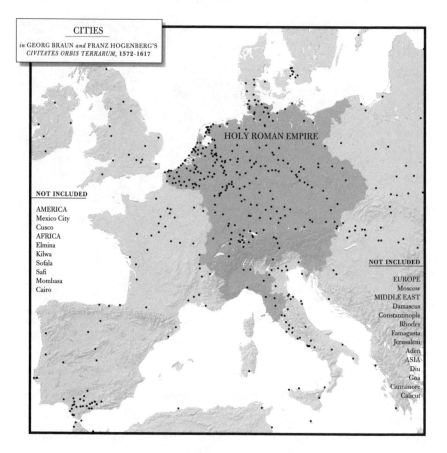

CITIES
in GEORG BRAUN *and* FRANZ HOGENBERG'S
CIVITATES ORBIS TERRARUM, 1572-1617

HOLY ROMAN EMPIRE

NOT INCLUDED

AMERICA
Mexico City
Cusco
AFRICA
Elmina
Kilwa
Sofala
Safi
Mombasa
Cairo

NOT INCLUDED

EUROPE
Moscow
MIDDLE EAST
Damascus
Constantinople
Rhodes
Famagusta
Jerusalem
Aden
ASIA
Diu
Goa
Cannanore
Calicut

Schedel had presented 30 original, or at least partly original, views in 1493 and Münster 60 in 1550, Braun and Hogenberg printed nearly 500 realistic views.[108]

The quality of the images was also better. Mapmakers, printers, and engravers had been exchanging observations and sketches across religious and national lines for decades, and in the process they had succeeded in raising the realistic city view to the status of art. By 1600, discriminating, paying consumers had also entered the scene. No longer satisfied with lifelike approximations of cities, they demanded greater fidelity to what the eye could see.[109] The travelers, merchants, armchair scholars, and patriotic citizens who bought the volumes received, of course, a mix of surveyorlike observation and painterly illusion, one's own city and the cities of the nation and of the world rendered in three dimensions, usually from on high. Stressing the fleeting nature of earthly disputes, Braun and

Hogenberg's *Civitates Orbis Terrarum* placed cities next to each other, as Ortelius's *Theatrum Orbis Terrarum* had nations. With respect to "our Germany," as Erasmus called it in his ambivalent letter to Reuchlin, this implied situating the nation among, not above, other nations. To the late-sixteenth-century humanists, the deepening appreciation of what constituted a nation was not an act of chauvinistic superiority. It was a way of imaging peace in a world slipping into war.

CHAPTER 3

THE TEARS OF STOICS

c. 1580–1700

*Such a dying, as perhaps there
never was in all of Germany.*

—SEBASTIAN BÜRSTER OF THE
CISTERCIAN MONASTERY IN SALEM
(NEAR LAKE CONSTANCE)

BETWEEN 1570 AND 1648, THE GERMAN LANDS WENT FROM A PLACE of flourishing learning to a decimated ruin. The annals of history scarcely disclose a similar descent. The most obvious comparisons remain the Black Death of the fourteenth century, from which central Europe took more than a century to recover, and central and eastern Europe in the first half of the twentieth century, which historians tellingly describe as having been visited by a second Thirty Years War.

Comparisons between the first and the so-called second Thirty Years War are, in fact, revealing. Although scholars differ on seventeenth-century population estimates, one approximation places the antebellum numbers of the people in the German parts of the Holy Roman Empire at around 16 million and by the end of the cataclysmic Thirty Years War at 11 million.[1] During the Thirty Years War, somewhere between 15 and 40 percent of the population met an early death, some (as many as a half a million) through siege and battle, but most through a horrifying panoply of hunger, privation, and disease.[2] Especially in the guise of plague and famine, the effects of war devastated populations severely. Some areas were largely spared, like the impassable mountains of Tyrol, Styria, Carinthia, and Carniola, as were parts of the northwest German flatlands, including East Friesland, Schleswig, and Holstein, and stretches of the Rhineland and Westphalia. Towns and villages far from major routes, and wayward valleys and forests, missed the worst of the damage, as did some well-protected cities like Cologne, Bremen, Hamburg, Frankfurt am Main, and Vienna. But in the diagonal from Alsace and Lorraine, through the Palatinate, Franconia, Hesse, parts of Saxony, Brandenburg, Mecklenburg, Pomerania, and along the Baltic coast, suffering persisted without mercy. Some lands lost as much as half their population.[3]

By comparison, the First World War ended in Germany with the loss of 2.5 million lives, with a further depletion of an estimated 4.5 million through a decline in the birth rate coupled with high rates of mortality. More devastating still, the Second World War cost 7 million German lives, or about 10 percent of the German population, with the German dead spread out among the soldiers (3.7 million), civilians (2 million) and the so-called expellees from the former eastern territories (1 million). Demographers estimate that a further population deficit, resulting from a decline in births and a general increase in mortality, accounts for another 7 million.[4] When both wars are taken together, these figures constitute extraordinary numbers, a historical catastrophe by any measure. Yet in the Second World War, the great death toll was in eastern Europe, where the invasion of German armies and killing squads resulted in a theater of terror that ended with well over 50 million lives lost. Here the apocalyptic end seemed near, as it did in parts of seventeenth-century Germany.

The Thirty Years War nevertheless devastated the German population, in terms of percentage, more extensively than both the First and Second World War together. The effects of the Thirty Years War also lasted longer. After World War II, West Germany achieved prewar levels of economic consumption within two decades, and in this time quickly replenished its population. East Germany registered similarly high birth rates, but lost its population to exodus, and after the erection of the Berlin Wall to a declining birth rate, a development paradoxically accelerated when the Wall fell.[5] By contrast, it took sixty to a hundred years after the Thirty Years War before Germany returned to its antebellum population.[6] Cities and towns expanded slowly in this period, losing power and influence to territorial rulers. Learning and literature also took more than a century to recapture their former luster.

To make matters worse, a half century of economic decline had already preceded the destruction of the Thirty Years War. In this period, the numbers of homeless rose dramatically. In the 1570s, the city of Nuremberg was still capable of distributing more than ten thousand loaves of bread on a single day.[7] But as grain stores declined and orphanages swelled, there were fewer and fewer alms.[8] The poor were the most likely to fall to illness, disease, and starvation, and the first to be shut out from emergency provisions in hard times. The dramatic decline in Germany's economic fortunes had many causes, but principally it resulted from shortfalls in the supply of food. Just as the population increased, a global cooling led to a series of terrible harvests. The consequence was intermittent hunger, even famine, and the ubiquity of the plague, which visited various regions of the German lands in every decade between the 1560s and the middle of the seventeenth century.[9] As the economy declined, social tensions increased throughout German cities, and food riots spread; in Magdeburg, more than two hundred people died in the course of one such revolt.[10] In the countryside, social conflict also sharpened. On many large farms east of the Elbe River, serfdom intensified, with lords expanding direct labor from two to three days per week and imposing personal jurisdiction in marriage and criminal law.[11] In the west, deteriorating conditions brought forth resistance and revolts, one after the next, especially in Upper Austria, the Lake Constance region, and along the Upper Rhine.

Telling too was the explosion of witchcraft accusations. Although occurring throughout Europe, they reached their greatest density in Germany, the "motherland" of witch hunts, as Friedrich Spee put it in his *Cautio Criminalis* of 1631.[12] Between 1560 and 1650, magistrates put to death as many as thirty thousand supposed witches, 80 percent of them women, with the greatest concentration of persecutions between 1585 and 1635, and many following downturns brought about by bad harvests and the plague.[13] Catholic territories proved especially prone to witch hunting on a grand scale, particularly the Electorates of Cologne and Mainz as well as the Bishoprics of Eichstätt, Bamberg, and Würzburg. Yet Lutheran districts in the north, like Mecklenburg, Pomerania, Schleswig and Holstein, and some Calvinist areas were not immune.[14] In addition to religion, the degree of state centralization suggested the likelihood of persecution, with weak states in the splintered regions of the Empire more susceptible than dynastic, well-consolidated strong states like Catholic Austria and Bavaria, or Protestant Brandenburg and Electoral Saxony.[15] Of course, the persecutions always pitted neighbor against neighbor, so that it seemed to one witness that "there is no more friendship on this earth."[16]

Witchcraft accusations suggested that a general crisis was near, and contemporaries, who assumed that history could easily be reversed, sensed the impending catastrophe. "Darkness and barbarism threaten and are spreading across the beautiful land of Europe," wrote humanist chronicler Marcus Welser in a 1586 letter to his friend Justus Lipsius.[17]

His friend was Europe's learned seismograph of troubled times. Although scholars insufficiently appreciated the influence of Justus Lipsius until after World War I, when collapse again loomed on the horizon, Lipsius's neo-stoicism shaped the thought of Europe cascading into economic crisis and religious civil war.[18] A professor at the University of Leiden and a philologist well-known for his painstaking edition of Tacitus (the most complete since Beatus Rhenanus), Lipsius saw the violent world of the Romans as a "theatrical representation of the life of today."[19] He wrote in a style reminiscent of Seneca and Tacitus, with virile short sentences, shorn of adornment. His most famous work, *De Constantia (On Constancy)*, was an international best seller; it went through more than forty printings in the original Latin and appeared in translation in a series of European vernacular languages. In *De Constantia*, a young man flees the war-torn Low Countries in search of peace. On his way to Vienna, he stops in Liège to converse with Languis, his good friend and wise interlocutor. "You must not forsake your country, but your affections," Languis says to him.[20] The age demanded endurance not flight, reason not emotion, and steadfastness not fickleness of feeling.

Lipsius defined "constancy" as "a right and immoveable strength of the mind, neither lifted up nor pressed down with external or casual accidents."[21] Strength of mind rested on reason, not opinion, and reason faced the exterior facts of the world with fortitude. Flickers of emotion, he taught, were no more helpful than wrangling on the decks of a ship in the midst of a storm. Lipsius also has his character Languis scorn sentimental attachments, including those to the nation, as if one were "wedded to one corner of the world."[22] One may love one's country, he conceded, but this love of country is not based on "that native soil which we first touched with our bodies and pressed with our feet." Instead, it is based on customs and ordinances, which together constitute "some one state, or as it were one common ship, under the regiment of one prince, or one law, which I confess we ought to love, to defend, and to die for."[23]

Lipsius would foreshadow the enlightened love of fatherland propagated in the eighteenth century by Joseph Addison in England and Thomas Abbt in Prussia.[24] In the 1580s, the immediate context was the carnage that ripped through the Low Countries as the Reformed Protestants fought for their religious and political independence from the Catholic House of Habsburg. At the time, Amsterdam and Antwerp, homes to Rembrandt and Rubens, were the cultural capitals of continental Europe, and Louvain and Leiden its greatest universities.[25] These places, as well as the smaller cities of Haarlem, Rotterdam, Dordrecht, Delft, and Utrecht, were great engines of social and intellectual change as surely as Venice, Milan, Florence, Genoa, and Padua had been a century before. Fueled by imperial rivalries and the nascent economies of the Atlantic world, these Dutch towns and cities anchored a triangular productive zone of advanced farming and still more sophisticated manufacturing that stretched south to Paris and west to London.[26] As Holland entered its seventeenth-century golden age, its townsmen became the merchants of Europe, its sailors the masters of the sea. The German lands, meanwhile, descended into decline and destruction.

II

In 1618, a comet visible to the naked eye streaked across the night skies of central Europe. To a society keen to see meaning in events like these, it seemed one of those sure "*signa antecedentia*" of "war, revolt, inflation, religious change, price increases, drought, and great death," as one broadside stated.[27] The portent seemed especially to cast a shadow over events in Prague, where, earlier in the year, delegates of the Protestant estates had tossed the Emperor's Catholic deputies out the third-floor window of the castle, which looked over the city from a considerable height. The defenestration was both a very real and a very symbolic event, signaling no less than the Protestant challenge to the Catholic-controlled imperial throne. The Bohemian estates had invited the Protestant elector of the Palatinate, Prince Frederick V, to claim the Bohemian crown, which would have had the effect of giving Protestant princes a majority of the imperial electors, with a future Protestant emperor a near certainty. But Prague was close to centers of Catholic power, and when Frederick V's Reformed court clashed with the city's multireligious culture, dissension followed, and the Catholics saw their chance. On November 8, 1620, the troops of Maximilian I of Bavaria, under the command of Count Tilly, routed the Protestant forces of Bohemia at the Battle of White Mountain, and soon commenced a Catholic offensive that would threaten the foundations of the Reformation world.

This was the beginning of what by the 1650s contemporaries already referred to as the Thirty Years War, but called the *"Teutsche Krieg,"* or *"bellum Germanicum,"* while it raged.[28] It centered on German religious and political questions and most of the destruction occurred in what people recognized as constituting the country of Germany. The German War, "brother against brother," was not, however, a civil war in any ordinary sense.[29] There were many foreigners involved, both as major belligerents and as mercenaries. One Bavarian regiment consisted, for example, of 534 Germans, 218 Italians, 54 Poles, 51 Slovenians, 43 Burgundians, 26 Greeks, and a number of assorted further nationalities.[30] Swedish armies consisted largely of German, Dutch, and the especially feared Scottish regiments. But they also drew heavily from the poor peasants of the Swedish and Finnish countryside, which experienced staggering depopulation as a result. In Bygdeå, a northern Swedish village from

Matthäus Merian, "Prague," in Merian, *Topographia Bohemiae, Moraviae Et Silesiae* of 1650, based on an original engraving by Karel Škréta.

which we have excellent records, 230 men were pulled into the crown's campaigns between 1621 and 1639—of them, only 15 survived, 5 as cripples.[31]

Within a decade, the war was almost over and the Catholic armies victorious. Emperor Ferdinand II had come to dominate a realm that stretched from the Alps to the gates of Stralsund on the Baltic shore. His hired general, Albrecht von Wallenstein, had an army of 134,000 soldiers, and this force, greater than any other Europe had ever known, systematically compelled Protestant armies to retreat. Once Christian of Denmark entered into negotiations with Wallenstein at the Peace of Lübeck, the Catholics had a strong position in the German lands, and some even speculated that Ferdinand supposed himself "master of Germany."[32] Following impressive victories in the field, Ferdinand issued the Edict of Restitution, which was to return the religious balance of landholding to the year 1552, just before the Peace of Augsburg. All spiritual properties taken over by the Protestants in the past three-quarters of a century were to be returned. The Archbishoprics of Bremen and Magdeburg and seven bishoprics were to become Catholic again, and over five hundred cloisters taken back into Catholic hands. Throughout the territories affected by the edict, Lutheran churches were either torn down or occupied, and Protestant municipal authorities and church officials summarily dismissed.

But fortune soon tipped in the other direction. In 1631, Gustavus Adolphus, the Protestant king of Sweden and a brilliant tactician, landed on the shores of Pomerania and counterattacked. A propaganda barrage accompanied the campaign, emphasizing the Swedish king's selfless devotion to German freedoms and the Protestant cause. Here the adjective "German" referred to the freedoms of the estates against Emperor Ferdinand II, just as the Magna Carta asserted the liberties of barons and the English church against King John. Yet on the question of the Swedish king's intentions, modern scholarship has whittled away at the propaganda of the era, revealing a "lion of the North" possessed by power and covetous of the imperial crown. His brilliance was in any case well funded, mainly by the powerful, scheming, and ruthless Cardinal Richelieu.[33] The absence of Wallenstein also enabled Swedish gains (Ferdinand had dismissed the Austrian general when the Catholic League, led by Maximilian of Bavaria, insisted Wallenstein had become too impudent and strong). Now the aged

Tilly led the Catholic forces, and he was no match for the young, innovative, and highly mobile king of Sweden. Moreover, since Tilly's ill-fated sack of Magdeburg, in which some twenty thousand civilians were ignominiously slaughtered or burned, public opinion, fired by hundreds of political broadsides documenting the event, had turned decidedly against the Catholics.[34] The electors of Brandenburg and Saxony both sided with the Swedish forces, and at Breitenfeld, just north of Leipzig, the armies clashed. The clash, which ended badly for Tilly, struck down the Catholic cause and put an end to Habsburg hopes of a unified Catholic empire in the German lands. At the same time, it prolonged the war and inaugurated one of the most destructive decades of German history—the 1630s.

III

The war brought forth a prodigious amount of testimony in the form of diaries and chronicles. Written by people ranging from pastors to local scribes, learned farmers to pious nuns, and even, in one remarkable case, by a common soldier, the surviving sources provide rare insight into the struggles of men and women in a time of catastrophe.[35] In these documents, the self interacts with the world in a very different way than the self of later centuries, when the question of one's inner state, or identity, became paramount.[36] As these are stoic documents, they mark the events that impinge upon life with exactitude, and sometimes note the gap between what words can and cannot describe. We feel the quiver and hesitation of their authors' quills, but the writers leave their inner states unaddressed.

The documents do, however, provide an image of the encounter between civilians and soldiers, allowing us to see the dimensions of these clashes and the destruction of land and people that followed. They also suggest the sheer fear of marauding armies, now nearly ten times larger than a century earlier and filled with hastily trained soldiers sporting pikes, swords, muskets, and pistols. "They pillaged, stole, burned, and broke into all the churches," noted Hans Heberle, a shoemaker near Ulm, "and chased everyone with wife and child out."[37] Likewise, a chronicle from the hamlet of Stausebach, near Fulda, reports that some soldiers stole from the fields, others from the village, and "in sum it was always too little for them."[38] The same chronicle also remarked on rape and civilian torture.

"Oh, how some women were violated. Oh, how some people lost their lives in miserable ways."[39]

Soldiers descending upon villages caused migration back and forth between the rural countryside and the cities, where walls provided protection from soldiers but not from disease and famine. In his *Time Register*, as he called it, Heberle reported civilians on the run, now from Swedish troops, now from imperial troops.[40] In these years, Germany was a land of constant movement. Between 1625 and 1649, Peter Hagendorf, a soldier involved in the siege of Magdeburg, marched an estimated 25,000 kilometers (about 15,500 miles), his wife and children in tow. They rarely except in winter rested in any one place for more than a week.[41] While en route, Hagendorf's wife, Anna, actually bore four children, three of whom were baptized, and all of whom died, as did she, by 1633.[42] In the great histories of the Thirty Years War, flamboyant generals like Tilly and Wallenstein occupy central stage. But women and their children also participated in the war. General Johann von Werth's Bavarian Cavalry Regiment moved as a mass of nearly two thousand people, only half of them soldiers, the rest women, children, stall hands, and servants of various sorts.[43]

Contemporary literature wasted few kind words on soldiers: "The soldiers of today are for the most part almost nothing but booty stealers, plunderers, peasant tormentors, oppressors of people, tribute mongers, torturers, cowards and deceits," the Saxon pastor Arnold Mengering complained.[44] Yet the life of a soldier was far from easy, and exceptions aside, only when soldiers went without pay did the plundering begin.[45] This occurred often enough, however, given that hunger stalked soldiers as ruthlessly as it pursued civilians.

Hunger, as much as pillage, resounded throughout the chronicles, with the 1630s especially dire, and one year, 1635, was particularly catastrophic. Sebastian Bürster, a monk in the Cistercian Monastery of Salem, went back to early entries in the monastery's chronicle documenting famine—for 1541, for example—and scribbled *post factum* that this hunger crisis "was nothing as compared to what happened anno 1635."[46] In Bietigheim, a town north of Stuttgart, the local scribe saw in the "coal-black bitter hunger" of 1635 "the whip of a just and angry God," with hunger "everywhere getting the upper hand."[47] He recounted that people were forced to eat grass and bark and to make flour from acorns, that dogs and cats had disappeared from the town, and that dying horses occasioned fights among starving villagers. More than three hundred people perished in the town that year, causing the scribe to appeal to Ezekiel: "Our bones are brittle, our hope is lost, and it is the end for us."[48]

It was not even hunger but rather the plague that was the most insistent cause of death. In the 1630s, it ripped through upper Germany with ferocity, its epidemiological path paved by decades of poverty, war, and famine. It devastated both the countryside and the city, where people from the land huddled together in great numbers seeking protection. A chronicler from Nassau reports of one town whose population declined from 600 to 20 and of another where death was so omnipresent "the hands were missing to bury the dead."[49]

The devastation left an altered landscape, changing the balance between man and nature. "No matter where one looked there was no dog or cat, but fields of rabbits and foxes," one scribe (echoing many others) reported.[50] In times of great death, corpses lay strewn in the fields, chewed and picked at by an animal population that flourished as the human population declined. This reversal of fortunes, the rule of nature over depleted man, also fascinated the writers of the age. One in particular attempted to make sense of a chaotic universe, in which the "ox butchers the butcher, the wildlife hunts the hunter, the fish devours the fisher. . . ."[51]

This was Hans Jakob Christoffel von Grimmelshausen, now easily the most famous German author of the seventeenth century. Having experienced war as a captured boy, then as a young musketeer, and finally as a regimental scribe, Grimmelshausen penned satirical stories with hard-biting social criticism and a great many autobiographical elements. In his *The Adventures of Simplicius Simplicissimus*, published in 1668, Grimmelshausen employed jarring storytelling, ribald comedy, and fantastic visions to show, as he put it elsewhere, that "war is a frightening and awful monster."[52]

Grimmelshausen's protagonist, who goes by the name of Simplicius, takes leave of his innocence and his hometown and encounters his country, its people, and the horrors of war. In *Simplicissimus*, as the novel is sometimes called, peasants see the world with particular clarity. In his often-quoted eyewitness report of an attack on a farm in the Spessart forest, for example, Simplicius describes in graphic detail how soldiers tortured peasants, noting, for example, the "captured wives, hired girls, and daughters" and that he "heard pitiful screams from various dark corners."[53] Far from signaling the Lord's punishment, as the moralists would have it, the protagonist blames these horrors on the earthbound actions of ordinary men. He also offers his insights as barely veiled social criticism, which, in one instance, is revealed in a dream of a tree that mirrors this war-torn world. The cavaliers on the top of the tree oppress the roots, the lowly people, who are at the bottom and struggling to get onto higher branches—but the trunk is slathered with grease, making the climb up virtually impossible. Against this world of hierarchy and wretchedness, Grimmelshausen offers pleasant visions. In one, the god Jupiter imagines a "German hero" who creates peace and unites the religions in amity. Grimmelshausen's *Simplicissimus* did not, like so many other treatments of the war, merely admonish men to repent; instead, it abjured them to end the violence. It was not only a book about the war, it was a book against war.[54]

IV

Like *War and Peace* and *All Quiet on the Western Front*, *Simplicissimus* was a postwar recounting. While the war raged, the literature that reflected the tenor of the time was the funeral oration. It enjoyed remarkable popularity throughout the early modern period, especially in Protestant areas, where it became a kind of devotional literature.[55] With learned prose and rhetorical skill, clergymen lauded the deceased, consoled the bereaving, and tried to impose order where meaning faltered and understanding broke down. The genre sometimes approached poetry, and in one author, Andreas Gryphius, the connection became explicit.

Born in 1616 in Glogau in Upper Silesia, Germany's most lyrical poet of the baroque era placed personal loss in the context of the war swirling around him; he lamented, for example, the "too early, much too early departure" of his mother amid "fire and death and plague and storm and sword."[56] In 1637 in the town of Lissa, a Polish publishing center for Protestant refugees from the Empire, he published a collection of poems containing thirty-one sonnets and an elegy to his recently deceased stepmother. Then, in 1638, at twenty-two, Gryphius enrolled at the University of Leiden, where he studied anatomy, philosophy, astronomy (especially the ideas of Copernicus) and politics.[57] It was in Leiden too that Gryphius became intimately acquainted with the neo-stoicism of Justus Lipsius. During this time, he also continued to write poetry. His *Sonnets: The First Book* included fifty poems, twenty-nine of them taken, often reworked, from the Lissa collection.[58]

As a poetic form, the sonnet contains the creativity of the poet in a single fourteen-line stanza—in German as in French poetry of the period, this was usually in alexandrine meter, six stresses, twelve syllables. Often there was a caesura in the middle, sometimes marking question off from answer, sometimes to introduce amplification, sometimes antithesis. By combining mosaic images to create a sense that misery confronts at every turn, Gryphius mastered the meter in such a way that it gave the alexandrine a bitter, lamenting tone.[59] This was achieved by circling around and converging on an adamant point.[60] Schooled combinations of images, not flow or the subtle expression of spontaneous feeling, gave baroque poetry force. "Much crying, acting mournful, showing as a woman, letting his heart go, that does not fit you," wrote Martin Opitz, the dean of seventeenth-century poetic style.[61] "Poets should provide reports of wisdom," he insisted in his *Poems of Consolation in Adversities of War*, and wisdom implied *constantia*, rational tranquility in the face of external fate.[62]

Gryphius penned what is now the most widely reprinted German poem of the baroque era. Originally entitled "Lamentation for a Devastated Germany," "Tears of the Fatherland" is arguably the first truly great poem written in German about Germany.[63] It initially appeared among the Lissa Sonnets, then, with its new title, in the first collection of poems Gryphius published in Holland. These were the lamentations of an expelled man looking in; and they bear closer examination.

Wir sind doch nunmehr gantz / ja mehr denn gantz verheeret!
Der frechen Völcker Schaar / die rasende Posaun
Das vom Blutt fette Schwerdt / die donnernde Carthaun /
Hat aller Schweiß / und Fleiß / und Vorrath auffgezehret.
Die Türme stehn in Glutt / die Kirch ist umgekehrt.
Das Rathauß ligt im Grauß / die Starcken sind zerhaun /
Die Jungfern sind geschänd't / und wo wir hin nur schaun
Ist Feuer / Pest / und Tod / der Hertz und Geist durchfähret.

Hier durch die Schantz und Stadt / rinnt allzeit frisches Blutt.
Dreymal sind schon sechs Jahr / als unser Ströme Flutt /
Von Leichen fast verstopfft / sich langsam fort gedrungen
Doch schweig ich noch von dem / was ärger als der Tod /
Was grimmer denn die Pest / und Glutt und Hungersnoth
Das auch der Seelen Schatz / so vilen abgezwungen.[64]

Entire, more than entire have we been devastated!
The maddened clarion, the bold invader's horde.
The mortar thunder-voiced, the blood-anointed sword
Have all men's sweat and work and store annihilated.
The towers stand in flames, the church is violated,
The strong are massacred, a ruin our council board,
Our maidens raped, and where my eyes have scarce explored
Fire, pestilence, and death my heart have dominated.
Here through redoubt and towns runs away new-let blood,
And thrice within six years our very rivers flood
With corpses choked has pressed ahead in tedious measure;
I shall not speak of that which is still worse than death,
And crueler than the plague and torch and hunger's breath:
From many have been forced even the spirit's treasure.[65]

The poem commences with "we," and the "we," given the original
title, can only mean the people in Germany who have suffered. Beginning with a general statement, "Tears of the Fatherland" proceeds, in
the next two alexandrines, to allegorical detail: the clarions calling forth
the apocalypse, the horde signaling the riders who commence devastation.[66] Gryphius structured the rhymes of the first quatrain *abba*, with
lines one and four the "we," the passive locus of devastation, and lines
two and three the activity of destruction. The second quatrain repeats this
rhyme scheme, except that it only amplifies the sense of devastation. The
images are more concrete, but allegorical nevertheless. The towers stand
for security, the church for spiritual life, the city hall for secular order. As
the pace of the poem quickens, each image outdoes the one preceding.
Then, lines three and four are coupled by an enjambment, forcing us fast
to the conclusion—in the elongated fourth line, which slows us down again

with three caesuras—that fire, pestilence, and death ruin not the flesh but the heart. Then a pause, as if exhausted with nothing further to say; then a tercet, a three-line unit that descends into images still more gruesome—rivers of blood, running not once but repeatedly, through to the last line, which will reveal what is worse than the foregoing, worse even than the four horsemen of the apocalypse—pestilence, famine, war, and death—and this is to have your soul (your "treasure") wrested away.

Critics do not agree on the meaning of the last line—whether it is a crestfallen recognition that all is lost, or an admonition to turn inward. Most likely, the "spirit's treasure" forced away is a barely veiled reference to the attempt to convert Lutherans to Catholicism in the wake of the 1629 Edict of Restitution. This process occurred across Germany and created a country of people in religious flight. Seen in this way, "Tears of the Fatherland" was a plea not just to end the war, but also to end the religious persecution that both caused and accompanied it. At the same time, the last line admonishes to remain steadfast in faith. The "tears" in the title are not, then, tears of emotion. Instead, they mark the genre, a lament for a lost loved one, a threnos, which, as one rhetorical handbook published in 1630 defined it, "is a lamentation for the destruction of cities and countries," written as another such handbook states, "with tears."[67] Bitter but possessing fortitude, these were the tears of stoics.

V

And still, the maw of war continued to demand its due. In September 1631, the Swedish victory at Breitenfeld succeeded in raising the hopes of the Protestant forces. But it also made the Emperor desperate, and he turned again to Wallenstein, who had retired to his ducal estate in Bohemia. The greatest military entrepreneur of his era, Wallenstein dramatically increased the size and fitness of Catholic forces in the field. Meanwhile, Gustavus Adolphus had made his way deep into German territory, reaching Augsburg in April 1632. The march to Vienna was now achievable, but Wallenstein could easily trap him deep in upper Germany, with no escape route north. To avoid a direct conflict with Wallenstein's numerically superior army, Gustavus Adolphus encamped his forces in Nuremberg, and Wallenstein laid siege to the city, hoping to starve the citizens and the Swedish army. The encounter proved a debacle for both sides. About 10,000 citizens and 20,000 soldiers would die on the Swedish side, another 20,000 on the Imperial. Most of the deaths, however, were caused by hunger, typhus, and scurvy. Decimated, the Swedish troops pulled out of the city, and Wallenstein's troops followed in pursuit, finally engaging the Swedish general in November, just south of Leipzig, at Lützen. In one of the great battles of the Thirty Years War, the Swedes took a nominal victory, but the death of the tactical mastermind Gustavus Adolphus over-shadowed all else.[68] And within two years, the Catholic forces, powerfully aided by the Spanish, reversed the course of the war once again, achiev-ing a decisive victory at Nördlingen. The Swedes retreated from southern Germany, and most of their German allies, led by the king of Saxony, made peace with the emperor.

Signed in May 1635, the Peace of Prague foreshadowed the more famous Peace of Westphalia, still thirteen years away. In Prague, the prin-ciple *cuius regio, eius religio*, "whose realm, his religion," was reaffirmed and the Edict of Restitution was shelved for the next forty years. The Prot-estant states agreed not to form an alliance against the Emperor, and the territorial order was restored to lines drawn in November 1627, with the exceptions that Brandenburg received Pomerania, and Saxony took Lusa-tia. The new balance of power was not lost on Cardinal Richelieu, King Louis XIII's powerful minister. Days later he declared war on Spain, the other, more menacing branch of the Habsburg line. From 1635 to 1648, when the German War dragged itself to an end, the central axis of conflict turned on the struggle for European supremacy between the French Bour-bons and the Austrian and Spanish kings.

VI

No one knew more about the course of the war than Matthäus Merian, whose printing house in Frankfurt am Main published the *Theatrum Europaeum*, a detailed account, concentrated on the German lands, of the political, moral, social, and natural events of the time. An eighty-one-year endeavor, which began in 1637, the twenty-one-volume *Theatrum Europaeum* reported on battles and sieges as well as comets and earth-quakes. In fact, it remains our most detailed textual and pictorial source of the war, and indeed of Germany in the seventeenth century. Yet for all its *militaria*, the intention of the work was not to stoke fascination with battles and bloodshed but rather its opposite: to cultivate peace as the "desired goal of all loyal patriots," as the author of the text of the first volume put it, and to mourn the "horribly plagued Germany," our "beloved fatherland."[69]

By the 1640s, Germany lay in ruins, its "beautiful form," in Merian's words, "now disfigured."[70] The destruction was everywhere in plain sight: in collapsed cities and razed towns, in destroyed churches and plundered monasteries, and in deserted villages and fallow fields as far as the eye could see. "When a traveler views the current Germany, and puts up against it what was a few years ago," Merian wrote, "he cannot view it without shedding hot tears."[71]

Along with his sons Matthäus the Younger and Caspar, Merian created an enduring monument to this disfigured country. Entitled *Topographia Germaniae*, its first volume appeared in 1642, and the last of its sixteen volumes in 1654, four years after the elder Merian's death. It is an astonishing work, containing more than seventeen hundred city and town views and detailed textual descriptions of some three thousand places, mainly written by Martin Zeiller, one of the most popular travel authors of the time. But unlike the *Theatrum Europaeum*, the *Topographia Germaniae* shows us little about the actual horrors of war. Instead, Merian hoped that by "evoking the previous happiness and wonder," he might spur new generations to "maintain what has remained, rebuild what has fallen, and bring back what has been lost."[72]

The artistic rendering of these small places was particularly breathtaking. In their many views, maps, and sketches of buildings and monuments, Merian and his sons portrayed Germany, city by city, town by town.[73] In the first ten volumes, covering south Germany and Westphalia, the elder Merian made most of the illustrations; thereafter, for northern Germany, his son Caspar drafted most of them.[74] Some of the engravings are downright copies—not a few taken from the more than five hundred colored panoramas compiled by Georg Braun and Franz Hogenberg in the *Civitates Orbis Terrarum*.[75] Yet when they are Merian originals, the signature is unmistakable. Even if a battle or a siege is portrayed, the sun is almost always near its apogee, the trees verdant, the clouds benign, and the water

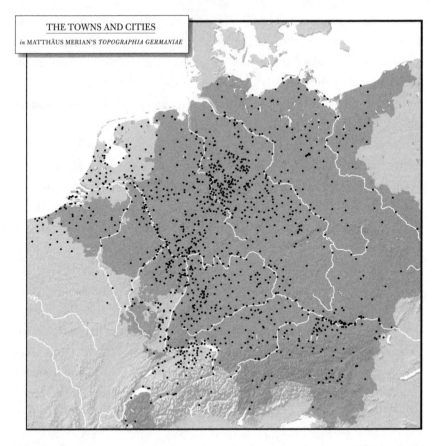

THE TOWNS AND CITIES
in MATTHÄUS MERIAN'S *TOPOGRAPHIA GERMANIAE*

placid. Some commentators have remarked on the absence of life in these images, yet what they might see as a desire to simplify is actually Merian's attempt to evoke a *locus amoenus*, a pleasant and peaceful place, against the *locus terribilis* of war and destruction.

The sense of naturalness and permanence that pervades the work was of course deliberate. An attentive student of Dutch landscape painting, Merian placed Germany's cities in the frame of serene nature, with commerce present but never distracting, and the panoramas generally wide and deep. He organized his compositions sometimes from a slightly elevated foreground, sometimes from a bird's-eye view, with the angles varying. We can see the port of Constance, for example, as if from a glider coming in from eastern lakeside, our view equally captured by the distant mountains and enveloping hills. We see not just a city but also a whole landscape, an effect created by Merian's division of his view into a clearly distinct foreground, middle ground, and background. The center of the city occupies the middle of the frame, but our eyes wander to where the Rhine trails off to the distant *Untersee*. Marked by exceedingly clear lines and conspicuous white spaces, Merian's engravings emphasized surface over solidity, giving them a peculiarly luminous quality.

As was the case with Ortelius's atlas, the luminous quality of Merian's cities and towns drew inspiration from a spiritualist vision that eschewed dogmatic strife. A native of Basel, Merian had sojourned extensively in Lyon, Paris, and the Netherlands, where he became close to dissenting and persecuted groups, especially the Huguenots. In Frankfurt am Main, he was a confidant of spiritualist circles and an anonymous publisher of their works, and in this context fell under the suspicion of the city's censors.[76] He was no hero, however. Merian stayed clear of the authorities, toned religious polemics down when they entered into the texts of his illustrated volumes, and chose instead to portray his fatherland, as he called it, in a state of repose.

The *Topographia Germaniae* proved an immense success. Some volumes went through five or more editions, with each edition printing between five and ten thousand copies.[77] Despite the intricacy of the work,

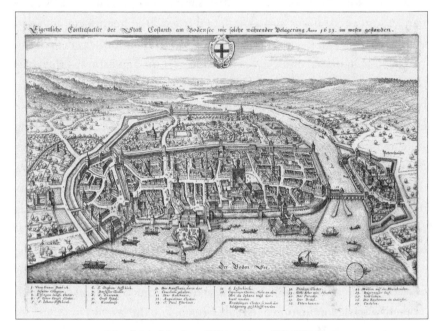

Matthäus Merian, "Constance," in Merian,
Topographia Sueviae, 1643.

and the rich text that accompanied the depictions, the volumes were only moderately expensive. Poor townsmen and peasants did not buy them, but as times improved well-off citizens did—so that two hundred years later they were still sometimes found as family heirlooms in German towns.[78] As Germans immersed themselves in Merian's landscapes, they came to see their towns and cities as belonging together—as part of a visual expression and a spiritualist longing for peace.

VII

When peace finally came in 1648, it was attended with high expectations and great fanfare. Negotiations in the Catholic town of Münster and the Protestant town of Osnabrück had been going on for five years, and during this time, the war ground on, with some of the final battles, like Freiburg in August 1644, Jankow in March 1645, and Zusmarshausen in May 1648, being among the bloodiest of the conflict.

In its final form, the Peace of Westphalia consisted of two treaties, the first between Sweden and the Emperor, the second between France and the Emperor, with both involving the allies as well. After proclaiming a "Christian and universal peace and a perpetual truce," the treaties commanded the warring parties to entertain, with respect to their former enemies, an "everlasting amnesia, amnesty, or pardon."[79] This amnesty was the basis for restoring ecclesiastical property to the baseline year 1624, thus nullifying the Edict of Restitution, which had played such a deleterious role in prolonging the war. Bavaria and the Habsburg crown lands, including Bohemia and Silesia, constituted exceptions to this rule, taking 1630 as their base year. The Counter-Reformation won back by force of arms was thus cemented in much of the south and east of Germany; the Hussite civilization of Bohemia was as a result shattered; and multireligious Silesia remained a ruin, save for three impressive "peace churches" where Protestants could worship. The treaty also reaffirmed the principle "*cuius regio, eius religio*," although it made exceptions for religiously mixed imperial cities such as Augsburg, and it recognized the Reformed (Calvinist) Church as a religious denomination of equal status before the law.

The Peace of Westphalia also made far-reaching territorial changes in the Empire, affecting both its external shape and its internal territorial order. Holland and Switzerland, de facto outside the Empire, were now also de jure independent of it. In recompense for its immense bloodletting, Sweden received western Pomerania, Stettin, Stralsund, Wismar, the dioceses of Bremen and Verden, as well as the islands of Rügen, Usedom, and Wollin. It consequently controlled significant sections of the north German coast and guarded the mouth of the Elbe, Oder, and Weser Rivers. Sweden also craved control over the Baltic, and, in doing so, elicited subsequent conflict with Poland and Denmark. In 1648 the threat of Swedish and Imperial power had induced France to support the territorial expansion of Brandenburg, still more pawn than player in the theater of European politics. As a result, Brandenburg received the eastern part of Pomerania and significant stretches of territory from the former bishoprics of Halberstadt, Minden, and Magdeburg. The feeble House of Hohenzollern, whose lands had been run over at will during the war, now emerged as a German territory second in size only to Austria. Its new prince, the (not yet Great) Elector Frederick William, had studied at the University of Leiden, was a devotee of neo-stoic political philosophy, and would soon raise a formidable standing army, making Prussia a significant regional power by the end of his reign in 1688. Saxony was the other regional power propelled to prominence after the war. During the war, it had supported the Emperor, then Sweden, and then the Emperor again. At the Peace of Westphalia, it received only Lusatia, which it had already taken a decade earlier. Over the next half century, Saxony's rulers spent considerable money on music and art, and by the end of the seventeenth century, Dresden was already becoming to Berlin as Athens to Sparta.

In the south and west, the struggle between the more formidable powers of France and the Habsburgs proved decisive. The peace treaty permanently destroyed the Spanish road, the route by which the Spanish Habsburgs marched troops to the Netherlands, thus allowing France to break the Habsburg encirclement. The Kingdom of France now occupied significant sections of Lorraine, parts of Alsace, and, straddling the Rhine at Breisach and Philippsburg, it soon became a constant threat for southwest Germany.[80] But the Habsburg emperor had retained patches of land as far west as Breisgau, and in protecting this territory, sometimes called

Anterior Austria, he would become the principal protector of southwest Germany against the further incursions of an increasingly powerful France.

The postwar German nation was not easy to define. In *The Present State of Germany*, first published in 1667 under a pseudonym and with a false place of publication, the famous jurist Samuel Pufendorf called it "an irregular body, like a monster, if at least it be measured by the common rules of politics and jurisprudence."[81] Pufendorf cleverly argued that Aristotelian political categories could not capture the complexities of the Holy Roman Empire—neither a "limited kingdom," nor "a body or system of many sovereign states and princes," but "something without a name that fluctuates between these two."[82] Pufendorf defended the Empire and wanted it strengthened against "furious diseases," the principal of which—in view of the threat of France—was that initiative had passed to the powerful states. The treaty conferred upon them the right to make foreign alliances, so long as not directed against the Emperor and the Empire; and it gave them far-reaching, if not quite absolute power over their subjects.

The Germany that emerged appeared very different from a century earlier, when Sebastian Münster had imagined Germania as illuminated by the vibrant cities of the south and west. With the exception of Cologne, no city west of the Elbe River had more than 30,000 inhabitants, while in the south only Nuremberg, Prague and Vienna had a larger population. By 1700, Germany's large urban centers were in the north: Hamburg, with roughly 70,000 denizens, Berlin with 55,000, Cologne with 42,000, and Dresden with 40,000. Two of these cities were capitals of powerful absolutist states, and two were ports with access to the Atlantic. German cities had by now fallen far behind their western European counterparts. With populations well over 500,000, Paris and London each outsized the ten most populous cities in Germany combined.[83]

Numbers, however, do not tell the whole story. Before the Thirty Years War, Germany's most powerful cities were fiercely independent. Some cities, like Hamburg and Bremen, successfully withstood princely power and maintained their freedoms. Most cities, however, paid dearly for the resistance they amassed. In 1664, the Elector and Archbishop of Mainz occupied Erfurt, accelerating its decline; and in 1681, France annexed Strasbourg, inaugurating a long process by which that city, once so central to German humanism, became part of the French kingdom. A similar fate befell Königsberg, a German city in ducal Prussia outside the Empire. When the Prussian crown pressed it for money in order to finance the Northern Wars, the citizens of Königsberg demurred, but Prussian arms swiftly broke their resistance. To Pufendorf, the general trend was evident. "Now the wealth of many [imperial cities] has been reduced," he wrote, "and we may probably enough conjecture that they will in some time be brought entirely under the yoke of the princes."[84] The future belonged with Vienna, Berlin, and Dresden, as well as with a series of smaller upstart cities like Stuttgart and Munich, Mannheim and Kassel, all depending for their luster on the fortunes of dynastic houses.

Finally, in the harsh, underappreciated countryside, where some three-fourths of the people actually lived, there were also significant shifts.[85] In the course of repopulation, people from the mountain highlands moved into the depopulated but fertile hills and valleys of Upper Germany. Some of this movement was religiously inspired, especially from Austria, where the Treaty of Westphalia meant the end of hope for Protestants who had not fled earlier. In other parts of Germany, significant migration took place from regions unaffected by the war to recently devastated and depopulated areas. In addition, princes, like the Elector of Brandenburg, purposely settled migrants, preferably from the Netherlands, on newly claimed land.

If migration was one side of the population story, fertility was the other. Historians estimate that averages of five to six children per family were necessary in order to achieve lasting population regeneration in this period. This assessment points to not only a high number of women dying in childbirth but also to levels of child mortality such that a third of the children still died in the first year, another seventh by the third, and barely half of children reached the age of twenty.[86] For those who looked closely, high rates of child mortality were as visible as destroyed castles and monasteries. One "sees children without end but few men old enough to serve in the military," noted an observant Italian traveler in 1662.[87] In these years, some families had few children, others more. Grimmelshausen fathered ten children; a pastor named Alexander Bosch, whose siblings had been torn away by the plague in 1629, sired sixteen. It was of course their wives who mightily struggled, first in bearing children, then in taking care of them.

VIII

The struggle was all the more remarkable since Germany had by no means escaped the valley of treacherous times. Various wars continued throughout the seventeenth century. The Dutch War of 1672 to 1678, the War of the Palatine Succession from 1688 to 1697, as well as the Northern Wars and the Turkish Wars—all had a deleterious impact on economic life. If it remains an exaggeration to collectively call these wars "the second Thirty Years War," the very comparison points to the impact of ongoing hostilities.[88] Fertility receded again, and some areas confronted significant devastation. Struggling Pomerania was again decimated in the course of hostilities between Sweden and Prussia. The Palatinate likewise witnessed dramatic depopulation in the last two decades of the seventeenth century. More ordinary problems also beset the population. The incidences of plague receded, if often imperceptibly. The price of grain, still the surest predictor of mortality, fluctuated erratically, and those fluctuations lasted well into the eighteenth century, periodically sending mortality soaring. As late as 1708–1709, an exceptionally cold winter, followed by rain, flood, and plague, reduced the population of ducal Prussia by a third.[89]

In these ways, the crisis of the long seventeenth century seemed to drag on interminably. The famous comet of 1664 struck fear of worse to come, moving Paul Gerhardt, next to Martin Luther the most popular hymnist in German Protestantism, to compose a song whose second stanza rings:

Die Zeichen in der Höh	The signs in the high
Erwecken Ach und Weh,	Wake pain and sigh,
Es hat in nächsten Jahren	In the coming years
Die ganze Welt erfahren	The whole world saw
Die brennenden Kometen	That burning comets
Sind traurige Propheten.	Are sad prophets.[90]

Evoking the prophecies of 1618, which brought Elector Frederick V of the Palatinate to Prague and marked the beginning of the Thirty Years War, Gerhardt suggests that the sad prophets have come once again, and that only repentance could save the people. A pastor in the St. Nicholas Church in Berlin, Gerhardt became the most limpid and lyrical voice of human suffering in the baroque era. Likening ordinary people to children wandering in the storms of plague, war, and fear, his songs moved the heart and demonstrated that the era remained steadfastly religious, seldom questioning, as did Grimmelshausen, how God could countenance such suffering.[91] But there was also optimism, buoyed by a religiosity that held fast to the bounty of nature and the mercy of the Lord. This optimism did not blind him to the injustices that beset his society or to the ravages of the land, which he lamented with force. But Gerhardt, like Gryphius, understood that his time on earth was ephemeral, as was the destruction that marred his country. As Gerhardt wrote:

Ich bin Gast auf Erden	I am a guest here on earth
Und hab hier kein Stand;	and have here no stand;
Der Himmel soll mir werden,	For me it is the life after,
Da ist mein Vaterland.	There is my fatherland.[92]

II

THE
COPERNICAN
TURN

HISTORY IS FULL OF EVIDENCE OF THE LINGERING POWER OF inherited authority. After the discovery of the so-called New World, more than a century passed before mapmakers stopped editing Ptolemy's ancient maps, which showed only Europe, Asia, and Africa. Copernicus's discovery that the planets revolved around the sun, revealed in his *De Revolutionibus Orbium Coelestium* of 1543, met a similar fate. Nearly a century later, cartographers, including the best among them, continued to hedge their bets. In the "Cosmographical Introduction" to his celebrated *Atlas Novus*, published in Amsterdam in 1635, Willem Blaeu put forward two contradictory theories, one that depicted Copernicus's heliocentric model, the other Ptolemy's planets moving in cycles and epicycles around a stationary earth.[1]

It was Willem's son, Joan Blaeu, who became one of the first commercial cartographers to embrace Copernicus without equivocation. In the background to the world map of his *Atlas Major* of 1662, he depicted classical gods representing planets, along with the two halves of the spherical earth, and made them all orbit Apollo, the god of the sun. Yet the younger Blaeu merely gathered knowledge, he did not create it. He never actually surveyed a territory himself, calculated the precise distances between towns, or traced the bend and bows of rivers. Instead, he bought copperplates, copied and then slightly changed the maps of predecessors and competitors, and paid other cartographers for their maps, which he then reproduced.[2] When he sided with Copernicus against Ptolemy, he simply put on a map what most scholars knew to be true.

Nevertheless, his *Atlas Major*, which comprised eleven volumes and contained nearly six hundred maps, was one of the most extensive and expensive atlases ever made.[3] Intended for wealthy patrons, the *Atlas Major* found its way into the libraries of leading universities, the houses of well-to-do merchants, and the castles of powerful princes. Indeed, the atlas was so lavish that some people, like Prince Johan Willem Friso, governor of Friesland, even had a special bookcase carved for it. Intricately detailed, the maps captivated their viewers by creating the illusion that by turning pages, one literally sailed the seas and traversed the land.

Was this, however, truly the way to know one's country? In a parable entitled "On Exactitude in Science," Jorge Luis Borges, the twentieth-century Argentine author, wrote of a fictional empire whose subjects had worked assiduously to perfectly map it at a scale of nearly one to one, so that "the map of a single province occupied the entirety of a city, and the map of the empire, the entirety of a single province."[4] Unfortunately, later generations, less enamored with cartographic ways of knowing, ignored the vaunted map of the empire and sacrificed it "to the inclemencies of sun and winters."[5]

Was Germany in the eighteenth century like Borges's imagined empire? As we have seen, the initial apprehension of Germany as a two-dimensional space, which occurred around 1500, resulted in a transition from an itinerary to a mapped sense of space. The subsequent period, spanning the next two centuries, witnessed a deepening in how Germans saw, portrayed, and represented their nation. Yet as the picture of the nation became increasingly reified and the mapping of Germany increasingly precise, it no longer told people what they needed to know. Instead, the German lands underwent fundamental political and ideological transitions, and these resulted in a paradigmatic shift in the way one knew and represented the German nation.

Part II argues that Germany in the second half of the eighteenth century resembled Borges's imagined empire. The time had passed when one could fathom the nation by an ever more accurate depiction of its cities, towns, and countryside. Like Borges's "later generations," Germans slowly turned to new modes of understanding their nation, and this "Copernican turn" completely changed how they knew and experienced their country.

The first innovation involved the advent of sacrificial patriotism, which deepened allegiances to states within Germany, and even created nascent nations. In the waning decades of the eighteenth century, Germany remained a geographical space, loosely framed by the Holy Roman Empire, in which a number of different countries seemed to be emerging—indeed, Prussia, Bavaria, Austria, and even Württemberg were sometimes referred to, and treated, as if they were nations themselves. Just as there are nowadays many examples of separate nations in which language does not divide countries, as is the case in much of Central and South America, so it was entirely conceivable then that central Europe north of the Alps would fracture into a series of nations, or fatherlands, each speaking German, or a dialect of it. This was not only conceivable; it is exactly what Germans anticipated.[6] It is telling that in the late eighteenth century (when utopias were first thought of temporally—imagined in the future rather than in another place), no one in the German lands sketched out the contours of a future German nation.[7] Rather, enlightened authors such as Wilhelm Ludwig Wekhrlin dreamed of a future state (he had Württemberg in mind) of "beautiful and well-built streets," "blooming fields," and "navigable rivers" in which the ruler, animated by physiocratic ideas, created a land of prosperity and peace.[8]

Chapter 4, "Partition and Patriotism," shows how new forms of patriotism in the German lands first took hold in territorial states—foremost Prussia and Bavaria, but also smaller places like Württemberg and Osnabrück—that were either threatened by, or subject to, partition. It was the specter of partition, with the tearing apart of Poland a chilling example, that fueled attachment to individual fatherlands. As a result of this new sentiment, Germany became a nation deeply divided, with powerful individual states vying to become countries of their own.

Looking back, nationalist historiography recalled this development as if it represented the nadir of the German national story. And in some senses, that historiography was right. Yet it is not clear that contemporaries were as troubled as later chroniclers. After all, some parts of the original space of German-speaking Europe had already turned Swiss and Dutch, and large parts were taken up by conglomerate states, like Prussia and Austria. No one disparaged these states because they were multiethnic. At the end of the century, German-speaking subjects constituted a numerical minority in Austria and around half the population of Prussia. Prussian patriots did not think less of Prussia because it was nearly half Polish-speaking, and no one, save for a small number of Polish nationalists, thought it untoward that the second largest city in Prussia was Warsaw. As late as 1800, there was no reason to make political space in the German lands match so-called nation-space.

The second breakthrough, largely occurring in the decades between

1770 and 1790, can be observed by noting what people saw when they traveled. Using the profusion of late-eighteenth-century travel reports, chapter 5, "The Surface and the Interior," begins by portraying travelers as they looked at cities, scrutinized the physiognomy of people, inspected churches and buildings, admired vistas, marveled at gardens, and viewed works of art: in short, as they saw the nation's surface. It then charts the transition whereby travelers came to seek out the nation's metaphorical interior: the country's basic rhythms in rhymes and folk songs, in the power of poetry, and in the feeling of the landscape, melancholic and tragic in turn. By the 1790s, young intellectuals, who would soon be called Romantics, were beginning to bring the two ways of knowing the nation together, creating a novel and interiorized sense of the country. This was a paradigm shift of immense importance. If nation was once something on the outside, a patch of earth to which one belonged, or an emblem of a culture one was proud of, it became during the era of early Romanticism something immanent, or inside, a statement of who one was. This breakthrough was no less significant than when Germany, around 1500, was first conceived as a two-dimensional mapped space. The new epistemology of nationhood, as it came into focus around 1770, is often mistaken for early nationalism. It certainly laid the foundation for nationalism. It was not yet, however, the thing itself.

Nationalism, the third shift, transformed the existential categories that had previously defined the nation in almost every fundamental way, altering how Germans imagined the past and future of their nation, redefining who belonged to the nation and who did not, and reordering conceptions of social hierarchy. Put schematically, nationalism changed the very notion of before and after, inside and outside, and above and below.

We can see the temporal dimension—redefining the relation of before, during, and after—of these fundamental shifts with greater clarity when we consider the long view. In 1500, when we began our story, nation describers evoked the distant past of Tacitus but projected virtually no idea of the distant future. By 1800, in contrast, nationalism infused nation thinking with a new sense of possibilities, especially with respect to the future. Delivered in Berlin in 1807–1808, Johann Gottlieb Fichte's famous *Addresses to the German Nation* drew their immense force from the attempt to galvanize a small coterie of intellectuals—*die Wissenschaft*—to train and rouse a nation to great deeds, which Fichte imagined would eventually culminate three centuries later in a nation-state called "the Republic of the Germans."[9]

The question of inside and outside was no less fundamental. Around the year 1500, inclusion and exclusion was mainly a spatial or geographical question. Was Trier a French or a German city? Johannes Cochlaeus asked in this time. We may recall that he answered himself, as if addressing an ancillary detail, by noting that "most ascribe Trier more to France than to Germany, although German is the local language."[10] In the early articulations of nationalism, some three hundred years later, such casual demarcations were no longer viable. The question of inside and outside, who and what belonged, was now of basic importance, turning on a conception of a coherent people, and not merely a space with diverse people in it. When Ernst Moritz Arndt appealed to the fatherland "as far as the German tongue sounds," he had in mind an aggregation of individuals into a group, and not a mere geographical space. Conversely, the other, the outside, was no longer thought of in additive terms—as side-by-side nations, as sixteenth-century humanists insisted that they were on maps and in the plan of God. Rather, nationalism projected emotions of love and hate onto one's own and other nations, making "inside" a limited "imagined community" that brought forth passion, devotion, and sacrifice, while "outside," or the "other," elicited curiosity or admiration, but as often aversion and even hate.

Finally, nationalism, as it developed around 1800, conceived of the social order as a horizontal kinship, the precise opposite of the early-modern caste system that could hardly imagine the peasant—the lowliest figure in this vertical order and in many places existing in states of bondage—as the repository of national virtue. Before the age of nationalism, Germans were pictured and labeled in costume books, on the margins of maps, and in descriptions of the world, as nobles or town dwellers. Only during the twilight of the old order would German intellectuals begin to conceive of the simple, rural *Volk* as standing for, and representing, the best of the nation.

Chapter 6, *"De l'Allemagne,"* demonstrates that nationalism came late to the German lands. In Germany, it actually had a limited sociological base, and became a genuinely popular way of thinking only when states, primarily Prussia, backed it with significant military and financial resources. Contrary to popular understandings, nationalism played virtually no part in the actual anti-Napoleonic war, and war was not the experiential ground of nationalism. Defeat was. The humiliation of a partitioned nation—Prussia—set nationalist intellectuals in motion, just as the larger context of nationalism was the dissolution of states and the fact that nearly 60 percent of the people in the German lands changed rulers in the course of the Napoleonic Wars.[11] Movement, change, the collapse of old structures, defeat in war more than victory: these were the essential conditions allowing German nationalism to flourish for the first time. Austria, in this period, would never know the same humiliation. Although a small group of German nationalists gathered around the Habsburg court, their brand of German nationalism, typically more strategic than deeply felt, lacked the added force of trauma. This cannot be emphasized enough. While isolated articulations of German nationalism existed prior to Napoleon overrunning Prussia in 1806, it was the defeated fatherland of Prussia that brought the new nationalism to the fore.

As a whole then, Part II, "The Copernican Turn," tries to explain how this dramatic change in the very meaning and significance of the term "nation" came about, and how it is that nationalism did not "engender nations," as the philosopher and social anthropologist Ernest Gellner famously argued, but rather emerged as a new and powerful answer to the old question of what a nation is.

CHAPTER 4

PARTITION AND PATRIOTISM

c. 1700–1770

What pity is it
That we can die but once to serve our country!

—JOSEPH ADDISON, *CATO*, ACT IV, SC. IV

• • •

The patriot can only seldom by death
be useful to his country.

—THOMAS ABBT, ON THE REASON

FOR WRITING HIS BOOK *ON MERITS*

THE PRUSSIAN ARMY ENCOUNTERED RUSSIAN AND AUSTRIAN FORCES in Kunersdorf, a village just sixty miles east of Berlin, on August 12, 1759. Amid deafening cannon shot and blinding smoke, Major Ewald von Kleist rode at the front of his battalion directly into a line of grenadiers. A shot hit his right hand, another his left; then three more shattered his leg and peeled him from his horse. In the night, Cossacks robbed him of his clothes and boots, leaving him to lie half naked and deserted in the mud of the moors of the Oder River. The next morning a Russian officer clothed him and ordered him carried to town, where a surgeon attempted to clamp together Kleist's shattered bones. In the night of August 22, Kleist's spliced bones split apart again, fatally rupturing an artery.[1]

A distant relation to the later and more brilliant Heinrich, Ewald von Kleist had achieved fame for "The Spring," a rococo poem that depicted life in a happy time, and for *Cissides and Paches*, an epic poem written in 1758. Ostensibly recounting a Macedonian battle against a far stronger Athens after the death of Alexander the Great, the poem was in fact meant as an allegorical reflection on the Prussian predicament during the

Seven Years War.[2] It tells of the two warriors trapped in a fortress, fighting to the death, when Paches gives the dying, wounded, exhausted, and thirsty Cissides blood, drawn from the bodies of fallen fellow fighters, to drink, making the army into a band of blood brothers. It was this quasi-aristocratic brotherhood, extended to the ordinary soldiers, rather than a chain of command, that held the beleaguered army together.[3] By the end of the poem, Cissides and Paches, as well as all their soldiers, die heroic deaths. Impressed with their courage, the victorious Athenian leader "has the ashes of the two friends preserved in an urn, and has for them an impressive monument built."[4] The leader then returns to Athens, but with his army so weakened that Macedonia survives. "And so was through the courage of the two friends," Kleist concludes, "the destruction of the Fatherland avoided."[5]

II

The Seven Years War was the last of a series of armed conflicts that had begun in 1740, when Maria Theresa assumed the Habsburg throne, and predatory rulers contested the ascension. Sensing Austrian vulnerability and seeing an early chance for attaining glory, Frederick II, who was soon to be known as "the Great," immediately marched into Silesia, a conquest that effectively doubled Prussia's population and dramatically increased its economic power.[6] Prior to the invasion, Prussia had the fourth largest standing army on the continent (behind France, Russia, and Austria) but was tenth in terms of area and thirteenth in population.[7] By all measures save one, Prussia was a power of the second rank, Austria of the first, and Silesia was one of Austria's most valuable lands. The resulting War of Austrian Succession, the bloodiest encounter on German territory since the Thirty Years War, dragged on for most of the decade, and concluded in 1748 with the Peace of Aachen, which granted to Prussia the territory of Silesia and to Maria Theresa the recognition as the legitimate heir of the Habsburg crown. Henceforth, however, Austrian political and military strategy would aim at regaining its lost territory and reducing, as the Austrian statesman Wenzel Anton von Kaunitz later put it, "the House of Brandenburg to its primitive state *de petite puissance très secondaire*."[8]

For Prussia, the certainty of renewed war after the Peace of Aachen accelerated the militarization of its society. Whereas many states spent half of their peacetime income on the military, Prussia spent more than 80 percent in that way, and fielded two times as many soldiers per capita as Austria, four times as many as France, and five times as many as Bavaria.[9] Even in peacetime, more than 4 percent of Prussia's male population was in the army—a figure surpassed only by the mercenary polity of Hesse-Kassel, whose dukes sold some 6 percent of the country's men off to serve what were often life terms in the armies of other states.[10] When measured as a fraction of the economy, the overwhelming force of the military in Prussia was daunting. One scholarly estimate puts the percentage of Prussia's national income devoted to the military at 35 percent in 1760—an enormous sum, far larger than that of any other major power.[11]

Prussia also bound its country to its army, a fact especially decisive for the scions of its noble houses. Whereas in other countries, the nobility constituted an independent power base and the officer corps remained an international mix, in Prussia the nobility found in armed service a calling, becoming, as Frederick II never tired of repeating, the "foremost and most brilliant estate of the state."[12] Throughout the eighteenth century, more than 90 percent of Prussian army officers were noblemen, almost all of them from Prussia itself. As a result, the Prussian officer corps enjoyed levels of social cohesion found nowhere else in Europe, and it was soon emulated, in spirit if not degree, in France, Savoy, and eventually, if less successfully, Austria.[13] Militarization also powerfully shaped the general ethos of the Prussian nobility. In the late eighteenth century, the majority of Prussian noblemen had served in the army, with the sacrifice of some families already severe. For example, when Ewald von Kleist fell at Kunersdorf, he was only one of twenty-three members of the Kleist clan who would die in the course of Frederick's Silesian wars.[14] And the Kleists were hardly alone: some fifteen hundred officers, almost all Prussian nobles, sacrificed their lives for Frederick, an immense aristocratic bloodletting.[15]

In Prussia, the sacrificial ethos of its aristocratic class, the Junkers, was reinforced by a rigidly militarist social order.[16] Since 1733, military recruitment had been at least in part organized according to the canton system,

with all men between sixteen and thirty subject to conscription, roughly
for twenty years, although actual military time was restricted to only two
to three months and the rest of the year was spent in unpaid leave working
the land of the noble estates. This "military-agrarian complex" allowed
noble families to replicate in the military sphere social structures of agrarian domination on the heath, whether as lord over serf or capitalist farmer
over hired hand.[17] In either case, the families who gave marching orders
were also the bosses on the farm. If the system did not blanket all of Prussia with the same intensity, the militarized barrack state proved crushingly
oppressive to the Prussian-born conscripted day laborers, craftsmen, and
former bonded serfs who made up the rank and file.[18] In addition, it placed
Prussia in the company of Russia, which had also developed a territorially
based recruitment system, if with less efficiency and more draconian military service; together, these two countries formed something of an eastern
zone of military states whose power depended on their ability to extract
human rather than financial resources.[19]

Given this oppressive system, it comes as no surprise that the patriotism espoused by Kleist did not reach down the ranks. On the contrary,
the Prussian army registered roughly eighty thousand desertions in the
course of the Seven Years War.[20] Prussian tactics took ample cognizance
of this fact by insisting on rigid formation (exact postures, broad lines
three deep, and precise synchronization when holding and reloading
rifles) and inhuman punishment (such as running the gauntlet, where a
man is slowly walked through two rows of soldiers who take turns whip-
ping him). Frederick the Great himself wrote, in his *Instructions for the
Commanders of Cavalry Regiments*, that "the common soldier should
have more fear of his officer than the enemy in front of him."[21] This was
saying a great deal. In the course of a battle, roughly a third of the soldiers
would be lost, some killed by musket balls that pierced far less cleanly
than today's rifles, others by the unsanitized scalpels of overwhelmed
and ill-trained surgeons.[22] Moreover, unlike Ewald von Kleist, few of the
soldiers received proper burials. Instead, their corpses were placed in
large pits and covered with dirt, or placed in a pile and burned, as if soldiers were no more honorable than witches or forgers, as one eighteenth-
century military manual complained.[23] In this context, it should hardly

surprise that no one stopped to count battlefield losses. Commanders just guessed at them. There were no detailed statistics, no letters or records, and the names of fallen commoners were not recorded.

Despite its militarization, Prussia was still no match for the coalition of countries that came together in 1756, when France, Sweden, and Russia joined forces with Austria. It is hard to overestimate the profound impact of the new alliance. Since the Thirty Years War, the duel for European dominance between Austria and France had determined the main lineups in the continental wars. For more than a century, Catholic France had sided with Protestant Prussia in order to weaken Catholic Austria and gain influence over the religiously mixed western areas of the Holy Roman Empire. As a result, continental warfare rarely replicated the religious division of the Reformation and Austria could act as the principal protector of the German Empire against an aggressive France. A great deal of the pro-Austrian sentiment, especially in the vulnerable western principalities, derived from the centrality of Habsburg arms to imperial defense against the powerful and rapacious neighbor across the Rhine. The reversal in 1756—with France now on the side of Austria—proved all the more decisive.

Sensing himself encircled, Frederick invaded Saxony that August, commencing a war whose campaigns ranged from Quebec to the Caribbean and from the coast of Africa to the plains of northern India. No one expected Frederick to win. Even in his limited European theater, sheer ruin seemed the most likely outcome. This was also what almost happened. "*Je crois tout perdu*," the great king famously wrote after the Battle of Kunersdorf.[24] As the short road to Berlin lay virtually undefended and his army dispersed, successful pursuit by Austrian and Russian troops would have meant certain defeat and the subsequent partition of Frederick's lands. Likely, this meant East Prussia being ceded to Russia, Pomerania to Sweden, scattered territories in the west to France, and Silesia back to Austria.[25] According to the calculations of the famous historian Jacob Burckhardt, Prussia would have retained only the Mark Brandenburg, a sandy territory the size of Saxony (but without that duchy's wealth), and its capital, Berlin, a city half as large as Vienna.[26]

But Frederick's enemies failed to take advantage of his debacle at Kunersdorf. Hobbled by the requirements of continental warfare and concerned about Prussia's remaining forces, they refused, like the Athenian king in *Cissides and Paches*, to pursue.[27] It was to be one of the many miracles of the House of Hohenzollern. Another occurred in 1762, after the sudden death of Empress Elizabeth of Russia, when Czar Peter III, a pro-Prussian Frederick enthusiast, ascended the throne and ordered the withdrawal of Russian troops. The fatherland, as the poem presaged, was thus saved.

III

In the era during and after the Seven Years War, "my fatherland" some-times referred to a locality, sometimes a region, and sometimes the nation. Increasingly, however, it evoked the attachment of elites to a modern ter-ritorial state.[28] In the course of the eighteenth century, the most import-ant of these states—Austria, Prussia, Saxony, Bavaria, and Hanover—had become increasingly sovereign relative to the Empire. Each pursued power for its own sake, not for a religious or national cause. In time, it bears repeating, these territories might have become German-speaking father-lands, countries, even nations, of their own.

Such fatherlands were especially important in the eastern half of the Empire. If a contemporary of Kleist had folded a map of the German Empire in half, creasing it at a line passing roughly through Augsburg, Erfurt, and Lübeck, the states of Prussia, Saxony, Bavaria, and the lands of Austria would practically take up the whole of the east. To the left of the fold there would be Hanover and Württemberg, with only the latter's ruler not having the status of one of the seven princes who elects the Emperor. In the northern part, western Pomerania north of the river Peene belonged to Sweden, while Holstein, including the city of Altona, belonged to the Kingdom of Denmark. In the southwest, close to 300,000 subjects lived in Anterior Austria under Habsburg control.[29] Modern, medium- and large-scale territorial states would, in other words, cover much of the map. Moreover, the great territorial states also housed the majority of the popu-lation. In the 1780s, Austria (within the Empire), Prussia, the Electorates of Bavaria and Hanover, the Kingdom of Saxony, and the Grand Duchy of Württemberg already accounted for nearly 20 million of the Holy Roman Empire's roughly 28 million people.[30]

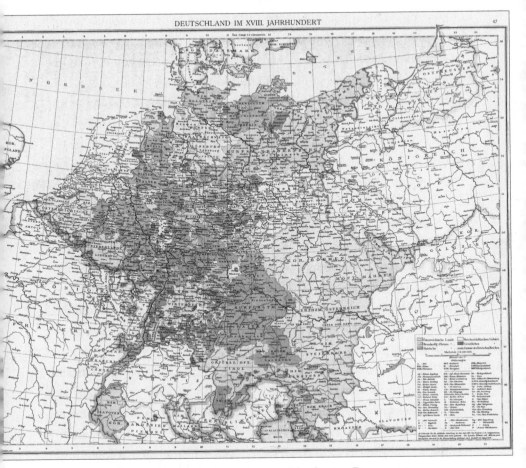

"Germany in the 18th Century," in Gustav Droysen,
Allgemeiner Historischer Handatlas (1886).

Much of the rest of the population lived in smaller states, like Hesse-Kassel and Hesse-Darmstadt, the Electorates of Cologne and of Mainz, the two halves of Mecklenburg, the Electoral Palatinate, and the Margraviate of Baden—all territories with an estimated population between 200,000 and 400,000 subjects. Below them was a string of smaller territories, and only a few of them were capable of financing significant standing armies. They were, however, wealthy enough to pursue enlightened projects and employ intellectual luminaries. Anhalt-Dessau, for example, was lauded and admired throughout the enlightened world for the stunning gardens at Wörlitz; Braunschweig-Wolfenbüttel employed the dramatist and apostle of tolerance Gotthold Ephraim Lessing as the curator of the Herzog August library; and Weimar hosted Goethe and Schiller.[31] All had a population of between 50,000 and 200,000. Below these territories were the patches of land ruled by the "free imperial knights," some 350 noble families whose properties domiciled as many as 400,000 subjects.[32]

Finally, there were the free imperial cities. Hamburg stood out, with a population of around 100,000; Nuremberg remained important, with a population of 50,000. Cologne and Bremen each had 40,000 inhabitants, and Frankfurt am Main and Regensburg, roughly 35,000. Thereafter the numbers dwindled. Augsburg, once a great humanist center, had become a provincial city of some 32,000 people. Ulm had half as many denizens, and Speyer half as many again.[33] Many of the fifty-one free "cities" had devolved into small towns, like Isny im Allgäu, or Gengenbach in the Black Forest, and collectively they had become specifically associated with the Empire. In Goethe's early version of *Faust*, written in the 1770s, a student in Auerbach's cellar in Leipzig calls out to the doctor, "You come from the Empire, one sees it in you," by which the student meant that he came from south Germany, the land of imperial cities.[34]

At least in the middle-sized and large states, territories assumed sharper, more pronounced contours. One index of this transition was the changing kinds of advice Veit Ludwig von Seckendorff gave in his influential *Teutscher Fürstenstaat (German Princely State)*, a handbook for rulers and their officials first published in 1656 and then reissued in a dozen new editions over the next century. A Dutch-influenced official of the Principality of Saxon-Gotha, Seckendorff admonished German rulers not to be satisfied with the rough geographic coordinates of the cosmographers, but to discern "how the [principality] is bordered, how the principalities and other lands are called that abut it, and at which localities of the principality such boundaries occur."[35] Seckendorff also insisted that princes ensure that borders are marked, whether "with rivers, stones and other boundary markers" that are permanent and "not with transient ditches, trees, and such things."[36]

His advice was seldom taken. Deep into the eighteenth century, many principalities continued to emphasize boundaries along routes, not peripheries, so that people imagined the extent of dynastic domains in linear terms, as length and width along roads, with borders serving merely as jurisdictional limits. Mapmakers likewise rendered borders imprecisely, essentially by drawing a pleasingly curved line around the outer edges of the farthest towns within a state's domain.[37] Descriptions often followed this inexact procedure. An eighteenth-century geographer described Thuringia as an "Earldom that borders toward the east on the Margrave of Meißen, but toward the west against the land of Hesse and on the so-called Eichsfeld."[38] Even the *Universal Encyclopedia* of Johann Heinrich Zedler, published in sixty-eight volumes between 1731 and 1754, described territorial states as a ruler's patrimony over a land that "at some time stops."[39]

As the eighteenth century progressed, however, a novel sense of territorial space set in. Anton Friedrich Büsching, a cutting-edge geographer and author of a tremendously influential *Description of the World*, argued that when evaluating the size of states, surveyors should calculate area rather than measure the distances traversed by intersecting diagonals. "Most useful to bring the state, as represented in the best land charts, into a square, or many squares," Büsching urged, "and to calculate its surface content according to geographic miles."[40] The splintered nature of German territories posed serious challenges to this procedure, because it required one to know the precise bow and bend of a territory's political borders, and most mapmakers chose the easy-to-outline imperial circles as the fundamental unit of analysis.[41]

An important exception was Nuremberg's Jean Baptiste Homann. He engraved nearly six hundred maps in folio size, half of them delineating territories in the Holy Roman Empire, and every one of them following the outlines of states or administrative units.[42] Homann's coloring schemes reinforced the strictly political image, darkly coloring the maps of political territories around the edges. The actual territory was washed in a lighter version of the same color, so that the territorial unit was highlighted on the sheet. The prominence of political toponyms, typically in uppercase letters for states, reinforced the importance of territorial divisions and suggested a Germany marked by a maze of interior borderlines.[43] Even Homann's city views, like his "Illustration of the imperial and commercial city of Frankfurt am Main, with its area and its borders," subordinated engraved skylines to depictions of the actual territories.

People also came to see states in depth, resulting in changing understandings of what territories contained. Seckendorff had suggested that each territory be divided into administrative units, and from there counted and appraised according to bailiwicks, towns, marketplaces, villages, individual farms, forests, rivers, and lakes; thereafter individual buildings,

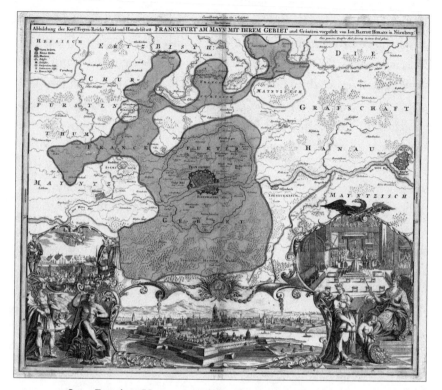

Jean Baptiste Homann, "Illustration of the Imperial and
Commercial City of Frankfurt am Main, with its Area and
its Borders," early eighteenth century.

and only then the people, divided into the three principal estates: nobility,
townsfolk, and peasants. The early editions of the posthumous "Seckendorff," as his handbook was called, celebrated the delicate equilibrium of
the feudal order. But in the course of the late seventeenth and early eighteenth centuries, absolute rulers registered significant gains at the expense
of the various estates beneath them, and by 1720 the editor of "the newest" and "with diligence improved" edition of "Seckendorff" excused the
seemingly apologetic tone of the first edition, which urged balance.[44]

Rulers, partly as a consequence of adopting innovative ways of evaluating their realm, began to shape their territories anew. Digging mines,
draining rivers and marshland, winning back arable land, and constructing
streets, they spurred economic activity and settled people.[45] The state itself
became larger and more significant. If it once sufficed to have a handful of
courtiers taking care of territorial business, specialists were now required,

leading to the growth of genuine bureaucracies. One should not overestimate their size. Excluding armies, even great powers remained small. In 1762, some 7421 officials in the direct employ of the crown administered the Austrian-Bohemian territories (excluding Tyrol and Anterior Austria), while in 1786 roughly half as many officials watched over Brandenburg-Prussia.[46] If modest in numbers, officials nevertheless tried to follow the advice of professors in the emerging field of *Polizeiwissenschaften*, or policy studies. Some scholars, like the Viennese Joseph von Sonnenfels, argued that the visible hand of the state should provide the order for society; others, like the influential Göttingen professor Johann Heinrich Gottlob von Justi, contended it was best to bring together the state's guiding hand with the mysterious workings of commerce. States, they both believed, could harness and control the passions and energies of the people while the land could yield wealth and the population soldiers.[47]

As the number of subjects a state possessed became more important, states began to count individual people. The novelty of this seemingly simple step bears underscoring, because in the long arc of human history, most people were never counted, registered, or even listed. The Church of Latter-Day Saints estimates that of the 26 billion people born between 1500 and 2010, only the names of 8 billion were ever recorded, while before 1500, all but the names of exceptional people have disappeared.[48] This is because at the beginning of the modern era, states and cities counted people only sporadically. Some German cities, usually before a siege, tallied their inhabitants once, as did Nuremberg as early as 1426 in anticipation of war with the Hussites.[49] Other cities counted subjects intermittently: for example, Speyer did so in 1470 and 1530, in order to regulate disputes over domains, and Cologne in 1570, to assess the number of religious refugees.[50] Religious institutions also did not count people. It was not until the sixteenth century that parishes began to keep records of baptisms and burials, first in Protestant lands, then—after the Council of Trent in 1545 and 1563—in Catholic territories as well. Yet the early parish registers remained patchy and unsystematic, and many were destroyed during the tumultuous Thirty Years War.

States began to count people because people mattered—not for themselves, but for the state. Sweden, Denmark, the Netherlands, France, and England had already calculated their populations, and in the course of the eighteenth century, major German states followed suit: Hesse and Prussia counted their subjects in the 1740s; the Habsburg monarchy (in the German-speaking lands) in 1754; Saxony in 1755; Württemberg in 1757; and Bavaria in 1777.[51] In this time, the term "statistic," first used in print by Gottfried Achenwall in 1749, came into general use, deriving its name not from numbers but, as the word itself betrays, from the description of states.[52] Achenwall depicted territorial states as ruling over land and people, and counted caste—the nobility, clergy, townsmen, and peasants—only with respect to political representation.[53] By the end of the eighteenth century, scholars who described states, like August Friedrich Wilhelm Crome, compared their territorial sizes with their population densities. The ratio of land to people was the best indicator of a country's civilization, Crome argued; he later extended this analysis to include financial resources and military might. Crome also devised tables that provided readers with a "sensory impression" of the relative population, wealth, and strength of the countries of Europe.[54]

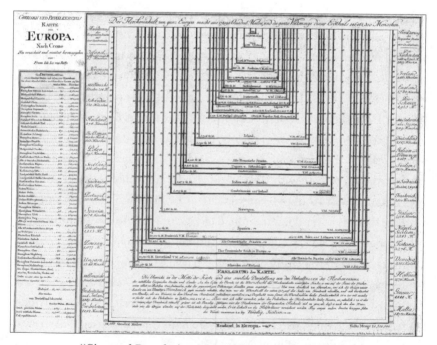

"Size and Population Map of Europe According to
[August Friedrich Wilhelm] Crome," redrawn and expanded
by Franz Johann Joseph von Reilly, 1794.

States, as the new science of statistics made clear, had become something more than merely the symbolic and spatial extension of dynastic houses. They had also become expressions of land and people, wealth and power.

IV

A young enlightener, barely twenty-three years of age, revealed the precise sinews of this new state-centered sensibility. Thomas Abbt was already a "professor of worldly wisdom" at the University of Frankfurt an der Oder, where the Battle of Zorndorf had raged just to the north, and the Battle of Kunersdorf just to the east. On the occasion of his daily walks, Abbt visited Ewald von Kleist's grave in the burial yard of the city church, and the postbattle atmosphere gave a sense of urgency to the scholar's work. Two years later, in 1761, he published *On Death for the Fatherland*, a clear-eyed work that rendered in prose sentiments what Kleist had already expressed in the more metaphorical language of poetry.

In his book, Abbt countered the opinion, first espoused by Montesquieu in 1748 in *The Spirit of the Laws*, that true patriotism was possible only in a republic, not in a monarchy. Abbt began from a different starting point: love and death—love for "the well ordered monarchy" and death, even a joyful death, of the sons for the fatherland. In a fatherland where the monarch is beneficent and the glory of the kingdom is dependent on the welfare of the subjects, these very subjects come to identify with the state, Abbt contended. If a war is then defensive and just, as seemed to him the case with Prussia, an intensified love for the fatherland followed, and this love—both natural sentiment and duty, both for the state and its regent—provided the source of the passion, even enthusiasm, that allows the individual subject to overcome the fear of death. Like the Spartans of old, the individual even perceives "the enjoyment of death" as a liberating sacrifice. As Abbt put it, echoing *Cissides and Paches*, it is "the blood, pulsing through our arteries, that our groaning fatherland drinks, in order to let it live again."[55] Moreover, the willingness to die for one's country had a crucial secondary effect: it transformed servile subjects into active, participating citizens.[56] Abbt did not make the point explicitly. Rather, Moses Mendelssohn, who being Jewish belonged to a religious group denied equal rights and privileges, underscored this "completely different standpoint." In his review of *On Death for the Fatherland*, Mendelssohn wrote:

> The evil that [war] brings with it is tied to an important advantage. . . . The distance between the different estates is reduced, and the citizens [*Bürger*] are brought close to a republican equality. In a warring monarchy, all are citizens, merit and not birth determines the estates, and the state becomes like a republic, which has elected the king as dictator.[57]

With mere argument, one had always to obey. But the deeds of war leveled the social edifice and opened the door to the participation of independent and willing citizens.

Criticism of Abbt's position did not surface until the conclusion of hostilities in 1763. The most prominent objection came from Friedrich Karl von Moser, a Württemberg Pietist and the eldest son of a distinguished jurist of the Holy Roman Empire. He argued that there was a narrow fatherland—"the land to which [the patriot] owes his sustenance and daily existence"—and a wider fatherland: the Holy Roman Empire of the German Nation.[58] In a tract entitled *On the National Spirit*, published in 1765, Moser wrote: "We too are a people of one name and one language, under one common ruler and one constitution, subject to the same body of law which determines our rights and our duties."[59] In the most vigorous statement written in the era of the Enlightenment detailing the general idea that Germany constituted a fatherland, Moser nevertheless admitted that Germany was beset with weakness: "Our constitution has been a puzzle for centuries, we have been the spoil of our neighbors, the subjects of their ridicule, a great and at the same time despised people."[60] Moser feared that Germans had become estranged from one another, cold and without empathy. He also worried that since 1740, when Frederick marched his troops into Silesia, the possibility of secession from the Reich threatened to tear the band that held Germans together.[61] At the core of the decline in German national sentiment was, then, according to Moser, the "military spirit of our time" and the "monstrosity of a military-patriotic governmental system"—in a word, even though he desisted from writing it, Prussia.[62]

The anti-Prussian thrust of the essay was, however, evident to Moser's contemporary readers. Unknown at the time was that Austria had paid for it.[63] Graf Johann Anton von Pergen, a protégé of Kaunitz, offered Moser a yearly pension of 1500 guilders, which Moser readily accepted despite his "shame."[64] Austria had also been instrumental in helping free Moser's father, who had languished in prison since 1759 for his outspoken opposition to the absolutist policies of Duke Carl Eugen of Württemberg. Even the title of Moser's tract, with the term "national spirit," was likely an Austrian invention suggested by Pergen.[65]

In the "national spirit debate," allegedly followed in "every half respectable tavern," the Prussians immediately fired back.[66] Abbt replied to Moser that there are Prussian and Austrian, but not German subjects: "When their princes have different interests, then it is no longer the duty of the Prussian or Austrian subjects to ask what the German Reich requires of him: but only what he owes to his fatherland, that means to that land, the laws of which protect him and make him happy."[67]

The qualifier "no longer" is revealing. In the period spanning the aggressive personal rule of the French king Louis XIV (1661–1715), or during the Second Turkish Siege of Vienna in 1683, the German Empire had once commanded a more unifying kind of allegiance and loyalty. But the "diplomatic revolution" of 1756 had forced Austria into an alliance with France, the traditional enemy of the Empire. When Prussia invaded Silesia immediately thereafter, the Empire failed to issue an imperial ban. And when imperial troops did fight against Frederick, they fared miserably. By 1761, many of the states that had contributed to the Imperial Army had drawn back their forces, crippling the Empire as a force for peace. As a result, a genuine patriotism for the Holy Roman Empire (*Reichspatriotismus*) fell to its nadir.[68]

V

The Seven Years Wars ended with a stalemate and a horrific toll of bloodletting. During its course, the war claimed the lives of well over a million people; in Prussia alone, more than 180,000 soldiers fell, and nearly twice as many perished due to privation and disease, bringing the total loss to roughly 10 percent of the population.[69] The other major combatants also bled profusely. Austria's military losses, which were at least as severe as Prussia's, included an estimated 32,600 killed on the field, another 93,400 who died from their wounds or from disease, 19,600 who were listed as missing, and 17,400 as crippled.[70] Saxony too was decimated.

Between the bloodletting and the exhaustion, the war also wrought a dramatic shift in the balance of power on the European continent. Before the war, there had been three major powers: Great Britain, France, and Austria. Now, significantly, there were five.[71] Russia and Prussia, hitherto powers of the middling order, advanced to powers of the first rank. Russia benefitted from its large population, abundant resources, skilled leadership, as well as the decline of both Poland to the west and the Ottoman Empire to the south. Prussia moved forward because of its military efficiency and sheer audacity. But Frederick the Great had lost his young-man's thirst for war, and Austria now became an increasingly volatile country. Frustrated at the loss of Silesia, Austria searched for compensation while a mountain of debt and the cumulative casualties of war pushed it to a more coercive, Prussian-style system of fiscal-military extraction. The result was the swift postbellum remaking of Austria into a menacing military might.[72] This shift occurred, moreover, as a power vacuum emerged in central Europe. France, which had previously acted as a financial and military counterweight to Austrian and Prussian aggression, amassed crippling military debts by the war's end, while Great Britain, having become master of the North Atlantic, decreased its overall continental engagement.[73] If there were now five powers, only three were active on the continent, and two of them, Prussia and Austria, had significant stakes in Germany, while the third, Russia, was pushing farther and farther west.

For the Holy Roman Empire, the external situation was nothing if not precarious. Internally too, ominous portents gathered. In the postbellum decades, the size of Austria's standing army grew to some 300,000 soldiers and Prussia's to just under 200,000; meanwhile, the next largest fighting force, the Bavarian army, mustered only 20,000 men, and Saxony—diminished and struggling with its debt—maintained a still smaller force. By 1777 the combined power of Austria and Prussia had become six times what the other German states put into the field, and, by 1790, this discrepancy increased yet again.[74]

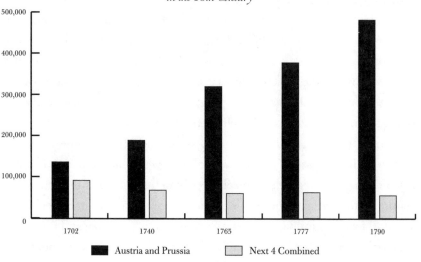

THE MILITARIZARION OF GERMAN STATES
in the 18th Century

The might of Austria and Prussia, and the relative decline of the rest of the German lands into political and military powerlessness, set the parameters of the course of high politics and diplomacy. But culture has a force of its own that does not always align with military might, and amid this heavily armed competition, a new public sensibility arose. Critical, enlightened, pacific, this new sensibility turned away from absolutist states and standing armies and looked instead to the small and medium-sized states, and even to the people of the countryside, as a source, however idealized, of social rejuvenation.

The historian and jurist Justus Möser of Osnabrück exemplified this postwar sensibility. "Where do we find the true German nation?" Möser asked rhetorically in a review of Friedrich Karl von Moser's *On the National Spirit*, and answered: "We certainly do not find it at the court of princes."[75] Instead, he started with the local—his Osnabrück, then a provincial city of 9000 souls and the capital of a territory of 120,000—and desired to write "a history of the people and its form of government with the ruler as an accidental circumstance."[76] Often portrayed as a conservative thinker, Möser in fact narrated history as if the people mattered more than the princes.

Beginning with the honor of independent landowning men, Möser

sought to render "a complete moving painting" of the history of Osnabrück, emphasizing the value of mixed rather than absolutist constitutions,
and showing the worth of local militias over the obedient soldiers of standing armies.[77] With great felicity, he also described the territory's natural
landscape—the moors and heaths, the hills and rivers, and the flora and
fauna—as well as the structure of local agriculture, the settlement of towns,
and the customs of the peasant population.[78] He even gave an account of a
typical Osnabrück woman, who from her hearth "keeps an eye on horses
and cows, guards cellar and pantry, spins and all the while cooks."[79]
Throughout the rest of the *Osnabrück History*, which remained unfinished during his lifetime and reached only to the middle of the thirteenth
century, Möser traced the relationship between property in the countryside and forms of military and state organization—"the natural history of
a nation's original contract through all its actual changes," as he put it in a
letter to the enlightener Friedrich Nicolai.[80]

It is impossible to read Möser's posthumously published *Osnabrück
History* without the Seven Years War as a backdrop. The work makes
repeated reference to the ruinous impact of military recruitment on local
populations and to the baleful effect of the historic shift from independent
militias to standing armies of servile soldiers. As the middle-aged but still
relatively unknown Möser researched and wrote the work, he also corresponded with the young and well-connected Abbt, who had likewise come
to realize that "he should write about life for the fatherland, because the
patriot through death can only seldom be useful to his country."[81] Abbt's
"immortal" work, *On Merits* (*Vom Verdienste*), was written in constant
exchange with Justus Möser, who in turn sent the younger man concepts
and drafts from his *Osnabrück History*. The two became so close, Möser
later recounted, that Abbt "had his own room in my house and was treated
like a son and brother when he visited us."[82] It is difficult to know what
direction Abbt's thought would have taken next: he died unexpectedly in
1766, at the age of twenty-seven. Möser saw Abbt's death as an "irreparable
damage to the sciences" and regretted that he did not reach the age when
experience and talent come together to form a great work.[83] Friedrich Nicolai and the young philosopher Johann Gottfried Herder also wrote moving
reflections about his death, with Herder calling for a memorial for "the
man Abbt, as a second Kleist."[84]

VI

After the conclusion of hostilities in 1763, Europe enjoyed nearly three decades of relative peace—or, to be more precise, the absence of a general European war involving more than two countries. But the rapaciousness of the great powers did not abate, and one power emerged as especially aggressive, even militaristic. This, as contemporaries understood, was Austria. To be sure, it was Prussia, not Austria, that set the standards for military-fiscal efficiency in the eighteenth century, and it was the challenge of the Prussian model that motivated Austrian reform.[85] Yet by 1780, when Joseph II ascended as the single regent to the throne (he had shared it with his mother, Maria Theresa, since 1765), "the Habsburg monarchy," as new research underscores, "was a highly militarized war machine, second only—if at all—to Prussia."[86]

The key to this reversal was Joseph II himself. In 1761, as the Seven Years War was winding down, he had advocated doubling the size of the Austrian army. Even when the conflict was over, he urged increased military spending, and looked to the Prussian model for how this could be done. In a memorandum on domestic reform, written at the age of twenty-four in 1765, he proposed that Austria introduce a cantonal system, with stricter discipline and a mandatory three-year service for nobles who expected to work in the state administration. Joseph was also the first to regularly wear a military uniform in court society, and he scarcely concealed his admiration for Frederick.[87]

But to others in Vienna, the militarization of the Habsburg monarchy was misguided if not downright dangerous. To Kaunitz, the state chancellor since 1753, this new militarization threatened to cover the monarchy with "a new kind of slavery" that would snuff out "industry" and undermine true patriotism.[88] As the engineer of the strategic reversal, Kaunitz argued passionately that it was the dilettantism of the Austrian leaders in the field, not the size of its army, that had caused setbacks, and that finances had first to be put in order before any enlargement of the military could be considered. Economic development depended on maintaining a balance between the civilian and the military spheres, he insisted, surmising that the ideal balance worked out to be a ratio of roughly 1 military person per 100 subjects. (By this standard, Austria's ratio was slightly worse, Prussia's ratio was much worse at 1:30, and Hesse-Kassel's outright deplorable at 1:15.[89]) Armies, Kaunitz argued further, are primarily shields and should not oppress what they are meant to protect. Since the peasants paid taxes and supplied soldiers, they were the starting point of Habsburg wealth and power.

Yet Joseph II, determined and tenacious, was not to be deterred, and by February 1770, he had persuaded his mother, Queen Maria Theresa, to order a census of all people and draft animals with the clear intention of introducing a new military conscription similar to the Prussian cantonal system. Accordingly, the census counted only men, tabulating their age, occupation, and height as well as noting whether the counted men were heads of their households. As if to reinforce the connection between the census and conscription, Austria began to affix numbers to houses, which had previously been distinguished, if at all, by a painted front illustrating a trade or given a name (such as "at the Black Eagle"). Initiated in the Austrian and Bohemian lands in 1770, the new enumeration of houses met with considerable resistance from nobles, who considered the undignified numbers affixed to their houses distasteful, and from peasants, who saw through its tie to the new military draft.[90] But the resistance remained sporadic, and the census revealed that the Habsburg crown had nearly as many subjects as France.[91]

The system of conscription, first introduced in the Austrian-Bohemian lands in 1770–1771, divided Habsburg territories into districts, each responsible for supplying troops for a regiment. It targeted men between seventeen and forty, allowed for fewer exemptions than in Prussia, and placed the onus of the draft on landless peasants too poor to pay taxes. As in Prussia, conscripts served for life, but with significant amounts of time in furlough, so that the rural labor pool was not decimated. The army would eventually designate nearly 40 percent of the male population in the Austro-Bohemian provinces and in Hungary as potential cannon fodder, resulting in an unprecedented militarization of rural society.[92] In one important respect, however, Austria did not follow Prussia's lead. A noble military elite, ready to spill blood for the crown, failed to materialize, causing at least one Austrian general to complain "of more a poverty than a surplus of young, patriotically minded people in the state."[93]

Joseph II oversaw all of this—quite literally. No European monarch traveled as assiduously. Covering some thirty thousand miles, he at first was accompanied by a royal retinue; later, there was less fuss, and he often preferred to ride saddle rather than coach. His first official journey was to Frankfurt am Main for his coronation as emperor—an office he dismissed as "disagreeable and useless" and the ceremony "a veritable comedy."[94] Then he undertook scores of trips to such places as Temesvár, Rome, the town of Neisse in Upper Silesia (where he met with Frederick despite Maria Theresa's misgivings), Budapest, and Prague.[95] Recording his observations in detailed reports, the young king used the information he gleaned from his travels to shape the reform policies he would implement in the 1780s. Royal travel, which once functioned as a mobile display of majesty and power, now served as a source of governmental knowledge. Unlike the itinerant Maximilian I, who in the early sixteenth century had to be seen in order to properly rule, nearly three hundred years later Joseph II needed to see the realm in order to properly rule it. The shift in the style and the purpose of travel also testified to a larger transformation from an Austrian conception of *Hausmacht*, dynastic power, to an understanding

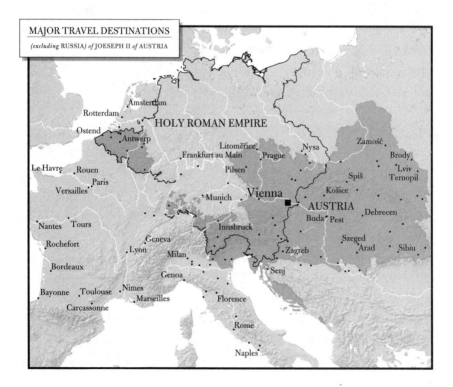

MAJOR TRAVEL DESTINATIONS
(excluding RUSSIA*) of* JOESEPH II *of* AUSTRIA

of rule centered on a territory and its populations, with the ruler following Frederick's example, as the first servant of the state. Moreover, the lands of Austria, not the German Empire, determined the coordinates of Joseph's journeys. If the routes and destinations of his travels show us what he cared about, then it is clear that the northern reaches of the Holy Roman Empire interested him little. From east to west, he reconnoitered almost every corner of the Habsburg lands; when he did travel abroad, he went to Holland, France, Italy, and Russia. Only on a few occasions did he pass through southern Germany, suggesting that Austria and Europe, not Germany, were the focus of this monarch's attention.

Austria was indeed in the process of becoming a modern territorial state, "a clearly defined empire with fixed boundaries and a distinct geographic shape," as one historian describes it.[96] The punishing trial of the Seven Years War had accelerated this territorial consolidation and, as a result, had also encouraged more sustained mapping efforts. After the war, Maria Theresa commissioned a detailed cartographical survey of the monarchy, which took twenty-three years to complete and ended by assuming the name of her son. The *Josephinische Landesaufnahme*, as it came to be called, covered nearly all of the monarchy in more than 4000 separate sheets at a scale of 1:115, and constituted a cartographical enterprise second in Europe only to the more scientific French efforts. The map reflected the centralizing dynamic of the Austrian government, and the monarchy's evolution into a territorial unit: a country, much like Frederick's Prussia, of its own.

VII

In 1769, when Frederick the Great and Joseph II actually did meet, in Neisse, the encounter augured troubled times, especially for the Polish-Lithuanian Commonwealth. Stretching from just east of the Oder all the way to the gates of Kiev, and from the Baltic Sea in the north to the Carpathians in the south, the Commonwealth was ruled by a king beholden to Russia and by an assembly of nobles that refused any and all concessions to centralized, fiscal-military policies. It thus happened that the third largest country in Europe, with the fourth largest population, had a standing army of a mere 26,000 soldiers. The balance of power had kept Poland's heavily armed neighbors from ripping it apart. But now Russian expansion

Allegory of the First Partition of Poland.

brought Austria and Prussia together, as they hoped to both satisfy and halt Russia and gain territory of their own.

The result was the First Partition of Poland in 1772, one of the most controversial acts of diplomacy in modern European history. During a time of peace, with no succession crisis on the horizon and without heed to questions of legitimacy, the three major eastern powers robbed Poland of nearly a third of its territory. Austria appropriated western Galicia and nearly 2.5 million subjects along with it. Russia took the largest but least valuable slice of territory (a major strip of land stretching from Latvia to the Ukraine), and Prussia seized the Netze district, the smallest, least populous, but economically wealthiest part of Poland.

VIII

The importance of the partition for the history of Poland, and for Polish-German relations, is well documented. Less appreciated, though, is its significance for the German Empire and the major states within it. Presciently, Edmund Burke, the great eighteenth-century British conservative, noted that "if the partition of Poland takes place in utmost extent, the existence of the Germanic body in its present form, for any length of time, will be a matter rather to be wished for than expected."[97] Germany's medium-sized states, each with armies more modest than Poland's, also recognized the danger, and turned to one another as well as to new protectors, generating feverish activity among the courts of Saxony, Bavaria, the Palatinate, and Württemberg. Some states, like Bavaria and the Electorates of Mainz and Trier, turned to a depleted France. Hanover at least had the protection of Great Britain (whose king, George III, was also the duke and prince-elector of Hanover). But throughout the Empire the question was where Berlin and Vienna would turn next.

The question was not misplaced. Prince Henry, a brother of Frederick the Great, immediately hatched plans for new partitions in the militarily "soft areas" of the Empire, while Joseph II, who played an initially passive role in the First Partition of Poland, turned to the possibility of sharing parts of Bavaria and Franconia with Prussia. Frederick proved reticent, however, worrying about his ties to England and the consequences of enticing France into a great-power feast of German territories.[98]

Then, another opportunity arose. In December 1777, Maximilian III Joseph, Elector of Bavaria, passed away without an heir, which ended the Bavarian line of the Wittelsbachs. The throne passed to Charles Theodore of the Palatinate branch of the family. In the eighteenth century, under the system of primogeniture, the deaths of childless rulers were welcome opportunities for rapacious territorial states and therefore primary causes of war. Austria, Maria Theresa's reticence notwithstanding, challenged the Bavarian succession and pushed the newly crowned Charles Theodore to cede significant parts of Bavaria in exchange for Anterior Austria, an archipelago of territories in southwest Germany, and a handsome sum of money. Bavaria, it was thought, could compensate for the loss of Silesia by adding to the Habsburg crown a contiguous block of territory rich in resources. The acquisition of Bavaria would have drawn Austria closer to Anterior Austria, and thus deeper into Germany. Given the pressure to consolidate territory, this would have brought Austria westward, with expansion across southern and western Germany a likely outcome. When Charles Theodore agreed, Austria sent troops through the Inn Valley and into Bavaria.

The action brought forth a hue and cry throughout the Empire. Seeing its chance to counter, Prussia, aided by the Saxons, sent its forces south to confront Austria. As a result, more than 400,000 soldiers faced one another in Bohemia, raising fears, as the British ambassador in Vienna put it, that "the two most formidable armies that have ever been seen in Europe for some centuries must decide the matter."[99] Ultimately, the War of the Bavarian Succession, as this episode in high-stakes brinksmanship came to be called, ended in a battle-less stalemate. In the subsequent Peace of Teschen, Austria received only a strip of land known as the *Innviertel*, whose most distinguished town was Braunau (the subsequent birthplace of Adolf Hitler), while Prussia received future rights to the principalities of Ansbach and Bayreuth. In the war of public opinion, Prussia certainly came out ahead, seeming like a David fending off an overweening Goliath.

The matter did not rest there. In 1785, Charles Theodore considered exchanging the whole of Electoral Bavaria for the Austrian Netherlands, which comprised Flanders, Brabant, and Luxembourg, and included the cities of Antwerp and Brussels. The exchange would have considerably increased the size and power of Austria, and it would have created a significant country in the western part of the Empire. In the end, however, the combined military threat of Prussia, Saxony, Hanover, and a series of mostly Protestant middling and minor powers (known as the League of German Princes) put a stop to this project. Some might argue that this Prussian-led alliance of mainly Protestant states against the Catholic house of Habsburg seems to foreshadow nineteenth-century developments. Yet at issue in 1785, as in 1778–1779, was not the eventual unification of Germany, but rather the question of how to curb the absolutist aggression of Austria.

IX

Throughout Europe in the second half of the eighteenth century, the aggressive politics of enlightened absolutism shifted borders and carved up countries. This feverish partitioning, whether as a threat or an actuality, also called forth patriotism. Starting with the Seven Years War and intensifying during the American Revolutionary War, new forms of patriotism were especially marked in the Netherlands, where in the wake of the disastrous Fourth Anglo-Dutch War (1780–1784), a group calling itself the Patriots temporarily ousted the Orangist stadholder. The Patriots would have established a state based on national-patriotic principles, had not Prussian and British troops intervened in 1787, forcing many of the Patriot leaders into exile. Still more dramatic were developments to the east of Germany, where the First Partition of Poland brought forth radically new forms of patriotism. In 1788, when a parliament known as the Great Sejm first convened, this newfound feeling had left behind older conceptions of Poland based on the gentry republic and embraced policies far more revolutionary than anything found in the German lands at the time.[100] Animated by partition-inspired, radical-democratic nationalism, Polish reformers extended representation to the propertied classes, abolished tax exemptions for the nobility, moved to create a standing army of 100,000 men, and, on May 3, 1791, passed a constitution that held that "power in human society derives from the will of the nation."[101] Unfortunately, a brutal Russian invasion, and the Second Partition of Poland, quashed this new constitution, the first in Europe and the second in the world (after the United States). There followed the costly Kościuszko uprising of 1794, in which thousands of townsmen, aided by many more peasants brandishing scythes, fought and perished in pitched battles with the absolutist armies of Russia and Prussia.

Poland, literally wiped off the map, was the feared prototype. And just as the partitions of Poland ignited national agitation there, the possibility that Austria might simply annex Bavaria brought forth the first stirrings of Bavarian patriotic sentiment. Catholic, reform-minded, mainly based in Munich but with some representation in provincial towns, enlightened Bavarians portrayed the Bavarian people as their true countrymen. Johann Georg von Lori, a high-ranking official associated with the newly formed Patriot Party, argued that while other nations were built upon dynasties, Bavaria had its roots in the folk, and was indeed primary among those nations, "which in Germany appeared as a primal people [*Urvolk*]."[102] Lori dedicated his *Chronological Excerpts of the History of Bavaria* of 1782 to his Bavarian countrymen, hoping it would bring forth "a certain pride, which ennobles the sentiments . . . and firms the national character."[103] Lori also offered a barely veiled critique of the new sovereign, Charles Theodore, who was all too eager to swap territory and people. Lori's contemporary Lorenz von Westenrieder likewise criticized the plans of the unpatriotic ruler. "The people see the disloyalty to the country as that for which every nation ought to see it, as a thing contrary to nature," Westenrieder wrote.[104] Deeply influenced by Justus Möser, Westenrieder composed his *Letters of Bavarian Mind and Customs* (1782) in order to celebrate the virtuous Bavarian, "who with a few thousand of the same could turn away the army of a Xerxes."[105] Unlike Prussia or Austria, which were artificially soldered together by dynastic marriage and military conquest, Bavaria, according to Westenrieder, was rooted in the permanence of a people, the uniqueness of its language and customs, and the natural beauty and bounty of the land. History and folklore—not dynastic power politics—held the keys to what these patriots ardently called the Bavarian nation.

These Bavarian intellectuals, most of them in the employ of the courts, first began to invent their nation in the 1770s and 1780s. They were hardly alone in their efforts. Throughout Germany, enlightened intellectuals constructed fatherlands, with Justus Möser as their guiding light. There appeared histories of Hamburg, Schleswig-Holstein, and the Duchy of Oldenburg. There was also a history of Hesse, written with the intention, as its author, Helfrich Bernhard Wenck, put it, of "making the subject more at home."[106] Ludwig Timotheus Spittler was surely the most noteworthy of these fatherland historians. He wrote analytically precise histories of his native Württemberg as well as of Hanover, in whose service he stood as a professor in Göttingen. "The Empire lives mainly in its territories," Spittler proclaimed. The medium-sized states, which he called "little states," were guarantors of "German freedom" in a system of states, the Holy Roman Empire, essentially defined by the balance of power.[107]

But would the balance of power hold? For the German states, there was another possible future; it involved the westward expansion of the superstates and the ultimate division of the German lands into two spheres of influence. As early as 1770, Austria and Prussia had discussed partitioning and dividing Germany between them.[108] But the mutual mistrust of the two powers, the threat of outside intervention, and residual loyalty to the institutions of the old Empire militated against partition. Prying Germany into two parts, one Prussian, the other Austrian, would have in any case involved gigantic compensations to France, Russia, and Great Britain, and may well have called forth an unsettling degree of state-based patriotism. Would it have called forth *Reichspatriotismus* at a time when national patriotism seemed, as the poet Friedrich Gottlieb Klopstock complained, like "a dying little daughter"?[109] It remains doubtful. Even Johann Stephan Pütter, the star of the Göttingen jurists and the erudite author of a three-volume account of the constitution of the Holy Roman Empire, conceded in 1787 that the "distinct and separate states, which stand almost in the same relation to each other as the different states of Europe," had acquired so much weight that the unity of the German Empire was "only immediately obvious" at the Emperor's court in Vienna, at the Reichstag in Regensburg, and in the Imperial Chamber in Wetzlar.[110] The German Empire, in this realistic assessment, had become a traditional political order held together by agreements of convenience among great powers.[111] Could it outlast another bout of concerted Austrian or Prussian aggression or survive a revolution in the organization and deployment of military force? Or would Germany go the way of Poland, ceasing to exist?

CHAPTER 5

THE SURFACE AND
THE INTERIOR

c. 1770–1790

*How necessary that the Germans
know their own land.*

—NICOLAI

I N HIS *MAPPA CRITICA* OF 1750, A SCIENTIST AND CARTOGRAPHER named Tobias Mayer ascertained anew the coordinates of twenty-seven German cities and the relative position of Germany's borders, and argued that previous mapmakers had situated Germany too far to the east—in some places on some maps by more than a degree. Like the poet Friedrich Schiller but before him, Mayer hailed from the small town of Marbach am Neckar. He had become a major figure in an international effort to figure out precise readings of longitude, and he was quite right about Germany's coordinates: Germany was closer to Paris and farther from Moscow than previously recognized. Moreover, distortion grids, which compare points on old maps to satellite-generated coordinates, show that early-eighteenth-century maps had become less exact even against Gerhard Mercator's Map of Europe of 1585.[1]

The *Germaniae Mappa Critica*, Mayer hoped, would launch the first concerted effort since the sixteenth century to map all of Germany with scientifically ascertained coordinates. Following the French model, the project, an enlightened *Germania Illustrata*, aimed to cover the whole empire, including the ten administrative units known as Imperial Circles and all the individual territories within it. The maps were to be in German, legally binding in territorial disputes, and accompanied with detailed descriptions of places.

Tobias Mayer, *Germaniae Mappa Critica*, 1750.

It was a bold plan that would take as much as half a century to complete, and major intellectual figures quickly got behind it. Anton Büsching, the most renowned geographer of his day, proposed "each state of the Empire should suffer a Cabinet-Atlas to be taken of its territory by the German surveying-office . . . and then permit a general chart to be engraved therefrom, which might be afterwards used for executing a chart for all Germany."[2]

But nothing ever came of it. The German Surveying Office existed only on paper, as a subdivision of the Cosmographical Society, founded in 1747 by mathematicians, geographers, and mapmakers in the employ of Jean Baptiste Homann.[3] Although modeled on the Royal Society of London and the Académie Royale des Sciences in Paris, the Cosmographical Society never amounted to more than a loose association of scattered scholars. It tried to raise money for its mapmaking project, first by selling globes, then by raffling off maps. The society also appealed to princes and rulers, albeit unsuccessfully. The Emperor considered the society's proposals but demanded the cartographers convert to Catholicism. In the end, few funds were forthcoming; no state, except occupied Saxony, suffered a survey of its territory; and no improved map of Germany was made.[4]

The Empire, to turn a scholarly phrase, did not see like a state. France, Great Britain, Austria, Prussia, Hanover, and even Osnabrück were in the process of surveying and mapping their territories. By contrast, no one felt responsible for Germany as a whole. Neither the Emperor nor the estates in Regensburg funded surveying projects, and despite seeming to be "the state of the German nation," as one historian calls it, the Holy Roman Empire never commissioned its own mapping.[5] At a time when serious cartography had become a matter for states, engineers, and armies, the mapping of all of Germany was relegated to foreigners, private companies peddling maps for amusement and study, or scholars like Tobias Mayer.

The relative decline in nation mapping reflected the persistent weight of Germany's splintered territorial composition—the "some three hundred larger and smaller states with special titles and constitutions," as the geographer and statistician Johann Ernst Fabri put it in his *Geography for All Estates*, published in Leipzig in 1786.[6] Yet for our purposes, it also marked the dusk of one method of conceiving the nation and the dawn of another. A way of envisaging Germany focused on cities, states, territories, and people—in short, a surface that is observable, measurable, countable, and mapable—ceded to an entirely new conception of the nation. Poetry, not politics, was the source of this new conception; sound, not sight, its primary sense; and the vernacular German, not geography, its principal idiom. The new way of knowing claimed that a nation was not merely outside, not just surface, but something interior, perhaps even (though the word was not yet used) an identity.[7] In the famous and often quoted distich of Goethe and Schiller—"Germany? But where does it lie? I do not know where to find it. Where the political begins, the spiritual ends"—the surface and the interior seem opposed. Yet a transformation was already under way, bringing the Germany one could see together with what contemporaries called its soul. The connecting tether was travel.

II

Travel was hardly a new way to get to know one's land. Sixteenth-century humanists counted on travel to make empirical observation. They walked or rode a horse from town to town, and when they arrived in cities, their first order of business was to climb the stairs of the high bell towers—332 steps in Strasbourg, 401 in Ulm—in order to see the city in the cradle of the land.[8] Humanists also surveyed, described, sketched, mapped, and painted the place they called "our Germany."[9] But after the initial "century of intense wonder," as Stephen Greenblatt calls the sixteenth century, a long period of decline and destruction cut into the curiosity that marked the humanist project of a *Germania Illustrata*.[10] There is no precise measure of this decline. Yet the small number of travel accounts, geographies, and territorial descriptions between 1660 and 1760 suggest a century-long dearth in interest and knowledge about the nation; after 1760, there was a greater interest, followed by an explosion of publications in the 1790s. One index of contemporary travel reports published by Germans about the German lands provides a rough measure: it lists three German-centered reports in the 1760s, twelve in the 1770s, twenty-eight in the 1780s, and sixty-seven in the 1790s.[11]

Like the first discovery of Germany in the sixteenth century, the second unfolded in the context of the immense interest in travel in the wider world. In what the historian Urs Bitterli calls the "second phase of the great maritime travels of discovery," it was particularly the Pacific Ocean that came more sharply into view.[12] By 1700, California was no longer thought to be an island—even as some mapmakers persisted in the error. By the 1740s, it became clear that no isthmus bridged Asia and America across the northern Pacific. By 1767, Samuel Wallis had set anchor in Tahiti. And by 1774, James Cook had mapped the contours of New Zealand, charted the eastern coast of Australia, and ascertained that no continent, save for one made of ice, existed at the southern pole.[13] Once thought to be a certain sentence of death, circumnavigating the globe had become, thanks to frequent land visits, cleaner decks, and more fresh food and water, a survivable voyage.[14]

The revolution in the experience of space was also evident in land travel.[15] As a humble friar following monastic directives, Martin Luther had walked across vast expanses in order to meet his adversaries, here and there hitching a ride on a wagon, but scarcely progressing faster than his Germanic forefathers. By the mid-eighteenth century, however, an intricate network of roads had been built, and the horse-drawn carriage had supplanted two human legs as the primary means of travel. The carriage was also much faster, the increase in speed as much as fourfold.[16]

In 1500, the trip from Hamburg to Augsburg took roughly thirty days, but by 1780, with coach routes crisscrossing the old Empire, that journey could be completed in eight.[17]

Space also became more legible. In 1500, there were only rudimentary maps to guide travelers; by the end of the eighteenth century, regional road maps proved essential in helping voyagers find their way. The firms of Jean Baptiste Homann in Nuremberg and Matthäus Seutter in Augsburg sold them in great quantities for the price of a tavern meal. Vended in some fifty German cities and peddled by itinerant map sellers, road maps found their way into homes as well, becoming among the most widely circulated representations of territorial space in the German lands.[18] Travelers also

Johan Peter Nell, "New, Expanded Postal Map Through All of Germany," 1788 (based on the postal charts of Jean Baptiste Homann).

carried distance displayers (*Meilenzeiger*), allowing them to see at a glance how far one city was from another. Along heavily trafficked routes, milestones marked out distances, and postal stations, where horses could be exchanged, greatly increased in number; by the 1760s, there were some nine hundred separate stations.[19]

A new sense of time accompanied the altered perception of space. In the age of Luther, most towns possessed public clocks. The bells tolling above the chaos of the day told people when to eat and when to pray, when to assemble and when to fight, and when to rejoice and when to mourn.[20] The more elaborate clocks ordered not just quotidian but also cosmological time. The enormous clock on the cathedral of Strasbourg, for instance, featured a moving calendar and an astrolabe documenting the changing position of the sun, moon, and planets.[21] Time, like space, must be cut into equal and measurable units in order to make sense of it, and just as artificial grids of longitude and latitude allow a visualization of an area's extent, the counting of time by hours, minutes, and seconds enables an estimation of duration. By the seventeenth century, clocks had been refined so much that their daily error decreased from fifteen minutes to fifteen seconds. Furthermore, around 1690 many new clocks came with minute hands, suggesting that time was not just intermittent—the sound of the hourly church bell— but constant and precise. Clocks were also no longer the preserve of church towers and municipal halls. In the early eighteenth century, the Black Forest had become a center for the production of pendulum clocks designed for homes, a small fraction of which were the famous cuckoo clocks. Pocket watches also became widely available, a de rigueur accessory for a man of standing.[22] A general increase in pace resulted, signaled by the proliferation of schedules, timetables, and enlightened admonishments not to waste time but to fill it with industry. Even barracked soldiers strode with greater purpose, their marching speed, at least in one army, increasing from 60 steps per minute at the beginning of the eighteenth century to 114 steps per minute a hundred years later.[23] By the end of the eighteenth century, carriages often left major cities many times a day; and in the densely trafficked roads of southern Germany, arriving could be calculated to the hour.

The day was also extended. By the beginning of the eighteenth century, major court and commercial cities, like Hamburg, Berlin, Vienna, Hanover, and Leipzig, installed public oil lanterns, providing sources of light to urban centers otherwise illuminated only by personal lanterns or when torchbearers walked by. One could not, as a student in 1690 claimed, "pass through the crowds of people just as in broad daylight."[24] But, to take one example, the roughly sixteen hundred lanterns that went up in Berlin certainly changed the habits of the city, allowing public life, albeit mainly for young men, to flourish into the hitherto dark hours. Taverns, coffeehouses, and evening salons thrived in the new zones of illumination.

The lighting remained restricted, however. Other cities adopted it only slowly. Frankfurt am Main did not put in public lighting until the Seven Years War, and a string of cities, including Augsburg, Trier, and Nuremberg, did not install lighting until the end of the eighteenth century. Many medium-sized cities, like Bonn, Naumburg, Giessen, and Erfurt, were not illuminated until the era of the Napoleonic Wars, and many smaller cities, like Lüneburg, Lüdenscheid, Schweinfurt, and Schwäbisch Hall, were not lit until after the conflict. Smaller towns often waited until the second half of the nineteenth century, when gas lamps were introduced. Light, spectacle, and perhaps in this sense enlightenment, still bypassed the rural world, where the vast majority of people still lived.

III

Until the 1770s, Germans traveling through this rural world rarely remarked on its beauty. Instead, they filled their travel journals with observations about cities and courts. Passing through Lower Saxony on his way to Holland and England in 1704, Zacharias Conrad von Uffenbach, for example, described curiosities like the Greenland geese, two tigers, and "a lion and lioness" in the possession of the Duke of Hesse-Kassel.[25] A scholar of some standing, he also remarked on the condition of libraries, noted particularly ingenious inventions, reported on newfound natural wonders, and listed artistic treasures, as if providing an inventory for future travelers.

Exceptions to this way of seeing were few but revealing. One was the unpublished journal of Albrecht von Haller, a young Swiss medical student now famous for penning one of the earliest poems praising the beauty of the Alps. In his journey through the German lands between 1725 and 1727, Haller was much impressed by the bounty of the countryside and the piety of the people of Württemberg. He also commented on the people's economic welfare, thinking they would benefit if the princes did not cordon off so much forest and land for their hunting amusement, especially because "wild boars and fallow and common deer are here so ubiquitous as tame domestic animals."[26] Another exception, in part, was the published travel report of Johann Georg Keyßler, an enlightened scholar of antiquities. Keyßler's account, *Travels Through Germany, Bohemia, Hungary, Switzerland, Italy and Lorraine,* published in 1740–1741, hints at a new appreciation of natural beauty, correcting the many travelers who see in Switzerland "little else than a confused chaos of barren rocks, craggy mountains, perpetual snows and gloomy valleys."[27]

Foreigners saw Germany in much the same way, although sometimes with a wider vision. When Lady Mary Wortley Montagu, an English aristocrat who has left us with detailed and perceptive accounts of the Ottoman Empire, traveled through Germany en route to Constantinople in 1717, she noted that Vienna "is inhabited by all nations" and that the "apartments of the greatest ladies and even of the ministers of state are divided but by a partition from that of a tailor or a shoemaker."[28] Unlike any other account from the time, her journal was sensitive to the situation of women: marveling at the Viennese ladies of court who openly "have two husbands, one that bears the name, and another that performs the duties," and expressing "much melancholy" about sprightly girls confined to nunneries.[29] Other foreign travelers focused on Germany's religious and political diversity. Montesquieu, soon to be author of *The Spirit of the Laws,* journeyed through the German lands in 1729, observing how religious denomination divided territories, towns, and even churches—like Heidelberg's Church of the Holy Spirit, in which a recently erected wall blocked off the Catholic nave from the Calvinist choir.[30] He also observed extreme cruelty, both to animals (noting how royalty hunted considerable quantities of deer conveniently brought to islands on the Rhine, where they could be shot at) and to men, reserving his most acerbic criticism for the "disgraceful tyranny" of the king of Prussia, whose forced military conscription caused parents to send young boys abroad or fathers to purposely mutilate their sons.[31] James Boswell, subsequently famous as the biographer of the even more famous Samuel Johnson, also offered searing commentary of Germany's ruling elite. Touring Germany in 1764, he left an inspired if often sardonic account of its courts and cities, portraying Germany's quirky or even mad small-time rulers (like the Prince of Zerbst, "a strange, wrong-headed being" enamored of his cannons) and the nation's impressive literati (such as "Professor Gottsched . . . who set a-going the true cultivation of the German language").[32] As did many traveler accounts of the old style, Boswell explicated the wonders of Germany's numerous and impressive libraries, like the "noble library" of Wolfenbüttel and "the great old room" of the university library in Leipzig.[33] He also chronicled his meeting with Frederick the Great, for whom he had "prodigious veneration" and "felt a shock of the heroic."[34] Yet aside from general glimpses of the countryside and complaints about the inns that house "the great Boswell" on straw spread out on the floor, he spoke little of the rural world or the people who lived there.[35]

IV

The enlightened philosopher Friedrich Nicolai was different. In 1781, when his son was old enough to travel with him, Nicolai set off on a journey whose "main goal was to observe people."[36] Packed with a host of inventions, including an odometer one could affix to the axle of a wagon, a writing table built into his coach, a folding bed, and "a kind of fountain pen one could carry in a pocket," Nicolai and his son took a land route south from Berlin, then traveled by barge down the Danube to Vienna, where they spent four weeks in the "capital" of the German Empire; they then doubled back toward Munich, Stuttgart, and Tübingen before heading southwest through the Black Forest and to the town of Schaffhausen on the Swiss border.[37] It was not yet the halfway mark of a journey, which lasted seven months, and for which Nicolai kept a journal, now lost.

The journal served as the basis for the twelve volumes of Nicolai's *Description of a Journey Through Germany and Switzerland in the Year 1781*, which concluded with his entry on Schaffhausen.[38] Even if only half complete when Nicolai ceased writing, it nevertheless represented the most ambitious attempt to understand Germany by observation and travel of its time. By discovering its commonalities, Nicolai also hoped to bring Germany's diverse parts together. "Germany consists of so many large and small countries, in which everything is different, position, climate, constitution, physiognomy and character of the inhabitants, religion, science, art, industry, and customs," he wrote.[39] Its people, moreover, "are full

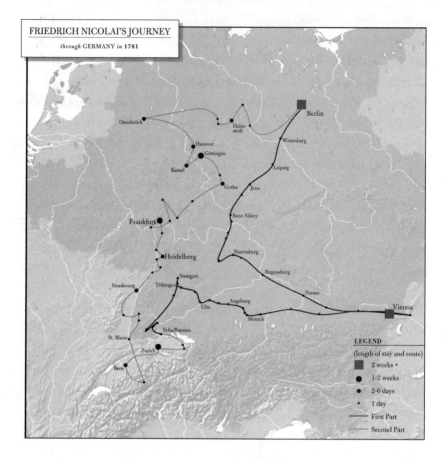

FRIEDRICH NICOLAI'S JOURNEY
through GERMANY *in* 1781

LEGEND
(length of stay and route)
■ 2 weeks +
● 1–2 weeks
● 2–6 days
· 1 day
—— First Part
—— Second Part

of prejudices, mostly unfounded, against each other, and even hate each other, without truthfully knowing why." Travel descriptions, he believed, would help Germans "bear and love one another."[40]

Lofty ambitions notwithstanding, Nicolai's account was marred, as is well-known, with religious prejudice. Protestant more in attitude than in piety, Nicolai perceived Catholics as dull-witted and superstitious, monks as vile creatures with faces "twisted and disfigured," and pilgrimages as "disgusting, uninteresting spectacles," in which "so much time is lost in such miserable pietistic idleness."[41] Prejudice also occluded Nicolai's view of ordinary people. Even as he wrote as much about commoners as dignitaries, Nicolai typically did little more than steal a glance at rustics as his coach sped through villages; when he looked harder, he usually saw only dull faces, miserable huts, indolence and idolatry. When two round-hatted Tyrolean peasants with brown vests and suspenders boarded his ferry in an Upper Austrian town, Nicolai "observed them long and precisely and hardly saw anyone so stupid and bigoted."[42]

He based his deductions on the "science" of physiognomy, defined in broad terms as the "talent to discern from the outward appearance of a person his inner constitution," as the Swiss pastor Johann Caspar Lavater put it.[43] With Lavater, Nicolai believed the world could be knowable by what appears to the senses, and that physiognomy, far from an exercise in prejudice, was a form of empiricism.

Nicolai saw the divisions of Germany as refracted through faces, especially of women, who he believed were not as mobile and therefore less likely to shade their "national physiognomy."[44] He noted of the Catholic city of Bamberg that the faces tended toward "the uniformity of a limited national physiognomy" whereas in neighboring Protestant cities of Nuremberg and Erlangen, more people possessed "perpendicularity in profile."[45] In the Austrian city of Linz, the young people had "something delicate, fine, soft," but "when the years of their youth have passed, something fleshy, the muscles more hanging than taught."[46] The closer he came to Vienna, the more feminine the physiognomy of the people seemed— a result, he reasoned, of their tendency to hedonistic pleasures. He contrasted the femininity of the Austrians with the more vulgar Bavarians, whose "lipless or very small lipped mouths" differed from Austrian "kiss lips."[47] Religion also influenced this "science" of physiognomy. In Augsburg, "the strangest of all the old cites," the denizen of the comparatively new city of Berlin observed, "the Catholics can be differentiated from the Protestants at first glance," with the "Protestants approximating the Swabian national physiognomy, the Catholics the Bavarian."[48] For Nicolai, "Swabian" connoted mainly positive characteristics of satisfaction, calm, and generosity. The beauty of Swabian women also impressed him.

Even if Nicolai's insights seem superficial now, they conformed to the common opinions of a period when silhouettes were a widespread fashion, and when the markers of a human diversity were not yet set. Physiognomy was but one expression of this indeterminacy. In the 1770s, European scholars also debated the importance of skin complexion as an inner marker of worth, with major figures, like the Swedish botanist Carl von Linné and the Göttingen naturalist Johann Blumenbach, dividing humanity into dermatological classes. In the 1795 edition of his influential *The Varieties of Mankind* (first published in 1776), Blumenbach referred to these differentiations as "the national differences of color," of which there were five: white, yellow, red, brown, and jet black.[49] Blumenbach also popularized the term "Caucasian," which he borrowed from his colleague Christoph Meiners, using it to refer to the "variety from Mount Caucus" from whence came "the most beautiful race of man" and "the first race of mankind."[50] Among well-powdered Europeans of the 1770s, white skin still had a specifically aristocratic association, and was only beginning to be connoted more widely in terms embracing European peoples to the exclusion of black Africans, Asians, and indigenous peoples in the Americas. Through the writings of the art historian and antiquities scholar Johann Joachim Winckelmann, who believed the whiteness of classical Greek statues reflected "the noble simplicity and quiet grandeur" of cultivated perfection, whiteness assumed a new aesthetic reification—in art, but also in the perception of human beauty, with the exterior reflecting an ideal of inner perfection.[51]

Focusing on facial shape, skull size, and skin color, as well as the relationship of beauty to virtue, the German discussion of human variety took part in a wider, transatlantic debate, conducted at the height of the slave trade and carried on in Latin, French, English, and Spanish.[52] A modern thinker, Nicolai traveled through Germany with eyes conditioned by the fundamental assumption of this wider debate, and this was, as Immanuel Kant put it in his piercing criticism of physiognomy, that one can "judge what lies within a man, whether in terms of his way of sensing or his way of thinking, from that which is visible and so from his exterior."[53]

Nicolai spent four long volumes of his journal on Vienna, the capital of Austria and easily the greatest city of eighteenth-century central Europe. Situated at the intersection of the Danube and the ancient north-south Amber Road, with the bluish Styrian Alps to its south and the Hungarian plain to its east, Vienna was twice the size of Berlin (without counting Berlin's barracked soldiers) and dwarfed all other cities in Germany. Fanning out from St. Stephan's Cathedral, Vienna's narrow streets and alleys bustled with porters, craftsmen, shopkeepers, hawkers, lackeys, and officials. Two decades earlier, Bernardo Bellotto had painted the city in luminous topographical detail, as if a guide showing the city's many squares, special corners, and little appreciated views. Like Bellotto, Nicolai may have observed sellers of dried herbs across from what was then the Kaunitz Palace, or disputing scholars and indifferent students standing in front of the Aula at University Place.[54]

If so, Nicolai desisted from including such details in his journal. He did, however, contrast Vienna's 3445 illuminated lanterns with scarcely lit Berlin, and conceded that Vienna's art museums contained fine examples of Dutch painting, including Van Dyck and Rubens.[55] Otherwise, he thought Vienna closed to outside developments, impervious to Enlightenment (except perhaps in music), hectic and cruel (he was particularly critical of late baroque animal baiting), and loud (the church bells tolled without interruption). In literature and drama, the Viennese had little to boast—not one writer, in Nicolai's opinion, merited the attention of the rest of Germany. The Viennese, his complaint continued, also engaged in constant gambling, eating, drinking, and merrymaking. In a word, they were shallow, and Joseph von Sonnenfels, perhaps the most prominent voice of the Austrian Enlightenment, was not wrong to call Nicolai's judgment a "national insult."[56]

Nicolai also commented on the aesthetics of town and country in Ger-

Bernardo Bellotto, *The University Square in Vienna*, circa 1760.

many. His descriptions were less sensitive and more predictable than those of talented contemporaries, such as Johann Kaspar Riesbeck, who in his pseudonymous *Letters of a Traveling Frenchman* (1783) depicted the mountain cliffs at the foothills of the Alps as sublime, or Georg Forster, who in his *Views of the Lower Rhine* (1791) hazarded an early, if guarded appreciation of the decidedly unclassical, and therefore unbeautiful, and as yet unfinished cathedral of Cologne.[57] Yet Nicolai more faithfully reflected enlightened ways of seeing. He deemed ugly what seemed raw and uncultivated, like the Thuringian Forest, its mountains covered with pine trees "giving a monotonous and cheerless view," or the Black Forest, whose "dense growths of pine and spruce" he dismissed as "unfathomable woods not in the least handled by scientific forestry."[58] The darkness dismayed him in particular, especially in towns, like Tübingen, where "the streets are very narrow, crooked, and badly cobbled, in the evening unilluminated, and not kept very clean."[59]

Almost without exception, beauty worthy of comment appeared as vistas, whether from the *Fasanerie* overlooking Vienna, "wonderfully illuminated in the evening sun"; or Dachau, which offered a "wonderful prospect" when bathed in the "falling sun"; or the "indescribable beauty" of the road from Esslingen to Stuttgart, where "vineyards alternate with fields of mayflowers."[60] He considered some vistas "romantic," as when a river valley nestled a village, such as occurred in the town of Camburg on the Saale River, and even adored Germany's higher mountains, like the Traunstein in Upper Austria, "which seemed to have delicate clouds flowing around it."[61] But what really arrested his attention was the scene of a church he saw in an opening along a forested path, where suddenly "in a narrow valley between high mountains covered with dark spruce, the great majestic building appears."[62] It was St. Blaise Abbey in the Black Forest. "The impression is indescribable," Nicolai effused, "to see in this raw region such a spacious, well-ordered building."[63] Evoking cool classicism, shorn of the ornamentation of high baroque, St. Blaise was nearly complete when Nicolai saw it in 1781. Ensconced in the lightless woods of the Black Forest, it was "the most beautiful church in Germany," he thought, because it demonstrated that the rays of reason could penetrate a region steeped in what he assumed to be superstition.[64]

The *Description of a Journey Through Germany and Switzerland in the*

Year 1781 was the most ambitious attempt of the century to consider Germany as a whole, even if it mainly represented a north German, Protestant perspective on the Catholic south. Initially popular, the work launched with over a thousand subscriptions, and its early volumes went into multiple editions.[65] Subsequently, however, its popularity waned, a result perhaps of its sheer bulk, but also because it came at the end of a way of seeing a nation. "Nicolai still travels, he will travel for a long time," Goethe and Schiller wrote in one of *Xenien*'s many caustic couplets directed against him, "but in the land of reason he can no longer find the way."[66] The winds of intellectual change had failed to move Nicolai, the young writers opined, and he remained the mortal enemy of all that was beautiful in the new art, poetry, and philosophy. Cuts deeper still came from the university town of Jena, where a young philosopher criticized Nicolai's travel journal for trafficking in banalities with regard to religion ("there are Catholics, and they really are Catholic") and for the presumption that the enlightener could comment on anything just by looking at it. "[Our hero] was simply incapable," the sardonic critic wrote, "to go even a line under the surface and to the interior of whatever object."[67] The critic was Johann Gottlieb Fichte, and his acerbic comments were not surprising, since Nicolai had written a series of pointed barbs, rendering ridiculous the new idealism, or "I philosophy," of Fichte and his friend F.W.J. Schelling.[68] The exchange, however impolite, got to the heart of the matter—whether a place can be known simply by examining its surface, as if moving along a life-sized map, or whether its interior, as expressed in its ideas and literature, must also be probed. Fichte's scorn was unchecked; he even wrote imaginary epitaphs for Nicolai's tomb.[69]

V

Unlike Nicolai, who meticulously planned his journey, the young Johann Gottfried Herder left his position as pastor in the Latvian city of Riga for a sailing voyage, "I do not know where to."[70] Beginning in March 1769, the voyage brought him to Copenhagen, through the Öresund, around the peninsula of Denmark, and south through the North Sea and the English Channel, ending in Paimboeuf at the mouth of the Loire, and from there by carriage to the city of Nantes, where he wrote a travel journal conspicuous for its complete lack of curiosity about the places he had seen. In *Journal of My Journey*, written in the same year but published posthumously, there are no depictions of the Baltic seaboard, no remarks on the sound separating Denmark and Sweden, no musings on the strong tides of the Channel, and no thoughts about the jagged coast of Brittany: only reflections on the self and considerations of educational plans. Herder then made his way to Paris, where he stayed another two months and wrote to his friend Nicolai that "the patriotism for Germany has become stronger in me."[71] From Paris, Herder traveled to Antwerp, and boarded a ship for Amsterdam; the ship breached a sandbar, and at this precise moment, as the vessel was being perilously battered by the waves, Herder supposedly took out his copy of *The Works of Ossian*—a cycle of poems that James Macpherson claimed to have translated from Scots Gaelic. As he was reading it, Herder arrived, according to his own account, at a double epiphany. He realized that the poets of old wrote and sung mainly about the storms of life, and that the origins of national literatures were to be found in songs, ballads, and odes, the poetry least freighted with rules.[72]

Both in Riga and at sea, then in Nantes and Strasbourg, Herder was beginning to develop a series of ideas that would ultimately reshape how Germans thought about themselves. His initial insight was about language, to which he assigned an independent power beyond its mimetic qualities. Words, far from just describing the world, allowed us to "feel from the inside," Herder wrote.[73] The idea was partly religious, deriving from a Pietism that emphasized "Christ within us" rather than "Christ for us," but it also reflected a new emphasis on the "deep interiority of the ear" as against "the clarity of the eye."[74] The inner language was the mother tongue, which was not defended for its laudable characteristics, or its ancientness, or even because it allowed one to understand the word of God. Instead, it was celebrated because it was the natural language. Inspired by Rousseau, Herder insisted that only the simple language of parents and children could lead poetry and literature in the German lands back to its source, an original, uncorrupted voice.

The path back led to the countryside and to "popular songs," which Herder translated for the first time in 1773 as *"Volkslieder"* (from which, translated back, we have the English term "folk songs").[75] He expected to find them both in print and on the streets, and he intentionally blurred the familiar distinction between their oral and written transmission. What mattered was the tone. Rough and unmannered songs, according to Herder, had survived with fewer foreign accretions; they would guide German literature back to a path of its own, not one dictated by the fashions of France or the metrics of the classics. Hewing close to life, the new literature would reflect how ordinary people loved and feared, and how they touched, saw, and heard the world around them.

Then, in late September 1770 in the French city of Strasbourg, one of the most fateful encounters in the history of German letters occurred. On the steps of the hotel *"Zum Geist,"* Herder met an unknown writer nearly five years his junior, the young Johann Wolfgang Goethe. An intense friendship followed, with Herder impressing Goethe as a man of immense intellectual fermentation and Goethe regularly visiting Herder in the near blackened room to which he was confined on account of an unsuccessful eye operation.[76] In this lightless venue, much that would become essential to the sound and direction of German poetry was first discussed. From Goethe's autobiography, *Poetry and Truth*, we know that Herder introduced Goethe to a wide field of learning and the newest thinking in literature and aesthetics, and that Goethe was a willing satellite, a "friendly moon of the earth," as he later wrote.[77]

Given Goethe's subsequent prominence, it is easy to forget that in the initial encounter Herder was very much the teacher. Born and raised in the modest town of Mohrungen in East Prussia, Herder, then twenty-six, had become a prodigious reader and a prolific, if polemical writer, equally versed in history, philosophy, and poetry. A remarkable polyglot, Herder had mastered a series of ancient and modern languages and was already deep into his thinking about rhythm and meter and national literature. By this time, Goethe, aged twenty-one, had only written a series of inconsequential poems and pastoral plays, many of which he had recently torched in an auto-da-fé.

We cannot re-create the conversations that transpired in the darkened room in Strasbourg, with Herder's eyes bandaged and Goethe listening intently. We know only that over the course of six months Herder steered Goethe's attention to the countryside as a place of a different kind of truth— sensual, original, and close to nature. For Goethe, who was then studying law in an enclave of German students in French-speaking Strasbourg, that

Daniel Bager, *The Young Goethe*, 1773.

truth was soon to be found in German-speaking Alsace, and in particular in the village of Sessenheim. It also appeared in the guise of an eighteen-year old girl, Friederike Brion, with whom Goethe fell, seemingly, in love. They first met in October 1770 and corresponded thereafter; he visited her in early 1771 and stayed with her family from May 18 to June 23. It is from this visit that we have Goethe's sensitive drawings of the village and his accounts of rural celebratory life. His extended stay no doubt suggested to the Brions that in accordance with custom he had become her fiancé, an expectation that Goethe rudely frustrated in August. In a letter written from his family home in Frankfurt am Main, he forbade her to contact him further, seriously compromising the standing of Friederike, who was then ill and who would never thereafter wed.

In the villages of France and Germany in the 1770s, marriage was not a private, sentimental association between two loving partners but rather a public, social tie, in which familial, communal, and occupational interests played a decisive role.[78] The amorous interlude revealed the young Goethe's blindness to rural realities and shed an unflattering light on his character. Yet it also inspired lyrical innovation. In one poem written for Friederike, entitled "Welcome and Departure," we hear Goethe evoke the rough, adventurous tones of Ossian, whose characters ride "wild like a hero to battle."[79] This was indeed the voice Herder sought—close to nature, masculine and assertive, and full of mystery.

Goethe also followed Herder's appeal to collect folk songs. In September 1771, Goethe sent him twelve songs he had collected "from the guttural of the oldest grandmothers" in Alsace.[80] They speak of knights and a beautiful maid who duels to get her captured lover back, of the pregnancy of an unwed noblewoman and the violence she endures at the hands of a count, of a cross-dressing prince who hopes to remain in his father's kingdom, and of a common carpenter who sleeps with a countess and is rewarded for his deed rather than sent to the gallows. Love and violence, transgression and rough justice, are the principal themes of these songs, the most famous being the last, "Rose upon the Heath," later put by Franz Schubert to music. Goethe claimed to have written it down from memory, though perhaps it was his own composition, drawn in part from a seventeenth-century songbook in Herder's possession.[81] It too is a simple ballad of love and violence, perhaps even rape. "I will pluck you," says the boy to the rose: "I will pierce you," the rose replies. "The wild boy broke / The little rose upon the heath anyway."[82] Herder included the composition in *Of German Character and Art*, published in 1773, and *Old Folk Songs*, originally scheduled for publication in the same year.

Of German Character and Art became the manifesto of the *Sturm und Drang* (Storm and Stress) movement, which emphasized the sway of emotions and the sensual experience of the world. In the volume, Herder included not just the songs of the north, but also the hymns of Luther—testimonies to an "original, fearless, free and manly language."[83] Goethe, in his contribution to the manifesto, likewise turned away from classicism and toward a rougher art. The established aesthetic rules had taught Goethe that elegance demanded lightness and simplicity, purity of form and harmony of elements, for which neoclassical columns stood as a marker. But columns are not part of our domiciles, Goethe maintained in his famous essay, "The Strasbourg Cathedral": "our houses are not constructed around four columns in four corners; they are built with four walls on four sides."[84] The wall, not the Greek, French, or Italian column, was the central German element. The late medieval architect of the cathedral, Erwin von Steinbach, had erected walls that, like "thousands of tree trunks and a million branches," strove inexorably to the heavens.[85] Yet despite its intricate details, the cathedral impressed itself on Goethe as an irresistible unity, whether at evening twilight, "when its countless parts melted into whole masses," or at daybreak, when the morning mist "enlivened the great, harmonious mass into countless small parts."[86]

When *On German Customs and Art* appeared in 1773, it achieved instant popularity, with Herder's call to search for "folk songs, provincial songs, and peasant songs" inspiring a young generation of German intellectuals.[87] They scoured the libraries and occasionally ventured into taverns in search of the authentic voice of common people. They also composed poetry of their own in the new, popular tone. Gottfried August Bürger, perhaps the most emphatic proponent of popular verse, read folk songs to his maid, hoped for the applause of the village schoolmaster, and declared the local tavern a better forum for his ballads than the court theater.[88] He was hardly alone. The elder Justus Möser waxed enthusiastic about collecting, as did the younger members of Herder's and Goethe's circles in Strasbourg: men such as Johann Heinrich Jung-Stilling, an eye surgeon from whom we have the first extended reflection on the religious feeling of *Heimweh*, or homesickness, and Matthias Claudius, who published ballads and folk songs in *Der Wandsbecker Bothe*, perhaps the first newspaper in Germany that deliberately cultivated the language of the people.

One quill was quick to censure this folkloric movement, and it belonged to none other than Nicolai. He had already criticized Herder's affinity for coarse rhythms and rhymes, asking rhetorically why poems should "breathe a martial bravado that is too raw even for our contemporary soldiers?"[89] He also felt nothing of the "national feeling" that his friend Herder sensed in the bardic tradition. "We live in palaces, wear golden and silk clothes, eat spiced foods and drink fine wine," he pointed out, "and our poets should take all of their descriptions and similes from oak forests, cliffs, and morning fogs?"[90]

In July 1773, Nicolai sent an extremely critical letter, no longer extant, to Herder about the manifesto, including Goethe's contribution to it. We know only that Herder was not amused by it, and "took leave for now and for some time" of Nicolai's journal, *The General German Library*.[91] This was no small step. Under the aegis of Nicolai, the journal was the clearest voice of the high Enlightenment in the German lands, and Herder risked a great deal by snubbing it.[92] In any event, the matter seemed to linger quietly until the summer of 1774, when Nicolai derided a new essay by Herder, as well as the new type of writing of the younger generation inspired by the philosopher. "I like to see language, like rivers that remain in their beds, giving clear water and carrying bountiful ships," whereas the young poets of *Der Wandsbecker Bothe* are of the opinion that "it would be better if [language] were like the Danube that tears everything with it, or a swelled up stream that breaks beds and dams, and in ripping floods rages through field and forest."[93] In a reply, Herder bid farewell to Nicolai's "unimaginative, enlightened, smooth genius."[94] "Who are you," Herder asked of the powerful organizer of the German Enlightenment, "and all your friends, who have proclaimed yourselves the norm of all knowledge and thought?"[95]

Nicolai's critiques, however sharply parried, nevertheless wounded Herder, and, along with delays at the typesetter, were responsible for holding up the publication of Herder's own collection of *Old Folk Songs*, which finally appeared in two volumes in 1778 and 1779, and showed the full breadth of his conception. The original plan had emphasized the affinity of German to British ballads, with the last part adding untamed Nordic songs into the mix. Its aim was to establish a national literary aesthetic, in which German literature would find a center of gravity in its own poetry and that of the peoples with whom it was most closely tied. In the later published version, Herder reached to all corners of Europe for the ideal rhythm, placing different national songs in counterpoint to one another. Among the songs included were a significant number from France, Spain, and eastern Europe, for Herder still imagined that Germany could profit by taking in other traditions. Indeed, he addressed those other traditions as if they played equal parts in a European symphony of poetic voices.

It was, however, the volcanic creativity of the young Goethe that imparted genuine expressive power to the new literature. In 1773, he published *Götz von Berlichingen*, a historical tragedy that takes place during the time of Luther and the Peasants' Wars and features as its main theme the struggle of an independent imperial knight to gain freedom against the designs of a covetous and powerful neighboring state. The play abounds with scenes and personalities, love affairs and betrayals. It also evokes the folk tone that Herder so greatly prized, while mimicking a rough-hewn sixteenth-century speech, which famously culminates in the hero's defiant but often censored "Swabian salute" to the besieging army ("Tell your captain, I have as always due respect for his Imperial majesty. But he, tell him, he can lick my arse.").[96] Herder thought it Shakespearean, if perhaps too consciously. It was also inconclusive, since Götz dies with the words "freedom, freedom" on his lips, but to what positive end?

The question of ends also haunted Goethe's other major literary contribution of the early 1770s. In 1774, Goethe published *The Sorrows of Young Werther*, an epistolary novel that explored the self-destruction of the sentimental, feeling heart. In the novel, Werther falls in love with Lotte, a beautiful, virtuous, soon-to-be married woman who shares Werther's contemporary poetic enthusiasms. Werther's love necessarily remains unfulfilled, the tie to Lotte becomes unbearable, and Werther cannot control his heart's feelings. Instead, his feelings consume him, leaving suicide as the only way out. The novel ends with Werther, who seems to get nothing right, amateurishly shooting himself and taking an agonizing twelve hours to die.

The Sorrows of Young Werther was a European sensation, and for most of his life Goethe would be regarded principally as the famous author of this novel. For German literary patriots, the book elevated Goethe to Promethean stature. "My heart swells with noble pride," wrote the poet, composer, and editor of the otherwise critical *Deutsche Chronik*, Christian Friedrich Daniel Schubart.[97] Not everyone was as pleased, however. An embittered Nicolai penned a satirical *The Joys of Young Werther*, in which the guardian of the Enlightenment took potshots at the new poetry and allowed Werther to get Lotte after all. Lessing, a more perceptive critic, could also not countenance the ending. "Do you imagine a Roman or a Greek youth would have taken his life in *that* way and for *that* reason?" he asked in a letter to Johann Joachim Eschenburg, a well-known translator of Shakespeare.[98] The tragic demanded something more elevated. The ancients, Lessing fulminated, would "have hardly excused in a girl" such immature obsessions.[99]

It was, however, precisely in bringing the tragic to the realm of the common, and in fact to a young woman, that the new literature of *Sturm und Drang* found its greatest expression. While Goethe was writing *Werther*, he had also begun work on the Faust story, the material that Lessing, in his *Seventeenth Letter Concerning the Newest German Literature*, had proclaimed worthy of a German Shakespeare. Reworked in England by Christopher Marlowe as *The Tragical History of Doctor Faustus*, the sixteenth-century German tale came back to the German lands by the end of the seventeenth century via chapbooks and puppet theaters. But far from counting as high literature, *Faust* had become a synonym for the superstitions of the unlearned. "Only the rabble drags around D. Faust and other such books," the critic Johann Christoph Gottsched, an arbiter of early-eighteenth-century good taste, remarked, emphasizing in his *Critical Art of Poetry* of 1730 that a serious German poet should desist from staging such popular spectacles.[100] Goethe had remembered the play from childhood—he may also have seen it performed by a traveling theater group in Strasbourg in 1771. In Goethe's hands, however, the material took on altogether new form.

In Goethe's early version of *Faust* (usually referred to as *Urfaust*), the protagonist has studied philosophy, medicine, and law, "and unfortunately theology too." He is "cleverer than all the doctors, professors, writers, and pastors," and later interpreters were perhaps not wrong to wonder whether Goethe did not in part base Faust on his friend Herder.[101] Faust, in any event, realizes that all his book learning has not brought him closer to "infinite nature," "the source of life."[102] He makes a pact with Mephistopheles, though as the manuscript remained a fragment, we do not learn of its precise stipulations. In the course of his quest, he meets Margarethe, whom Faust will soon call Gretgen (Gretchen in *Faust* I and II), "a wonderful beautiful child / who has fired something within me."[103] She is modest, decent, and pure, and Faust asks Mephistopheles to obtain her for him. She falls for Faust, even though he does not know God but insists "feeling is everything."[104] Nevertheless, she mistrusts his companion and cannot pray in his midst. Gretgen therefore longs to be alone with Faust, but her mother sleeps lightly, making any nighttime meeting nearly impossible. This leads Faust to lend Gretgen a bottle, telling her to give her mother only three drops. The mother, in this way, is accidentally poisoned to death, and Gretgen becomes pregnant with an illegitimate child, leading to her being shunned in the village. Finally, Gretgen murders the child.

This act of infanticide was resonant for Goethe. When he returned from Strasbourg to Frankfurt am Main in the late summer of 1771, Goethe followed the trial of an unmarried barmaid, Susanna Margaretha Brandt, who had killed her infant, for which she was decapitated by sword in the following January. Brandt had been incarcerated a mere two hundred yards from Goethe's house, and Goethe read about her trial with intense interest. No doubt, he also had in his mind what might have been the fate of Friederike Brion, whom he had recently left behind. After their parting, if we can believe his autobiographical account in *Poetry and Truth*, he felt a "somber remorse."[105] In the play, Faust focuses his anger on Mephistopheles, as Gretgen, like Brandt, languished in jail, with her execution planned for the next day. "Who was it that pushed her to ruin, I or you?" Mephistopheles replies to Faust.[106] In his fury, Faust attempts to free Gretgen, but she has become mad, and stays to face her executioner, as Faust rides off with Mephistopheles.

Modulating a variety of characters and situations, not only in content but also in sound, the play constantly changes its metrical rhythms. Its opening rhymed couplets mimic sixteenth-century vernacular poets, like Hans Sachs, master of popular verse, while Wagner, Faust's assistant, speaks with rhetorical pretention in counterpoint to his master's subjective and inspired free verse, reflecting his rule-unbound genius. Similarly, when Gretgen timidly encounters Faust in the garden, it is with careful alexandrines; later, she speaks in short, distraught, irregular lines, echoing, according to one interpreter, the sound of the weaving spindle in her room.[107] In the eighteenth century, one rarely read poetic writing silently, and when read aloud the shifts in rhythm were particularly poignant. Rather than following a predetermined artistic way of talking, rhythm expressed the real-life force behind speech, bringing the artistic and the natural, the high and the low, together—overcoming, in the process, what Erich Auerbach famously called the "separation of styles," by which social realism is excluded from high tragedy.[108]

The intellectual embrace of the natural and the popular is, if one may hazard an interpretation, simultaneously at the center of the tragedy of Faust, a character who (like Herder and Goethe) was no longer satisfied with elevated formulas and pious rules of art. Faust finds the natural in Gretgen, a humble, pious, and domestic girl, and one need not insist on biographical interpretation to see the story of Goethe and Friederike as backlighting the love between the two characters. The collision between the two worlds comes to a head in Faust's dialogue with Gretgen about religion, when Gretgen expresses her disbelief at Faust's lack of belief. Goethe, one may speculate, evokes the inability of *Sturm und Drang* intellectuals, including himself, to comprehend the simple godliness of the people. The work suggests that, in the end, Gretgen possesses greater powers of perception, since she, not Faust, first mistrusts Mephistopheles. Yet the play begs the question of whose tragedy the play recounts, since both Faust and Gretgen fall to ruin. We may well ask if *Sturm und Drang*, the first major encounter in German literature with ordinary people since Grimmelshausen in the nineteenth century, was not, in Goethe's own interpretation, ? 17 e. tragic. This sense of the tragic is heightened when we consider that Goethe portrayed people of idyllic villages only. The very poor of the cities—like the orphaned barmaid Susanna Margaretha Brandt, who served the Jews of the Frankfurt Ghetto and whose class made up most of the infanticide cases—remained for him unrepresentable.[109]

VI

Genuine interest in the people was hardly self-evident. In early modern times, the people of a nation comprised different estates, with the mass of the people, the peasantry, constituting the lowliest and least important caste. Rustics might be pitied for their burdens or examined for their exotic customs, but never extolled for their virtue. This had been true at the time of Luther and Erasmus, and a quarter of a millennium later little had changed. Travelers saw the common people from their fast-moving coaches: Boswell ignored them, Keyßler pitied them, Lavater studied their shapes, and Nicolai reflected on how to ameliorate their lot. No enlightened thinker wished to step out of his coach and walk among them.

Yet in the Europe of the 1770s, the decade in which *Sturm und Drang* came to the fore, a more sympathetic appreciation of the people had begun to set in. One can see this in the contented, industrious English peasants in the paintings of Thomas Gainsborough, or in the depictions of upstanding French families rendered by Jean-Baptiste Greuze. Again, it was Rousseau who inspired the new sentimentality, which also drew on the encounter with peoples in the South Pacific. One may speculate that the "agricultural revolution," aided by the beginnings of a general warming, also contributed to a sense that the rural population was finally winning its battle against harsh nature. In England, where artists often painted yeoman farmers in unthreatening landscapes, widespread undernourishment and even famine visited the countryside less and less.[110] The result, as the historian Wolfgang Hardtwig has suggested, was the waning of a division between a prosperous urban civilization and the raw struggle for subsistence that characterized the countryside. Now, for the first time, denizens of cities could imagine their rural compatriots as part of the same cultural universe.[111] As a result, new possibilities for belonging began to open. For the "imagined community" of the nation, horizontal comradeships were extended, and the circle of inclusion widened.

In the last two decades of the eighteenth century, a significant increase in the number of travel journals describing the German lands reflected the new interest in both place and people. Books rolled off the press explaining how to travel, where to stay, and what to see, "since only a few years ago have people begun to understand that it is also beneficial to travel Germany."[112] Even as some travel journals continued to describe courts and cities, others mixed the urban focus with a new attention to the rural world. In *My Travels in the German Fatherland*, published in 1799, Johann Christoph Friedrich GutsMuths, a prophet of the physical education movement, wrote detailed comments about Dresden and Prague, penned reflective accounts of the isolation of the Riesengebirge, and wrote of the miners in the Ore Mountains, even mentioning the pittances children earned working in the shafts.[113]

Spurred by the French Revolution, a number of travel journals assumed a decidedly critical stance: this was famously the case in Georg Forster's *Views of the Lower Rhine*, which chronicled his journey with the young scientist Alexander von Humboldt through the Rhineland and into revolutionary Holland and France. It was true too of the unheralded Johann Ludwig Ewald, a court pastor in Detmold who appended to a travel journal a reverie about a future—in 1898—when countries would have arrived at an understanding of how to maintain peace and standing armies would be mainly engaged in civilian work.[114] Some travel accounts even pursued the hidden secrets of village life. Inspired by the literature of *Sturm und Drang*, and by the travel writer Johann Kaspar Riesbeck's injunction that "one has to mix with all classes of people who one wants to get to know," young people ventured from cities and university towns into the rural countryside.[115] In his unpublished manuscript of his wandering with a friend into the gentle hills outside Tübingen, Friedrich Köhler, a theology student, noted the appearance of the people and the condition of their dwellings, customs of rough justice, what people ate, and the style and color of regional costumes worn on Sundays and on special holidays.[116]

VII

In 1793, as Nicolai composed the final volumes of his travels through Germany, a nineteen-year-old student named Wilhelm Heinrich Wackenroder wrote a series of letters documenting his more modest trips to the forests, mountains, and cities of Franconia. A starker contrast between ways of seeing is difficult to imagine. Whereas Nicolai had traveled speedily along well-trodden roads in a horse-drawn coach, Wackenroder rode on horseback or walked with his friend Ludwig Tieck. The two galloped along paths, trekked up mountains, wandered through back alleys, and climbed into caves. A major intellectual figure, Nicolai intended his weighty volumes for an enlightened audience he had helped to create. Wackenroder, enrolled at the provincial University of Erlangen, often wrote to his parents asking for money. Announced with great fanfare, Nicolai's volumes found an eager audience, and were debated with esprit; by contrast, Wackenroder's letters remained locked in his family's papers and closed to the world.

Yet it is the travel letters, first published nearly a century after Wackenroder's untimely death from typhus in 1798, that signaled a turn in the imagination of place no less important than the first sixteenth-century depictions of Germany as a mapped space. As in the autumn of the Middle Ages, the Romantic turn involved a heightened attention to the senses. "Sensual beauty for the eyes can only be experienced completely by the eyes, in the original nature, or in the copying of the paintbrush," Wackenroder wrote.[117] His comparison of the experience of nature with art proved revealing. Four years later, Wackenroder and Tieck would publish one of the most important early documents of German Romanticism, *The Heartfelt Effusions of an Art-Loving Monk,* in which the young authors insisted that the true love of art is necessarily opposed to systematization. To them, great art was of divine origin, and the experience of seeing art akin to the act of prayer.

Hoping to experience nature with a comparable intensity, Wackenroder and Tieck climbed the rounded peaks of middle Germany, such as the Ochsenkopf in the Fichtel Mountains, from which the two friends could see all the way to the source of the Main River. Precisely when the details were far and indistinct, the expansive views seemed especially "sublime," as if observing paintings in a gallery.[118] The son of a jurist interested in mineralogy and an eager reader of *The Works of Ossian,* Wackenroder was also fascinated by the jagged caves of Franconian Switzerland, of which the recently discovered Rosenmüller Cave had become quite well-known for its stalactites and stalagmites.[119] Whereas Nicolai had favored the flattened vistas of a well-ordered landscape, Wackenroder was drawn

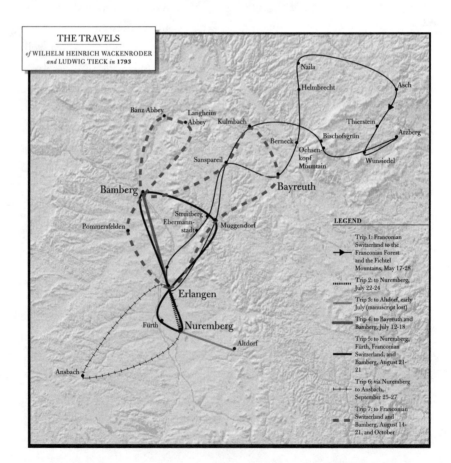

THE TRAVELS
of WILHELM HEINRICH WACKENRODER
and LUDWIG TIECK *in* 1793

LEGEND

Trip 1: Franconian
Switzerland to the
Franconian Forest
and the Fichtel
Mountains, May 17-28

Trip 2: to Nuremberg,
July 22-24

Trip 3: to Altdorf, early
July (manuscript lost)

Trip 4: to Bayreuth and
Bamberg, July 12-18

Trip 5: to Nuremberg,
Fürth, Franconian
Switzerland, and
Bamberg, August 21-
21

Trip 6: via Nuremberg
to Ansbach,
September 25-27

Trip 7: to Franconian
Switzerland and
Bamberg, August 14-
21, and October

to unpredictable, sometimes threatening, vertical formations. He did not long for nature unspoiled, however. Both he and Tieck also sought out the ruins nestled among the craggy rocks and hills, such as those of Burg Neideck, its medieval walls clinging to a cliffside.

The artistic preference for the jagged mountain and not the flowered field, ruins and not palaces, the medieval and not the modern, the suggestive and not the complete, defined some of the elemental differences between the young Wackenroder and the elder Nicolai. Remarkable too were their varying perceptions of the people, something especially noticeable in their divergent treatments of Catholic Bamberg. Although Wackenroder followed Nicolai in the enlightened critic's insistence that there was a Catholic physiognomy, he took an altogether different tone toward pious Catholics, giving us a surprisingly sympathetic account of the faithful attending holy services.[120] In these passages, Wackenroder marveled at the activity in the crowded cathedral in Bamberg. "Some read abidingly in their prayer books, others prayed standing at the rosary, and still others knelt piously quite close to me," he recounted, "and the ceremonies, which changed every minute, made a stronger and more wonderful impression on me the more mysterious and incomprehensible they were."[121] Influenced by Goethe's aesthetics, Wackenroder also gazed at the many towers, spires, walkways, and statues of the late Romanesque structure, even though he omitted mention of the celebrated Bamberg Rider, perhaps because the cathedral's baroque craftsmen had painted the horse white and the king's belt and crown gold.[122]

Wackenroder was also among the first to rediscover the Franconian city of Nuremberg. Travelers, including Nicolai, had formerly passed through Nuremberg reading the polymath Christoph Gottlieb von Murr's famous description of the imperial city's curiosities, which listed all of Nuremberg's scholars and artists, and many of its buildings, churches, and cloisters, reflecting evident pride in the city's achievement. But von Murr's account remained silent, as Nicolai complained, about Nuremberg's decline while being embarrassed about its crooked streets and late medieval gothic visage.[123] Wackenroder, in contrast, was drawn precisely to that which was old. "I cannot but sufficiently wonder at the city," he wrote, "because one cannot find a single new building, but many old ones, from the tenth century onward, so that one feels placed in ancient times and one expects to meet a knight or monk or a townsman in old costume."[124] Wackenroder called the city "Romantic"—for "with every step one has a view of ancient times and of a work of art in stone or color."[125] Nuremberg boasted an abundance of fountains—Nicolai had counted 112—"some with small towers and many figurines," and endless crooked streets and alleys flanked by houses confusedly shoved into one another.[126] Wackenroder also admired Nuremberg's churches, especially St. Lorenz, its middle nave narrow and high, and its windows almost all stained glass, "so that the colors seem to burn."[127] And of course he was astounded by its early-sixteenth-century artists, especially Albrecht Dürer, whose *Four Apostles*—in a seventeenth-century copy—showed Dürer to be a genuine genius, "a German Raphael."[128]

This turn to the medieval world of knights and ladies, combined with a nostalgic longing for the past and praise of raw landscape, would soon take on more programmatic, even national implications. In 1799, the year after Wackenroder's death, a remarkable group of young intellectuals came together in the small university city of Jena. This group of scholars and writers included August Wilhelm and Caroline Schlegel; his brother Friedrich Schlegel and Friedrich's future wife, Dorothea; the visionary poet and Romantic novelist Friedrich von Hardenberg (better known by his pen name Novalis); and the avid collectors of folktales and sagas, Clemens Brentano and Ludwig Tieck. There were also philosophers among them: Fichte, who had settled here in 1794, and would remain until 1799, when his subversive ideas about religion proved too radical for Duke Karl August of Saxe-Weimar; Schelling, who took idealism in a transcendental direction; and Hegel, who came to Jena in 1801, and was at that time known mainly for mediating between Fichte and Schelling.

The intellectual hothouse of Jena would dissolve in 1801, principally with the early death of Novalis. The following January, Friedrich Schlegel would leave Jena and travel to Dresden, where he had first encountered classical art, and on to Leipzig, Weimar, and across middle Germany en route to Paris. In a series of epistles intended for Ludwig Tieck, Schlegel described this trip as a personal journey, a *Bildungsreise*, in which he discovered his self and a new sense of his country, Germany. As he traverses the landscape, he knows he cannot describe each view, only a few stark impressions, of which the first and most lasting was the sight of Wartburg Castle, perched upon "a single mountain surrounded by forest and enveloped by cliffs and valleys and hills."[129] Forsaking empirical description, he relates what the scene conjures—"the memory of the times, when poetry was here in full bloom and in all of Germany there was a general sense of life, love, and gaiety," and "one still had a fatherland."[130] Crestfallen that contemporary Germans, huddled in ordinary houses around country roads, had abandoned their heights, their poetry of old, and their life on the cliffs, he conceded that "patience has become our primary national virtue and next to this modesty."[131]

The only other vista that evoked such nostalgia was the first sight of the Rhine. Foreigners—whether the Gothic romancer Ann Radcliffe in her *A Journey Made in the Summer of 1794 Through Holland and the Western Frontier of Germany*, or Abbate de Bertola, an Italian poet, scholar, and mediator of the new German literature—had already written about the river as if in painted, Romantic hues. In his *Voyage on the Rhine*, Bertola had described the colors and shades, shapes and turns, of the middle Rhine, much as would a "guide through an art gallery familiar to him."[132] Schlegel, however, rendered the river as a source of "memories of that what the Germans once were, and what they could become."[133]

The romanticization of landscape evoked an interior, subjective, national feeling—not mere pride in the outstanding features of a country, but a deeper sense of an identity between subject and object, person and place. If the prosaic starting point of this romanticizing of the land was Rousseau, its philosophical source was the "productive imagination" of Fichte, and its faithful mirror was Schelling's transcendental idealism, which assumed, in contrast to Fichte, that there really were objects out there, and that they had an existence independent of the mind. The philosophy gave the new view its shape, just as poetry gave it expressive voice. "The world must be romanticized," wrote Novalis, in order to find again "its original meaning" and "to give the common a mysterious visage, the known the grandeur of the unknown, and the finite the appearance of the infinite."[134] From the very first, this was an operation of salvage, a project of recovery. The Romantics stood for, and pushed forward, a shift in the conception of nationhood from an exterior object of identification—the country pictured, counted, and described from the comfort of a fast-moving coach—to an interior identity, which one felt, and to which, however haltingly, one began to say, "This is who I am."

CHAPTER 6

DE L'ALLEMAGNE

c. 1790–1815

German greatness does not claim victory with a sword,
but presses into the realm of spirit,
wresting away and laying aside prejudice.

—SCHILLER

• • •

The basic symbol of citizens, arms.

—FICHTE

ALTHOUGH BLESSED BY "PAINTERLY VIEWS" AND "MAJESTICALLY
beautiful rivers," the Germany of Madame de Staël was above all a land
of poets and dramatists, critics and philosophers.[1] In her epochal work
De l'Allemagne, she described the country's peculiar genius as Romantic,
as deriving more from Christian-medieval than from classical influences.
Rather than adherence to society's rules, enthusiasm for the truth distinguished Germany, *"la patrie de la pensée,"* from other modern nations. For
her, Lessing, Winckelmann, Goethe, Schiller, Christoph Martin Wieland,
Herder, the brothers Schlegel, and Immanuel Kant were leaders of a phalanx fighting for national rejuvenation. By contrast, her native France
adhered to the pedantry of classicism at a time when *l'esprit humain* was
elsewhere. In the wake of the Terror, her country had become calculating
and cynical. By the time of Napoleon, it had lost its taste for liberty. Like
all great works on other countries, *De l'Allemagne* reflected back on the
author's own.

The author was no minor figure. The daughter of Jacques Necker,
finance minister of the deposed and guillotined Louis XVI, Anne Louise
Germaine de Staël-Holstein had already written a prolific number of plays,

journals, reflections, and political tracts, including a plea for Marie Antoi-
nette that harbored a general critique of the condition of women in France.
In 1796, she published *A Treatise on the Influence of the Passions upon the
Happiness of Individuals and of Nations*, in which she argued that passion,
which fixes most forcefully on what does not yet exist, enables societies to
move forward but is injurious when pursued without consideration for the
misery passion can cause.[2] Composed in the shadow of the guillotine, the
book signaled her abhorrence of the increasingly ruthless politics of the
French Revolution, which she had initially supported, but whose authoritarian drift she came to distrust. With the advent of Napoleon's rule, her
erstwhile optimism collapsed. On November 9, 1799, nearly a decade after
the start of the Revolution, Napoleon overthrew the Directory and replaced

Marie-Éléonore Godefroid, *Madame de Staël*, 1813.

it with a consul, of which he was to become the first member, two years later instating himself in this position "for life." For de Staël, these were central acts in a drama of liberty's demise. Napoleon rightly saw her thinking and writing as seditious, and in the summer of 1803 he signed an order banishing her "to forty leagues distance from Paris, with an injunction to make [de Staël] depart within four and twenty hours."[3]

This was the beginning of Madame de Staël's decade in exile. With a "violently agitating pain," as she reported in her journal, she left for Germany in November 1803.[4] Forced to say "a last *adieu* to this France, my country," she reluctantly crossed the Rhine from Metz. She visited Frankfurt, where the literary engagement of women impressed her, and traveled on through the horrible roads of Hesse into a more agreeable and cultured Saxony; then to Weimar, "the slumber of the ideal in the real," where she first met Goethe, Schiller, and Herder. From Weimar, she pressed on to Prussia, "a country that does not inspire the imagination," and its capital, Berlin, where she remained unimpressed by the culture of the city's salons, disparagingly noting that especially for women time seemed to have stood still.[5] It was nevertheless during this trip that Madame de Staël conceived of the idea "of writing a book about Germany," which in her letters she sometimes referred to as a work that was to introduce German literature to the world.[6] It was in fact the realm of the imagination that fascinated her. "A strange people, these Germans!" she wrote her father. They were not as sensitive as the English, as graceful as the French, or as emotional as the Italians. Yet "in the most peaceful way they possess a completely Romantic imagination."[7]

Madame de Staël returned to her château in Coppet, near Geneva, in May 1804, having stopped in Würzburg, Ulm, and Zurich. A second trip brought her to Munich in December 1807; she then spent the spring in Vienna, thereafter sojourning in Prague, Dresden, and Weimar before traveling back in June 1808 to her Swiss exile, where she began the writing of *De l'Allemagne*.[8] Modeled on Voltaire's *Lettres anglaises*, and slyly critical of France, the manuscript was originally entitled *Letters on Germany*. By the time of its completion in 1810, it had ballooned to more than a thousand pages, becoming a vast political and literary description of a country that existed in the mind of its beholders but not on the map of Europe shaped by Napoleon's military conquests.[9]

The manuscript immediately and understandably aroused the censor's suspicion. The book supposedly advanced "injurious suppositions" that "abdicated the glory of her country and accorded to Germany superiority in education and thinking."[10] Conversely, its criticisms of Germany seemed treasonable to French authorities, especially her judgments that "Germany paid too much attention to France and does not have enough military spirit," that "it possesses too much indifference to independence and liberty, and that it had harmfully neglected its national power."[11]

Madame de Staël had indeed written, "The Germans have too much respect for foreign countries and not enough national prejudice."[12] She believed that "the nation [of Germany] as a whole has become less bellicose," and that in the first decade of the nineteenth century, "martial spirit and love of fatherland, both sources of the sacrifice of self, hardly exist for contemporary Germans, when taken as a whole."[13] She argued that the Germans were insufficiently independent, and that they "by no means possess *that*, which we call character." They may be virtuous as private persons, and dutiful in their public roles, but their "accommodating eagerness to serve power embarrassed."[14] Germany remained a contemplative land, not a country of deeds, Venus rather than Mars. "No nation is more capable of feeling and thinking," she wrote, "but when the moment arrives, when one must act, the modest conception of character undermines their decisiveness."[15] While these criticisms reflected the depleted condition of German states overrun by the Grande Armée, they could also be interpreted as exhortations to rise and resist. This was, in any case, how Napoleon and his new chief of police, General René Savary, read them.

Napoleon was convinced of the book's seditious nature, and on September 25, 1810, he ordered troops to surround the printer's office. Desperate to stave off a raid, Madame de Staël implored the Emperor to at least look at the book. He had actually seen the manuscript before; now he leafed through it again, read a few passages, and according to one report tossed it in the fire.[16] Savary was no less forthcoming, and he asked of Madame de Staël's son, "Do you think that we have made war for fifteen years in Germany, and that a person of such celebrity as your mother should print a book upon it, without saying a word about us?"[17] He also objected to de Staël's implicit contrasts. "We are not yet reduced to looking for our models in the peoples you admire," he wrote on October 3, warning, "This book shall be destroyed and the author deserves to be sent to [the prison of] Vincennes."[18]

Twelve days later, soldiers broke the printer's plates, and pulped the 5000 copies of volumes one and two as well as the 2000 copies of volume three.[19] In an instant, perhaps the greatest book ever written on Germany was turned into "a perfectly white box on which not a trace of human reason rested," as Madame de Staël bitterly complained.[20]

II

For the development of German nationalism, the German response to the French Revolution was, as Madame de Staël understood, absolutely crucial. A string of Germans, like the circumnavigator Georg Forster, threw their whole being into the event. A few, like the writer Matthias Claudius, opposed it from the start. Yet the preponderance of opinion throughout the German lands shuttled between fascination, as if mesmerized by a spectacle, and skeptical, passive observation.

A generation of older intellectuals tended to the latter position. Close to the end of his life and less sharp than in earlier years, Justus Möser, the popular enlightener of Osnabrück, took the most oppositional stand, arguing against the "book theory" of natural rights upon which the Revolution was based.[21] Friedrich Nicolai, halfway through his travel tomes, proved more representative of enlightened opinion: he distrusted revolutions and hoped that a well-conceived constitution would arise from the turmoil in France, but ultimately saw the initial events in the context of the reform politics of the major German states.[22] Herder, the guiding light of the *Sturm und Drang* movement, also presented the unedifying spectacle of a mind whose great insights came in his younger years. He had intended to write about the French Revolution in his *Letters Concerning Humanity* but—perhaps wisely—chose to leave in the drawer the two letters that addressed the events directly. In those unpublished letters, Herder likened the Revolution to a shipwreck that one could watch from shore and hoped that the turmoil would be fleeting.[23] "Humanity is older and greater than France," he maintained, and it will persevere when "one no longer talks about the ephemera of this Revolution."[24] From Goethe's quill, there was mainly revulsion. "All apostles of freedom, they have always been abhorrent to me," the author of *The Sorrows of Young Werther* wrote.[25]

The more typical reaction was one of enthusiasm giving way to dismay.

This was the reaction of the young, gifted, not yet conservative philosopher Friedrich Gentz, who initially saw in the Revolution "the first practical triumph of philosophy" and "the hope and consolation for so many old ills under which humanity groans."[26] Likewise, August Ludwig von Schlözer, one of Germany's best-informed political observers, initially embraced the Revolution, but when its bloodshed seemed to veer out of control, his confidence diminished. "Reforms, but no revolution," he insisted, is "the solution for the thoughtful German."[27]

To be sure, some, especially among the young, hoped for much more. Hegel, as a nineteen-year old, experienced the Revolution as "a glorious sunrise," while the poet Friedrich Hölderlin, like Hegel still a student in Tübingen, composed hymns to the concept of freedom and the nation of France, and never wavered thereafter, justifying that "Robespierre had to let heads roll."[28] Then there was the constellation of early Romantics—Ludwig Tieck and Wilhelm Wackenroder, Friedrich Schlegel and Novalis—still in their teens and united in their initial enthusiasm. By contrast, more experienced commentators usually took a calmer view, hoping that the French National Assembly would bring forth a monarchy with genuine representation, something more akin to England's Glorious Revolution of 1688.

One of these experienced commentators was Christoph Martin Wieland. Like many of the figures of the German Enlightenment, he had initially supported the French Revolution, imagining it "the greatest and most interesting of all dramas that have ever been played on the world stage."[29] But with the arrest, trial, and beheading of Louis XVI, Wieland knew that a path of moderation was no longer possible.[30] The "second major revolution," as he called it, involved the leveling of the social edifice and the rendering of all equal before the law. "Such a democracy," he declared, "the world has never seen," all previous democracies having been confined to small cities, tiny patches of land, or colonial outposts.[31] Wieland also predicted, correctly, that the revolution would come to Germany by force of arms, and in his essay "On German Patriotism," written in the early months of 1793, he considered the German response.

He likened the German disunity of his day to that of the Greek states on the eve of the Persian invasion in the fifth century BCE. Unable to repel Persia individually, the countries of Hellas, led by the Athenians and the

Spartans, had to band together and fight "as brothers for the preservation and freedom of the *common fatherland*."[32] But thereafter the Greek states would return to their private interests while the Athenians and Spartans continued to compete for local hegemony, offering one or another state a strategic alliance, which the states accepted or rejected according to their advantage. Fighting off the common Persian aggressor nevertheless created a "certain common patriotic spirit," which in Hellenic Greece was reinforced by knowledge of familiar customs, a history of great artistic and scholarly achievements, and the experience of a shared past.[33]

Was this not Germany as it faced revolutionary France? Were the Prussians and Austrians not the Spartans and Athenians? Wieland warned, however, that the Germans should not flatter themselves too quickly. Patriots abounded in Prussia, Bavaria, Saxony, Württemberg, and in large cities like Hamburg and Frankfurt am Main. "But German patriots who love the whole German Empire as their Fatherland above all else?" Of these, there were fewer, and of those "ready to offer a considerable sacrifice: where are they?"[34] Even in the various states, patriotism grew at a hesitant pace and Wieland wondered whether it would ever be capable of bringing forth that "beautiful passion" called "love of fatherland" characterized by readiness "to suffer and to sacrifice."[35]

Wieland's reflections seemed quaint and cautious when juxtaposed with the speed of events in France and the radical utterances emanating from Paris, where the very meaning of such terms as "nation" and "patriot" seemed almost daily to be undergoing powerful transformation. The subsequent history of German nationalism should not obscure this point: it was in the France of the 1790s, not in the German lands, that nationalism first crystallized into its modern, portentous form. "The nation exists before everything; it is the origin of everything," the Abbé Sieyès wrote in *What Is the Third Estate?*; "its will is always legal; it is itself the law."[36] In Germany, political ideas had remained beholden to a sense of nation founded on legitimate institutions and the historical past. In France, Sieyès pushed aside this "historical" argument and, following Rousseau, derived legitimacy from a "social contract" that rested on natural rights and was logically prior to any written constitution.

The radical redefinition of nation did not stop with Sieyès. In the course of the French Revolution, the burgeoning national ethos came to color social and political life as never before, and knew no parallel in the German lands. The historian David Bell is surely correct to say that, in this context, one may properly speak of nationalism as something more than merely a warm attachment to the cultural and political institutions of a country. Instead, nationalism is a political ideology that operates with a clear distinction between friend and foe and that attempts to form the people into active citizens for whom the nation stands above other loyalties.[37]

III

In Germany, by contrast, the major powers, far from developing national sentiment, still schemed how best to partition the country. In 1793, Johann Amadeus von Thugut, director of Austrian foreign affairs, considered a vast reorganization of the western German lands because "the Empire is lost and can only hope to be saved by Austria and Prussia."[38] He envisioned the dissolution of the Ecclesiastical Electorates of Mainz, Trier, and Cologne along with a series of minor principalities. Prussia would receive Luxembourg and patches of Westphalia that would allow it to stretch uninterruptedly westward; Austria would receive parts of Bavaria (south of the Danube) and would extend Anterior Austria all the way to the Rhine. The key to the reorganization was the considerable enlargement of the Electoral Palatinate. With Austrian and Prussian military aid, the newly enlarged Palatinate could serve as a bulwark in central Germany. Two hegemonic states, Prussia in the north, and Austria in the south, would then dominate the German lands, with a subordinate role for militarily viable, medium-sized states. In one version of this calculus, dating back to the ruminations of Joseph II, Austria even considered offering Tuscany to the Grand Duke of Württemberg, and Modena to the Grand Duke of Baden, in exchange for making Stuttgart and Karlsruhe and their surrounding lands an integral part of a supersized, Austria oriented to the west.[39] In this scheme, leading middle-sized states would be assimilated by larger powers, and Germany, rendered impotent by powerful states within it, would essentially cease to exist.

The reorganization reflected Vienna's lack of commitment to the territorial integrity of the Empire; it also never came to pass.[40] Instead, the estates convened in Regensburg and demanded an end to the costly war with France. By early 1795, French troops had overrun the Dutch Republic, and in this context, Prussia also stopped fighting. At the Peace of Basel, the left bank of the Rhine was ceded to France, thus marking the first time since the wars against Louis XIV that the Empire had lost significant portions of German-speaking territory to a foreign power. The theater of war soon shifted to south Germany, while Austria fought France virtually alone. In the meanwhile, Prussia and north Germany embarked on a decade of peace.

It was this peace that Immanuel Kant would defend in his essay "On the Possibilities of Perpetual Peace." This famous essay has such force and clarity that one is tempted to see it as a timeless statement against war. Written in 1795 and amended for a second edition in 1796, its more immediate context was the French annexation of the Rhineland and Prussia's exit from the war. One may reflect on the absence of national feeling in the German lands of the 1790s, such that a principal response to the annexation was an appeal to "perpetual peace." The paradox is lessened when we realize that Kant, like most Germans, thought in terms of states, not nations. Prussia, not Germany, was his kingdom. This becomes obvious with respect to the essay's second context, which was Russia's (and Prussia's) bloody repression of the revolutionary Kościuszko uprising in Poland in 1794. Then, just as the first edition of Kant's essay was going to print, Austria and Prussia scrapped their earlier partition plans in the west and turned their whole attention to the east. In the Third Partition of Poland, agreed upon in October 1795, Austria would acquire the rest of Galicia and parts of central Poland, while Prussia took a small area of so-called New Silesia between Cracow and Częstochowa and a large swath of northern Masuria, which included Warsaw. In area and population, Prussia as a result straddled two nationalities, with German-speaking subjects barely outnumbering Polish-speaking subjects.[41] The whole center of gravity of German politics now shifted east, as the two major powers in the *Reich* dramatically expanded their territory outside the German Empire. Prussia and Austria staked their claim in conjunction with a third power, Russia, which since the Peace of Teschen in 1779 had replaced France as the de facto external guarantor of the Empire.

Aaron Arrowsmith, map of Europe, 1796, after the disappearance of Poland.

We like to think of Kant's essay as forward-looking. In reality, it reflected the events and discussions of the eighteenth century.[42] Within Kant's admonition that "no treaty of peace shall be held valid in which there is tacitly reserved matter for a future war," for example, one can hear reverberations from 1740, when Frederick the Great first invaded and then annexed Silesia, inviting the future wrath of Austria.[43] In Kant's insistence that no state "shall come under the dominion of another state by inheritance, exchange, purchase, or donation," one may recognize the distant echo of the Bavarian succession crisis and the First and Second Partition of Poland.[44] And in his plea to abolish standing armies, one can discern a common critique that perceived the maintenance and costly upkeep of these increasingly large forces to be a principal cause of war between states.

But in Kant there was also something more: "To pay men to kill or be killed seems to entail using them as mere machines and tools in the hands of another [the state], and this is hardly compatible with the rights of mankind in his own person."[45] In the ideal state, subject-citizens were endowed with human rights, which the state could not violate. Kant believed this condition, in which subjects were treated as ends and not as mere means, could adhere in republican governments based on a constitution of law and in which the executive and legislative powers were separate. He did not mean France, which in his eyes had devolved into a democracy that collapsed the two branches of government, making it "necessarily a despotism."[46] Moreover, Kant genuinely feared the new kind of war unleashed by French revolutionary sentiment; he called it "a war of extermination, in which the destruction of both parties can result," making lasting peace possible only "in the vast burial ground of the human race."[47]

IV

Kant was not wrong to be troubled. In 1796, French revolutionary armies crossed the Upper Rhine into south Germany, inaugurating a protracted period of German history marked by war, occupation, and destruction. This time period, which ordinary contemporaries registered not as the dawn of a new age but as the reincarnation of the periodic scourge of war, would last for nearly two decades.[48] In south Germany, townsmen and peasants hoped that the French would merely wage war on the castles of the aristocrats. But soon the more general plundering began, and hardly a district in Swabia, Anterior Austria, Franconia, or Bavaria was spared. The French occupying armies of 1796 were larger than the absolutist armies of the eighteenth century, more dependent on requisitioning their own food supplies, and they were encamped in towns and in the countryside, not in garrisons or in garrison cities. Often undisciplined, French forces extorted civilians for money and supplies, assaulted people in the streets and in homes, and committed untold acts of rape, the sheer number of which is difficult to say. In one area near Augsburg, eight of forty-three parishes reported incidents.[49] If the archival finding can be generalized, it points to a widespread phenomenon, whose truth historians have only begun to consider. Certain, however, is that the initial encounter with French troops significantly and justifiably dampened enthusiasm for the Revolution.

Certain too is that nationalism played no role in the south German response to French occupation. This was true of the elites, and it was true of common people, who dealt with the encampments of various armies—first the French, then the Austrians—much as peasants and townsmen had done for centuries: by lying low, praying to God and hoping the armies would go away. Virtually no one in the 1790s responded to these French incursions with a German appeal to take up arms in order to save the German fatherland. If anything, the opposite occurred. There was remarkably little sense of France as the "absolute enemy," and missing completely was the blood-soaked rhetoric that so conspicuously marked the antagonism between Great Britain and France during the First and Second Coalition Wars.

This hardly changed with the turn of the new century. In the Peace of Lunéville, signed in February 1801, France extended full de jure sovereignty to the left bank of the Rhine, taking into the French hexagon the historically German cities of Speyer, Worms, Mainz, Koblenz, Bonn, Cologne, Trier, and Aachen. The Rhine, once a broadly coursing German river tying together innumerable small territories, had suddenly become the German border, with the German-speaking lands to the west now containing "our former countrymen" (*Landsleute*), as one descriptive guide to the Rhineland put it.[50] And still, the reaction of the Germans remained mute.

One remarkable document, which comes to us from the poet and dramatist Friedrich Schiller, testifies to an almost melancholic resignation. It consists of prose paragraphs written on three separate sheets of paper (two of them filled front and back) in light brown ink, paired with what seems like a later attempt at versification in a darker impression in the right margin. Discovered posthumously in Schiller's papers, the poetic fragment was published for the first time in Karl Goedeke's critical edition of Schiller's works in 1871. But it was not until 1902, in a more avowedly nationalist time, that Bernhard Suphan, the director of the Goethe and Schiller Archive in Weimar and editor of the collected works of Herder, imparted to the newly discovered fragment its artificial yet grandiloquent title, "German Greatness."[51]

The poem was actually a statement of political despair. "The German lives in an old house that is about to collapse," Schiller wrote, "but is himself a noble denizen."[52] Although the precise date when Schiller composed the poem is difficult to determine, it seems likely that it was written after Lunéville; in any case, the poem reflects on the dismal political realities of central Europe during Napoleon's conquests.[53] As Schiller saw it, France and Britain would conquer the world while Germany would remain territorially subservient. Only in the cultural realm could Germans still count among the great peoples: this was Germany's great consolation. "German nation and German Empire are two kinds of things," Schiller wrote, "and the majesty of Germany never rested on the crown of its princes." Instead, the Germans possessed "intrinsic worth," and, as he put it, "when the Empire comes to an end, the intrinsic worth of the German remains unchallenged."[54] This worth was based on German culture, a tender plant growing "among the gothic ruins of an old barbarian constitution."[55] As if to foreshadow Madame de Staël, Schiller called the Germans a young nation, expressing "the youthful Greek and the modern ideal."[56] That ideal started with language, a mirror of the nation, and this language, as well as the humane culture it brings forth, would be the true German contribution to the world. To the fragment's later and more bellicose Wilhelmine interpreters, that contribution led to and culminated in the creation of a national state. To the full-fledged nationalist interpreters during World War I, who took it upon themselves to complete Schiller's fragment, that state became a fighting state.[57] But circa 1800, Schiller evidently had something else in mind: "German greatness does not claim victory with a sword, but presses into the realm of spirit, wresting away and laying aside prejudice."[58]

Victory with a sword was a distinction belonging to none other than Napoleon. But Germany's medium-sized states consumed the spoils. In the wake of the Peace of Lunéville, the Imperial Mediatization, an assembly of princes in charge of compensating those who had lost their territory west of the Rhine, rationalized what remained of the many splinters of territory east of that august river. The result was the demise of worldly territories in the patrimony of the Roman Catholic Church, the secularization of countless abbeys and cloisters, the dissolution of the domains of the so-called imperial knights, and the end of the autonomy of numerous imperial cities.

The caesura was dramatic, and was especially severe in the religious realm. From one day to the next, thousands of monks and nuns were deprived of a vocation; sacred books and objects of art were packed up and sent to capital cities or sold on Saturday markets; and pilgrimages and special processions were abruptly terminated—as happened, for example, with the famous "Blood Ride" in Weingarten, then the largest horse-mounted procession in the world.[59] The break was also felt in urban life. Of Germany's free cities, all but six lost their sovereignty. Some relinquished it more than once, like Ravensburg near Lake Constance, which belonged first to Bavaria, then to Württemberg. Others surrendered unceremoniously, like Schwäbisch Hall, purchased by Württemberg with a modest bribe.[60] And whether free or unfree, many cities demolished their ramparts for fear of enticing bombardment, siege, and occupation, putting a decisive end to a once venerable tradition of urban self-defense.[61]

The result was a major shift in Germany's political topography, one that mainly redounded to the benefit of the medium-sized states. Collecting nine times more territory than it lost, Baden enriched itself spectacularly; Württemberg became nearly a third larger; and Bavaria increased in both size and population, as did Hanover, Oldenburg, and, if modestly, Prussia. Austria forfeited the most, losing in the space of a decade all of its western lands, first in the area of current-day Belgium and Luxembourg, then in southwestern Germany. Austria was slowly becoming an eastern power, separated from France only by a belt of middle-sized German states that owed their newfound prestige and wealth (grabbed from the riches of the secularized churches) to the pressure of Napoleon's armies. But even this reorganization could hardly hold up the pace of events and territorial changes, which circumspect cartographers now followed with "interim maps."[62] Then, in May 1804, Napoleon proclaimed himself emperor of France, and in November the Austrian king followed suit, as Francis I, demonstratively rendering secondary his position of *primus* of the Holy Roman Empire.

With these decisive gestures, the supporting walls of what Schiller had called a "gothic ruin" began to topple. In December 1805, Napoleon achieved a devastating victory over the tactically outmatched Austrians and Russians at Austerlitz. Against the background of four decades of partitions, perspicacious observers, like the traveler and formerly impressed Hessian soldier Johann Gottfried Seume, worried that "we are the Poles of the years '64–94."[63] Instead, the major middle states formed the Confederation of the Rhine, and in the following summer bid formal adieu to the German Empire. On August 6, 1806, the Emperor set down the imperial crown. On this day, the Holy Roman Empire of the German Nation ceased to exist. The old house had collapsed.

V

German nationalism played an insignificant role in the first decade of warfare against French forces. Not anger, or hatred, but melancholy and resignation characterized the German reaction to French occupation between 1792 and 1806. With the exception of those officials whose employment was directly threatened, few possessed even this sense.

Yet in the protracted period of war and occupation, a genuine German nationalism did, in fact, appear for the first time. It broke through at the end of a remarkable journey by the son of a formerly enserfed peasant, a twenty-eight-year-old subject of Swedish Pomerania, who had abandoned his studies at the University of Jena and his career as a pastor. Starting in 1798, he wandered "on foot, wagon, and ship" through southern Germany, Italy, France, and then back to Germany again. The wanderer was Ernst Moritz Arndt, soon to become one of the most prominent and widely read German intellectuals of his day. He chronicled his one-and-a-half-year journey in a five-volume journal, which revealed a young man sensitive to Romantic ways of seeing the world and imbued with a welling sadness about the fate of Germany and Europe under Napoleonic hegemony. By the journey's end, sadness turned to humiliation and anger, and anger to enmity.

In his travels, Arndt explored the caves and countryside of Franconia and discovered the old German charms of Bayreuth, Regensburg, and Nuremberg. He indulged a fascination with brush-covered ruins, the houses and churches of the late medieval period, and the sixteenth-century engravings of "Albert [sic] Dürer." Arndt also noticed something else. The major cities seemed depopulated shadows of their former selves. He first observed the decline in Nuremberg, where grass grew through cobblestoned central squares once humming with humanistic activity. He also saw it in Italy, "tyrannized under the name of fraternity," where the cities lay in ruin and refugees crowded the roads, causing him to wonder about his own country, "poor Germany," similarly "torn asunder."[64] And he observed it in the great cities of provincial France, such as Nice, which "offers a very deathly view," and Avignon, where "the best streets, plazas, and houses" evoke "death and depopulation."[65]

Armed with a keen eye for social injustice, the young Arndt by no means despised the French, though he deplored the "bloody fist of revolutionary turmoil" and the "tyranny" of France's armies, who arrogated to themselves "the right to make infallible their new-Republican faith."[66] Like most young intellectuals of his generation, Arndt had initially embraced the Revolution, but then recoiled when it resorted to regicide and drew back in dismay when pools of less exalted blood began to spill. But even in 1799, with the Terror passed, Arndt's observations fused horror with fascination, and the fascination was not, as it once had been, for "liberty, equality, and fraternity," but for national conscription, the French *levée en masse*, which he saw as decisive for the creation of a modern nation. With "this one phrase, every citizen is a born soldier of his fatherland and has to fight if necessary," France was able, according to Arndt, to mobilize "a nation of 24 to 30 million people."[67] He also wondered how other states could possibly resist an army of up to a million men.

In contrast to France, one nation had become "the ridicule of Europe." This "folk of thirty million people," the north looking dispassionately at the military occupation of the south, and the whole "lacking a national spirit," was, of course, the German nation.[68] The fate of the left bank of the Rhine seemed especially chastening. Occupied since the Peace of Basel in 1795, divided into four administrative districts known as *départements* since 1798, the left bank had become part of a France whose natural borders, as Georges Danton had put it in a speech to the National Assembly, extended along "the banks of the Rhine, the shores of the ocean, and the line of the Alps."[69] Arndt had discerned an eerie sullenness throughout occupied Europe and in the provincial cities of France. He now recorded the same gloom in what he thought of as his own country. Aachen, he claimed, resembled a "desert." Cologne, he recounted, exhibited "great emptiness." And in Bonn, where the university was "nearly destroyed," Arndt sensed that the "aspirations of many centuries had been trampled upon."[70]

Arndt registered genuine discontent. The French had stationed nearly 200,000 troops in the Rhineland, more than 10 percent of the local population. Just in requisitions, the occupying army constituted a colossal burden. The armies extracted considerable levies ("a well-organized looting," as one historian put it); they commandeered extensive labor forces for building roads and fortifications, closed down universities, and appropriated significant artistic and cultural treasures.[71] The local economies, already weakened by the loss of the trade in services and luxuries associated with the princely courts, fell into penury.[72] At the same time, the occupying forces demolished the intricate system of economic regulations and safeguards of the old regime, from trade guilds to poor relief, and dispensed with the once proud independence of Rhenish cities. With the economy in tatters and so many of the old institutions obliterated, the ranks of the poor swelled and the crime rate soared. A German Robin Hood by the name of Schinderhannes, who operated mainly in the Eifel district, was perhaps the most colorful representative of this flourishing banditry—even though his real story was more mundane and sordid, and often involved targeting Jews as especially vulnerable victims.[73]

The steep decline in the Rhenish economy of the 1790s helps explain part of the "emptiness" that Arndt apprehended. But it alone does not clarify why, as Arndt put it, "the French name has become a curse."[74] By the time Arndt arrived in the Rhineland, the administrative integration of the province into the French nation was in full swing, with the majority of governing officials coming from France, especially bilingual Alsace.[75] Revolutionary attacks on the Catholic Church—whether church desecrations, suppression of popular piety, or the incarceration of priests—also intensified, bringing forth a religious countersurge. Led by an embittered clergy, mass pilgrimages increased in number and constituted the visible manifestations of anti-French sentiment. Unlike south Germany, which had not been annexed to France, the Rhineland experienced the direct force of military occupation, and the resulting social, economic, and political turmoil elicited genuine anti-French animosity.

That animosity, it should be understood, was not inspired by nationalism. It is true that historians sometimes argue the reverse, pointing to a number of nationalist pamphlets and a nearly ritualized invocation of

German virtues against French persecution.[76] But the production of pamphlets that could be called nationalist remained marginal, flaring up just briefly in 1793 in reaction to the brief effervescence of the Jacobin Republic of Mainz. The considerable number of German travelers who crossed the occupied areas en route to Paris saw the occupation as the ordinary result of eighteenth-century cabinet warfare.[77] Arndt, who was certainly sensitive to the matter, witnessed little evidence of national sentiment. Instead, he assumed that in a generation's time the people of Cologne, Aachen, Trier, and Koblenz would be speaking French as their mother tongue.[78]

It was nevertheless in reaction to the French occupation of the Rhineland that Arndt first formulated a German nationalism that could go by no other name. It built on an emotional animosity that went far beyond the cultural aversion of earlier anti-French sentiment. "In France I loathed some Frenchmen, criticized most of them, did not value them, and loved some," he wrote. "Here I learn to hate them as enemies and destroyers of my people, and hardly do I see one more, and my cheeks flush hot with blood."[79] Fueled by a sense of national humiliation, Arndt's hatred focused not on the French state or on French culture, or even on the radical thrust of French politics, but, in fact, on the French people. In his view, the French had degraded the citizens of the Rhineland, torn asunder the institutions of the Holy Roman Empire, and debased the German people. Pairing his hatred with a political program, he posited a German nation in terms opposing the French doctrine (and now reality, regarding the Rhine) of natural frontiers.

In *Germanien und Europa*, published in 1802, Arndt sketched out the precise shape of a Europe defined by natural geography and linguistic borders.[80] In Arndt's Europe (see map), the Iberian peninsula was one country, as was Scandinavia, while Russia stretched from the Baltic to the Black Sea. In this Europe of nations, Italy was restored to its putative cultural unity of the Renaissance, while France was returned to its borders at the time of Louis XV (with Lorraine but not Alsace).[81] Poland, that "beautiful country," would regain a measure of its former luster, with the Vistula as its western border and comprising ducal Prussia and Courland, so that it would again become a sea power.

ERNST MORITZ ARNDT'S EUROPE
as IMAGINED *in* 1802

Arndt envisioned Germany in a Europe organized according to nations. The country would stretch from the Adriatic and the Alps to the Eider River and the Baltic Sea and from the Vistula to the English Channel, incorporating current-day Belgium and Holland, the latter supposedly a "screaming injury to Germany's natural borders."[82] Language sometimes counted as the marker of the border separating Germany from other nations—as the subsequently famous line in Arndt's 1813 song "The German Fatherland" ("as far as the German tongue sounds") has long informed us. However, the borders of Arndt's Germany also cleaved to historical markers, taking in French-speaking Flanders and French- and Italian-speaking Switzerland, for example, and hewed to physical barriers, like the Vistula, part of a German imaginary since the days of Conradus Celtis. This nonlinguistic dimension becomes especially evident in urban geography. Polish-speaking Warsaw was, for example, situated on the west bank of the Vistula, and therefore would be part of Germany, while

German-speaking Königsberg would lie squarely in Poland. The political aspect is also important for the question of which countries would survive. As the old European balance of power lay in shambles, nations, according to Arndt, had to be large, populous, and sufficiently endowed with national spirit to repel invaders. Small countries, like Sicily and Savoy, Bavaria and Saxony, would cease to exist.[83]

In 1802, Arndt's ideas scarcely reverberated.[84] Instead, the vast majority of Germans cooperated with the new regime, especially as it settled into the routines of governing. In south Germany, army provisions and discipline became more efficient, and in the Rhineland, the French administration began to integrate the local elite. Moreover, the French administrative presence was only part of the story. The more significant transfer of rule occurred within Germany. In the course of the territorial realignments occasioned by the 1803 Imperial Mediatization, more than three million inhabitants assumed new rulers. Most Germans became subjects of larger states such as Prussia, Austria, Bavaria, Baden, Württemberg, or France.

VI

Diplomatic and military events hardly stood still. After Napoleon knocked Austria out of the war, he forced Russia to pull back its troops. Meanwhile, the new Confederation of the Rhine, which Napoleon had intentionally strengthened, sealed a military alliance with France. Napoleon now contemplated French expansion to the Baltic Sea. Fearing French presence on its western border, Prussia joined a coalition with Britain and Russia and declared war on France.

It was a catastrophic miscalculation. On October 6, 1806, Napoleon's agile forces routed the once vaunted, still disciplined, but logistically hapless and tactically timid Prussian army at Jena and Auerstedt. Not expecting Napoleon to march his troops and heavy cannons through the woods and up to the high plateau above the old university town under the cover of night, the Prussian commander, Prince Hohenlohe-Ingelfingen, found his troops badly outnumbered and at severe disadvantage on the morning of battle. When the reserves failed to materialize, the French army simply slaughtered the Prussian forces, killing and wounding in some estimates as many as ten Prussian soldiers for every man that fell for the Grande Armée, a casualty ratio of 25,000 to 2500. At nearby Auerstedt, Prussian resistance, supported by superior numbers, proved more determined, but taken together the collapse was total, and the army ruined "more completely than any army has ever been ruined on the battlefield," as one young officer, Carl von Clausewitz, later wrote.[85]

Within two weeks of Jena, Napoleon arrived in Berlin, having on the way captured the cities of Erfurt, Halle, and Magdeburg as well as a string of Prussian fortresses. In Berlin, Napoleon strutted down Unter den Linden, the main avenue leading westward from the center of the city, and instructed his soldiers to dismantle the *Quadriga*—Johann Gottfried Schadow's bronze sculpture of four horses pulling the Goddess Victoria that sits atop what had been officially proclaimed in 1792 as the capital's "Peace Gate" (now known as the Brandenburg Gate).[86] Fourteen years later, Napoleon had the ensemble packed in crates and shipped to Paris. He also stopped in Potsdam to visit the tomb of Frederick the Great, stealing his sword.[87]

By then, the pusillanimous Prussian king, Frederick William III, had already fled along with his court to East Prussia, where in the city of Tilsit Napoleon imposed a punishing peace. Prussia lost nearly half of its territory, agreed to reduce the size of its army to a paltry 42,000 troops, and paid a huge indemnity.[88] It was fortunate not to have been erased from the map entirely, or remolded into a completely new polity, as was rapidly becoming common practice. In the same year, Napoleon created the Grand Duchy of Berg, took over the administration of Hanover, and conjured the new Kingdom of Westphalia, with his brother Jérôme as regent. Westphalia was larger than Saxony but smaller than Prussia; it boasted the first written constitution in the German lands, set up a congress of popular representation, abolished serfdom, and emancipated the Jews. "What people," Napoleon asked, "will wish to return to the arbitrary rule of Prussia when it has once tasted the benefits of a wise and liberal administration?"[89]

VII

"Not us," a very small number of Germans answered. Prior to the defeat at Jena, there had been a few nationalist pamphlets, many of them anonymous. There had been various halfhearted official efforts, mostly by the

Austrians and typically self-serving, to shore up national resistance in the western parts of Germany. And there was the unheralded Arndt, who just before the Battle of Jena had published another tract, *The Spirit of the Time*, in which he complained that "cosmopolitanism" was still held in higher esteem than "nationalism," and humanity was more sublime than the people, "*das Volk*."[90]

Patriotism attached to a territorial state, like Saxony or Austria, still came more naturally, and was by all accounts a sentiment more widely shared. The year 1806 nevertheless remains an important marker because for the first time in German history a handful of intellectuals began to write in an unmistakably nationalist mode. In less than a decade, there would be hundreds, their hectic pens scribbling in the service of national renewal.[91] But even at the height of their activity, nationalist intellectuals remained a minority, confined primarily to the educated bourgeoisie and the lower nobility, and more likely to be found in north Germany than in the south. Mostly, they were young men—hardly any of the major figures were over forty. Not a few of them wrote in desperate circumstances, with the hope to overcome their economically precarious circumstance by contributing to the larger patriotic cause. But it would be a mistake to underestimate their idealism, however much we now dislike its expression. It would also be shortsighted to belittle their influence. They set into motion a revolutionary idea, German nationalism, that changed not only Germany, but also Europe, and indeed the world.

Johann Gottlieb Fichte, born in 1762, counted among the earliest public intellectuals who explicated the new nationalism. He was an unlikely candidate. An ardent admirer of the French Revolution, even as it turned violent, he considered the whole spectacle "a rich painting about the great text: the right and value of human beings."[92] In a series of lectures in Berlin in 1804, he argued that the contemporary period witnessed a great transition, and that it was, in fact, the axial age of human history, at whose end man no longer needed external authority in order to live the virtuous life.[93] Like Hegel and Marx, but before them, Fichte looked back not in order to reach into the store of human experience, but to divine the direction of history.[94] He also posited that when the end of history was reached, the state could wither away.

Until 1806, Fichte's entire political thinking still assumed this world of states, not nations. Not with the end of the Holy Roman Empire, but with the crushing defeat of Prussia, this all changed, and in his "Patriotic Dialogues," composed in Königsberg in June 1807, Fichte sharply outlined the shift. In one of the dialogues, he has the so-called speaker A talk about the old patriotism, speaker B about the new.

> **A**: I don't want to be a German. I am a Prussian, and a patriotic Prussian at that.

> **B**: Now, understand me correctly. The division of Prussia from the rest of the world is artificial, based on haphazard and fortuitously erected institutions; the division of Germany from the other European nations is founded upon nature.[95]

"Patriotic Dialogues" was not, however, chauvinistic in an ordinary sense. Rather, it advanced a case for the importance of intellectuals to the education of the German nation. The thought seems otherworldly, especially in the face of Napoleonic power. Fichte reasoned that if this national education had transpired after 1792, there would not have been an 1806. Led by intellectuals, the new, highly educated patriots would have taken up arms and "could never have been defeated by a mortal power."[96]

Even if the political dimension of Fichte's nationalism was directed against the French, it was nevertheless inspired by the French Revolution. We can see this inspiration in an unpublished fragment, likewise written in the summer of 1807, entitled "The Republic of the Germans at the Beginning of the Twenty-Second Century." It is a remarkable document—an imaginative description of the first nationalist utopia, perhaps the first utopia in the nineteenth-century sense of the term (in which the course of history inevitably brings utopia about). Fichte centers his imaginary three-centuries-away Germany in the north, with Magdeburg as its capital city. It includes Holland, Belgium, Silesia, Bohemia, Moravia, Austria, and Switzerland, reaches in the east to the Vistula and in the northeast to the Memel; to the north it is bordered by the Eider River, the coasts of the Baltic and North Seas, and the English Channel. Tied together by a system of waterways connecting the Danube to the Rhine, and the Main to the Elbe via the Weser, this Germany boasted a port in Trieste on the Adriatic and held the Rock of Gibraltar.[97]

More than Arndt, Fichte developed a mapped sense of the German nation based on his understanding of what was necessary for modern states: infrastructure, strategic position, and access to trade routes. He also paid more attention than Arndt to the shapes of historically German states. He brought in Königsberg and East Prussia, for example, and extended Germany's northeast borders to the Memel, while describing the Vistula and the Warthe as the country's eastern extensions. Fichte's future Germany is a leading nation of Europe, and as in Arndt's vision, the small countries have been extirpated, although for Fichte that includes Poland. Left are "England, the Nordic Empires, Italy, Spain, Russia, and the French," with Europe stopping at the Hungarian border.[98] In this Europe of nations, each "race" is equal and free to develop according to its own laws of development.[99] Germany, once established, would have no territorial ambitions.

J. G. FICHTE'S REPUBLIC OF THE GERMANS
at the BEGINNING *of the* 22ND CENTURY

In Fichte's Germany, "only the German can be a citizen," and all male citizens over twenty serve as soldiers. Other nationalities, like the Poles, either have been assimilated or have emigrated; similarly, Jews have either joined the church or left for a "highly interesting state in Palestine."[100] The church in question is called the Christian Church; it has "the Bible as its national book," and Jesus Christ as its founding figure.[101] But it is otherwise a church of reason animated by nationalism.

This becomes clear in Fichte's description of the church and its liturgy. The men who enter the church visibly carry "the basic symbol of citizenship, arms."[102] The walls are likewise covered with weapons, as well as the urns containing the ashes of the dead. Those urns, presumably on shelves, are arranged according to service to the nation, the highest rung reserved for those who died in war, followed by those who counseled the nation, then "good house fathers and house mothers," and, finally, in unmarked urns, those who neither served the nation nor bore children. For the conception of a nation, rituals of birth and death are particularly revealing, because they sanctify the connection (conceived of as an identity) between self and country. In Fichte's imagined Republic of the Germans, the men commemorate the recently deceased, and the women consecrate the newborns. The "eldest and most worthy" women approach the altar with infants in their arms. When a child is blessed, a woman with the child in her arms (not the mother) steps forward and the child is named, and the name is placed in the citizen's book; the community then repeats the name, symbolizing the child's inclusion as a member of "the whole Fatherland of the German Nation."[103]

In this striking liturgy, the strict separation of male and female spheres is at the center of religious life, with women cultivating "love and empathy," men the "heroic virtue" of those ready to die.[104] The new conception of separate spheres—assigning to women a solely domestic, nurturing, passive role, and men a public, independent, assertive position—determined the meaning of public sacrifice and with it the gendered possibilities of citizenship.[105] The nation guaranteed immortality to men, who sacrificed for it, regardless of station or rank, and that immortality was to be inscribed as a name on a public monument. Conversely, desertion, an ordinary practice of soldiers in the old regime, brings "without exception at every rank a death sentence," and thereafter the soldier's "memory is eradicated, his land returned to the earth."[106] If sacrifice was marked by naming and brought immoralization, cowards were "dead forever."[107]

Both Fichte's "Patriotic Dialogues" and his "Republic of the Germans" remained unpublished. In the summer of 1807, when they were written, they revealed what was possible to think rather than what was widely thought. But in a series of lectures courageously delivered in French-occupied Berlin, Fichte would soon sound a clarion call for the new ideology of nationalism. In his famous *Addresses to the German Nation*, delivered in the following winter, he declared that national rebirth, "the means of salvation," involved "the fashioning of an entirely new self," a new man; and that a bond of brotherhood defined a nation, "an organic unity in which no member regards the fate of another as the fate of a stranger."[108] He also proclaimed that nobility is achieved not by birth or station but by sacrifice for a people.

Fichte, like many of the early German idealists, did not reach a wide audience. In the first year of publication, not more than six hundred copies of his famous *Addresses* were sold. But through his lectures, he deeply influenced key personalities, including Baron vom Stein, the intrepid reform minister; Rahel Levin, a Jewish intellectual whose salon was for a time the center of Berlin intellectual life; and Carl von Clausewitz.

VIII

A brilliant young officer, Clausewitz had been a military cadet at the age of twelve, graduating at the top of the elite Institute for Young Officers in Berlin, and was but twenty-six at the time of Prussia's disastrous defeat. For Clausewitz, the defeat at Jena seemed all the more catastrophic because he had belonged to a group of reformers who advocated extricating Prussia from a soporific neutrality that in their opinion had given it ten years of peace at the price of political paralysis. In Clausewitz's analysis, the defeat, which could have been avoided had there been an energetic reserve, "robbed us of our beautiful hopes" and severed "the whole magnificent relation between us and Germany."[109] The "us" referred to the Prussians of his immediate fatherland. It was in captivity and exile in France, when his Prussia was defeated and downtrodden, that he, like Arndt, turned increasingly to Germany.

At the beginning of the nineteenth century, a European code of civility still reigned in noble circles, and Clausewitz's "captivity" involved extended stays as guests of the French government and among its prominent families, including, upon his release after the Peace of Tilsit, a two-month sojourn in Coppet as a guest of Madame de Staël, who had already conceived of her book on Germany but not yet set pen to paper. We have little documentation of their precise exchanges, but Clausewitz's letters to his fiancée, Marie von Brühl, reveal him impatiently enduring Coppet's salon life of pleasant if cerebral conversation, in which Madame de Staël granted that Germans possessed poetic originality but scoffed at their martial spirit.

At first, Clausewitz feared she was right. Writing from Coppet on September 11, 1807, he deplored the "pathetic" spirit of the Germans, and complained of "an eruption of such lack of character and a weakness of disposition that the tears well up in our eyes."[110] Yet he believed it was an error to see the "hated French nation" as possessing an inherent national advantage deriving from the civic enthusiasm and the "military tendency" of the Revolution; instead, the brutality of the Terror, the precise opposite of real republicanism, was forced outward, and then it was hardly an accident that the overwhelming numbers of French forces momentarily achieved victory in battle. Moreover, neither national character nor the energies of the Revolution could sustain the string of conquests resulting in French rule over much of continental Europe. According to Clausewitz, these triumphs were instead "the work of a brilliant and fortunate leader," aided by the "talent of his generals."[111] Leadership, élan, energy, and the genius of a single man gave the French their decisive advantage.

In "The Germans and the French," an essay written after his return to Berlin in November 1807, Clausewitz argued that it was not the French, but rather the German experience that constituted the ideal precondition for genuinely republican governments. While the French evinced a propensity to political obedience and bureaucratic uniformity, the Germans distinguished themselves by their inclination to criticism and their history of diversity. Nevertheless, small republics could not survive the military challenges of the age. In the Germany of the early nineteenth century, Clausewitz hints, expelling the invaders would fall to the one state with a great military tradition and "character" in the sense that Madame de Staël intended the term. His concentration returned to Prussia.

Clausewitz hoped to participate in Prussia's renewal, and he received a chance when Gerhard von Scharnhorst, a dedicated, methodical reformer, asked him to take part in the reorganization of the Prussian military, now purged of discredited officers. Scharnhorst's new army would emphasize streamlined command at the top and the promotion of officers by merit rather than birth or royal favor. It would use flexible tactics in the field, an open order of battle, and territorial militias as reserve units in major encounters. Finally, it would introduce universal military conscription.

In August 1808, Scharnhorst proposed these sweeping reforms to Frederick William III with the intent, as Scharnhorst put it, "to raise and inspire the spirit of the army, to bring the army and the nation into more intimate union."[112] Over the next two years, considerable progress was made in all areas except the draft. General conscription—the elixir of modern warfare characterized by increasingly large engagements—was put off. In fact, the Austrians made greater progress, actually implementing conscription in Bohemia and in the hereditary lands of the Habsburg crown. But if the Prussians shied away from a *levée en masse*, they modernized their state in other, crucial ways: abolishing serfdom, emancipating the Jews, outlawing guilds, restoring municipal autonomy to cities, restructuring education (including the founding of a university in Berlin in 1809), and loosening restrictions on labor and trade. Perhaps most important, "subjects" became "citizens," equal before the law, and the citizens were, in the words of the king, "to replace for the state through spiritual power what it has lost in physical terms."[113]

IX

Trying desperately to contribute to this sudden welling of spiritual power was a young writer, not unappreciated but hardly enjoying general acclaim. A retired lieutenant in the Prussian army, Heinrich von Kleist looms far larger in our current imagination of the period than in the horizons of his contemporaries. Goethe had spurned him, especially after one of Kleist's plays, *Der Zerbrochene Krug* (*The Broken Jug*), proved a debacle on the Weimar stage. Madame de Staël left him unmentioned. And even major Romantics, like the poet-philologist Schlegel brothers, failed to appreciate his work. As was true of his writing, his patriotism was ill starred. Like

Clausewitz, Kleist could not think about Jena without shedding tears, and he disliked the French, an opinion that did not become more favorable during his nearly six months in French captivity. In the summer of 1807, he returned to Germany, taking up residence in Dresden, the bustling but beleaguered capital of Saxony.

Dresden drew together a remarkable cohort of German Romantics. It was here that Caspar David Friedrich first exhibited paintings more revealing of a religious and a national temper than an actual landscape. Dresden was also the temporary home of Adam Müller, who in his lectures on aesthetics, science, and politics first adumbrated a notion of the state as an organic whole, as opposed to its being merely a machine in the service of wealth and power. Earlier in the decade, Friedrich Schlegel, the most gifted of Romantic critics, lived in Dresden. So too did Ludwig Tieck, the poet, translator, and assiduous collector.[114] But the mood in Dresden was far from nationalistic. Saxony was still neutral, and the public was divided between those for Napoleon and those against.

In Dresden, likely at some time in summer of 1808, Kleist's thinking took a decidedly nationalist turn, especially evident in his play *Hermann's Battle*.[115] With no surfeit of subtlety, the play attacked the conciliatory stance of German princes and conjured an imaginary scenario in which the various Germanic tribes, led by Hermann the Cherusker, put aside their differences in order to route General Varus and his Roman legions in an apocalyptic battle in the Teutoburg Wood. The theme was not unfamiliar to German audiences. Wieland and Klopstock had tried their hand at it, and scholars have seen aspects of proto-nationalism in each of their plays. Kleist's rendition was remarkable for its obdurate cruelty. In one scene, the Romans rape the daughter of a blacksmith, and as the father sees the rape as a mark of shame, he turns on the girl and stabs her to death. Hermann, however, wants revenge; he tells the blacksmith to take his daughter's corpse into a tent and cut it into fifteen pieces, one for every German tribe. Messengers then take the body parts on horseback to each of the chiefs, whose hatred, ember hot after seeing the sliced-up and violated German virgin, is forged into a single, unified, national fervor.

Kleist drew the gruesome image, intended to summon the centrality of archaic sacrifice to the creation of what intellectuals of his generation thought of as the oldest nation in the world, from the Benjaminite War as told in the Book of Judges.[116] The Old Testament story likewise brutally asserts the coming together of a manly nation through the tearing apart of a female body, an assertion underscored when we recall that in Judges 19, the angry crowd of men first demanded the sacrifice of a man "so they could have intercourse with him," and only to save himself did the Levite offer a woman as sacrifice. Finally, just as the ancient war concluded with Israel's near extermination of the Benjaminite tribe, Kleist's furious drama ends with sacrifice and annihilation. As if in imitation of the angered Israelites, the German tribes in *Hermann's Battle* unleash their fury on the foe, pursuing the Romans all the way to the city of Caesar, "until nothing but black smoke flutters from a desolate heap of rubble."[117]

Kleist's nationalist engagement, further evidenced in a series of essays, proclamations, Spanish-inspired catechisms, and plays, remained largely without influence in his lifetime. Yet with more precision than the works of any other author, Kleist's writings open a view onto the imaginative sinews of early nationalism, revealing the proximity of idealism and brutality, democratic aspirations and war, and overtly masculine fantasies of aggression and violence, triggered by the realities of military and political weakness.

Not a few of the intellectuals drawn to this imagined violence gathered weekly in Berlin at the so-called German Table Society. Established in January 1811, its members included Achim von Arnim and Clemens Brentano, founders of Heidelberg Romanticism; Fichte, who later that year would become rector of the new University of Berlin; the city's preeminent architect, Karl Friedrich Schinkel; the founder of modern German legal history, Friedrich Karl von Savigny; and the theologian Friedrich Schleiermacher.[118] Carl von Clausewitz and a coterie of Prussian officers belonged as well—perhaps Kleist too, although the evidence is inconclusive. In any case, the Table Society discussed the fortunes of Prussia and of Germany and the shape of the new patriotism. It also descended, briefly if ominously, into anti-Semitism, reminding us that the birth of German nationalism was from the beginning tied in complex ways to anti-Jewish sentiment.[119]

Whether or not Kleist belonged to the Table Society, his nationalism reveals something of considerable significance. And this is that in its initial phase German nationalism, however problematic, drew from a coruscating burst of intellectual power and creative energy, making it at once particular and universal, sanguinary and utopian. Placing emotions of love, hate, and fear in the service of state power, German nationalism became one of the most potent and, in the end, lethal political ideologies of the nineteenth and twentieth centuries.

Nevertheless, the requirements of historical balance and analytical precision force us to acknowledge two important caveats. The first is that far from all of the major German intellectuals went over to the new nationalism. There was of course the skeptical Goethe, whose "conservative pacifism," as Gustav Seibt has aptly called it, caused him to immerse himself in his theory of colors and turn to his autobiography, *Poetry and Truth*, itself a story of a Germany of the spirit not the sword.[120] Some of the major philosophers also retained their distance from nationalism, including Schelling (by now a professor in Munich) and Hegel, who on the eve of the catastrophe at Jena had completed all but the preface to the *Phenomenology of Spirit*, but then spent two largely unproductive years writing for a local newspaper, the *Bamberger Zeitung*. There were, moreover, intellectuals who pleaded for peace. Perhaps the most prominent was the novelist Jean Paul. In 1808, he published *Peace-Sermon to Germany*, which urged his countrymen to embrace the good sides of the French and pursue moral and political renewal because, as he feared, a long winter of permanent war would otherwise supplant the springtime of everlasting peace.[121] One of Germany's most popular yet serious authors, Jean Paul had originally intended to dedicate the sermon to Karl Theodor Anton Maria von Dalberg, Prince Primate of the Confederation of the Rhine—a fact that reminds us that during the years of Napoleonic occupation, there remained alternative possibilities for political loyalty.

The second caveat concerns the influence of intellectuals who propagated nationalist ideas. Despite a widening of the public sphere, it remained limited. By 1800 book production had increased fivefold since the mid-eighteenth century, and literacy had increased apace. Yet the war years dented this development considerably. The British blockade of the continent, put in place soon after Napoleon's victory in Jena, undermined the economy and wreaked havoc on the book market, which plummeted by 1813 to nearly half its antebellum production of titles.[122] Censorship— emanating from the French government and from German regents, especially the anxious Hohenzollerns—exacerbated the problem, making it risky to publish nationalist writings. As one Nuremberg publisher, Johann

Philipp Palm, learned, the risk was more than financial. When he refused in 1806 to name the writer of *Germany in Its Deepest Humiliation,* a pamphlet whose authorship remains to this day unknown, Napoleon had him hanged. From the demand side, the situation was also not auspicious. The ability to sign one's name on a marriage register, the historian's index of literacy, does not mean that people can read extended prose, and Jean Paul, who had a gifted writer's sense for what the market could bear, estimated the real reading public as no larger than 300,000 people, or about 5 percent of the Empire's adult population. In 1809, nationalist writings hardly counted as significant even to this limited public, as Ernst Moritz Arndt conceded in the second installment of his *Spirit of the Time.*[123] Before 1813, nationalist writings, including the works of Arndt and Fichte, reached an audience of a few thousand readers—not more.

X

The turn began in 1810—not from the force of ideas but as a result of changing diplomatic fortunes. The relationship between Napoleon and Czar Alexander I began to deteriorate when the French emperor, in defiance of the Peace of Tilsit, annexed the Duchy of Oldenburg, whose sovereign, Duke Peter Friedrich Wilhelm, was the czar's uncle. Alexander responded with a boycott of French goods, excepting silk and wine, and over the course of the next year, tensions mounted. When a French invasion of Russia seemed imminent in the early months of 1812, Napoleon forced Prussia to enter into an offensive alliance, essentially supplying the French emperor with soldiers and opening Prussian garrisons to French forces.

For some Prussian patriots, the disgrace was too much, and they did the unthinkable: they deserted their king and sided with Russia. Some, Baron vom Stein the most prominent among them, now embraced Germany as their fatherland. "I have one Fatherland, it is called Germany," he wrote to a friend in Hanover in December 1812 from his exile on the Neva, emphasizing that "I can devote myself with my whole soul only to the one, and not a part of it."[124]

Napoleon's Russian campaign, which began in June, faltered within the first two months, as desertion and disease decimated the French army

"Europe at the Time of Napoleon's Greatest Extension of Power"
(just before his invasion of Russia), in Gustav Droysen,
Allgemeiner Historischer Handatlas (1886).

far more effectively than the cannons and muskets of enemy forces. By the
time of the first major battle, at Borodino, the Grande Armée was at half
its initial strength; by mid-September, when Napoleon's troops entered
the charred and deserted city of Moscow, the largest invasion force ever
amassed was a mere shadow of its former self. Short on supplies and facing the onset of winter, Napoleon and his army were soon forced to retreat
from the city and begin the cold, Cossack-harried, trek back westward. It
was indeed arduous, and the French emperor, according to one soldier's
account, seemed "indifferent and unconcerned over the wretchedness of
his soldiers."[125] Frozen and famished, Napoleon's depleted armies staggered across the Memel and into East Prussia in January 1813. Prussia, still

fighting on Napoleon's side, was treaty-bound to halt the Russian advance, and in this way save the remnants of the Grande Armée from total ruin.

At this time a second, equally decisive insubordination occurred. Upon the urging of Clausewitz, General Graf Yorck von Wartenburg, who had commanded an unwilling Prussian Corps in Napoleon's service in Russia, agreed to neutralize his troops for two months, allowing the Russian army to continue its pursuit of French forces. It was an act of high treason, and on January 3, 1813, Yorck wrote King Frederick William that he would await his bullet calmly and without remorse, emphasizing that he was speaking the "words of a loyal old servant" and "that these words are almost universally the words of the nation."[126] He meant Prussia, the true object of his loyalty, higher, even, than the king himself.

The king and his court in Berlin hesitated. When rumors abounded that the French would take the king prisoner, Frederick William moved the court to Breslau, and it was here, in the Silesian capital, that he slowly began to turn against Napoleon. In early February, the king had already called Scharnhorst out of retirement, and on February 8, the king agreed to allow the formation of volunteer units of riflemen. It was not enough. Berlin had already lost control of East Prussia, and Baron vom Stein, along with Yorck, had already persuaded the provincial estates to raise a fighting force. By mid-February, the king was faced with the possibility of a genuine revolutionary uprising. Only then did he switch sides, signing a treaty with Russia later in the month that would guarantee that Prussia would be returned to its 1806 borders in the event of victory against France. Then, on March 17, 1813, the king issued "To My People," a genuine, Prussian-national call for arms.

Drafted by Gottlieb von Hippel the Younger, a close friend of the fabulist E. T. A. Hoffmann, the call represented the first time a Prussian king made a national appeal to the people in order to justify a policy. By "my people," he meant the subjects of the Prussian crown: "Brandenburgers, Prussians, Silesians, Pomeranians, and Lithuanians." The Kingdom of Prussia, the regent proclaimed, faced an alternative: either "an honorable peace or a glorious downfall." Germans were also addressed, as an afterthought and as if an extension of the Prussians, and like them facing the question of whether they will continue to exist.[127] "To My People" was, then, only obliquely a document of German nationalism—and certainly not a nationalist proclamation as Arndt, Kleist, and Fichte would have imagined it.

XI

The Prussian reversal placed the resources of a warring state behind the patriotic press, with the consequence that this patriotism—part Prussian, part German—expanded dramatically. As never before, nationalism now reached beyond small coteries of intellectuals in Berlin, Vienna, and Dresden. Backed with the money of the state and the encouragement of energetic Prussian officers, Ernst Moritz Arndt, for example, peddled his appeals to the elemental emotions of love, hate, and taking revenge in broadsides printed in tens of thousands of copies.[128] In this time, genuine war poetry arose, with young bards, soldier-poets like Theodor Körner, propagating a nationalist war spirit in the style of the late Heinrich von Kleist. Körner, who would be martyred in the war, admonished his comrades:

Und sauft euch satt in Blut!	Drink yourselves satiated with blood!
Und wenn sie winselnd auf den Knien liegen	And when they whimper on their knees,
Und zitternd Gnade schrei'n,	And tremble screaming for pardon,
Laßt nicht des Mitleids feige Stimme siegen,	Do not cave to sympathy's cowardly voice,
Stoßt ohn' Erbarmen drein!	Stab into them without mercy![129]

This was the "magnificent poetry of hate," as the lyricist Joseph von Eichendorff called it, its blood-soaked imagery and archaic combat metaphors no less powerful as they flowed from the pen of a dashing twenty-two-year-old man in the face of death. In Körner's verse, the French are stripped of their humanity, rendered not as mere enemies but as animals and criminals.[130]

Such sanguinary poetry was also put to song, and it is in the form of song that the new nationalism rung so plangently in the ears of eager troops and supporters of the war. Among the most popular of the songbooks was *Die deutschen Wehrlieder* (*The German Army Songs*), compiled by the eccentric, aging semiprophet Friedrich Ludwig Jahn, known as Father

Jahn, the organizer of a gymnastics movement for young men training to liberate the fatherland. The songbook, which went through no less than nine editions during the war, propagated "songs of masculinity," as Jahn put it.[131] This was no timeless male bravado, however. Implicitly rejecting the machinelike choreography of cabinet-war marching music, Jahn's book included songs from Arndt and Körner and emphasized the passion, individual initiative, and elementary emotions of a new kind of man, the warrior-citizen.

The nationalist movement burst on the scene in the summer of 1813, when Napoleon's troops were desperate and on the run. Contrary to conventional opinion, this new nationalism did not grow out of the actual experience of war, but from the preparation for it, as well as from the mobilization of state resources behind an idea and a sentiment. Only now it was more than just a sentiment. Some took up arms on their own volition, a phenomenon hitherto more discussed than practiced.

All-volunteer units, such as the Lützow Riflemen, thus revealed a new willingness to sacrifice one's own life for a patriotic cause. The Riflemen counted some three thousand men and at least twenty-three women who disguised themselves as men. One of them, Eleonore Prochaska, was martyred at the Battle of the Göhrde and was treated as no less than a "German Jeanne d'Arc."[132] Mainly from Prussia and northern Germany, the riflemen (and women) included many artisans (40 percent), some farmers and landless peasants (15 percent), a significant number from the educated middle class (12 percent), and students (5 percent).[133]

The student fighters have received the most attention. Roughly half of all Prussia's college students participated in the war, and they left a trail of poetry and art telling of genuine idealism.[134] Although some may have been motivated by a royal proclamation claiming that those who served would receive advantages in subsequent state appointments, it would be unreasonable to assume that all of them, or even most of them, risked their lives for cushier positions. The voluminous memoirs and correspondences from this period suggest a deeper commitment. Moreover, one might well emphasize the lasting effect on young people—the future leaders of Germany—of fighting and ultimately winning a war defined as a war for the freedom of the Prussian nation. Circumspect observers are right to criticize the nationalist idea that the whole nation, inside and outside of Prussia, rose up. Certainly, it did not. But for the first time, a significant portion of educated young people believed—passionately and with deeds following their conviction—that they had a fatherland to die for.

No less novel, and too often overlooked, was the public sacrifice of women. In *On Death for the Fatherland*, one of the founding documents of both Prussian patriotism and the ideology of separate spheres for women and men, Thomas Abbt had limited the active participation of women in war to childbearing. In this conception, women too have a fatherland but only in the context of family.[135] Sons may bring honor to mothers, but active sacrifice, or enthusiasm in the face of death, was reserved for men, with important repercussions for the gendering of modern citizenship. Yet in 1813, and as a supplement to King Frederick William's "To My People," Princess Marianne of Prussia, admired for her love of literature and scholarship, summoned the "women of the Prussian state" to sacrifice not only sons but also money, jewelry, and clothing, and, if circumstances allowed, "to care for the wounded."[136] She also called for the establishment of patriotic women's organizations. Between 1813 and 1815, nearly six hundred were founded throughout Germany, their ranks swelled by noble and middle-class women.[137]

What such engagement meant for women can be gleaned from an unlikely source: the letters of Rahel Levin, the Jewish intellectual known throughout Europe for the critical, cosmopolitan atmosphere of her engaging "open house." She well understood the dangerous, exclusionary logic of early nationalism. The patriotic German Table Society had excluded Jews and women from membership, and not a few of her once regular visitors—including Achim von Arnim, Clemens Brentano, and Adam Müller—had, as a result, shunned her. "My German friends . . . are all gone . . . as if they had died," she lamented, bitterly, in January 1808.[138]

Yet by 1813, she too was engulfed in the patriotic upheaval, whose energy she characterized as a "moving stream of emotions and lightning thoughts."[139] That summer, she fled Berlin for Breslau, and then found herself in Prague, the city closest to the front, staying at the home of her friend the actress Auguste Brede. Following the Battle of Kulm at the end of August, streams of wounded entered the city. "I saw our whole country here," she wrote to Sophie von Grotthuß, a fellow Jewish writer and *salonnière* who was then in Dresden. "My heart swelled. Our downpour-soaked streets were covered with unhoused wounded. My countrymen [*Landsleute*]! I fell on my knees and screamed to God."[140] Levin set up her "true Prussian office" in Brede's home, where she cared for the wounded, "distributed and sent shirts, socks, food, and money," wrote letters to find lost comrades, and informed mothers of their sons' deaths.[141] There can be no doubt that in this moment she felt a certain pride at being Prussian and "being able to serve the soldiers."[142] A "Prussian *Chevere* woman," she called herself, alluding to a Hebrew term for a female comrade.[143] Like so many other intellectuals, she had never actually seen the monstrous, bloody side of war, and her Prussian patriotism notwithstanding, she also felt deep empathy for the soldiers of other fighting nations. A follower of Fichte not Arndt, Levin remained a European, and imagined less martial futures. In a rumination that at once expressed and critiqued the new separation of spheres, she wrote Karl August Varnhagen, her future husband, "I have such a plan in my heart to summon all the women of Europe to resolve to never partake in war; and together to help the suffering; then we could be peaceful, from one side, we women, I mean. Shouldn't something like this work?"[144]

XII

In the summer of 1813, the new nationalism remained largely a Prussian phenomenon. Then, in a fateful encounter, Klemens von Metternich met Napoleon in Dresden and offered to mediate between the warring parties. The Austrian foreign minister suggested France retreat to its natural borders and keep the left bank of the Rhine, but Napoleon saw that such a retreat essentially robbed him of all French conquests since 1796. Furious, Napoleon threatened with what remained of the Grande Armée. "I've seen your soldiers," Metternich replied, "they are no more than children."[145] Napoleon's hat fell, or he flung it, and Metternich refused to pick it up. "You know nothing of what goes on in a soldier's mind," Napoleon raged. "I grew up on the field of battle. A man like me cares little for the lives of a million men."[146] When Metternich chided him for sacrificing the men of France for his imperial ambition, Napoleon dismissed the criticism, pointing out that in Russia he had spared the French, who counted for only a tenth of the casualties, and sacrificed instead the Poles and the Germans. "You forget, sire, that you are addressing a German," said Metternich.[147]

Austria reentered the war on August 11, 1813, and the stage was set for a numerical mismatch. Metternich had surely exaggerated when he dismissed the French emperor's forces as "no more than children," but most of Napoleon's men were, in fact, new, hastily trained recruits, and the bulk of them were Germans from the Confederation of the Rhine and Poles from the Duchy of Warsaw. As Austrian, Russian, Prussian, and Swedish troops bore down on French positions in Saxony, Napoleon's situation became extremely precarious.

Two months later, on October 16, the armies clashed outside of Leipzig, where Napoleon had concentrated close to 180,000 men north and south of the city. In over three days of fighting, the injured and dead counted as many as 38,000 men on the French side and 54,000 on the allied side, making the *Völkerschlacht* (the Battle of Peoples, or Nations), as it came to be called, the largest military engagement in western history when it occurred and the deadliest single military encounter in Europe or North America until World War I. In the course of the battle, positions changed slowly, sometimes imperceptibly, with the French gradually falling back toward the city, and the casualties especially severe on the third day. When a contingent of Saxon troops defected to the allies and turned their rifles on French forces, the balance finally tipped. With his army decimated, Napoleon retreated under cover of night and early morning to the west, even as thousands of men remained defending positions in Leipzig in one last stand.

Napoleon's tenuous rule in Germany thereafter crumbled like a dried-out castle of sand. Bavaria had already switched sides before the battle started. In its aftermath, Baden, Württemberg, Hesse, and Nassau followed suit. Almost immediately, the political constellations of the past years came undone. By November, Jérôme, king of Westphalia, returned to Paris, his departure virtually unnoticed. And triumphantly, in the other direction, came "our horses," as Levin called them, referring to the *Quadriga*, which King Frederick William III reclaimed from its pedestal in the Louvre and the Prussian army proudly paraded back through northern Germany.[148] En route, the horses received an enthusiastic reception. And when they arrived in Berlin, their chariot driver, the goddess Victoria, was given an Iron Cross, the medal of Prussian bravery and courage, before the ensemble was hoisted back atop the Brandenburg Gate.[149]

The era of French predominance in central Europe was over, but war would erupt one last time. In late February 1815, Napoleon escaped from exile on the island of Elba. Within three months he gathered an impressive force in order to face his opponents one last time. But then, on June 18, at Waterloo, just south of Brussels, allied armies commanded by the Anglo-Irish Duke of Wellington, and reinforced by the Prussian General Gebhard von Blücher, finally and decisively defeated the French emperor. A quarter century of war was thus brought to an end.

XIII

Easily overlooked amid the smoke and fury of military campaigns was the publication of *De l'Allemagne* in London on November 4, 1813. The book, which painted the Germans as a poetry-loving, Romantic, and peaceful people, would go on to powerfully influence French attitudes toward their neighbors throughout much of the nineteenth century. When de Staël first drafted the manuscript, she had somehow hoped that literature would unify Germans otherwise beset with division, calling forth a culture capable of defying the destructive maw of the Napoleonic military machine.[150] Indeed, her anti-Napoleonic intentions reverberated throughout the work, even influencing specific interpretations. *Faust*, in her hands, had become an allegory of struggle between good and evil rather than the boundless and hubristic striving for knowledge, while Schiller's dramas were all about the protagonist's struggle against tyranny; in 1810, when she had originally written the manuscript, this could only be understood as the tyranny of Napoleon.[151] She had also offered a general appreciation of the German propensity for enthusiasm, which she considered "the defining characteristic" of the German literary nation.[152] And she distinguished enthusiasm, which is open and all-embracing, from fanaticism, "an exclusive passion whose object is an opinion."[153] If Germans had one thing to teach other nations, she believed, it was this open-to-the-world enthusiasm; the French, by contrast, had succumbed to an ever narrower fanaticism, which, when teethed with military force, left only destruction.

It is difficult to think of a passionate panegyric so little loved and so widely criticized. Madame de Staël had overlooked the Romantic intellectuals of the younger generation, and in 1813, her image of a country of poetic dreamers without patriotism neither flattered nor made sense. Rahel Levin pronounced "a lyrical sigh," dismissing the idea that anyone could learn something about Germany from it.[154] By the twentieth century, with German militarism pronounced and its bellicosity in plain view, de Staël's analysis would even come to seem positively naïve. Yet one should not lose sight that the book, before it was censored and pulped, had captured the thoughts and aspirations of a mainly pacific nation before the advent of nationalism. And one should perhaps not forget that for another half century, until the 1860s, Germany (including Prussia) would count among the least bellicose of major powers, and that the Romantic spirit Madame de Staël had once conjured continued to inform how Germans imagined their nation.

III

—

THE AGE OF NATIONALISM

IN HIS APARTMENT IN THE RUE DU FAUBOURG POISSONNIÈRE, NOT far from Paris's Gare du Nord, the poet Heinrich Heine wrote *Germany: A Winter's Tale*, a series of "versified travel pictures, a completely new genre," as he called it.[1] Beginning the long poem with a high-minded, prose preface that announced his "patriotism," Heine reassured his readers that he had no intention of handing over the Rhine to France, and that, like any man who loves his country, he will give his "heart's blood" for a free Germany. Laden with pathos, the first cycle functions as a counterpoint to the false song of a harp-strumming girl, whom Heine encounters at the border, and who sings of self-denial on earth and happiness in the hereafter. Heine knows the song and its hypocritical author ("who preaches water and drinks secretly wine"), and offers us instead:

Ein neues Lied, ein besseres Lied	A new song, a better song
O Freunde, will ich	Oh Friends, I want to
Euch dichten!	proclaim to you!
Wir wollen hier auf Erden	We want already here on this
schon	earth
Das Himmelreich errichten.	To raise the Kingdom of Heaven.[2]

Heine's much improved song speaks to the disappearance of misery and the dawn of abundance, symbolized in a time of dearth by bread and sugar peas, torts and cakes, flutes and fiddles.

But then, abruptly, Heine encounters a Prussian customs official, and the utopian flight narrows into a constricted reality, which the poet can answer only with irony and satire, and the crestfallen recognition that the censor now guards the borders of the German spirit. Then the actual "travel pictures" begin—first to Aachen, a dull town of stiff Prussian soldiers whose uniforms and pointed helmets are new but whose mindless servility is the same as in the disciplined days of old; then to Cologne, where the agents of darkness are busy trying to complete the old cathedral, the symbol to Heine not of a great nation but of a "giant prison in which German reason languished"; its construction, he proclaims, was rightly stopped in Luther's time.[3] Then a pause to talk with "Father Rhine," weighted down by indigestion caused by stupid patriotic songs, both German and French; and a reflection on German feather beds, where, "in the airy empire of dreams," the good German reigns.[4]

From the river, Heine travels to Hagen, where the smells of sauerkraut waft amid the company of Westphalians, "sentimental oaks," as he calls them. Then the poet heads into the Teutoburg Wood, where Hermann the Cherusker, now with a monument of his own, led "German nationality" to victory, saving Heine's hapless contemporaries from having to live up to the higher standards set by the Romans. Pushing farther east, to the Kyffhäuser Mountain, Heine stops to argue with the fabled Barbarossa,

Moritz Daniel Oppenheim, *Heinrich Heine*, 1831.

Germany's sleepy savior, whose red beard has grown longer from snoozing his way through war and revolution, and where an impatient Heine tells Barbarossa that Germans no longer need an emperor.[5] Then he proceeds to Minden, Hanover, and finally home to Hamburg, nearly half of it burned down in the fire of 1842. There, in a vivid daydream, Heine meets Hammonia, goddess of Hamburg, who fills him with yearning for the Germany of his senses—village odors, German tobacco smoke, the songs of nightingales—so that he nearly sheds tears and calls the "foolish longing," the surprising emotion, "love of Fatherland."[6]

In *A Winter's Tale*, Heine combined random recollections of a real trip from Paris to Hamburg, where his mother still lived, with a poet's sense for the *lieux de mémoire* of a historical landscape and an exile's heightened awareness of the sights, sounds, and smells of his homeland. In Heine's Germany, there is not a river, a wood, a castle, or a cave without national significance. The sheer preponderance of his national allusions—often, though not always, satirical—is astounding. If we can trust the results of digital searches of critical editions of collected works, Heine employed the word "Germany" twice as often as Goethe, even though Heine's period of literary productivity was half as long.[7]

Yet even as no major poet wrote as much about Germany as a symbolic landscape as Heine, he felt the constant need to reassure his readers of his love of country and to set himself off from those "rogues" who "put their patriotism out for show."[8] Heine did not, however, call them "nationalists," nor did he identify "nationalism" as their creed—those terms were rarely used in the nineteenth century. On occasion, he called them "Teutomaniacs," sometimes "the so-called national parties."[9] Whatever their name, Heine felt they had to be addressed.

In fact, Heine lived in an age of nationalism—in the sense that Kant intended the term the "age of enlightenment," while distinguishing it from "an enlightened age."[10] Just as enlightenment in Kant's time was not yet the prevailing form of reason, nationalism was in the age of Heine a particular, not yet dominant way of thinking about what the nation was, is, or could be. Moreover, for much of the age of nationalism, nation conceptions as well as nationalism were discussed and fought over in the context of a vast sea of indifference. For most people, other allegiances (or a number of allegiances) were primary.[11] In this sense too, nationalism was, like the enlightenment in Kant's time, far from being the dominant discourse.

Chapter 7, "Developing Nation," evokes the age of Heine. It tells of the attempts of writers and painters to define a modern Germany of history, literature, and nature; to make it a place of poetry and art; to turn it into a nation of constitutional governments that could ameliorate the worst forms of poverty; and to do all of this against the constant threat of repression. This thesis is hardly original. Wolfgang Menzel, a historian and critic, dismissively advanced it in the 1820s, complaining that Germany had become a country of writers not doers. While France pursued valiant deeds, and England commerce, Germany sat back, smoked, and dreamed through its books. In Germany, according to Menzel, history had passed from the heroic to the literary age in which the sword was exchanged for the pen and the manly pursuit of war gave way to the all-too-gentle cultivation of peace.[12]

One need not share Menzel's negative valuation. Yet the early nineteenth century, the so-called Biedermeier era, has long endured disparagement, even though it represented significant advances in core indexes of human welfare—health, wealth, literacy, education, and cultural production—and elicited new social, political, and national aspirations, including sympathy for the common people, even the poor. During the Revolution of 1848, many of these issues came to the fore. Basic social changes were introduced. Economic reforms were promulgated. Rights were guaranteed. And who actually belonged to the nation was defined, even if the precise shape of the nation remained a hotly contested question. But the sword—more precisely, the Dreyse needle gun—quickly became mightier again, turning economic, social, and national aspirations into a blood-soaked calamity. Heine watched this mid-nineteenth-century spectacle from his adopted home in Paris.

The bloody end to the Revolution notwithstanding, the age of nationalism was an era of relative peace for Germany. Following the conclusion of the Congress of Vienna in 1815, Germany minus Austria had virtually no military engagements. After the 1860s, the relationship was reversed, and it was Prussia, then Imperial Germany, which proved more bellicose—but mainly in the colonial sphere. Altogether, across a span of ninety-eight years, the United Kingdom, France, and Russia were at war in roughly three times as many years, according to the data of the conflict catalogue, as Germany or Austria.[13] Until the 1860s, it was precisely this relative peace that allowed nation describers to address questions of poverty, social change, and the welfare of the people. Peace, or at least the absence of major conflict, enabled the economist Friedrich List to argue for tariffs to protect infant industries, for example; or for the writer and activist Bettina von Arnim to address the poor as the authentic "*Volk*"; or for the playwright Georg Büchner to present dramatic fragments delineating the tragic dimensions of the lowborn. Conversely, the return of war elicited new understandings of nationhood and made clear that states, not nationalist dreams, would determine the shape of the nation.

Chapter 8, "Nation Shapes," explores concepts of nationhood and the ideology of nationalism in the postrevolutionary period, when states returned as primary movers and war again became the arbiter of history. Yet German unification was never a foregone conclusion, nor was it the only or even the predominant issue for those who thought about the nation. As important was the effort to understand the transformation of the German lands. Becoming modern and industrial, and increasingly urban, Germany altered irreversibly in this period. So too did its political shape, as small and medium-sized fatherlands lost autonomy, and Austrian lands were severed. In the end, of course, Prussia, not Austria, won the wars of the 1860s, and the consequences for subsequent German history, as is well-known, were profound.

The Second German Empire, established in the Hall of Mirrors at Versailles in 1871, was the first German polity to deliberately and persistently mold its citizen-subjects into Germans, making attachment to the nation-state a sentiment shared among broad strata of the population. National allegiances did not as a result displace other loyalties: regional attachments continued to be strong and even deepened as a sense of national belonging intensified.[14] However, there was no denying that profound identification with the objects of nationhood—whether monuments, memorials, postcards, street signs, or every possible form of monarchical and nationalist kitsch—gave Germans in the Second Empire the unmistakable sense of being a member of a modern nation.

Chapter 9, "Objective Nation," explores the tension between everyday forms of national attachment and the pull of ideological nationalism. As a political doctrine that posits the congruity of people and space, places nation above other loyalties, and makes voluntary sacrifice of life the measure of worthy national citizens, nationalism was still framed by broader, almost banal kinds of attachments to the nation. These attachments, it is argued, sometimes supported, but as often stood in the way of nationalist bellicosity. Yet it was also true, as prescient observers noted, that German nationalism had become "more fanatical" after the turn of the century, and that by 1914 the boundary separating the age of nationalism from the more brutal nationalist age had, in fact, become porous.

—

CHAPTER 7

DEVELOPING NATION

c. 1815–1850

Literature has become the most distinguishing
trait of our nationality.

—WOLFGANG MENZEL

• • •

Who are the subjects of the state? The poor are!

—BETTINA VON ARNIM

"RARELY HAS A GREAT WRITER BEEN MORE THOROUGHLY FOR-gotten," Hannah Arendt observed in 1947.[1] She was referring to Friedrich Gentz, a rhetorically gifted, politically prescient author, the translator of Edmund Burke's *Reflections on the Revolution in France*, and an *avant la lettre* conservative. Like Burke, Gentz stressed the accumulated benefits of tradition over the violence of abstract reason as applied to the obstinate rhythms of everyday life, and, as was true of the best of this philosophical tradition, he brooked no apology for callous absolute rule. In 1797, when he was just thirty-three, he brashly appealed to the new king of Prussia, Frederick William III, to grant freedom of the press, arguing that publicly defended truth sufficed to blunt the spread of falsehood. He also defended the American Revolution, calling it a "defensive revolution" for granted rights as opposed to the "offensive revolution" of France.[2] In subsequent writings, Gentz often took Great Britain as the model of good government, and this fact commended him to Prime Minister William Pitt the Younger, who paid Gentz modest sums of money to write against portentous developments on the continent.

Gentz was also one of the first intellectuals to argue for the necessity of an alliance of the great powers against Napoleon. In the subsequently famous preface to his *Fragments on the Balance of Power in Europe*, published in the summer of 1806, Gentz urged "Germans, worthy of your name," to take leave of their "self-imposed defenselessness" and gather the "national will."[3] France, he thought, was a militarist country that was mainly interested in expansion, and only Austria could lead Germany and Europe to a durable peace. Unlike Baron vom Stein and Ernst Moritz Arndt, Gentz did not envision a Europe stripped of small countries; on the contrary, the legitimacy of the international order depended on the collective defense of the small nations against the large. Following Burke, Gentz even questioned whether the carving up of Poland had not been the beginning of the descent of Europe.[4]

Steeped in the writings and sometimes enjoying the company of intellectuals like Immanuel Kant and Christoph Martin Wieland, the Schlegels and the Humboldts, Johann Gottlieb Fichte (whom he detested), and Adam Müller (whom he admired), Gentz personified the promise and disenchantment of early-nineteenth-century conservatism. Like Kant, Gentz understood humanity as crooked timber—imperfect and difficult to shape. Influenced by the statesman-scholar Wilhelm von Humboldt, Gentz imagined a restrained government releasing rather than confining creativity, while following Müller, he came to see the state as more than just a machine.

Gentz was deeply involved in the literary and aesthetic discussions of the age. He also frequented Berlin's salons, and met and developed a consuming relationship with Rahel Levin. When the French occupied Berlin, she burned many of Gentz's letters in order to protect him, and he did the same with her correspondences, so we are left with only traces. "You are an infinitely productive creature, I am an infinitely receptive one; you are a great man, I am the first among women," he wrote to her—contravening our expectations—in one of the correspondence's few surviving letters.[5] The passage is often commented upon as reinforcing, even while reversing, what had already become a strict separation of gender spheres.[6] We may also see it as evidence of a time when the hardened political oppositions of the nineteenth century had not yet become fully apparent. Isolated moments of nostalgia aside, Gentz soon took leave of what had once been a shared intellectual and emotional world. At the Congress of Vienna, Levin saw him as he hurried up the steps to one of the grand salons. As if denying their common past, Gentz simply passed her by.[7]

II

As Prince Metternich's personal secretary, Gentz was the chief impresario of the tough negotiations and patiently wrought concessions that characterized the reality (although not the popular image) of the Congress of Vienna. In nine months of seemingly interminable meetings between September 1814 and June 1815, Gentz and his colleagues shaped a central European peace that lasted nearly forty years, until 1853, when war broke out in Crimea. The Congress brought about this peace by creating a balance of forces that left none of the great powers dissatisfied; even the loser of the war, France, came to accept the fundamental legitimacy of the new order.

The Congress set France back first to its 1792, then to its 1790 borders, and created an anti-French *cordon sanitaire* of small states, running from Holland through Prussia, the Palatinate, Baden, Switzerland, and into the Kingdom of Sardinia. It also furthered Austria's withdrawal from the Austrian Netherlands (making up much of current-day Belgium), Anterior Austria (in southwest Germany), and Bavaria. Instead, Austria shifted east and south, into the Illyrian lands and into Italy, where Austria ruled over the Lombardo-Venetian kingdom with greater rigidity than anywhere north of the Alps. It was, moreover, in Italy, far more so than in Germany, that Austrian troops would engage in the bloody business of repression: in Naples and Piedmont in 1821, in central Italy in 1830, and infamously under the command of Joseph Radetzky in northern Italy in 1848.[8]

For Prussia, the essential question was its east-west orientation. Once Russia retained the greater part of what came to be known as "Congress Poland," it deprived Prussia of significant territories and populations, much of it Polish-speaking, that it had acquired during its eastward expansion in the 1790s.[9] For compensation, Prussia looked to the Kingdom of Saxony, one of the most urban and densely populated states in Germany. The Saxon ruler had been loyal to Napoleon nearly to the end, and Prussia felt entitled to the territory—even Rahel Levin hoped Prussia would at least receive a large stretch along the Elbe, "the most cultured river in Europe."[10] Gentz was less sure. A Silesian by birth, distrustful of Berlin, Gentz argued that Prussia had entered the war very late and now pursued "an extravagant wish to extend her possessions at the expense of all."[11]

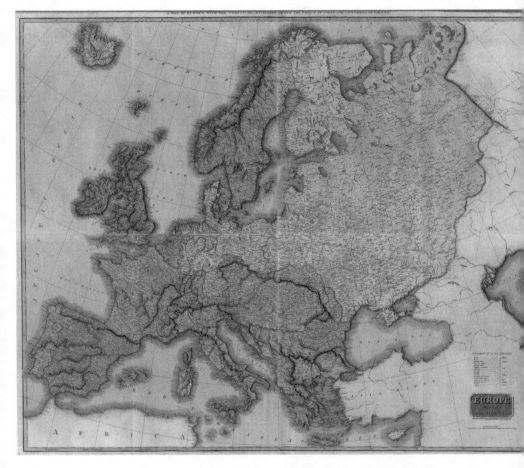

John Thomson, "A map of Europe with the political divisions
of the Peace of Paris and the Congress of Vienna," 1816.

In the end, Prussia settled for 60 percent of the land of Electoral Saxony
and 40 percent of its people, and turned for further compensation to the
"soft" areas of the west, where the Duchies of Jülich and Berg, the Mosel
Valley, the west bank of the Rhine, the cities of Aachen, Cologne, and
Düsseldorf, and various smaller patches combined to make a territory of
significant size.[12]

The importance of Prussia's territorial shift from an eastern to a western
orientation can hardly be understated. In 1813, Wilhelm von Humboldt
had still conceived of the Elbe as the western border of Prussia, insisting
only that Prussia retain the fortresses along the river.[13] Prior to 1806 (and
for many prior to 1813), there was nothing disturbing in Prussia's large

Polish population. Nor was it strange to consider Prussia, like Austria, as a multinational country of its own.

Suddenly, Prussia became mainly a German power, even if its two territorial clumps were not contiguous, and stretches of Hanover, Hesse-Kassel, and Braunschweig now separated the new western territories from Prussia's older eastern lands. What the territorial change meant was by no means clear. Metternich reckoned that the separation of the Hohenzollern realms (plus its two-front exposure to France and Russia and its new population of recalcitrant Catholics) would count among Prussia's weaknesses. Gentz feared the opposite. As Austria looked to the south and east, Prussia would consolidate its lands along an east-west axis in the north—the first step, Gentz assumed, "in a series of operations through which [the Prussians] hoped sooner or later to acquire most of north Germany."[14] Gentz worried that the division, not the unification, of Germany would follow.

As the Congress of Vienna shifted Prussia west and Austria east and south, it also transformed Germany's exterior and interior borders into more precise lines—a less commented on but equally important achievement. Prior to the Napoleonic Wars, Germany's borders had been defined by territorial enclaves and complicated sovereignties. At the Congress, the bewildering patchwork of the border of the state of Baden with Switzerland took on, for example, its current form—with the exception of the Swiss canton of Schaffhausen, whose German borders would not be finally regulated until 1964.[15] The new border between Prussia and the Netherlands was likewise clarified, despite what seemed to German nationalists to be its artificial character. In the north, Denmark lost direct control of Holstein, which it had acquired when the Holy Roman Empire unraveled in 1806. Yet the king of Denmark retained it in personal union within the new entity known as the German Confederation, thwarting those few who already thought Holstein should be divided along its ethnic-linguistic borders, with its German-speaking side reverting to Prussia.[16] Internally, the borders between Bavaria and Württemberg, Prussia and Saxony, Saxony and Thüringen, as well as those between many other states, were also fixed, often in difficult, sometimes disappointing negotiations. Bavaria did not receive Frankfurt am Main, as it had hoped, and Denmark did not get Hamburg and Lübeck, as it had expected.[17] And like its exterior borders,

Germany's interior lines of demarcation remained set until renewed Prussian expansion in the 1860s.

The new lines of demarcation were also important in another, more abstract sense. For the first time at a major international conference, countries and polities were conceived in purely spatial terms. Whereas the negotiators who had worked out the Peace of Westphalia in 1648 had produced diplomatic documents that delineated territorial extents by describing a prince's jurisdiction over towns, persons, or institutions, the envoys in Vienna drew exact borders on scaled maps.[18] As a result, the states shaped at the Congress of Vienna contained virtually no overlapping sovereignties and, save for a few exceptions like the Hessian town of Wimpfen in Württemberg, the new states were largely devoid of exclaves and enclaves.

Finally, the Congress debated whether there should be a new German state and what form it should take. The possibilities ranged from the creation of a unified nation-state (usually thought of as under Prussian leadership) and the resurrection of the Holy Roman Empire (an idea that garnered little support, even in Austria) to the creation of an empire governed binationally (as Austria-Hungary would become in 1866) and a far looser confederation of states bound together in a security alliance and based on the principle of dynastic legitimacy. This last concept emerged as the most workable. As agreed to in June 1815, and reaffirmed in 1820, the German Confederation was an association of "sovereign princes and free cities" whose purpose was "lasting security and independence."[19] Austria and Prussia supplied nearly two-thirds of the German confederate army.[20]

III

This new Germany enjoyed little popular acclaim. German nationalists, like Baron vom Stein and the firebrand Joseph Görres, left Vienna dismayed; leading members of the Prussian army scorned the proceedings of the Congress for lack of principle; and many educated Germans, mainly in the north, had hoped for a loftier, more resounding conclusion to decades of war. Young people were especially chagrined. In October 1817, nearly five hundred fraternity brothers and members of gymnastics societies gathered at Wartburg Castle, where they celebrated the tercentennial of Luther's 95 theses and the fourth anniversary of the Battle of Leipzig. For the first time in history, idealistic students and oppositional politics came together in a mass public demonstration.[21] On a hill in the nearby town of Eisenach, students consigned sheets of paper with the titles of condemned books to an auto-da-fé. It is likely that the list had been supplied by Father Jahn, the elder, idiosyncratic gymnastics leader, and that the students hardly knew which works they were consigning to the flames.[22]

Gentz seized on their youthful inexperience, admonishing that it is wiser to study books than to burn them. He also abhorred a national celebration that combined a religiously divisive symbol with the Battle of Leipzig, the "final act," he argued, in a two-decade-long anti-Napoleonic struggle that Prussia mainly watched from the sidelines, and for which regular soldiers of dynastic states, not volunteer units of students, proved decisive.[23] However, the "false fire" of Wartburg was not without consequence.[24] Once a defender of freedom of expression, the increasingly Machiavellian Gentz now argued that the government should exercise control over public controversy. He saw his opportunity when, on March 23, 1819, Karl Sand, a nationalist fraternity student, stabbed the best-selling playwright August von Kotzebue to death, claiming that Kotzebue was a traitor to the fatherland.[25] At a famous meeting later that year in the Bohemian spa town of Carlsbad, the monarchs and ministers, with Gentz as their main adviser, agreed to install state-appointed overseers at the universities and remove professors they deemed hostile to public order. They also banned the gymnastics movement, drove the fraternities underground, and set up a special committee to investigate "the facts relating to the origin and manifold ramifications of the revolutionary plots and demagogical associations."[26]

Professors were fired and public figures denounced. The police interrogated hundreds of students and arrested a sufficient number to cower all but the most dedicated into a more covert existence.[27] Censorship was tightened as the German states, whose patchwork geography had previously offered endless hideouts for contraband publishing, coordinated their efforts for the first time. A new and more menacing atmosphere of suspicion pervaded the German lands, and the best and brightest of contemporaries felt the change: there was nothing left, Clausewitz declared, "but to withdraw indignantly into one's own innermost being and to shut oneself off from the world."[28]

Then, one last omen surfaced: the first major occurrence of sustained anti-Jewish violence in Germany since the expulsions of the late Middle Ages broke out. Erupting in early August 1819, the Hep Hep Riots engulfed scores of cities and towns, first striking in southern and central cities, then spreading north all the way to Hamburg and even Copenhagen. Townsmen threatened, beat, and abused Jews, smashing the windows of Jewish houses and stores. Ludwig Robert, Rahel Levin's brother, lamented that many held the riots "to be less important than they were," and conceded that it "constricts his heart."[29] Levin, still in relatively tranquil Berlin, was crestfallen. The new anti-Semitism, along with the increasingly religious tenor of the times, she wrote, "stirs up the people to the only atrocity in which it remembers its old liberties—attacking the Jews."[30]

IV

We often see the period after 1819 as marked by political quiescence. Germans, it seemed, withdrew into an inner realm, preferring the private over the public, the province as against the outside world. The Biedermeier became an era of small-mindedness, a retreat, as the historian of culture, Hermann Glaser, put it, into "homely shelters against the winds and storms of a radically changing world."[31] Coziness, *Gemütlichkeit*, prevailed over public courage, and calmness, *Ruhe*, became the first duty of the citizen.[32]

Whatever the merits of this view of the Biedermeier period, it must also be taken into account that a long war had just ended, and that Germany, like other war-torn societies, required an extended period of peace. In that light, the idyllic longings of the period, which seem to us naïve, must be set against nearly two decades of destruction, while the utopian schemes that would reemerge later in the century alarmed many of those who witnessed the destructive fury of the French Revolution and the Napoleonic conquests that followed.[33] It is true that Germany, by 1820, became a repressive society, and that the provincialism of its towns and rural villages, where some 70 percent of the people still lived, was all too evident. But without belittling the importance of the Carlsbad Decrees or justifying myopia, it must also be admitted that other forces were at work.

The Biedermeier period, its name deriving from a fictional Swabian schoolmaster and poet caricatured in the 1850s for his small town-horizons and naïve verse, was an era of the book more than the sword. In the German lands, the number of books published increased sixfold in the thirty years following 1813, when the war brought book production to a nineteenth-century low.[34] In this prolific period, the number of books printed in Germany outstripped those of France and England, making Germans seem like the people of *Dichter und Denker*, poets and philosophers, a term suggested by Madame de Staël but coined in 1828 by Wolfgang Menzel.[35] Fifty thousand men lived in Germany, Menzel calculated, "who have written one or more books."[36] The most widely read literary critic of the time, and later an embittered and even anti-Semitic opponent of the poet Heinrich Heine and the authors of the Young Germany movement, Menzel found little to applaud. Instead, he lamented that German history had passed from the heroic to the literary age, exchanging the sharp sword for the busy pen. The Germans do not do, Menzel complained, they write.

He was not entirely wrong. Benefiting from technological advances in print and papermaking, the printed word, image, and music sheet reached more and more people. By 1841, according to one count, more than 300 cities and towns in the German Confederation boasted bookstores, while five years later Prussia alone housed over 600 lending libraries.[37] Through colporteurs, books even found their way into the countryside, where the book market was concentrated on bibles, hymnals, devotionals, pocket books, and *Volkskalender* (almanacs), some of which attained print runs as high as 50,000 copies.[38] Newspapers and magazines also blanketed Biedermeier Germany. More than a quarter of the German population, and half the men, regularly read newspapers and magazines—typically in public places.[39] And those who did not read were read to by those who could.[40]

Books, magazines, and newspapers reached a population on its way to achieving nearly total literacy. The baseline statistics reveal large swaths of Germany ahead of European norms, not only in eastern and southern Europe, where literacy rates remained disheartening, but also in France and England. In 1836, a startling 90 percent of Prussian recruits could sign their name. However, significant differences still existed between Prussia's literate west and less literate east, and figures for higher levels of literacy, including the number who had the ability to write sentences and fluently read printed text, remained more modest.[41] Because of the many divisions of Germany, it is difficult to find comparable statistics for other parts of the country. Generally, it is thought that the Catholic lands were less literate—although detailed studies suggest a wide array of exceptions.[42]

Some historians have seen in Prussian primary schools sites of discipline and drill, "the first modern dictatorship of the mind," as one has put it.[43] Contemporaries, though, especially foreigners, were of a completely different opinion. Disparate luminaries, like the American educator Horace Mann, the English critic and poet Matthew Arnold, and the French philosopher Victor Cousin, came to Prussia to see the most advanced primary school system in the western world, where, as Mann put it, schoolchildren "were taught to think for themselves."[44] Along with Baden and Saxony, Prussia became one of the most educated places in Europe, if schools are any measure. Between 1816 and 1848, the percentage of children enrolled in the elementary grades rose from 54 to 78 percent.[45] No doubt, village schoolteachers, although well trained by contemporary standards, were badly paid. The clergy sometimes exercised deleterious oversight. Rural parents reluctantly released their children from farmwork. And the whole system was designed to ensure obedience among Prussian subjects. But when literacy, numeracy, and an educational commitment to general knowledge combined with a broader availability of books and newspapers—as well as not a few impoverished, idealistic, liberal-minded instructors—a radical, revolutionary dynamic unfolded. It was no accident that Frederick William IV, who succeeded his father on the Prussian throne in 1840, later fulminated at teachers who "destroyed the loyalty in the bosom of my subjects and turned their hearts against me."[46]

While literature, literacy, and learning progressed, the military stagnated.[47] Between 1820 and 1850, the portion of the state budget that Prussia spent on its military declined, dropping from 45.6 percent to 37.8 percent, while its regular army hovered between 125,000 and 135,000 soldiers.[48] Given that Prussia's population increased by more than 150 percent in these thirty years, this meant that the percentage of its population serving in Prussia's regiments was reduced by roughly a third, falling to less than 1 percent.[49] By comparison, Frederick the Great had put more than 3 percent of his total population in uniform, and nearly 20 percent of Prussia's gross national product into the military.[50] In the Biedermeier period, the opposite was the case, and, though precise calculations are

THE DECLINING IMPORTANCE OF THE MILITARY
in Prussia

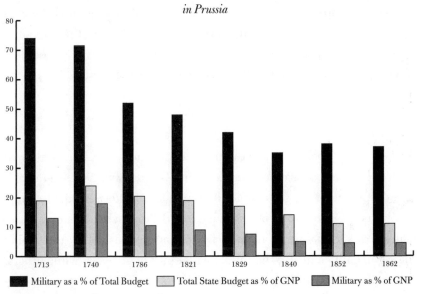

Military as a % of Total Budget   Total State Budget as % of GNP   Military as % of GNP

difficult, it seems that no more than 5 percent of Prussia's GNP went to the support of the army.

Conscription also seems to have gone badly, especially in Prussia's western provinces. In Aachen in 1817, authorities targeted five hundred men for conscription, but could enlist fewer than a hundred. By the 1830s, the problem had become endemic, and the army was actually only enlisting about a third of available recruits—by the 1840s, as few as a quarter.[51] Enthusiasm for the *Landwehr*, the citizen militias, was not much greater. Even though military training did not entail long stays in barracks away from home, resistance was tenacious. Nor can civil-military relations be characterized as placid. By one count of violent disturbances in Prussia between 1815 and 1848, scuffles between soldiers and civilians were more numerous than food riots.[52] The Rhineland was particularly in turmoil, and confrontations often involved considerable bloodshed.[53] Even Berlin, with its militaristic sensibility, witnessed scores of clashes between contentious citizens and garrisoned soldiers, the number of violent incidents per year nearly tripling between 1820 and 1838.[54]

The situation was similar in Austria. The resources that Austria apportioned to the military also declined, although not as precipitously as in Prussia. The slice of the state budget spent on the military dropped from

51 percent in 1780 to 33 percent in 1840.[55] Following a trend prevalent throughout Europe, these declining military outlays redefined states as more than just machines of war. Nevertheless, the decisive tipping point, when countries spent more on civilian than on military tasks and on debt servicing, would not come until the second half of the century.[56]

V

As the military declined relative to the civilian sector, and as peace allowed for economic and educational development, Germany witnessed a remarkable deepening of the sense of itself as a nation. Historians like Leopold von Ranke, Georg Gottfried Gervinus, and Friedrich Christoph Dahlmann began to make nations, not civilizations (as was widely the case in the eighteenth century), the fundamental unit of analysis, while others, like Freiherr vom Stein, oversaw the publication of crucial editions of original sources—most notably, the *Monumenta Germaniae Historica*, which first began to roll off the press in 1826.[57] Nor was the turn to history just an academic affair. In this period, preservation societies proliferated from Vienna to Osnabrück. Their amateur members eagerly unearthed local relics, dug biographies out of archives, and repaired and restored old castles, churches, towers, and sagging houses.[58]

History, moreover, was just one domain in which the new national sensibility was apparent. In architecture, a national aesthetic was visible in the return to the sturdy Romanesque arches, as in the portals of the Bavarian State Library in Munich or the sandstone-fronted Polytechnic in Karlsruhe. The revival of high medieval gothic was also national in aspiration. Beginning with the renowned architect Karl Friedrich Schinkel's plan to build a red-bricked "liberation cathedral" on the newly named Leipzigerplatz in Berlin, the revival culminated with the all-consuming effort to complete the Cologne Cathedral, whose unfinished steeple had become a symbol of an inchoate nation.[59]

The deepening national sensibility was also evident in the ardent search for characteristic German art. One example involved the ceaseless activity of the brothers Sulpiz and Melchior Boisserée, who in the years of Napoleonic occupation, when secularized churches and monasteries were forced to discard sacred art, had amassed a breathtaking collection. It included more than two hundred Dutch and German paintings from the late Middle Ages and the early Renaissance, among them works from Rogier van der Weyden, Stefan Lochner, and Hans Memling.[60] Another such collector was Gustav Friedrich Waagen, who wandered through southern Germany, Switzerland, and Alsace, cataloguing religious and secular buildings and documenting the paintings and sculptures that had survived Napoleonic art raids. Believing that art expressed place and time, Waagen championed the architectural riches of medieval towns like Regensburg, with its numerous monasteries and churches, and Rothenburg ob der Tauber, whose "many towers and old buildings" appealed to "the friends of old German customs and art."[61]

While the brothers Waagen and Boisserée collected and catalogued art, others followed Johann Gottfried Herder's injunction and gathered up and published folktales. Works with titles such as *Westphalian Legends and Stories* (1831) and *The Austrian Magic Horn* (1834) flooded the German book market. Some of these tomes resulted from the labor of love of dedicated dilettantes. Others were the work of great men of erudition, like the brothers Jacob and Wilhelm Grimm, who first published their *Fairy Tales* in two volumes in 1812 and 1815, and then again in an expanded edition in 1819.

In the tradition of Herder, the Grimms imagined themselves as researching poets hewing close to oral tradition but bending it to speak to the present. Crisscrossing the countryside of their native Hesse, they claimed to have gathered roughly hewn German peasant tales "transmitted from one generation to the next."[62] They thought of the tales as "sleeping texts," articulating the wishes and the life experiences of the common people, especially the downtrodden, across long periods of time.[63] As it turns out, a large number of the original tales came from a small group of well-educated middle-class women, most of them from French-speaking Huguenot families, none of whom were mentioned by name in the first editions. In later editions, the Grimms cut out tales like "Puss in Boots" and "Bluebeard," which had been drawn too directly from Charles Perrault, the seventeenth-century French author of *Mother Goose Tales*. The Grimms also inserted folksy-sounding turns of phrase, deleted overtly sexual references, and smoothed over hard-edged violence. Wilhelm Grimm also softened endings, so that the protagonists would live "happily ever after."[64]

VI

The nationalization of German culture brought forth an astonishing output, whose wide arc can only be suggested. There was, for example, an ever-deeper pride taken in Germany's natural surroundings: the curvature and flow of its rivers, the slopes and shapes of its high elevations, and the hush of its forests. This new sensibility, pairing nation and nature, derived from the late-eighteenth-century appreciation of picturesque countrysides and the early Romantic valorization of raw landscapes. Powerfully shaped by European perceptions—especially British ones—it was also made possible by the advent of modern tourism.

The Rhine serves as an illuminating example. In the first decade of the nineteenth century, at least nine separate tourist books described the Rhine. Three of them were Dutch, three British, and only one was actually German: Joseph Gregor Lang's supposedly Romantic but actually schematic and practical *Travel on the Rhine*, originally published in the year the French Revolution broke out.[65] Picture books likewise came mainly from abroad. It was the Englishman Richard Gordnor who first popularized aquatinting, a form of etching that uses powdered resin instead of a needle to create a more diffuse sense of tone. While German engravers were still reproducing Matthäus Merian's seventeenth-century images of the Rhine, Gordnor made thirty-two new aquatint etchings depicting the river against silhouettes of abbeys and castles and fulminous skies. When steel engraving was introduced, the technique also came from England, and among its first commercial successes was William Tombleson's *Views of the Rhine*, published in 1832 and replete with dramatic images of castle ruins. Tombleson's rendering of the ruins of Stolzenfels, a crumbling castle on the middle Rhine, seems, for example, to emerge from the granite rock and bend with the curve of the Rhine just as unquiet clouds threaten the placid river.[66]

By the 1830s, German publishers followed the English example and began to saturate the market with picture books, panoramas, and albums, leading one author to complain that "between Mainz and Cologne there can hardly be found a house or a tree that has not already set a pen or grav-

William Tombleson, "Ruins of Stolzenfels," from *Views of the Rhine*, 1832.

ing tool into motion."[67] Many of these books simply appropriated old pictures. Half of the images of Karl Geib's *Malerische Wanderungen am Rhein*, published in 1838, were lifted from Tombleson.[68] But whether borrowed or original, these pictures created visual expectations for the prodigious numbers of tourists now seeing the Rhine by boat. In 1828, the *Concordia*, the first passenger steamship to navigate the Rhine, transported more than 18,000 passengers; by 1840, more than 600,000 sightseers, travelers, and traders passed through the middle Rhine each year.[69] Often outfitted with small libraries and modest restaurants, the steamships could bring passengers from Cologne to Mainz in a day. Tourists could also take longer if they wished, resting in "the most excellent hotels in Germany," as the early Baedeker guides called the Rhineland lodges.[70] As the guidebooks suggested, sightseers could amble through the crooked streets of St. Goar, or view the curving banks of the Rhine through the gothic ruins of the St. Werner Chapel in Bacharach. "A special, new and yet *heimatliches* feeling" is how Carl Gustav Carus, a German painter, experienced it, as if "I had for the first time found a fatherland, my fatherland."[71] For the other tourists, half of whom were still British in the 1830s, souvenirs helped sentimentalize the landscape. For the well-off, there were vases, porcelain plates, beer steins, and wineglasses, all adorned with images of the Rhine, while for more modest middle-class budgets, there were illustrated albums or copies of individual engravings.[72]

In this period, characterized by a general warming of average annual temperatures, mountains also became objects of fascination and identification. As glaciers began to recede in the late eighteenth century, it was again English travelers who first came to see the Alps as majestic, giving "a feeling," as the poet prodigy Lord Byron wrote in *Child Harold's Pilgrimage*, opposite "the hum / of human cities."[73] In the Byronic Alps of 1812, the highland populations were poor and cities distant.[74] The Austrian and Bavarian Alps remained especially undeveloped. The Tyrol region, save for the city of Innsbruck, counted among the most economically backward regions in Germany, a fact attested to by the annual spring trek of *Schwabenkinder* over the treacherous Arlberg pass and down into the Lake Constance basin, where the youngsters sold their summer labor to the highest bidder at the "children markets" of the lakeside towns.[75]

It was the modest peaks of middle Germany, more even than the audacious Alps, that inspired the imagination—one thinks, for example, of Caspar David Friedrich's Riesengebirge landscape, its bluish, pre-cubist layers of triangular peaks replicating in immense dimension a peaceful church steeple.[76] The Brocken, central Germany's highest mountain, may even have been Germany's first natural tourist attraction.[77] At a mere 3747 feet, its unimposing summit is believed to have been scaled as early as the fifteenth century, though the first climber whom we know by name—the mapmaker Tilemann Stella—did not make the ascent until 1562.[78] Thereafter, the list of men who climbed the mountain is long and illustrious. When a young Goethe made his first "pilgrimage" to the Brocken in 1777, he was different only in having hiked to the snowcapped summit in early December. Nevertheless, he experienced the "purest pleasure," gazing upon "the region of Germany below me all covered in clouds."[79]

Most encounters with the summit were less exalted. For years, it was expected that the students of Halle and Göttingen would ascend the Brocken; by 1800, there was a full-fledged stone-walled inn at the summit, and by 1820 more than two thousand hikers trekked to the top every year. On one otherwise unremarkable Monday in 1824, at least thirty-six men and one woman climbed the mountain.[80] They jostled for pilsner and wine, elbowed one another in crowded rooms, sang songs, and left their thoughts in a guest book, which for posterity recorded an unending stream of sentimental platitudes about the mysteries of nature, theological flights about the smallness of man and the greatness of God, and complaints about the weather and the cloud-obstructed view. There were also scattered comments, especially after 1815, about the German nation, as well as a great deal of nonsense.[81] "The whole book smells of cheese, beer, and tobacco," one writer observed.[82]

That commentator was Heinrich Heine, whose first major work of prose, *The Harz Journey*, mocked the new nature tourism that brought people to such previously forbidding sites as the mountains of central Germany. As Heine has an enduring place in a pantheon of politically progressive authors, it is necessary to recall that it was *The Harz Journey*, published in 1828, that first made him famous, and that the charm of the book lay in its subtle combination of characteristically sensitive Biedermeier descriptions of nature and sardonic asides about philistine mountaineers and inebriated gymnastic students.[83] It also parodied unimaginative guidebooks, in particular Friedrich Gottschalk's otherwise competent and not altogether un-Romantic *Handbook for Harz Travelers*, and lampooned tourists who, in Heine's words, saw nature as if looking at "a clearly drawn and distinctly colored map."[84] Yet for all the satire of Heine's *Harz Journey*, one cannot escape fully the sense that the young author experienced a sense of community on the top of the mountain. Heine, after all, sang Ernst Moritz Arndt's "Song of the Fatherland" with the other tourists, most of whom were students from Halle. He also reflected, perhaps satirically, on the nationality of the mountain. "The Brocken is a German," he wrote, "in its calm, sensible, tolerant character."[85]

The most enduring Romantic symbol of Germany was, however, not the Rhine River or the Harz Mountains, nor the coastline of the North and Baltic Seas (which Heine was the first major poet to describe in verse). Rather, it was the slowly disappearing woods. Population growth, indiscriminate cutting, and the extension of fields had chipped away at the woods for decades. One can see it in late-eighteenth- and early-nineteenth-century engravings: hills and plains, forested in our day, were bare and bleak, and forests, unless newly planted, seldom abutted towns.[86] Deforestation in Germany was certainly less devastating than in England, even before the mills of Lancashire began to fire, and less severe than in France, Italy, Spain, Portugal, or Holland.[87] Some areas of Germany, such as the Sauerland, experienced significant deforestation; other areas, like the Teutoburg Wood, seem to have been spared.[88] And in many parts of Germany, foresters experimented with new types of trees. In the Prussian and Saxon woods, for example, they planted so-called normal trees (*Normalbäume*— Norway spruce or Scotch pines) in neat, countable rows, so that the trees' collective yield could be tabulated.[89]

The German fascination with woods is often combined with a supposed militarist character. In his brilliant but idiosyncratic *Masse und Macht* (*Crowds and Power*), published in 1960, the Nobel laureate Elias Canetti claimed that the "mass symbol of the Germans was the army," but "the army was more than the army, it was the marching woods."[90] What the ocean was to the British, the Revolution to the French, the mountains to the Swiss, the matador to the Spanish, the woods were to the Germans, Canetti proposed. Like the ideal German soldiers, the trees stood parallel and upright, clean and separated. Of course, such clean parallel woods resulted from the eighteenth-century application of enlightened forestry, not timeless and untouched German landscapes, and the military doctrine of the day emphasized not soldiers marching in rows but the ability of light brigades to show courage and initiative.

When Germans of the Biedermeier era imagined woods, they typically thought not of conquest but of the individual experience of stillness, for which there existed a Romantic bon mot: *Waldeinsamkeit*. In the poems of Joseph von Eichendorff, who employed the term a number of times, it suggested longing for solitude in the early evening among the timbers. Solitude was also the implied subject of an eight-line poem scrawled by the young Goethe on a board in a wooden house on a hill near Ilmenau in Thuringia. Written in 1780 but first published in 1815, "*Über allen Gipfeln*" ("Above All Peaks") remains "perhaps the finest expression yet given to the sense of resignation inspired by the sublime calm of nature," as George Eliot put it after she hiked to the house in the spring of 1855.[91] In the poem, quiet comes from God, or nature, and descends through the tops of trees, then to the birds, and finally to us, the least significant of all, the unstressed "*du*" in the final line, *Ruhest du auch*.

VII

By the mid-1830s, major figures passed from the stage, including Adam Müller and Friedrich Schlegel in 1829, Carl von Clausewitz and Baron vom Stein in 1831, Goethe and Gentz in 1832, and Rahel Levin Varnhagen in 1833. In their stead a generation of young people came of age for whom the tribulations of the Napoleonic Wars belonged to the experiences of their parents. Impatient with what they saw as the suffocating stillness of the 1820s, and having little idea how much worse things could be, they romanticized violence and railed against an oppressive system and its main personification: the "detested and dreaded" Prince Metternich.[92] It seemed to these young authors that hardly a letter went unread, or a critical book not suppressed, especially in Austria, where "every footman in a public house is a salaried spy," as Charles Sealsfield, an exiled Austrian author, put it.[93] But measured by the standards of Russia or Spain at the time, censorship in 1820s Germany was either haphazard or too sophisticated (Jacob Grimm, being a librarian in Kassel, also worked as a censor for Hesse).[94] Nor were the police omnipresent. Both Britain and France had larger forces than Austria, and Prussia's police was smaller still. Altogether, some sixteen hundred policemen (*Landgendarmen*) watched over Prussia's vast rural spaces; in the tumultuous Rhineland, there was but one gendarme for every fifty square miles.[95] In other parts of Germany the situation was similar. The police forces of Bavaria, Saxony, Baden, and Württemberg remained minuscule, and in still smaller territories nearly nonexistent. The German Confederation could not fill this gap. It gathered details on hundreds of political suspects, but it had no judiciary authority, and virtually nothing ever came of its efforts.

Germany actually counted among the quieter places of Europe. Uprisings had occurred in Spain and Portugal in 1820, in Piedmont and Greece in 1821, and in Russia in 1825. In the summer of 1830, the impetus to revolt came from Paris, where citizens overthrew the reactionary Bourbon ruler Charles X and erected a constitutional monarchy with Louis-Philippe as king. Those "July days" in France ignited further revolts: in Brussels, Warsaw, and central Italy, where Austrian troops, at the behest of the Vatican, swiftly suppressed the uprisings. In Germany, the decline in artisanal wages, the deleterious effects of customs wars, rising peasant debt, and the high price of bread fueled a series of protests, particularly in middle and northern Germany. Frightened for their lives, rulers of small states granted a series of constitutions.[96] But Prussia conceded little and Austria conceded less, while the German Confederation, still under Metternich's control, strangled progress at the national level.

Conservative intransigence succeeded only in frustrating those who had hoped for progress through persuasion and in encouraging young radicals for whom violence was the only conceivable way forward. On April 3, 1833, some 50 students, most of them from underground fraternities, tried to incite a revolution by attacking a Frankfurt jail housing political prisoners. Quashed within an hour, the uprising led to 7 rebels being killed, 24 wounded, and the majority arrested; and of those, 16 were sentenced, 11 (including 10 students) for life.[97] The state of Prussia reacted to the event with particular severity. For the crime of belonging to a fraternity, which became not only illegal but treasonous, Prussia sentenced 39 students to death (4 by means of the wheel, the rest with the executioner's ax), and 165 received either life in prison or significant time. A shocking verdict, it was slightly vitiated in 1836, when death sentences were commuted to life or thirty years in prison. (But when Frederick William IV ascended to the Prussian throne in June 1840, he granted a general amnesty to the students still languishing in jail.)[98]

For the first time in its modern history, but not the last, Germany drove many of its best and brightest into exile—to communities in England, Belgium, Switzerland, France, and the United States.[99] Home to the major figures in the Young Germany literary movement, like Heinrich Heine and Ludwig Börne, Paris would soon harbor the sixth largest German-speaking population in the world.[100] To make matters worse, on Metternich's directive, the censors banned outright the works of the Young Germany authors, and constricted the flow of books from foreign presses. Some regional German governments pursued the bans, issued in 1834, with great vigor, others with less. Austria stood out, staunching the flow of new poetry, political newspapers, and radical pamphlets. Austria had already barred foreign students from attending its universities, and it had prohibited young Austrians from studying anywhere but in Austria itself.[101] As one petition of authors, which included the dramatist Franz Grillparzer, complained, Metternich's repressive policies gutted Austria's literary and cultural life.[102] The German Confederation was dragged down with it. Although hardly a bureaucratic behemoth, the Confederation increasingly focused its activity on the coordination of repressive policy.[103] The policy poisoned the public sphere and embittered the young, who saw the Confederation, as the British envoy in Frankfurt observed, "as being bent upon the total destruction of the liberties of Germany."[104]

The dramatist Georg Büchner, born in a Hessian village in 1813, belonged to this generation of young men. Deeply frustrated by the outcome of the Revolutions of 1830, he had barely finished *Gymnasium* when, in 1834, he penned *Der Hessische Landbote*, a pamphlet proclaiming taxation a "blood tithe," the new constitutions "empty straw," law the property of the "superfluous classes," and the government "the father of lies."[105] Earnest and bitter, full of statistics and yet rhetorically powerful, the *Hessische Landbote* threatened that "whoever lifts the sword against the people shall be slain by the sword of the people."[106] In fact, the opposite occurred. The authorities seized the pamphlet and arrested Büchner's co-conspirators, including Pastor Friedrich Ludwig Weidig, who had edited the eight-page tract and actually softened its language. In a Darmstadt jail, a drunken overseer tortured Weidig so insistently that the pastor committed suicide. Some of Büchner's other friends did not survive the ordeal either. Although Büchner managed to escape, he was stricken by guilt and traumatized by the specter of a slow, silent death in prison.

Incarceration became his metaphor for the acute social and political claustrophobia of the Biedermeier era. In *Woyzeck*, Büchner's subsequently famous and posthumously published dramatic fragment, a poor, discharged soldier is subject to the petty torments of a local garrison commander and an amateur scientist. To Woyzeck, the hapless protagonist, the oppressive sense of confinement is heightened by the forced diet of nothing but peas, the insipid clichés of the captain, and the scientist's pseudoscientific, half-Latin drivel that proclaims freedom while crushing it. Perhaps recalling an imprisoned Gretgen in Goethe's *Urfaust* (the forerunner of Gretchen in *Faust*), the crazed Woyzeck sees the world caving in on him with jarring clarity. It is, however, the bloated drum sergeant who robs Woyzeck of Marie, the one person he has left. She too belongs to the poor, and like Gretgen speaks and sings in the sound of folk song and biblical verse.[107] As Woyzeck is too weak to beat the well-fed sergeant, he cannot control his rage at losing her. His suffering causes him to stammer and slur syntax. He cannot even afford a pistol. Ultimately, Woyzeck stabs Marie repeatedly with a knife, unable thereafter to wash the blood from his murderous clothes.

Arguably, Büchner's *Woyzeck* constitutes "the first real tragedy of low life," as the critic George Steiner has asserted, fulfilling what was genuinely original about the early versions of Goethe's *Faust*: that commoners are treated as tragic subjects, eliciting our outrage, not at the person, but at the mean conditions of life.[108] The connection of low tragedy to the history of the nation may seem overly subtle. But to contemporaries, it was not. To conceive of the people of all castes as kin, as the modern imagination of the nation implied, necessarily extended empathy to the lowborn as well as the high. And in literature, there was no more telling index of this than the admission that the poor or marginalized were capable of being understood in tragic terms—a category traditionally reserved, as Aristotle put it in his *Poetics*, for those "better than the ordinary man."[109]

VIII

The condition of the poor became more pressing as rural poverty worsened. In the 1840s, the German countryside had not yet escaped the shadow of Thomas Robert Malthus, who calculated that population would grow faster than food production. Before 1770, most of Europe was locked in a Malthusian trap in which death rates fluctuated like sensitive seismographs to the slightest changes in the food supply. Thereafter, starting in the last decades of the eighteenth century, nutritional diversity and the introduction of the caloric-rich potato added as many as 500 calories per day to a protein-poor diet.[110] For many poor artisans and day laborers, this was the difference between malnourishment and the energy to work. However, the broadly prevalent increase in caloric intake also succeeded in reducing the average age of marriage and extending the window of female conception, resulting in larger families and eventual overpopulation. In the early nineteenth century, war and economic setbacks still kept the population in check. By the 1840s, however, two decades of slow economic growth, mainly spurred by increased agricultural productivity, led to population expansion. Thus, when crop failures and potato blight struck, widespread misery ensued. Armies of the indigent were forced to rely on imperfectly organized systems of charity; in Barmen, the birthplace of Friedrich Engels, nearly 10 percent of the population depended on soup kitchens to survive.[111]

Germany remained a developing nation. It was decades behind Great Britain in key economic indicators, like the use of steam power and the production of coal, iron, and textiles. In per capita levels of industrialization, it trailed Belgium, Switzerland, and France, whose economies were set to take off. It may even have lagged behind the European average.[112] Germany's estimated GNP per capita barely eclipsed Spain's and the gulf between Britain and Germany was larger than that between Germany and what economists hazard as an estimate for nineteenth-century Vietnam.[113]

Other indicators of individual economic well-being also revealed widespread misery. In some regions, real wages did not genuinely improve until the second third of the nineteenth century. The wages of German construction workers in the 1840s trailed the earnings of similar workers in Britain and France, and were just beyond what a worker in Japan or the Yangtze Valley in China might earn.[114] Life expectancy was similarly dismaying. Infant mortality in Germany remained among the highest in western Europe, with nearly 30 percent of children dying before the age of one (in part, this was a result of the southern German practice of breastfeeding babies for only a short time, or not at all).[115] Germany's high rate of infant mortality actually worsened, especially in cities, in the mid-nineteenth century.[116] These rates also dragged down figures for life expectancy, which in 1820 hovered at thirty-three years, placing Germany behind the United States, Great Britain, France, and Sweden, and just ahead of the lands of Italy and Poland.[117] Finally, there is the dismal evidence from human height. Recruits in Württemberg, for example, record no signs of growth in height (circa 5'4") until the 1850s and 1860s; then there is moderate growth, with measurable increases only beginning in the 1890s.[118] Evidence from Austria and Bavaria, where male recruits from the 1830s averaged closer to 5'5", also suggest that poverty systematically stunted growth, placing the physical stature of Germans in midcentury at a par with the poor of southern India today.[119]

IX

Intellectuals of the Biedermeier era confronted this impoverished state more directly than historians have allowed. Friedrich List, for example, began his ill-starred, subsequently famous career as a critic of economic backwardness. Born in the Württemberg town of Reutlingen, List wrote a long memorandum in 1819, when he was a thirty-year-old civil servant, reproaching incompetent officials who were unwilling to alleviate the suffering of destitute subjects emigrating to the Americas.[120] As he lodged more criticism in the coming years, his superiors eventually had him fired, arrested, and jailed. In 1825, as part of an agreement to lessen his prison time, List went into exile, eventually becoming a citizen of the United States, where he worked as a farmer, businessman, journalist, and political propagandist. In the 1830s, the United States had thrown up high tariffs, justified by economists of America's "national school" who insisted that young nations needed protection in an international environment where the terms of trade were stacked against them. Although counting himself a liberal, List made precisely this argument about his own country, which he now thought of as Germany, not just Württemberg.

With greater intellectual passion than anyone before him, List argued that Germany, as a developing nation, needed to be safeguarded against the unfair invasion of foreign goods. A customs union was a first step, List argued, and he conceived of it originally for Germany's small southern states. But Prussia, then already sprawling, pursued the idea first, erecting low tariffs in 1818, then extending favorable conditions and entry to its neighbors, and eventually uniting other German states behind a common tariff wall in the 1830s and 1840s.[121] List thought that wall was too low, especially in view of the dominant position of British industry. "It is not yet safe for the lamb to lay with the lion," he wrote in 1837.[122] In *The National System of Political Economy*, his celebrated treatise on economic development, published in 1841, List described what he saw as the three stages of economic growth: a country is initially dependent on agriculture, albeit with some trade; next, it acquires infant industries; and third, industry becomes prevalent. Tariff levels, he maintained, should conform to these stages of economic development. The book also possessed polemical bite.

Denouncing "cosmopolitan economics," List derided tariff agreements
that made Germany "into a British India."[123]

As surely as common tariffs increased a nation's wealth, the railroad,
according to List, could tie a nation together.[124] In a series of essays, List
sketched out railroad grids that would unify Germany economically and
liberate it from "the plague of war, inflation and famine, national hate and
unemployment, ignorance and laziness."[125] He energetically promoted the
Leipzig-Dresden line, the first between two major cities, as the beginning
of a Leipzig-based network, which he mapped out in 1833 as a proposed
"German railway system." List's sketch excluded Vienna but not Prague,

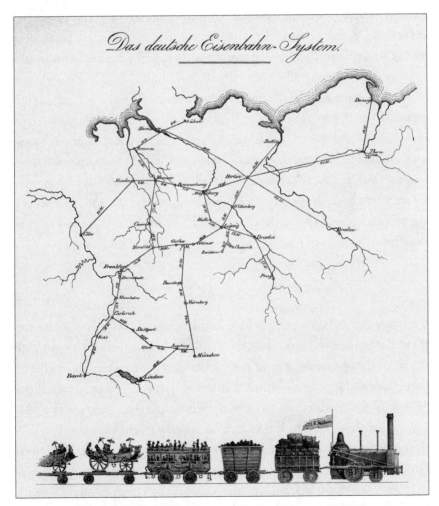

Friedrich List, "The German Railway System," 1833.

reflected a western and northern orientation, and was centered on a triangle between Leipzig, Magdeburg, and Berlin. List also argued for a route from Karlsruhe through Stuttgart to Ulm (and thus to the Danube) that would "make Baden a flourishing land" and even connect "western Europe with the southeast and with Asia." Finally, he advocated that Prussia, with its territories like pinned wings crossing the north of Germany, should establish rails between Berlin and the recalcitrant Rhineland.[126]

For German economic development, List offered a simple, powerful prescription: eliminate internal tariffs and erect external duties, standardize money, invest in infrastructure, and establish mass education. Even today, these are the fundamental building blocks of a sound development strategy. There was also a nationalist dimension to his prescription. In the event that Germany rose in the ranks of manufacturing nations, patriotism would strengthen, List believed, and the so-called German lamb would eventually be able to pull close to the "British lion."

Widely applauded for his insights, List became a sought-out, celebrated author in the 1840s. Yet earning a living by writing was no easy matter, and his decades-long search for permanent state employment, after once running afoul of the authorities, ended unsuccessfully. Moody, quarrelsome, and unreliable, List got into an argument with his publisher, Georg von Cotta, who unceremoniously cut off ties. Despondent and without a secure source of income, List wandered off in late November 1846. He was found dead near Kufstein in Austria, with only a pistol by his side.

X

Thinkers throughout the ages have contemplated how to ameliorate the lot of the poor. Even absolutist governments have attempted to mitigate the worst destitution—for example, Frederick the Great famously ordered that potatoes be planted rather than rye. However, it was not until the 1770s that the productive potential of the industrial economy made it possible to think, at least in England, that poverty might someday be eradicated.[127] In central Europe, the new attitude toward poverty followed circuitous routes, and by List's time had become the common property of groups ranging from utopian socialists to religious reformers. Indeed, by the 1840s, hundreds of Christian and Jewish groups dedicated their energies to helping the poor. They collected money, food, clothing, and coal for heat, engaged in educational work, and cared for orphaned and neglected children. Meanwhile, books, pamphlets, petitions, and articles on what came to be known as the "social question" proliferated. Writers ranged from influential Prussian officials to dismayed county commissioners, engaged priests and pastors, and even to rough-edged novelists, like the Swiss author Jeremias Gotthelf. They included early advocates of state social welfare, like Karl Biedermann and Robert von Mohl, and radical economists such as Bruno Hildebrand. Then too there were the iconoclasts, like the ecumenical Catholic theologian Franz Xaver Baader, the progressive Ruhr industrialist Friedrich Harkort, and Wilhelm Wolff, a now obscure schoolteacher to whom Marx dedicated *Das Kapital*.[128]

This early, national, conversation about the poor informed Bettina von Arnim's often overlooked intervention in the debate. A Romantic author and a vital presence on the Berlin intellectual scene, she became concerned with the fate of a community of some twenty-five hundred people, mostly migrants from the poverty-stricken Vogtland of southern Thuringia. They resided in a settlement on the northern outskirts of Berlin, just beyond the Hamburg Gate. Reminiscent of the pitiless suburbs of Glasgow or the makeshift textile slums of Łódź, the Vogtland, as Berliners called the settlement, packed an endless flow of the rural poor into a dismal series of dank, badly ventilated, and sparsely furnitured tenement houses.[129] Probably, von Arnim never went there herself, but she sent a young Swiss schoolteacher named Heinrich Grunholzer to talk to families and inspect conditions, and included Grunholzer's written observations, little altered, in an appendix to the work she published, *This Book Belongs to the King*. Unsparingly documenting the condition of aging soldiers without bread, and the fate of underemployed spinners and weavers unable to pay their rent, it told of widows and widowers desperately trying to feed their children, and of workers whose injuries and illnesses kept them from securing a livelihood.[130] In her depiction, the *Vogtländer* were loyal to their ruler and ashamed of their own poverty. Yet when the book was published in 1843, its evocation of the humble poor, far from moving the authorities, actually angered them. It also put von Arnim out of favor in court circles.

She nevertheless pressed on and gathered more reports, this time from Silesia. In what came to be called her *Armenbuch (Poor People's Book)*, she gathered a whole range of statistics, family stories, newspaper clips, and interviews concerning the fate of Silesia's linen weavers and spinners. Von Arnim paid particular attention to their dwellings, recounting how many people slept in a room, what they ate ("mostly soup from dark flour, a bit of bread and small amounts of potatoes"), and what they wore, noting they "are seldom in possession of a Sunday dress, which is why so many are hindered from participating in holy services."[131] Challenging the Biedermeier veneration of the small family and the walled town, von Arnim depicted one desperate household after the next, often with one parent and multiple children in squalor, the money that they had earned from spinning going into the pockets of landlords and factory owners.

There was also something novel about the *Armenbuch*. Its author saw the spinners and weavers of Silesia not as the margins, or as a class apart— but as the people.[132] "Who are the subjects of the state?" Bettina von Arnim asked rhetorically, answering herself with a resounding "the poor are!"[133] The rich, by contrast, derived their virtue from luxury, were blind to the poor, and had no real attachment to the fatherland. "When I talk to poverty, I talk to the people, *das Volk*," she insisted.[134]

In June 1844, in the very Silesian towns whose poverty von Arnim chronicled, an uprising occurred. Directed at factory owners and their merchants who bought homespun cotton at depressed prices, the Silesian Weavers' Revolt was neither an early proletarian revolution nor the desperate cry of the hungry, as it is often depicted. Rather, as the historian Christina von Hodenberg has demonstrated, this uprising was in essence a demand for a just price for the workers' homemade products.[135] Unlike the linen spinners who populated von Arnim's text, the cotton weavers still lived within four sturdy walls and wore untorn clothes on their backs (which their arrest reports detailed). In any case, soldiers shot eleven protesters dead, wounded twenty-two, and arrested and jailed more than a hundred. Initiated by inexperienced troops, a callous officer, and a government consumed by fear of revolution, the harsh reprisal transformed a limited protest into a full-blown tragedy. The uprising also meant that von Arnim's text would never be published in her lifetime.

A German poet exiled in Paris hoped for more: that the "Silesian Weavers," as Heine's immensely popular poem was titled, wove a "threefold curse . . . , a shroud" for "the false fatherland."[136]

XI

To the forces of order, this threefold curse appeared in the guise of the Revolution of 1848, which was itself made up of three interrelated, chronologically overlapping revolutions with different goals, geographies, and temporal frames of reference. The first revolution, about subsistence, bore close affinity to the conflicts of the old regime. Its protagonists looked back to a world of custom, not the capitalist market of the future, and argued for the just price of goods essential for survival. Occurring mainly in a diagonal of poverty from Baden and Württemberg through Franconia and Hesse, Thuringia, Brandenburg, and Pomerania, the protests peaked early in April and May 1847, and then again between March and May 1848.[137] During the second peak, hunger riots lent a middle-class, constitutional revolution urgency, as did local revolts against the rich and powerful, rebellions against communal governments, anti-Semitic uprisings (especially numerous in northern Baden, rural Hesse, and the Province of Posen), and peasant insurrections against landlords and the residues of serfdom.[138]

The second revolution—for citizens' rights and democratic institutions—aspired to set up arrangements in which people and their rulers shared sovereignty. Modeled on contemporary Great Britain more than revolutionary France, its temporal horizon, to borrow the language of Reinhart Koselleck, was the present of the mid-nineteenth century. It aimed to create monarchical governments constrained by constitutions and beholden to the representatives of the people, or at least the propertied classes. Following an altogether different geography than the agrarian uprisings, the second revolution took place mainly in towns and cities and aspired to secure democratic procedure in law. The so-called Pre-Parliament, which met in St. Paul's Church in Frankfurt am Main from March 31 to April 3, 1848, set elections for the "whole of the German people."[139] At the time, no one knew whether universal male suffrage would benefit radicals or royalists, and not a few delegates harbored reservations about the "dangerous experiment."[140] In the end, roughly three-quarters of adult men were eligible to vote, and in May 1848, in the first German election ever, about half the nation's men went to the polls.[141]

At the subsequent Frankfurt Parliament, which convened later that month, the delegates quickly turned to pressing issues. Within six weeks, a newly appointed constitutional committee issued a draft on basic rights, recommending that the government guarantee freedom of expression, religion, scholarship, teaching, assembly, and association to all those born in Germany, as well as ensuring all Germans freedom from unlawful search and seizure and due process. The committee also urged the Parliament to guarantee equality before the law, to make property inviolable, and to abolish the remaining vestiges of bondage.[142] This catalogue of basic rights, as it came to be called, was passed by the constitutional committee on June 1, and the committee wasted no time forwarding it as a recommendation to the Frankfurt Parliament. There it was first discussed in plenum on June 19, and then many times again, eliciting impatient assessments, famously from the poet Georg Herwegh, who denounced the assembly as a "Parla—Parla—Parliament," where "talking never ends."[143]

Meanwhile, the Revolution failed to solve what the historian Thomas Nipperdey called its "basic conflict," the question of force.[144] As the Frankfurt Parliament worked out the basic laws in the summer of 1848, Austrian military forces regrouped, shifting the spatial center of gravity of the Revolution (or at least its violent dimension) to the south and east. In June, General Alfred zu Windischgrätz, an unreconstructed loyalist who had distinguished himself by his ruthless repression of a textile worker strike in 1844, attacked Czech students and artisans in Prague, causing more than a hundred casualties and showing that enthusiastic citizens were no match for well-armed, disciplined soldiers of the line, especially when their field commanders understood how to combine cavalry and artillery to bear on weak points of the insurgency. Ominously, not a few German nationalists applauded the repression—thinking it a Teutonic victory over Slavic presumption.[145] Then, in late July, in the First Battle of Custoza, the Austrian General Graf Joseph Radetzky emerged victorious against the Piedmontese army in an encounter that brought about the Austrian occupation of Milan and augured the end of northern Italy's secession attempts.[146] In Hungary, the armies of General Josip Jelačić, who did Austria's bidding in order to win Croatian independence from Hungary, plundered the countryside and turned the Hungarian Revolution into a desperate, nation-against-nation struggle.

The savage spiral of violence radicalized the streets of Vienna. When in

October more Austrian troops were ordered to march on Hungary, a German battalion, the Richter Grenadiers, mutinied, and the resulting struggle between loyal and insurrectionary soldiers forced the Emperor to flee for Olmütz. As the Revolution hung in the balance—in Vienna, not Berlin—a small minority of the democratic left in the Frankfurt Parliament sent a delegation, headed by the charismatic, left-leaning Robert Blum, to mediate. There was little he could do. Artillery bombardments, cavalry charges, and infantry assaults overwhelmed the ill-trained, tactically hapless army of radical artisans and angry workers. Casualties were heavy. One estimate places over a thousand dead on the ledger of the Imperial army and four to six thousand on the side of the revolutionaries.[147] Meanwhile, on the night of November 8, a military tribunal condemned Blum, who as an emissary of Parliament should have enjoyed immunity, and executed him the next morning.[148]

If the first revolution was about the poor, the second about rights and constitutions, the third, coterminous with the second, was about nationalism. Its core questions were how far would Germany stretch, who would rule it, and who would be included.

When Germans began to think of the territorial shape of their nation, their ideas and proposals crisscrossed the heart of Europe: some recommended a Germany that included parts of the Balkans but not Posen; others a Germany that included Denmark and Holland; and others still a Germany that also incorporated Belgium, Alsace, and Switzerland. There were proposals for a Bavaria-centered small and neutral third Germany (outside of Austria and Prussia) and for a large Germany with an immigrant-absorbing colony in the principalities of Moldavia and Wallachia. More typically, Germans imagined their country as the German Confederation plus Schleswig, Posen, and East and West Prussia. Most of the imagined Germanies that surfaced during the Revolution assumed there would be German kings, conceiving of some kind of rotation—for example, the regents of Prussia, Austria, and Bavaria alternating every five years. Capital cities were also to be charted anew. Some writers envisioned new capital cities in Nuremberg, Bamberg, and Regensburg. Others placed the new capital of Germany at Erfurt or Gotha, while one writer proposed a brand-new capital city near Hof in Bavaria.[149]

The most vexing problem involved determining borders. In areas such as Posen, as the Frankfurt delegates quickly realized, it was "impossible to draw precise, continuous borders between the nationalities."[150] Towns were mixed, people switched back and forth between languages, and many were indifferent to nationality, which was, in any case, one among multiple ways of marking human groups. The international committee of the Frankfurt Parliament proposed that most of Posen, especially in the north and west, be recognized as German territory, and that a line of demarcation, heavily favoring the Germans, come with guarantees for the protection of nationality on both sides of the border.

The subsequent debate showed that few nationalists understood the complexities involved in ethnic partitions, and some were hostile to any concessions made to other nationalities. In what became one of the most often quoted speeches in the Frankfurt Assembly, the writer Wilhelm Jordan argued that one cannot simply place a half a million Germans under foreign rule and that anyone who proposes such a measure is an "unconscious traitor to the nation."[151] An enthusiastic Prussian, an undistinguished journalist, and a still worse poet, the young Jordan had been arrested earlier in the decade and was counted among the left-leaning constitutional monarchists. Born after the end of the Napoleonic Wars, and not yet thirty years old when he gave his speech on July 24, 1848, Jordan assumed that his nationalist position was as yet unpopular. Yet he felt that the tide of "cosmopolitan idealism" had begun to ebb.[152] "Germany fears no one, and needs fear no one," he intoned, insisting "it is finally time for us to awaken" from "dreamy self-abnegation" and embrace "a healthy national egoism."[153]

Whether this "healthy national egoism" reflected the sentiments of ordinary people, such as peasants, craftsmen, and small-town store owners, remains an open question. The best evidence suggests otherwise.[154]

The shape of Germany would not be left to the Frankfurt delegates to decide, however. With victories of the center over the periphery, and of powerful states over divided minority nationalities, the old order had already begun to roll back revolutionary gains. When the Frankfurt Parliament voted overwhelmingly in late October for the creation of a Germany that included the German-speaking lands of Austria, a revived government in Vienna, led by Prince Felix of Schwarzenberg, declared Austria a European power, its sovereignty indivisible. This Austrian rebuff then gave leverage to a group of Frankfurt delegates who were derisively dubbed the "small Germans." Looking to Berlin, not Vienna, they hoped that King Frederick William IV would accept the crown, and that Prussia would unify Germany.

The vote in the Frankfurt Parliament to offer the crown to the Prussian king was extremely close—290 to 284, with 29 absent—and it largely reflected old geographic and religious lines of demarcation.[155] Delegates from Protestant areas of north Germany supported handing over crown and scepter to the Prussian king, while in the Catholic Rhineland and in south Germany (except for Protestant Franconia) they resisted. The fit was not perfect, however, since Protestant areas of Württemberg remained "large German," and Catholic Silesia "small."[156] The vote, in any case, came to naught. When the Frankfurt Parliament offered the crown to the conservative Prussian king on April 3, 1849, Frederick William scorned it as "a dog collar" and privately sneered that "against revolutionaries only armies are of use."[157]

The parliamentarians were crestfallen. Over the course of a year, they had worked out a new constitution that envisaged a limited monarchy with the separation of powers, a document of basic rights, and a catalogue of reforms safeguarding a nascent capitalist order. Twenty-nine of the smaller states, mainly in the southwest and the center of Germany, adopted it. But the major states dismissed it contemptuously.

One last series of uprisings, however, played out like an encore before the curtain came down for the last time. Between late April and July 1849, barricades went up again in the Rhineland and in Silesia, as well as in Saxony and in southwest Germany, where rulers again fled. But the armies of the major states had in the meantime found their calling in the application of superior force against civilian militias, mutinied soldiers, and energetic but untrained and insufficiently armed revolutionaries. The uprising in Dresden was the first to be crushed, with some 250 casualties. Skirmishes in the heavily citadeled Rhineland followed. These spilled into the Palatinate and came to a head in Rastatt, a Badenese town where the Prussian army, aided by troops from Bavaria and Württemberg, outmaneuvered and outgunned the revolutionary forces.[158] Casualties were high and reprisals harsh. The best estimate places the toll for the Prussian soldiers and allied armies at 150 dead and 750 wounded, while casualties suffered by the revolutionary army were three times that.[159] Overall, nearly a thousand people faced execution and imprisonment, and thousands more emigrated.

In the end, however, the fate of the wider Revolution of 1848 was not sealed in Frankfurt am Main, Berlin, or Rastatt. Rather, it met its demise in Italy, where democrats still had tenuous control over Tuscany, Rome, and Venice, but lost their hold after republican France refused to aid them, and in Hungary, where the conflict assumed altogether different dimensions. The historian István Deák estimates that "about 50,000 Hungarian soldiers died and about the same number of Austrians."[160] Nineteenth-century figures, based on estimates of battle casualties, range lower, and include the wounded, but nevertheless suggest daunting dimensions, especially on the Hungarian side (close to 30,000 casualties).[161] By comparison, revolutionary deaths in Vienna likely numbered fewer than 5000; in southwest Germany, fewer than 1000; and in Berlin, Prague, and Dresden, in the hundreds.[162] If death tells a story, it suggests that the most violent centers of the Revolution were not in the country we think of today as Germany—but to the south and east of it.[163]

XII

In the summer of 1848, Heine was still living in Paris.[164] Suffering from a debilitating, undiagnosed illness—probably a form of lateral sclerosis combined with muscular dystrophy—he was confined to his bed and a recliner, with his legs lame and his jaw partly paralyzed. What letters survive from this period tell of a poet admitting that "he was not a Republican" and was not about to become one. The letters also reveal that he preferred "to flee the frightening agitation of public life" and take refuge in "the everlasting spring of poetry."[165] In his writings, he did not reference the embryonic constitution, with its catalogue of the "Basic Rights of the German People," and its guarantee of religious freedom, including Jewish emancipation; nor did he mention the men, women, or children killed or wounded by the troops of the regular army. He did, however, comprehend the dangers that the nationalists posed. "Our enemies," he complained, "the so-called national parties, the Teutomaniacs, are strutting about with an insolence as ridiculous as it is brutal."[166]

After the Revolution, Heine dictated a poem, which he called "In October 1849." Heine hoped his publisher, Julius Campe, would print it immediately as a broadside. But Campe did not reply to any of Heine's entreaties once the Revolution began, and the poem was instead printed a year later under the title "Germany / From Heinrich Heine / In October 1849."[167] Describing the return of peace and the perpetuation of family happiness, disturbed only by occasional gunshots reminiscent of firing squads, the poem tells of heroism and cowardice, and informs that in Hungary, not Germany, the epic of 1848 and 1849 came to a Nibelungen-like conclusion. After the Revolution, wolves, swine, and hounds rule, and Heine prudently admonishes himself to keep silent. The pen did not prove mightier, as he had once predicted, and for the poet the bitter end cruelly expanded out to a period of seven years, as Heine lay immobile, condemned to what he called his "mattress grave."

CHAPTER 8

NATION SHAPES

c. 1850–1870

*The period which culminated about the middle
of the nineteenth century was therefore
one of unexampled callousness.*

—ERIC HOBSBAWM

N THE 1850S, THE ENGLISH NOVELIST GEORGE ELIOT, ALONG WITH her partner, G. H. Lewes, author of *Life of Goethe*, made two extensive visits to Germany. In the first, they spent three months in Weimar in the fall of 1854, followed by four months in cold, "dry and bracing" Berlin. They worked on their books, strolled through parks and up and down boulevards, and met and discussed with the cultural luminaries of their day, such as the composer Franz Liszt ("the first really inspired man I ever saw," in Eliot's words) and Karl August Varnhagen, the widower of Rahel Levin.[1] Their first German sojourn marked the beginning of their unconventional, unmarried life together; it also drew them deeply into the world of postrevolutionary Germany, which they embraced as fervently as had Madame de Staël a half century earlier. Like de Staël, Eliot was attracted to the serious passion, shorn of pretension, shown by the Germans, who "to counterbalance their want of taste and politeness, are at least free of bigotry and exclusiveness."[2] She considered that Germany "has fought the hardest fight for freedom of thought, has produced the grandest inventions, has made magnificent contributions to science, has given us some of the divinest poetry, and quite the divinest music, in the world."[3]

She might have added theology and philosophy. Eliot was the translator of David Friedrich Strauss's purely historical *The Life of Jesus*, and of Ludwig Feuerbach's radically materialist *The Essence of Christianity*. It was, moreover, in the pages of the *Westminster Review*, the star-studded liberal quarterly she secretly edited, that the once obscure philosopher Arthur Schopenhauer was rediscovered. In the course of this initial visit to Germany, Eliot also deepened her admiration for Heinrich Heine, who, though "half a Hebrew," was "as much a German as a pheasant is an English bird, or a potato an Irish vegetable."[4] She thought him an even better writer of prose than Goethe, but maintained that Heine's greatest strength lay in his short, swift flights of lyrical poetry, his songs "all music and feeling," evoking a sublime thought, or a landscape rich with picturesque symbolism.[5]

In their second trip, in 1856, Eliot and Lewes stayed in romantic Nuremberg before moving on to Munich, where they admired its handsome if distant mountain vistas, mingled with scholars and artists, and perused the city's rich museum holdings. Perhaps following an afternoon in the Alte Pinakothek (set off as of 1853 from a "new picture gallery," the Neue Pinakothek), Eliot wrote her famous plea in *Adam Bede* for narrative fidelity to life as it is, praising the "rare, precious quality of truthfulness" of Dutch landscape paintings, "these faithful pictures of a monotonous homely existence, which has been the fate of so many more among my fellow-mortals than a life of pomp or of absolute indigence, of tragic suffering or of world-stirring actions."[6] The English couple's journey then took them south, traveling by horse-drawn omnibus through the highlands of Bavaria and Tyrol, past villages "with picturesque wide gables," to Vienna and Prague, and from there north by rail through Saxon Switzerland, "with its castellated rocks and firs," and onto Dresden, where they spent the next six weeks strolling around the baroque city, visiting almost daily the paintings in the Royal Gallery, and writing.[7]

If Dutch painting inspired Eliot's aesthetics of truthfulness, the new, closer-to-life attitude toward the countryside gripped her empirical imagination. In England, she complained, painters still painted ploughmen jocund, shepherds peaceful, and villagers merry.[8] In Germany, by contrast, "linking the higher classes with the lower" occurred with greater honesty and less exclusivity.[9] The task was more pressing than ever, as Germany, like England, was undergoing sweeping social and political transitions. How, in this context, should writers describe changes in a nation's landscapes so as to include the industries that employed people, and the cities that domiciled them? Who was to be included in descriptions of the nation? And who left out? As Eliot thought about these questions, she especially admired the work of one man, Wilhelm Heinrich Riehl, "a model for some future or actual student of our own people."[10]

II

Born in 1823 in the small town of Biebrich, Riehl remains one of the most controversial figures of the nineteenth century, alternately praised as a champion of the common people in their diverse hometown settings and vilified as a conservative precursor of the Nazi idealization of the *Volk*.[11] Like many midcentury figures, Riehl had initially embraced the Revolution of 1848. In Wiesbaden, where he was a newspaper editor, it unfolded on March 4 on the Palace Square, where a throng of people implored the Duke of Nassau to guarantee basic rights, abolish the last remnants of serfdom, and issue a constitution. From the balcony of the royal castle, the duke actually granted these requests, and Riehl thought it a great moment in the history of the duchy. But thereafter the people became politicized and divided into parties, some supporting a republic, others a monarchy.[12]

By his own admission, it was in the course of the Revolution that Riehl became "for the first time consciously conservative," and his first major postrevolutionary work, *Die bürgerliche Gesellschaft* (*Civic Society*), exemplified his new outlook.[13] There were estates of permanence and of movement, Riehl argued. Peasants and memebers of nobility belong to the first, townsmen and workers to the second, and it was the duty of a modern prince and his officials to bring the four estates together in productive harmony. Especially novel was Riehl's portrayal of the peasants. They were, he claimed, sedentary, devout, and deferential. They distrusted politicians and city people, and, within their patterns of daily life, they harbored a hidden, living archive of German ways and habits of thought. When he wrote *Civic Society*, which he had wanted to call "The Four Estates of the Modern State," 70 percent of the German population still lived in communities of less than two thousand people and the majority of Germans still found their employ in agriculture.[14] Idealizing a rooted peasantry, Riehl suffused the Indian summer of this world with warmth and imbued it with innocence.

Civic Society became Riehl's most read and reprinted work, often overshadowing his less heralded, more empirical writings. These were based, since 1843, on a peripatetic ethnography of people living in what the historian Mack Walker, following Riehl's research, called "German hometowns . . . , the kind of place where nearly every modern German has felt, somehow, that his origins as a German lay."[15] Suspended between village and city, usually with populations between two and ten thousand, these modest communities ranged from old Imperial cities enjoying significant, statelike autonomy to territorial towns defending what shreds of special privilege they still had.[16] No one knew them as well as Riehl. Whether traversing the Tauber Valley, walking along the banks of the Lahn River, or crisscrossing the Palatinate, Riehl paced out his observations and patiently took in the diverse manners and customs he observed.[17] And unlike the travelers of previous centuries, he talked to ordinary people.[18]

Riehl also had a method. Before he left on his walking tours, he studied town descriptions and topographical maps; then he traveled, usually by train or coach, to a starting point. He rarely walked for more than a week—typically by himself, sometimes with his dog, and always with a blank notebook in his knapsack. When he arrived in a town he ascended, following a tradition familiar to the sixteenth-century humanists, the stairs of the local bell tower in order to see the settlement situated in its surrounding landscape. When he came back down, he sought out townspeople, talked to them, and allowed them to tell their stories, listening and later in the evening recording what he had heard in his notebook. Once Riehl returned home, he deepened his knowledge of the places he had visited by reading histories published by local historical societies, which by the 1850s were omnipresent and in his opinion more trustworthy than the histories written by university professors.[19] Gathering his notes and sketching out paragraphs, he then "freely composed" scenes of hometown country life, much as would an artist guided by what Riehl called the "landscape eye."[20]

"The Landscape Eye" was the name Riehl gave to his short history of how the Germans saw their own country. It begins in the sixteenth century, a time, according to Riehl, when folk songs and folk books supplanted paeans to the king and emperor; paintings depicted towns and peasants, not just castles and courts; and humanists described country and people in detail. Sebastian Münster, Riehl thought, was the most painstaking and comprehensive of these early describers of the nation, and his

Cosmographia the first complete, comparative, well-ordered depiction of Germany.[21] Riehl also counted Matthäus Merian's *Topographia Germaniae*, the "Old Merian," as among the great house books of the German people, passed down in family heirlooms from generation to generation and, like the *Cosmographia*, still found in the household libraries of south Germany.[22] These books demonstrated that the culture of the sixteenth and seventeenth centuries hewed closer to the common man than did both that of the Middle Ages and the eighteenth century. Riehl derided the latter epoch as the "pony-tail period" and thought the maps of Jean Baptiste Homann characteristic of it. Framed by coats of arms, crowns, and miters and decorated with handsome cartouches, Homann's maps nowhere represented ordinary people—as earlier maps had done, if only in stereotyped costumes.[23] The eighteenth century also did not know the pleasures of simply walking; it therefore had no eye for Germany's rolling mountains or dense forests, and deemed them inferior to wide-open, closely sheared, easily traversed, and precisely cultivated landscapes.[24] It was not until the nineteenth century, according to Riehl, that a sense for the beauty of untamed nature and a genuine interest in the people returned. But by then, the land and its rural people were threatened. Riehl wrote ruefully about the growth of bureaucratic states and sprawling cities, the expansion of roads and the advent of rails, and the nascent industrial revolution.

He poured many of his insights into *Country and People*, first published in 1854. In this work, his most imaginative and veracious, Riehl conceived of Germany as a landscape of three parts. There were two great parallelograms: one giving shape to the sparsely populated, underdeveloped, flat German plains in the north and northeast, the other encompassing the high, remote elevations of the south and southeast. Between these two parallelograms lay the densely towned hills and plateaus Riehl called "individualized Germany."[25] It formed a rough triangle from Lake Constance in the south to Breslau in the east and Aachen in the west.

Riehl actually conceived of Germany as a modern mapmaker would. The three landscapes—the north German flatlands, the high elevations in the south, and individualized Germany—constituted the base map. New layers then reshaped the lands and its people. Soldered together by war and peace treaty, "artificial states" constituted the first layer, imposing unnatural political boundaries on rooted mentalities. Bavaria, for example, now possessed territories, like the Palatinate, distinguished by a progressive political culture alien to its conservative heartland. Baden mixed Lutheran, Calvinists, and Catholics together in a jumble, and Württemberg had taken on a Catholic population estranged from its religious traditions. Prussia, the most artificial state of all, contained vastly diverse populations but not a single people.[26] New roads also restructured the land, constituting a second layer. Especially in areas of significant population density, the *Chaussees*—well-drained highways paved with crushed rock—tied together cities and market towns, allowing for significant increases in travel speed and reliability. Yet they also circumvented the curvature of country roads, bypassing the natural weave connecting German hometowns.

The final layer, the railroad grid, was the newest addition to the German landscape; it dramatically compressed the country, reducing the duration of the trip from Hamburg to Augsburg from eight days in 1840 to two and a half days a decade later.[27] Cutting linear lines through the landscape, the rails drew town and country into the orbits of cities, further blurred the distinction between the urban and rural worlds, and reinforced the status of the new palace cities as against older urban centers—the court city of Wiesbaden against the Carolingian city of Limburg, for example.[28] They also changed how Germans experienced the landscape. Riding in trains, people saw the countryside as fast-moving panoramas punctuated by the rapid passing of fence posts. Genuine contact came only at the end points of journeys, when trains stopped at stations, usually built on the outskirts of towns. As a result, the slow transition between regional and national cultures, a central component of the earlier experience of travel, quickly dissipated. To those traveling the "Holland line" from Oberhausen to Arnhem, for example, the gradual change in the visage of German to Dutch towns became barely perceptible.[29] Riehl, discussing his concerns about the limited experience of travel in trains, noted that since early trains could not easily climb steep hills, rails had the effect of flattening the landscape. Finally, the rails contravened the country's physical features. An insistent student of maps and an avid reader of geography, Riehl noticed that the railroad grid pushed into the background the Germany of rivers, mountains, and plateaus, and that the emerging industrial zones of the Rhineland and Westphalia were more densely crisscrossed with rails than the drainage basins of the Elbe and the Weser.

German railway map, 1855, from Gustav Droysen,
Allgemeiner Historischer Handatlas (1886).

Riehl's remarkable analysis of the shapes and contours of the Germany
of his day captures with admirable precision the structure of small-town
life just as industrialization was poised to transform it. Unfortunately, his
observations about the genuinely rural world are less acute. He came to the
countryside: he was not of it. He had very little to say about the changes
occurring in actual farming. He neglected any mention of the fallow land
hard won under improved plows, or better field rotations, aided by the plant-
ing of clover, or new crops, like the potato and sugar beet, which in the 1850s
dramatically increased agricultural productivity. He also did not describe
the significant increase in livestock, especially hogs and cattle, that transformed what the countryside looked like, and what it produced. In the end,
Riehl was interested in landscapes, not farming, and, as the critic Raymond
Williams has pointed out, "a working country is hardly ever a landscape."[30]

The resulting rural mystification also distorted Riehl's view of one of the most momentous changes then taking place in the German countryside: emigration. In the 1850s, economic dislocation forced a mass exodus that surpassed two million people per year at its peak. Germans, most of them from Riehl's individualized country, boarded ships in Hamburg and Bremen destined for the United States, where they settled in New York, Philadelphia, Baltimore, St. Louis, Cincinnati, and Chicago, as well as on the plains of the Midwest.[31] In some American cities, like Milwaukee, the German-born population constituted more than a third of the local inhabitants, and by the 1860s Germans had become the largest immigrant group in the United States. About two-thirds were men, and in the 1850s some 7 percent came back.[32] The vast majority, however, stayed, creating émigré populations clustered in communities, typically centered on a church, that cultivated German language and customs and supported German-speaking social and political clubs.[33]

Little interested in this momentous change, Riehl refused to see that human movement had become part of the rural landscape and missed how mass emigration to North America altered village and hometown horizons. Instead, he held fast to nineteenth-century platitudes about emigrants rejecting national traditions. He also drifted into anti-Semitic prejudice. Although appalled by the riots against local Jews that accompanied the Revolution of 1848, Riehl nevertheless believed that "stock market Jews" were responsible for the deleterious impact of capital in the countryside, empathizing with the peasant's "natural hostility" to the "alien intruder."[34]

Finally, Riehl's praise of the virtues of rootedness also colored his understanding of home life. In *The Family*, published in 1854, Riehl insisted that a well-ordered society rested upon hierarchy, inequality, and a strict division between the sexes. Advances in civilization, he maintained, brought sexual differentiation, not androgyny. Conversely, the advent of women writers (he singled out Rahel Levin and Bettina von Arnim) was an "abnormality in the psychological climate."[35] Charlotte von Stein was the better example of a true German woman, because she put her intelligence in the higher service of Goethe's creative genius. Women should not assert, Riehl opined, they should support. "If the Greek goddess carries a spear, the German goddess wears a dress."[36] He was of course speaking in clichés. As urban centers grew, they attracted mainly male labor, and left behind countrysides in which women outnumbered men and took on ever more work in the fields. Women carried water and wood, scythed and threshed—in addition to everything else.

III

Most Germans still lived in small towns and in the countryside, and, like Riehl, Germany's best authors mainly wrote about the denizens of these modest places. There was the Austrian author Adalbert Stifter, who enveloped enduring love stories in austere, striking landscapes; the Swiss author Gottfried Keller, whose short stories like "Romeo and Juliet in the Village" told of tragic love and the dark abyss of family life; and the north German Theodor Strom, who in his *Immensee* turned the barren Holstein heath into a bleak canvas of unfulfilled longing. There was also the Jewish author Berthold Auerbach, who in his immensely successful *Black Forest Village Tales* recounted earthy stories of life in the Jewish-Catholic town of his youth (Nordstetten, near Horb, on the Neckar) and shellacked them with a sheen of sentimentality thick enough to smother even the slightest hint of rural anti-Semitism. Other authors explored the poverty-stricken countryside, such as Jeremias Gotthelf, who sketched the changing visage of the Emmental (in the Bernese highlands), while Fritz Reuter, who had languished for seven years in a Prussian jail in the 1830s, wrote harsh dialect poetry and prose depicting the difficult conditions of rural laborers on the large farms of his native Mecklenburg. Stifter, Gotthelf, Reuter, and Auerbach were from the countrysides they wrote about; their knowledge of the rural world was precise, and in the case of Reuter unsparing.

Yet even here, it has been argued, there was a deficiency of vision. In *Mimesis: The Representation of Reality in Western Literature*, written in German-Jewish exile in Istanbul and first published in 1946, the great twentieth-century literary scholar Erich Auerbach contended that German novelists of the nineteenth century remained confined "to the narrow realm of the local," depicting the "economic, the social, and the political as in a state of quiescence."[37] Compared with Honoré de Balzac's and, later, Émile Zola's sharp-edged, close-to-life portrayals, German authors disappointed, and their failure, according to Auerbach, revealed a general reluctance to see things as they really were. Even a writer like Stifter, Auerbach complained, rendered coarse, impure peasants as delicate, charming figures. Moreover, German authors rarely attempted that "radical mixture of styles," high and low, that became a staple of French realism. Instead, according to Auerbach, they avoided "serious representation of contemporary everyday social reality" and nowhere brought together "a forceful realism with a tragic conception of the problems of the age."[38]

Auerbach was surely right in seeing that the German realist novel neither portrayed life in the emerging industrial zones nor depicted the big city truthfully, as Victor Hugo had rendered Paris or Charles Dickens had described London. In the German lands, the diminished capacity to see ugly realities with clear eyes characterized writers and poets, politicians and pundits, left and right.

It thus came to pass that in the age of capital, Germany possessed virtually no public window onto its own early industrial revolution. In the 1850s and 1860s, there were no critical novels recounting the backbreaking days and the makeshift quarters of vast numbers of railroad workers, the lowest rung of the industrial working class. There were no extended exposés giving a sense of the long hours and dangerous conditions of Ruhr Valley miners, still made up mainly of first-generation Westphalian peasants. And there were no major critical works telling of the heat, sweat, and toil of the formers and puddlers in the giant steel mills of Essen. Germans continued to write many books, but in the crucial first two decades that saw industrialization take off in the German lands, those books ignored the gigantic swarms, often thousands strong, of laborers wielding pick, ax, and shovel in order to move earth and tunnel into it so that railroads could be built. Nor did they penetrate the dark Saxon textile mills that bound their workers to a merciless pace, and that, despite stringent labor laws, still chained children to spinning machines.[39]

The working poor, in short, were without their describers.[40] To a significant extent, this was a forgotten casualty of 1848. With thousands of central European revolutionaries in exile, the native German tradition of industrial description went underground, and the 1840s explosion of writing on the working poor—from Friedrich Engels to Bettina von Arnim— all but disappeared. One extensive bibliography on German writings on the "propertyless" lists five titles from the 1820s, fifteen from the 1830s, seventy from the 1840s, and only nine from the 1850s—when the indus-trial revolution actually kicked in.[41] Riehl, often cited as a counterexample, devoted an extended essay to the fourth estate—but in it he offered only vacuous analytical differentiations and hoary platitudes.[42] When it came to industrial workers, he briefly discussed only the miners of Westphalia, whom he praised for their traditionalism, political quiescence, and prayer.

The occluded vision also constricted the sense of the urban world.[43] The only pre-unification novel centered on Berlin, Wilhelm Raabe's *Die Chronik der Sperlingsgasse* (*The Chronicle of Sparrow Lane*), confines the city to a side street in the angled and contorted Märkisches Viertel, with an attic window allowing the protagonist, an old poet, a sheltered vista onto a cramped world in which "memory has taken the place of hope."[44] Excur-sions to other parts of Berlin are few, timid, and imprecisely rendered, making the novel—unlike the works of Balzac or Dickens—impossible to trace out and map.[45] Urban complexity is acknowledged and the rich and poor are mentioned, but they are described as bland, binary background, as if Raabe, then a young author, simply lacked a language for it.

Yet in the two decades after the Revolution, the population of Ger-many's major cities grew dramatically. The populations of Breslau, Ham-burg, Dresden, Leipzig, Stuttgart, and Munich more than doubled. Vienna became a city of over a million people and Berlin nearly tripled in size, surpassing its Danubian counterpart in population and becoming the third largest city in Europe. For the first time in Germany's long history, big-city populations altered the country's demographic profile. Between 1830 and 1870, the percentage of people living in communities with over 100,000 denizens more than doubled.[46] Concentrated in the Rhine-Ruhr basin, new cities like Barmen, Elberfeld, Dortmund, and Essen became small-scale Manchesters, replete with smog-belching towers. The physiognomy of cities also changed. Rails penetrated cities that had only recently (or in Nuremberg's case not yet) lost their protective walls, and, as a result, trav-elers no longer arrived at city gates but in the city, often at stations situated in impoverished urban peripheries.[47]

There were exceptions to this general tendency to avert one's eyes to the harsh new conditions of industrial life and the chaos in Germany's new cities. One was the statistician Ernst Engel, who in the 1850s and 1860s published precise statistical accounts of the wages of workers in Belgium and Saxony, and who calculated what has come to be known as Engel's law: "the poorer a family is, the larger the part of its total expenditures must be utilized to procure food."[48] Another was the painter Adolph Menzel.

IV

In his day Menzel was celebrated as an illustrator of books on Frederick the Great and as a painter of court and military life. Born the son of a lithographer in Breslau in 1815, Menzel moved to Berlin with his family in 1830 and apprenticed in his father's shop. His real gift, though, was drawing, and it was to drawing, and later painting, that he devoted his life. A solitary man, conspicuously short, Dutch-bearded, moderate in habits, and disciplined beyond ordinary measure ("no day without a line," he liked to say), Menzel spent most of his years standing in seclusion at his easel or hunched over the hundreds of sketches in his expansive studio.[49] When he did venture out, it was mainly to observe and draw. No one looked at things from as many angles. No one saw as insistently.

Menzel was the first German, perhaps even European, painter to depict industrial workers as genuine individuals. He painted them as he observed them—not as comical figures in the shadows of picturesque scenes, or as props for perspective, or as charming additions to back- or foreground. Instead, he put them front and center as a matter of fact. In *Head of a Bearded Workman in Profile*, painted in 1844 just after the Weavers' Revolt, Menzel placed the subject in profile pose, and, by applying the oil colors thickly, suggested his subject's determination, steadfastness, and even defiance. In a manner reminiscent of Rembrandt (whose drawings Menzel had been assiduously studying), Menzel also reddened the workman's eyelids, softening stoicism with sadness. Moreover, unlike other painters and writers, Menzel did not turn away from painting lowly subjects when the radical forties gave way to the political disappointments of subsequent decades. In 1855, he returned to the portraiture of workers with a study that similarly lends weight and dignity to an unnamed member of the fourth estate. In *Head of a Worker Wearing a Cap*, Menzel explored a workingman's facial contours, emphasizing deep ridges and exaggerating features like the chin and ears, in order to give an impression of the worker's years of steadfast toil.[50] Contemporaries would soon call this way of rendering ordinary

Adolph Menzel, *Head of a Bearded
Workman in Profile*, 1844.

people and ordinary scenes "empathetic seeing"—it offered no political
program, no transcendence, just immediacy.[51]

Menzel left behind a largely hidden body of work that revealed a stringent commitment to the realistic portrayal of the quotidian in modern life.
Yet most of his early paintings of common subjects were out of the public eye until 1906, when the art historian Julius Meier-Graefe posited two
Menzels: one, the public artist close to the court and much feted; the other,
hidden from view, with a modern sensibility for everyday dignity that foreshadowed French impressionism. Menzel's surviving correspondence was,
however, largely silent about the early "modernist" paintings Meier-Graefe
celebrated. And it does not even hint at a double life. In the end, most of
the paintings never sold. Menzel just stacked them up in the dark corners
of his immense studio.

V

The aftermath of the Revolution transformed the political landscape. Most critically, martial law remained in force in Baden until 1852 and in parts of Austria until 1854. A state of siege (*Belagerungszustand*) became, as the political writer Ludwig August von Rochau noticed, part of public life. It was, as he put it in his awkward neo-Hegelian formulation, the "actualization of the sharpest tip of the concept of dictatorship."[52] Authorities arrested hundreds and dismissed thousands of civil servants, including a significant number of dedicated and politicized schoolteachers. Liberals were purged from state bureaucracies and conservative-minded men put in their stead, and many of Germany's best and brightest fled.

The collapse of the Revolution of 1848 did not just leave ruin, however. Over the next two decades, a remarkable phase of association building began.[53] Nationalist organizations—like the gymnastics societies, shooting clubs, and singing societies—mushroomed. So too did economic interest groups, religious societies, and women's associations, such as Louise Otto-Peter's General German Women's Society, founded in 1865. Elite political organizations, such as the German National Association, also flourished, and indeed ad hoc religious, economic, and political organizations soon transformed into a durable, five-pillared system of political parties, representing the range of public opinion from conservative to socialist views. But in the various parliaments of the German states, political parties could still only limit power; they did not yet have it, with executive power remaining firmly in dynastic hands everywhere.

The German Confederation, as one historian observes, was "awash" with monarchies—thirty-five to be precise—and they marched with the times and retained popularity, not as mere extensions of dynastic households, but as genuine fatherlands.[54] Emphasizing the beneficence of the regent and the justness of the constitution, dynastic states erected monuments to the ruling family and staged sumptuous celebrations on royal birthdays; they also subsidized immensely popular folk festivals, like the Oktoberfest in Munich and the Cannstatter Volksfest just across the Neckar from Stuttgart; and they opened parks and welcomed wider publics to rich art holdings, especially striking in Saxony and Bavaria. They also supported state-based historical societies and pursued an active propaganda campaign in print, pictures, and commemorative kitsch. Moreover, developments that seemed to further nation building often benefited dynastic states within Germany. Receipts from the customs union accounted for nearly 20 percent of some state coffers, for example. Railroads, which Friedrich List had imagined would tie together the nation, also covered individual states in a lattice of railed infrastructure.[55] As a result, monarchical sentiment deepened. In Bavaria more and more people named their children after monarchs and other members of the royal family.[56]

If subjects of states felt like they counted, it was partly because states began to actually count them. Prussia established its first statistical bureau in 1805, Bavaria in 1808, Württemberg in 1820, and Saxony in 1831.[57] Typically manned by only a few people, the new offices nevertheless counted individuals as if they had equal worth.[58] States also began to map people. When it appeared in 1828, the *"Administrativ-Statistischer Atlas vom Preußischen Staate,"* a choropleth map that used hand-colored shades of brown and yellow to show human densities, was one of the earliest population maps ever published.[59] Counting language as an index of nationality was also a nineteenth-century invention. In Prussia, the statistics bureau began tracking mother tongue in the 1820s, but only in the eastern districts of Gumbinnen and Königsberg, and then again in the 1830s in select districts of Posen and West Prussia. It was not until 1843 that Prussia added a column devoted to language to its general census, counting the language spoken by the family, which in practice meant the head of the household. In bilingual Prussia—with a great deal of intergenerational and linguistic fluidity, interlinguistic marriage, migrant workers, and non-German domestic servants—this method cloaked significant inaccuracies. Richard Böckh, who would become head of the Prussian statistical bureau, contended instead that each individual had to be counted, assigned a mother tongue, and represented by an integer.[60] Although Böckh's method improved accuracy, it also came at a cost. People who spoke two or more languages with equal or near facility were wiped out as a statistical category. Fractioned identities and shifting ethnic allegiances fell away. And national indifference—likely the most widespread position—was colored over.[61]

In the case of the statistical and cartographical representation of nationalities in the Austrian lands, the coloring over was quite literal, especially

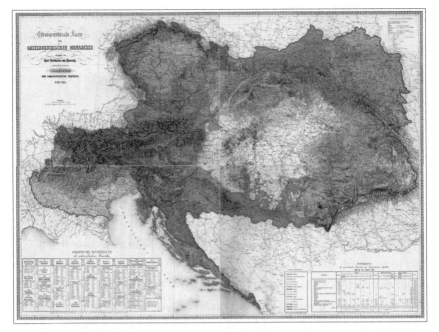

Karl von Czoernig, "Ethnographic Map of the Austrian Monarchy," 1855.

in the mapmaker Karl von Czoernig's "Ethnographic Map of the Austrian Monarchy." Realistic seeming, stunningly detailed, based on 306 smaller charts, Czoernig's four-part map, in which peoples are shown to have areas and borders as territorial states did, was the result of an immense effort in data collection, questionnaire distribution, and statistical tabulation.[62] It nevertheless proffered a fiction that Austria's nationalities mainly resided in discrete areas bordered by language frontiers. Bi- and trilingual zones found imperfect expression. Jewish settlements were not even counted. And instead, the kind of counting and tabulating that had long marked "seeing like a state" found its way to the representation of nationality.

Finally, states also became richer. Between 1840 and 1860, the state budgets of Prussia and Austria more than doubled, as did the number of people each employed.[63] While Prussia significantly increased the size of its police, Austria, as one critic quipped, bloated into "a standing army of soldiers, a sitting army of officials, a kneeling army of priests, and a creeping army of denunciators."[64] Moreover, in both Prussia and Austria, military budgets, long in decline relative to total state budgets and GNP, increased, as did military personnel as a percentage of the young male population.[65]

It was no accident, then, that the major political issue of the 1860s turned on the control and organization of the army. In Prussia, it ended in a constitutional crisis and a second defeat for the liberals.

In its political outlines the crisis is well-known. In 1860, Albrecht von Roon, the minister of war, proposed that Prussia expand the size of its army, extend the term of service to three years, and abolish citizen militias. Liberals deemed the expansion unnecessary and expensive, believed militias expressed a close connection between the people and the army, and discerned in the privileging of the regular standing army a reinforcement of the crown's main instrument of repression. Intensified by the electoral successes in 1861 of a new left-liberal Progressive Party, the standoff came to an impasse in September 1862, when the crown called in a new prime minister, Otto von Bismarck. Not known for his conciliatory politics, Bismarck informed the Landtag that if it did not approve of the military budget, the ministers would "take the money where we find it."[66] The constitution, he further noted, did not envision deadlock. Instead, there was a "gap" in it, forcing the government to operate without parliamentary approval. "Not through speeches and majority decisions will the great questions of the day be decided," Bismarck told the budget committee of the Landtag in his first speech as prime minister of Prussia, "but by iron and blood."[67] The speech was not well received; even hotheaded pro-Prussian liberals like Heinrich von Treitschke thought it crass and boorish.[68] But when Prussian arms won swift battles against Denmark and Austria, bringing unification close to reality, the majority of liberals acquiesced. After a royal concession about the legality of it all, the liberals approved the budget retroactively.

The conflict was about who controlled organized force in an age when states could draw on industrial technologies, resources, and infrastructure. The Prussian parliament held veto power over the army's budget but the crown maintained complete *Kommandogewalt*, deciding when and how the army was to be used, with what weapons and what tactics, and who was to be promoted within its ranks. The Prussian nobility, a militarized class that drew its identity and social cohesion from a long tradition of sacrifice in battle, still made up more than 90 percent of officers in the infantry and cavalry. The crisis essentially cemented the class character of the army, undermined the ideal of the fighting citizen, and defeated liberal efforts to nationalize the fighting force of the state. Liberal fantasies of war had also been sanguineous—but citizen participation in battle drew on the assumption that when citizens fought and sacrificed, the fatherland was itself transformed. Now the reverse dynamic began. Centered on the harsh, disciplined rule of the barracks, the new "school of the nation" inculcated military values. Not the nationalization of the military, but the militarization of the nation followed.[69]

VI

In the 1850s and 1860s, war had returned as an arbiter of history. Across the globe, it reappeared in three extremely destructive wars: the utterly cataclysmic Taiping Rebellion, with deaths of more than twenty million people; then the Crimean War, which demonstrated the destructive capabilities of superior British firepower against slow-moving, tactically hapless columns of Russian soldiers; and finally the American Civil War, which unfolded the "red business," as the poet Walt Whitman called it, of highly mobilized, industrial, mass warfare, killing over 200,000 men in combat and more still from wounds and disease.[70]

In central Europe, the return of war as an arbiter of history made it abundantly clear that states at war, not nationalists in debating clubs, would determine the space of nations. But which states? Of the four hundred pamphlets addressing the question of the territorial shape of central Europe published between the Treaty of Villafranca, which ended the Austro-Italian War in 1859, and the Battle of Königgrätz in 1866, the greatest number had assumed that both Austria and Prussia would determine the new order, slightly fewer that Prussia alone would be the driving force, with only a handful imagining Austria in this role.[71] Remarkable in this phase of polemic are the flare-ups of rhetorical violence. One anonymous pamphleteer, for example, called for a united Europe to fight the France of Napoleon III and, "however bloody the war," to end it with the "annihilation [*Vernichtung*] of the archenemy."[72]

Nationalists on both the left and right had come to understand that states, not nations, possessed armies, civil servants, police, statistical bureaus, and financial resources, and that armed inter-state conflict, not the altered optics of nationality, would reshape central Europe north of the

COMPARISON OF EUROPEAN POWERS, 1863
Prussia=100

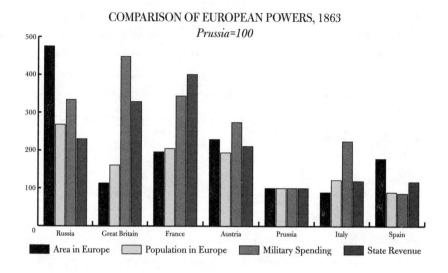

Alps.[73] The future contours of the region were not easily predictable, however, and in 1863 it was hardly obvious that Prussia would be the state to reshape the German lands. According to the tabulations of the contemporary statistician Otto Hausner, Prussia's military spending looked average, coming in a distant sixth in comparison with other European countries, while its police budget put it behind France, Austria, Russia, Spain, and Italy. Austria was clearly the more formidable power, and it was the second largest country in Europe in terms of land and the third largest by population. Parliaments did not slow it down either, and its military and police budgets, both in absolute and per capita terms, outstripped its neighbor to the north.[74]

In the clash of forces, however, unknown factors often play a larger role than statistical certainties. And in the brief war against Austria in 1866, largely over Prussian control of Schleswig-Holstein, Helmuth von Moltke, the Prussian chief of the general staff, coordinated forces more precisely and with greater speed than any commander before him. Using the rails to race separate armies into position where they could strike in near unison with breach-loading rifles against Austrian muzzle-loaders, Moltke surpassed in organizational acumen and otherwise outpaced his Austrian opponents. On the morning of battle, the Austrian general Ludwig Benedek possessed a dramatic superiority in numbers—240,000 Austrian troops against Prussia's 135,000. He made no use of it, however. Instead, Prussian infantrymen, the best shooters in Europe, ripped apart the Austrians, whose soldiers suffered casualties three times higher than their opponents endured. When Moltke's second army finally arrived, the Austrians retreated in panic. As Moltke's armies bore south and closed in on Vienna, Emperor Franz Joseph conceded the fight.[75]

VII

From Crimea to the American South, the new technology of photography documented the grim reality of midcentury warfare. However staged many battlefield scenes were, the photographs of the likes of Mathew Brady, James Gardner, and Roger Fenton shocked the public. Because the war between Prussia and Austria ended so quickly, photography did not play a comparable role. If unknown at the time, a record did remain, however. It was from Adolph Menzel's recording eye and faithful brush.

Menzel, whose life spanned one of the most peaceful periods of European history, had actually never seen battle. For a painter who insisted on close observation, this fact embarrassed him, and for reasons of "general artistic duty," Menzel left for Bohemia "to sense the stuff—what war is."[76] As the clash between the Prussians and Austrians unfolded, he traveled to Königgrätz, arriving just after the decisive Prussian victory. But hostilities were still in progress, and between the towns of Sadowa and Chlum, where a large cavalry confrontation ended in carnage, he got his first taste of war's "horror, misery, and stench," as bodies, limbs, dead horses, knapsacks, caps, and helmets were strewn by the roadside.[77] In three works of pencil and watercolor, he portrayed dead soldiers as they lay on straw, in a military hospital, and on a barn floor. The last was especially jarring. In *Three Fallen Soldiers in a Barn*, we come upon the dead bodies, as if having just opened a door, and we see them at our feet. They are not arranged in a heroic pose, and, as if to underscore the fallen soldiers' extreme vulnerability, Menzel left their lower extremities naked. Like Francisco Goya, whose *Los desastres de la guerra* had been published in book form for the first time in 1863, Menzel refused to ennoble this war or suggest that the suffering was somehow connected to a higher sacrifice.

Adolph Menzel, *Three Fallen Soldiers in a Barn*, 1866.

Menzel's realism did not diverge from prevailing sentiment as much as
is often supposed. Germans by and large greeted the outbreak of the war
in the summer of 1866 with dismay.[78] A swift Prussian victory was hardly
a foregone conclusion, and reports of the American Civil War, which had
ended with a horrendous casualty count only a year before, gave them cause
for concern. In most newspapers, a tone of solemn duty predominated, and
as far as can be ascertained, common people on both sides displayed little
enthusiasm. But when the war concluded, intellectuals went about giving
it meaning, and opinions diverged. Prussian historians like Heinrich von
Sybel, Heinrich von Treitschke, and Johann Gustav Droysen saw the battle
as a providential victory of Protestant Prussia over Catholic Austria, and
represented the year 1866 as the logical consequence of a chain of events
starting in 1517, when the Reformation began. The die, they believed, was
now cast for the achievement of German unity.[79]

The Austrians, by contrast, accepted the result of the battle as if it were
the chance outcome of a duel, not a verdict of providence.[80] There were few
Austrian nationalist outcries, and little sense that a very long history of Austrian primacy in the German lands had abruptly come to an end. Instead,
Austrian liberals turned to the question of a constitution, the absence of

which they claimed caused low morale and ultimately defeat. Attending to its larger problem, Hungary, the government in Vienna offered a series of concessions that culminated in the Austro-Hungarian Compromise of 1867, making the House of Habsburg into a so-called dual monarchy with its geopolitical compass set east and southeast.[81] Bismarck made this easier by making no territorial claims on Austria and instead merely securing its assent to Prussia's annexation of Schleswig-Holstein, Hanover, Hesse-Kassel, Nassau, and Frankfurt am Main. Prussia now completed its historical shift west, tying its flanks together and making the Prussian state virtually synonymous with north Germany.

It could have turned out otherwise—as not a few commentators expected, Friedrich Engels among them. As the terms of Austria's secret negotiations with France prior to the war suggest, the shape of Germany, perhaps even of German history, might have turned out very different. In the event of Austrian victory, Venetia was to be ceded to Italy, Silesia to Austria, and Prussia's western territories severed and made into an independent German state.[82] Although unclear how, the southern German states were also slated to accrue additional territory—continuing a process of medium-sized state enlargement that began with Napoleon. The Germany that would have emerged (mapped out for the first time below) would have established medium-sized German states between France in the west and Austria and Prussia in the east. When Belgium and the Netherlands are brought in, the emergence of a viable group of such states in northern and western central Europe would come into focus. In this counterfactual outcome, Austria would have retained its eastern orientation, and Prussia its army but not its coal and iron (almost all of which was mined and produced in areas Prussia would have lost in the event of defeat). Relations of power between north and south, Prussia and Austria, would have returned to a balance, as France once again played Prussia and Austria against each other, giving the medium-sized German states a reprieve.

Instead, the German Confederation was dissolved and the North German Confederation formed in its stead. In a familiar pattern, Prussia now pushed to extend its hegemony, applying economic, political, and military pressure on the southern states. The eastern parts of Prussia that were outside the German Confederation, including the cities of Danzig, Posen,

GERMANY

after counterfactual AUSTRIAN VICTORY
over PRUSSIA *in* **1866**

and Königsberg, were now part of a German polity. Of greater moment, however, was the departure of Austria from Germany. The exit meant not just the loss of Vienna but also of Innsbruck, Salzburg, Graz, Linz, Klagenfurt, and multiethnic Trieste, with its port on the Adriatic. It involved the forfeit of Prague, as recently as 1848 a majority-German speaking city but now populated by more Czech speakers, and it occasioned the departure from the Bohemian lands, with their long, complicated, relations to Germany. And of course, Germany lost the rugged Austrian Alps, and its highest mountain, the Ortler.

The geopolitical revolution also meant that Germany's medium-sized states would not survive as sovereign countries.[83] Historians might be skeptical of the sociologist Charles Tilly's notorious calculation that in 1490 Europe contained roughly five hundred states and half a millennium later, in 1990, barely thirty.[84] Yet Bismarck's contemporaries were certainly cognizant of the process of territorial consolidation. In December 1866, one satisfied German nationalist noted that, "of the fifty-nine states of Europe, eighteen have disappeared in the last few years."[85]

Nevertheless, in the mid-1860s, the scope of this territorial consolidation was unclear. In terms of both area and population, many of Europe's medium-sized states—including Romania, Serbia, Greece, Denmark, the Netherlands, Belgium, Portugal, and Switzerland—remained alive and well.[86] At the time, Bavaria and Hanover also belonged to this group, as did, if on its smaller end, Baden, Württemberg, and Saxony. Indeed, to some observers, the demise of Germany's medium-sized countries seemed a European anomaly.[87]

No one saw the impact of the disappearance of medium-sized German states with as much clarity as the iconoclastic, liberal historian, Georg Gottfried Gervinus. As other historians embraced Prussian power and *Realpolitik*, Gervinus argued that Prussian militarism would devour liberty and independence in Germany. In 1866, Germany's medium-sized states had sided with the Confederation; after Prussian victory over

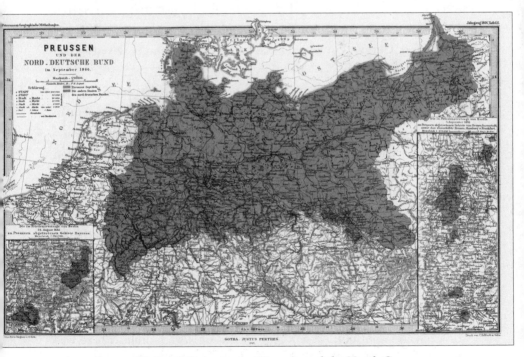

August Heinrich Petermann, "Prussia and the North German Confederation in September 1866."

Austria, Bismarck either took them over or forced them to join the North German Confederation. "The fate of the annexed lands tormented me almost as if I were a citizen of each," wrote an anguished Gervinus.[88]

From Gervinus's perspective, worse was still to come. In the summer of 1870, Bismarck maneuvered an overconfident Napoleon III into declaring war on Prussia. Armed with superior chassepot rifles, the French actually bested Prussian troops in the initial battlefield encounters, but the Prussians possessed a general staff, organized troops more efficiently, and brought to bear more streamlined logistics, sharper operational sense, and better artillery. As a result, the Franco-Prussian War was a mismatch, culminating in the Battle of Sedan in early September. After capturing Napoleon III, Prussian troops, aided by armies from the south German states, then took Strasbourg and Metz and besieged Paris. In the Hall of Mirrors at Versailles, as the siege continued and the population of Paris faced famine, German generals and princes proclaimed a new German empire with William I as emperor.[89] The French provisional government capitulated at the end of February 1871—even though a final peace was not reached until May. Meanwhile, French troops massacred Parisian workers and artisans in revolt. As the blood of the Paris Commune dried, Germany annexed Alsace and Lorraine and imposed a giant indemnity on France.

The war transformed nationalist sentiment. The divisions that had marked the Austro-Prussian War had evaporated. Catholics, silent in 1866, supported the war in 1870. In the North German Reichstag, only two lone Socialists, Wilhelm Liebknecht and August Bebel, refrained from voting for extraordinary war credits. In Baden, with its Catholic majority and long border with France, the parliament was not even convened.[90] And in Bavaria, Catholic particularists, who wanted Bavaria to be an independent country, found themselves increasingly isolated.[91] Elsewhere, Catholic voices competed with the nationalist press in proclaiming enthusiastic support for Bismarck and the unification of Germany under Prussian leadership.[92] It was a moment of genuine, unabated German nationalism, not unlike the sentiment that welled up in Prussia in 1813.

A few, if important, dissenting voices were also audible. There was Johann Jacoby, a steadfast liberal whose resistance landed him in jail—again. There was Ludwig Windthorst, a defender of Hanoverian and

Catholic interests whose reticence about the war and the annexation of Alsace-Lorraine was conspicuous.[93] And there was Gervinus.

Shortly before his death in 1871, Gervinus wrote a "Memorandum on Peace," which he addressed but never sent to the newly coronated Kaiser William I. The Austrian War of 1866, Gervinus wrote, "tore Germany into three bloody parts."[94] Far from laying the path to unification, it constituted an act of violence against the decentralized, peaceful spirit of Germany, transforming it into "an ever-ready, offensive, war power," a "military dictatorship."[95] But as Prussian arms were victorious, it fell to her rulers to "unmake what has already happened."[96] Quixotically, he requested that the Kaiser give autonomy back to the medium-sized states and restore the regional character of the country. Only in this way, Gervinus reasoned, would Germany again become a peaceful power achieving conquests in the realm of the spirit and the domain of science, and thus fulfilling the true mission of the failed Revolution of 1848. The cosmopolitan city of Hamburg, a "German London," could be the capital, he added.[97]

The shape of Germany was to be otherwise. As Prussia won the subsequently named wars of unification, it kept the coal-, steel-, and iron-producing areas of both Silesia and the Rhineland, and these areas fueled a rapid industrialization that in a generation would almost triple per capita GNP in Germany, as well as double the real wages of the many workers who toiled in the regions' mines, foundries, and smelting factories. These territories, and the immense wealth they produced, also supported a military-industrial complex that made Germany into a formidable power on the international stage.

By its own constitutional definition, the new Germany was not, however, a nation-state. Rather, it was "a permanent alliance" of the sovereigns of the individual states "for the protection of "federal territory" and "the care of the welfare of the German people."[98] Historians have long argued that Imperial Germany was an "incomplete" nation-state because it was divided religiously between Protestants and Catholics, because there were many Germans outside of it, and because it contained ethnic and religious minorities who were not fully integrated.[99] This is to adopt an overtly nationalist analysis. On its own terms, the new empire simply shied from deriving its legitimacy from either the nation or the people. In the constitution, the word "nation" is completely missing, while the term "people" appears only one other time as a noun—in Article 29, defining the role of parliament, the Reichstag, as a representative institution. Even the noun, "German" or "Germans" appears only in three articles, two setting rules for military conscription, and one guaranteeing Germans freedom of movement within the country and protection outside of it. The term "Germany" (*Deutschland*) hardly fared better. It was mentioned four times, twice with respect to railroads and defense, once in regards to customs and tariffs, and once in order to declare that a subject from one state, like Prussia, was not to be considered a foreigner in another, such as Bavaria. Otherwise, "German" appears throughout the constitution merely as an adjective, typically modifying "empire" (eleven times) or "army" (seven times).[100]

Yet in the nearly half century of continental peace after the founding of the German Empire, Germans would celebrate and internalize their new country as a nation. They would explore its history and gather together its artistic treasures. They would construct monuments and stage festivals. And they would flood the markets with all manner of national kitsch, making Imperial Germany, however rooted in the legacy of the dynastic territorial state, seem, with time, "an objective nation" with a definite shape.

CHAPTER 9

—

OBJECTIVE NATION

c. 1870–1914

No ideas but in things.

—WILLIAM CARLOS WILLIAMS

S TARING ACROSS LOCH LEVEN FROM THE SCOTTISH TOWN OF
Kinross, Theodor Fontane gazed at the ruins of the local castle. It was
the summer of 1859. Like Herder a century earlier, Fontane adored the
bardic tradition and had fallen in love with its blend of nature, history,
and legend. At the time, he was a middle-aged journalist and the author of
a few unremarkable books on Great Britain. The Loch Leven transfixed
him. As he observed the fortress across the water, shimmering with tales of
recalcitrant barons and the defiant Mary, Queen of Scots, who was imprisoned there, images of another castle, Rheinsberg, cross-dissolved into his
imagination.

Was that castle northwest of Berlin, where Frederick the Great had as
crown prince spent the happiest years of his life, any less filled with legend
and history? "No," Fontane answered, and resolved to walk through the
landscape of his home province and learn of its sagas and stories, nature
and people.[1] He began his wanderings in 1861 and continued for nearly
thirty years. He visited and revisited such places as his native Neuruppin,
a broad-avenued garrison town and the birthplace of star architect Karl
Friedrich Schinkel. He also visited nearby Karwe, where old Field Marshal Karl Friedrich von dem Knesebeck planted twenty-one fir trees when
he heard the news of Napoleon's death on the island of St. Helena; and the

town of Wust, west of Berlin, where the young, cosmopolitan Hans Hermann von Katte, the intimate boyhood friend of Frederick the Great, lay buried (having been executed by Frederick's father, the callous Frederick William I, who forced his son to watch the beheading).[2]

Nowadays, Fontane's renown derives from a series of novels that treat such themes as the Prussian nobility in decline, the myopic provincialism of Prussia's moneyed parvenus, the constricted moral visions of its leading classes, and the claustrophobic mental life of its administrative capitals. The most famous of them, *Effi Briest*, is about a young woman confined by social corsets and archaic honor codes. Yet as late as the 1890s, Fontane's fame still rested on his beloved *Wanderings Through the Mark Brandenburg*. Like his searing, ironic novels, his travel sketches suggested something of significance about Imperial Germany—that buildings, monuments, memorials, memorabilia, and all manner of things provided mortar for local and national identification.

Like Fontane's Brandenburg, Imperial Germany was marked by its objects, making the new nation less into a "daily plebiscite," as the French philosopher Ernest Renan famously described a nation in 1882, than into "a daily reminder," with objects constantly reiterating the national past and announcing its reality to the present.[3] These objects of nationhood also give us entry into an analytical space between what historians have called "national activists" on the one side and a more banal sense of nationhood on the other.[4] The former have been researched extensively. In the meantime, nearly every major nationalist of the era has been studied, dissected, the logic or illogic of his worldview exposed. Yet it was the commonplace, clichéd reminders of nationhood, more even than the frenetic activity of the ideological nationalists, that made the nation seem to ordinary Germans as natural as the air they breathed.[5]

II

Ironically, the new nation-state got off to a slow symbolic start. In 1871, there was no national anthem. The national flag remained a source of contention. There was no motto, no official national holiday, and debate continued about the national tree, between the mighty oak or the elegant linden.[6] It took three years for the new currency, the imperial mark, to replace the older thaler, guilder, and kreuzer, and the coin showed images not of the new nation but rather of the rulers of the individual states on the front and the imperial eagle on the back. Stamps suggested symbolic hesitancy as well. Starting in 1872, new imperial stamps replaced a plethora of state stamps, most of them printed for the first time in the 1850s. Stuck on letter envelopes and postcards, the stamps sported everywhere (except Bavaria and Württemberg) the same white imperial eagle with the Kaiser's shield. Not until the late 1890s did the Imperial Post Office begin issuing more varied stamps, emphasizing national prowess with an image of a strong-willed *Germania* on a stamp of 1897, for example.[7]

Imperial Germany's symbolic hesitation should not, however, obscure the importance of fundamental changes. If timidly, stamps at least circulated in the space of the new nation. First introduced in the North German Confederation in 1867, unified postal rates replaced charges calibrated by distance or defined by state borders, making it as cheap to send a stamped letter from the southwestern German city of Mannheim to distant Königsberg, not far from the Russian border, as it was to ship it to nearby Karlsruhe.[8] Under its energetic first director, Heinrich von Stephan, the Imperial Post Office built hundreds of postal stations throughout the Empire, so that in every little hometown people knew, as one contemporary recorded, "when I stand here, the German Empire stands here."[9] Railroads likewise tied the country together, if primarily by buttressing the regions. By 1890, the number of passengers riding rails had tripled, but in Bavaria and Saxony, more than 95 percent of the passengers still traveled within the borders of their home states, mainly sitting on the hard wooden benches of third-class cars or standing in fourth class.[10] Moreover, as with post offices, the proliferation of new rail stations underscored the coincidence of the national, the regional, and the local. Especially in the south German states, municipalities built railway stations with care. They frequently boasted locales for eating and drinking, and towns advertised them on postcards, which circulated in prodigious quantities.

Objects of nationhood were also kept on one's person. When traveling abroad, citizens increasingly carried the passport of the German Empire— with states listed directly underneath, followed by the person's name, occupation, and place of birth, and on the next page a series of identifiers, including age, height, hair and eye color, facial shape, and special characteristics helping to match the document and its bearer. There was as yet no photograph and the nationality and religion of the passport holders were not identified.[11] As with stamps and rail travel, what changed was how passports situated people within the nation's space.[12] Before unification, Germans were subjects of Saxony or Bavaria and carried passports from these states, not from the German Confederation. The new passports made movement within Germany borderless, and marked off what was foreign in new ways. To a Bavarian, Austria-Hungary, not Württemberg, was now a different country.[13] Still, with the exception of travel from Russia, the passport regime was lax in Imperial Germany. There were no elaborate border controls and people came and went with an assortment of identity papers.[14] It was World War I that brought the passport controls familiar to us now, making nation-states into monitored communities, with guards at entry points, and all who crossed the border required to have a passport and visa on their person.[15]

III

Nation-space quickly became palpable and tangible, and the history of travel illustrates the transformation. From the late eighteenth to the early nineteenth century, German travelers had experienced eastern and western borders as slow transitions from one culture to another, while rarely expounding, either when coming or going, on Germany as home.[16] By the 1840s that had begun to change, and by the 1880s travelers were already registering a sharper sense of transition when crossing national lines. They also reflected on Germany as their home country, and those reflections were typically ballasted, especially in the east and the south, by a conviction of the strangeness and inferiority of the other.

One such traveler was Heinrich von Treitschke. Part public intellectual, part scholar, Treitschke was a professor of history at the University of Berlin and easily the most influential German nationalist of his time, "the prophet of our empire," as one contemporary called him.[17] In a profusion of articles, commentaries, books, and electrifying lectures, he propounded the idea that Prussia was the preordained unifier of modern Germany. He also put forward a series of political principles that shaded into nationalist prejudice. These included seeing power, not culture, as determining the

fate of nations; authorities, not the masses, as the shapers of history; Protestantism, not Catholicism, as animating the German spirit; and men, not
women, as the true subject of history. These assumptions also infused his
historical writing. Carried along by a singular, confident, narrative, Treitschke's five-volume *German History in the Nineteenth Century* was a state-
centered national history every bit as confident in the inexorable unfolding
of the future as Karl Marx's *Das Kapital*, published over a decade earlier.

As a traveler, Treitschke was as little interested in the uniqueness of
other places as he was in the pastness of the past. In his letters—written
from abroad to his fiancée, and then wife, Emma, in the 1870s and
1880s—Treitschke ceaselessly compared and judged. In his opinion, for
example, the harbor at Bordeaux did not match the activity of Hamburg,
the wine hills of the Dordogne could not compete with the Rheingau,
and the countryside of Lazio did not seem "musical-lyrical like ours."
Similarly, he thought Grenada merely a "southern Heidelberg," coastal
Pula in Croatia a "southern Kiel," and Norwegian painters but "valiant
Düsseldorfers."[18] Often, Treitschke saw the grandness of a place not in its
foreignness, but in its Germanness—the luxurious visage of Budapest, for
instance, revealed coarseness except in the essentially German castle on
the Buda side of the city.[19]

Particularly in the east, the experience of crossing borders suggested
sharp breaks. In a journey through Upper Silesia and Austrian Galicia taken
in the late summer of 1871, Treitschke encountered a landscape he could
describe only as fundamentally "other." When he crossed the border at
Three Emperors Corner in Mysłowice (where the German, Russian, and
Austrian Empires met), the contrasts were particularly jarring. In Galicia, "a
new world begins," Treitschke wrote, "industry immediately disappears,"
rows of monotone houses replace quaint villages, and "beautiful Silesian
forests" give way to "anonymous, pitiable, neglected woods." The passage
was like "a theater effect," he wrote to Emma, and "the great difference"
taught him to appreciate "what Prussia means for the civilization of humanity" and to thank the Lord for "the undeserved fortune of being born a German."[20] Even the wealthy Renaissance city of Cracow proved unsettling.
The German population had markedly declined, according to Treitschke,
the Polish population remained desolate, and life seemed only to pulse in
the Jewish quarter of Kazimierz, where he discovered "a whole new world,"

"full of deceit."[21] To Treitschke, whose anti-Semitism was not yet public, Kazimierz seemed a "Brueghel's hell, only that no paintbrush could render the disgusting stink that hovers over this band [of Jews] like a cloud."[22]

This was nationalism beginning to hate.[23] Generally speaking, early-nineteenth-century nationalists had encouraged assimilation and saw culture as the key to bringing diversity under the generous tarp of nationality. In Herder's time, and throughout the nineteenth century, Germans imagined that nations would coexist like flora in a garden. By the time of Treitschke, however, some began to envision nations as desperate species struggling against one another in the hour of their extinction.

This new, harsher, social Darwinist conception of nations also informed Treitschke's observations on Jews. In "Our Prospects," a notorious article published in the *Preußische Jahrbücher* (*Prussian Yearbooks*) in November 1879, Treitschke addressed what he called the "German-Jewish question."[24] He had been traveling again, and it was likely in the East Prussian seaport and border town of Memel (now Klaipėda in Lithuania) in the summer of 1879 that he witnessed, as one German-Jewish rabbi put it, "our Russian coreligionists" who sold their wares from cellar windows and on the market street.[25] "Year after year from the inexhaustible Polish cradle," Treitschke infamously wrote, "a swarm of ambitious pants-selling youngsters forces its way across our eastern borders, and their children and children's children will one day control the German stock exchange and its newspapers."[26] Warning against the emergence of a "German-Jewish mixed culture," Treitschke maintained that a deep division existed between the Semitic and the western essence: "There would always be Jews who are nothing but German-speaking Orientals."[27]

The subsequent debate opened the dam to the first major flood of postemancipation anti-Semitism. At first Jews stood nearly alone in countering Treitschke. German history must include the bloody facts of anti-Semitic persecution, the historian Heinrich Graetz insisted. The nation was in its essence diverse, made up of tribes, among whom were Jews, argued the philosopher Moritz Lazarus. Finally, Jews should embrace their German fatherland not because Germany served a higher ideal but simply because it was the home of their fathers and forefathers, the young neo-Kantian Hermann Cohen contended. Non-Jewish critics joined the condemnation only in the summer of 1880, when leading Berlin dignitaries—including the historians Theodor Mommsen and Johann Gustav Droysen as well as the Lord Mayor of Berlin, Max Forckenbeck—warned of the "racial hatred and medieval fanaticism that has been called into existence and directed at our fellow Jewish citizens."[28] Mommsen, in particular, worried about the "calamity" of a "civil war of the majority against a minority" and insisted that the young nation-state must remain unified.[29] Jews were essentially Germans who belonged to a religious group whose rights were to be protected, Mommsen insisted. "What does it mean," he asked Treitschke, "that they [the Jews] should become German? . . . They already are so, as much as you and I."[30]

IV

Historians know a great deal about nationalism and less about the nation. We have long researched the ideological contexts as well as the organizational patterns and political programs of German nationalism. But we know comparatively little about how people, places, and things assumed national characteristics, essences, and boundaries—how, for example, forests and meadows became not green but German, French, or Polish.[31] The two categories—nationalism and the sense of nation—were at once separate, overlapping, and in tension. German nationalism, as Treitschke expressed it, sharply differentiated what was inside from what was outside, denigrated what was foreign, and encouraged aggression. At the same time, the banal sense and stuff of the nation, especially as manifest in objects, admitted a symbolic opening and supported—but just as often stood in the way of—nationalist aggression.

In the first three decades after the foundation of the German Empire, objects of nationhood became a central feature of German material culture—and in this culture, virtually no object seemed as omnipresent as the monument. There were, to begin with, the spectacular, giant monuments, often ensconced in lush countrysides. They include the Monument to Hermann, victorious over the Romans at the Battle of the Teutoburg Wood, consecrated in 1875; the Niederwald Monument, commemorating the unification of Germany by standing guard at the border of the Rhine just north of Rüdesheim, and finished in 1883; and the Kyffhäuser Monument of 1896, located southeast of the Harz Mountains, and celebrating an amalgamation of the great medieval Emperor Barbarossa, Kaiser William I, and German veterans of war. There were also urban monumental landscapes, like the impressive Victory Boulevard in Berlin, completed in 1901 and including nearly a hundred statues of Prussian heroes. Taken together, these monuments show a country shaping a martial self-image, commemorating in granite, bronze, and marble its battles and heroes.

While many Germans went on pilgrimages to the great national shrines, most were more likely to encounter the far more modest monuments in their own cities and towns. Such monuments were also more numerous. Contemporary observers wrote of a "monument craze," a "monument mania," or even a "monument plague."[32] Tracking mainly monuments to Kaiser William I, Otto von Bismarck, and Veterans' and Victory Memorials, one author counted 875 monuments in 1904.[33] His numbers, it seems, were far too low. Credible inventories of monuments to the Kaiser alone count 322 in 1902 and place monuments to Bismarck at around the same number, while the number of monuments to the veterans of the German wars of the mid-nineteenth century surely ranges in the thousands.[34]

The multitude of monuments to William I suggested Imperial Germany's dynastic more than its militarist character. Ranging from modest columns costing 10,000 marks to elaborate and expensive statutes such as those in Essen, Leipzig, and Berlin, which cost as much as 500,000 marks, they began to be erected in earnest only after the monarch's death in 1888, reached a high point with the centenary of his birth in 1897, and then declined significantly thereafter. Close to 80 percent of them were built in Prussia; some could be found in Saxony and Thuringia, but they were rare south of the Main River and were completely absent in Bavaria (since they would have seemed an affront to the Bavarian royal family).

A world of monarchical kitsch, as important as the monuments themselves, buttressed this building craze.[35] Images of Kaiser William I were found on silver spoons, ceramic plates, plaques, and commemorative medals, as well as on a range of commercial goods, including stationery, tobacco boxes, chocolate bars, Christmas hams, and champagne bottles. As most of this kitsch was sold by hawkers or in small shops, it could not easily be controlled, and government-sponsored initiatives often faltered. Kaiser William II's attempt in a much-heralded speech in 1897 to affix the epithet "Great" to his grandfather foundered not on popular dislike for

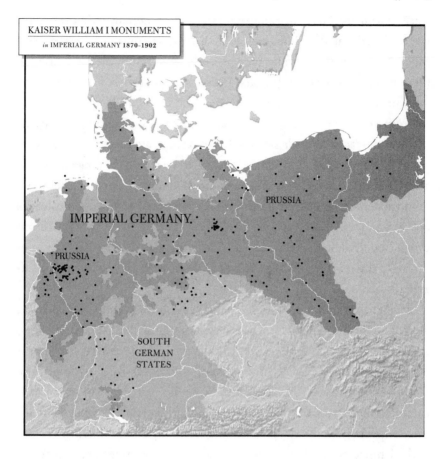

KAISER WILLIAM I MONUMENTS
in IMPERIAL GERMANY 1870-1902

PRUSSIA

IMPERIAL GERMANY

PRUSSIA

SOUTH
GERMAN
STATES

the old emperor but on the failure of the new image—that of the supposedly true military genius behind unification—to gain traction. Instead, the image of a wise monarch, above the fray, captured the imagination, and it did so mainly through the mass circulation of sentimental images: first in large-format photographs costing roughly twenty marks, and thus within reach of the middle classes; then through smaller, more modest *cartes de visite*, which became widely available; and finally as dirt-cheap images pirated by taking pictures of the pictures. Images were collected in albums and the albums were displayed on dining room tables, with basic albums costing as little as half a mark.[36]

It was, however, with the postcard that the image of Kaiser William I really gained wide circulation and visibility. Developed in the 1870s, postcards, at three cents each, achieved mass circulation in the following decades. According to one estimate, approximately 250 million postcards

were sent in the German Empire in 1900.[37] Essentially, what the letter
was to the educated middle class, the postcard was to wider social circles.
Since the mail was picked up numerous times each day, the circulation of
these images was fast and furious. People sent postcards when they were
away on a railway journey and from weekend resorts, which were already
emerging on the outskirts of cities at the turn of the century. Postcards
marked life stages—people sent them, for example, to the attendees at wed-
dings.[38] And in cities they were sent across town to make arrangements. By
1900, postcards covered an enormous range of subjects, picturing flowers,
erotic material, human curiosities, local scenes, and much else. Postcards
of the emperors, William I and still more William II, made up a significant
category in this broad array, and of those pictures, the vast majority, and
certainly the most popular, were family pictures of the powerful Hohenzollerns at home.

It might be argued that monuments dedicated to Otto von Bismarck,
more than those intended for Kaiser William I, provide an index of aggressive nationalism. Certainly, their spatial patterns were different. Just over
10 percent of towns with monuments to Bismarck had also erected a
monument to Kaiser William I, and those municipalities were not concentrated in Prussia.[39] In fact, enthusiasm for Bismarck monuments flourished especially in the states of middle Germany and in the liberal cities
of the Rhineland; in Bavaria, it took root in largely Protestant Franconia;
and in southwest Germany, it was confined to predominantly Protestant
cities, university towns, and isolated centers of liberal Catholicism. Conversely, there were virtually no monuments in the industrialized Ruhr and
very few in Upper Silesia. Bismarck's legacy of anti-Catholic legislation
during the Kulturkampf of the 1870s and 1880s and the antisocialist laws
made it difficult for Catholics and workers to see him as a figure of national
identification.

Nevertheless, Bismarck monuments and the cult of the Iron Chancellor rivaled the attention paid to the ruling family, just as Bismarck kitsch
barely took a second seat to the proliferation of royal objects. Some 370
German towns and cities offered Bismarck honorary citizenship and
countless squares and streets were named for him. There were Bismarck
hotels and restaurants, and Bismarck lent his surname to both a torte and
a style of pickled herring. Upon his retirement in 1890, well-wishers sent

him a stream of letters and greeting cards, with one estimate placing the number at half a million individual mailings.[40] Postcards also pointed to the sheer scope of turn-of-the-century political adulation. Some pictured Bismarck and his famous pronouncement "We Germans fear God but nothing else in this world."[41] But not all had overtly nationalistic messages. Also popular were postcards with Bismarck and his Great Danes, Tyras II and Rebecca, the *Reichshunde.* Other postcards attempted to make Bismarck into the wise grandfather of German statecraft. And a large number pictured the Bismarck monument in this or that town or city.[42] As with Kaiser William monuments, a stream of kitsch—Bismarck steins, busts, medallions, and bracelet charms—followed in the wake of the monuments. Even with Bismarck, whom the aggressive nationalists attempted to appropriate as their own, the circulation of objects points by no means in a single direction—and certainly not just in the direction that many nationalist ideologues hoped.

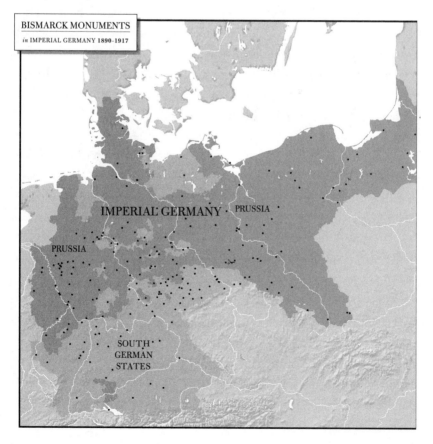

BISMARCK MONUMENTS
in IMPERIAL GERMANY 1890-1917

IMPERIAL GERMANY · PRUSSIA ·

PRUSSIA

SOUTH
GERMAN
STATES

Finally, there were the monuments to Germany's veterans. Constituting by far the largest number of monuments in Imperial Germany, they only reinforced the mixed messages of the nation's object culture. Most were simple columns, some had an eagle on top, and a smaller number featured a sculpture of Germania or the Goddess of Victory. Just a few actually showed soldiers with weapons (more often sword or flagstaff than rifle).[43] Costing between 6000 and 10,000 marks, these simple monuments could even be found in Catholic regions, working-class towns, and bilingual areas.[44] Erected by the popular veterans' associations, which counted more than 2.8 million members by 1913, these monuments called forth "an uninterrupted sequence" of patriotic festivals that followed, as one contemporary complained, "one another like frames in a cinematography theater."[45]

Like the imposing Kaiser and Bismarck monuments, the monuments to Germany's veterans generated a world of objects, the best known of which were the regimental beer steins. As enlisted men passed from active duty to the reserve, some 10 percent of the soldiers bought the steins from colporteurs.[46] Intended to commemorate the period of active duty, the steins typically came ringed with the colors of the state—green and white for Saxony, white and blue for Bavaria, and black, white, and red for Prussia. They sported a pewter top, often in the shape of an eagle, a cannon, or a soldier at attention or offering a *prost*. When they first appeared in the 1880s, they were mainly hand-painted, but demand was so vigorous they were soon industrially produced. Some were made of ceramic, others of porcelain.[47] After 1900, they became more and more ornate and were decorated with scenes from a soldier's life: those made for cavalry units typically displayed soldiers on horseback riding through agreeable landscapes and those for the infantry featured kind-faced soldiers marching in step. Pleasingly painted, with the reservist's name, unit, and period of active duty inscribed, the steins probably spent most of the time on fireplace mantels or prominently displayed on cupboards. Heirlooms somewhere between folk art and mass-produced kitsch, they showed the army, the nation, and service as an expression of harmony. Reservist pipes sported similarly painted scenes of military life: soldiers socializing in taverns, or a soldier at attention in front of a guardhouse, or trotting on horseback, or, most tenderly, leaving his lady or returning back to her safely.

Regimental stein
of the author's
great-grandfather.

V

Such symbols of the nation may seem trite. And perhaps they were. But to one young student from abroad, they suggested novel, if for him unattainable, possibilities of national belonging. That student was W. E. B. Du Bois, who would become a major philosopher, historian, sociologist, and civil rights activist, arguably the most influential African-American intellectual of the first half of the twentieth century. In the summer of 1892, as a young Harvard graduate student, he crossed the Atlantic in a steamship, arriving in the Netherlands before "ascending" the Rhine, where "every castle has its tale of the Thirty Years War, the French Revolution or the ruthless march of the wonderful Napoleon."[48] He then traveled on to Frankfurt am Main before taking the train to Eisenach, where he spent the summer studying German, learning the ways of the land, and feeling "more at home with cultured white folks than I had before in my life."[49]

Even before coming to Germany, Du Bois had been a keen observer of German intellectual and political life. He had imbibed the philosophy of Hegel and Schopenhauer, read the *Germania* of Tacitus, and studied the "national economist" Friedrich List.[50] As an undergraduate, he had also delivered a valedictorian address at the historically black Fisk University in Nashville, Tennessee, on the subject of Otto von Bismarck and the unification of Germany. With rich and resonant rhetoric, he unfurled his unbounded admiration for the chancellor, praising "the man of iron, one of the strongest personalities the world has ever seen." Bismarck was "a man with one idea," Du Bois told his audience, and that was to turn Germany from "a handful of petty quarreling principalities" into a genuine nation.[51]

In October 1892, Du Bois departed for the University of Berlin, where he would hear the lectures or participate in the seminars of some of the most important German intellectuals of his time: in political economy, Adolph Wagner; in constitutional history, Gustav Schmoller; in the history of philosophy, Wilhelm Dilthey; in sociology, two younger scholars, Georg Simmel and Max Weber; and in modern political history, one professor he thought especially impressive: "the well-known von Treitschke."[52] According to Du Bois, Treitschke was always arriving late for lectures, "in dark grey or blue cutaway with cylinder hat, gloves and the all-pervading German cane." He was "stone-deaf with a slight impediment in his speech," Du Bois reported, and had "a sort of breathless way of speaking."[53] Du Bois nevertheless listened attentively to Treitschke's lectures, including his remarks on Jews, and to his declaration that "mulatoes [sic] are inferior."[54] It was, Du Bois felt, as if Treitschke "were pointing me out."[55]

In the late nineteenth century, foreign students, like Du Bois, came from all over the world to Germany. They hailed from Japan—"there are a hundred times more Japanese students in Berlin than Danes," complained one journalist from Denmark.[56] They made the voyage from India, especially young nationalists who perceived Imperial Germany as a geopolitical counterweight to the British Empire.[57] A large number were from Russia— students like the young novelist Boris Pasternak, who found temporary refuge from czarist oppression in the neo-Kantianism of his Marburg teachers.[58] Students also came from France, Italy, Spain, the Austro-Hungarian and Ottoman Empires, and the United States. Although one of the very few African-Americans to make the journey, Du Bois was in fact among thousands of American college students who flocked to German universities in the late nineteenth century.[59] And, like many American students who preceded and followed him, Du Bois learned as much by travel as by study.

Du Bois traveled with eyes more open than did Treitschke. He enjoyed both "red-tiled villages" with "homely homes all full of love and sorrow," as well as large cities like Hamburg, its harbor "a busy sea of masts and small boats" and its streets "as crooked as Boston's but broader."[60] As was still touristic fashion, Du Bois also wandered through the Bode Gorge of the Harz Mountains and climbed the Brocken.[61] Humming Friedrich Schiller's "Ode to Joy" and singing, "All men become brothers," he no doubt felt a great affinity for the country, if one occasionally punctuated by the aggressive curiosity that sometimes caused "a burst of anger, and a general feeling of forlornness and homelessness that is terrible."[62]

W. E. B. Du Bois
as a young
student.

Du Bois nevertheless found Germany's patriotism moving. Berlin, he wrote, marched in "half military stride," at the head of a country where all over the place one sees "banners gaily flying," and hears "trumpet" and "drum!" It thrilled Du Bois, who even grew a mustache in the style of the new kaiser, William II. "The march of soldiers, the saluting of magnificent uniforms, the martial music and the rhythm of movement stirred my senses," he wrote.[63] It also caused him to think about his own country, where "in the south, fellow Negroes simply did not speak or think of patriotism for the nation which held their fathers in slavery for 250 years."[64] When Germans sang *"Deutschland, Deutschland über alles,"* Du Bois "realized that they had something he had never felt and perhaps never would."[65]

National symbols, Du Bois realized, could in fact help integrate outsiders. He certainly saw the possibility for the integration of Socialists, although he did not reflect on it for the Catholics, because he imagined Germany as built on the spirit of Luther. He also did not reflect on it from the standpoint of Jews.[66] Instead, common shibboleths of anti-Semitism marred his otherwise cogent analysis of Imperial Germany. "The great capitalists of Germany, the great leaders of industry, are Jews," Du Bois wrote. "They practically control the stock-market, own the press, fill the bar and bench, are crowding the professions."[67]

The place of anti-Semitism in Du Bois's analysis of Germany deserves careful treatment. It was endemic to his milieu—both at Harvard and the University of Berlin. Inspired by Treitschke's lectures, nearly half of all Berlin students had signed a petition in the early 1880s demanding limits on the immigration of foreign Jews, the exclusion of Jews from positions of public authority, a restoration of the Christian character of public schools, and a statistical accounting of the Jewish population. By 1892, the atmosphere had not improved. On the contrary, anti-Semitism was at a high-water mark. Du Bois blamed the "recrudescence of anti-Jewish feeling in a civilized state" on the supposed Jewish control of the economy. He also blamed the anti-Semites, even as he accepted, as did many progressives in his day, key components of their analysis. He did not see any parallel between the situation of the Jews in Germany and that of his own race in America. In his mind, Jews were integrated and guaranteed fundamental rights, including due process of law. They participated in all manner of social clubs, especially patriotic ones. They did not endure grinding poverty, and they were not lynched.[68]

VI

Kaiser William II, whom Du Bois so admired and who had ascended the throne in 1888 and dismissed Bismarck in 1890, spent much of his time crisscrossing the country, giving speeches, attending ceremonies, and literally making a spectacle of himself. In the age of nationalism, royal travel assumed new functions. Four hundred years earlier, the itinerant emperor Maximilian I went on the road to project power. In the eighteenth century, Austria's Joseph II toured his country to know his land and its people.[69] Kaiser William II traveled to be seen, celebrated, and to shore up support for the dynasty. He also hoped to bind the nation together. His appearances in German cities and towns were of course selective, concentrated mainly in Prussia and north Germany. Most of his dedications and speeches redounded to the benefit of dynastic monuments or military happenings (such as maneuvers, the jubilee of this or that regiment, or the dedication of a ship). The Kaiser also graced the festivities of student fraternities, feted cities, attended sporting events, and celebrated technical achievements (like the opening of the Elbe-Trave Canal in Lübeck or a new bridge crossing the Rhine at Mainz). When the young kaiser arrived, whether by yacht, train, coach, or (by the turn of the century) automobile, cities declared "emperor days," and intensely planned for the occasion. Sometimes William II made the main speech, and other times he responded briefly to remarks from the *Bürgermeister* or some other dignitary. In either case, tens of thousands of people showed up. Streets and houses were bedecked with banners and flowers. Local organizations presented themselves in formation. Singing clubs accompanied the Kaiser with patriotic song. Tents and pavilions were erected. And business in binoculars, trinkets, busts, plates, medallions, and commemorative spoons ballooned.[70] The event, moreover, was reproduced in newspapers, on postcards, in photos, and eventually in moving pictures, making "Filmhelm," as one sardonic critic dubbed William (or Wilhelm), the world's biggest new-media celebrity.[71]

William II's new style of rule, combining dynastic presentation with modern transportation and communications, projected a nation of restless energy. That energy also came with a massive naval buildup. First approved by the parliament in 1898, and enthusiastically supported by the Kaiser, the German naval fleet embodied Germany's new imperialism. By dint of the sheer number of ships Germany could build and put into the North Sea, the fleet was meant primarily to challenge its neighbor Great Britain. Since Britain could summon only two-thirds of its ships for defense of the island nation (the rest were defending faraway possessions of the empire), the German fleet, it was hoped, could force Great Britain to cede colonies as part of a deal, allowing the rising power Germany to pursue world imperialism on a grander scale. Quixotic, dangerous, and costly, the naval program succeeded only in fueling an arms race. It also stoked colonial fantasies and caused Germans to think that territorial expansion was the natural way of the world. Embracing this high-imperialist mind-set, Bernhard von Bülow, the foreign minister and soon-to-be chancellor, declared in 1899 that in the coming century Germany would be either a hammer or an anvil.

It is sometimes asserted that Imperial Germany stood on the sidelines of high imperialism, and that colonialism was not central to it. In fact, Germany was third, behind Great Britain and France, in new territory gained. Moreover, by the turn of the century, a plethora of colonial images, objects, and spectacles had come to permeate everyday life, reinforcing the nation of things with a message about imperial destiny. Nearly every small German city had its "colonial store" that sold sugar, rice, coffee, tea, spices, cocoa, tobacco, cigars, chocolate bars, illustrated coffee cups, and trinkets—even if most of the goods were not from German colonies but from Central and South America.[72] There were men in the employ of the German Colonial Society, a pro-imperialism pressure group, who traversed the country, armed with wall maps, photographs, and colonial products, lecturing about the benefits of empire. There was instruction in schools, and geography lessons with maps showing Europe at the center of global communication and transportation networks, and telling which European country controlled which overseas colony. High imperialism also pervaded the nascent but powerful world of commercial advertising, which purveyed stock images of exotic and sexualized Pacific Islanders and bestial Africans, while influencing the fashion of children's clothes, especially in the form of naval costumes.[73] There were board games and trading cards collectible with the purchase of certain coffees, soaps, and cocoas. There were also "People Shows" featuring Africans (typically flu-ent in German) reenacting supposedly native life and dance; tens of thou-sands of people, perhaps more, attended them—as did the Kaiser at the Hamburg Zoo in 1909.[74] Altogether, a frenzy of activity and exhibits, a world of things, and "a pictorial ocean" of images combined to make col-onies, empire, and racial hierarchy seem as natural and self-evident as nationhood.[75]

Imperialism (or *Weltpolitik*, as it was called at the time) also had a domestic component. In order to ensure a broad base for its naval buildup, the government had to bring the Catholics into the imperialist consensus. There was nothing obvious about this. In 1871, Catholics had accepted the new empire with hardly a murmur. But in the subsequent Kulturkampf, Bismarck attacked the church and liberals condemned popular devotion, while both denounced what they thought of as an unholy Catholic alliance of politics and piety. As a result, Catholic enthusiasm for the new nation palpably subsided, and in the 1870s and 1880s, the faithful began to cultivate alternative histories and turn their backs on nationalist symbols.[76] They also showed less enthusiasm for invented national holidays, such as Sedan Day.[77] Initially organized by patriotic Protestants and intended to commemorate the Prussian encirclement of French troops on September 2, 1870, Sedan Day brought forth protracted Catholic resistance, especially in the Rhineland and south Germany, ultimately making it into a holiday celebrated only by liberal Protestants.[78] Fueled by a general suspicion of the powerful, modern, secular state, the Empire's Catholics cultivated a distinguished tradition of antimilitarist discourse and held firm against the excesses of aggressive nationalism.[79] Nevertheless, they gave the new imperialism their qualified support.

The other political subculture, possessing still greater fortitude, belonged to the free trade unions and the Socialists. Unlike the Catholic Center Party, their numbers, far from merely holding steady, expanded dramatically so that by 1912 the trade unions encompassed more than two million members, while the various Socialist parties captured more than a third of the electorate. Their subculture was also more distinct than that of the Catholics. Not only did Socialist workers desist from attending Sedan Day celebrations, they also set up alternative festivals: first the March Festival, celebrating the outbreak of the Revolution of 1848 and, for a time, the Paris Commune, then the May Day celebrations of the Second International.[80] When German nationalists gathered to deliver paeans to Bismarck, Socialists sang hymns to Ferdinand Lassalle, the colorful leader of the German Workers Movement in the 1860s. They also altered patriotic songs, changing "fatherland" to "free people," and adopted progressive rather than militaristic patriotic tunes: Max von Schenkendorf's "Freedom That I Love" instead of Max Schneckenburger's "Watch on the Rhine," for example.[81] Socialists read different books—not Marx's *Communist Manifesto*, which sold only a few thousand copies, but August Bebel's *Women and Socialism*, which sold hundreds of thousands, and Otto Corvin's *Priest Mirror*, a scurrilous anticlerical tract that was also a best seller.[82] And they had their share of maverick historians, like the unjustly forgotten Franz Mehring, who at every turn challenged academic consensus, insisting, for example, that when military historians describe battles, they should also narrate the sufferings of ordinary men.[83] Finally, the Socialist subculture also made its mark on politics. The Socialists tirelessly censured the imperiousness of barrack sergeants, the corpselike discipline demanded of the army ranks, the disproportionate amount of military service demanded of the poor, the army's disregard for civilian law and local practices, and the army's inhumane prosecutions of war, especially in the colonies.[84]

The culture of patriotism was complicated by gender as well. From eighteenth-century formulations on, the idea that one's country was something worthy of dying for assumed separate spheres for men and women, assigning to men the agonal, productive public, and to women the nurturing, reproductive home. Laws reinforced these dichotomies, permitting women to participate only in organizations dedicated to charity, which, in the main, reproduced the basic register of virtues that separate spheres of ideology promoted. It was not until the promulgation of an empire-wide unified Law of Association in 1908 that this situation changed, allowing women to become members in organizations with political intent. Even before, women, if mainly of the upper class, had formed auxiliary branches to such organizations as the Colonial Society and the Navy League.[85] By 1907, there were already seventy branches of the Women's Naval Association, for example, and by 1910, the Women's Colonial Association was nearly half as large as the men's.[86] Women's engagement for nationalist causes, however, did not go uncriticized. Some men insisted on the foundational nature of separate spheres and "the domestic tradition of the German wife and mother."[87] Not a few women embraced this position as well, while others saw nationalist engagement as an avenue to widening political participation.

VII

By 1910, national objects colored the landscape, marked places, and saturated the symbolic environment. They also invited active participation. This was particularly true of historical objects and their preservation. Throughout Germany, members of preservation societies buried themselves in local archives, revived local sagas, unearthed dusty histories, and restored historic buildings, including castles, half-timbered houses, churches, and what remained of dilapidated old towers and ramparts torn down a century ago.[88] Writing about local history also proved immensely popular. Beginning in the Biedermeier era, historical associations had spread across Germany (more densely in the south and middle than in the north), setting teachers, priests, pastors, rabbis, and county officials to work writing regional and hometown histories. By 1910 there were more than 250 separate organizations, many with their own journals or regular newspaper inserts.[89] Only World War I, and then the Nazi period, halted this century-long, abiding interest in collecting, celebrating, and passing on knowledge about local history.[90]

Late Imperial Germany also saw major efforts to collect, collate, list, and describe Germany's artistic monuments.[91] Between 1905 and 1912, the art historian Georg Dehio organized and described thousands of buildings, sculptures, and paintings—"monuments in their place, not in museums," as he put it.[92] In five volumes, Dehio described some ten thousand objects. He offered brief depictions of monasteries and churches, commenting upon their altars, carved statues, stained-glass windows, and ornate pulpits. He elucidated the characteristics of city halls, castles, opera houses, and towers and gates. Conceding little to touristic titillation or nationalist narratives, Dehio attempted to describe monuments in neutral language, omitting, for example, mention of Martin Luther in his portrait of the Wartburg.[93] An expert on sacral architecture, Dehio was particularly pathbreaking for giving prominence—for the first time in the context of a national review of art objects—to the great churches of Catholic Bavaria, like Dominikus Zimmermann's Steinhausen and Die Wies, Munich's St. Michael's, and the Abbey of Ottobeuren.[94]

Finally, Germany's natural landmarks and landscapes also required preservation, especially as industrialization advanced, cities grew, and "natural monuments," as they were called, came under threat.[95] To German tourists, the Rhine was still the most admired of nature's creations, even if its fabled twists and arresting turns, striking vistas and unpredictable swirls had largely been straightened and smoothed.[96] Tourists continued to throng to the towns of the middle Rhine, drawn there by restored castles, gaudy hotels, endless trinket shops, cheap wine, and the comfort of the rails.[97] Forests were also frequently visited, even if they too were hardly holding up, and now covered barely a quarter of Germany's land area (down from an estimated 40 percent in 1700).[98] Often following easily available guides and well-marked trails, thousands of men and women, organized in regional and national hiking associations, tramped through German woods and fields and trekked to patriotic monuments or nationally symbolic heights, like the Schneekoppe in the Giant Mountains of Silesia or the Brocken in the Harz.[99] Centered on hiking, song, and camaraderie, the so-called *Wandervogel* made these excursions into the woods into a spiritual experience, and saw youth a force for revitalizing the nation.

· VIII ·

In the end, it was, however, the man-made monuments that revealed Imperial Germany's story about itself with particular clarity. Most monuments valorized dynastic dignitaries, great leaders, and valiant fighters. Nevertheless, stone statues of poets, philosophers, writers, scholars, intellectuals, musicians, artists, and scientists had also come to symbolize the nation. Monuments to German intellectuals had been erected as early as the 1760s—a slumping Hercules representing Ewald von Kleist, poet of friendship and fatherland, was among the first.[100] Yet it took nearly a century for the pace of building to accelerate. The centenary in 1859 of Friedrich Schiller's birth buoyed the first wave, then building slowed until the 1880s, when civic organizations raised money to honor intellectual celebrities, above all Martin Luther, who was feted as the spiritual founder of Germany and as a model family man.[101] It was in the three decades beginning in the early 1880s that the greatest number of monuments to intellectuals were erected. Centered in the south of Germany, not the north (excepting Berlin), the distribution of monuments to "spirit" was almost the opposite of those to "power." Both types are well represented in the middle states, especially Saxony and Thuringia (in part because of the many Luther monuments built there), and many university towns erected statues of Bismarck as well as of scholars. The relative paucity of monuments to intellectuals in Prussia certainly suggests that it had come to prize power over spirit, while the balance between these two forces remained more complicated in the rest of Germany.

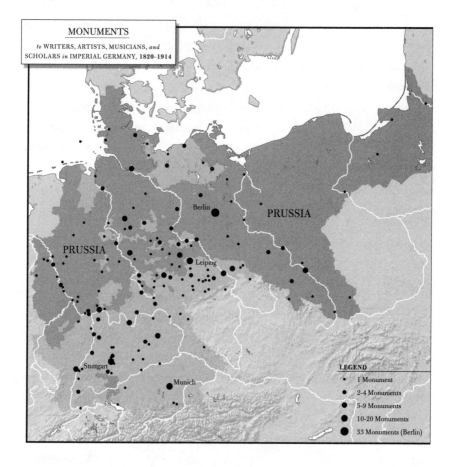

MONUMENTS
to WRITERS, ARTISTS, MUSICIANS, and
SCHOLARS in IMPERIAL GERMANY, 1820-1914

LEGEND
• 1 Monument
• 2-4 Monuments
● 5-9 Monuments
● 10-20 Monuments
● 33 Monuments (Berlin)

The question of who was actually commemorated proves a telling indicator of how the nation had come to shape literary sensibilities. Authors
who were often commemorated included Theodor Körner, whose youthful, blood-soaked lyrics still fanned martial fantasies; Max von Schenkendorf, whose poetic voice was subtler but still war-enthused; and Friedrich
Rückert, who wrote heartrending lamentations about the death of his
children as well as anti-French poems and songs. Celebrated as well was
Hoffmann von Fallersleben, his body of clean-rhymed, plain-language
verse already overshadowed by one composition, "*Deutschland, Deutschland über Alles,*" which would become the anthem of the Weimar Republic in 1922. The monuments indicate that although the Germans of the
Empire still thought of themselves as constituting a nation of "poets and
philosophers," it was the poets who really captured their imagination.

Monuments to the great thinkers—such as Gottfried Wilhelm Leibniz, Immanuel Kant, Johann Gottlieb Fichte, and G. W. F. Hegel—remained sparse.

In late Imperial Germany, monuments, like nationalism generally, reflected and reinforced major fault lines of class, gender, and religion. It is hardly surprising that there were no monuments to such colorful champions of the working class as Karl Marx, Friedrich Engels, Wilhelm Liebknecht, or even Ferdinand Lassalle, whose status as a folk hero for the workers far outstripped the prestige of his more theoretical comrades. Excepting queens and princesses, there were also very few public monuments to women: one was to the writer Annette von Droste-Hülshoff, but it was tucked away in the courtyard of her family's castle; another, in Tübingen, was to Ottilie Wildermuth, an unheralded author of short stories about Swabian life. Thereafter the trail goes cold. Hildegard von Bingen—mystic, visionary, and one of the most important religious figures of the Middle Ages—received a plaque in the Walhalla, built in 1842, but no secular monument in the imperial period. Anna Louisa Karsch, patriotic poetess of the Seven Years War, had already been rendered in stone during her lifetime, but her monument began to deteriorate and no one in the separate-spheres nineteenth century thought to repair it.[102] Major figures of Catholicism were also commemorated sparingly. There were at least twenty-six public monuments to Luther (not counting fountains) but none to Erasmus (who had by this time fallen out of fashion with Catholics as well). Of the popular authors of the contemporary Catholic milieu, only the almanac writer Alban Stolz received a monument, although not until 1913; of the politicians, Ludwig Windthorst and a number of minor conservative Catholics were commemorated, but not the great statesman Klemens von Metternich.

For Germans of the late imperial period, the question of how to include Jewish figures proved especially vexing, with Heinrich Heine the revealing touchstone for gauging the persistence of anti-Semitic attitudes. By the centenary of his birth in 1897, there was in all of Imperial Germany only a bronze engraving on a house where he had lived in Hamburg.[103] Düsseldorf, the city of his birth, contracted the famous carver Ernst Herter to sculpt a major monument, but the project ran into the opposition of anti-

Semites, who considered Heine "through and through a real Jew, not an authentic German."[104] Similar attempts also failed in Mainz and Frankfurt, and Herter's sculpture (of Heine's Lorelei) ultimately found a home in the Bronx, where "thousands of Germans who gladly called themselves Americans," as the *New York Times* put it, attended the unveiling.[105] Not until shortly before the outbreak of World War I were two modest monuments built to Heine in Germany: one by Social Democrats in the city of Halle, the other by the citizens of Frankfurt am Main.[106]

IX

In 1913, less than a year before the beginning of the conflagration that would become World War I, Germans erected an enormous monument commemorating a nationalistic falsehood—that the Prussian reentry into the war against Napoleon and the Battle of Nations at Leipzig had constituted a common struggle of the German people against Napoleon.[107] Weighing half a million tons, 90 percent of it pure cement with an outside layer of granite, the *Völkerschlacht* (Battle of Nations) Monument outsized New York's Statue of Liberty and was the largest such structure in Europe.[108] Pairing Romanesque solidity with modernist emphases, the architect, Bruno Schmitz, designed the great stone statue to evoke three temporal dimensions: a war memorial for fallen soldiers in the crypt, a heroes' hall for the German people of the present in the central section, and inspirations for future generations in the cupola.[109]

The unveiling was full of fanfare, lasting three full days and drawing hundreds of thousands of visitors. Newspapers, magazines, advertisements, postcards, and even the new medium of film portrayed it as revealing the depth and breadth of spontaneous national sentiment. In reality, one had to pay one hundred marks to even listen to the speeches—some of which, despite the presence of prominent foreign dignitaries, made it seem as if the Germans, and particularly the Prussians, had defeated Napoleon all alone.[110] The parade, which wound from the train station to the grounds, counted numerous military organizations, hundreds of university students, and thousands of schoolchildren, their overuse in a nationalist ceremony drawing murmurs and criticism.[111] Songs, cheers, and "hurrahs" were organized in advance. The city council even bought many of the "private" decorations that lined the streets and made sure, by arresting those they thought were vagrants, that the streets appeared clean and orderly. The council also forbade posters or advertisements criticizing the celebration. Banned, for example, were Social Democratic placards pointing out that Germany's princes had eagerly served Napoleon and broadsheets deriding the festival's overblown commercialization.[112]

For German nationalism, the Battle of Nations was at best an ambivalent touchstone. Germans had fought for and against Napoleon, and most of the men fighting in the battle were conscripts, not volunteers. There was also no general uprising. And yet for genuine nationalists, 1813 had become a heroic mirror before which the Germany of the present, often bested in world politics, seemed to pale. In a series of encounters with other powers—first in Morocco in 1905, then at the subsequent Conference of Algeciras in 1906, then in Bosnia in 1908, and in Morocco again in 1911—Germany had found itself increasingly isolated, with France on the side of Britain, Russia alienated, and only Austria-Hungary as an ally. Moreover, as Germany fell into greater isolation, it became apparent that it had gained little in the scramble for colonial empire. Instead, it had fought two brutal wars—the Maji Maji War in German East Africa and the Herero Wars in German Southwest Africa. Fewer than a thousand German soldiers fell. But German troops killed nearly a quarter of a million African men, women, and children.[113]

The immediate years before World War I witnessed a palpable militarization of German society. While hardly representative of broader public opinion, General Friedrich von Bernhardi's *Germany and the Next War*, published in 1912, signaled this ominous turn. He saw war as unambiguously positive, a form of regeneration, and a fact of human life that contributed to biological, social, and moral progress. As the public sphere became increasingly militarized, exaggerated masculine rhetoric, hardly confined to men alone, became more audible. Baroness von Spitzemberg, a sensitive seismograph of the prewar conservative scene, complained, for example, that society was becoming socialistic, modern, and effeminate. Other groups were also not exempt from the militarization of German society. Reaching through the Catholic Center Party and even into the ranks of the Social Democrats, a broad coalition supported the army expansion of 1913, agreeing to pay for it with a onetime patriotic "defense contribution."

It was in this context of a society "organizing itself in and for war" that Heinrich Class published *Wenn ich der Kaiser wär* (*If I Were the Kaiser*).[114] Chairman since 1908 of the ultranationalist Pan-German League, the Treitschke-inspired Class saw the state as a mere means serving the ends of a racialized German nation.[115] Drawing on eugenic proscriptions for keeping the race healthy, including sensible nutrition, outdoor activity, and efforts to eradicate alcoholism, Class's nationalism waxed ominously modern. He argued, for example, for a legal system based on "the service of the individual for the collectivity," as well as for a constitution that gave the Reichstag, elected by men of property and education, the right to appoint ministers and counselors to the Kaiser. The purpose of such an arrangement, according to Class, was to bring the Kaiser and the people closer together, and enable the Kaiser to emerge as a genuine "Führer."[116] Class also raised the possibility, in certain kinds of defensive war, of expelling non-German populations from German-occupied territories in order to make the German nation an ethnically homogeneous space. But in 1912, Class still pulled back from this precipice, as he deemed such expulsions brutal and inhumane.[117]

There were other such books; one journalist counted thirty-two in 1913. Some authors argued that the nation was to be conceived in racial terms. Others claimed that war—beautiful, reinvigorating, a source of creativity, a maker of states, and part of the divine order—would save the German nation. The journalist who counted them was Georg Brandes, an influential Danish literary critic, a Jewish mediator between Nordic and Germanic cultures, and an acute observer. Comparing France and Germany, he pointed out that "the Germans are called a people in arms, but the French are it," referring to the fact that France had a higher percentage of its men in uniform.[118] The real difference between the two countries, he argued, was in the organization and ideology of German nationalism. Countless associations rallied millions of members to push for nationalist causes, while innumerable authors extolled the virtues of the martial nation. Turning away from Goethe, Schiller, Wagner, and Marx, the Germans, Brandes believed, had recently embraced the "blood men" who, as military leaders, "sacrificed thousands of lives."[119] Born of diplomatic and imperialist frustration, the shift in mentality was significant. More than a century before, Madame de Staël had written that enthusiasm distinguished the Germans, fanaticism the French. Perhaps recalling that passage in *De l'Allemagne*, Brandes wrote that in France love of fatherland has become "enthusiastic," in Germany "fanatical."[120]

Brandes was not right for all Germans, even in the feverish few years before World War I. However, he did see that in the tug between a bellicose, exclusionary, even "fanatical" nationalism and a more ordinary, banal, object-centered attachment to the nation, the ideology of Treitschke and his heirs had gained in strength and influence. But even this new nationalism had by and large developed during peacetime. War, and still more postwar reflections on it, would soon shift the very parameters, ideological and practical, of this nationalism, and bring the country out of what we have called the age of nationalism and into the nationalist age. For Germany, and for millions of other Europeans, it was a catastrophic development.

IV

—

THE
NATIONALIST
AGE

I N 1949, ERNST KANTOROWICZ, A CONSERVATIVE-MINDED GERMAN-
Jewish émigré to the United States, delivered a characteristically erudite lecture at Mills College in Oakland, California, entitled "*Pro Patria
Mori* in Medieval Political Thought." In feudal Christianity, Kantorowicz
explained, one sacrificed for an eternal fatherland, a *patria aeterna*, not
the temporary fatherland of the here and now. When a knight gave his life
defending a seigneurial lord, the sacrifice was personal, not public. It was
for the individual king or prince, not for his property, land, or territory.
The crucial turn, Kantorowicz argued, came at the end of the thirteenth
century, when King Philip IV of France taxed "for the defense of the native
fatherland" (*ad defensionem natalis patriae*).[1] The new emphasis on sacrificing for a territory as opposed to a person was not merely a classical
borrowing, as might be supposed. Rather, Kantorowicz contended, this
novel concept of sacrifice derived from the martyrdom of Crusaders, who
were usually thought to be defending the Holy Land, and from the terri-
torialization of the Christian community. These deep religious connections, according to Kantorowicz, elicited profound emotional resonances,
although only in wars that were thought to protect the Holy Land, or the
fatherland, or in some other way to be just. "If the soldier's death in action—
not to mention the citizen's death in bomb struck cities—is deprived of any
idea encompassing *humanitas,* be it God or king or *patria*," Kantorowicz
insisted, "it will be deprived also of the ennobling idea of self-sacrifice."[2]
"It becomes," he emphasized, "a cold-blooded slaughter."[3]

Chapter 10, "Sacrifice For," documents the centrality of sacrifice to the
experience of World War I, Germany's first cataclysmic war in nearly three
hundred years. It shows that the dynamic center of the nation shifted to the
question of how to conceive, represent, and live with the sacrifice given it,
and maintains that this question dominated not just the four years of the

war, but even more profoundly the subsequent period of peace. Weimar culture, which the sociologist Karl Mannheim would in retrospect compare with the flourishing of literature and art in Periclean Athens, was, it is argued, in no small measure an extended reflection—in literature, painting, sculpture, and film—on the meaning of war and the sacrifices it demanded.[4] It was, moreover, in the postwar mediation of the war, less than from the direct experience of the war itself, that a form of nationalism developed that had little to do with dying *ad defensionem natalis patriae*, and centered instead on *völkisch* categories infused with racist logic. While not without roots in the nineteenth century, the new radical nationalism represented an ideological departure that deprived, in Kantorowicz's words, "the ennobling idea of self-sacrifice . . . of any idea encompassing *humanitas*."[5]

Nationalism, then, became the dominant ideology of the age not during the First World War but in a Germany shattered by its fallout. As we have seen, the period roughly between 1815 and 1914 was an age of nationalism in the sense that Kant famously defined his time as an age of enlightenment and not yet an enlightened age. In the early and mid-nineteenth century, nationalism had taken hold in some places and among some groups of people—but it had yet to unfold its full destructive dynamism.[6] Even in the Second Empire, "nation," a term largely absent from the constitution, did not serve as the legitimating ground of state power. Moreover, despite Otto von Bismarck's famous claim to have forged the nation in "iron and blood," Germany, when considered comparatively, had not experienced a truly major war.[7] On the German side of the Franco-Prussian War, for example, some 40,000 men died, as compared with more than ten times that number in the American Civil War. World War I, defeat, and collapse would change that. Before 1914, perhaps even before 1918, Germans lived in an age of nationalism. After 1918, they lived in a nationalist age.

In essential ways, then, war shaped and defined this nationalist age. Between 1914 and 1945, actual war took up only one decade of three but the effects of large-scale killing dominated the other years of so-called peace and blurred the line separating the two, making at least the early years of Weimar Germany less an anteroom to the Third Reich than a postwar society in which high levels of violence persisted.[8] Although the war ended in western Europe in 1918, it continued in the east with brutal ethnic, political, and even international warfare. It is true that the victims of postwar violence in the newly constituted Germany numbered in the tens of thousands rather than, as in eastern Europe, in the hundreds of thousands, or in Russia, where civil-war deaths ranged in the millions. Yet in many ways Weimar was closer to the eastern experience of violence than the western story of gradual recovery. A loser of the war, an occupied country, an economic calamity, with secessionist movements prevalent, Weimar struggled—economically, politically, and culturally—with the consequences of the war. Indeed, it took five years, until 1924, before the Republic fully satisfied Max Weber's famous, if rather martial, definition of a viable state, articulated in 1919, as a "human community that successfully claims the monopoly of the legitimate use of physical force within a given territory."[9] Conversely, in its ideology, social and economic priorities, and front-generation rhetoric, Hitler's Germany was to a significant degree structured by the fallout of the First World War, along with the preparation for the Second. If much of Weimar may be considered a postwar society, it seems hardly amiss to think of the first six years of Nazi Germany as a prewar society. Nor is the emphasis on the peacelessness of the age a present-day interpretation alone. The years 1924 to 1929 were "the only genuine period of peace that my generation in Germany has experienced," recounted the jurist and journalist Sebastian Haffner in his pseudonymously and posthumously published memoirs, but this period of peace, in which Germans were enjoined to concentrate on their private affairs, "was not," according to Haffner, "what was wanted."[10]

The bleeding of war into peace was also expressed in the foregrounding of the military state. Clichés about militaristic Prussia aside, the new centrality of the military state was a reversal of a historic trend. In the first half of the long nineteenth century, Prussian military spending had actually declined in relation to both civilian outlays and as a percentage of GNP, reaching a low plateau in the 1840s, and rising slightly after the Revolution of 1848.[11] As was true of other European countries at the time, Prussia had ceased to be a state whose main purpose was fighting and had become instead a state in which the civilian tasks of government outweighed the military. Although this process of demilitarization was interrupted by the wars of the 1860s, the military outlays of Prussian-dominated Imperial Germany remained rather average by contemporary standards for another

MILITARY AS % OF STATE BUDGET AND NET SOCIAL PRODUCT
1872–1961

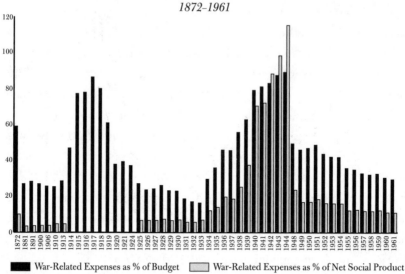

■ War-Related Expenses as % of Budget   ▢ War-Related Expenses as % of Net Social Product

half century, with the military constituting some 30 percent of the federal budget, and trending from 3 to 4 percent of GNP.[12] The arms race immediately prior to World War I registered a palpable increase in military outlays.[13] But an altogether higher and persistently significant level of spending did not occur until the First World War.[14] After "the great seminal catastrophe of this century," as the diplomat-historian George Kennan called the war, Germany's military expenditure remained high. Close to half of military outlays went to pay benefits to the disabled and injured and to the widows of fallen soldiers.[15] Not until 1928 did the military budget actually decline, but the downturn was reversed in 1934, when Hitler began to rearm. The result was a thirty-year fusion of state, war, and economy. By 1944, the cost of the war exceeded German productive capacity, even when aided by some eight million foreign laborers, many subsisting in slavelike conditions.[16] Only by stealing, robbing, and emptying the occupied territories of their livelihood could the National Socialists sustain this civil-military polity.

The destructive fusion of the military with the modern state resulted in an immense amount of death. With the exception of the 1630s, when war, plague, and famine conspired to rapidly depopulate vast areas of northern central Europe, the death toll of the first half of the twentieth century was simply unprecedented.[17] When combined, the two world wars were five times deadlier than any series of armed conflicts in modern Europe, and the proportion of those who died from the primary violence of war, and not its secondary effects (such as disease and unintentional famine) was much higher than in earlier centuries.[18] Moreover, soldiers fell at roughly the same rate across the two world wars, if somewhat higher in the first. One estimate places the daily death toll for German soldiers at 1303 per day in the First World War and 1083 in the Second.[19] At the start and end of the First, and at the end of the Second World War, the numbers were higher still. For German soldiers, the highest mortality came in the summer of 1944, especially August, and in the first months of 1945, when between 10,000 and 15,000 German men died per day, mainly fighting against an advancing Soviet army.[20] In earlier wars, battlefield casualties had been comparable—but the great battles of the past usually lasted a day or two. The Battle of Nations, fought in Leipzig in 1813, was an exception. It raged for four long days, and prior to the First World War, it was the deadliest confrontation in European or North American military history. During World War I, however, battles continued on for months, making the Battle of Verdun in 1916 nearly ten times more lethal than Leipzig, and the Somme deadlier still.[21] And when total deaths, military and civilian, are counted together, the Battle of Stalingrad, to take the most lethal single encounter on the eastern front during World War II, exceeded the death toll even of the Battle of the Somme.

The new conditions of war also shaped the profiles of those who died. In World War I, the young died in disproportionate numbers. Roughly half the soldiers who died in the German armies were between nineteen and twenty-five; and in the last two years of the war, boys eighteen to twenty years old accounted for a fourth of those killed.[22] The male death toll among the soldiers of World War II was also a lament for the young. Roughly a quarter of a million German men perished in almost each of the birth years of those who were fourteen to thirty when the war began. For those men who were nineteen when the Second World War started, 40 percent fell to their deaths as a result of the war.[23]

As the character of German society changed, so too did the ranks of those who sacrificed their lives. In the First World War, it was still primarily men from the countryside who fell.[24] While the rows of industrial workers who died ranged dismayingly long, rural people were drafted in greater numbers and died disproportionately. By the Second World War, this was no longer the case, as employment in German industry was by then nearly twice as large as in agriculture. But both wars reflected the conditions of the industrial era, including callousness toward human life, mass formations, rapid-fire weaponry, and soldiers who understood their roles as industrial laborers whose "work," as Ernst Jünger put it in 1925, "is called killing."[25]

It was, in fact, the industrial dimension of the wars that made them so lethal. In World War I, men fell to the relentless patter of guns shooting five hundred rounds a minute, with artillery fire causing over 70 percent of deaths in the German army. By comparison, the light arms of the infantry brought about less than 20 percent of all deaths, and hand-to-hand combat—with knives, sables, and bayonets—less than 0.1 percent.[26] World War II was fought in a more advanced industrial period. Air warfare, armored vehicles, and radio communication broke up rigid formations and made rapid mobility possible. Especially in the east, where the most intense fighting occurred, the war was fought in vast battle spaces, in which the distinction between the front and rear army was not always clear, zones of conflict stretched across huge territories, and the decisive fighting formation was not the long line of men in trenches but small groups, constantly in motion, with a great deal of cohesion and the ability to strike the enemy in close quarters.

The greatest difference between the two world wars was not, however, technology or battlefield formation. Rather, it was the centrality of civilian killing to the Second World War. In one estimate, 58 percent of all dying in World War II was civilian death on the Allied side—with Nazi Germany by far the greatest killer of civilians. World War II, at least in eastern Europe and in China, was a war of peoples, not just armies, and one in which civilian deaths were not merely unfortunate and incidental byproducts of war.[27] Certainly, in eastern Europe, civilian death tolls induced by Nazi Germany were startling: in Yugoslavia, at least a million civilian deaths; in Poland some two million non-Jewish civilians and some three million civilian Jews; and in Russia, the epicenter of the civilian catastrophe, some sixteen million civilian deaths, including over a million Jews. Genocide occurred precisely in, and was a part of, this mass killing of largely defenseless civilians. Too often thought of outside the context of the Second World War, the Holocaust alone accounted for more civilian killing than occurred in all countries, on all fronts, during World War I.

II

Two German terms help illuminate the brutality of this new epoch and allow us to differentiate what we are calling "sacrifice for" and "sacrifice of." The first is the noun "*Volksgemeinschaft*" ("national community"), the second the adjective "*völkisch*" (depending on context, translated as "ethnic," "racial," or "popular"). In the first decade of the Weimar Republic, *Volksgemeinschaft* constituted an appeal to national unity—it was placed on the banner of almost all major political parties, ranging from the Socialists to the Catholic Center and the progressive democratic parties, and in the Republic's first years even to segments of the overtly nationalist parties.[28] Initially, it suggested that a nation that had sacrificed in World War I remained unified across differences of politics, region, religion, and class. In early Weimar, the term had yet to assume ethnic or racial meaning. Instead, it simply stressed how sacrifice for the nation solidified the community. *Völkisch*, by contrast, divided, and was meant to divide. It was a prewar term that experienced a spike in popularity in 1917, and radical nationalists employed it during the Weimar Republic to distinguish their particularly hard-edged positions from conventional, moderate, nationalism, centered on *Volksgemeinschaft*.[29] One of the most often used qualifiers in Hitler's early speeches, the adjective "*völkisch*" also counts among the terms he most often employed in *Mein Kampf*. With regards to the radical nationalist scene, the word "*völkisch*" functioned as a flag, or a signifying practice; it was essentially an early-twentieth-century dog whistle.[30] Within the radical nationalist milieu, it was understood as meaning that a racially pure German nation could be achieved only by the sacrifice of groups within it.

The ascendancy of the adjective "*völkisch*" over the noun "*Volksgemeinschaft*," and the infusion of the latter term with the ethnic and racial meaning of the former, signaled the beginning of Germany's descent into a new kind of exclusionary politics. The descent began in Weimar, with the introduction of Aryan lineage statutes in a series of radical nationalist organizations, including the enormously influential Stahlhelm, originally an organization of former frontline soldiers. These statutes, which basically served to exclude Jews, undermined the principle that sacrifice in war guaranteed national belonging. However hesitantly pursued at first, the National Socialist persecution of war veterans—if those veterans were Communist, Jewish, or confined to psychiatric hospitals—likewise showed that "sacrifice of" had taken on greater weight than "sacrifice for." It was, however, when radical nationalists seized power, as they did on January 30, 1933, that the descent gathered momentum.

This new, radical-nationalist politics can be traced along three conceptual axes: before and after, inside and outside, and above and below. This interpretive grid is adopted from the insights of the late historian Reinhart Koselleck; it allows us to see something of the fundamental structure of German nationalism during the Nazi era.[31]

The first axis, the temporal dimension, refers to radical nationalism's simultaneous derivation of the nation from a deep past and its projection forward to a dystopian future. Radical nationalists of this era thought in genealogies and geopolitics, the inheritance of race and the ethnic reordering of continents.[32] They were not interested in arguments about the here and now; realism, which focuses on the immediate, was not their optic. *Mein Kampf*, for example, did not explain Germany's distant past, or the actual present, or even much about Hitler's own life. The deep past had only mythic value for Hitler, the proximate past served as a battleground for debates with other nationalists, and Hitler's life history, as told in *Mein Kampf*, was, as we now know, largely a fabrication. For radical nationalists like Hitler, the temporal stress fell, instead, on the future—and not some very distant future (as Fichte had imagined "The Republic of Germans at the Beginning of the Twenty-Second Century"), but rather the proximate, ostensibly shapable, future. Despite the millennial grandiosity of Third Reich rhetoric, Hitler thought in decades, not centuries, in continents, not the world. His *Second Book*, written in 1928 and not published during his lifetime, brimmed with practical prescriptions about how to remake German foreign policy to achieve its ultimate goal, the securing of living space for Germany's growing population. To Hitler, this meant continental hegemony, not the imperialist empire as conceived before 1914. If Hitler had a model, it was the vast tracts of land possessed by the United States in the American west, which Germany would pursue with the aim of enabling Germans "to lead a life comparable to that of the American people."[33] In the near future, Germany was to be a land empire "in the one and only place possible: in the East."³⁴ Thus, Hitler's agenda was expansion and domination, and the conquering of vast if still delimited spaces in eastern Europe. This is what he aimed for, and what he believed he could accomplish.

The second axis—inside and outside—points to processes of inclusion and exclusion in the construction of the national community. Like no other political party in German history, the National Socialists understood how to bind people across a broad stratum to coalesce around collective goals. From fostering participation in its state-run leisure organization, "Strength Through Joy," to the sense of purpose encouraged by the Hitler Youth, the Nazis engendered a compelling sense of community. Yet while these integrative initiatives were pursued with vigor, they remained essentially static in their social impact.

By contrast, exclusion, especially of Jews, radically changed society, overturned its laws and rules, and made ordinary Germans complicit in the persecution of their neighbors. This was because Nazi Germany did not defend, modernize, or reinvent a past racial order, as occurred in South Africa and the Jim Crow South of the United States. Rather, it created a new racial order where no such order existed, or where segregation based on religion had been abolished at least half a century earlier. To achieve their aims, the Nazis literally had to tear apart a modern society. They had to identify Jews as Jews and stigmatize them as separate. They had to strip them of their status as German citizens and deprive them of protections. And they had to marginalize Jews into social spaces where they were often at the mercy of others. All of this left virtually no institutions untouched, and no neighborhoods unaffected. Even integrative activities, like draping the German flag from one's balcony, took on exclusionary meanings, especially after laws barred Jewish participation.

The corrosive quality of Nazi exclusion policies—creating personal, social, and spatial distance between non-Jewish and Jewish Germans—cannot be underscored enough. In the personal dimension, these policies entailed conceiving loving relations between Christians and Jews as miscegenation. In the social sphere, they meant making neighbors into strangers, and placing them outside ties of human empathy and solidarity. An "inclusive exclusion," to use the philosopher Giorgio Agamben's term, such exclusions involved the active abandonment of a group inside the community to the mercy of their oppressors.[35] The active abandonment formed a national "we" in relation to a banned, denationalized "they." It also constructed a new relation between inside and outside in a space outside law, in which dominion over the abandoned culminated in the ability to kill without committing homicide.

Chapter 11, "Sacrifice Of," considers radical nationalism in power primarily in its exclusionary logic and practice. It focuses on Germans eliminating Jews from personal, social, and community space, severing ties of friendship, solidarity, and compassion, and tacitly coming to a consensus that there was a "Jewish question," and that expulsion was its "final solution." By the time of the November pogrom in 1938, commonly known as Kristallnacht, the logic of inclusion and exclusion had already come to take on important elements of hierarchy. In more than 1200 communities throughout Germany, a ritual of denigration was played out, with a well-known impact on the lives of German Jews. Less reflected on is that the event also initiated hundreds of thousands of non-Jewish Germans into a brutalizing ritual of German domination and Jewish submission, inaugurating a transition from persecution fueled by processes of inclusion and exclusion to one centered on the third axis in our grid, vertical relations of power.

This third axis, above and below in Koselleck's scheme, came more prominently to the fore during the war. The occupation of Poland in 1939 saw repetitions, with greater violence, of patterns of power and domination established during the November pogrom, including the destruction and desecration of a large number of synagogues and the humiliation and sometimes murder of local Jewish populations. But in this initial phase, ethnic Poles (especially of the intelligentsia)—not Jews—were the primary target of Nazi Germany's murderous policies. In the first mass killings of the Second World War, ethnic German militias (made up of Germans resident in the Polish territory of 1919–1939), typically aided by the Nazi SS, murdered a large number of their fellow Polish citizens, targeting especially lawyers, doctors, officials, clergy, and an enormous number of schoolteachers. Then, as the occupation deepened, Nazi occupiers pushed Jews into ghettos, restricted their access to food, and exposed them to sickness and disease. As spatial confinement narrowed, the brutality of the vertical relations of power and domination intensified, leaving Jews vulnerable to the ravages of German occupiers and their auxiliary forces.

If, to borrow from Max Weber, power over another is the ability "to carry out one's will even against resistance," then Nazi military occupation represented an extreme form of power over others.[36] Moreover, it was a form of power in which killing constituted the only further extension of that power—although with the paradoxical effect that in the moment the other is killed, the relation of power, defined by the ability of one person to lord it over another, necessarily vanishes.

III

The genocide of the Jews, the subject of chapter 12, "Death Spaces," began unequivocally in the summer of 1941, and occurred in the context of other mass killings. Best known are the so-called euthanasia killings, the murder of the mentally ill. The Nazis murdered some 70,000 at designated killing facilities and at least as many in helter-skelter murders in occupied Poland before Clemens August von Galen, the Catholic bishop of Münster, publicly called for their cessation. Larger still were the number of non-Jewish Poles murdered. By June 1941, the SS and ethnic German militia groups had gunned down close to 200,000 Polish civilians.[37] The invasion of the Soviet Union brought about killings of an entirely different dimension, however. Between June 1941 and January 1942, the German army eradicated some two million Soviet prisoners of war, while the death rates of all Soviet soldiers, including those POWs, reached as high as 600,000 per month.

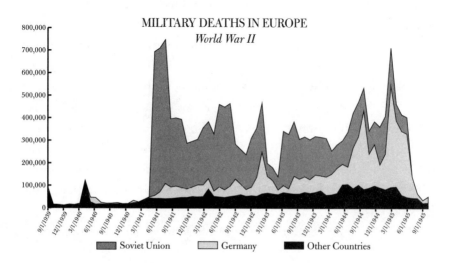

MILITARY DEATHS IN EUROPE
World War II

Soviet Union   Germany   Other Countries

304 || GERMANY: A NATION IN ITS TIME

The genocide of the Jews, as can be seen in preceding chart, began in the context of an enormous increase in wartime lethality, and included an unprecedented amount of killing of captured soldiers. It also began with bullets. In countless (and in fact still now not fully counted) cities, towns, villages, and out-of-the-way hamlets throughout the Soviet territories of eastern Europe, the Nazis and their accomplices killed Jews by shooting them. In the first six months of the invasion of the Soviet Union, the *Einsatzgruppen*, the mobile killing units of the SS, alone murdered at least a half million Jewish men, women, and children.[38] This means that genocide had already taken place before the German government made a centralized decision, typically thought of as Hitler's order, to kill all the Jews of Europe. Moreover, by December 1941, when this centralized decision likely fell, new ways of killing had already altered the operational logic of the genocide, shifting its focus and increasing its daily lethality. In addition to killing Jews in the places they lived, Nazis now also sent Jews to killing centers, the so-called extermination camps. By mid-1942, the pace of the killing had increased dramatically, and by mid-February 1943, some 75 percent of all Jews who would be killed in the Holocaust were already dead. When as many as four million Jews had perished, Auschwitz-Birkenau began to take in unheard-of numbers of transports, and became, in the final year of its operation, before the liberation of the camp, the largest factory of death the world had ever seen.

No single, satisfactory answer exists to explain the emergence of the Nazi genocide of European Jews. Yet two kinds of explanations, when braided together, bring us closer. The first involves the proximate context of war. Almost all the Jews killed—more than 99 percent—were murdered during wartime. "No war, no Holocaust," as the historian Yehuda Bauer has observed.[39] War provided an alibi and a cover to mass killing, not just of Jews but of a whole range of civilian groups in the "bloodlands" of eastern Europe, where National Socialist killing broke through all norms of civilization.[40] Nevertheless, while the genocide occurred in time of war, it did not result from direct combat, threadbare justifications about fighting partisans notwithstanding. Instead, it was mainly a phenomenon of a military occupation.

The second explanatory strand involves the dynamics of occupation and Nazi conceptions of racial hierarchy. Hitler had long insisted that only conquered land, not conquered people, would be made a part of the racially conceived, territorially expansive German nation. A new and portentous concept, Hitler's "land policy of the future," as he termed it in *Mein Kampf*, envisioned for non-German populations only expulsion, slavery, and extermination. Sometime in the period between August 1941, in the midst of Nazi jubilations of early victory, and December, when the eastern front began to falter and the United States entered the war, Nazi leaders came to see only the latter two of these two possibilities, slavery and extermination, as viable for Jews.[41]

Slavery is a relationship of domination over an individual, implying the ability of one person to determine the name, educational level, work, location, conjugal relations, and procreation of another person; it also involves the right, reinforced by law, of the master to inflict bodily harm on the slave and, in limited cases, to kill him or her. It may seem self-evident, but it is also important to underscore that the relationship presupposes the personal presence of the master and the slave in the same place. This holds for postslavery systems of racial domination as well. Despite legal codes of segregation reinforced by violence, neither white South Africa in the era of apartheid, nor the white southerners of the segregated parts of the United States could afford black flight. Racial domination of this kind required proximity, because it implied a personal and an economic relationship, and, from the standpoint of the masters, economic dependency on the subordinate other.

Nazi Germany was, in this sense, different. Radical nationalists wanted Jews ineradicably out. And they wanted Jews out from the very beginning. To the radical nationalists of the early Weimar Republic, the Germanic race, far from being an abstract category, essentially meant Germans, with Jews excluded. Point four of the Nazi Party's twenty-five-point program of 1920 put it candidly: "Only a member of the race can be a citizen. A member of the race can only be one who is of German blood, without consideration of creed. Consequently, no Jew can be a member of the race."[42] In *Mein Kampf*, Hitler downplayed the importance of the Party's original program—but not on this matter. By answering the question of who was German *ex negativo*, the vocabulary of race significantly sharpened nationalist discourse and made Jews into the dialectical opposite of Germans. The arcana of the word "Aryan" only underscored this exclusion; Hitler began to use the term as early as August 1920, first as an adjective, paired with "blood," then as a noun, set off against "Jew." "Aryan" was hardly a descriptive term, especially because few people agreed on who was included. Rather, it just signaled exclusion. "The most powerful opposite of the Aryan is the Jew," Hitler wrote with unmistakable bluntness in *Mein Kampf*.[43] Policies that derived from the opposition were also clear enough. They entailed unmixing, beginning with segregation and denaturalization laws, and ended with expulsion.

Expulsions, whether from official positions, organizations, or communities, constituted the basic template. This made Nazi Germany different from other societies based on racial domination. In the months after the November pogrom of 1938, as Jews left the communities where their forefathers had often lived for generations, one after the other local mayor gleefully announced his village or town to be free of Jews. During the war, in the many communities of eastern Europe, the dynamic was similar. The Germans came in and established new ethnic hierarchies, and Ukrainians, Lithuanians, Latvians, Poles, and others participated, pushing Jews to the lowest rung, and confining them to ever smaller, more constricted spaces. In the context of war and occupation, the Nazis considered whether Jews, like Russian POWs, were even worth feeding. Eventually, Nazi starvation policies created a Jewish population "unfit to work," outside the law, and utterly without protection—in a word, killable.[44] At the local level, when the Nazis introduced the term "unfit to work," extermination was near. Whether Chełmno, Bełżec, Sobibór, or Treblinka, the early death camps were essentially regional killing installations, decimating, in the main, the Jews of Poland. Auschwitz, the *ultima ratio* of radical nationalism, was intended on a larger scale for the Jews of Europe.

Part Four attempts to understand Germany during the nationalist age, and to take measure of the catastrophe it wrought. It is animated by the conviction—as Primo Levi, a survivor of Auschwitz, wrote in *The Drowned and the Saved*—that "the greater part of historical and natural phenomenon are not simple, or not simple in the way we would like."[45] The following three chapters nevertheless try to advance a coherent interpretation of the turbulent years 1914–1945 by emphasizing the dynamic between the mass sacrifice for the nation and the eventual sacrifice of groups within the nation. It also attempts to use the categories of Koselleck—before and after, inside and outside, and above and below—to understand the essential structure of radical nationalist thought and practice. Finally, it looks closely at the contexts in which Germany became, during World War II, a genocidal nation.

SACRIFICE FOR

c. 1914–1933

*Only one circumstance makes
all of this bearable, the willing
acceptance of sacrifice.*

—KÄTHE KOLLWITZ, SEPTEMBER 1914

• • •

*My untenably contradictory position
on the war. How did I come to it?*

—KÄTHE KOLLWITZ, AUGUST 1916

IN *THE NOTEBOOKS OF MALTE LAURIDS BRIGGE,* PUBLISHED IN 1910, Rainer Maria Rilke described the death of Malte's grandfather, chamberlain Christoph Detlev, who passed away in his manor on the outskirts of a Danish town. The grandfather did not pass silently. For two long months, one could hear the bellows of the old man all the way to the edges of his expansive estate. His was an individual death just it had been an individual life, the dying occurring where the living had happened. Rilke juxtaposed the grandfather's singular death in quiet Denmark with the countless factory-style fatalities in Paris's aptly named Hôtel Dieu, where in five hundred and fifty-nine beds "a death of one's own" will soon "become just as uncommon as a life of one's own."[1]

Rilke wrote loosely associated prose poems, rather than linear narrative typical of the nineteenth-century novel, in his search for literary forms that could adequately mirror life and death in a demystified industrial age. The search would, however, soon prove itself more difficult than even Rilke imagined. This was perhaps because in the new era, the ubiquity of mass death by machine gun, aerial bombing, and gas made dying in the Hôtel Dieu seem insignificant by comparison.

II

The new era began with optimism, at least in some quarters. From the balcony of the Hohenzollern Castle in Berlin, Kaiser William II declared on the evening of August 1, 1914, that he "no longer recognizes political parties or religious denominations," for "today we are all German brothers, and only German brothers."[2] In the central districts of Munich, Cologne, Hamburg, and other cities, throngs of people greeted the Kaiser's words effusively, leading one historian to call the day the war started "the actual founding moment of the nation."[3]

Nevertheless, the working classes were absent from the crowds; the denizens of Germany's small cities and towns were quiet; and in the countryside, rural people fell mainly silent. In German border cities, like Freiburg im Breisgau, Königsberg, Trier, and Aachen, the inhabitants were noticeably anxious, while the national minorities—the French in Alsace, the Danes in Holstein, and the Poles—were dismayed. Resisting in significant numbers, the Poles had to be forced by the police to the conscription office. They, however, were the only ones.[4] Trains otherwise ran on time, strikes ended, and young men showed up at the barracks. Not enthusiasm but a sense of duty characterized the reaction of most citizens of Imperial Germany to the outbreak of the war.[5]

Besides, there were a significant number of volunteers: newspapers claimed more than 1 million men.[6] The actual number was closer to 200,000, but the army was a conscript army, and men on draft rolls could not volunteer. This left boys under seventeen, men over fifty, anyone with an exemption, and reservists whose division had not yet been called up. As a result, the composition of the volunteers was skewed. Motivated by a mix of idealism and peer pressure, more than half of the eligible pupils in German *Gymnasia* volunteered. If not already assigned to a regiment, college students likewise signed up in droves, as did significant numbers of tradesmen and businessmen, and a good many workers.[7] In the absence of a draft, the numbers would have been higher. Great Britain, the major power without compulsory military service, relied mainly on volunteers, and they signed up in daunting numbers: 1 million by December 1914, and 1.5 million in the following year—nearly 40 percent of men in the eligible age range.[8] Nothing suggests that Imperial Germany, with its more robust military culture and more muted pacifist crosscurrents, would have been any different. But this should not be confused with aggression or bellicosity.

It was about sacrifice. This necessity of sacrifice for the defense of the nation belonged to the unwritten code of male citizenship. Few thought "it sweet and fitting to die for the fatherland," as the Horatian adage had it. Germans, however, did believe that sacrifice in war was required of men. They also had no idea what was to come. With the exception of those serving in colonial armies, the callow young men who marched to battle in 1914 had never known war. Neither had their fathers. The generation that had fought in the Franco-Prussian War were grandfathers by now.

At the outbreak of World War I, German nationalism had become a tacit social contract whose core postulate was neither hate nor expansion but rather the duty to defend and die for the fatherland. Even if such a contract seems age-old, it was, in fact, comparatively new. In the Seven Years War of the eighteenth century, appeals from leaders and intellectuals to die for the fatherland had set the parameters of sacrificial patriotism; in reality, these had very little influence over the practice of warfare, which relied on forced draft, harsh discipline, and interminable drill. Even in the vaunted war against Napoleon, Prussian volunteers, who numbered some 3000 soldiers, hardly altered the conduct of a war in which major encounters often had casualty lists of over 60,000 dead and wounded. Roughly a half century later, little had changed. In Europe, unlike the United States, the wars of the middle decades of the nineteenth century pitted conscript army against conscript army, with those killed in battle "shoveled into the ground and so forgotten," as the English writer William Makepeace Thackeray noted with respect to the 45,000 British soldiers who died in Crimea.[9] In the Franco-Prussian War of 1870, there were not quite 10,000 Prussian volunteers—more than in 1813, though not significantly higher when adjusted for population growth.[10]

During World War I, however, a new sense of obligation came to the fore. Implying the necessity of defending the nation from attack, the word "duty" appears in countless soldiers' letters. The other word that appears often is "sacrifice." Containing the dual meaning of suffering and of renunciation of the self in the service of the collective, no idea proved more important to giving meaning to the immense amount of dying that occurred.[11]

The tacit social contract—the duty to defend and die for the nation—also helps explain why soldiers continued to support the war, even when it became clear, as it did very quickly, that it would be long and bloody. Soon after the war commenced, the German government published daily casualty lists, which registered the dead, missing, wounded, and those taken prisoner. Divided by region and regiment until December 1916, thereafter by last name, the lists transfixed the public.[12] They also revealed that the first months of the war, even before the armies settled into trench warfare, were far more lethal than what followed.[13] In these incipient months, bright idealism yielded to gloom and dismay, and the numbers of volunteers dissipated.[14] And yet there was no public resistance. Fueled by a genuine commitment to defend the fatherland, soldiers showed up when called, and a "second acceptance," as scholars call it, set in, pairing "sacrifice," or *Opfer*, with "stoic resolve," or *Durchhalten*.[15] Even the sociologist Max Weber, who throughout the war wavered between patriotic and critical instincts, understood the public force of the opinions of those ready to "die for" their country.[16] Moreover, the knowledge that others had sacrificed bound people to the cause. "They were better than we were," a boy in Ernst Glaeser's novel *The Cohort of 1902* says of his absent, distant father and his comrades at the front; "after all they were risking their lives."[17]

III

The war unleashed a torrent of testimony—as no war had ever done before. Mainly a result of the sheer number of soldiers fighting, the plethora of letters, sketches, photographs, and diaries also reflected the reality that soldiers were now literate and educated citizens. This had not been true of the Seven Years War, or of the Napoleonic Wars, and consequently both conflicts left scarce testimony from ordinary men.[18] In central Europe, the number of soldiers who wrote letters did not increase until the Franco-Prussian War; one estimate places the number of German letters, postcards, and packages sent during that conflict at half a million per day. World War I dwarfed this number. Historians estimate that there were 28.7 billion pieces of mail sent: on average 9.8 million items were sent per day to the front, 6.8 million from it.[19] One commonly thinks of the nineteenth century as the great age of letter writing, but nothing compares to "the rebirth of the letter," as one contemporary called it, that occurred during World War I.[20]

For most soldiers, the experience of war was more mundane than heroic. Surviving letters reflect the raw conditions of war, the boredom of trench life, and tell of long bouts of homesickness. Some depict the landscapes—the cratered, treeless stretches of no-man's-land, or the recalcitrant grandeur of damaged but defiant landmarks, like the French cathedral of Reims. Especially in letters, the touristic dimension of the experience was palpable, and it forced not a few to realize, often for the first time, that "we have really learned to love our Germany."[21] A few letters vividly described the horror, but, because of governmental censorship and the soldiers' desire to keep loved ones from worrying, most writers smoothed over the experience with a prevailing language of euphemism and convention. Indeed, many soldiers outright lied about the dangers they faced.[22]

Convention also shaped notions of heroism and sacrifice, not least when families received notice that their boy had met "a heroic death for the fatherland," to cite the standard formula written on the army's condolence card.[23] Occasionally, a nationalist sense of sacrifice also animated the letters of ordinary soldiers. "Today we are going as heroes into battle," wrote a fearless Sargeant Hugo Frick from the Somme to his family on September 29, 1916; the following February, he again reassured his mother, that "if he falls, he will die a beautiful death for the fatherland."[24] Such forthright statements were rare, however. And Frick fell three months later.

More typically, letters registered a steady litany of complaints: that some families sacrificed their sons many times over; that fathers of young children were too often placed on the front lines; or that respite, in the form of leave or vacation, was too seldom granted. Not a few letters decried how officers maltreated enlisted men, requisitioned the best food, and enjoyed too many privileges. There were also the obligatory grumbles about the mail and its surveillance, especially vexing to husbands writing to their wives, and complaints that loved ones wrote too seldom or failed to send cigarettes. Toward the end of the war, vitriolic criticism increased sharply: that ordinary people, especially workers, were being used as cannon fodder; that doctors were maliciously misdiagnosing soldiers to hurry them back to the front; or that, far from leveling class differences, the trenches actually accented them. There was also an incessant clamor about food rations. In the final stages of the war, hunger had become "by far the most important issue in a soldier's life," as one report on troop morale put it.[25]

Letters from the home front, mainly from women, were also preoccupied with hunger. "For us terrible times are beginning, there are no more potatoes," wrote Hedwig Lauth to her husband in the first months of 1917.[26] Caloric averages plummeted precipitously as a food crisis, the dimension of which had not been known for nearly a century, descended on major cities.[27] In some communities, mortality rates shot up by as much as 60 percent, with tuberculosis, dysentery, and other diseases wreaking havoc on civilian populations.[28] By the third year of the war, "the whole thinking is now only concentrated on what we can eat," as Lauth put it.[29] Much of the correspondence concerned the flour, dried vegetables, and biscuits the soldiers included in the aid packages sent from the front. But the letters also revealed startling accounts of domestic revolts, mainly centered on food, and brutally repressed.

Finally, the "burning desire to end this butchery," as one enlisted soldier put it, became ever more audible, and was even evident in published death notices.[30] In the first years of the war, terms such as "fatherland" and "heroic death" animated the obituaries.[31] By 1917, however, another phrase, "sacrifice of the war," entered into the announcements. No higher purpose, no transcendence, the new notices intimated—just the maw of war demanding its due.

IV

No artist struggled as much with the sacrifice war demanded as Käthe Kollwitz. Prior to 1914, she had been widely known for her charcoal sketches of the poor, including a moving series focused on the Peasants' War of 1525 and another, depicted in six consecutive images, of the Silesian Weavers' Revolt of 1844. Stirred by genuine indignation and by a fascination with tragic uprisings, Kollwitz's art had been dynamic, bold, and righteous. The war shattered her artistic confidence, not because she opposed it, but because she struggled to find meaning in it. Although she had been pro-international and antiwar like many other socialists, she had come to draw inspiration from the youth-movement idealism of her younger son, Peter, who thought the materialism of his society shallow and war potentially transformative. When the conflict broke out, Kollwitz, like her son, hoped that the war would midwife a new age with values worth fighting for. But she also grieved, worrying that "the soaring of the spirit will soon be followed by the blackest despair and rejection."[32] She nevertheless helped her son, who in August 1914 was still in school, to get his father's consent to enlist voluntarily.

The first wave of young volunteers fell at rates twice as high as ordinary enlisted men, and that November, Peter Kollwitz was killed at Diksmuide in Belgium. When news of his death reached Berlin, Käthe Kollwitz was consumed by unremitting anguish and wished she had sacrificed her own life instead.

In December, she turned back to her art in the hope of creating something lasting out of loss. "The monument would have Peter's form, lying stretched out, the father at the head, the mother at the feet," she wrote.[33] It was to be dedicated to young volunteers who met a "sacrificial death," and she imagined schoolchildren at the consecration, singing words such as "we come to pray" and "there is no more beautiful death in this world than to be killed by the enemy."[34] In a letter to Hans, her other son, she even promised he would be part of the monument in the event that he also died a heroic death.[35] Obviously, she did not want her other son to fall in battle. However, she struggled with the problem of meaning and was slow to emancipate herself from religious and idealistic ways of thinking. She was also convinced that only when she submerged herself into the world of Peter's idealism could she sculpt a monument adequate for him.

Initially, Käthe Kollwitz's thoughts for the sculpture reflected a mix of Christian and modern ideals of sacrificial patriotism. The granddaughter of a celebrated, though controversial pastor in Königsberg, she was deeply influenced by Christian ideas of duty, and this religious sensibility informed her artistic search for meaning and shaped her thoughts about the monument. She imagined the parents kneeling, hands clasped, over Peter's slain body, as if the ensemble was to be a modern pietà.[36] According to the historian Regina Schulte, Kollwitz even experimented with versions of the sculpture that envisioned Peter as Christ and she as the heavenly mother.[37]

It was not until the late summer of 1916, deep into the slaughter of the Somme, that she began to question this approach. On August 27, she wrote in her journal:

> My untenably contradictory position on the war. How did I come to it? Because Peter sacrificed his life. What I saw so clearly then and what I wanted to preserve in my work now seems to be once more so dubious. . . . Now the war has been going on for two years and five million young men are dead and more than that number again are miserable, their lives wrecked. Is there *anything at all* that can justify that?[38]

She nevertheless believed that "life must be subordinated to an ideal," observing that young German boys, including Peter, had "subordinated their lives to the idea of the love of fatherland"—as had young men in Russia, Britain, and France.[39] Her ideas at this time spiraled in many directions at once. In July 1917, she considered putting a relief of grieving parents at the cemetery gate where Peter was buried, pondering various possible inscriptions for it: "Here lies German youth," or "Here lie Germany's finest young men," or "Here lie the youthful dead," or just "Here lie the young."[40]

V

Kollwitz was hardly alone in her conflicted views. Among artists, the list of those expressing support for the war was long and illustrious. It also reached deep into what came to be the political left. It included the painters Max Beckmann, who experienced the war as a "wonder," a heightened form of life, even as he sketched it, in etchings and woodcuts, with a sharp eye for war's dislocations and utter frightfulness; and Franz Marc, who recorded in his diary that he "felt the deeper meaning, behind the battles, behind every bullet, so strong that the realistic and material completely disappeared."[41] Perhaps more surprising is that Otto Dix, later to be known for jarring depictions of the horror of war, counted among the initial enthusiasts. He volunteered in August 1914, was assigned to an artillery regiment, and became a noncommissioned officer in November of the following year. As his company's MG 08 machine gun fired some 500 rounds a minute, Dix counted among those who killed enemy soldiers in great number. Although commonly thought of as a pacifist, he left little evidence of wartime soul-searching. After extended engagements in Champagne, Flanders, and at the eastern front, Dix voluntarily participated as a shock- or stormtrooper in the final offensive of March 1918, received a neck wound in early August, yet was back at the front at the end of September.[42]

There were, of course, artistic depictions of war that emphasized loss, mainly from women. One thinks of the haunting drawings of bereavement by Käte Lassen and the eerie colored battle lithographs of Katharina Heise.[43] Like Kollwitz, they were caught up in the idealism of the war only to be engulfed by the sorrow of losing sons.[44]

In general, artists neither simply affirmed nor recoiled from the war. If previous wars had engaged artists mainly as official painters or chroniclers of the heroic, the First World War challenged independent artists to render what they felt and saw. With precious few exceptions, they created forms of realism that expressed the energy, excitement, tediousness, and unrelenting brutality of war. It was also true that never before had so many artists met death, or lost loved ones.

Writers of prose and poetry contributed as well to the torrent of war testimonials. According to one estimate, some 15 percent of Germany's writers had signed up for the war voluntarily.[45] Some wrote during the conflict, although most of those who survived published only after the armistice. Between 1918 and 1933, some three hundred "war novels" appeared, most in the late Weimar Republic. During the war, Germans penned a prodigious number of poems of widely varying levels of quality. At the beginning of the conflict, in the late summer and early fall of 1914, the *Berliner Zeitung* received some five hundred poems a day—a popular literary outpouring without precedent in German history, and before which the famous poetic effusions of Prussia's war against Napoleon in 1813 simply paled.[46]

Like ordinary soldiers, Germany's writers, intellectuals, and artists were drawn into the war, and attempted to fathom its meaning. The pattern of support, resistance, and interpretation was by no means simple, however. Neither one's generation, nor profession, nor whether or where one served satisfactorily predicted support or resistance.

Gender was, however, significant. Of the major female intellectuals, only Gertrud Bäumer and Helene Lange, leaders of the women's movement, unequivocally supported the war from start to end. Bäumer especially embraced the conflict's gendered division of labor and, in a famous address in 1914, lauded the male soldier who "at all times finds it sweet and sublime to die for the fatherland."[47] Some middle-class women were more critical. The historian Ricarda Huch—brilliant, long overlooked, and immensely popular in her time—had just published the third and final volume of her prescient *History of the Thirty Years War* (originally entitled *The Great War in Germany*) and in August 1914 distanced herself from the prevailing hysteria. She did, however, think the war would be short and that German arms would swiftly prevail.[48] Thea Sternheim, among the most insightful diarists of the twentieth century, felt the impact of the war from its inception, and retained an ambivalent position.[49] For her part, the Socialist firebrand Rosa Luxemburg refused any and all concessions to the war effort, spending most of the war in prison.

Generational differences also make up part of the pattern of support and resistance, and they were in some cases pronounced. Older male intellectuals tended to support the war for its duration. Of those who in 1914 were roughly forty to sixty years old, a few, like Thomas Mann, were more active in the production of war propaganda. Some, like the modernist poet Richard Dehmel, the influential art critic Julius Meier-Graefe, and the innovative historian Karl Lamprecht, volunteered for active service, for which Lamprecht paid with his life. Others, like the sociologist Max Weber, the theologian Ernst Troeltsch, the renowned historian Friedrich Meinecke, and the political authors Maximilian Harden and Friedrich Naumann, initially supported the war but came to understand that its price would be the democratic reform of Imperial Germany. Finally, some from the older generation opposed the war outright. They included leading lights of the left, such as Karl Liebknecht, Gustav Landauer, and the revisionist Eduard Bernstein, as well as left-liberals, such as the novelist Heinrich Mann and the theater critic Theodor Lessing, whose wartime *History of Making Sense of the Senseless* belongs to Germany's philosophically radical, uncompromisingly anti-historicist, and often forgotten antiwar documents.[50]

Younger male intellectuals were more divided still. The resisters included the physics prodigy Albert Einstein, who joined the pacifist group "New Fatherland" when the war broke out, and the Dadaist poet Hugo Ball, who offered searing, surprisingly realist criticism from exile in Zurich. Other examples were the theater critic Siegfried Jacobsohn, who rebranded his journal *Die Schaubühne* (*The Theater Stage*) in 1918, making it into the critical *Weltbühne* (*World Stage*); and the young Walter Benjamin, who was still studying at the university as the war broke out, working on early sketches of what would later become "The Origins of Baroque Tragedy." But in opposition to this group was a much larger number who enlisted, and then recoiled when the realities of war set in. The most famous of them included the novelists Alfred Döblin, Erich Maria Remarque, Arnold Zweig, and Hermann Hesse, whose wartime letters were especially poignant. There were also a number of exceptional expressionists, like the painter Ernst Ludwig Kirchner and the dramatists Walter Hasenclever and Ernst Toller.

Many intellectuals, ranging from artists to writers to public figures, came to see war as defining modernity. Some, like Ernst Jünger, became nationalists—not during but after the war; others, like Otto Dix, looked back critically at the war. Not all survived. Walter Flex, the author of the best-selling *Wanderer Between Two Worlds*, fell in October 1917, and his book—a silk of inspirational idealism draped over a reality of ennui and death—received much praise, but few imitators.

The war decimated the ranks of expressionists in painting and poetry with particular severity. Prominent among those who perished were the painters August Macke and Franz Marc and, of those who wielded a pen, Ernst Stadler, Gustav Sack, and August Stramm.[51] Exploring new literary and artistic forms, they attempted to apprehend the experience of war without belying its complicated emotional ramifications. They eyed war clearly, not just in what they told, but also in the form of their telling.

In a series of pitiless short poems, August Stramm, for example, eliminated adjectives, adverbs, and interpunctuation in order to echo the sheer frightfulness of war. Composed shortly before his death in September 1915, "Storm Attack," reads:

Aus allen Winkeln gellen	From every corner screams
Fürchte Wollen	fear wanting
Kreisch	Screech
Peitscht	Whips
Das Leben	Life
Vor	For
Sich	Ward
Her	To
Den keuchen Tod	Gasping death
Die Himmel fetzen.	The skies shred.
Blinde schlächert wildum das	Blindly butchers wildly all
Entsetzen.	around the horror.[52]

The first line evokes hesitant, fearful soldiers emerging from their hiding corners and running. Subsequent lines are single words, except the fourth, "life," which in the German original takes a definite article but hardly interrupts the poem's central axis, a word tunnel propelling soldiers forward into inexorable death, spread out in a three-word line, then dispersed across the skies. Then there is a pause, indicated by a period, before the poem spills onto its last line, whose final word is "horror."

Stramm actively participated in the horror. He saw war as a workplace and killing an occupational task. "I want to murder murder [sic] then at least I am one with what is around me," he wrote in a remarkable series of letters to his wife, in which he portrayed himself as a volitionless killing machine. "I murder coldly and incite others coldly, hard, raw," he told her, adding: "I cannot ask why and to what end!"[53]

Others, however, did ask why. As the war mercilessly dragged on, the chasm widened between the purpose of the war, as conceived at home, and its meaning as experienced on the front. "Our soldiers are not dying for the ideas we thrash out on the home front," conceded Max Weber in a speech in the summer of 1916, adding, "one cannot now speak of ideas, and our soldiers cannot now die for them." According to a newspaper report (we no longer have the original), he then asked: "What, then, are they actually dying for?"[54]

Like most scholars, Weber had initially joined in the chorus of war enthusiasm, supporting the German government's war aims and believing that the war would transform his nation's place within Europe and the world. But after the battles of Verdun, the Somme, and Passchendaele, he came to see the futility of it all, and that only a negotiated peace could end the war. He was not alone in this insight. Shared by socialists, liberal politicians, and a wide array of intellectuals, this realization led to the passing of a Reichstag resolution in July 1917 renouncing territorial annexation and calling for the immediate cessation of hostilities.

VI

The hostilities nevertheless continued, and conservatives responded to the Reichstag resolution with the founding, in September 1917, of the German Fatherland Party, whose aim was to agitate for a victorious peace based on extensive territorial demands. Attracting hundreds of thousands of members as if almost overnight, the new political party signaled the public reemergence of radical nationalists imbued with social Darwinist ideas about fighting to the death and ominous plans in the event that Imperial Germany should win the war.

From the very beginning of the war, these radical nationalists had been waiting in the wings for their opportunity. The pan-German leader, Heinrich Class, was one such man. In a memorandum completed in early September 1914, he proposed annexing Belgium and the industrial areas of northern France, seizing the Baltic provinces from Russia, and making Africa "in its northern two-thirds" into a series of German colonies.[55] Exceeding all previous conceptions of Germany as a territorial space, Class's annexationist vision stipulated that Germany expel local populations and turn those who refused to go into helots.[56] In the history of German nationalism, the idea of forcibly moving whole ethnic populations had surfaced before the war, and indeed Class, as we have seen, was one of the few people to put the idea forward. But before the war, expulsion evoked a sense that a dangerous bridge was being crossed.[57] Even during the war, Class still possessed misgivings with regards to Belgium and northern France. The east, though, was altogether different. Class proposed to drive Russia back to its borders before the rise of Peter the Great, while annexing Lithuania, Latvia, and Estonia, and then creating a new Poland situated farther to the east and stretching to the Dnieper River. According to the pan-German leader, such a territorial rearrangement would entail the expulsion and exchange of some

GERMANY AND THE NEW EUROPE

in HEINRICH CLASS'S WAR
AIMS MEMORANDUM *of* 1914

Stockholm

SWEDEN

DEN-
MARK   Copenhagen

Hamburg

Pskov

Riga

Danzig   Königsberg

Minsk

HOL-
LAND   Berlin   Posnan
Amsterdam   IMPERIAL   Warsaw
              GERMANY
              Leipzig
Cologne   Dresden   POLAND
Brussels
      Trier   Frankfurt   Prague
              Nuremberg
Paris   AUSTRIA-
      Metz   HUNGARY
FRANCE   Munich   Vienna

Zurich SWITZ-
        ERLAND

ITALY

EXPULSONS AND RESETTLEMENTS

**"Ethnic field cleansing"
(approx. 7 mil. people)**
French Speaking Belgians to France
White Russians to Russia
Volga Germans to Baltics
Poles in Germany to Poland
Germans from Poland to Germany
Lithuanians to eastern Poland
Jews to Palestine

seven million people with the effect of creating as "pure as possible national states."[58] Within this ruthless policy of "ethnic field cleansing" (*völkische Feldbereinigung*), as Class called it, the Jews, some one million in his calculation, would be banished either to Russia or to Palestine (where they would live in a Jewish state under Turkish dominion).[59]

German occupation of territory during World War I brought Class's vision in closer proximity to reality than is commonly supposed. By the end of 1916, Germany had already come to occupy an area nearly the size of its prewar territorial holdings, with almost 16 million people under its direct control, and another 3.4 million under a puppet government in Romania.[60] Of its various occupation regimes, the most brutal was Ober Ost, a military government set up by General Erich Ludendorff in 1915 and encompassing Courland, Lithuania, and Białystok-Grodno. Run nearly unfettered as a colonial occupation, Ober Ost imposed "a rigid suffocating order," as one contemporary observed, on close to 3 million people.[61] The German occupiers inventoried local possessions, requisitioned agricultural produce, denuded forests, and conscripted impoverished men and women into work camps, barely feeding them enough to survive. They also combed the countryside for laborers in "regular hunts," as one account of abuses put it.[62]

An unexpected set of events soon made German hegemony in the east a near reality. In the winter of 1916–1917, a struggling Russian army began its hunger-induced dissolution, and the February Revolution, which dethroned the Romanovs, brought the provisional government of Alexander Kerensky to power. Aware of the territorial stakes, Kerensky chose to continue fighting. The German high command responded with a daring and dangerous measure. In a deliberate provocation intended to create domestic unrest, the German army transported a revolutionary by the name of Vladimir Ilyich Lenin in a sealed boxcar from his exile in Switzerland across German territory to Finland Station. His appearance in the Russian capital radicalized the revolution, and his party, soon to be named the Bolsheviks, took power in October 1917. Almost immediately, the Bolsheviks ended Russian participation in what seemed to them an imperialist war.

Urged on by the radical nationalist lobby, Germany took full advantage of the collapsed empire. With the signing of the Treaty of Brest Litovsk on March 3, 1918, the German Empire dramatically expanded its eastern reach, directly annexing territory that stretched to Kaunas in Lithuania, Grodno in White Russia, and Lublin in the southern parts of what would become Poland. More remarkable still was what Germany took away from Russia. It deprived the old czarist empire of a quarter of its population and stripped it of Finland, Estonia, Livonia, Poland, Ukraine, and Crimea. This area, containing Russia's major industrial centers, coal reserves, and roughly a third of its agricultural land, was three times the size of prewar Imperial Germany.[63] Only eighty-five miles now separated German-controlled Narva from St. Petersburg (now renamed Petrograd), while Moscow lay just over three hundred miles from German-held Mogilev. Moreover, anyone looking at a map could see the proximity of Germany and its satellites to the Black and even Caspian Seas, and could even imagine a concentrated German foray into the Middle East. As the ensuing Russian Civil War raged, and the western periphery of its old empire threatened to break away, Germany contemplated, in the words of the historian John Darwin, a "vast reordering of the whole Eurasian landmass."[64] In dimension, the reordering was nothing less than Napoleonic. Even the comparison with the still larger territorial extent of the Third Reich at its zenith is not amiss.

It is worth recalling that in March 1918, when Germany forced a prostrate Russia to accept punishing terms at Brest Litovsk, no one knew how the war would end. Perhaps Germany could move troops to the western front to deliver a knockout blow before the Americans arrived. Perhaps trench warfare would continue to count its gains in yards and meters, even with the Americans fighting on the side of the Allies. Or perhaps, as happened, the infusion of men and matériel from the United States would allow the Allies to overwhelm the Central Powers.

In this context, Germany's decision to erect an imperial presence in the east when it badly needed troops in the west proved catastrophic. Partly, this decision was determined by Germany's heavy-handed occupation, which elicited considerable resistance, especially in Poland and Lithuania. It also reflected the failure of client states, like Ukraine, to requisition the grain necessary to feed its starving citizens and military.[65] Whatever the reason, the German army kept an astonishing fifty divisions in the east, and not a few of those soldiers who were transferred to the west jumped from their transport trains, defected on the spot, or mutinied—according to one estimate, one-tenth of the men transferred to the west abandoned their units.[66]

The situation was hardly better in Flanders Fields, where, beginning in July 1918, thousands of soldiers walked home, got on hospital trains for the lightly wounded, or simply stopped following the orders of their commanders. By late summer, this "hidden military strike," as it has come to be called, had seriously compromised the fighting ability of the western army. Internal memoranda estimated the number of "shirkers" at close to a million, and the estimates of historians—working with letters, journals and memoirs, the records of medical units, and state documents—confirm, at least in dimension, these official guesses.[67] The largest number of men had faked illnesses, delayed returning to the trenches, temporized behind the front lines, and avoided where possible the nets of control stations and military police. Others inflicted wounds on themselves and still others walked into enemy capture. By August 1918, the hidden military strike had become a mass phenomenon, even though censorship kept it from the wider public. The war was lost, and most soldiers just wanted to go home.

VII

As the war continued into its fourth year, a revealing document found its way to the German public. Drafted by the German ambassador to London, the Lichnowsky Memorandum, as it came to be called, showed that Great Britain had gone to the utmost to prevent the outbreak of the war while German military leaders had goaded Austria-Hungary into irresponsible bellicosity.

Käthe Kollwitz interpreted the revelations as showing that the Great War was neither a defensive war nor one fought for higher ideals. It was a betrayal. "That is what changes everything," she wrote in March 1918, when the memorandum was debated in the Reichstag, "the feeling that we were betrayed then, at the beginning."[68] Crestfallen, she now realized that "Peter would still be living had it not been for this terrible betrayal," adding, "Peter and millions, many millions, of other boys. All betrayed."[69] By the beginning of October—extremely late, given that thousands had already abandoned the front and a new civilian government was already in place—she wrote, "Not another day of war when all is lost."[70] Two weeks later, she drafted her first essay against the war—but the Socialist newspaper *Vorwärts* did not publish it. At the end of the month, she wrote a second letter, and this time it was published. Young men still alive might yet be saved, she told the readers of *Vorwärts* on October 30, 1918, and their loss "would be worse and more irreplaceable for Germany than the loss of whole provinces."[71] Shuttling between a national and a European perspective, she was still trying to make sense of the war in terms that made Germany a nobler country. "Germany must make it a point of honor to profit by her hard destiny, to derive inner strength from her defeat, and to face resolutely the tremendous labors that lie before her," she wrote.[72]

She was right that ending the war would bring a prodigious saving of life, and not just in the obvious sense. Even as late as that month, German military leaders were discussing a "battle unto annihilation," in which they projected German casualties as high as 20,000 to 25,000 citizen-soldiers per day over the next six months, or four million dead on the German side alone.[73] Fortunately, Prince Max von Baden, the new civilian leader, along with the Reichstag majority, opposed this draconian plan. And when the German navy decided on its own version of a last apocalyptic battle, sailors in Kiel mutinied and arrested their officers.

VIII

The uprising ended a war already lost and toppled a regime bereft of legitimacy.[74] As General Ludendorff slinked off to Sweden and the Kaiser, who abdicated on November 8, to Holland, revolutionaries established councils of workers and soldiers and proclaimed various versions of a democratic republic. Large crowds occupied public spaces in major and minor cities to discuss political possibilities.[75] Rosa Luxemburg, who had been recently released from jail, hoped to lay "the basis for work with women and for education," for which "we," meaning the Socialists, "are weak"—and indeed days after the revolution broke out, the nascent republic declared equal suffrage for men and women over twenty.[76] Meanwhile, some seven million soldiers were demobilized, with roughly a third of the troops having abandoned their units to return home.[77]

The German Revolution of 1918 shadowed Russia's revolution of the previous year but for a crucial difference. In Russia, the provisional government's decision to continue fighting opened a space for takeover in October by men who had little time for the niceties of democratic procedure. By contrast, the advent of peace granted Germany a reprieve and saved it from descending into a large-scale civil war. Instead, Germany's new Socialist leaders announced a constitutional assembly and set elections, even as the far left, to the dismay of Rosa Luxemburg and Karl Liebknecht, voted to boycott the Constitutional Assembly.[78] The subsequent Spartacus Uprising, which the two fabled leaders opposed, was in full swing when Friedrich Ebert, representing the Council of People's Deputies, appointed Gustav Noske, a Socialist military officer, to restore order. Employing recently demobilized "Free Corps," Noske put a swift end to the revolt, killing at least two hundred revolutionaries, injuring many more, and staining the new republic with political fratricide. In the midst

of this bloodshed, right-wing henchmen murdered Luxemburg and Liebknecht, throwing their corpses into the Landwehr Canal, which flowed
placidly through the center of the capital.

Since the leaders of the new republic believed a constitution could
not be worked out in violent and tumultuous Berlin, they established the
assembly in Goethe and Schiller's tranquil city of Weimar. The new constitution began by proclaiming the nation as sovereign. Article 1 announced
that the state derived its power "from the people"—and in its initial formulation, it read "from the German People."[79] For the first time in German
history, with the brief exception of 1848, the nation was declared the principal ground of state legitimacy. The Weimar Constitution employed the
substantive "*Volk*" eight times and used it as a prefix more than thirty times.

The novelty of this declaration, the nation as sovereign, can hardly
be stressed enough. Since the fall of the Roman Empire, some form of
monarchy or nobility-centered arrangement had been the standard form
of political organization in Europe. In the nineteenth century, large-scale
monarchical empires, with vast tracts of territory, still covered the continent. Imperial Germany had defined itself as an empire for the people,
not a nation-state of the people. The Weimar Republic, as established in
1919, was, by contrast, a sovereign nation-state. The timeline is telling
and important. In the great transition from a world of empires to a world
of nation-states, Germany was not a "late nation," as the political philosopher and sociologist Helmuth Plessner famously argued, but rather
became a de jure nation-state at roughly the halfway mark, when empires
covered slightly less than 50 percent of the earth's landmass.[80] Every bit as
profound as the concurrent Russian Revolution, the nation-state revolution after World War I completely transformed the European continent. It
fractured it into smaller pieces, hardened borders between countries, and
bound people into sovereign and separate communities. It also created a
world where nationality counted, and national belonging mattered, especially for minorities outside the national community from which the state
now derived legitimacy.

This was because just as nation-states granted rights, they could also
take them away. Article 48 of the Weimar Constitution gave the President
the power to restore order, "if necessary with the help of the armed forces,"
when "public security and order were significantly disturbed or endan-

gered." It also allowed the president to temporarily suspend guaranteed rights, such as the inviolability of person and home, the right to privacy in communication, freedom of speech, expression, assembly, and association, and the right to vote in a free election. The emergency powers provision, as it was termed, proved fateful. In the Republic's second year, 1920, the Socialist-led coalition of political parties unequivocally committed to the new republic failed to win a majority in a free election, and the Socialists, as democratic ethos requires, handed over power to political parties whose commitment to democracy was less secure. Thereafter, governing coalitions came and went at a dizzying pace, changing some twenty times, with the average duration of a government less than eight months.[81] The President—elected by popular vote but intended, much like the Kaiser, to be above the party fray—allowed the chancellor to govern by constitutionally granted emergency decree, intermittently between 1920 and 1924, and continually after March 1930.[82]

IX

As a result of the deliberations of the peace conference at Versailles, Germany's actual contours changed. The victorious Allies stripped Germany of 13 percent of its prewar continental territory and 10 percent of its population. In the west, France regained Alsace and Lorraine and took the Saar (until 1935, when citizens could decide in a plebiscite), and Belgium received the German-speaking districts of Eupen and Malmédy. In the north, Denmark recovered parts of Schleswig and Poland received a corridor of land carved into the former district of West Prussia, so that it could have access to the Baltic Sea.[83] In the east, Poland also received Posen and parts of Silesia, while Danzig was made into a free city under the auspices of the League of Nations. Finally, in the south, although Austria hoped for unity with Germany, the victorious powers at Versailles disallowed it.

Collectively, these proved to be the most significant changes to the shape of Germany since the Austrian exit from the German Confederation in 1866. One consequence was that a large number of German speakers—some 20 million—now lived just outside German borders, and would later constitute a significant breeding ground for aggressive nationalists.[84] The Treaty of Versailles also reduced the size of the German army to 100,000 men, of whom only 4000 could serve as officers; it scuttled the navy and banned the construction of an air force; it stripped Germany of overseas colonies; and it issued the infamous Article 231, the War Guilt Clause, which mainly served to justify the imposition of a financially crippling indemnity.

The Versailles *"Diktat"* gave the otherwise spent and exhausted ideology of nationalism new life. Major politicians, even of the left, refused to sign the treaty, while on the right, Versailles fanned fantasies of revenge and fueled the *Dolchstoßlegende*, the myth that Germany had been stabbed in the back by revolutionaries, Jews, and democrats.

Making matters worse, political violence marred the streets.[85] The sheer litany of bloody conflict was daunting—from the Spartacus Uprising of January 1919, in which Luxemburg, Liebknecht, and as many as 200 others were viciously murdered; to the March general strike two months later, which in some estimates led to the death of 1200 workers in Berlin; and to the revolutionary uprising in Munich in May, put down brutally by the Bavarian army with a death toll close to 1000 people. There was also the Independent Socialist demonstration in front of the Reichstag in January 1920, in which the Prussian security forces, in a rain of bullets, killed 42 people and wounded more than 100, followed by the right-wing Kapp Putsch of March 1920, and the historically unprecedented protest of 12 million workers who struck against it. The violence seemed to see no end. A senseless Communist uprising shattered the peace in middle Germany in March 1921, and some 200 workers died in the fighting. And as this turmoil threatened to spread, violence devastated the east. Germany's provisional army killed roughly 2500 Poles in the First Silesian Uprising in August 1919, nearly 50 during the Second Silesian Uprising almost a year later, and some 3000 during the Third Silesian Uprising, occasioned by a plebiscite in May 1921.

The first years of the Weimar Republic were deadlier than anything Germans had experienced in modern-era peacetime, likely surpassing even the fatalities in the German Confederation during the Revolution of 1848.[86] In the second half of the nineteenth century and the early years of the twentieth century, Germany had been spared revolutionary unrest— unlike France, which had witnessed a massacre of its own citizens in the Paris Commune in 1871, or Russia, which had experienced a massive and deadly uprising in 1905, or even Spain, which had actually fought a series of bloody civil wars. Just as large-scale war had been outside the lived experience of Germans before 1914, domestic violence during peacetime was outside their experience as well. Moreover, the Republic was rife, as Germany had never been before, with instances of individual political violence. Emil Gumbel, a mathematician and political activist, analyzed 354 cases of political killings from the right, and 22 from the left, demonstrating that the courts had a blind eye to right-wing murder.[87] The major political assassinations were in any case all on one side of the ledger; they included, most prominently, Hugo Haase, the chair of the Independent Socialists, in October 1919; Matthias Erzberger, leader of the Catholic Center Party and the man who had signed the armistice ending World War I, in August 1921; and Walther Rathenau, the farsighted, German-Jewish foreign minister, in June 1922.

However, the most dangerous threat to the Republic was still to come. In the course of the war, the German mark had lost nearly half its value, and during the first years of Weimar it tumbled further still. The inflationary trend—advocated by German businesses to weaken the power of organized labor and by the government so it could pay cheaper reparations—worsened in the winter of 1919–1920, went into free fall in the autumn of 1921, and took on catastrophic dimensions in the second half of 1922, collapsing, by the end of the year, to 7500 marks to the dollar.[88] When Germany defaulted on reparations payments, French and Belgian troops occupied the Ruhr, the heartland of German industry, leaving the government no recourse but to call out passive resistance to the occupation. Initially a hugely popular measure, passive resistance sent a powerful pulse of nationalism through the young republic. At the same time, the currency, following nearly a decade of depreciation, became essentially worthless, raising the runaway inflation of 1922 to the hyperinflation of the fall of 1923. Germans—the images are now iconic—carried wheelbarrows of money to buy essential foods and stuffed worthless million-mark bills into their heating stoves. Hobbesian chaos accompanied the currency free fall: Communist uprisings in Saxony, Thuringia, and Hamburg; deadly encounters with occupation forces in the Ruhr; anti-Semitic riots in the Scheunenviertel of Berlin; and the threat of secession in the Rhineland. There was also an attempted putsch in Munich, with a planned march on Berlin, on November 9. When the putsch was eventually put down, its incendiary anti-Semitic leader, Adolf Hitler, was jailed, if for barely more than a year.

X

During the duress and chaos of early Weimar, Käthe Kollwitz ceased working on Peter's monument and imagined her loss and Germany's loss as somehow alike. "As I kiss Peter's face and bid goodbye to the work," she wrote in her diary on June 25, 1919, "I thought of Germany. For Germany's cause was his cause, and Germany's cause is now lost as my work is lost."[89] Slowly, she turned to other projects.

In the early 1920s, she made a series of woodcuts, called *The War*, and arranged them, as if carefully considered poems, in an album published in 1923. It begins with an image of sacrifice, the mother begrudgingly handing her child over to a demanding god, as once the biblical Abraham had. The active figure is the naked mother while the child, an infant, is defenseless. We might see this image as a psychological manifestation of Kollwitz's feelings of guilt, since she supported Peter's patriotism against her husband, Karl Kollwitz, who wanted to keep Peter away from the front. Another interpretation, however, might suggest that this was the gendered role that sacrificial patriotism assigned to women, and that the mother simply yet tragically gave up her son when asked.

Other prints depict the misery of mourning, including parents bent into one another in inconsolable sorrow, images of grief-stricken widows beyond any earthly redemption, and mothers desperately seeking to protect children.[90] Unlike Kollwitz's earlier efforts, the album suggests no beneficial effects, private or public, of sacrifice. Crucially, the series also includes an image of volunteers: young men, full of enthusiasm, led by the skeleton of death to the beat of a cynical drum. It is the most complicated and unsuccessful of the prints. The idealism of 1914 is inadequately expressed, the manipulation too evident, the element of free choice negated, as the combatants, the first being Peter, were already in the skeleton's clutches.

Perhaps Kollwitz herself sensed the problem. In any case, she turned back to Peter's monument in January 1924, only this time, she thought, it would just be a portrayal of the grieving parents.[91] The boy, who had fallen in the first months of war and whose likeness Kollwitz struggled to render as a universal idea, was now absent. Because there was no purpose to his death, there could be no idealism. This was the real novelty of her sculpture, the reason it represents a break in the tradition.[92] There was no dying for something. There was only dying. And mourning.

XI

In Germany, as in other countries devastated by the war, the circles of mourning were multiple and varying. Between death on the front, and disease and weakened immune systems at home, one in every six German families endured the death of a loved one during the war years.[93] War widows were, as a result, ubiquitous. More than 600,000 women, roughly two-thirds of them less than thirty years of age, had lost their husbands. Most of these young widows had children, typically under six years old, and the overwhelming majority required financial assistance.[94] Pensions were tied to military rank, so that the widows of enlisted soldiers, who made up 98 percent of casualties, received about a third of the income of skilled workers.[95] This was difficult in the best of times, but devastating during the inflation of 1923 and would be again once the depression of 1929 started. Moreover, the tribulations of war widows were not only financial. Only a tiny minority of these women had been able to say final words in the presence of the deceased, and trips to northern France, where nearly 700,000 German soldiers lay buried, were expensive and actively discouraged by the government.[96] What was encouraged, however, was dignified composure, pride in the sacrifice of their sons, and "silent mourning"—*stille Trauer.*[97] For many women, the grief was overwhelming. Two-thirds of the women who lost a husband never married again.[98]

Parents were a still larger group of the grief-stricken. This too constituted a historic reversal. Medical, hygienic, and nutritional advances in the nineteenth century meant that natural death had become associated with the elderly. But during the war, the young died and the old were left to grieve. Fallen soldiers—many of them young men who were unmarried and without children, and with a full life before them—typically resided with their mothers and fathers. The twenty- to twenty-four-year-olds were the worst-hit age group, making up 39.8 percent of all losses.[99] In most cases, the parents never knew how their sons died. With no ritual to consecrate death, threadbare patriotic clichés and stilted fatherland sayings could hardly console. Traditional religious succor helped more. Still, the death of an older child, as the historian Oliver Janz notes, counts in psychological terms as a "maximal trauma," and it can only be assumed that the war left many parents who never again fully knew joy.[100] Some historians link higher rates of elderly mortality, especially in urban areas, to the trauma of losing sons and grandsons.[101]

There remained, of course, the persistent issue of the wounded. Altogether, they approached five million, a horrifically high number. Roughly a third of all the German men who had been mobilized were wounded in the war, and about one in every ten was listed as "permanently disabled."[102] Classification was nevertheless imprecise.[103] One account—based on more than 700,000 veterans—lists 6.2 percent of the men as having lost a leg (and 0.2 percent both legs), 2.9 percent an arm, 0.3 percent their sight, and 0.8 percent their sanity.[104] In another count—drawn from an insurance office in Aachen—15 percent were amputees.[105] The statistics are impersonal and do not convey the degree to which the disfigured and impaired came to haunt the streets, workplaces, and even the art of Weimar Germany.

Yet most wounded war veterans did not want to be "living war memorials," as the perceptive and acerbic writer Joseph Roth called them.[106] In fact, disabled veterans often felt betrayed by a country that seemed to deny them recognition for their losses and respect for their wartime sacrifices. If there was bitterness in the complaint, there was also irony. The Weimar Republic had made veterans' benefits the state's "foremost duty," as Friedrich Ebert, now the president of the Republic, called it. The government used nearly 20 percent of the national budget to pay for war pensions.[107] It had also passed legislation that entitled the disabled to occupational training and free health care for war injuries.[108] Yet civilians often looked at disabled veterans as if they were fortunate beneficiaries of an overgenerous welfare state. Sensing public ingratitude, the disabled took the streets, asking, "Where is the fatherland's thanks?"[109] The wounded veterans demanded public recognition of their sacrifices, less government red tape, and a central place in a national narrative. But as Weimar did not give it to them, the disabled turned into disaffected democrats. Not a few turned to the right.

One kind of disability went dramatically undercounted. This was the incidence of individual psychological trauma. During the war, some 500,000 men were treated for "war neurosis," many with the so-called Kaufmann method, which involved re-creating the traumatic moment with persistent applications of electrical currents in "high voltage lazarets."[110] After the war, German psychiatrists essentially hid the phenomenon. Fearing the costs to the state (one estimate from 1922 put the amount at a billion marks annually), psychiatrists willfully misread a mass psychological condition as a form of individual weakness.[111] By the mid-1920s, the state-employed psychiatrists almost universally opposed compensation for war-induced nervous disorders.[112] Instead, they counseled hardness.[113] Veterans who could not be treated were placed in psychiatric asylums, where, in the course of the euthanasia campaign, the Nazis later murdered some 5000 former soldiers, mostly men diagnosed with schizophrenia.[114]

Finally, the situation of Germany's younger generation of children was also vexed. During the war itself, a great number of children grew up in a "fatherless land."[115] As mothers assumed the double burdens of work and heading the household, children had to take on responsibilities and confront shortages and absences with fortitude. But far from feeling cold or indifferent toward their absent parent, most children idolized their fathers at the front as brave warriors eager to fight and die for country from the purest motives.[116] Young boys especially felt they had something to prove to them. It should come as little surprise, then, that an idealized war captured the imagination of this fledgling generation. Too young to fight but old enough to hope to show their mettle in battle, the boys and later young men of what the historian Detlev Peukert called the "superfluous generation" proved fertile recruiting grounds for paramilitary associations, like the Free Corps, and filled the ranks of extreme parties, especially of the right.[117] There were, moreover, a great many of them. In terms of numbers, young men born between 1900 and 1910 made up a historically unprecedented 23.1 percent of the total male population in 1925.[118] Facing a slumping economy and high unemployment, they were politically socialized in the near civil-war conditions of early Weimar, and they participated in and became inured to the violence that marred its streets.

XII

The futility of "sacrifice for" the nation came to haunt Weimar culture. It backlit the sketches and paintings of Hannah Höch and George Grosz, which depicted killing machines crushing struggling workers while jaundiced old men smoked cigars. It echoed in Bertolt Brecht's verse, especially "The Legend of the Dead Soldier," a poem about a corpse declared k.v. (*kriegsverwendungsfähig*, capable of being used for war) and paraded through city and town before being sent off to die a hero's death. And it informed some of Weimar's greatest films—like *The Cabinet of Dr. Caligari*, *Nosferatu*, and *Metropolis*—which the film scholar Toni Kaes has recently described as "shell shock cinema," movies obsessed with the trauma of mass death but unable to deal with the war directly or treat it with recognizable realism.[119]

When it came to war, realism was by no means an exclusive property of the left, however. And nor was the search for the meaning of sacrifice. The greatest war novel of the Weimar era, Ernst Jünger's *Storm of Steel*, first published in 1920, did not, for example, start as a nationalist work. Instead, it sought to document modern war characterized by masses of men and industrialized killing, and to show that, its anonymity notwithstanding, twentieth-century warfare still opened spaces for the heroic. Dedicated to "the fallen," the book rehearsed Jünger's mantra that there was a higher meaning to the death of soldiers in war—only, in the first edition, he believed that the "meaning" would be revealed in time. The word "Germany" barely appears in the first edition of the book, the word "national" still less. Instead, war seems like a natural event, a volcanic eruption, destroying but also allowing for new creation. It was not until the third edition of the work, the first one to be issued by a larger publishing house, that Jünger sharpened the analysis of the battle-steeled front soldier as presaging the "new man" of a more brutal, ruthless, mechanical age. Against the backdrop of the French occupation of the Ruhr, multiple putsch attempts, secessionist movements, runaway inflation, and his own departure from the Weimar army, the Reichswehr, Jünger underscored— for the first time in the new preface to this new edition of 1924—what the soldiers fought for: "over all that is base, there is one great, clear, and unifying idea: the Fatherland, in its widest sense. For it we are all ready to die. In the passing of time, this is what separates us from others: We are willing to sacrifice."[120]

Without equivocation, Jünger made fatherland the object of sacrifice. In the text, he addressed the question in new ways, writing that before the war, the nation had been an empty concept beclouded by garish symbols. But as he watched his fellow soldiers perish, he knew that they could only have sacrificed for a greater idea. The war had taught them "to stand for something, and, if it had to be, to fall for it, as men ought to," he wrote.[121] To further distinguish this third edition, he added a conclusion with a nationalist appeal. In place of the Kaiser conferring on Jünger the "*Pour le mérite*" medal, thus hewing close to autobiographical truth and patriotism in the old style, Jünger wrote as "we" and declaimed that the front soldiers will ensure that "Germany lives and Germany shall not die."[122] No longer merely backward-looking, the work of memory now gave meaning to the fallen, formed national community in the present, and pointed the way to the nationalist politics of the future. In the second edition of his novel *Fire and Blood* (*Feuer und Blut*), published in 1926, Jünger described the kind of state that the "new nationalism" implied: "Love of fatherland, camaraderie, courage and discipline will be expressed by it," he wrote. "In other words, it has to be organized as national, social, armed, and authoritarian."[123]

A conservative intellectual, Jünger never reached mass audiences with his "new nationalism." Yet his nationalism revealed a persistent question about social cohesion in the new nation-state, and a tendency to see that cohesion in terms akin to the experience of men in arms. The propositions Jünger arrived at in the course of the Weimar Republic expressed core ideas of National Socialism. But they were not the thing itself.

XIII

In April 1931, Käthe Kollwitz finally finished the sculpture she had struggled to create for more than fifteen years. Removing her son altogether, the sculpture features two figures: the mother, arms hugging herself trying to contain the sorrow, her head bent down; and the father, positioned on a separate base, his arms stiff by side as he stares forward with aggrieved

Käthe Kollwitz, *Mourning Parents*, 1931.

stoicism. In early 1932, Kollwitz displayed the figures in an atrium of the National Gallery in Berlin—to mixed reviews. The far left thought them insufficiently critical of the imperialist character of the war, while the nationalist right deemed them unpatriotic. That July, just seven months before the Nazi seizure of power, Kollwitz installed *Mourning Parents* at the Roggevelde Cemetery in Flanders, where Peter and hundreds of German war dead lay buried, and not far from them the graves of countless British and Belgian soldiers. In the end, she represented Peter in the only form she could, as an absence. And she embraced him in the only way she knew how, as a grieving mother. "I stood in front of the woman, saw her—my own—face, cried, and stroked her cheeks," Kollwitz would note in her diary.[124]

CHAPTER 11

SACRIFICE OF

c. 1933–1941

*The problem, the personal problem, was not what
our enemies did but what our friends did.*

—HANNAH ARENDT

W HILE RECUPERATING IN A POMERANIAN MILITARY HOSPITAL, Corporal Adolf Hitler overheard fellow comrades speak of the perfidious November criminals. As the Revolution of 1918 raged, and Hitler faced the possibility of permanent blindness due to a gas attack, he made a decision that would change his life and the historical destiny of his country. He resolved to go into politics.

This was Hitler's story about himself. The evidence does not support it. Instead, as recent research shows, Hitler was in desperate straits during the turbulence that marked early Weimar, and only his demobilization unit kept him from falling into complete and utter penury. As an artist he had been a failure, as an architect he had promise but did not get far, and as a soldier, he was actually only a dispatch runner. Moreover, his regimental comrades, far from lauding his bravery, described him as an *"Etappensch-wein"* (literally, a rear area pig) who was exceedingly covetous of military distinctions and constantly badgered his superiors, one of whom was Jewish, in order to get them.[1] At the end of the calamitous war, Hitler was no doubt disappointed about the fall of the Empire and the abdication of the Kaiser. But these events did not keep him, as it did others, from briefly working for Kurt Eisner's revolutionary government in Munich, and even putting himself up for election as his military unit's representative in the

Republic of Councils (he came in second).[2] Then, after the collapse of the leftist regime, Hitler was transferred to a new regiment, the Bavarian Reichswehr Group Commando No. 4, which was to watch, inform on, and reeducate the army. In these tasks, Hitler succeeded, and it was the first genuine success of his life. Moreover, he was particularly successful in one aspect of this new existence: that of giving speeches.[3]

Hitler became foremost an orator with a keen sense for telling his audience what they wanted to hear. And his first audience was the radically truncated army, the Reichswehr, reduced from 500,000 to 100,000 men, making it smaller than the new army of Poland, or the fighting force of tiny Belgium. Brimming with resentment, bursting with fantasies of revenge, the young men of the Reichswehr became convinced of Communist treachery and the role of Jews in stabbing Germany in the back. And it is, in fact, from a report on a speech to these disgruntled soldiers, which Hitler delivered on August 25, 1919, that we have the first unequivocal evidence of his racial anti-Semitism.[4]

Hitler, it seems, did not develop this form of anti-Semitism before or even during the war. Instead, new research suggests that this racial anti-Semitism emerged in the venomous echo chambers of a postwar radical nationalist milieu in the Munich of the Weimar Republic. In its precise blueprint, it first appears in a letter of Adolf Gemlich, who was also employed in reeducating soldiers, from September 16, 1919.

In this letter, Hitler insisted that there is anti-Semitism based on emotion and anti-Semitism based on facts, and first among the facts is that "Jewry is absolutely a race and not a religious association."[5] By race, Hitler meant nationality determined by what he imagined to be immutable genetic characteristics. Jews have lived among Germans "as a non-German, alien race which neither wishes to nor is able to sacrifice its racial character," Hitler averred, even as they "possess all the political rights we do."[6] The first object of a rational anti-Semitic policy must, therefore, "lead to the systematic legal combating and eliminating of all privileges of the Jews."[7] Thus, Hitler already conceived of a program in which Jews would be subject to so-called exceptional laws (laws that apply to one group only). In addition, he wrote of an "ultimate objective."[8] In the letter to Gemlich, he called it "the irrevocable removal of the Jews in general."[9]

Hitler developed his radical nationalist ideas, and the racial anti-

Semitism on which they rested, in the course of hundreds of speeches he delivered between 1920 and 1923. He then explicated these ideas in the first volume of *Mein Kampf*, written in 1924 in the "comfortable hotel" of Landsberg Prison, where he was incarcerated after the abortive Beer Hall Putsch of November 9, 1923, and in *Mein Kampf*'s second volume, written mainly in Obersalzburg in 1926.

Hitler began with a truism: "The domestic mouse pairs with the domestic mouse, the wolf with the wolf, and so on."[10] He then proceeded to apply it not to different animal species, but what he claimed were genetically distinct populations of individuals, which he called races, within the same species. To this conceptual error he added an additional falsehood: namely, that nature will punish any variation of racial purity with weakness, for when higher beings, as he called them, bred with lower ones, reduced resistance to disease and loss of fertility would result.[11] As the Germans were the higher race and Jews the lower, it followed in Hitler's twisted logic that inbreeding or mixing was the principal cause of German decline, which only the physical removal of Jews could arrest.

Hitler wrote *Mein Kampf* primarily for his radical nationalist base. The initial print run of the first edition of volume one, published in July 1925, was a modest 10,000 copies. It sold out in a few months, and a second printing was needed. The second volume, published in December 1926, did less well; it took two years for a second printing to appear in 1929 (It would not be until 1930 that the two volumes would be published together in a less expensive popular edition).[12] Mainly, he wrote the book to reassert his claim to lead the nationalist right. Reassuring his base after the ill-conceived Beer Hall Putsch of 1923, Hitler essentially put together a manual showing the way forward, with himself at the center. This is why he stressed the power of the spoken over the printed word, announced the importance of propaganda for manipulating the masses, and offered ever more grandiose visions of German destiny.[13] He was ranting to his base, not speaking to the nation as a whole.

Yet when the two volumes of *Mein Kampf* came onto the market, Hitler's aggressive poses stood in awkward contrast to the actual impotence of Hitler and the National Socialists. In the Reichstag election of December 1924, the Nazis barely received 3 percent of the vote, and for the next five years, they would do no better.

340 || GERMANY: A NATION IN ITS TIME

II

As the modest initial sales of *Mein Kampf* suggested, there was nothing inevitable about the rise of National Socialism. However, the rise of the Nazis was part of a larger drift to authoritarianism and radical nationalism that came to define European politics in the interwar years. According to one count, twenty-six of twenty-eight European countries were parliamentary democracies in 1920—yet by 1938, thirteen had become authoritarian regimes.[14] In roughly the same period, according to another count, sixteen right-wing coups occurred, dramatically altering the political map of the continent.[15] Of those countries that remained democratic, all but two, Czechoslovakia and Switzerland, belonged to the comparatively rich northwestern Atlantic rim of Europe. Of those that fell, every country except Germany was in the relatively poor east and south.[16]

Of the countries that turned away from democracy, Germany was the greatest power, with the most educated population and the most dynamic economy. Moreover, its new nationalism, poisoned by social Darwinist racial theories, enjoyed higher levels of popular support than anywhere else in Europe, outstripping the Iron Guard of Romania, the second most popular radical nationalist party, by a margin of two votes to one.[17] The National Socialists, it is true, never won a majority of the votes in a free election. But the German political system did not require this—just as in the United States the final tally of the popular vote is immaterial to the election for the presidency. The Nazis did, however, receive the second highest voter tally in the Weimar Republic's brief history when, in June 1932, they captured 37.3 percent of the vote. They also drew support from a wide array of social classes. Ranging from the working classes, especially skilled workers, to white-collar workers, Nazi voters also included the solid bourgeoisie and a significant percentage of Germany's upper class. While polling better among Protestants than Catholics, the Nazis nevertheless bridged religious divides more successfully than any other party. Women, who were scarcely represented in the Nazi Party's various organizations, voted for Hitler in nearly the same proportion as men, while students supported the National Socialists in overwhelming numbers.[18]

Like other radical nationalist parties, most of whom flourished among

This National Socialist propaganda poster reads, "National Socialist / Or the Sacrifices Were in Vain."

the vanquished of World War I, the Nazis appealed to frustrated nationalism, and to the prevalent desire to recapture Germany's status as a great power. They also appealed to militarism, although not of the old kind. The Nazis glorified the unheralded commoner who had fought on the front line and given his life to the fatherland, not the generals embodied in the stone monuments of Imperial Germany. They also reveled in the myth of the front generation, imagining soldiers who had been steeled by the experience of war and who emerged with deeper insight into the true meaning of modern life. Finally, the Nazis underscored the personal dimension of the sacrifice, suggesting that only they understood that without Germany's return to great power status, the sacrifices of so many young men would have been in vain.

The allure of National Socialism was not just ideological, however. The Nazis also exploited middle-class fears of socialism, rural hopes for agricultural subsidies, and lower-middle-class anxieties about falling further down the social ladder. Like a hall of shifting mirrors, Nazi electoral appeals seemed to allow each group to see its own interests reflected in what the Nazis said they stood for. In the context of the Great Depression, with unemployment hovering around 30 percent, the Nazis offered hope, perhaps more than any other party. To a divided and immobilized society without a compass, they radiated future, authenticity, and power.

Finally, National Socialists incorporated a virulent brand of anti-Semitism into their campaigning. Leaving little doubt that they believed Germans and Jews were locked in an existential struggle, the Nazis proclaimed that if Germany were to reclaim its status as a great nation, it would have to marginalize and ultimately get rid of the Jews. By approving, condoning, or ignoring the brutality of the movement's hatred of Jews, a wide sample of Nazi voters signaled their willingness to accept this conception of Germany, including the degraded place to which the Nazis intended to consign the Jews. Outside of those who shared the vitriolic anti-Semitism of the Nazis, many Germans would come to believe that there was, indeed, as the Nazis never tired of explaining, a "Jewish question."

III

The Nazi seizure of power on January 30, 1933, is one of the most minutely documented events of modern German history, but it was, in a narrow sense, a transition from one authoritarian regime to another. For more than two years, the Weimar Republic had already been governed in an authoritarian fashion. The three previous chancellors—Heinrich Brüning, Kurt Schleicher, and Franz von Pappen—had all governed through the emergency decrees stipulated in Article 48 of the Weimar Constitution, and they were thus essentially shielded from the pressures of a democratically elected Reichstag. Moreover, the majority of the German people had come to feel indifferent about the Republic's slow slide into authoritarian rule. In the elections of July 1932, the two explicitly antidemocratic parties—the Communists and the Nazis—received more than 50 percent of the votes. In this sense, Hitler did not put an end to Weimar: it had effectively committed suicide already.

Still, the death of democracy and the descent into dictatorship are two different things, and the Nazi takeover is an object lesson in what can happen when democracies allow those who intend to subvert it to assume power. January 30, 1933, may have marked a transition from one authoritarian regime to the next, but that night Hitler's followers, carrying torches and marching on the street, announced a new brand of politics based on terror and lawlessness.

The new politics began in earnest a month later, when the Reichstag went up in flames, and the Nazis used the conflagration as justification for a new, and more permanent, emergency decree. The so-called Enabling Act, valid for four years, essentially allowed Hitler to govern without the Reichstag and to set aside any number of basic rights and legal protections. Wasting no time, the Nazis proceeded to arrest thousands of Communists, whom they blamed for the fire, as well as ransack the Communist Party headquarters and suppress Communist newspapers.

Virtually no one, outside the Communists and some Social Democrats, protested. On the contrary, Hitler held an election soon after, on March 5, 1933, in which the Nazis won 43.9 percent of the vote. It was not the overwhelming majority the new chancellor had hoped for. The votes of the Socialist and the Catholic Center parties held firm. However, a mere six weeks after the seizure of power, the liberal, moderate nationalist vote completely migrated to the Nazi camp. The crackdown on the left, it seems, was welcomed. And in the absence of public protest, this consensus gave Hitler tacit permission to dismantle what remained of Weimar's threadbare democratic institutions. That July 14, less than six months after the Nazi seizure of power, Hitler banned all parties save for the National Socialists themselves.

The German descent into dictatorship was marked by brutality, mainly directed at the left and applauded by the right. Only days after the seizure of power, Hermann Göring, the new minister of the interior, deputized as an auxiliary police force some 50,000 men from the SA (Sturmabteilung, or stormtroopers), the SS (Schutzstaffel, or Protection Squad) and the Stahlhelm (Steel Helmet, a right-wing organization of former front soldiers), and in the coming months and years, these men would be responsible for a horrific amount of unofficial violence.

Moreover, in the first year, the Nazis arrested, detained, and imprisoned some 200,000 people. This fact immediately distinguished Nazi Germany from other fascist countries, like Italy, and from populist regimes, like Poland, though not from the Stalinist Soviet Union, whose Gulag harbored a much larger population of political and class "enemies."[19] Like the

Communist behemoth to its east, Nazi Germany quickly became a carceral state; it expanded police prefects and ordinary jails, converted workhouses into holding prisons, and created all manner of detention centers. In Berlin, the Nazis set up some 170 camps alone, according to the historian Niko-laus Wachsmann.[20] Members of the SA and SS, men who had typically not fought in World War I but only in the internecine strife of Weimar, served as guards and beat and brutalized prisoners, most of whom were Commu-nists and Socialists. In the early years of the regime, the Nazis arrested few foreigners, few women, and few Jews, except in their capacity as mem-bers of left-wing groups. Because the camps were extremely brutal places, knowledge about the cruelties that occurred behind their walls seeped out, albeit selectively. More people knew about the abuses in the cities, where most camps were set up, than in the countryside; the working classes knew more than the middle classes, who often dismissed news of beatings and torture as Communist propaganda; and Germans on the left knew more than those on the right, if only because released prisoners talked.

The camps were the most extreme, violent, and visible mechanism of repression. Less spectacular yet more public were the executive decrees and discriminatory laws, especially those targeting Jews. A monthly time line of these discriminatory laws—drawn from the most extensive (if still far from complete) corpus of anti-Semitic ordinances, laws, and decrees—shows that during the first six months of Nazi rule, there was a veritable onslaught of measures, largely focused on the expulsion of Jews from posi-tions in federal and state bureaucracies. The most important of these was the Law for the Restoration of the Professional Civil Service, which dis-missed Communists and Jews from their positions as judges, professors, and teachers in the employ of the state. Especially for Jews with advanced education, the measure was devastating. Victor Klemperer, a professor of French literature and one of Germany's most insightful diarists during these years, missed the worst of it because the law provided exemptions for former front soldiers.[21] But others were hit very hard. Roughly half of all state-appointed Jewish judges and prosecutors lost their jobs overnight, as did a third of all Jewish lawyers.[22] Moreover, the onslaught did not remain confined to the halls of federal and state governments. There were also local anti-Semitic ordinances, not counted in the timeline below. Among the hundreds of such ordinances, one finds such a decree as in Cologne that denied Jewish athletes access to public sport arenas, or an ordinance in Frankfurt am Main stating that Jewish-owned stands could not display Christian symbols during Christmas.[23] Nongovernmental entities issued their own exclusionary statutes. Needing little encouragement, professional organizations, such as the German pharmacists and the German lawyers, introduced "Aryan" paragraphs into the requirements for membership. So too did all varieties of social clubs, like the Singers' Union and the Pan-German Chess Club.[24]

The historical time line, as seen below, shows peaks and ebbs of anti-Semitic legislation. Just as accelerations—in early 1933, late 1935, and throughout 1938—reveal intense phases of persecution, there were slower periods that sent mixed signals. The first round of anti-Semitic persecution was, for example, hardly an unqualified success.[25] During the government-sponsored boycott of Jewish businesses in April 1933, many non-Jewish Germans continued to shop at Jewish stores, even going out of their way to patronize shops menacingly guarded by paramilitary thugs.[26] Nor was the ultimate trajectory of Nazi policy self-evident. In November 1933, a report compiled for the Württemberg Ministry of the Interior speculated about how the Nazi government in Berlin would approach the "Jewish complex." The author dismissed the possibility of pogroms and what he described

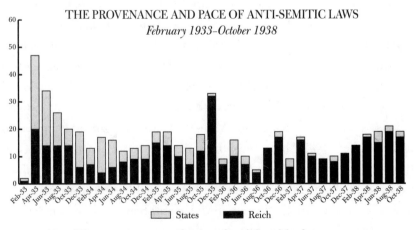

The provenance and pace of anti-Semitic decrees,
February 1933–October 1938 (according to the inventory in
Joseph Walk, *Das Sonderrecht für die Juden
im NS Staat*, 2nd ed.).

as transplantations to other countries, and he assumed the Jews would be consigned to a "special form of civic existence similar to that of a national minority."[27] Part of the reason he thought this likely was that exclusionary laws were hardly unprecedented, and other countries, like the United States, had them as well. In any case, by the last quarter of 1933, the pace of anti-Semitic legislation had indeed slowed down, and for a brief period, the regime's attention seemed to lie elsewhere.[28]

On January 30, 1934, Hitler announced he would triple the size of the army; five months later, he ordered the slaughter of hundreds of regime supporters, including Ernst Röhm, his main rival and chief of the Nazi stormtroopers, and Gregor Strasser, a prominent Nazi advocate for a more thoroughgoing social revolution. The Night of Long Knives, as this purge of June 30 to July 2 is called, was reassuring to army leaders, who saw the stormtroopers as a growing threat to its monopoly on the state's legitimate use of force, and to conservatives who feared the anticapitalist, populist wing of the Nazis. On August 2, 1934, the day after Paul von Hindenburg, the aged president, World War I hero, and the very embodiment of old monarchical Germany, passed away, Hitler united the offices of chancellor and president in his person, becoming the de jure as well as the de facto supreme figure of the Third Reich.

Yet Hitler remained beholden to the adulation of his radical nationalist supporters. One result, especially evident in the first years of his rule, was the constant back and forth between his attempt to consolidate more power and the pressing demands of his anti-Semitic base. In 1934, as he focused on rearmament and curbing the influence of the SA, Nazi activists became increasingly impatient that Hitler seemed to be doing so little to address the "Jewish question." Their discontent soon took the form of "individual actions," which, as Interior Minister Hermann Göring complained in December 1934, "have recently multiplied to an exceptional extent throughout the Reich."[29] In fact, these actions were still mostly confined to Hesse, an area with a history of anti-Semitic politics dating to the 1880s, and to Franconia, another region in which anti-Semitic rivers ran deep.

What began in a small cluster of communities in Hesse and Franconia was soon replicated in multiple towns and cities, often taking the form of public anti-Semitic demonstrations, locally staged boycotts, and wanton desecration of synagogues. The actions were often downright frightening.

In the Hessian town of Wehrda, not far from Marburg, a band of nearly twenty masked people armed with clubs barged into the synagogue on March 22, 1935, and bludgeoned a group of praying Jewish men, injuring a number of them critically.[30] In Breslau, the SA marauded through the city carrying posters with the names and addresses of German women who were involved with Jewish men, while in Karl Marx's hometown of Trier, according to a June 1935 report, people smeared Jewish "windows and store fronts with human excrement."[31] Traveling through Germany in the summer of 1935, an astonished Virginia Woolf noted with dismay that in some areas, "every village had a painted sign, 'Jews are not wanted here.' "[32]

The anti-Semitic actions, which spiked dramatically in 1935, elicited few public expressions of solidarity with Jews. It is true that Gestapo reports still made occasional reference to the lack of support for anti-Jewish measures, especially in Catholic areas, and noted with chagrin that in some rural communities, Christians still attended Jewish funerals.[33] There were also individual shows of support—a visit to the house of a Jewish neighbor, or someone crossing the street to talk to an acquaintance. In Germany, Jews quickly learned to distinguish between non-Jews who went out of their way to shake hands or buy at Jewish stores and those who were deliberately unkind. By 1935, however, fewer and fewer vestiges of elementary kindness and civility could be discerned.

Instead, violence, both real and symbolic, polarized communities, sharpened separation, and forced people to take sides. It had the desired effect of separating Jews from local communities. The Berlin rabbi Joachim Prinz called this state of affairs a new kind of ghetto—different than the medieval one, because Jews now felt completely isolated on the open streets and in the busy market squares. "The fate of Jews is," he stated in a lecture delivered in April 1935, "to be neighborless."[34]

IV

This powerful anti-Semitic surge "from below," as one historian calls what were literally hundreds of "individual actions," activated Hitler's radical nationalist base, made neighbors into strangers, and pushed leading Nazis in Berlin to consider reformulating, with Hitler's approval, the legal codification of German national citizenship.[35] The Nuremberg Laws of September 1935 were the outcome.

The first Nuremberg Law defined citizenship in terms of "racially related blood" and made non-Jewish Germans "the sole bearer of full political rights" (*Staatsbürger*), while stripping Jewish Germans of their status as Reich citizens and degrading them to second-class "members of the state" (*Staatsangehörige*).[36] The second Nuremberg Law criminalized extramarital intercourse and forbade marriages "between Jews and nationals of German blood"—no small intervention considering that roughly a quarter of Jewish men and 16 percent of Jewish women were married to Christians.[37] Indeed, precisely because of this high rate of intermarriage, the framers of the Nuremberg Laws had to admit distinctions, and for this they looked to the United States, "the global leader," as one scholar has recently called it, "of miscegenation law."[38] Noting that the American "one-drop rule" was too extreme (it stated that anyone with one "non-white" ancestor was black), radical Nazi jurists nevertheless wanted a definition akin to "one quarter colored," which would make a person with one Jewish grandparent Jewish in the eyes of the law. Ultimately, the makers of the Nuremberg Laws compromised and settled, in the main, on three Jewish grandparents, and added two categories of *Mischlinge*—Jews with two grandparents (first degree) or with one grandparent (second degree).

The Nuremberg Laws thus produced two kinds of laws, one that drew its legitimacy from the national community, the other that defined the diminished legal status of outsiders. As the distinguished German-Jewish jurist Ernst Fraenkel observed in 1941: "The conception that the community is the sole source of law corresponds with the teaching that there can be no law outside the community"—an understanding, he further noted, that creates a duality between "peace, order, and law" for those inside, and "power, struggle, and destruction" for those outside.[39]

The laws also shaped how non-Jewish Germans documented national identity. If Germans wanted to marry, they had to prove their so-called Aryan status to a justice of the peace, much as those who wanted to join the Nazi Party had to document non-Jewish lineage. A genuine craze for genealogical research resulted, one that went far beyond what the law required. Germans eagerly bought up literally millions of "ancestor passports," small, inexpensive booklets in which to fill out the names and vital information of one's family tree. Almost overnight, genealogy became one of the most popular pastimes of the Third Reich, as virtually every middle-class household raced to document their bloodlines in these passports, while archivists everywhere worked hard to help non-Jewish Germans prove their racial purity. In the new legal and mental templates, Germans began to conceive of nationality as something one could calculate in fractions and percentages, and marital ties to Jews in terms of racial defilement.[40] Indeed, denunciations for race defilement poured forth the moment the Nazis criminalized intercourse between Christians and Jews. In Berlin, they soared from 35 denunciations in 1935 to 1242 in 1936.[41]

V

In the years subsequent to the promulgation of the Nuremberg Laws, a surprising number of prominent or soon-to-be prominent writers traveled to the Third Reich. For example, Albert Camus, then still a young student, came to Germany with his new wife in July 1936. He still admired the "little Gothic cemetery of Bautzen" and the "long, relentless, barren plains of Silesia," but the student, who would become one of the most astute observers of the human predicament in the age of extremes, generally felt the "dizziness of those who have gazed too long into a bottomless pit."[42] Thomas Wolfe, the American author of the dazzling semiautobiographical *Look Homeward, Angel*, spent the summer of 1936 in Berlin. Germany was "the geography of my heart's desire," Wolfe wrote. Yet after he witnessed the Gestapo apprehending a Jewish man on a train, he was happy to be "out," as he put it in his novella *I Have a Thing to Tell You*.[43] For many writers, it was, in fact, the noisome air of a society based on persecution that shocked them.

Among the most trenchant commentators was W. E. B. Du Bois, the author of *The Souls of Black Folk* and most recently of a scathing historical indictment entitled *Black Reconstruction in America*. Departing in early June 1936, from New York on the not yet infamous MS *St. Louis*, Du Bois crossed the Atlantic to the English port city of Southampton, and from there traveled, via London and Brussels, to Berlin, which he reached in the early hours of July 1. Ostensibly there to research industrial organizations and institutions of higher education, and to draw lessons for African-Americans, Du Bois also went to Hitler's Germany in order to see what had changed from his visit thirty years earlier.[44]

Du Bois reported a vast and deep consensus behind the Führer, and pegged Hitler's support at 90 percent of the population—certainly an exaggeration, but a telling one nevertheless.[45] After a lost war, a failed revolution, a tumultuous experiment with democracy, and repeated bouts of economic calamity, the fervent German desire, Du Bois believed, was for order.[46] A brilliant sociologist, he also emphasized Hitler's ability to satisfy the workers with what he called "the Russian method": low unemployment, homes, roads, public health, old-age insurance, and state-sponsored vacations.[47] It was however propaganda that enabled Hitler to weave a new philosophy into German consciousness, with the superiority of the German race, the menace of the Jews, the threat of communism, and the necessity of world empire being its ideological mainstays. "The majority of the German people believe these propositions," Du Bois claimed, even as they hated certain aspects of Nazi rule, especially its spying and the loss of liberty.[48]

Despite his liberal philosophy and his own experience with subjugation, Du Bois still counted Germany as one of the few countries in the modern world—France and to a lesser extent England were the others—where "colored citizens are appearing as citizens with equal rights at least on certain occasions."[49] In a widely discussed and criticized newspaper article, he insisted that he had "been treated with uniform courtesy and consideration" and that "it would have been impossible for me to have spent a similarly long time in any part of the United States."[50] He did note that Nazi anti-Semitism constituted an example of a public campaign of prejudice that "surpasses in vindictive cruelty and public insult anything I have ever seen, and I have seen much."[51] He even compared it to "such horrors as the Spanish Inquisition and the African Slave Trade."[52] Nevertheless, Du Bois retained an essentially positive impression of a society that had embraced him in the 1890s, and, it seemed, did so again. "I cannot get over the continual surprise of being treated like a human being," he wrote toward the end of his report on his five months in Nazi Germany.[53] Perhaps he felt that the record of his own country—where African-Americans were lynched and their basic rights denied—was still worse.

VI

While the Nuremberg Laws had redefined the very meaning of the terms "German" and "Jew," the pogrom of November 1938 irrevocably altered German-Jewish relations. A changed diplomatic context—the Anschluss with Austria in March and the invasion of the Sudetenland in the same month—set the stage. When foreign governments, most prominently Neville Chamberlain's Britain, reacted tepidly to Hitler's aggression against Czechoslovakia, the Nazis realized they could act with impunity toward their own citizens. In late October, the Nazis actually deported some 17,000 Polish Jews, sending the "expellees," as one survivor, Jacob Littner, called his group, into a future in which "most of us only vaguely comprehended what was in store."[54] By this time, individual acts of violence against Jews in the small cities and towns of central and southern Germany had noticeably increased. Just as widespread anti-Semitic acts in 1935 had brought about the promulgation of the Nuremberg Laws, this new spike in anti-Semitic violence foreshadowed the destructive pogrom of the second week of November.[55]

On November 7, Herschel Grynszpan, a young Polish Jew whose parents had recently been deported, shot Ernst vom Rath, a German attaché in Paris; two days later the diplomat died of his wounds. This was the alibi the Nazis needed. Gathered at the famous *Hofbräuhaus* in Munich to celebrate the fifteenth anniversary of the Beer Hall Putsch, the leaders of the Party took the opportunity to unleash the first nationwide pogrom in the German lands since the late Middle Ages.

Virtually no city, town, or village with Jewish residents was exempt from the reign of terror. Contemporary reports listed 191 synagogues burned, of which 76 were totally destroyed; historians have now documented at least 1200 synagogues that were either destroyed or desecrated.[56] The extent of destruction and the degree of desecration remain difficult to determine. In Bavaria, some 41 synagogues were partly or fully destroyed, and 134 desecrated, which typically meant Torah rolls torn apart, sacred objects defiled, and furniture demolished.[57] The Nazis also damaged a great many businesses, broke into scores of houses, and bludgeoned, kicked, beat, and humiliated Jews; and in communities throughout Germany, neighbors simply watched, often cheered Nazi thugs on, or participated in the violence.

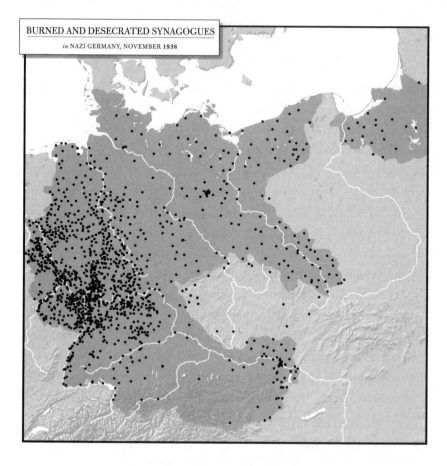

BURNED AND DESECRATED SYNAGOGUES
in NAZI GERMANY, NOVEMBER **1938**

This physical violence, and its widespread approbation, was more prevalent than historians, who have long worked with official statistics, have allowed. Nazi figures, which listed 91 Jews killed, did not take into account those who eventually died as a result of being brutally beaten, or those who committed suicide during and soon after the pogrom—one historian, Raphael Gross, has counted between 300 and 500 suicides for November alone.[58] The official figures also do not give a sense of the sheer terror of the pogrom. In a significant number of places throughout Germany, Nazis with hammers and axes broke into people's houses, pounded and demolished tables and chairs, smashed windows, tore fixtures from the ceilings, and ripped paintings from the walls, while Jews, who were hiding and huddled inside, had no idea "if we would survive the night," as Marga Silbermann Randall from a small Rhenish town put it.[59] The violence did not even spare old people. In Neustadt an der Weinstraße, stormtroopers chased the elderly out of an old age home, and then torched the building, while in Emden in East Fresia, they forced the seniors to march past the burning synagogue and then perform gymnastic exercises in the schoolyard.[60] Parentless children were also targeted. In Esslingen, west of Stuttgart, men bearing axes and clubs stormed the local orphanage, while Nazis destroyed another orphanage in the Rhenish town of Dinslaken, and then made sure that the Jewish children, some thirty-five of them, were deported.[61]

On the night of November 9, the vast majority of perpetrators belonged to Hitler's base—Nazi Party activists and the SA. The next morning, however, the circle of culprits widened to include a great many young people. Even whole classes of schoolchildren sometimes participated in the attacks, as was the case in Großen-Linden, a Hessian village in which some two hundred children, encouraged by their teacher, joined in.[62] Weaned on nearly six years of propaganda and overtly racist and anti-Semitic instruction, teenagers formed a particularly large contingent who tormented Jews and damaged their property. Looters, young and old, also made up a large number of the participants. Despite prohibitions, they eagerly pillaged private homes, taking away carpets, furniture, silver, linen, men's and women's clothing, paintings, mirrors, candlesticks, and toys of all kinds.[63] They also plundered stores—with some reports recounting that women fought over lingerie and shoes.[64]

The role of women in these violent crowds is difficult to pin down. In subsequent testimonies of German Jews, very few non-Jewish women actively engaged in the physical act of destruction are mentioned. One exception was in the village of Freudental in Württemberg, where women of the National Socialist Women's League, the women's arm of the Nazi Party, participated in the violence and stole sacred objects from the synagogue.[65] While there were other cases as well, the existing documentation points to less enthusiastic participation by women.[66] However, this aversion to physical violence did not stop women from looting or from taunting Jewish men subsequently arrested and sent to concentration camps. It also did not prevent women from actively cutting off ties to Jews whom they knew. "We somehow lost contact" was a typical, passive formulation.[67]

In reality, ordinary Germans responded in a variety of ways to the November pogrom. Some internal sources suggest strong disapproval of the wanton destruction of property and at the spectacle of people, especially women, children, and old people, being beaten.[68] This dismay seemed especially noticeable in Catholic regions, where, according to a summary report of the SD (*Sicherheitsdienst* or Security Service), there was "a clear rejection of the entire operation."[69] Some priests even landed in prison or in concentration camps for evoking the Sermon on the Mount on the following Sunday.[70] There were also reports of Protestant pastors who prayed for the Jews and reminded their parishioners of the imperative of neighborly love.[71]

Nevertheless, the paucity of such documented resistance suggests that disapproval was a minority response. Closer to the mark was one Jewish witness who reported that "the population spoke out against it in isolated cases and only in secret."[72] Certainly, state terror rendered the German population quiescent, but their passivity also resulted from a widespread resignation that had increased in the nearly six years since the Nazis came to power. Moreover, during the November pogrom, more Germans than ever before crossed a threshold of violence, participating, actively or passively, in the brutalization of a minority population. Once this threshold was crossed, it became hard to step back and articulate anti-Semitic measures as intrinsically wrong. Instead, many Germans justified them.

Burning the furnishings and ritual objects from the synagogue
in Mosbach in Baden on the town square, as a large audience watches,
on November 10, 1938.

For German Jews, the lack of public resistance became the writing on the wall, even for the most patriotic among them. One was Willy Cohn. Born in 1888 and named after the Kaiser, he came from an assimilated Jewish family in Breslau and fought at the Battles of the Marne and the Somme.[73] In chronicling his experience of war, revolution, economic and political turmoil, and the rise of National Socialism, Cohn's diary also presents the story of a patriot who gradually loses his sense of belonging. Like other Jewish veterans, he had joined the *Reichsbund jüdischer Front-soldaten* (the Jewish war veteran association and the second largest Jewish organization in Germany), and had marched in parades, wearing his Iron Cross proudly. For Cohn, the Nazi seizure of power cut deep into his sense of self. "What goes on in one's mind after having sacrificed so many years for Germany cannot be expressed," Cohn wrote at the end of March 1933. He was equally shaken by the anti-Semitic surge of early 1935, reflecting that "on the one hand this is the land in which we were born, whose development we have followed over the decades, on the other, we have been excluded from it and made alien."[74]

Cohn knew, however, that the "*Novemberpogrom* was a turning point of a different kind."[75] And he was hardly alone. "I always thought, now we have reached the worst point," Luise Solmitz, a conservative Hamburg schoolteacher married to a baptized Jewish man, conceded: "But now I see it was always just a prelude to the next thing." Her husband, Fredy—a civil servant even before World War I and a soldier who had fought in thirty-three separate battles during the war—"also admitted it: we are destroyed."[76]

During the next few days, the regime rounded up Jewish men and marched them in broad daylight to train stations and from there sent them to concentration camps. Surviving photographs present images of rows and rows of onlookers, some with cameras, documenting the trek of mainly older, established men, who had clung to an illusion that their standing would shield them from persecution. In all, some 26,000 Jewish men were sent to concentration camps, with only those with war injuries and holders of the Iron Cross First Class exempted, if only after the ordeal of their arrest.[77] Together, these arrested men constituted roughly 20 percent of the male Jewish population, and overnight they doubled the number of inmates in the camps.[78] Previously, Jews, mainly of the left, had constituted some 5 percent of the camp population. Now they made up the majority, and in short order overcrowded the holding capacities of Dachau, Sachsen-hausen, and Buchenwald.[79] Violent and corrupt guards tormented the new prisoners and killed some 469 Jewish men in November and December alone. In order to hide perimortem beatings and torture, the concentration camp guards sent only urns with ashes back to the wives and families.[80]

Yet within a few weeks of the pogrom, the camps began sending recently arrested Jews home, starting with the disabled, elderly, and sick; then war veterans were released, followed by men who agreed to relinquish their businesses or emigrate immediately. By the outbreak of the war in September 1939, the Jewish population of the camps had actually decreased to 1500 people, roughly 7 percent of the some 22,000 inmates.[81]

The incarceration of Jewish men after the pogrom was never meant to be permanent, but rather to shock and humiliate, and if emigration rates in late 1938 and the beginning of 1939 are an indication, they did precisely that. Realizing they were unwanted and extremely vulnerable in their own country, the remaining German Jews tried to escape as fast as they could. Not all made it. After being roused from her house and lined up outside, Rosa Hecht Weil, an elderly woman in Fürth, asphyxiated herself by forcing her head into an oven on Christmas Day 1938; she was unaware that two British visas, one for herself, the other for her husband, who would successfully flee, had just been mailed from London. Such heartbreaking stories abounded, most never to reach the public eye. Even for those who did escape, the sadness was profound. "We loved Germany, as one can love only one's home," an émigré named Elisabeth Freund wrote from Havana in early 1941, yet "we had to leave the country, whose language we speak, whose songs and poems we grew up with, and whose forests and mountains we wandered through."[82]

This last wave of German Jews left mainly for other European countries, especially England, the Netherlands, France, and Poland. They also departed in great numbers for North and South America.[83] As the situation became increasingly desperate, the United States took on fewer refugees—a fact underscored by the dramatic voyage of the MS *St. Louis* in May 1939, the same transatlantic liner on which Du Bois had crossed the Atlantic three years before. Departing from Hamburg with 937 passengers, almost all of them German Jews, the *St. Louis* arrived in Havana on May 27, but only a few passengers were allowed to get off, and when the ship turned to the United States, it was denied refuge. Eventually, the *St. Louis* was forced to return to Europe, with most of its passengers still on board. Of them, 288 were allowed to disembark in England, while the rest—620 passengers—were forced to return to the Netherlands, Belgium, and France. In the end, 254 of these German Jews, ranging from children of six to old men of eighty, would be killed in the genocide.[84] Perhaps more remarkable was that so many survived, often by sheer chance. For instance, young Rudi Dingfelder, upon being ripped out of the trains at the ramp on Auschwitz, lost his glasses and could hardly see—but because the Nazis sent all Jews with glasses into the gas chambers, Rudi counted among the 2 percent of Jews on that particular transport who were selected to work, and did not meet imminent death.[85]

VII

The Jews, moreover, were hardly the only group targeted. By September 1939, some 300,000 people within Germany had been sent to the camps, although fewer than 5000 people, mostly men, had died as a result of "starvation, freezing, shooting, or the effects of abuse," as one camp survivor described it.[86] In the early years, Communists and a significant number of Socialists constituted the largest number of concentration camp inmates. In addition, there were more than 10,000 gay men in the camps, and several thousand Jehovah's Witnesses, while Christian clergymen, most of them Catholic, numbered in the hundreds.[87] Before the outbreak of war, there were also roundups of "social outsiders," and their death toll, totaling more than 1200 men between January 1938 and August 1939, was disturbingly high.[88] By this time, the Nazi regime had forcefully sterilized some 300,000 men and women whom the Nazis diagnosed with hereditary illnesses, which ranged from "chronic alcoholism" to the "congenitally feeble minded."[89] The regime had also abrogated a series of diplomatic treaties, had brought Europe repeatedly to the brink of war, and had placed the German economy in the service of massive rearmament.

However, as the historian Christian Gerlach reminds us, in the first half of the twentieth century, Germany was one among a number of extremely violent societies and, in fact, "at that time, many much bloodier regimes ruled in Europe and elsewhere."[90] The Ottoman Empire had already persecuted the Armenian population to a degree as yet, in 1939, unknown in Germany. Likewise, the Soviet Union was already guilty of far greater persecution, having forcibly starved whole populations and incarcerated millions of people in Gulag prisons. The brutality of the Japanese occupation of China, culminating in the Nanjing massacre of 1937, already outstripped the crimes amassed by Nazi Germany by the summer of 1939. The point here is not to practice what the historian Peter Gay once dismissed as "comparative trivialization," whose "historical function is to cover over the special horror of German barbarity between 1933 and 1945 and to divert attention from studying that barbarity in its own—that is to say, its German—context."[91] Instead, it is to draw attention to a stark fact: of Jews killed in the genocide, more than 99 percent were murdered *after* September 1, 1939.

VIII

The Second World War, unlike the First, began solemnly. "On the streets one does not notice any kind of patriotic enthusiasm, as in 1914," noted Willy Cohn in his journal on the evening of August 28, 1939.[92] Instead, Nazi Germany invaded Poland with an overwhelming force of 1.5 million men, and within six weeks the military campaign was essentially over. By October 7, Cohn even conceded a "certain greatness" to Hitler for his ability to dramatically reshape world politics.[93] Cohn followed the news closely in the subsequent weeks and months. He had read that the Nazis had begun to transfer populations and settle Poland with ethnic Germans. He had also heard rumors of atrocities.[94] Yet Cohn hailed from a German-Jewish family whose service record dated all the way back to the Battle of Königgrätz in 1866. The grim forebodings—"of these things that are happening in Poland—did *not* come from the military," he assumed.[95]

Unfortunately, Cohn's confidence was woefully misguided. From the start, Hitler had encouraged all the branches who took part in the occupation to take a merciless course, and in a closed-room speech to his generals on August 22, 1939, he laid bare his radically new concept of occupation. "Destruction of Poland in the foreground, aim is to remove living forces," Hitler told his military leaders, adding, "hearts closed to empathy . . . extreme severity."[96] From the diary of General Franz Halder, we know that on that day Hitler insisted on the "physical annihilation of the Polish people," and from the notes of Field Marshal Fedor von Bock, that he vowed that "Poland would be depopulated and settled by Germans."[97]

Hitler intended to eradicate the Polish elite and to reduce the remaining Poles to an uneducated mass of servants to their German overlords. Having long ago abandoned what he considered old-style Germanization, which entailed assimilating minorities to the dominant culture, Hitler aimed to create a social order with Germans as masters, Poles as helots, and Jews as the banished. Hesitantly floated as an idea before 1914, the expulsion and transfer of peoples in order to create ethnically homogeneous spaces had gained traction, as we have seen, during the First World War and remained a popular idea among radical nationalists in the 1920s. Hitler's views were in this regard unoriginal. Only now there was the possibility of actually putting them into practice, especially as a phalanx of eager administrators saw their own advancement in terms of the progress made toward the Germanization of space in the sense that Hitler envisaged it.

Arthur Greiser, the Gauleiter (party leader and district governor) of the Warthegau, the new German province created from parts of the Polish provinces of Poznań and Łódź, was such an administrator. "A model Nazi," as his biographer calls him, Greiser eagerly turned the annexed area into a testing ground for population policies and the remaking of ethnic space.[98] He ordered street signs changed into German, renamed parks and squares, and tore down statues and monuments that valorized Polish history.[99] In order to enforce strict segregation, he commanded that beaches, pools, public baths, playgrounds, and park benches be separated; he also divided restaurants and hotels along lines of nationality, and staggered food-shopping times so that German consumers could enjoy easier access to meat and vegetables. Cultural institutions like museums, concert halls, theaters, and libraries became off-limits to Poles. Greiser even considered making it mandatory that Poles deferentially bow to Germans on sidewalks. Basic symbolic practices and rituals that accompanied birth and death were not spared either. Just as Jews were forced to add "Israel" and "Sara" to their names, all newborn Poles were to have their names supplemented with "Kazimierz" or "Kazimiera," so that they could be identified as belonging to a subservient ethnicity. And beginning in October 1941, Germans and Poles could not be buried in the same cemeteries.[100]

Although not widely used as a term at the time, this was nothing less than legal apartheid, institutional segregation reinforced by terror. Its aim was not to protect an existing discriminatory society, but to create an entirely new order defined not only by separation, but also by hierarchy and subjugation. To achieve this new order, the Nazi occupiers resettled roughly a quarter million Germans from eastern Europe into the Warthegau and nearly 200,000 Germans from the Reich, some of them, like the young Martha Michelsohn, full with "youthful pioneer spirit."[101] Because the Nazis had no intention of building new houses, the new settlers occupied the homes and requisitioned the furniture and goods of Poles and Jews who had been expelled, or in some cases murdered. During the war nearly a half million Poles were sent west as forced laborers from the Warthegau to the Reich, while nearly 300,000 Poles and about a quarter million Jews were pushed east into the General Government, the part of Poland occupied but not annexed in 1939.[102] This, however, did not make the Warthegau the "blonde province" of Nazi Germany that Greiser had hoped for.[103] It would eventually change the province's ethnic balance though, from roughly 6 percent German in 1939 to 23 percent in 1944.[104]

Throughout annexed and occupied Poland, the number of people expelled and transferred actually dwarfed those who were killed by orders of magnitude. The killing was nevertheless considerable, and from the very start it accompanied the ethnic reshaping of space and the forced movement of peoples.

In the first two months of the invasion, the German army accounted for the murder of at least five hundred non-Jewish civilians, sometimes in brutal fashion, as in the village of Longinówka, where the army burned some forty Poles in a building and shot those trying to escape; or in the city of Częstochowa, where soldiers herded a large number of Polish men into a park and executed them; or in the small town of Złoczew, where the military murdered some two hundred civilians, including women and children.[105] Much of the killing resulted from exaggerated reprisal, and sometimes these reprisals targeted Jews. On September 12, 1939, in the small town of Końskie, north of Kielce, snipers shot four German soldiers, and the army forced twenty-four Jews to dig the graves, and then, when a few Jews tried to leave the scene, shot them all.[106] A horrified Leni Riefenstahl, who was there to make a movie about the war, witnessed the atrocity.[107]

The Nazi filmmaker Leni Riefenstahl witnesses a massacre of
Jewish men in the Polish town of Końskie, September 12, 1939.

It was, however, not the army but the so-called self-defense units (*Volks-
deutscher Selbstschutz*) of Germans living in Poland that decimated Polish
and Jewish civilian populations with particularly disturbing impunity.[108]
Working closely with the SS, these ethnic German militias sometimes killed
Poles immediately, and sometimes arrested and incarcerated them in makeshift concentration camps, taking them later in trucks to killing sites (usually
woods or a ravine) and shooting them. Few recall these killing sites today.
But they demand our attention. The massacre in Piaśnica Forest—where
ethnic German militias shot some 13,000 Poles, Kashubians, Jews, and
handicapped people in the winter of 1939–1940—was, for example, arguably the first mass killing of the European theater of the Second World War.
(It was more than half the size of the infamous Soviet massacre of Polish
officers at Katyn Forest in the spring of 1940.) Some of the killing in other
places was of similar dimension. In the fall of 1939 and into the first months
of 1940, self-defense units killed at least 10,000 "Poles and Jews" at the edge
of gravel pits near the small town of Dragacz (Dragaß), and with the complicity of the German army, they murdered around 8000 people in woods
fifty kilometer south of Chojnice (Konitz).[109] There were also many smaller
murder events; one study counts more than 350 separate killing sprees.[110]

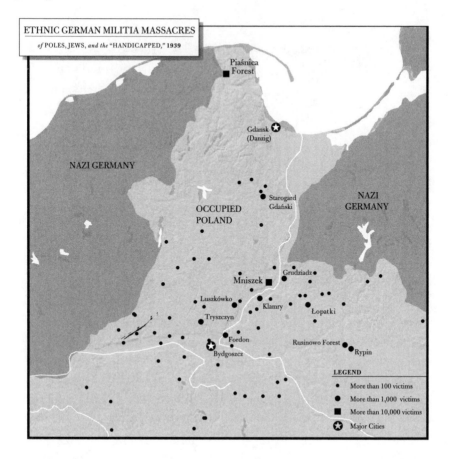

ETHNIC GERMAN MILITIA MASSACRES
of POLES, JEWS, *and the* "HANDICAPPED," 1939

Piaśnica
Forest

Gdansk
(Danzig)

NAZI GERMANY

Starogard
Gdański

OCCUPIED
POLAND

NAZI
GERMANY

Grudziadz
Mniszek

Luszkówko
Klamry
Lopatki
Tryszczyn

Fordon
Rusinowo Forest
Bydgoszcz
Rypin

LEGEND

• More than 100 victims
● More than 1,000 victims
■ More than 10,000 victims
✪ Major Cities

In the months after the invasion, the German army also engaged in the wanton destruction of religious structures and symbols. Although historians have paid less attention to such desecrations, their impact on the rural communities of Poland cannot be underestimated. German soldiers torched, burned, detonated, or otherwise razed at least seventy synagogues. They chopped up historical wooden houses of worship and used the boards for firewood. They desecrated other synagogues by making them into horse stalls or marketplaces. They also demolished cemeteries, and in a number of towns crushed the stones and used them to pave roads. Reminiscent of the November pogrom of 1938, this second destruction, carried out in the fall of 1939, was mainly the work of the German army, although in some instances the Gestapo or the SS drove the destruction forward.

These rampages hardly stopped with synagogues. In dozens of places, German soldiers sought out Orthodox men and shaved their beards and side locks. They forced Jews to collect and then burn their *tallis* and *tefillin*, beating those who resisted. These assaults often occurred on Jewish holidays. On Rosh Hashanah (September 14, 1939), Germans forced Orthodox men in the town of Mogielnica into the market square, shaved their beards and locks, made them dance and sing songs, and lit bonfires to burn holy books and Torah scrolls—all the while, according to one testimony, the German and Polish witnesses laughed and applauded.[111] Similar scenes transpired during Succoth holidays in Sochaczew, west of Warsaw, and in Sierpc on Yom Kippur.[112] Even Christian holidays failed to give respite: on Christmas Eve 1939, the army set the synagogue in Siedlce ablaze, and the soldiers stood by, watching it burn down.[113]

In this context of violence and desecration, the Nazis began to erect Jewish ghettos. There had not been a specific order to create them, and they were not a planned stage in the unfolding genocide. Prior to the Nazi invasion of Poland, the Nazis hardly even mentioned the word. In *Mein Kampf*, Hitler had referred to ghettos only as a historical phenomenon. In the nearly four thousand surviving secret Nazi reports measuring popular opinion in Germany, the term itself appears fewer than ten times.[114] When the Nazis rolled into Poland with tanks, there was no order to surround Jewish streets in cities, towns, and villages with barbed-wire fence. Even Reinhard Heydrich's infamous *Schnellbrief* of late September 1939, often seen as the beginning of the ghettoization process, only gave the *Einsatzgruppen* guidelines for moving Jews from the countryside into the larger cities and for setting up Jewish Councils. It referred to a ghetto just once, and then only as an urban concentration of Jews in a certain area, from which it might be necessary, for reasons of security, to restrict Jews from leaving in the evening hours.[115]

The preponderance of historical research has focused on the two largest ghettos, Łódź, sealed in April 1940, and Warsaw, cut off from the surrounding city in mid-November. Housing roughly 20 percent of the Jewish population of Poland, these ghettos were shocking experiments in human segregation, economic exclusion, and control. The Warsaw Ghetto, for example, pressed 30 percent of the city's population into less than 3 percent of its area, isolating Jews behind walls ten feet high and topped with barbed wire. The Nazis forced the Jews inside to endure soul-destroying hunger, allowing the general Jewish population of the ghetto just over a thousand calories per day and the less fortunate even less, so that by the end of 1941 thousands were literally dying in their rooms and in the streets. "In the public assistance shelters, mothers are hiding their dead children under the beds for eight days in order to receive larger food rations," noted Adam Czerniakow, the head of the Jewish Council in the Warsaw Ghetto, in his diary on November 19, 1941.[116]

The vast majority of Jews—some 80 percent—were, however, in smaller ghettos. Some of these ghettos were open, while others were sealed with barbed wire and fences. The first ghetto of any significant size was set up in the central Polish city of Piotrków Trybunalski, de jure by decree on October 8, 1939, de facto with fences and wire by January 24. Many more

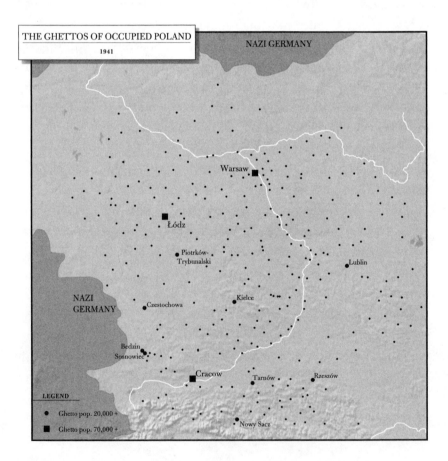

THE GHETTOS OF OCCUPIED POLAND
1941

NAZI GERMANY

Warsaw

Łódz

Piotrków-
Trybunalski

Lublin

NAZI
GERMANY

Kielce

Czestochowa

Bedzin
Sosnowiec

Cracow

Tarnów

Rzeszów

LEGEND

● Ghetto pop. 20,000 +

■ Ghetto pop. 70,000 +

Nowy Sacz

followed over the next two and a half years, with the pace accelerating in the summer of 1940 and the spring of 1941.[117] When these ghettos were guarded, it was typically to keep Jews from trading with the local population, or else to prevent typhus, a bacterial infection carried by ticks, lice, fleas, and mites, from reaching the contiguous communities.

This process of enclosure should be seen not as planned but as gradual. It began with the establishment of the Jewish Councils, the *Judenräte*, typically set up in Poland in late 1939 and in the first months of 1940. Composed of a few men of authority in the local Jewish community, the councils struggled to ameliorate the severity of Nazi measures designed to demarcate, dispossess, demean, and demonize Jews. Its leaders worked, often heroically, to stave off the worst consequences of Nazi barbarity. As in prewar Germany, persecution often began with identification—the requirement, for example, to wear the yellow star. This was generally followed by the confiscation of Jewish-owned shops and businesses, the imposition of arbitrary and onerous levies, the recruitment of Jews as slave laborers, the stealing of their personal property (especially furs and gold), and the restriction of movement in and out of communities.

A severe harshness came to cloud every facet of daily life, spurred on by the unpredictability of German authorities, and the satisfaction that Germans and Poles derived in lording it over Jews. Such brutality often took the form of arbitrary beatings and killings. Sometimes it involved sexual violence and rape, a more widespread phenomenon of Nazi occupation than previously supposed. These cases rarely found their way into the documentation. Yet we know that in dozens of Jewish communities, SS soldiers, German police, and Polish auxiliary forces took advantage of their power over Jews and raped Jewish women and girls.[118] We have only scattered evidence of this during the first year of occupation, but as the conditions of the ghettos deteriorated, rape became a regular occurrence, finding its way into the historical record.

The early ghettos were not, however, mere anterooms to destruction. It was only in the second half of 1941 that ghettos would take on this still more sinister purpose. By then, the Nazis had begun to separate ghettos into two parts, with those capable of working for the Nazis crammed into the one, small children and the infirm packed into the other. The purpose of the division was all too evident.

IX

Unbeknownst to the outside world, a secret clause had accompanied the Nazi-Soviet nonaggression pact that allowed Hitler's troops to march into Poland unopposed by Russian military forces. Signed in Moscow by foreign ministers Joachim von Ribbentrop and Vyacheslav Molotov on August 23, 1939, the treaty, and the codicil that accompanied it, partitioned Poland and indeed much of eastern Europe into German and Soviet spheres of influence. Essentially, it had opened the door first to Nazi, then to Soviet aggression, with the Wehrmacht invading Poland from the west and the Red Army from the east. Both occupations, as the historian Timothy Snyder has underscored, were extremely brutal, involving a great deal of civilian killing.[119]

Yet from Hitler's standpoint, the arrangement was always only temporary. While historians may debate whether *Mein Kampf* laid out genocidal policies directed against Jews, its programmatic implications for Russia were clear enough. In the penultimate chapter of *Mein Kampf*, "Eastern Orientation or Eastern Policy," Hitler states:

> Germany will either become a world power or it will cease to exist. . . . We are stopping the perpetual Germanic march towards the south and west of Europe, and turn our eyes towards the lands of the east. . . . We are shifting to a future policy of the soil. . . . When in Europe we speak today about the new policy of the soil, we have in mind, in the first order, Russia and its vassal border states.[120]

There was little ambiguity in these words, written in the mid-1920s. In June 1941, Hitler would amass the largest invasion force ever recorded, some three million men, in order to invade the Soviet Union. Stalin could not believe they would launch the invasion without winter gear.[121]

CHAPTER 12
—

DEATH SPACES

c. 1941–1945

History counts its skeletons in round numbers.
A thousand and one remains a thousand,
as though the one had never existed.

—WISŁAWA SZYMBORSKA, "HUNGER CAMP AT JASLO"

• • •

The sun was never beautiful.

—EDITH P. (SURVIVOR)

THE WAR AGAINST THE SOVIET UNION BEGAN WITH A DRAMATIC
increase in lethality (see page 303). The Soviet army lost more men in the
first three months of the Nazi invasion than did France, Great Britain, and
the United States combined—on all the fronts and for the duration of the
war. Genocidal escalation was not, however, a mere by-product of the brutality of the war against the Soviet Union. In crucial ways, the dam holding
back genocidal impulses had already been breached before the invasion
even began.

II

The so-called Barbarossa Decree, which consisted of guidelines for the
German army dated May 13, 1941, stated that civilians aiding the enemy
were to be dealt with ruthlessly while political commissars were to be shot.
The decree also stipulated that towns and villages suspected of aiding the
enemy were to be subject to collective reprisal.[1] Never before had soldiers
been given such latitude to kill noncombatants. Codes of military conduct,
which had still defined fighting during the First World War and which had

largely remained in place on the western front in the Second World War, were to be left behind.

Logistical planning also contributed in crucial ways to the emergence of mass violence. In the spring of 1941, Herbert Backe, then second in command in the Ministry for Agriculture, wrote a chilling memorandum describing the projected food situation for the upcoming invasion of the Soviet Union. In a discussion of the implications of this memorandum in a meeting of May 2, 1941, the Economic Command Staff East concluded that an invasion could succeed only if the "entire German army is fed from Russia during the third year of the war" (i.e., in 1941).[2] The planning staff then issued a directive urging the cordoning off of the central black earth region in southern Russia and the "non-supply of the whole wooded zone including the essential industrial centers and Petersburg."[3] Alluding to "unbelievable hunger," the planning staff's directive soberly predicted the death by starvation of thirty million people.[4]

In these preliminary discussions, one easily overlooked organizational change would have dire consequences for the Jews. General Wilhelm Keitel, chief of the Armed Forces High Command, conceded to Heinrich Himmler, the head of the SS, that the SS could "carry out special tasks for the Führer" in territories that came under German dominion. During the occupation of Poland, the SS still had to report to the army. In the conquered territory of the Soviet Union, this would no longer be the case. Instead, one particular branch of the SS, the Reich Main Security Office (RSHA, *Reichssicherheitshauptamt*; with its director being Himmler's direct subordinate, Reinhard Heydrich), was essentially given the green light to pursue its policy of destruction. The timing of the organizational change was also significant. As the invasion of the Soviet Union approached, Himmler and Heydrich were beginning to envision the Soviet Union, and not merely the constricted areas of Poland, as the primary space for what Heydrich called the "final evacuation."[5]

The new grant of bureaucratic autonomy to the SS, and in particular to the RSHA, also had the effect of giving wide latitude to the *Einsatzgruppen*, the mobile killing units of the SS. Divided into four battalion-sized units, the *Einsatzgruppen* consisted of some 3000 men who were responsible, as Heydrich put it, for executing Communist "functionaries" at various levels, "Jews in positions of party and state," and "other radical elements."[6] Historians once argued that the *Einsatzgruppen* likely received an order at the beginning of the invasion of the Soviet Union to kill all the Jews in the newly occupied territory. However, since the *Einsatzgruppen* did not begin to kill Jewish women and children regularly until mid- to late August, this contention no longer seems plausible.[7] Instead, it is now widely thought that in late June Heydrich communicated a set of general categories, encouraging his officers to decide for themselves who counted in these categories, and thus who was to be executed.[8]

The new legal, logistical, and operational conditions, plus the speed with which German forces advanced into Soviet territory, enabled a campaign of murderous fury. So too did the actual discussion about the territory that Nazi Germany would soon occupy. Less than a full month after the start of the invasion of the Soviet Union, Hitler, in a meeting with leading Nazi officials, outlined his plans for a territory that stretched from the Baltic in the north to the Volga in the east and the Crimea in the south and which, the Nazi dictator insisted, would "become part of the German Reich."[9] The occupation of what was essentially all of European Russia, which "we will never leave," necessitated unimaginable brutality, and involved, according to Hitler, "first the rule, second the administration, and third the exploitation" of these lands.[10] Others present at this meeting concurred. "Naturally, the gigantic space has to be pacified as quickly as possible," Hermann Göring added, and pointed out that "this was best achieved by shooting dead anyone who even looks askance at us."[11] General Keitel also emphasized that since it was "not possible to put a guard at every train station and barn," it would be necessary to involve the local population in German rule, and to kill anyone who did not cooperate.[12] "Shooting and resettlements," Hitler insisted, were in any case necessary to achieve the "final order."[13] Moreover, since the Russians had announced partisan warfare behind the lines, they "have given us the possibility of exterminating [*Ausrotten*] whatever stands against us." The pretext, Hitler believed, "has, in turn, its advantages."[14]

III

It is impossible to know what "advantages" Hitler had in mind. What we know is that Soviet POWs were the first extremely large victim group. The

killing of the Soviet POWs was not, as is often thought, mainly an incidental casualty of an insufficiently supplied, fast-moving German army unable
to support huge numbers of captured soldiers.[15] Instead, the overwhelming
body of documentary evidence points to a conscious policy, formulated
before the invasion began, of starvation. The premeditated nature of the
killing also comes to the fore when we analyze the geographical pattern of
death, noting the enormous number of Soviet POWs starved, frozen, or
just plain shot in the rear areas controlled by German civil authorities.[16]
Christian Streit, whose *Keine Kameraden,* published in 1978, remains
the pathbreaking work on the subject, estimated that the German army
murdered some 1.2 million Soviet POWs on Soviet territory, as many as
500,000 in the General Government of Poland, and as many as 400,000
in the German Reich.[17]

The death rate in the Reich itself reveals that the murder of Soviet
POWs was by no means a matter of military exigency. Between July 1941
and April 1942, nearly half of all Soviet prisoners brought to the Reich
died there, mainly of starvation and typhus. Some died in camps that later
assumed notoriety, like Bergen-Belsen. Others lost their lives in less familiar ones, like Stalag XD 310 in Wietzendorf, where 16,000 Russian soldiers perished, or in the village of Oerbke on the Lüneburg Heath, where
30,000 Russian prisoners dug holes in the ground to protect themselves
from the elements and ate grass and bark in order to survive; those who
perished lay buried in a mass grave sparsely marked by a few stones in a
"Cemetery of the Nameless."[18]

As one moves east, we know less about what happened, whether in
the camps of Pomerania and East Prussia, or in the camps of the General Government—such as Stalag 307 in Biała Podlaska or Stalag 327 in
Jarasłow—where it is estimated that some 290,000 Russian POWs perished between June 1941 and April 1942.[19] In these regions, graves are
hardly marked, and we are left with little more than imprecise or highly
rounded-off numbers. Historians know, for example, that there were some
200,000 prisoners in Stalag 319 in the eastern Polish town of Chełm, and
that about 90,000 died there and are buried in the nearby "forest of skeletons." They also know that in Stalag 318 in Lamsdorf in Upper Silesia,
POWs "turned to cannibalism" once they could find no more grass, flow-

SELECT GERMAN ARMY POW CAMPS
for SOVIET SOLDIERS, 1941-1942

ers, or raw potatoes to eat.[20] Such an occurrence was not isolated. Hearsay and credible testimony are, however, difficult to separate.[21] Streit, having read through the mass of documentation, cautiously affirms that in the winter of 1941–1942, cannibalism "seems to have occurred often."[22]

Closer to the eastern front, there were still more holding pens: places like Stalag 305 in Kirovohrad and Stalag 352 in Minsk—cold, shelterless sites that temporarily housed as many as 100,000 men each, and allowed most of the men to perish.[23] There were also transit camps like Dulag 184 and 230 in Vyazma, northeast of Smolensk, where there are estimates of close to 80,000 dead. Many soldiers never even got to the camps, since the death rate of prisoner transports ranged as high as 20 percent.[24] Here too we lack precise figures and have only imperfect documentation. A Red Cross doctor working near Smolensk noted in his diary the "nightmarish"

One of the many camps in which the German army
held Soviet prisoners of war, August 1942.

sight of four to five trains passing daily, with "20–50 freight cars, some
open, some closed," carrying Soviet POWs of all nationalities, and the
tracks littered with corpses of dead soldiers.[25] When trains or trucks could
not be organized, the army forced prisoners to march, and shot those who
could not—often "in front of the eyes of the civilian population," as one
German official complained.[26]

The murder of Soviet POWs unnerved German soldiers. Some Germans felt pity while others wondered about the consequences should they
themselves fall into captivity. Not a few had absorbed propaganda dehu-
manizing these Soviet fighters as not being worthy of the resources the
army needed to divert in order to keep them alive, and were thus indifferent to their fate. Even a sensitive German army soldier like Willy Reese, an
aspiring author whose idol was Rainer Maria Rilke, wrote that he "felt no
anger at the ill treatment of these helpless men, and no sympathy either."[27]
A few did, however. In a letter to his wife, Freya, the young Helmuth James
von Moltke, the great-grandnephew of the field marshal whose military victories in the 1860s essentially unified Germany, wondered what the "heca-
tombs of corpses" meant for his own country.[28] "A blood guilt that cannot
be atoned for in our lifetime," was his answer.[29]

IV

At the beginning of the invasion, the German army and the SS advanced into areas that had already witnessed immense amounts of killing. Internal German reports, one after the other, tell of piles of corpses left by the Soviet secret police after Russia withdrew from the occupied territories of eastern Poland. In turn, the Russian retreat spurred a further series of ethnic, religious, and political killings, as people, encouraged by nationalist associations, settled scores with real or supposed Soviet collaborators. Historical ethnic antagonisms ran deep in much of this region, with anti-Semitism the most persistent and prominent. It was expressed not just as latent prejudice but also as active hatred that periodically erupted with horrifying violence.[30]

The German SS intentionally incited this hatred. This too was planned with deliberation. On June 6, two weeks before the invasion, Heydrich instructed the heads of the *Einsatzgruppen* that "self-cleansing efforts," by which he meant pogroms, "are to be triggered leaving no traces whatsoever."[31]

Pogroms often began well before the SS arrived and became bloodier the moment local killers understood that they had clearance from the Germans. On June 30, 1941, for example, *Einsatzkommando* 1B noted that "the population of Kaunas killed about 2500 Jews during a spontaneous uprising," even though only a fraction of the Jews had been killed before the Germans arrived.[32] Other *Einsatzkommandos*, smaller units of the mobile killing groups, reports stated, more truthfully, that "pogroms have been started," as was the case on July 16 in the Latvian city of Riga, where the SS recounted that "400 Jews were killed during pogroms."[33] In still others, the SS claimed that "pogroms are being initiated," as was reported from the White Russian city of Grodno, or in a string of Ukrainian cities, like Sambor, where "50 Jews were killed by the enraged crowd," or in Chorstkóv, "where 110 Jews were slain by the population," or Tarnopol, where as many as "600 Jews were killed in pogroms."[34] The list of pogroms, which historians are still reconstructing, is long and complicated, just as the documents underlying them are equivocal on the question of responsibility and vague about the "efficacy" of pogroms from the standpoint of the German killers.[35]

In northeastern Poland (the districts of Łomża and Białystok), there were some forty-two pogroms, and of these, Jedwabne, Radziłów, and Wąsosz conformed most closely to so-called classic pogroms in which neighbors murdered neighbors with iron bars, picks, shovels, and axes, while those not already dead were immolated in barns.[36] In many of these cases, the degree of German instigation remains a matter of dispute, though it can be safely asserted that the mere presence of the SS sufficed for Poles to turn on Jews. Indeed, the evidence increasingly points not to spontaneity but to a general pattern of collusion between German authorities and local Polish elites. In the infamous case of Jedwabne, for example, the local mayor played an important role in the organization of the pogrom.[37] Collusion appears in other areas as well. In eastern Galicia and Volhynia (now western Ukraine), scholars estimate the number of pogroms to be between 35 and 140, and the number of victims between 12,000 and 35,000.[38] Here too German SS and reserve police units were a conspicuous driving force, but armed groups of Ukrainian nationalists, not simply revengeful peasants, did most of the killing—especially in the large urban pogroms that occurred in Lwów, Tarnopol, and Zolochiv.[39] A surviving film of the Lwów pogrom shows that, amid dense crowds of people, Ukrainian nationalists armed with sticks and clubs brutally beat Jews, including women whose clothes had been torn off their back, as young German soldiers attempted to keep order while taking pictures with their Leicas.[40]

Sadistic pogroms transfix the moral imagination, but militias proved to be far more lethal.[41] By the end of July, when German civilian authorities replaced the military administration, Lithuanians, for example, had killed roughly 1100 Jews in pogroms, but some 18,000 in militia shootings.[42] Here too Germans and local people shared culpability. As the Germans took over the area, the killings increased in incidence and magnitude and came to include women and children, commencing unequivocal genocide.

Any number of documents reveal this genocidal escalation. The notorious killing register of *Einsatzkommando 3*, commanded by the SS colonel Karl Jäger, is particularly instructive. Jäger listed the number of Lithuanian Jews his company executed, day by day, town by town, and whether or not they were men, women, or children, or belonged to a non-Jewish category, such as the mentally ill or Red Army commissars. When Jäger's men began killing in early July 1941, they murdered mainly men, but by early August they killed a significant number of women, and by the middle of that month they began executing women in roughly the same number as men. By this time too, Jäger reported the murder of children.[43] "The list is the origin of culture," the novelist Umberto Eco once said.[44] Here, the list was a document of unmitigated barbarism. A small excerpt will suffice:

4.8.41	Panevezys	1312 Jews, 4602 Jewesses, and 1609 Jewish Children	7523
18 to 22.8.41	Rasainiai Co.	466 Jews, 440 Jewesses, 1020 children	1926
25 and 26.8.41	Obeliai	112 Jews, 627 Jewesses, 421 Children	1160[45]

The list thus trails on. In all, there are 111 entries in the Jäger report, documenting sixty-three separate sites of murder. For each entry, Jäger tabulated the numbers of Jews killed in each massacre, as if he were creating an account ledger. He added the numbers up, gave a preliminary total at the end of each sheet, and at the end of the sixth sheet calculated that altogether 137,346 Jews had been killed by December 1, 1941. He noted, on the seventh sheet, that "the distance from assembly point to the graves was on average 4 to 5 km," and on sheet eight, he concluded that the "Jewish action" was "more or less terminated as far as *Einsatzkommando 3* is concerned."[46]

While accurately representing the scale of the killings, the list is often factitious in terms of the precision of its details. Jäger laconically noted, for example, that in the Lithuanian town of Eyshishok (to use its Yiddish name) on September 27, 1941, "989 Jews, 1636 Jewesses, and 821 Jewish children" were killed.[47] Yet we know that the slaughter took place over two days, not one—that on September 25 men were murdered, on September 26 women and children—and that the victims were not just from Eyshishok but also from surrounding villages. We also know that the Nazis killed more than 4000 people, not 3446, and that some 720 Jews, mainly men, escaped.[48] The numbers seem abstract; in the case of this particular town, one can begin to reimagine it because Yaffa Eliach, a historian from the town, later collected photographs of its Jewish population and copies of these pictures now make up the three-story-tall "Tower of Faces" at the U.S. Holocaust Memorial Museum in Washington, D.C. The numbers do, however, allow us to see patterns. And when one evaluates the Lithuanian evidence from the standpoint of communities instead of from the kill reports produced by the murderers themselves, one particular pattern prominently emerges. In many towns and villages, men were taken on one day and shot in a nearby wood—while days, weeks, or even a month later, the Nazis and Lithuanian nationalists came back for the entrapped women and children.

The systematic killing of women and children cannot be confused with antipartisan measures, as Nazi propaganda claimed. It was outright genocide. Within a month of the occupation, the magnitude of the killing increased throughout all the eastern territories. The summer and early fall of 1941 witnessed an explosion of massacres that involved over a thousand Jewish victims. A large number of killings, a concatenation of bloody events, involved more than five thousand deaths. There were also a series of massacres, typically occurring over a few days, in which the Nazis killed ten, twenty, and in one case more than thirty thousand Jewish men, women, and children.[49]

As with the Lithuanians, the people of Ukraine were equally caught up in the Nazis' genocidal fury, partly as accomplices, partly as victims. Here too, large-scale massacres commenced in mid- to late August.[50] The first was in the city of Kamenets-Podolskii, where—in coordination with German Reserve Police Battalions, local police forces, and regional commanders of the German army—the SS murdered at least 20,000 Jews over a three-day period. Similar mass killings occurred soon thereafter in Lwów and Berdichev, each involving a significant amount of planning and a wide array of complicit organizations.[51]

A month later, on September 29–30, 1941, the Nazis killed more than 33,000 Jews in the wooded ravines of Babi Yar. In one of the most "successful" cooperations between the German army and the SS, the Germans forced Jews to march from the Jewish cemetery in Kiev to the northern outskirts of the city, where they were made to run through a gauntlet of Nazi soldiers to the edge of what was essentially an enormous gorge. The SS then gunned them down with machine guns. Even in this part of Europe,

DEATH SPACES || 377

which had only recently witnessed untold human suffering, such brutality and indifference to human life was shocking. After the war, Babi Yar, whose pits eventually swallowed 100,000 victims, mostly Jews, would become the Soviet Union's primal symbol of Nazi cruelty, just as Auschwitz embodied it in the west.[52] And yet in dimension, the immense ravine of Babi Yar had its siblings in the late summer, fall, and early winter of 1941.

V

All of this was no longer simple atrocity in the sense of an exceptional occurrence. These mass killings were daily work, with a lethality many times higher than in the early "pogrom" phase of killing. These mass murders involved all manner of gruesome experimentation. Murder methods included lining up Jews at the end of a ditch and shooting them; executing them with the so-called Jeckeln method (by forcing Jews to lie facedown on the layer of people who had just been shot and shooting them in the neck); burying them alive, as happened in a number of cases with children; burning them in a synagogue, granary, or barn; and throwing grenades into a barrack or a prison in which Jews were trapped. There were also cases of drowning Jews in a river, freezing them in an ice box, suffocating them in a sealed cellar, and, as was first put into practice in southern Ukraine in November 1941, rerouting exhaust pipes into a locked chamber of moving "gas-vans."[53] Many of the killings happened in the nearby woods, as Jews from the surrounding area were brought to a single place to be shot, their corpses covered thinly by dirt and lime. Germans also killed Jews in plain sight. Since partisans often had strongholds in the woods, it was sometimes safer for the Nazis to kill in city centers, often in the courtyards of schools. In Ukraine alone, there were some two thousand killing sites, and for all of Nazi-occupied eastern Europe, including the former Yugoslavia, estimates range up to five thousand sites in total—many of them long since hidden, others marked only by a rudimentary stone or cross, sometimes not even mentioning that Jews lay beneath the surface.[54]

The killing utterly altered landscapes, transforming forests into fields of extermination and towns and villages into microeconomies of death. Large numbers of local people, many more than in the infamous extermination camps, were drawn into the killing operations.[55] Some volunteered, others worked for vodka or furs, and still others were requisitioned at gunpoint. From Lithuania to Crimea, people dug, covered, and disinfected pits; they pried out gold teeth; they gathered clothes and placed them in piles; and they brought tools to the murder site and prepared meals and fetched water for the executioners. Thousands of towns and villages became places of varying shades of complicity. "One day I woke up and we were all wearing Jew clothes," one Ukrainian woman recalled, echoing what might have been said in almost every town and village in the region.[56] Not a few of the requisitioned were young girls and boys who knew the names of their classmates being killed, yet were powerless to help them. Others were forced to do things that stayed with them for the rest of their lives. Decades after the war, an elderly woman from Ternivka, a town in southeast Ukraine, recounted that as a young girl she was forced to be a barefoot "presser," packing dirt and lime on the layers of just murdered (and half-murdered) Jews in a giant ditch: "You know, we were very poor," she confessed. "We didn't have shoes."[57]

Throughout eastern Europe, the killings were visible and audible. Townspeople watched murders transpire from across fields and from the tops of hills, from the attics of forest cabins and from the windows of buildings. Especially in the summer and fall of 1941, the killings were carried out in front of the curious, sometimes approving public. Yet the events also shocked and frightened spectators, including many children.[58] People heard the rapid-fire "tics" of machine guns or the "tic, silence, tic" of Mauser rifles, and they heard the screams.[59] When Jews were led out of town to a nearby wood, there was no ambiguity. After the Germans left, local people often went to the sites to hunt for valuables the Germans had not already taken. And in many, many places—cities, towns, and villages in Ukraine, the Baltic countries, and Poland—people quickly forced their way into Jewish houses, procuring new beds, tables, chairs, lamps, drapes, candlesticks, cutlery, boxes and bowls, as well as the obligatory furs and jewels. Some items were kept, others traded and sold on flourishing black markets of Jewish goods. The genocide enabled an enormous acquisition of possessions, a far more lucrative transfer of goods, one may surmise, than any revolution could have realized. In Stanisławów (now Ivano-Frankivsk, Ukraine), an SS officer stopped the shooting in the Jewish cemetery at nightfall and sent the remaining Jews back to their homes, which their neighbors had already emptied "of anything of any value," as one survivor, Jeannette Nestler, recalled.[60] In Otwock, a Polish town, Calel Perechodnik, a member of the Jewish Ghetto Police, was the only one of his family to live through the liquidation of the small ghetto. He could understand why the Poles came and took his tables, chairs, pots, pans, pants, and suits, leaving only old Hebrew books behind.[61] But then he saw a young Polish woman pushing his daughter's stroller, and his legs buckled.[62]

When Nazi units began to slaughter German Jews, whom the Nuremberg Laws still defined as subjects (*Angehörige*) of the Third Reich, there could no longer be any pretense that the murders were occurring in the context of antipartisan warfare. The first mass murder of German Jews occurred in Serbia, on October 12 and 13, 1941, when the 342nd Infantry Division of German soldiers shot some 400 German-Jewish men in a "reprisal action." Along with their families, these Jewish men had tried to escape the Reich in 1939 and immigrate to Palestine, but they got no farther than the city of Šabac, which the Nazis had turned into the site of a concentration camp.[63] The second such killing of German Jews, in Lithuania, extended to women and children and was not in any way associated with supposed military exigency. In his entry for November 25, 1941, Karl Jäger claimed his men had murdered "1159 Jews, 1600 Jewish women, 175 Jewish children" from transports originating in Berlin, Munich, and Frankfurt am Main. These are the earliest dated entries revealing that the German-Jewish "resettlers" (*Umsiedler*), as Jäger still called them, were in fact being killed.[64] Yet Jäger ordered the killing of German Jews on his own initiative; he had no special instructions from Berlin, and the transports arrived at Kaunas only because they were redirected from their original destination of the Riga ghetto, which the local SS commander, Friedrich Jeckeln, claimed was already too full.[65] Upon arrival, the German Jews were beaten and brutalized, and marched up a long hill to Fort IX on the outskirts of Kaunas. The killers then forced them to stand before a large ditch, previously dug by Soviet POWs, before an SS machine gunner shot them down.[66]

In his report, Jäger tersely noted that on November 29 his executioners had also gunned down "693 Jews, 1155 Jewesses, 152 Jewish children" from transports from "Vienna and Breslau."[67] Willy Cohn was on that second train, along with his wife, Trudi, and his two daughters, nine-year-old Susanne and three-year-old Tamara.

VI

While fueled by hate and cruelty, the brutal killings of the *Einsatzgruppen* also followed a bureaucratic logic: Himmler and Heydrich, along with the men of the SS, hoped to demonstrate that with their methods they could make whole zones of eastern Europe "*judenfrei.*" Franz Walter Stahlecker, the ranking SS officer in charge of *Einsatzgruppe* A, even created a rudimentary map, sketching out the number of Jews that his men had killed in the Baltic countries and in White Russia, appending it to a report sent to Heydrich on October 15, 1941. Stahlecker, or the man who made the map for him, actually employed coffins to symbolize the dead, and already labeled Estonia "free of Jews."[68]

When zealous Nazi administrators attempted to clear their own areas of eastern Europe of extant Jewish populations, a second kind of murderous logic, leading to different methods of killing, unfolded. During the occupation of Poland, ridding areas of Jews mainly involved expulsion. But in the summer of 1941, it came to embrace outright murder. As with the Soviet POWs, the hunger crisis, not the brutality of the war, provided the alibi. And it was again the Warthegau, far from the front, that took the lead. The idea, "in part fantastic," but nevertheless "thoroughly feasible"—as Major Rolf-Heinz Höppner described it in an infamous and often cited memorandum of July 16, 1941—involved the deportation of "all the Jews of the Warthegau" in such a way that those capable of labor would be employed in barracks guarded by the SS, while the women would be sterilized ("so that the Jewish problem may actually be eliminated completely with this generation").[69] Höppner appreciated that not everyone could work, and given the food shortage expected in the winter of 1941–1942, he calculated that "not all of the Jews can be fed."[70] Instead, he suggested another approach. "One should weigh honestly, if the most humane solution might not be to finish off those of the Jews who are not employable by means of some quick working device," and added, "at any rate, that would be more pleasant than letting them starve to death."[71]

Höppner outlined a possibility, but he did not give an order. A change of plans, however, soon brought Höppner's scenario closer to reality. Hitler had originally wanted to wait to expel the German Jews until after the war with Russia. But in mid-September, amid the jubilation of the early victories of the Wehrmacht, he changed course and accelerated efforts to make Germany and the occupied territories "free of Jews." After a meeting with Himmler on September 17, Hitler ordered the expulsion of all Jews from Germany and the Protectorate of Bohemia and Moravia.[72] The first transports departed the Reich in mid-October, and the first twenty trains carried some 20,000 Jewish men, women, and children to Łódź, the largest ghetto in the Warthegau and the second largest in Poland—with 40,000 more to come. It will be recalled that Arthur Greiser was the Gauleiter of the Warthegau, and that he and his men counted among the most eager officials working to create a "blonde province" free of Jews. Thus, with this new turn of events, Greiser's hopes to become the first Gauleiter to create a completely Aryan eastern province were dashed. He therefore shifted gears, hoping to make the Łódź Ghetto productive by using Jews as slave labor to support the voracious needs of the German army, all the while reserving the possibility to give "special treatment," as it were, to the estimated 100,000 Jews Greiser had deemed unproductive. It seems that Greiser had essentially asked Himmler for permission to kill them.[73] And Himmler assented to the request.

The question remained how to carry out this mass-murder campaign. It so happened that Greiser had an employee by the name of Herbert Lange, who had worked on the euthanasia program and had killed more than 10,000 handicapped people, mainly by locking them in mobile gas vans (where they were killed by either tossing gas pellets inside the vans or rerouting the carbon monoxide exhaust into the sealed compartment). As the *Einsatzgruppen* in Lithuania, Latvia, White Russia, and Ukraine were already killing men, women, and children in disheartening numbers with bullets, the step taken in the Warthegau to kill with gas seemed merely one of method.

The decision to situate the killing in one place—Chełmno, some forty miles north of Łódź—was, however, a new element. It meant transporting Jews to a permanent killing site, rather than having the killing squads going to the various places where Jews lived and killing them there. Lange received the first transports at Chełmno on December 7, and in the next six months his men killed 100,000 Jews by rerouting gas into the back compartments of sealed vans. Nevertheless, when the murders in Chełmno began, it was not yet, as recent research has shown, part of a general or systematic plan to kill all the Jews of Europe. Rather, it was a case of second-level Nazis handling what they perceived as a "local problem"—in this case, how to rid the Warthegau of its Jews.[74]

VII

In June 1941, just after the invasion of the Soviet Union started, Hitler began to spend much of his time in the "Wolf's Lair" near Rastenburg in East Prussia. These new military headquarters were, of course, used primarily to monitor the eastern front. But it also put Hitler in close proximity to the genocide, and in particular it was Himmler who kept him apprised of the latest developments. Although Himmler's appointment calendar is missing for the critical period from June 25 to August 12, it is apparent from other sources that he constantly traveled back and forth between the Wolf's Lair and the killing fields of Latvia, Lithuania, White Russia, eastern Poland, and Ukraine. For example, he went to Białystok on July 8 and conferred with Kurt Daluege, the head of the Order Police, just before Police Battalions 316 and 322 murdered some 3000 Jewish men.[75] He also met with Hans-Adolf Prützmann and Heinrich Lohse, high-ranking SS officers in Riga, at the end of July, just as their killing units in Latvia and Lithuania began to shoot an increasingly large number of women and children. Then, on August 15, Himmler witnessed a mass execution of Jewish men and two Jewish women in a village outside Minsk, although whether he thereafter ordered the killings of all Jewish men, women, and children in the Soviet Union, as historians once thought, remains unclear—and is actually doubtful. What is certain is that by the next afternoon he had flown back to Rastenburg to lunch with Hitler at the Wolf's Lair.[76] In early August, Himmler had lunch or supper with Hitler almost every other day.[77] It is hard to imagine that the genocidal escalation—in the second week of August—occurred without Hitler's full approval and encouragement.[78]

Paradoxically, there is little evidence that Hitler had fundamentally abandoned his policy of expulsion from German-occupied territory. The original charge to Reinhard Heydrich—made in January 1939—had been to pursue, "by emigration or evacuation, a solution of the Jewish question."[79] The "solution," as envisaged before the start of the war, was to make the Third Reich, including the recently incorporated Austria, "free of Jews."[80] On July 31, 1941, two and a half years later, Heydrich was given the task of "making all the necessary organizational, functional, and material preparations for a complete solution of the Jewish question in the German sphere of influence in Europe."[81] The note, signed by Göring but drafted by Heydrich himself, is sometimes seen as the order to kill the Jews of Europe. Yet even in this note, drafted after the beginning of the invasion of the Soviet Union, there is no mention that the end goal—forced emigration and evacuation—had changed. Circumstances had, however, altered dramatically. The sphere of German influence was greater and the number of Jews in German-ruled territory larger. The scope of the armed conflict had also expanded. In this context, the memorandum gave the SS the go-ahead to pursue the "complete solution" in the midst of war, and not to postpone it until afterward.

What did "complete solution" actually mean? Our first instinct is to assume that it meant killing all the Jews of Europe. Yet if we consider the course of the war until the end of July 1941, it becomes clear that the Nazis, exalting in the heady initial victories of the first six weeks of their Soviet invasion, would not have imagined that the war would drag on for another four years. Probably, they thought it would end much sooner, and the possibilities of expulsion—to somewhere in the east—would remain open. The note also asked Heydrich to submit "an overall plan." As Christopher Browning, the eminent historian of the genocide, explains, this was essentially a request for a "feasibility study."[82] But for what, exactly? For genocide? For the expulsion of the Jews to a place of certain death? It bears recalling that before the invasion of the Soviet Union began, Nazi leaders had already assumed the mass death of millions of Soviet civilians by starvation. Why, two months later, would a "complete solution" involve anything less?

A feasibility plan is not, however, a decision, and the precise context in which leading Nazis thought about Jews within their dominion would soon change again. With the first harsh winter setting in, the blitzkrieg grinding to a halt, and German losses mounting, it became apparent that the war in the east was far from over. It was also evident that the conquered territories were draining resources. "When we shoot the Jews dead, let the prisoners of war perish, subject a large part of the population of big cities to death by starvation, and in the coming years will also lose part of the rural population to hunger," an economic adviser to the occupation of Ukraine noted, "then the question remains unanswered: who is supposed to actually produce economic value here?"[83] The question framed a reorientation of regime policies, especially the use of millions of POWs for work. Although an untold number of Soviet prisoners were still to perish, Hermann Göring's directive, issued on November 7, to exploit their labor signaled the beginning of a policy shift, especially as it came just before central decisions about Jewish policy were made.[84] The policy involved a choice to utilize one group, Soviet POWs, at least for the time being, while sacrificing another group, the Jews, despite the obvious fact that in many areas Jews continued to work as slave labor.

By mid-November, the highest level of Nazi leadership was considering the fundamental decision of whether to kill all the Jews of Europe. In a speech delivered on November 18, 1941, two nights after meeting with Hitler and Himmler, Alfred Rosenberg, Reichsminister for the Occupied Eastern Territories, wondered whether it was now still necessary "to push them [the Jews] across the Urals or to bring about in some other way their eradication."[85] The precise articulation of the two possibilities—expulsion or the "biological eradication of all Jewry in Europe" (as Rosenberg put it)—was itself new, and Rosenberg equivocated as to which direction Nazi leadership would pursue. The very next day, Himmler and Rosenberg reached a modus vivendi, which allowed for closer cooperation in killing operations between the SS and the civil administration in the occupied territories.

Various ministerial and regional leaders now attempted to draw Jewish policy into their own bureaucratic domains. Rosenberg insisted that Jewish questions, even when taken care of on the ground by the SS, were nevertheless to be pursued in "the context of the overall policy" of the ethnic reshaping of the east, which would have the effect of placing it under his direction. Hans Frank, the Gauleiter of the General Government in Poland, tried, as one SS officer complained, "to pull the management of the Jewish problem completely to his sphere." Himmler, meanwhile, wrote in his appointment calendar on November 24 that "Jewish questions belong to me."[86]

It was largely in order to demarcate administrative territory and adjudicate disputes that Reinhard Heydrich, Himmler's right-hand man, sent out, between November 29 and December 1, invitations for a meeting scheduled for December 9, 1941, at the offices of the International Criminal Police Organization, or Interpol.[87] But after the Japanese attack on Pearl Harbor on December 7, the United States declared war on Japan, and Germany responded, on December 11, by declaring war on America. During this period, Heydrich postponed the meeting until January 20, 1942, and relocated it to an opulent villa serenely overlooking the Wannsee.

It is likely that Hitler around this time decided that the "final solution," involving the eradication of the Jews of Europe, should commence immediately.[88] Hitler raised the specter of extermination on seven occasions between October 19 and December 18, and five of these occasions fell within days of December 11.[89] On December 13, Joseph Goebbels, the notorious propaganda minister, noted in his diary that Hitler had decided to "make a clean sweep."[90] The connection in Hitler's mind between what we have termed "sacrifice for" and "sacrifice of" was in this decisive instance intimate. "We are not here to feel empathy with the Jews," Goebbels paraphrased Hitler as saying, "but to have empathy with the German people," and in particular with the soldiers sacrificing their lives on the front.[91]

Other high-ranking leaders expressed similar sentiments. "We want to have compassion only for the German people," announced Hans Frank a week later before a gathering of district officials in the General Government on December 16, "otherwise for no one in the world."[92] As to the fate of the Jews, he declared that he would "proceed only on the assumption that they will disappear."[93] Frank's recent trip to Berlin had underscored that there was no longer any place for the Jews farther east. As he paraphrased it, Frank was essentially told to "liquidate them yourselves."[94] He reminded his audience—a third level of Nazi hierarchy—to surrender any vestiges of compassion: "We must destroy the Jews wherever we encounter them and wherever it is possible, in order to preserve the entire structure of the Reich."[95]

There is also compelling evidence from Himmler's appointment book that a decision had been made to accelerate the killing process. In his meetings with high-ranking officials involved in the euthanasia campaign, Himmler explored ways to step up the efforts to use gas to kill Jews.[96] Within two weeks, euthanasia technicians appeared in Bełżec, a death camp that had been under construction since November but was not yet in operation. A note from December 18 in Himmler's appointment book mentions a meeting with Hitler at Wolf's Lair. It states tersely: "Jewish question | as Partisans to exterminate."[97]

VIII

Nazi Germany killed noncombatants in three ways. One was by confinement, essentially starving to death Soviet military prisoners and Jews concentrated in ghettos. A second way—until recently insufficiently researched by historians—was by bullets. Gas was the third way. It was this last method that was largely responsible for the explosion in Nazi murder rates in 1942, especially in Poland.

To place this shift in context, it is necessary to recall the horrific ledger of Nazi war crimes. By mid-January 1942, some three million Soviet POWs had been captured, and through a policy of deliberate starvation more than two million of them were already dead. The siege of Leningrad was entering its first fatal winter—there too the deliberate encirclement of the city and the starvation of the population had already caused the death of hundreds of thousands of civilians. Dystrophic ghosts seemed to stalk the city, as people killed for ration cards and hid the bodies so as to collect the dead's allotted shares.[98] By this time, the Jews had also been decimated. The *Einsatzgruppen*, the German Order Police, units of the Waffen-SS, and some regular army units had by now killed more than 500,000 Jews in central Europe—the vast majority with bullets. As previously noted, they killed not just men, but women and children, now in numbers commensurate with men. In the six months after the invasion of the Soviet Union began, Germany had committed mass murder on a scale without comparison—either in its own history or in the history of non-Russian Europe.

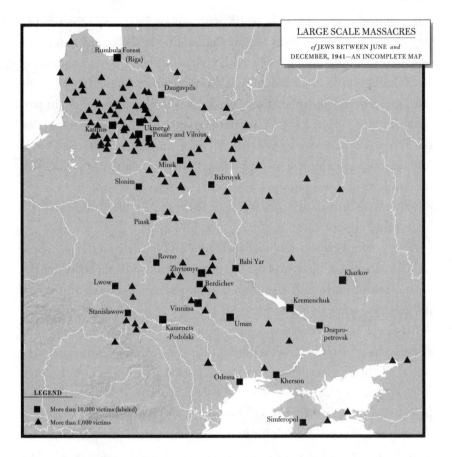

LARGE SCALE MASSACRES
of JEWS BETWEEN JUNE *and*
DECEMBER, 1941—AN INCOMPLETE MAP

LEGEND

■ More than 10,000 victims (labeled)

▲ More than 1,000 victims

In January 1942, the killing strategy began to shift, and it was the Wannsee Conference, which convened on January 20, that inaugurated the change. The conference widened the geographical scope of the genocide from Nazi-occupied areas to Jewish communities in all of Europe. Evacuation was no longer a "final solution," as earlier documents intimated, but at best a "provisional option . . . in view of the final coming solution of the Jewish question."[99] While the Wannsee Protocol did not make absolutely clear that Nazi Germany would kill every last Jew in Europe, it did abandon the policy that primarily focused on making places and regions under Germany's control "free of Jews." It also authorized the deportation of central and western European Jews to the east while selecting some Jews to work, "in an expedient manner in the course of the final solution."[100] The Nazis intended on immediately exterminating those not selected to work.

The protocol does not use the word "exterminate," yet in the absence of a deportation option, this was the only possibility left.[101] In any case, ominous hints to this effect were contained in the summarized comments of Josef Bühler, Hans Frank's deputy at the conference. Bühler implored the Reich to proceed with the "final solution" as swiftly as possible, in part because of the outbreaks of typhus in the ghettos of Poland, and urged that the final solution begin in the General Government, where transport was less complicated, and where—according to his calculation—"of the 2 1/2 million Jews in question, the majority of the cases were *unfit to work*."[102] There can be little doubt that everyone at the table understood what was being said.[103]

The conference secured the acceptance and formalized the participation of a series of ministries of the German government in the mass murder of the Jews of Europe. It also placed the leadership and coordination of the genocide squarely in the hands of Himmler, Heydrich, and the SS.[104] What the meeting, or at least the protocol of it, did not do, however, was address the specific method of killing. The document contained no mention of Chełmno, already in operation, or Bełżec, then under construction, or Auschwitz, a place where gas in the form of a pesticide named Zyklon B was already being used to kill Soviet POWs. Rather, the protocols of the meeting, drafted by Adolf Eichmann, who would soon organize the deportation of the Jews of Europe to the death camps, and reworked by Heydrich, summed up the results of the conference in the form of general guidelines. We know that thirty copies were made, and as many as three hundred Nazi officials saw the protocol.[105]

IX

Wannsee marked the beginning of the end of the Jewish ghettos of Europe. Previously, there had been essentially two models: those in central and western Poland, caught between Nazis trying to both utilize the ghettos to turn a profit while eliminating the resident Jews by attrition, and those of eastern Poland, Lithuania, Latvia, Estonia, White Russia, Russia, and Ukraine, where ghettos were typically holding pens before massacres.[106] Following the Wannsee Conference, new ghettos were mainly anterooms for death.

The liquidations of Jewish ghettos and the subsequent deportations of Jews to killing centers were extremely violent affairs. We know from reports from the great urban ghettos, like Warsaw, that tens of thousands of Jews hid in holes and sewers, and in the cracks between walls. In Łódź, Chaim Rumkowski, the head of the Jewish Council, turned over thousands of children in a desperate gamble to keep the rest of the ghetto alive. By contrast, we know comparatively little about the struggles of the Jewish ghettos in the smaller cities, towns, and villages.

Depending on the size of the community, the Nazis usually encircled such ghettos with hundreds of forces, typically drawn from Polish, Lithuanian, Latvian, or Ukrainian auxiliary troops, gendarmes, or police units. In some communities, the Nazis began by killing the ill, the old, and even the children in nearby forests; in others, they killed them in the middle of town; and in still others, like Pajęczno, a small village north of Częstochowa, in a churchyard. As many of the rural ghettos were not on railway lines, the Jews were sometimes stuffed into trucks or horse-drawn wagons, and delivered to distant railways stations or to the next largest ghetto. In a number of small towns, like Limanowa in southern Poland and Radzymin on the outskirts of Warsaw, the Nazis forced the Jews to fast-walk or even run to the next town, city, or train station. They shot those who did not make it.

The Nazis killed an astonishing number of people this way. Along the twenty-five miles of road from the village of Łosice to the town of Siedlce in eastern Poland, the Nazis gunned down roughly a thousand Jews. Likewise, "the entire highway from Biłgoraj to Zwierzyniec" in southeastern Poland was, according to one witness, "littered with the bodies of Jews."[107] Moreover, in many places, there was not just one deportation. Especially in such medium-sized cities as Rzeszów, Tarnów, and Zamość, the Nazis organized the deportations in installments, each time decimating the ghetto by a few thousand people. In a variation, as occurred in Nowy Sącz, the Nazis created one ghetto for the Jews who would be killed, and another for those who might yet work. After the whole ghetto was finally liquidated, the Nazis used the empty buildings as holding places for new transports from the region—before ultimately shipping the entrapped Jews to Bełżec.

The ghetto liquidations were extremely violent operations, in no small measure because they met ferocious, desperate resistance, especially on the part of young Jews. This point bears emphasizing. This was not an orderly, rational procedure, and Jews were not passive. It was mayhem, and there was a great deal of resistance, even though much of it was not well organized.[108] The resistance often started the night before, when the Nazis reinforced the ghettos with barbed wire, which both townspeople and Jews understood as a sign that deportation was imminent.[109] In town after town, Jews escaped to the forests, hid in buildings, paid Poles to hide them, or tried to fight off their oppressors with hastily made weapons. The portion of Jews who resisted in these ways was as high as 10 percent throughout occupied Poland. Given that there were still 2.5 million Jews alive in Poland at the beginning of 1942, this indicates that as many as 250,000 Jews either fought or went into hiding.[110]

The outcomes of organized resistance differed from place to place. In Mińsk Mazowiecki, a small town in central Poland, roughly a thousand Jews, a third of the Jewish population, resisted deportation but ended up by being shot. In the southeastern Polish village of Tyszowce, about a fifth of the population staged an ill-fated revolt. But these were isolated incidents. In eastern Poland, which had been occupied by the Soviet Union between 1939 and 1941, armed resistance was more prevalent—largely because of the greater density of Zionist and Communist organizations, which resulted in networks of underground groups that were essential for successful revolt. But even in this part of Poland, organized and armed insurrections staged during the liquidations proved sporadic—there were only twenty-three cases, according to the calculations of the scholar Evgeny Finkel.[111]

Nonetheless, a great deal of spontaneous resistance arose, as can be seen from the sheer magnitude of violence and chaos. Writing about the liquidation of the ghetto in the town of Szczebrzeszyn, southeast of Lublin, Zygmunt Klukowski, an unusually observant Polish doctor, described that Nazis, as well as the Polish "blue police" in SS employ, took Jews from their "houses, barns, cellars, attics, and other hiding places." By midafternoon, there were some nine hundred Jews assembled—but between four and five hundred had been killed, and, according to his information, "approximately two thousand people are in hiding."[112]

To many Jews, hiding, despite its dangers, seemed preferable to revolt. In the eastern Polish town of Międzyrzec Podlaski, nearly two thousand Jews broke away as the ghetto was being dissolved; in the town of Radzyń in the Lublin District, roughly half of the population went into hiding; and in Łaskarzew, southeast of Warsaw, some eight hundred Jews found their way into the forests, occasioning a monthlong "Jew hunt." Going into hiding was generally easier for assimilated Jews, who knew the local Catholic environment, than for Orthodox or Hasidic Jews, whose survival chances were abysmal in 1942.[113] It was, of course, easier for the young, who could run, than for the old. And it was a strategy more used by men than by women, who were less willing to leave their children or elderly parents. But even if Jews escaped deportations, they still faced the subsequent sweeps of the Nazis and the prolonged hunts of their neighbors. Nevertheless, the countryside held out a glimmer of hope. In the ghettos of Warsaw and Łódź, walls, barbed-wire fences, and legions of guards kept Poles and Jews separate. In the rural areas, where ghettos were sometimes open and sometimes closed, ties between Jews inside and Poles outside often remained intact.

Yet these ties seldom held. In the summer of 1942, the Nazis began to enforce the death penalty for those concealing Jews, and as a result thousands of Polish peasants turned out Jews who had been paying for their hiding places. Sometimes the Poles were motivated by fear of the Nazis, sometimes by anti-Jewish hostility, especially when they handed over the Jews they had harbored instead of letting them flee into the woods. More lethal still was the so-called Jew hunt. In Dąbrowa Tarnowska, north of Tarnów, an official statistic records that 286 Jews were discovered and killed in such hunts, and that local Poles turned in 200 of them.[114] They essentially tipped off SS men, or the German Order Police, or the Polish "blue police," or even the Jewish Ghetto Police, who then took up the leads and ferreted out Jews in abandoned sheds, makeshift holes in the earth, or underground tunnels. Poles also took the initiative and hunted down Jews by themselves—in no small measure because the Germans paid them for their efforts: in *zloty*, with vodka and sugar, and with the clothes of the victims.

Deaths in the ghettos, including liquidations, are estimated at between 500,000 and 800,000 lives—roughly 10 percent of the Jews killed in the genocide. Those who survived were packed into boxcars and transported to extermination camps whose main purpose was simply to kill Jews. This new strategy of transporting victims to killing sites brought the railroads, the classic nineteenth-century technology for controlling large areas of territory, centrally into the destruction process.[115] Ghetto liquidations, in coordination with the railroads, became a daily part of Nazi murder operations, and would involve a new circle of bureaucrats with knowledge of, and complicity in, what was happening. Because the Nazis never set up a specific budget for the destruction of the European Jews, the SS had to pay for the transports, as if Jews were like any other kind of cargo. As the trains traveled through various countries with varying currency units, the financial and logistical transactions were often complex. This process typically involved SS captains having to deal with otherwise unimportant railway officials—"ordinary men," as the historian Raul Hilberg put it, "performing extraordinary tasks."[116] Moreover, the train schedules typically required very low security clearance, if one at all, so all stationmasters on a given route, who would receive the schedules, could literally envision the path of the transport train, heavy with some twenty to fifty cars, arriving at places like Treblinka or Bełżec, and then returning, as one could see from the detailed schedule, unburdened with empty cars a few hours later.

The trains were known as *Judenzüge*, "Jewish trains."[117] Between 1942 and 1944, some two thousand trains transported well over two million Jews to death camps—a small number compared with the total passenger traffic of the German *Reichsbahn* in these years. Yet from testimonies of peasants and Jewish survivors, we know that people in villages abutting the rails heard the screams of the thirsty, doomed passengers as they passed on their way to the extermination camps.[118] When the trains stopped—which happened often given the confusion of military transport, death traffic, as well as ordinary freight and passenger trains—a market for water sometimes came into being, as Jews trapped in cattle cars paid Poles and Ukrainians for sips of water.[119] In the Polish town of Szczebrzeszyn, a young woman exchanged her wedding ring for a cup of water for her child.[120]

By 1942, the newly erected extermination camps dictated the timing and geography of ghetto liquidations. This was an entirely new development. Until December 1941, the camp system had been marginal to the genocide.[121] The number of Jews killed in the camps paled in comparison with those who had been shot to death. Then, places like Chełmno became the model. Built to accelerate the Warthegau's progress toward becoming "free of Jews," Chełmno commenced operation on December 7, which allowed the Nazis to dissolve the rural ghettos in its immediate vicinity and kill Jews deemed "unfit to work." In Chełmno, Nazis forced Jews into sealed vans, then drove them on a set route for about forty-five minutes with exhaust pipes rerouted into a sealed compartment. In this way, they killed all the Jews trapped inside the van, typically seventy people at a time. They then emptied the vans in a nearby wood and forced local Poles to bury the bodies.

X

For the Nazis, Chełmno was not nearly fast enough. In March 1942, Bełżec opened its gates. In May, Sobibór started to kill Jews. And in July, Treblinka began its murderous operations. The new extermination centers possessed astonishing killing capacity. Some 120 men, all experienced killers, who had already murdered more than 70,000 people with disabilities, ran these killing centers.[122] At any given time, each of the camps consisted of roughly twenty Nazi guards, eighty Ukrainian or other Eastern European helpers, and as many as five hundred Jews forced to aid the process before they themselves were killed.[123] The Nazi guards were almost never "ordinary men." Of the SS members, three-quarters were "old fighters" (men who had joined the Nazi Party before 1933), most were between twenty-eight and forty-two (and thus belonged to the generation of men too young to have fought in World War I), and almost all were true believers in National Socialism.[124]

It was, in fact, in the death camps of Bełżec, Sobibór, and Treblinka that the vaunted efficiency of the Nazis came into full view. Typically, trains with some fifty boxcars or cattle cars pulled up to ramps. German and Ukrainian guards hurried the famished and thirsty Jews from the trains, beat and whipped them, and falsely informed them that they were in a transit camp. Desperate, most Jews clung to the illusion. The guards then reinforced the deception by separating the Jews, men to one side, women and children to the other, and telling them to undress for purposes of disinfection. Sometimes, to make the ruse seem real, the Nazis made Jews in special units shave the heads of other Jews. The guards then rushed the Jews down an enclosed road, or "tube," where they were forced to wait, naked, before being pushed, men first, into the gas chamber, the doors locked behind, as stationary motors pumped carbon monoxide into the sealed rooms. Thereafter the women and children were shoved in. Those Jews who arrived too weak to walk were taken to a special barrack, or the *Lazarett* ("hospital") as it was cynically called in Treblinka, and shot immediately.[125] In the late summer of 1942, the Treblinka guards, working from sunrise to sunset, murdered an average of eight thousand Jews daily.[126]

Commentators often focus on the precision of the killing operation, yet from the Nazi standpoint, it was the disposal of the bodies, not the killings, that required technical precision and effective solutions. In Operation Reinhard (the code name for the attempt to kill most of the Jews of Poland in three extermination camps), the Nazis buried the bodies of murdered Jews: in Treblinka and Sobibór, they dug precisely calculated rows behind the gas chambers, and in Bełżec, Jews were dumped into large, helter-skelter mass graves (thirty-three of them, according to recently conducted archaeological research).[127] In Treblinka, the sheer number of buried bodies caused the grounds to buckle, forcing the Nazis to open the pits—after late summer 1942 with excavators—and burn the corpses on huge open pyres. "Tongues of flame" rose "into the night," one witness from outside the death camp recalled.[128] But even this process was not as thorough and precise as is sometimes imagined. When the Nazis closed the camps of Operation Reinhard in 1943, they had to keep local scavengers from digging up corpses and searching for gold teeth. After the war, the fields of Treblinka—as Rachel Auerbach, a survivor who returned to the grounds in November 1945 attested—were "sown with human bones," the earth "torn up and dug up," and replete with "all sorts of objects," testifying to a postliberation "Treblinka gold rush," as she called it.[129]

Like Chełmno, the extermination camps of Bełżec, Sobibór, and Treblinka were essentially regional killing factories—voracious engines of death that emptied the Jewish ghettos in the villages, towns, and cities around them.[130] We can see this pattern clearly by plotting the liquidated ghettos of the parts of Poland occupied by Nazi Germany in 1939 against the death camps to which Jews had been sent. The camps essentially drew in from the nearby regions: Bełżec from southern Lublin, Cracow, and Galicia; Sobibór from eastern Poland and from northern Lublin; and Treblinka from the districts of Warsaw, Radom, and Białystok.[131]

The dimensions of the killings have lost none of their capacity to shock our sensibilities. In Treblinka alone, between July 1942 and October 1943, some 800,000 Jews were killed in "ten small chambers, hardly enough space, if properly furnished, to stable a hundred horses," as the Soviet writer Vasily Grossman observed. Among the dead were over 300,000 Jews from the Warsaw Ghetto, more civilians than immediately perished in Hiroshima and Nagasaki combined.[132] The Jews of a great many smaller places were also put on this "vast executioner's block."[133] When Grossman came upon Treblinka with his unit of the Red Army in September 1944, he thought the world had never before created such a hell.

Three months later, the Soviets approached Auschwitz.

XI

As the Red Army neared, Auschwitz guards feverishly began sending inmates back into the interior. They put one young girl, not yet sixteen years old, into a cattle car destined for Bergen-Belsen, by now a disease-ridden camp overflowing with prisoners. The girl, a mere shadow of her former self, arrived at Bergen-Belsen, where, overcome with hunger, cold, and exhaustion, she died, likely of typhus, just weeks before British troops arrived.

The girl was, of course, Anne Frank. Her diary allows us to imagine the two years of her life in hiding with great precision—until she was denounced, captured, interrogated, imprisoned for a week, and then interned with her family in the disciplinary barracks of Westerbork Transit Camp in the Netherlands. Her subsequent fate is more difficult to reconstruct. Between 1942 and the summer of 1944, the Nazis organized eighty-five separate transports from the Dutch transit camp to the east, sixty-six to Auschwitz, the rest to Sobibór. Anne Frank and her family were crammed in to the last train to Auschwitz. Over an arduous two days, the train traversed north Germany via Bremen, Berlin, and Breslau, before it entered the gates of Birkenau late on the night of September 5, 1944. Having turned fifteen a few months earlier, Anne Frank was not sent, as were all those under fifteen, immediately to her death. Instead, she was selected for work, disinfected, and forced to have her head shaven and a number painfully punched onto her forearm. With her mother and sisters, she was housed in Block 29 of the Birkenau Women's Camp, just beneath Crematoria II.

Thanks to the diary, and surviving photos, the world recognizes the face of Anne Frank. For reconstructing the fate of so many others, it is the preservation of the individual name in precise records that has been decisive. Here the difference between the genocide in eastern and western Europe is important. The mayhem and chaos that characterized the shootings and the pogroms in the east were not, as a rule, duplicated in western Europe, where the Nazis, working with their collaborators, documented the arrests and deportations of the west European Jews with far more precision.

The story of the family of Arno Klarsfeld is in this sense illuminating. When the Gestapo attempted to round up the Jews of the French city of Nice in the fall of 1943, Klarsfeld, along with his wife and two children, hid in their apartment. The Gestapo found the father, but not the mother, son, and daughter, who remained concealed inside a false partition. After interning Klarsfeld at the concentration camp in Drancy, north of Paris, the Nazis put him on a convoy that departed for Auschwitz on Thursday, October 28, 1943, and arrived two days later, the Jews trapped inside the cattle cars already dying of thirst. Of the one thousand Jews on the transport, the majority of them were sent immediately to the gas chambers, while the rest were given numbers, 159546–159817 for the men, and 66451–66553 for the women. Arno Klarsfeld, prisoner number 159683, survived the brutal ordeal of the ramp, and was selected for work in the so-called *Fürstengrube*, a subcamp of Auschwitz. In this I.G. Farben–owned coal mine, SS guards worked him to the edge of death, before sending him to the gas chambers of Birkenau.[134]

We know this because the rest of Arno's family—mother, daughter, and son—survived not only the Gestapo raid but the war itself. When the family came out of hiding, they remained in Nice for the winter months, before leaving for Le Puy-en-Velay in the Haute-Loire, where, it was said, Gestapo presence was minimal. The Klarsfelds then moved to the nearby village of Saint-Julien-Chapteuil, and the denizens of this small town quietly shielded them, along with a dozen other Jews, from the Germans.[135]

Arno's son, Serge Klarsfeld, who was only ten when the war was over, went on to study history and political science at the Sorbonne. Eventually he used his historian's training to figure out his Romanian father's fate, deducing it from transport lists, tattoo numbers, and infirmary records. Serge also began to use those transport lists to reveal the full magnitude of the Nazi crime. In *Le Mémorial de la déportation des Juifs de France*, published in 1978, he reproduced the lists for each of the trains, providing the names of the deported (in alphabetical order), the dates and places of birth (if available), and in some cases the nationality of each person. Somewhere in the middle of the unpaginated book, under convoy 61, one entry, as laconic as all the others, tells of his father: "Klarsfeld, Arno, 20.01.05, Brailia."[136] Typing up the names from the original deportation lists, Klarsfeld tabulated 75,700 names in all, the majority killed within hours after entering the gates of Auschwitz.

Later in life, Klarsfeld explored another "dark and little known corner" of the genocide, "the murders of 11,402 Jewish children who were arrested in France and deported to Nazi concentration camps," of whom only some 300 survived.[137] With the deportation lists as his starting point, Klarsfeld pursued the stories of these children, one by one, over a period of twenty years. He also assiduously tracked down photographs, drawing up short biographies to run with them. The resulting work, the *Mémorial des enfants juifs déportés de France*, was published in 1995. As Klarsfeld wrote in the preface, "The eyes of 2,500 children gaze at us from across the years in these pages."[138]

XII

When the German Sixth Army surrendered at Stalingrad in February 1943, 75 percent of the Jews who would be killed in the Holocaust were already dead. Although historians continue to debate the effect of Stalingrad in bringing the war to an end, in Germany itself an unmistakable fear that the war could drag on or even be lost took hold. The new pessimism also pervaded letters from the front. Writing in late January 1943, a cavalry captain was already blaming the downfall of the army on cruelty toward the peasantry, unfettered corruption, the murder of so many Russian POWs, and the "solution of the Jewish question."[139] By mid-1943, this common concern became more desperate, and by August 1944, fear of revenge and even annihilation had come to suffuse the letters of soldiers. "If we lose this war," one worried sergeant wrote, "we are done for decades, alone because of the revenge of the Jews," while another considered that "the Jews will then fall on us and exterminate whatever is German."[140]

This kind of anxiety, reflected in the letters of ordinary recruits, reveals that many soldiers knew about the mass killings of Jews.[141] This was especially true of the largest massacres, like Babi Yar, the news of which, "reached us like a wildfire in 1941 at the front behind Kiev," as one young German officer recalled.[142] Clandestinely taped conversations of captured German soldiers in British POW camps also document that German soldiers knew about the genocide, often down to the details of the "wagons" used to transport Jews to their death.[143] This evidence, derived more from officers than enlisted men, demonstrates that soldiers understood they could partake in shooting if they wanted to; that many engaged in a kind of execution tourism; and that the large killings, like Babi Yar, typically happened with significant army support. The taped conversations also disclose that rape was usually condoned, and that it typically ended by executing the woman.[144] In contrast to their accounts of the killing of Russian POWs, the captured soldiers betrayed little indignation about the murder of Jews, with the exception of some cases of Jewish women and children who were killed.[145]

Soldiers also passed along knowledge of the genocide to others. During the war, gossip abounded and rumors seeped back to the home front—so many, in fact, that Nazi courts stepped up their efforts in 1942 to punish anyone who spread them.[146] Nevertheless, murmurs about mass murder increased dramatically in this time. "Horrible stories are going around that the Jews, with women and children, are being killed en masse in open graves and on open fields," noted a master artisan in Hamburg in his diary, adding, "You can hardly hear it anymore, it makes you sick."[147]

In Germany, the knowledge of what was happening was far more widespread than is often assumed. In September 1942, when Friedrich Kellner, an anti-Nazi, midlevel official in Mainz, heard that "the last Jews were being deported from his district," he knew "from well-informed sources, that all the Jews were being brought to Poland and there they would be murdered by formations of the SS."[148] Rumors of mass murder proliferated. Kurt Dürkefälden, an ordinary draftsman in Lower Saxony, would encounter such rumors on multiple occasions. In February 1943, a soldier on a train told him about the mass murder of Russian POWs; in June his brother-in-law confessed that he had witnessed the mass execution of Jews in Ukraine; soon thereafter, his boss disclosed that he had heard from his own son that entire villages were being decimated in Białystok; and finally, his mother-in-law, a nurse in a military hospital, confided that one of the wounded soldiers there had bragged, "We have whacked ten thousand Jews in Russia."[149]

It was once thought that few Germans knew what was happening in the east. Now scholars debate whether the portion of adult Germans who knew about the mass murder of Jews was over a third or just under a half.[150] The killings were impossible to hide, especially given the enormity of the crimes, the many cities, towns, and villages in which they occurred, and the numbers of Germans and others who were perpetrators, accomplices, or direct witnesses. It is nevertheless entirely possible that the soldiers as well as civilians on the home front did not know about Treblinka or Auschwitz. Reinhart Koselleck, the young officer (and future historian) who claimed that news of Babi Yar had spread through the front like "wildfire," insisted he had never heard of Auschwitz until the Soviets, who were holding him captive, forced him to walk through the extermination camp and a Polish man accused the Germans of having gassed the Jews.[151]

The number of people directly involved in the murders is also much higher than previously imagined, even if the total number of Germans implicated in one or the other task of destruction remains a matter of speculation, as is the number of non-German accomplices throughout Europe. Some numbers, however, are instructive. In the Lublin District, for example, roughly 2000 German policemen participated in the deportations, while in one town alone in the District of Lwów, some 450 German civilians helped liquidate the local ghetto, or witnessed it, and subsequently signed an oath of secrecy.[152] But of course there were thousands of such towns.

At the end of the war, the Allies meted out sentences to some 100,000 Germans accused of crimes, although most were not related directly to the genocide.[153] Perhaps twice that number served as camp guards, mainly in the satellite camps, which mushroomed in number in the last years of the war. At least 3000 men were killers in the *Einsatzgruppen*, but those SS units constituted "only the thin cutting edge of German units that became involved in political and racial mass murder," as one historian has noted.[154]

Some 50,000 Germans served in the Police Battalions, which killed about half a million people in the east (though less than fifty of the men ever received prison sentences).[155]

Nor was military occupation exclusively a man's world. Some 30,000 German women worked for the SS, the Gestapo, and for police units in the east, while 10,000 served in the civil administration, and 3500 as camp guards.[156] From soldiers who assisted in massacres or observed shooting, to men who operated the trains or organized schedules, and women who typed up the orders and organized starvation rations—they all were complicit to various degrees. Most participated in one way or another, even if they did not pull a trigger. Perhaps some did not know there was a general plan to kill all the Jews of Europe, but there can be no doubt that they knew that the Jews in their field of vision would be either killed immediately or worked to death.

This was especially true in Poland. There was simply no way to hide the fact that in the course of a killing spree concentrated in the second half of 1942 the cradle of Jewish civilization in eastern Europe was turned into a graveyard of immense scale. Like the Germans, the Poles certainly knew.[157] They witnessed the liquidations in their hometowns—some helped Germans, others helped Jews, and many enriched themselves. All the German tourists who went to Warsaw, often with a newly issued Baedeker guide for the General Government in hand, were cognizant of it—because Warsaw's number-one tourist attraction, the Ghetto, was all of a sudden razed and it was without people.[158] All those who worked in any capacity in the occupation government also knew it—including the many thousands who worked in myriad private businesses in the east. Virtually no one could fail to notice the almost complete disappearance of the Jews in the course of the war. In 1939, Jews constituted about 10 percent of the population of Poland; for comparison, the African-American population makes up roughly 13 percent of the United States today.

In the last year of the war, awareness of the enormity of Nazi crimes increased significantly. Especially inside the Third Reich, concentration camps proliferated, and the number of Jews and eastern workers siphoned off from more hellish fates grew apace. The postwar emphasis on the famous camps to the east has obfuscated the importance of this expansion. Thus, by August 1944, Buchenwald and Dachau each had more than seventy satellite camps. Nearly 60 percent of all "Buchenwald" inmates were in the satellite rather than the main camps, and far more visible to civilians. As the satellite camps opened as fast as they closed, the total number of such camps is difficult to estimate. One scholar puts the number as of January 1945 at close to 560.[159] These camps dotted the map of Germany with *punctums*, to use Roland Barthes's term for the disturbing detail of a photo that reveals a visible inhumanity.[160]

The ever-growing concentration camp system transformed whole areas of Germany. For example, the camps of Mittelbau-Dora, itself a subcamp of Buchenwald, reshaped the Harz Mountains. A countryside that had once been evoked through bluish peaks in the paintings of Caspar David Friedrich became a landscape pocked by sites of exploitation, torture, and murder.[161] East of the Danubian city of Linz, the concentration camp of Mauthausen incarcerated a prisoner for every five civilians, transforming the otherwise idyllic hills of this area into a heavily guarded facility.[162] Unlike earlier stages in the evolution of the camp system, toward the end of the war the concentration camps employed people outside their walls, often with overseers who were not ideological SS guards but ordinary policemen or veterans who could no longer be deployed at the front. As the SS officers put more and more inmates in private firms, on roads, or at work clearing the rubble from destroyed cities, they had to constantly move the prisoners from camp to camp. One survivor, Nechama Epstein-Kozlowski, told David Broder, an American psychologist who conducted some of the earliest interviews with liberated Jews, of how she had been shipped to Majdanek, then to Auschwitz, back to Majdanek, then to Płaszów, back to Auschwitz, then to Bergen-Belsen, then to Aschersleben (a satellite camp of Buchenwald), and finally to Theresienstadt.[163]

XIII

Even as the war was in its final throes, the Nazis pushed on with the genocide. In May 1944, the first deportations from newly occupied Hungary arrived in Auschwitz. The killing operation worked at an unbelievably frenetic pace, putting to death some 20,000 Jews every day. When a train full of Hungarian Jews arrived in the camp, they were shouted at, beaten, and tormented, and within the span of four hours, most—in fact, 95 percent—

were sent to the gas chambers. As the crematoria that incinerated their bodies could hardly handle the flood of corpses, special commandos of prisoners worked day and night, feeding the furnaces. The ashes rose, as the poet Paul Celan later wrote, to "a grave you will have in the clouds," where, the poet sardonically added, "one lies unconfined."[164]

Of the some 1.1 million people killed in Auschwitz, 900,000 were Jews. Of the victims, 70 percent never received a number or had their name entered in a book. Nevertheless, individual names of the dead were in many cases still recorded during World War II. Even for Soviet soldiers who were captured, the German army created identity cards for roughly half of them—although this meant that the death of more than 1.5 million still went undocumented.[165] Such identity documents were also extant for Jews from western Europe, Jews from the Reich, and of course for any Jew who could work. Even in Auschwitz, guards made lists of those who survived the selection (on average, such prisoners lived for another three months). And still, most never received such a number—an omission tantamount to their erasure.[166] In Bełżec, Treblinka, and Sobibór, there were no such lists, and the *Einsatzgruppen*, in their furious activities, did not make them either.[167] Today, historians continue to try to find the exact locations of all the places where Germans and their accomplices murdered Jews.

Although still incomplete, these efforts allow us to glimpse a continent scarred by concentration camps, ghettos, and killing sites. According to scholars from the U.S. Holocaust Memorial Museum, the National Socialists and their allies erected more than 1500 concentration camps, while the Nazis alone created some 1100 ghettos (almost all of which they liquidated between 1942 and 1943, killing nearly all the Jews who could not escape).[168] The number of killing sites is every bit as daunting. In a still incomplete register, the Yad Vashem Memorial Foundation has provided descriptions for almost 2700 places where the Nazis and their accomplices killed Jews on the lands of the former Soviet Union alone, and of these, at least 1000 involve the murder of more than 100 people.[169] A seemingly endless number of airfields, antitank ditches, clay quarries, meadows, vacant plots, riverbanks, and town squares became sites of murder—and as many as a third of them remain unmarked.[170] Taken together, the camps, ghettos, and death spaces remade Europe and created a map of a continent disfigured by murder, death, and loss.

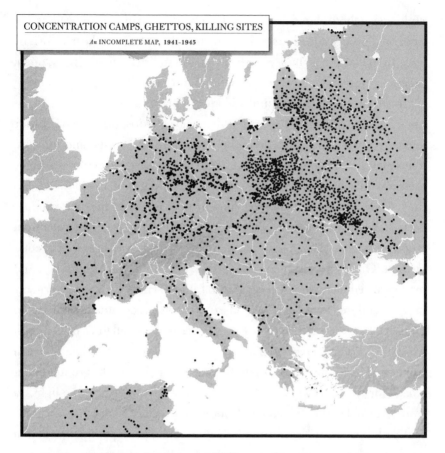

CONCENTRATION CAMPS, GHETTOS, KILLING SITES
An INCOMPLETE MAP, **1941-1945**

An incomplete map of concentration camps of the Nazis and their allies, of Jewish ghettos, and of major killing sites where Nazis killed Jews in the Soviet Union, 1941–1945.

XIV

The poets who tried, however hesitantly, to come to terms with this scarred continent looked, as the baroque poets once did, to inversions of the natural and man-made world. In "Aspen Tree," first composed in 1945 (though perhaps as early as 1943), then reworked and published in 1950, Paul Celan wrote of his mother, Friederike (Fritzi), whom the Nazis murdered in the winter of 1942–1943 in an obscure concentration camp about a hundred miles southwest of Kiev. Celan contrasts the leaves of the aspen tree "glancing white into the dark" with her hair, never allowed even to gray; and imagines the dandelion-filled green of Ukraine, which she could no longer behold. He describes a dry cloud hovering over a well as she wept, and evokes a Jewish star in tandem with her "ripped heart," torn by lead. In the last lines, he sees only an oak door, lifted off its hinges, open, except to "my gentle mother," who "cannot return."[171]

It is no accident that naturalistic images preoccupied the poetry of the time. Save for those incarcerated in the major ghettos, the Jews of Europe looked out and saw a rural world of farms, fields, forests, and villages. Those Jews who had been able to go into hiding tried desperately to make their way in a largely rural landscape, in which the winter cold tormented them (they could not make fires for fear of being seen) and the summer heat produced thirst so urgent that many died drinking stagnant water from muddied puddles. Some Jews wandered, with no refuge, in search of compassion. Others buried themselves in the ground, or built a bunker, and mainly stayed there. For instance, Jacob Littner, who, exiled from Germany in 1938, endured as an "expellee" in eastern Europe, eventually sequestered himself (along with his wife) beneath a house in the small town of Zbaraż in western Ukraine.[172] His experience was many times repeated. In a village in southern Poland, the Golds, a family of eight, repaired to the ground under a barn for twenty-seven months. "On sunny days we had some light," a seven-year-old survivor recounted, "otherwise complete darkness."[173]

Of all images, the sun turned black became, perhaps, the most often employed metaphor of Holocaust poetry. In Abraham Sutzkever's "Stalks," the sun gathers back its light, just as in Nelly Sachs's "O the Chimneys," it welcomes the smoke from the crematoria.[174] The blotted-out sun also haunts less schooled reflections. Edith P., the youngest in a family of six children from a devout Jewish family in eastern Hungary, evoked the same dark sun as it rose in the early morning above Auschwitz. In a filmed testimony in the 1980s, she remembered that when the sun rose, "it was not like the sun," it was "not bright," it was "always red to me, it was always black to me, it never said—never, never was life to me."[175] She also recollected a later time when she saw the sun from inside of a boxcar on a train that had departed Auschwitz and was halted, momentarily, somewhere in Germany. A friend helped her up so that she could see out of a "little window, with bars," and Edith P. then saw that "the sun was bright and vivid," and that "there were three or four people outside, one woman with a child, nicely dressed up." "Paradise must look like this!" she thought.[176]

Her testimony reminds us that the Nazi imposition of "living space" created a corresponding death space for most of Europe's Jews. Forty years later, Edith P's voice still trembled with barely suppressed rage at her confinement. As if it were a recent memory, the older woman could still recall the young girl's one desire. "I had such yearning to live, to run, to just run away and never come back."[177]

V
—

AFTER
NATIONALISM

B ETWEEN THE BATTLE OF STALINGRAD AND THE FALL OF BERLIN, Germans went from being lords of humanity to being a defeated and despised nation. They had started the most destructive war in European history. They had enabled the first genocide in Christian Europe. They had committed war crimes that the Prussian generals of old could not have even conceived.

As Soviet, British, French, and American forces occupied Germany, enormous shock and disorientation ensued. "We didn't know about any of this, any of it" is how conversations with occupying soldiers often began, only to concede, "there were times at the front incompatible with honor," or comrades "had heard things from the Poles."[1] According to Julius Posener, a German-Jewish architectural historian who had fought on the British side, the conversations typically ended with the assertion that, "the German soldier was clean."[2]

Outsider attempts to change hearts and minds only encouraged distrust and denial. Conducted amid the ruins of the once proud imperial city, the Nuremberg war trials looked a lot like the ex post facto application of laws while the actual process of de-Nazification tended to ensnare the little man while letting the worst Nazis go. In the Soviet zone of occupation, the situation was even worse. The occupiers issued summary sentences to former Nazis, those suspected of being one, or simply those who opposed Soviet rule. On the grounds of Buchenwald and Sachsenhausen, and in a series of other places, the Soviet secret police erected "special camps" that bore disturbing affinity to Nazi concentration camps. In these camps, the Soviets interned an estimated 150,000 Germans, mainly men, roughly a third of whom did not survive, with most of the dying occurring in 1946–1947, largely from isolation, cold, malnourishment, and its attendant afflictions.[3] It was nevertheless the case that some Germans attempted to make a break with the past in order to find "the starting point for a dignified national life," as Willy Brandt, the future German chancellor who had become a Norwegian citizen in 1940, put it in *Forbytere og andre tyskere* (*Criminals and Other Germans*), published in Oslo in 1946 and long left untranslated.[4]

Chapter 13 briefly considers how Germans attempted to reconstitute this "dignified national life," despite the disorientation, desperation, and difficulties of the immediate postwar years. Amid the ruins and rubble, it is argued, a renaissance in thinking about the nation occurred, involving a turn to realism in the assessment of what Nazi Germany had wrought.

Then, beginning in 1949, two countries claimed German allegiance. In one, its capital in East Berlin, the Communist Party ruled. Elections were a sham, and by June 1953, four years after the founding of the German Democratic Republic, large segments of the population rose up and opposed the regime—but Soviet tanks crushed the revolt. An exodus thereafter commenced. In daunting numbers, young people, skilled workers, and academically trained professionals fled west, causing a significant decline in the adult population. Only a wall, clandestinely erected on the night of August 13, 1961, halted an out-migration of historic proportions, which in per capita terms was far larger than the great German migrations of the nineteenth century (although still significantly smaller than the exodus of German Jews in the 1930s).

As East Germany descended into a second dictatorship, internal documents revealing the mental dispositions of the people became increasingly opaque, making it difficult to write the history of how East Germans actually felt about their life under the Communist Party and about Germany's recent genocidal past. The East German government compounded the problem for the less than 20 percent of the German population it claimed to represent by issuing blithe pronouncements that the west, not the east, was the true heir of German fascism, and therefore bore the cross of guilt. "Here in the DDR we have no historical legacy to overcome," Arnold Zweig, the author who had become a member of the People's Chamber, stated. "The past goes on living in the west. But here we are all done with it. We didn't overcome it. We puked it out."[5]

By contrast, West Germany, its capital in Bonn, wrestled with the legacy bequeathed to it by Nazi rule from the start, and that struggle, along with the work of erecting Germany's first continually functioning democracy, constituted the core of the West German achievement, however marked by a constant shuttle between memory and forgetting, illumination and blindness, honesty and lying, empathy and indifference.

Of course, real history is messier than our analytical differentiations allow, and there were many people in East Germany who grappled with the past just as in the west there were many who ignored it. Moreover, some indicators suggest that the two histories show remarkable parallels. We know, for example, that in the first two decades after the camps were restored and opened to the public, the numbers of visitors to Buchenwald in the east and Dachau in the west were roughly equal, with first spikes in visitor interest at the end of the fifties, followed by stagnation, and even decline, but then a rise in the number of visitors to Dachau that was never matched at Buchenwald.[6] Yet a precise comparative study, below the level of official pronouncements, would take us too far afield, and the primary sources in the east just do not yield insight in the same way. Especially for a study of changing mentalities, the West German case simply offers the his-

Occupied Germany, 1947.

torian better clay to shape an analysis. This study therefore concentrates on the western zones of occupation and on Federal Republic.

Chapter 14, "The Presence of Compassion" tells of the long, difficult road to becoming a nation that looked to its past with "empathetic seeing," as the art historian Robert Vischer called a particular approach to realism a century earlier. There were periods of clarity, when Germans sometimes glimpsed the past with relative honesty. The immediate postwar period was such a time, despite the demonstrable persistence of nationalism and anti-Semitism in the general population. So too were the late 1950s and early 1960s, when events, including an anti-Semitic smear campaign and public trials of Nazi criminals, forced German society to introspection. There were also periods of dim perception, typically characterized by the obfuscating importance of other, seemingly more pressing matters, like the rebuilding of Germany's economy in the 1950s, or the utopian visions of the late 1960s and early 1970s. Finally, there were periods when seeing the past increasingly coexisted with realism and compassion for both those Germans who had suffered through dictatorship and war, and for those who had been persecuted, exiled, and murdered. More than historians have allowed, the 1980s and 1990s represented the decisive decades when Germans came to understand the dimension and specificity of suffering caused by a once genocidal nation. Yet, precisely in these decades, Germany would shed its ethnic homogeneity and confront a new nationalism that, while having an affinity with the old, was essentially a reaction to an increasingly fluid, global world.

CHAPTER 13

A LIVING CONCEPT
OF FATHERLAND

c. 1945–1950

In a thousand years was her beauty built,
in one night was it utterly destroyed.

—ERICH KÄSTNER, ON DRESDEN

THE BRAVE BUT FAILED ATTEMPT OF YOUNG CLAUS SCHENK GRAF VON Stauffenberg is well-known. On July 20, 1944, he tried to kill Adolf Hitler by placing a bomb in a map room where the dictator and his officers were discussing strategy. At the time, 80 percent of the Jews killed in the genocide were already dead and the vast preponderance of Russian soldiers and civilians who died in the war had already perished. The same was not true of German soldiers. By contrast, when Hitler arrested and executed von Stauffenberg, and many of his co-conspirators, Germany had lost only 30 percent of the soldiers who would die for the fatherland. Then, in August, the month after the failed plot, nearly 350,000 German soldiers fell to their deaths.[1] In the last months of the war, as the Red Army pressed from the Vistula in central Poland to the Oder River just east of Berlin, and as the western Allies pushed through the Ardennes and into the Rhineland, German casualties mounted at an alarming rate. In January 1945, Germany lost 450,000 soldiers, nearly as many as the United States on all fronts during the whole war. From January to April 1945, German military deaths averaged well over a quarter million per month, with most of the dying occurring in the *Endkampf*.[2]

Civilian death tolls also rose dramatically. In the last two years of the war, the aerial bombers of the United States and Great Britain destroyed more than a hundred cities and towns in Germany, killing at least 300,000 civilians and badly wounding twice that number, with women, children, and old people the hardest hit.[3] "Hamburg was the first big city to be annihilated," as the writer Hans Erich Nossack put it in his sparse eyewitness testimony of the events of July 1943, "mile after mile there was not a single living house."[4] Later in 1943, the city of Hanover was laid to waste, as it would be again in January 1945, so that, as one occupation officer later noted, by the end of the war, "you could walk for miles without seeing a building left with a wall higher than your thigh."[5] Save for the cathedral, Cologne was likewise a complete ruin, causing one cultured observer to lament that "later generations will know a whole school of medieval architecture, the late Rhenish Romanesque, only from books of art history."[6] Many smaller cities also became "corpse towns," as the British author Stephen Spender called them.[7] Münster, for example, survived the Thirty Years War but not the Second World War; 80 percent of its houses were destroyed.[8] In Pforzheim, a medium-sized city in Baden, "skeletons of houses stand next to skeletons of houses and behind the skeletons, a chaotic mass of rubble," the novelist Alfred Döblin wrote in his travel journal.[9] Then, of course, there was the Dresden of the satirist Erich Kästner; in

Potato harvest in Berlin, with the Reichstag
(German Parliament) in the background, 1945.

mid-February 1945, when the city was bombed, it was filled with refugees, mostly women and children. And there was Berlin. Once a bustling vibrant metropolis, it had become the victim of its political leaders' pretentions to world power, and in the spring of 1945, it was reduced to dust and ash.

Probably, the German population of the east suffered even more than Germans in cities. As urban Germany lay in ruins, the largest expulsion of humans in history began. The eviction involved Germans from Poland, Russia, Romania, Czechoslovakia, Yugoslavia, and Hungary—and from regions like Pomerania, Silesia, and East and West Prussia that had, in some form, long counted as German lands. The total numbers are staggering. In three distinct waves, some twelve million people, disproportionately women, children, and elderly, left their homes with what they could carry or pull in a cart. As Nazi Germany neither planned for nor sanctioned retreat, a first wave of some six million Germans had already taken matters into their own hands and fled pell-mell as the Soviet armies approached.[10] The second wave occurred when the Red Army arrived. Soviet soldiers rounded up ethnic Germans, told them to gather their things, and marched them to the borders. Throughout eastern Europe, local violence and staged anti-German demonstrations shadowed the exodus; in some cases, such as in Brno, Czechoslovakia, the violence burst into large-scale killings.[11] Direct ethnic violence, however, was responsible for only the smallest portion of death. Instead, lack of food and water and the attendant diseases of malnutrition, like diphtheria and typhus, were the primary fatal factors. In the third wave of expulsion, after the Potsdam Conference in the summer of 1945 issued directives for an "orderly and humane" evacuation, the number of deaths probably declined. Yet during this time, a system of camps arose, often on the ruins of the very camps that the Nazis had abandoned, with some, like Auschwitz and Theresienstadt, repurposed from their wartime use. The number of camps, and ethnic Germans interned in them, is difficult to pin down. The historian R. M. Douglas has mapped out more than sixty of them, with a quarter of them housing more than five thousand inmates.[12] Sites of torture, beating, and deprivation, the camps also witnessed, according to the Red Cross, a great deal of sexual violence.[13] Altogether, the forced labor, the marching, the deprivations, and the internments led to the deaths of a half million ethnic Germans.[14] However, the number of expellees unaccounted for is very large, some 1.5 million (meaning that the general number of two million deaths, long used, may still hold true).

To make matters worse, war-torn Germany did not exactly celebrate the arrival of the "expellees," and one can understand why. In the four occupation zones, the standards of living had declined precipitously: food was scarce, and rationing was tight. In the winter of 1946, occupation authorities limited Germans to foodstuffs that barely amounted to 1000 calories daily. Many people, especially women, spent the day shoveling away rubble but hardly had the caloric intake to sustain themselves. One result was astonishing malnutrition, worse than even in the most calamitous years of the early Weimar Republic.[15] Beyond food, other necessities of life were also hard to come by. On account of the destroyed roads and rails, coal remained in short supply, and people spent countless hours rounding up fuel for their stoves so they could stay warm. Sickness followed. Easily spread in conditions of crowding and malnutrition, the rates of typhus, tuberculosis, and diphtheria spiraled, filling Germany's hospital wards with legions of patients.[16]

In the midst of the dislocation, hunger, and disease, German women endured mass rape by soldiers of the occupation armies, especially the Red Army.[17] The dimensions are difficult to comprehend fully, particularly east of the Oder, where, as the Russian author Aleksandr Solzhenitsyn wrote, "every village—is now a fire," and many times over, "a girl's been turned into a woman / A woman turned into a corpse."[18] The largest number of sexual assaults probably occurred in East Prussia, Pomerania, Silesia, and the parts of Brandenburg east of Berlin.[19] Of elderly expellees polled fifty years later about their childhood experiences, half related that they had witnessed rape, and of the girls and young women, 14 percent reported that they had themselves been raped.[20] In the Soviet zone of occupation, the incidences of rape reached "shocking proportions" in some areas and persisted well after the initial spike in violence in April 1945.[21] In the first six months of 1946, the district of Merseburg, for example, reported 162 cases of rape "carried out by persons in Soviet uniform."[22]

The most shocking information, however, documents the prevalence of rape in the German capital, Berlin. Contemporaries guessed that soldiers raped almost every second woman, and that the offense became so commonplace that the women themselves sometimes referred to it as if a secondary consideration. "Imprisoned by the Russians for 14 days, had been raped but well fed" is, for example, how the journalist Margret Boveri referred to what had happened.[23] Some rapes were extremely brutal: gang rapes by soldiers, sexual assault by knife or gunpoint, and subsequent shooting and even mutilation of women. There were also spheres where women were coerced into becoming agents of the crime: mothers acceding to the violation of their own bodies in order to protect their daughters, for example, or a woman taking in one soldier to protect herself from worse ones. This last situation was described in *A Woman in Berlin*, a revelatory anonymous account first published in an abridged form in English in 1954 and as a full text in German in 1959, when critics derided the book for "besmirching the honor of German women."[24]

One estimate puts the total number of women raped in all of postwar Germany at 2 million, and 2.6 million when the eastern territories ceded to Poland and the Soviet Union after the war are also considered. This approximation focuses on Russian soldiers as the main aggressors. A second estimate, calculated from birth statistics, places the number at 860,000, and shifts the focus from rape committed by the Russian army to the soldiers of other occupation forces, particularly American GIs, who, according to one historian's calculations, committed 190,000 rapes.[25] In either case, the magnitude of sexual abuse that occurred during the war and the initial occupation was astonishing. In addition to the trauma itself, rape resulted in high rates of sexually transmitted diseases, which were often left untreated, leading to countless sick women who were often ostracized by their friends and family. Rape also led to pregnancies, which many women had aborted, even though abortion was costly, illegal, and dangerous—in Berlin alone some 6000 women died per year from botched abortions.[26]

Mass rape permanently altered the gendered experience of war and transformed relations between men and women.[27] In the diary of an anonymous woman, we read about German men:

We feel sorry for them. They seem so miserable and powerless. The weaker sex. . . . In earlier wars men could claim that the privilege of killing and being killed for the fatherland was theirs and theirs

alone. Today we women, too, have a share. That has transformed
us, emboldened us. Among the many defeats at the end of this war
is the defeat of the male sex.[28]

It takes no great leap of the imagination to understand that this was one
reason that it took until the 1990s for there to be a sustained scholarly
and public discussion about rape at the end of the war and during the
occupation.

II

The end of the war also brought a transformation in the relations between
Germans and the inmates of concentration camps. In the closing months
of the war, the Nazis forced many of those interned in the camps to march.
Most notorious are the death marches, in which the SS murdered as many
as 250,000 people, almost all on German territory. Yet soldiers of the SS
were far from the only Germans who murdered civilians. In the helter-
skelter chaos of the final months, *Volkssturm* soldiers, police, Hitler youth,
local Nazi fanatics, and ordinary citizens also killed inmates, sometimes
with SS encouragement, sometimes on their own initiative—"zebra shooting," as it was called in popular parlance, on account of the victims' striped
prison clothes.[29]

Despite such rampant brutality, many inmates broke away during the
marches and transports of the last months, becoming "free people but not
liberated," as one survivor put it.[30] One estimate puts their number at over
100,000.[31] Fending for themselves along roads and in forests, the prisoners
hoped to stay alive amid a generally inhospitable population. Some Germans just averted their eyes and withheld help. As Allied soldiers drew
near, other Germans thought that any association with the inmates might
be compromising.[32] A small number of escaped prisoners found townspeople who took them in, or gave them clothes, or brought food to the edge of
a road or field.

Jews were a special group within the larger population of survivors.
Some 50,000 had been freed from camps and death marches, and in
Germany roughly 15,000 had lived out the war in hiding. At first, occupa-
tion authorities, especially in the east, directed Jews to share quarters with

Germans, and immediately after the war many Jews spent weeks, months, and sometimes even longer in the households and on the farms of their persecutors. "We didn't speak to them," recounted Mary Wishnic, a survivor of the Stutthof camp, whom Russian soldiers put up, along with other survivors, in a large German house. "We didn't look at them" because they were guilty, and they said "we didn't know" or "we were too young to know."[33] Jewish suspicion of their German persecutors often ran deep. On the other hand, most Germans resented sharing their quarters, worried about the spread of illnesses, feared the wrath of inmates, and found the living reminders of Nazi persecution unsettling. Some Germans were obtuse, others attempted kind gestures, and still others knew the occupation authorities were watching. "They were nice," recounted Adam Sulkowicz, a survivor of a subcamp near Hamburg. "They had to be nice."[34]

Nevertheless, because most Jews wanted to live with other Jews, they soon entered hastily erected Displaced Persons (DP) camps, which both the local and the Jewish populations expected to be temporary. But while other nationalities were quickly repatriated, Jews could not as easily return, especially to Poland, where local postgenocide pogroms, of which Cracow and Kielce were only the most notorious, took as many as 1500 Jewish lives.[35] Like the Germans, the Poles had occupied houses and enriched themselves immediately after the Nazis took Jews away to be killed; now the Poles hardly wanted to relinquish what they had stolen. Instead, the nearly quarter of a million Jews who had fled east from Poland into the Soviet Union trekked in the reverse direction, west through Poland and into Germany, where, bitterly and ironically, they found refuge in DP camps. Moreover, this vast migration of Jewish survivors, still insufficiently researched, emerged just as U.S. immigration quotas and British blockades of passenger ships to Palestine made other possible exits difficult. For the next few years, then, Jews, mainly from eastern Europe, settled in camps, concentrated in the American sector, principally Bavaria, Württemberg, and Hesse. There were also DP camps in West Berlin; in December 1945, *Der Tagesspiegel*, the newspaper of the American sector, already felt it necessary to abjure its readers not to "make these homeless Jews . . . responsible for the aggravation of the Jewish problem."[36] In the rest of the American sector, the in-migration of huge numbers of Germans expelled from the east created further drains on local resources, causing some Germans to resent the new influx and others to feel that priority should be given to the expellees over the Jews.[37]

In this context of deprivation, chaos, and rebuilding, the occupation authorities made sure that Germans understood what had happened under Nazi rule. In cities and towns near concentration camps, occupation forces marched townspeople through local terror sites, forcing them to see how the Nazis had piled up corpses or buried them in pits. The authorities also published photographs of the camps in newspapers and posted them on billboards, and the pictures often showed not just bodies but Germans looking at the bodies, so that both the witnessing and the crime were brought together, imparting to the images a forceful "presumption of veracity," to use Susan Sontag's term for the claim of a photograph to represent truth.[38] The revelations were also broadcast over radio, at the time the most popular media, reaching close to 80 percent of the population in 1948.[39] As the number of movie houses increased, it was also possible to show German audiences what had happened on film. *Death Mills*, for example, a documentary short directed by Billy Wilder, who had fled Nazi Berlin in 1933, reached over a million German viewers.[40] In the style of a newsreel, Wilder juxtaposed harrowing images of recently liberated camps with placid German landscapes, having the narrator declare, "There are no German cities far from the next concentration camp."[41] The movie certainly left an indelible impression. One report on Bavaria told of downcast eyes, crying women, murmuring about camp-guard bestiality, and incredulity about how SS men tortured, abused, and murdered children.[42] But the statistics of broadcasts of the movie theaters also reveal the desire to turn away. In the American sector of Berlin, the movie houses showing *Death Mills* were initially half full; but with multiple showings, they were soon empty.[43]

It is difficult to comprehend how Germans, trying to make their way at war's end, confronted the enormity of the crimes their country had committed. Guilt, a term associated with the propaganda tussles of the interwar years, seemed to be something imposed from outside, however carefully philosophers like Karl Jaspers attempted to parse it into logical categories. Shame, a less political term, possessed more experiential immediacy.

It is explored in Dorothea Zeemann's remarkable memoir, no less revealing even though its venue is postwar Vienna, which, like Berlin, was occupied by the four Allied powers. Zeemann's feelings of shame depend on personal knowledge, and they surface when she watches a Soviet-made movie about the concentration camp Mauthausen. Like so many Germans, Zeemann knew Jews personally. One of her Jewish friends, Ella, had even offered to exchange her precious silverware for gold coins, which she thought she would need when sent east to work for the Reich. Zeemann "could not know but clearly suspected" that Ella faced a worse fate, which Zeemann described in hindsight with Auschwitz acting as a synecdoche for the entire world of the concentration camps.[44] As Zeemann watches the gruesome film about Mauthausen, tears running down her face, frame after frame of skeletons, children with distended bellies, corpses, hair, shoes, and eyeglasses flicker in front of her. But Zeemann manages to see only that "from every empty pair of glasses Ella stares at me."[45]

The film then shows an *Einsatzkommando* shooting Jews in a ditch. Zeemann reports that a person runs out of the movie theater screaming, "It is not true; that's faked."[46]

Zeemann replies, "It is true, I saw it in Lemberg."

At the same moment we see her estranged husband throwing up in the theater and his new lover holding and comforting him. Immediately, Zeemann's thoughts flash to her broken marriage. She thinks not about Ella but about herself, the person who has survived her own travails, and still wants to live.

III

No peace treaty would be signed, and for four years after defeat, Germany was the very opposite of a sovereign nation. There is nothing very remarkable about this—unless seen against the backdrop of World War I, when a revolution brought democratic forces to power, and a young republic established its sovereignty with the first constitution in German history to derive state legitimacy from the will of the people.[47] In its first four years, the Weimar Republic had faced street violence, secession movements, hyperinflation, and an attempted Nazi putsch; it had also choked under the weight of the Treaty of Versailles, especially Article 231, which established German guilt for the outbreak of the war, and used this supposed guilt as a justification for exacting harsh reparations. The Republic never quite recovered from the trauma of its first four years, and few people looking back ever longed for its return.[48] Yet the Weimar Republic had somehow unleashed enormous bursts of creative energy, especially in the first years after the war. By contrast, as Stephen Spender pointed out, "You can't have failed to notice that the Nazis have laid German culture just as flat as the ruins of the Rhineland and the Ruhr."[49]

Following the war, the great figures of German culture either had been killed, had committed suicide, or were in exile: insiders as outsiders again. They included Germany's greatest prose authors, Thomas Mann and Alfred Döblin; Germany's most renowned poets, including Nelly Sachs, Bertolt Brecht, and Else Lasker-Schüler, who died in Jerusalem just before the end of the war; as well as a battery of Germany's most penetrating intellectuals, many of them Jewish, like Theodor Adorno and Hannah Arendt.

By comparison, the German cultural scene seemed compromised and inconsequential. In a secret report written for the U.S. Office of Strategic Services in late 1943, Carl Zuckmayer, a German writer living in exile in rural Vermont, delivered devastating "characterological" accounts of those artists and intellectuals who were "active Nazis or evil accomplices," "naïve accomplices," or "indifferent or helpless." He also offered keen insights into the small number of "conscious bearers of inner emigration," of whom there were few of wider prominence.[50] The illustrious publisher Peter Suhrkamp and the humorist Erich Kästner counted among them, as did some—like Ernst Jünger, the actor Emil Jannings, the dancer Mary Wigman, and the film director G. W. Pabst—whose relation to the Third Reich Zuckmayer found difficult to categorize. But if the cultural life of postwar Germany grew from arid soil, it nevertheless represented a remarkable renewal, distinguished, as in the early years of the Weimar Republic, by the search for artistic forms adequate to the catastrophe.

Neither silence nor "empty, cold, forgetting," as Adorno later characterized it, descended on Germany.[51] Instead, there were concerted efforts to renew a critical German culture. One sees the renewal in the earliest postwar films, like Wolfgang Staudte's *The Murderers Are Among Us*, which premiered in October 1946 and narrates how love in the ruins opens a space for truth.[52] One senses it in the urgency and seriousness of purpose of literary and intellectual journals, such as Dolf Sternberger's *Die Wandlung* (*Transformation*) or the left-leaning and Catholic *Frankfurter Hefte*

(*Frankfurt Notebooks*), edited by Eugen Kogon and Walter Dirks. One encounters it in genuine attempts to save a language contaminated by Nazi-speak, as evidenced by the publication, in 1947, of both Victor Klemperer's *LTI* (*Lingua Tertii Imperrii*) and Sternberger's *From the Dictionary of a Nonhuman.* Indeed, the renewal stressed a new honesty in naming practices—calling a thing by what it is: a documentary collection in *Die Wandlung* not on "euthanasia" but on "The Murder of the Mentally Ill," for example.[53]

The new insistence on realism, on precise naming, was crucial to the emergence of a more honest German literature. It can be seen in essays and in short stories, like Elisabeth Langgässer's "The Beginning of the Season," which subtly describes a spa town full of anti-Semitism, and "Gone Underground," which explores with unsentimental precision the mixed motives of a German woman hiding a Jewish woman.[54] Centered on short rather than long artistic forms, the new realism tended to be laconic and precise, devoid of "calligraphy," as the journalist and cultural critic Gustav René Hocke described excessively beautiful writing.[55] There was no hour zero, as the myth had it. There was, however, an hour of sparseness. Critics lauded poets who employed bare words, such as those in Günter Eich's poem "Inventory," which named each of his possessions in an American POW camp: cap, coat, shaver, plate, cup, socks, pillow, cardboard bed, pencil, notebook, tarpaulin, towel, and twine.

In this time, German authors were particularly drawn to autobiography. Between 1945 and 1949, according to one scholar's counting, German authors published 237 autobiographical works, with 1946 and 1947 peak years, sliding back in 1948 and 1949, and falling off dramatically in 1950.[56] In the beginning, the lion's share came from Germans who had been in the camps, mostly Communists, with many following the model of Wolfgang Langhoff's prewar *Moorsoldaten* (*Peat Bog Soldiers*), which depicted the struggles of politically active workers in the Börgermoor camp near the Dutch border. Shining a harsh light on the brutality of the camps, the left-leaning accounts tended to be heroic in tone. Other autobiographical documents were more cautious. Originally wanting to entitle her journal "*Nein,*" Ruth Andreas-Friedrich, for example, evoked hesitation in the face of injustice, the fear involved in hiding Jews, and the ubiquity, at the end of the war, of rape.[57] There were also testimonies from people who had gone into "inner emigration"—a term the essayist and novelist Frank Thiess claimed in order to juxtapose the hardship of those who stayed as against those, like Thomas Mann, who radioed in civic lessons to Germans in devastated cities from comfortable circumstances.[58]

Less appreciated are remarkable works of testimony that emerged from voices that had once been close to—or even a part of—the Nazi regime. One example is Eugen Kogon. Born of a Ukrainian-Jewish mother but raised as an adopted child in a Catholic family in Munich, Kogon had been a supporter of the Nazis in the early 1930s but turned away soon after he witnessed the regime's terror unfold. Arrested by the Gestapo in 1938, Kogon was interned first in Dachau, then in Buchenwald.[59] After liberation in April 1945, the U.S. army enlisted former inmates, led by Kogon, to gather evidence and issue an extensive report, which Kogon wrote in four weeks, and subsequently expanded into *The SS State: The System of Concentration Camps*, easily the most influential book on the subject for more than a decade to come.[60] Selling 135,000 copies in 1947, the book put forward a systematic analysis of the camps, focusing on their purpose and structure, the treatment of prisoners, work and everyday life, and the psychology of both guards and inmates.[61] Kogon concluded the book with a reflection, moral and religious, on German guilt, not as a collective phenomenon, but as far too many individual failings. Germans knew what was happening and turned away, he asserted. Many refused to help, and some even shot Jews and others when told to. The only way forward, Kogon insisted, was honest, individual self-examination.

Even the dead seemed to offer this counsel. One of the most read works of poetry in those years was from Albrecht Haushofer, son of Karl Haushofer, the geographer who gave scholarly sanction to the term *"Lebensraum"* (living space). During the war, the younger Haushofer had ties to the opposition; he was arrested in December 1944, thrown into Berlin-Moabit prison, and executed the following April as the Russians were entering the city. His brother Heinz later found his body, and in Albrecht's coat pocket a poem, which, with others found later, were then published as the *Moabit Sonnets*. Using a form derived from baroque laments, Albrecht Haushofer wrote powerful, plain-language verse, in a rhyme scheme of *abba*, in which he describes unrecognized injustice and blameworthy inaction. The second stanza of one of the poems, entitled "Guilt," reads:

Doch schuldig bin ich anders	But I am guilty differently
als Ihr denkt	than you think
Ich musste früher meine	I had to recognize my duty
Pflicht erkennen;	sooner;
Ich musste schärfer Unheil	I had to name evil
Unheil nennen—	evil more precisely—
Mein Urteil habe ich zu lang	My judgment I reined in too
gelenkt . . .	long . . .[62]

Responsibility started with naming the crime. The precise, exact voice, expressing what was known: this was the kind of courage that would have made the difference in the Nazi period.

Some autobiographical accounts, especially of German-Jewish survivors, disclosed a far bleaker vision. Unlike his extended family, including his wife, Gertrud, Hans Günther (H. G.) Adler managed to stay alive through internments in Theresienstadt, Auschwitz, and two satellite camps of Buchenwald. Determined to document what he had experienced, Adler sketched out in December 1945 a project for an uncompromising portrayal of life behind barbed wire, high walls, and watchtowers. In the mid-1950s, this would become his penetrating study of Theresienstadt.[63] Presaging Primo Levi's concept of the gray zone, where there is no "why," Adler insisted that great suffering did not make better people. On the contrary, for many prisoners, the only answer to persistent brutality, especially if one wanted to survive or help others, had been deception. But what light could one steal from the reign of darkness, and how could that flickering light contribute to humanity? If time spent in the camps was not to become empty and lost time, survivors, Adler insisted, had to confront this problem.[64]

The problem for non-Jewish Germans was, of course, very different: they had to confront what Max Frisch called the other side of death in war, namely killing.[65] Bringing the fact of the dead and the act of killing together, and remembering what they most wanted to forget, was a daunting, existential challenge on its own terms. So too was the building of a new nation amid the embers of nationalism. As we will see, this did not entail a turning away from the nation. It did, however, mean, as Dolf Sternberger put it, the development of "a living and not a deathly concept of fatherland."[66] It also meant bringing forth a nation in which one sensed the presence of compassion.

CHAPTER 14

—

THE PRESENCE OF
COMPASSION

c. 1950–2000

*In the long run, our discussion of what kind of writing
should be appropriate to the age of Auschwitz is totally irrelevant,
if it touches on issues of genre alone and does not look
for the presence of compassion.*

—PETER DEMETZ, "ON AUSCHWITZ, AND ON
WRITING IN GERMAN: A LETTER TO A STUDENT"

THE FEDERAL REPUBLIC OF GERMANY BEGAN AS AN INWARD-TURNED, ethnically homogeneous society, in which Germans had a great deal to hide, and foreigners constituted just over 1 percent of the population. Germany was hardly the only country that emerged from the tumultuous and ruinous 1940s in this monochrome and inwardly turned form. Italy and the Netherlands also had negligible minority populations, while Poland, which in the interwar years possessed significant minorities, was now even more homogeneous than the two German states, and largely without Jews.[1] The same was true of Hungary and Czechoslovakia, and a number of lands within the Soviet Union, including the no longer sovereign country now called the Lithuanian Soviet Socialist Republic, and its capital city, Vilnius. Once humming with the sounds of spoken Lithuanian, Polish, German, Russian, and Yiddish, the streets of Vilnius, like those of so many other central and east European cities, would become largely monolingual in the second half of the twentieth century.

This new, neatly tessellated but culturally impoverished Europe was, of course, the result of war, genocide, ethnic cleansing, and population movement. It also reflected the heightened isolation of what economists now call deglobalization. As a technical term, deglobalization refers to a sustained drop in the relation of a country to indexes of international trade, circulation, and communication. Foreign trade as a percentage of gross national product is the usual way to measure this, and Germany, by this yardstick, did not recapture its former heights, reached in 1913, until the late 1950s.[2] Other indexes suggest an even longer isolation. Excluding those sent back and forth between the front, the number of letters Germans sent to people in foreign countries declined precipitously during World War I, never fully recovered in the first years of the Weimar Republic, turned down again in mid-decade, and continued its steady decline into the Third Reich. Not until the mid-1960s would West Germans be as fully integrated into the international circulation of letter writing as they had been before World War I.[3]

In this period, Germans also did not go abroad in significant numbers. In 1950, some 70 percent did not know a foreign language, and in 1955, nearly 80 percent of West Germans did not possess a passport—meaning they had not traveled beyond Germany's borders during peacetime.[4] Of those who had been abroad, the vast majority, mainly men, had been to other countries only as soldiers and occupiers. By contrast, 70 percent of German women reported that they had never been outside Germany.[5]

The country was turned inward in other ways too. In the Federal Republic, sympathy for the Third Reich remained profound and reached across the political spectrum. Polling people on the streets about their opinions of National Socialism four years after defeat, one modest study, conducted by the Allensbach Institute at the behest of Northwest German Radio, showed that 57 percent of the people affirmed the statement "National Socialism was a good idea but was carried out badly," while comparatively few negated it.[6] The persistence of support for National Socialism surprised the analysts of the institute, a newly formed polling organization loosely based on the American Gallup Company.[7] Of the people who had been members of the National Socialist Party, 65 percent still thought Nazism in principle a good idea but so too did 49 percent of those who had not been party members. Of the nonparty members, only 36 percent said National Socialism was not a good idea, and 15 percent did not know.[8] The precise content of the "good idea" proved more difficult to determine. Almost all respondents praised National Socialist "order"

428 || GERMANY: A NATION IN ITS TIME

and damned "the disorder" of the Weimar Republic. What they did not like about the Nazi period was its excess, its "nationalistic radicalism," as the Allensbach commentators called it.[9] Few respondents defended the ideals of the "Greater German Empire" or the concept of *Lebensraum*, just as nearly everyone thought that the Nazi persecution of the Jews went "too far."[10]

In the early 1950s, these attitudes would change only slowly. In October 1951, 40 percent of Germans polled believed that 1933 to 1939 represented the best years of recent German history, while almost everyone else responded with "Imperial Germany"—meaning that very few felt nostalgia for Weimar. Reflecting a similar mind-set, a third of the German adult population in 1952 thought that Hitler was either "the greatest statesman" of the twentieth century or believed he was an "outstanding leader of state," even if he had made some mistakes. A second group, around 40 percent of the respondents, believed that Hitler had done some good but that the negative consequences outweighed the positive achievements. Only 28 percent believed that Hitler had brought about an unremitting theater of horrors.[11] Germans also had favorable views of other Nazis. According to the Allensbach polls, 46 percent had a "positive opinion" of Admiral Karl Dönitz, head of the German navy, while 37 percent gave high marks to Hermann Göring, the second most powerful Nazi leader.[12] Conversely, only 3 percent admitted to having a "positive opinion" of Heinrich Himmler.[13]

Widespread disapproval of Himmler and the SS, however motivated by the politics of being an occupied nation, suggests that there was a general condemnation of genocide. Yet this condemnation hardly undermined the basic prejudices and beliefs undergirding National Socialism.[14] Moreover, the fundamental understanding of nationhood, as codified in the Nuremberg Laws of 1935, still shaped how Germans viewed Jews. Even the Nazi understanding of the "Jewish problem" still held significant sway—both in the way pollsters asked questions and in the way Germans answered. Echoing Third Reich rhetoric that there was indeed a Jewish problem, the Allensbach Institute asked, in August 1949: "Do you think Israel is a solution to the Jewish question?" Two-thirds of the respondents answered in the affirmative, and a further fifth were not sure.[15] Only 14 percent said no, suggesting that a very small percentage of Germans imagined Jews in their country in positive terms. The institute never repeated the question in quite this way. But throughout the 1950s and into the 1960s, it tracked responses to a question with very similar implications. "Would you say it is better if Germany did not have any Jews in the country," the institute asked in December 1952. To this remarkable question, 37 percent answered in the affirmative, 24 percent were not sure, and only 20 percent answered no. Over the course of the next decade, the desire to have a Germany free of Jews abated, and by 1965, only 19 percent responded that it would be better if there were no Jews, although 47 percent were still not sure.[16] Altogether, the Allensbach polls revealed a German population that still perceived Jews as a race apart. Even into the 1960s, Nazi-defined templates of racial difference held sway. In April 1961, 74 percent of West Germans affirmed that Jews were of a different race than Germans while only 10 percent said the same of the English.[17]

II

In 1959, Carlo Levi, the Italian artist and author famous for his memoir *Christ Stopped at Eboli*, embarked on a tour of the Federal Republic to discover the spirit of the new Germany that he believed lay beneath the glittering sheen of its economic recovery. "Where they threw themselves into their work, fabulous amounts of goods and riches emanated from their busy hands," he wrote of the Germans:

> The destroyed cities have arisen again; the cars drive swiftly along the most beautiful highways of the world, houses reflect the calm waters of the rivers, young lovers sit hand in hand, and the woods offer a sense of the eternal peace of nature. . . . But it is a wounded land without autonomy, an offended land, offended by itself, not by others: a land of closed, obdurate eyes.[18]

It is typically thought that the *Wirtschaftswunder* (economic miracle), in which West Germany doubled its GNP in the space of a decade, allowed those "obdurate eyes," as Levi called them, to remain closed to its past. However, good evidence points to the opposite conclusion—namely, that the creation of wealth and leisure enabled the emergence of an informed critical distance to the Third Reich. Through the 1950s and the early

1960s, Germans recognized the economic recovery as symbolic of a new era, and one, moreover, that seemed better than the prewar years of the Third Reich. By the end of the 1950s, less than 10 percent of Germans polled still thought the prewar period of the Nazi regime counted among Germany's best years.[19]

For good reason, public debate about German rearmament is conventionally seen as one of the major catalysts for a critical appraisal of the recent past. The debate, which took place in the mid-1950s, certainly transfixed the West German public, as a broad coalition, ranging from church organizations to trade unions, warned against the dangers of a remilitarized German society. Insisting that the new German army, the Bundeswehr, be kept under stringent parliamentary control, these groups passionately endorsed a military program that trained its soldiers to be "citizens in uniform," armed with modern weaponry as well as with the duty to refuse to carry out patently unethical orders. In conception, then, the Bundeswehr personified the rejection of Prussian and Nazi traditions of drill and obedience. In practice, however, much of the old order remained, since a significant percentage of the officers of the Bundeswehr (some 80 percent at the end of the 1950s) had served in the Wehrmacht, and more barracks were named for generals in Hitler's army than for officers of the resistance.[20] Moreover, when West Germany introduced the draft in 1956, almost every young man showed up, and very few registered as conscientious objectors.[21]

Every bit as profound as the debate surrounding the reconstitution of a German army was the appearance of Anne Frank's journal. First published in Holland in 1947, *The Diary of Anne Frank* was translated into German in 1950, but achieved widespread acclaim only when two Americans, Frances Goodrich and Albert Hackett, adapted it as a play in 1955.[22] In the next half decade, the play was staged more than two thousand times in West German theaters. From Hamburg to Freiburg, Trier to Passau, directors worked with actresses and their supporting casts to reenact the dramatic story of Anne Frank's final two years in hiding—before being denounced, captured, and deported. The play, which some two million Germans saw, does not end with her death in the spring of 1945. Instead, the final scene shows her father finding the diary, opening it, and hearing Anne whisper, "In spite of everything, I still believe that people are really good at heart."[23]

Probably, the audiences did not want to know more. In 1959, the diary was made into a Hollywood movie, and in West Germany at least a million viewers watched it; it too ends with Anne's soft, optimistic voice.

A transnational story, the popularity of Anne Frank's diary also bore testimony to the growth of a rapidly expanding, West German media culture. Between 1952 and 1965, the number of newspapers sold and books published in West Germany nearly doubled, as did the circulation of illustrated magazines, like *Stern*, *Der Spiegel*, and *Quick*, while the number of plays performed and radios purchased increased by a third.[24] Only visits to the movie theaters declined, mainly because of the introduction of televisions into German homes. In 1953, a mere 5 percent of Germans had even seen a television program, but by the end of that decade nearly 30 percent of the population had a TV in their living room, and a far larger percentage watched with friends, in pubs, or through store windows.[25]

Popular media, ranging from mass-market books to network television, contributed more than is often thought to a rethinking of the past. It was, for example, by reading the inspired, conversational, almost Anglo-American style of Golo Mann, son of the famous novelist, that a large number of Germans first encountered a new form of critical historical writing. In his *German History of the Nineteenth and Twentieth Centuries*, published in 1958, Mann lauded the adept leadership of Bismarck and Konrad Adenauer, the first chancellor of the Federal Republic, as fervently as he denounced the racial mania of National Socialism. With a perceptive sense for how much the Germans could take in, he also hinted at the enormity of Nazi crimes while avoiding their deeper exploration. Selling more than a million copies, the book explained to its readers in a calm, benevolent voice that the caesura of 1945 was deeper than any other in German history, and for this reason, "we" Germans had a historic chance to become a nation among nations again.[26]

Germans also learned of their past through illustrated news magazines, like *Stern*, which printed articles on this or that royal rendezvous alongside essays on the recent past, often by authors like Sebastian Haffner whose narrative power was considerable. *Der Spiegel* was likewise "obsessed with contemporary history," as the Israeli journalist Amos Elon put it in 1965, and it too paired energetic prose with evocative photographs.[27]

Indeed, it was through their illustrations that these magazines brought the photographic record of Nazi crimes to the broader public. It was in the pages of *Stern* and *Der Spiegel* that many Germans first saw the devastating images collected in Gerhard Schoenberner's *The Yellow Star*, which, at the time it was published in 1960, was the only photo book exclusively focused on the Nazi persecution and annihilation of the Jews. Its most poignant images included harrowing photographs of ghetto liquidations, gruesome pictures of inmates subject to medical experiments, and distressing scenes from Auschwitz.[28] Once compiled in these magazines, the images took on a life of their own in the public consciousness, and it was the mass media— first magazines, then television—that sent them into the wider world.

Mass media was not, then, silent about genocide. Instead, it brought together consumer kitsch and images of genocide, unwittingly challenging the glitter of the economic miracle with clear-eyed accounts of persecution and killing. This was especially true of early television programming. Even as the new medium mainly featured light comedy, quiz shows, news, and sports, it also ran documentaries on Germany's dark history. For example, in 1957 Bavarian Broadcasting showed, if with limited success, French director Alain Resnais's *Night and Fog*, a film replete with shots of corpses from Nazi camps liberated in 1945.[29]

It was nevertheless not until 1960 that German TV broadcast its first sustained program on the Nazi period. Directed by Heinz Huber and Artur Müller, the fourteen-part series, simply entitled *The Third Reich*, began airing that October and continued through May 1961. According to an Allensbach poll, more than 70 percent of the population knew about it, and the individual segments drew an average of nearly 60 percent of all German TV viewers.[30] The first six episodes covered the prewar years, and the eight others the war and the persecution of the Jews. Throughout its fourteen installments, the series left little doubt that Hitler was solely responsible for the outbreak of World War II, and that the German army, under his explicit direction, conducted the war with unprecedented brutality. The eighth episode, entitled "The SS State," addressed the camp system and genocide, and received, when it was rebroadcast in 1964, the inaugural Adolf Grimme Award, an accolade established for the rapidly expanding medium of television. While the series still depicted the genocide as mainly a product of Hitler's racial mania and Heinrich Himmler's blood-soaked empire, and even though it reproduced a great deal of propaganda footage, it nevertheless put forth a wide array of images of deportation trains, ghettos, concentration camps, and Auschwitz. It also addressed, if hesitantly, the question of knowledge and complicity. "As millions of Jews were killed in the ghettos and concentration camps, the millions of Germans did not know about it," the narrator of the series explains. "But in the beginning of the path that led to the extermination camps stood the German people—we stood—we stood by and let it happen."[31] Placing "we" in such close proximity to genocide was remarkable for the time, especially when four out of five adults in the Federal Republic still believed that Nazi leaders, and not the Germans themselves, were responsible for the near extermination of the Jews of Europe.[32]

III

It was in this context of a gradually evolving sensitivity to the Germans' complicity in the Third Reich's crimes that a series of trials of Nazi war criminals in the late 1950s and throughout the 1960s accelerated the rise of public consciousness about the actual genocide. Unlike the Nuremberg trials, which were held right after the war, the Ulm *Einsatzkommando* trial in 1958, the Eichmann trial in Jerusalem in 1961, and the two Frankfurt Auschwitz trials, which ran from December 1963 to August 1965, put the genocide squarely at the center of public attention. And alongside these larger-scale public trials, a significant number of smaller trials of execution squads, in places as diverse as Bonn, Dortmund, Bielefeld, and Tübingen, constantly reminded the German public of the extent of Nazi war crimes.[33] Focusing on the genocide in eastern Europe, the trials showed that the justice system had barely scraped the surface of the breadth and depth of Nazi crimes and made it evident that German society only dimly envisioned individual perpetrators behind the abstract statistics of killing.[34] Dramatic public discussions about the statute of limitations for murder— begun in 1960, climaxing in 1965, and rehearsed again in 1969—further sharpened a sense that courts were to play a central role in the constitution of a postgenocide society that claimed also to be a just society. As Ernst Benda, a Christian Democratic representative and later supreme court justice, memorably put it in a historic speech in the West German parliament in 1965, "A nation's sense of justice would be corrupted, with all of the

434 || GERMANY: A NATION IN ITS TIME

negative consequences, if horrific murders that could be prosecuted were not prosecuted."[35]

Benda both shaped and reflected emerging public opinion. More Germans in the early 1960s than was the case in the 1950s thought it right to try people who had committed crimes against Jews.[36] When the Israelis captured Adolf Eichmann (the man who had organized death transports during the genocide) on May 11, 1960, roughly two-thirds of the Germans who had followed the event believed that, if found guilty, he should receive either the maximum jail sentence or the death penalty.[37] But nearly as many were concerned about how the trial, which was held in Israel, adversely affected the reputation of Germany, and a significant percentage simply wanted to put the whole burdensome past behind them. Germans, they thought, should focus instead on the present and future.[38]

IV

The present was itself dramatic. Since 1953, East Germany had been losing citizens in extraordinary numbers. Attracted by West Germany's relative prosperity and freedom, some two million East Germans, roughly 12 percent of the population, crossed the zones of demarcation and settled in the west. Mainly, they were young, skilled, and well-educated workers and professionals, and East Germany could scarcely afford to lose them. Indeed, the exodus created a crisis of legitimacy for East Germany, and one with no obvious solution. On June 15, 1961, Communist Party Chairman Walter Ulbricht declared, "No one has the intention of building a wall."[39] Two months later, on August 13, the Communist government did exactly that, and by October, a so-called Anti-Fascist Wall effectively divided Berlin.

The Wall had a significant effect on the fortunes of German nationalism. In the short run, it made the question of German division into a central issue of the Cold War, as more than 60 percent of West Germans thought the partition of their country "unbearable."[40] The consternation was short-lived, however. As the 1960s wore on, anger subsided, and fewer people thought they would live to experience Germany unified again.[41] West Germans stopped visiting the east, even though they still had friends and family behind the wall.[42] Over time, more and more people in the west, especially the young and educated, began to believe that there were "two states of the German nation," as Willy Brandt, who became chancellor in 1969, put it.[43]

The eastern territories beyond the Oder River also faded from mental horizons. In 1956, only 9 percent of West Germans thought that Germany should recognize the Oder-Neisse River, the post-1945 line of demarcation between Germany and Poland, as the eastern boundary of the German lands. But in subsequent years, these numbers rose significantly, from 12 percent in 1959, to 46 percent in 1967, and to 58 percent by 1970, when Chancellor Brandt signed the Treaty of Warsaw, officially recognizing the borders.[44] The recognition meant the abandonment of maps that still depicted territories such as Silesia, eastern Pomerania, parts of Posen, and the old East and West Prussia as "at this time under Polish or Russian administration."[45] It also countered the insistent lobbying by leaders of German expellees who argued that their constituents had a right to their homeland. And it acknowledged that the expulsions of 1945–1946, however much suffering they caused, were responses to Nazi aggression.

The lingering solidarities of the nation at war remained powerful, however. Throughout the 1950s, the majority of Germans refused to concede that Germany bore the principal responsibility for the outbreak of World War II, and most Germans clung to the belief that the soldiers of the regular German army had conducted themselves in an exemplary fashion.[46] Throughout that decade, and even beyond it, rhetorical appeals to the community of arms still resonated with the broad public. In 1961, West Germany's defense minister, a man soon to be leader of the conservative-minded Bavarian Christian Socialist Union, could still ask of Konrad Adenauer's opponent in the Federal election: "We must be allowed to ask Mr. Brandt, what did you do abroad for twelve years?" And added: "we know what we did inside."[47]

By the late 1960s, however, the "invention of peace," to cite the eminent historian Michael Howard, was nearly a quarter century old, and war was no longer seen as a natural state of affairs.[48] Germans now lived in a welfare state, not a warfare state; fighting power was not the only index of national strength, and combat fitness ceased to be the principal measure of the worth of men. Instead, consumption, not conquest, indicated success, and the proliferation of schools, not the number of barracks, gauged progress.

By 1970, real GNP had tripled, and the money the Federal Republic spent on education and scientific research outstripped defense spending, just as it had decades earlier in the Weimar Republic.[49] As in other European countries, very few citizens saw spending on defense as a high political priority.[50] During this period, the number of conscientious objectors choosing civilian over military service surged dramatically. In the first decade of the draft, they averaged fewer than 5000 per year. Starting in 1968, these numbers doubled, and within a decade nearly 70,000 conscientious objectors would choose civil over military service every year.[51]

By the 1970s, the axioms of the nationalist age began to seem archaic, and the symbols of nationalism outdated. Some thought the national anthem, "*Deutschland, Deutschland, über alles*," unnecessary, and many could not recite the text, even of the innocuous third verse, hymning a blossoming fatherland.[52] National holidays were likewise hardly a matter of consensus, save that most Germans thought it was better to celebrate quietly.[53] In the West Germany of the early 1970s, flags were seldom flown, monuments were rarely built, and movies showing brave Germans fighting with dignity, still popular in the 1950s, began to disappear. In 1971, when Germans were asked if they were proud to be German, only 42 percent offered an unconditional yes. The less educated felt more pride than the well educated, and the old said yes much more readily than the young.[54]

The names Germans gave to their children, particularly when seen against names given in the first half of the twentieth century, provide a revealing index of this growing aversion to the nation as conceived during what we have described as the nationalist age. In 1900, Germanic names, like Helga or Dieter, constituted less than 20 percent of given names; by 1940, they had risen to over 50 percent, and came to predominate over traditional names, like Lisa or Michael, or innovative names, such as Marina or Hugo, or the names of saints. The Second World War marked both the zenith of Germanic names and the beginning of their decline. The name "Adolf," to take an obvious example, fell precipitously after defeat at the Battle of Stalingrad, and never recovered thereafter.[55] Horst did somewhat better, but not much. In general, Germanic names continued their downward trajectory, even if some, like Helmut, were artificially propped up by chance events (in this case, a soccer player named Helmut Rahn scoring the winning goal in the World Cup final in 1954). By the late 1970s, Germanic names had fallen to 10 percent; by 1990, to a negligible 5 percent.[56] In its basic outline, the curve follows the rise of the nationalist age, its apotheosis in the destructive 1940s, and its subsequent denouement.

Polling data likewise follows this trend of increasing distance from the nation as nationalists had once conceived it. The perception that the prewar Nazi period was the best period in German history, and that Germany would be better off without Jews, was already falling off in the second half of the 1950s, but instead of falling further, these trend lines actually leveled out in the 1960s. Similarly, the number of Germans who thought Hitler would have been considered the greatest statesman of the twentieth century were it not for the war fell significantly in the late 1950s and early 1960s. So too did the number of people refusing to recognize the borders drawn in 1945, and hoped instead for a return to the status quo ante bellum.

The generational revolt of 1968 no doubt shifted attitudes in West Germany, and some measures, such as the number of young men seeking status as conscientious objectors, suggest the emergence of a genuinely critical disposition toward Germany's militarist past. Yet the sound and fury surrounding the myth of a revolutionary 1968 also obscures the sig-

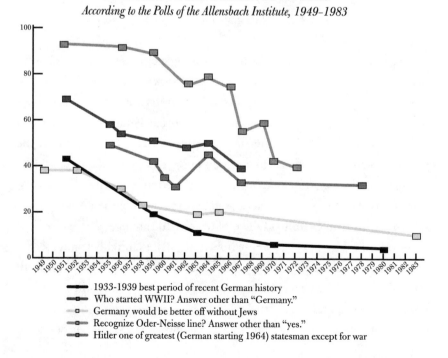

CHANGES IN WEST GERMAN ATTITUDES
According to the Polls of the Allensbach Institute, 1949–1983

— 1933-1939 best period of recent German history
—■— Who started WWII? Answer other than "Germany."
▫ Germany would be better off without Jews
—□— Recognize Oder-Neisse line? Answer other than "yes."
—□— Hitler one of greatest (German starting 1964) statesman except for war

nificant public opinion shifts that occurred much earlier. Moreover, as the historian Christina von Hodenberg has recently shown, the myth of '68 was focused more on young men than on young women, who tended to experience the 1960s as a series of private struggles, often with men their own age, for gender equality. The idea that the period was driven by sharp generational differentiations also hides meaningful and sincere cooperation across age groups. Even photos from the summer of 1968, showing demonstrations against the government's use of emergency laws, reveal scores of older people marching alongside the young.[57] Likewise, while young people certainly imagined their parents' generation as perpetrators, few households actually witnessed generational conflict based on a parent's Nazi past—and, in any case, most radical '68ers came from households that were already politically left-leaning.[58]

It was, rather, the conservative politicians with a tarnished past who elicited public ire—people such as Hans Globke, Adenauer's chief of staff who had written commentaries on the Nuremberg Laws, and Theodor Oberländer, minister for displaced persons, refugees, and victims of war, who had earlier urged the expulsion of Jews from Poland and the expropriation of their property, and whose units had participated in the Lwów Massacre in the summer of 1941. The second president of the Federal Republic, Heinrich Lübke, also had a National Socialist past, as did the third chancellor, Kurt Georg Kiesinger, whom a young Beate Klarsfeld slapped in the ear, exclaiming that he stood for the "revolting face of ten million Nazis."[59]

During the late sixties, Beate Klarsfeld, along with her French husband, Serge, belonged to the few who pressed further to reveal the extent of Germany's genocidal past and its continued presence in contemporary German society and politics.[60] Whether most young Germans, as a result of the events of 1968, came closer to a more honest and precise understanding of what actually transpired during the era of National Socialism is unclear. Most remained content with mere slogans about the depth of Nazi infiltration in the Federal Criminal Office, the German Intelligence Service, and in the police.[61] More extensive research, much of it eventually conducted by '68ers, would not occur until the quieter late 1970s and early 1980s. With the exception of the trials of war criminals, Auschwitz was still a symbol, not a research agenda. It disturbed political dreams and negated a better world. It was the young republic's negative utopia, but hardly more.[62]

V

In 1967, two psychoanalysts, Alexander and Margarete Mitscherlich, published *The Inability to Mourn*, one of the most influential books of the postwar era. The two authors—he had written a banned work on the postwar trials of Nazi doctors; she was a former student of Anna Freud and Melanie Klein and one of the Federal Republic's early feminists—diagnosed an "emotional immobility" (*Gefühlsstarre*) in the face of Nazi crimes.[63] They reasoned that with the fall of the Third Reich and Adolf Hitler, its main figure of identification, Germans confronted overwhelming feelings of guilt, shame, and fear. Ordinarily such emotions call forth contrition, the need for atonement, and the process of mourning. But the ideals and sense of self-worth of a whole generation were bound up in the racially conceived *Volksgemeinschaft*; and when it collapsed, the resulting psychological trauma caused a "de-realization" of the whole dark era.[64] Unable "to work through" feelings of guilt and shame and possessing habits of mind left over from the Nazi era, Germans, according to the Mitscherlichs, erected a series of defense mechanisms, such as repression, displacement, and denial, to shield themselves both from the truth and from the ability to mourn loss.

Were Germans, then, in a state of de-realization? Could they not mourn loss? The evidence is at once complicated and revealing. Yet public markers of death, loss, and victimhood do, in the main, disclose a chronology that conforms in important ways to the Mitscherlichs' discerning insights.

Consider memorials dedicated to the German soldiers who died in World War II. They make up by far the largest number of public markers of loss in the Federal Republic. An online project to list and tabulate them for purposes of genealogical research allows us to count nearly thirty thousand such monuments, including those markers where the names of the World War II dead were simply added to the names of those who died in World War I.[65] It is not, however, their numbers but their placement that is instructive, especially when compared to the confident memorial culture of Imperial Germany. In the aftermath of the Second World War, memorials were almost uniformly erected in sacral rather than secular spaces. It will be recalled that in the Imperial period, memorials to veterans were meeting sites for nationalist associations, foci for patriotic festivals, and places where military parades took place. They were conspicuous objects, which, as we have also seen, generated even more objects, often in the form of souvenirs and kitsch. In the postwar period, by contrast, they were almost always situated in churchyards and cemeteries, and the garish commodification, so prevalent for the monuments built before World War I, did not occur for the memorials to the fallen after World War II. Instead, memorials were often hidden, and their visitors tended to be reserved and quiet.

By contrast, the markers dedicated to the so-called expellees were far more public than those erected for the fallen. By 1950, the expellees had settled in thousands of cities and towns in East and West Germany. Initially, the east took in proportionately many more "new citizens," but the Communist government later forbade the creation of any political organizations representing the special interests of the expellees, and it prohibited the erection of monuments and memorials to lands the expellees perceived as having been lost. By contrast, some fifteen hundred memorials to the expellees dot the landscape of West Germany.[66] The first major wave of these markers occurred in the 1950s, with roughly a third of them placed in sacred spaces, like churchyards and cemeteries. The rest were situated in secular spaces, such as town squares, marketplaces, or at the roadsides on the outskirts of towns. After an initial surge, building slowed down in the second half of the 1950s, and came to a near standstill in the 1960s and early 1970s. Then, in the late 1970s, there was a second uptick, and a great many new memorials were erected in the 1980s.

To many commentators, expellee memorials appear to signal the persistence of nationalism in the Federal Republic. Certainly, some made nationalist appeals, although these were couched in the language of universal rights, typically informing, for example, that the "right of self-determination is also for Germans."[67] Often, however, expellee memorials simply mourned those who had lost their lives during the expulsion, or lamented the loss of the lands they once called home. Some communities erected signs that pointed to and noted the distance in kilometers to such places as Stettin, Breslau, and Danzig in Poland, or Königsberg in Russia.[68] A few communities, like the Hessian town of Bad Arolsen, put up engraved maps of Germany with its antebellum borders, and divided the nation into three parts: West Germany, East Germany, and the lands still under Polish or Soviet administration.

Yet even before Willy Brandt signed the 1970 treaty that recognized the border with Poland, it is unclear whether most expellees actually expected to return to their homeland, or have their homeland annexed into the Federal Republic.[69] For the expellees, the deeper problem was the loss of cultural memory. For despite all the markers, monuments, and commemorative signs, the general population of western Germany, including the children of expellees, were starting to place these names somewhere in the deep recesses of their mind, making them into *Names That No One Names Anymore*, as Marion Gräfin Dönhoff, editor of the weekly newspaper *Die Zeit*, entitled her nostalgic evocation, published in 1962, of these once German landscapes.[70]

Mourning the loss of family, friends and even a vanished *Heimat*, or homeland, is one matter, but commemorating the loss of those whom the Nazis had persecuted quite another. Between 1950 and 1968, West Berlin, to take a focused example, put up fewer than twenty markers commemorating the war years, and even renamed or tore down some that had been put up earlier.[71] In this period, monuments tended to bundle different groups of victims together or render violence abstractly. This was certainly the case for West Berlin's first major monument "to the victims of the Hitler dictatorship." Erected in 1952 in Plötzensee Prison, the monument blurred the distinction between victim groups but nevertheless "honored those millions of victims of the Third Reich who, because of their political convictions, religious beliefs, or racial origins, were vilified, abused, deprived of their freedom, or murdered."[72] Soon thereafter, the first major monument to the conservative resistance was consecrated; it featured a sculpture of a young, naked man with his hands bound, symbolizing the shackled potential of the abstract "other Germany."[73] Regarding the treatment of the Jews, there was mainly silence. The only notable exception in West Berlin in the 1950s was a plaque at the site of the Jewish Old Age Home in Wilmersdorf, which obliquely stated that "the National Socialists took the home illegally in 1941 and sent away its occupants."[74] In fact, the nursing staff and all the residents were transported to concentration camps and killed. Reacting to the eruption of anti-Semitic desecrations in 1959 and 1960, a number of monuments commemorated victims but refrained from naming names. The district of Zehlendorf, for example, erected a stone memorial, which read "To / The Victims / 1933 / 1945," while Charlottenburg built one to the "terrifying places of world history."[75]

It was not, in fact, until the second half of the 1960s that a small number of memorials accurately and precisely commemorated the persecution of the Jews. Most notable and controversial was a simple sign erected in 1967 at the entrance to the Wittenberg subway station. Under the phrase "places of terror that we must never forget," the sign listed the names of ten camps in yellow letters on black slats, starting with Auschwitz and ending with Bergen-Belsen.[76] Recalling the expellee signs pointing east, the slats were in plain sight, and they named places of death that Germans had only begun to name again openly.

Street signs, the most ordinary markers of the past, confirm the general pattern of silence about Jews killed in the genocide. Of nearly 250 streets in West Berlin named or renamed for historical figures between 1945 and 1968, only two squares and less than 10 percent of the streets named bore the names of Berlin's once vibrant population of Jews.[77] Generally, famous Jews, not necessarily those who were victims of the genocide, were honored with street names. Right after the war, these included men such as Karl Marx, Walter Rathenau (the Weimar foreign minister), and the prominent publisher Rudolf Mosse. Of the Jews for whom streets were named in the 1950s, only Albert Einstein belonged to the Jews forced to flee, and only Ottilie Pohl, an elderly socialist who had hidden resisters and died in Theresienstadt, counted among those murdered in the genocide. The next round of Jewish street names did not occur until 1966, when three Socialist politicians, including the reformist Eduard Bernstein, received street names, as did the famous director Bruno Walter and the rabbi and theologian Martin Buber, who had passed away in Jerusalem one year earlier. Taken together, the names fell short of the number and the types of street names used in East Berlin, which unequivocally took up the critical literary heritage of Jewish Weimar, and gave street names to the satirist Kurt Tucholsky, the dramatist Ernst Toller, and the anarchist Erich Mühsam, none of whom survived the Nazi years. In the 1950s, East Berlin named twice as many streets as West Berlin for people murdered in the camps, and only in the 1960s, after the construction of the Wall, did West Berlin begin to name more and more streets for people killed by the Nazis.

Was there, then, an inability to mourn? In greater measure than Alexander and Margarete Mitscherlich imagined, Germans took great pains to mark the absence all around them and mourn the dead and the places they came from. But they mainly mourned their own loved ones, principally in private and sacred spaces, not public and secular spaces, with the expellees a partial exception. In spheres of mourning that required compassion with others, there was a de-realization of the past, a lack of specific imagination, and an inability to mourn. Even as attitudes changed in the late 1950s and early 1960s, commemoration, perhaps also compassion, lagged well behind. Moreover, despite the cultural eruption of 1968, the presence of compassion and the ability to mourn others would remain conspicuously absent for at least another decade.

VI

In one very important respect, however, the 1960s did change the face of West Germany. Throughout western Europe, foreign labor migration had begun to alter a continent of ethnically homogeneous countries. This change was especially marked in the Federal Republic.

Recruitment of foreign labor began with Italian workers in 1955, but it then expanded dramatically when the Federal Republic began recruiting workers from Greece and Spain in 1960, Turkey in 1961, Portugal in 1964, and Yugoslavia in 1968. The voracious appetite of the growing West German economy required ever more workers, especially after the building of the Berlin Wall in August 1961 essentially dammed the flow of East Germans pouring into the Federal Republic. Deprived of this labor supply, which totaled more than three million people between 1949 and 1961, West Germany was forced to look abroad with even more vigor.[78] It turned to Turkey, and signed a formal agreement with Istanbul to send workers to the Federal Republic.

The relentless realist Max Frisch described the situation astutely when, in a caustic satirical piece about his native Switzerland in 1965, he wrote, "one called for workers, and people came instead." The German media quickly applied his turn of phrase to the Federal Republic, while leaving out the sardonic sentence preceding it: "A little master race believes it is in danger."[79]

National Socialism cast its shadow over the whole process of labor recruitment. The problem started with the name—*Gastarbeiter* (guest worker)—an attempt to circumvent the Nazi term *"Fremdarbeiter"* (foreign worker), even though, as Frisch pointed out, the Nazi word was more honest, given that the young Italian or Spanish men who came to Germany or Switzerland were hardly treated like guests on holiday. On the contrary, once they arrived, their conditions were often oppressive. In the early period, most foreign workers found housing in company-constructed dormitories or cramped military barracks, including some quarters that had once served as housing for Nazi slave laborers.[80] The barracks and dorms were severely overcrowded. Emine Sevgi Özdamar, a German-Turkish author who was among the early guest workers, described staying in otherwise single-person rooms that were expected to host up to six people.[81] At work too, conditions were hardly optimal. The men labored in mines, steel mills, auto factories, kitchens, and on farms, and the women, who made up about a third of the foreign workforce, joined cleaning crews or assembly lines, and toiled in kitchens and on farms as well. Both women and men often encountered domineering bosses, suspicious coworkers, and discrimination of all types. In factories, they were forced to work double shifts, or were summarily fired after just one sick day kept them from coming to work.[82] Moreover, once the workday was finished, their German coworkers rarely extended an invitation to come drink at the pub. More typically, the Germans went their way, the foreigners theirs. On rare occasions, foreigners ventured to the one pub that actually served them, but when guest workers populated a locale, Germans typically avoided it. In 1974, a decade after the first major waves of guest workers, an Allensbach poll reported that only 13 percent of Germans could say they met with foreigners outside of work, and, tellingly, only 7 percent said that their children played with the children of guest workers.[83]

In order to understand the extent of the segregation, West Germany's most famous muckraker, the journalist Günter Wallraff, went undercover for a whole year, pretending to be a guest worker named Ali. He came away from the experience believing that, as he wrote, "a piece of apartheid is right in the middle of us."[84] As a German, Wallraff admitted that he could not truly experience the "daily humiliations, enmities, and hate" in the same way as a real guest worker would, but he came to understand, and to share, what the foreign worker "has to bear and just how far contempt for other people can go in this country."[85] Indeed, far from experiencing the kindnesses of a host society, guest workers experienced immense isolation.

The loneliness was especially palpable on Sundays, when the stores were closed, the streets empty, and Germans were sitting in cafés or enjoying *Kaffee und Kuchen* at home. On countless streets, forlorn men from Italy, Greece, Spain, and Portugal walked aimlessly, dressed in their Sunday best. By the early 1970s, the sight of these men, conspicuously without their families, had become emblematic of the visible life of German towns and cities as was the spectacle of German invalids from the war—more than a million men, now in their late forties, fifties, and early sixties, their empty sleeves and pant legs stark reminders of the sacrifices made for Hitler's aggression.

VII

As German cities cleared rubble and started constructing new edifices, one type of building continually haunted the streets. Before the war, over a thousand synagogues had once stood on the territory of the Federal Republic. Roughly a third were destroyed during the November pogrom in 1938, while others were wrecked during the war, and almost all of them were eventually abandoned. Yet in town after town, village after village, hundreds remained.[86] Since synagogues typically occupied prime real estate in the centers of cities and towns, they were either repurposed, as shops, banks, schools, or churches, or torn down. In many cases, other structures, such as parking garages, shopping centers, hotels, or new town halls, were built on the sites where synagogues once stood.

At first, there was a prevailing, almost systematic silence surrounding the erasure of Germany's synagogues. Baden-Württemberg, for example, had been home to roughly one hundred and fifty synagogues before the war. By 1960, only five communities had even erected the barest commemorative plaque. Typically, the early plaques employed the passive tense, stating only that the synagogue "was destroyed in the period of National Socialism."[87] As *Wirtschaftswunder*-driven urban renewal advanced in the 1950s and 1960s, more and more synagogues were razed, and commemorative plaques were put up in greater number as old structures were torn down. By this time, some plaques began addressing what had happened with greater realism. A plaque placed in 1969 in the town hall of Etten-heim, for example, stated that Jews had been "humiliated, expelled, and carried off." It added that their temple was "destroyed," their ritual objects "desecrated, burned, or stolen," and abjured, "We want never to forget the suffering that our fellow Jews endured."[88]

The early 1970s, if the number of plaques in Baden-Württemberg is any indication, fell into silence again, followed later in the decade by renewed attention. In the late 1970s, a veritable surge began and gathered force in the mid-1980s, with almost three-quarters of commemorated synagogues in Baden-Württemberg receiving plaques during and after this burst. Other states, like Bavaria and Lower Saxony, show similar trajectories.[89] Only in the eastern states, like Brandenburg and Thuringia, do we see a different trend line, with very few commemorations until 1988, the fiftieth anniver-sary of the pogrom.[90] In the west, as the language of the plaques reveals, it had taken decades before communities wrung their way to formulations that treated the pogrom as if it were more than a mere occurrence. Once the transition occurred, however, grassroots commitment made commem-oration a permanent feature of West German cities and towns. A number of communities even went so far as to replace older plaques with newer ones that more accurately described the building's history. In Emmendin-gen, a small city in the southwest of Baden-Württemberg, the town had put up a plaque for the synagogue in 1968 that simply stated: "1821 newly built—1922/23 expanded—1938 destroyed." Twenty years later, the town replaced the innocuous old plaque with one that emphatically affirmed that the synagogue was "demolished and torn down by the citizens of Emmendingen," and that the "Jewish community was extinguished."[91] The language in 1988 was more precise, the focus on the community more truthful, and a sense for the tragic dimension of what had happened palpable.

Commentators typically date the surge in West German interest in the persecution of the Jews to around 1979, when the American television series *Holocaust* aired in the Federal Republic. While the evidence from the com-memorations of synagogues suggests a slightly earlier shift, it is nevertheless true that this series, watched by more than 60 percent of the adult popu-lation and discussed in endless panels and covered in countless schools, accelerated the trend and, more successfully than any historian ever could, brought the Holocaust to a mass audience. Indeed, Germans, who had hitherto spoken of "the killing of the Jews" or the "final solution," now began to use the term "Holocaust" when they referred to the genocide.[92]

The series managed to achieve the significant cultural impact it did by exploiting simple yet highly effective strategies of viewer identification. The plight of the Jewish Weiss family, whose members are portrayed as honest, educated, and caring, is intertwined with the story of Erik Dorf, a callous SS careerist whose "banality of evil" is matched only by that of his morally obtuse wife, Marta. The fictional Erik Dorf becomes the right-hand man of the very real Reinhard Heydrich and eventually becomes a key decision maker in the implementation of genocide. Even as the series intertwines the fate of the two families, it consistently portrays the Dorf family, with the exception of one uncle, in such diabolic terms as to totally prohibit any identification. Instead, the German viewers were led to mourn the Weiss family, whose qualities evoked Germans' own sense of their better selves, and identified with the German woman who married into the Weiss family, Inga. Portrayed by Meryl Streep, Inga is beautiful, brave, and unflagging in her devotion to her Jewish husband, Karl, an artist. In especially difficult scenes, Inga submits to being continually violated by Heinz Müller, a vile SA man and friend of her own family, in order to smuggle letters to her incarcerated husband in Buchenwald. When Karl is transferred to Theresienstadt, Nazi guards torture him and crush his hands, and then send him to Auschwitz, where Karl tragically dies bent over a final sketch. The camera also follows the infinitely kind mother, Berta, into the gas chambers as she comforts a young woman who had lost her sanity. Anna, Berta's own daughter, also became mentally ill following the trauma of being raped by Nazi thugs, after which she was murdered in a "euthanasia action."

The German and American versions of the series feature two differing endings: one of denial and one of redemption. In the German version, the final scene focuses on the Dorfs: Uncle Karl, the one sympathetic Dorf who had helped Jews, visits Marta, Erik's wife, and their children. Karl tells them that Erik, who has since taken a cyanide pill, was a cold-blooded killer of millions of innocent women and children. Marta refuses to accept the news and forces Karl to leave the house and never return. The series thus ends with denial, implicitly challenging Germans to take the oppo-

The Weiss family in the television series *Holocaust*, 1978 (U.S.) and 1979 (Federal Republic of Germany), portrayed by (from left) Fritz Weaver, Meryl Streep, James Woods, and Rosemary Harris.

site approach and confront their past honestly. In the original, as shown in the United States, the ending is redemptive, properly aligning with the identifications the story established from the beginning.[93] In this version, Rudi Weiss, Karl's intrepid younger brother and the only member of the Weiss family to survive, finds Inga after the war. His sister-in-law says, "You can hate me, if you wish, for being one of them." Rudi replies, reminiscent of Anne Frank's whisper at the end of the theater adaptations, "I don't hate you."[94] By this time, Inga has birthed Karl's son, naming him Josef after the loving father of the Weiss family. Barely more than a toddler, the young boy holds a paintbrush in his hand, suggesting that viewers are meant to believe that he will continue the artistic work of his murdered Jewish father. Effectively, they are also meant to understand that Inga has become a member of the Weiss family. As Rudi departs, she says, "Goodbye, little brother."[95]

Certainly, there is much to criticize about this film's treatment of the Holocaust—the color rendition and continual summer weather and blue skies gives it the feel of a *Heimat* movie; historical documents, especially photographs, are blatantly misused and jumbled chronologically; and some historical events, like the clearing of the Warsaw Ghetto, are rendered without the extreme violence that accompanied them, while others, like the killing at Babi Yar, give no real sense of the actual dimensions of the massacre. Perhaps most disturbing is that Jews, with the exception of one member of the Weiss family, are constantly portrayed as meekly cooperating in their own demise and suffering, when, in fact, Jewish resistance across eastern Europe was tenacious, widespread, and bloody. Elie Wiesel, the survivor and best-selling author, decried the series as "untrue and offensive," agreeing with many other critics who felt it trivialized Jewish suffering.[96] Nevertheless, the series portrayed some aspects of the genocide that had not been central to public discourse at that time: the persecution and killing of Jews in the first years of the occupation of Poland, for example, or the sheer magnitude of thievery and sexual violence that accompanied the Nazi occupation of Europe. Decisive, however, was that it allowed an irresistibly sympathetic Jewish family to stand as the victims. The series thus brought Jews, centrally and unmistakably, into the German circle of mourning. What *Holocaust* lacked in realism, it made up for in recasting the genocide in a light that highlighted Jewish suffering and encouraged German compassion.

This act of extending compassion was also the main theme of one of the most profound and popular political speeches of the postwar era: President Richard von Weizsäcker's address to the German parliament, entitled "May 8, 1945—40 Years After." Directly following the war, the controversial political philosopher Carl Schmitt had argued that although the winners of wars write history, it is the losers who make the better historians; he used Alexis de Tocqueville as his prime example.[97] Weizsäcker's speech was Germany's de Tocqueville moment, in which the acceptance of defeat led to deeper insight. It remains remarkable to this day for the way it resonated with an evolving sensibility about the German past. Weizsäcker started the speech by affirming that May 8, 1945, was not, for Germans especially, a day to celebrate. But because it marked the end of the tyranny that began on January 30, 1933, it was a moment of hope and a chance for renewal.[98] Nazi rule, he told his listeners, began with "the bottomless hatred of Hitler of our Jewish fellow citizens." He also contended, less veraciously, that only a few Germans carried out the crimes.[99] Nevertheless, he

Richard von Weizsäcker in the Bundestag, May 8, 1985.

underscored that ordinary Germans, motivated by a range of sentiment from "cold indifference to concealed intolerance to open hatred," consciously averted their eyes from Jewish suffering, leaving themselves with a heavy historical burden: "all of us, guilty or not, old or young, must take on this past."[100] Germany's history was not then something to escape or to master in order to make it disappear. Rather, it was a source of a different kind of strength.

Weizsäcker's reflections were printed, distributed, and sold in hundreds of thousands of copies and replayed countless times on radio and television. "The speech" (*"Die Rede"*), as it was sometimes called, brought forth widespread and deeply felt approbation. It also provoked criticism, the most vociferous coming from the sharp-tongued Bavarian politician Franz Josef Strauss. Appealing to the shibboleth of a "normal nation," Strauss contended that this "endless mastering of the past in the form of ongoing national contrition paralyzes a people."[101] Nations are not empty vessels, however, and the attempt—forty years after Germany had committed genocide—to ignore this history rung hollow, even more in the mid-1980s than it had in previous decades. It is perhaps for this reason that the speech would later become a touchstone for separating a kind of conservative national position, one which took pride in the accomplishments of the Federal Republic and did not seek to make light of the genocidal past, from a new radical nationalism that viewed any kind of national self-criticism as betrayal.

VIII

This new radical nationalism cannot be understood simply as old prejudices held over from National Socialism. Instead, it emerged as a forceful reaction to the vagaries and anxieties of a postwar world undergoing increasing globalization. By 1970, the worldwide level of international trade had finally returned to the prewar levels attained in 1913. Germans began routinely traveling abroad as never before. At the same time, the influx of guest workers into industries like mining, steel, and automaking, as well as into food services, approached a million people per annum, even as many would soon return to their countries of origin after working in Germany.

The global turn would soon reveal the precariousness of the postwar economic recovery. In October 1973, the Arab oil embargo crippled western nations, causing the growth rates even of high-performing, export-oriented economies like that of the Federal Republic to slow down and unemployment to pick up. Sensing popular anxiety, the Brandt government responded by putting a moratorium on the entry of new guest workers on November 23, 1973. By that time, guest workers constituted over 4 percent of the West German population—some 2.6 million people. When the government announced the ban, it soon became clear that guest workers from nations outside the European Economic Community (the forerunner of the European Union), could no longer leave Germany and expect to return safely. It was in this context that a new German government under Helmut Schmidt began to develop policies to integrate migrant families, including enacting legislation that allowed families of guest workers to come and live in the Federal Republic. Taking into account Germany's Nazi past, the Schmidt government recognized the moral significance of not separating families or deporting workers and argued vigorously for what Heinz Kühn, Schmidt's minister of foreigner affairs, called "unconditional and permanent integration."[102]

In the late 1970s, more foreign workers came to Germany (in sectors for which the moratorium foresaw exceptions), and a substantial number of the families of guest workers were reunited. By 1980, the population of foreigners in West Germany had increased to roughly 4.4 million, or a little more than 7 percent of the total population, just as unemployment rose to troubling heights, approaching 8 percent in 1982. To make matters worse, "unconditional and permanent integration" began to encounter substantial socioeconomic obstacles. More than a quarter of all foreign children had left school without a degree. Some 70 percent of the foreign workers remained unskilled or semiskilled laborers. And nearly three-quarters of all foreign workers earned less than their German counterparts.[103]

Most foreigners living in Germany had come to the Federal Republic through the guest worker program, but by 1980, the number of asylum applications, which had hitherto averaged less than 10,000 applicants per year, suddenly shot up to 100,000. Germans now became palpably anxious about the sheer number of foreigners in their midst. In 1982, the Allensbach Institute surveyed how Germans felt about what it called the "foreigner problem." Rather astonishingly, more than 80 percent of the respondents thought there were already too many foreigners in their country.[104] Among supporters of the two main conservative parties (the Christian Democratic Union and the Christian Social Union), nearly 90 percent thought there were "too many" foreigners, and even 60 percent of the newly constituted environmentalist Green Party agreed.[105] In addition, more than 70 percent of the total respondents believed that the Federal Republic was too generous in granting asylum, while 28 percent supported striking the asylum clause from the constitution, and only 16 percent believed that the applicants had actually suffered political persecution.[106]

The political fallout seemed unavoidable. Helmut Kohl, the new Christian Democratic Chancellor, who had taken office in October 1982 when the coalition supporting Helmut Schmidt collapsed, promised to reduce the number of foreigners living in the Federal Republic by half. In March 1983, he won the Federal election by vowing to stop West Germany from becoming what he called an immigrant nation. Kohl, when in office, moved quickly to pass a law that offered a payment of 10,000 marks (and an additional 1500 marks for each child) to foreign families who went home. The newsmagazine *Der Spiegel* called it a "take your premium and get out of here" policy.[107] Yet the "re-migrant incentives," as they were officially called, hardly made a dent in reducing the non-German population. Instead, the vast majority of foreigners, many of them with families already in the second and third generation in Germany, chose to stay. Whether or not Germans wished it, their country was becoming a de facto immigrant nation.

One reaction to this new de facto identity was an emergent nationalism that held fast to the ideal of ethnic homogeneity. In 1981, a group of scholars, including some with significant Nazi pasts, had composed the so-called Heidelberg Manifesto. Arguing that the immigration of millions of foreign workers was undermining "our language, our culture, and our ethnicity," the manifesto's authors painted what was for them a gloomy, dystopic picture of a "multiracial society," in which the ethnic purity of the German people would be compromised.[108] The manifesto earned far more criticism than support. However, groups like the Republicans, a new right-wing party founded in 1983 in order to combat multiculturalism, appropriated its alarmist message. Franz Schönhuber, the most visible Republican leader in the late 1980s, eagerly supported radical nationalist positions like those held by Robert Hepp, a sociologist whose cynically titled *The Final Solution of the German Question* (1988) contended that current rates of immigration would "end with 'the disappearance of the German people' and 'the end of German history.'"[109]

IX

Germans were not disappearing, but Germany did remain divided between east and west, and by the 1980s that division, reinforced by apathy and the passage of time, seemed to have hardened. Even after Mikhail Gorbachev, a reform Communist, came to power in the Soviet Union in 1985, the sense that the Wall was there to stay had become an article of faith on both sides of the border. In a subsequently famous speech delivered in Berlin on June 12, 1987, U.S. President Ronald Reagan challenged "Mr. Gorbachev" to "tear down this wall." With some notable exceptions, the West German media, more interested in perpetual peace than genuine change, largely ignored this address, while the newsmagazine *Der Spiegel* called it "the work of amateurs."[110]

Some West Germans knew better. For years, Ilse Spittmann, an editor for *Deutschland-Archiv*, a conservative political journal, had been writing prescient essays about the hollowness of support for the East German regime and the corrosive effect of the pervasive surveillance of the Stasi, its internal security apparatus. By 1989, the Stasi was far larger than the Gestapo had been during the Nazi period, and significantly surpassed all other comparable postwar east European regimes. East Germany was, in fact, one of the most spied-on societies in history. In the late 1980s, between 100,000 and 200,000 citizens worked full-time for the Stasi or served as informants.[111] The Wall had also become more menacing: it was now a wide strip, replete with watchtowers, barbed-wire fences, antitank ditches, a disheartening number of abused and angry dogs, and nighttime illumination one could see from outer space.[112] At least 140 people died trying to get across the Wall, mostly young men, the greatest percentage of them during the 1960s.[113] The Wall effectively stopped the exodus, but it also left the regime despised, and when a route to the west temporarily opened up through Hungary in August 1989, young East Germans rushed through it en masse.

It is perhaps no accident that Albert O. Hirschman, a man whose early life centered on exodus, provided the most insightful explanation for the East German Revolution of 1989 and the fall of the Berlin Wall.[114] The scion of an assimilated, patriotic, and Jewish family, Hirschman had served as the right-hand man of Varian Fry during World War II, helping to direct the Emergency Rescue Committee, which was responsible for creating escape routes for many European intellectuals, such as Hannah Arendt, Marc Chagall, Siegfried Kracauer, Golo and Heinrich Mann, and the publishers Helen and Kurt Wolff. After the war, he moved to the United States, where he had a brilliant career as a developmental economist. In his *Exit, Voice, and Loyalty: Responses to Decline in Firms, Organizations, and States*, published in 1970, he posited a seesaw or hydraulic effect especially between exit and voice. Where the possibility of exit exists, he argued, the urgency of voice declines.[115]

Much of East Germany's short forty-year history seemed to support this hypothesis. After the spectacular failure of voice in 1953, exit increased, and never significantly slowed, until 1961, when repression brought exit to a halt and the show of state power quieted voice as well. In this moment,

Hirschman conceded, the model was less illuminating. But in 1989, "exit and voice," as Hirschman put it, suddenly turned into a "joint grave-digging act."[116] What happened, he argued, was the exact reverse of 1961. Exit and voice, the private and the public script, conspired to put an end to the state with remarkable speed.[117] The key to the interpretation was the way that a private activity, exit, imparted energy and élan to a public activity, voice.

The subsequent history of the revolution and unification is too well-known to require a full recounting here.[118] By January 1990, the rallying cry of "we are one people" began to drown out the younger, more inno-cent, braver, and resolutely oppositional "we are the people." But this was not the nationalism of old, as some commentators feared; instead, East Germans pursued what the philospher Jürgen Habermas called "*DM [deutschmark] Nationalismus*," appropriating the language of nationalism in pursuit of better material outcomes.[119] Seeing a political opportunity, Chancellor Helmut Kohl advanced a program for quick unification, and in the first free election on East German soil since November 1932, East Ger-man voters embraced Kohl's proposals, turning their backs on the coalition of forces that brought about the revolution in the first place.

In the spring of 1990, East Germany actually looked more like a coun-try that had lost a war than one that had won a revolution. Offices had shut down, industrial plants were grinding to a halt, the state was dissolving, and West Germans, some with good intentions, were flooding into the east. Fearing a popular backlash, Kohl made the necessary but devastating decision to allow East Germans to exchange their currency for the West German mark at a 1:1 ratio, with a savings ceiling of 2000 marks, and thereafter at 2:1. East Germans drew a sigh of relief, but almost overnight the East German economy was obliterated, and the west essentially took it over. On October 3, 1990, West Germany declared the country unified; in reality, the two countries did not merge together, but rather five east German states joined the Federal Republic. In any event, on the day of unification, the city of Berlin piped Beethoven into speakers along Unter den Linden. People strolled back and forth, stopping here or there to eat *Currywurst* or *Döner Kebab*. Some listened to solemn speeches; others ate at one of the many ethnic restaurants that had begun to appear in West Berlin in the 1970s and became ubiquitous in the 1980s.[120]

Within a few short years, the introduction of West German capitalism into East Germany would bring forth what the Communist government could not: East Germans who had a strong sense of East German
identity. In a 1995 poll, the Allensbach Institute surveyed whether Germans felt "primarily German" or "primarily East or West German." Since
unification, the proportion of people from the new five eastern states who
reported identifying as "East German" had actually increased from 37 percent to 49 percent, but in the west, the opposite was true: two-thirds of the
West Germans polled said they felt themselves to be "primarily German,"
with lower numbers showing in Bavaria and West Berlin, where regional
identity ran high. Overall, however, the first five years of unification made
West Germans feel more nationally German, and East Germans less so.[121]

X

National unification washed away the anti-immigrant Republican Party but
not popular anger directed against foreigners. As it became increasingly
clear that unification would be both difficult and expensive, a new wave of
xenophobia targeted foreign workers and political asylum seekers. Beginning in cities in the east where unemployment was high, prospects bleak,
and experiences with foreigners limited, pogromlike attacks occurred in
Hoyerswerda, Dresden, Rostock-Lichtenhagen, and many other communities, soon spilling into West Germany. On November 22, 1992, in the
Schleswig-Holstein town of Mölln, xenophobes set a house ablaze, killing
a Turkish woman, her granddaughter, and her grandniece. Six months
later, in May 1993, a similar arson attack occurred in the Rhenish city of
Solingen, killing a woman, a teenage girl, and three children, all of whom
were Turkish. It was as yet the most heinous, but not the last, instance
of postunification violence against foreigners. By 2000, according to one
estimate, antiforeigner extremists would murder more than a hundred
non-Germans.[122]

Even as these anti-immigrant attacks escalated, an untold number of
protesters, men and women of all ages coming from varying walks of life
and political persuasions, proclaimed their unified opposition to the resur-
gent violence. Indeed, after the attack in Solingen more than three million
Germans joined candlelight vigils across the country, opposing the vio-

lence and mourning the victims.[123] In the 1990s, Germans did what they did not do in the early 1930s, and what they would have likely not done in the 1950s either: they went out en masse and protested for someone else, revealing the presence of compassion. They also symbolically affirmed a society and a democratic polity built, in part, on the lessons learned by a country that allowed radical nationalists into power and enabled them to commit genocide.

In fact, in the 1990s, Germans turned to precisely that past with considerable resolve. Synagogues continued to be commemorated, satellite camps of concentration camps were restored, and there was a great deal of public history and commemorative work on other victim groups, including Roma and Sinti, homosexuals, and men targeted by the German army's ruthless military justice. The veritable boom in memory work can also be seen in the breaking of taboos—one thinks of the discussion following the release, in the early 1990s, of Helke Sander and Barbara Johr's book and documentary film *Befreier und Befreite* (*Liberator and Liberated*), which, through a series of interviews, brought out women's voices and made credible claims about the ubiquity of mass rape.[124] One also thinks of the 1995 Wehrmacht exhibit, which contained more than 1400 photographs of regular army soldiers, often with a grin and a smile, observing, aiding, or committing war crimes. After the exhibit opened that March, it attracted long lines of viewers, as well as protests and counterprotests, and eventually a sustained debate in the German parliament. By the late 1990s, a kind of commemorative realism had permeated all corners of the Federal Republic. In Baden-Württemberg, for example, only three major sites of memory concerning Nazi crimes predate the 1980s, according to an official count, while eight are from the 1980s, nineteen are from the 1990s, and twenty from the first decade of the 2000s.[125] Other places, like Hamburg, mirrored the experience of the southwest, so that when the numbers and timelines are generalized to all of Germany, the late surge of memorial sites and its attendant public consciousness becomes evident.

Indeed, a vast, decentralized, commemorative landscape had come into existence. In 1997, the Federal Office for Political Education published two thick volumes inventorying and describing all the memorials in the Federal Republic for the victims of National Socialism. Traveling to hundreds of cities, towns, and even villages, the compilers questioned mayors, priests, pastors, and rabbis; they interviewed schoolteachers and local historians; and they spoke with scores of professionals and volunteers. Some even found themselves in the countryside, "pulling back weeds and ivy to reveal hidden stones and weathered epigraphs."[126] After sifting through thousands of entries for memorials, sculptures, and gravesites, Ulrike Puvogel, the inventory's scholarly editor, remarked that local interest in Germany's dark history began "relatively late, not until the end of the 1970s, the beginning of the 1980s," and that this process was, in both east and west, "fought for from below."[127] The result was a greater attentiveness to the tragic dimensions of the country's past than exists almost anywhere else.

Germans also began to separate out the prejudices of nationalism from their sense of belonging to a nation. One can see this when bringing different polling questions together. On the one hand, there are the numbers that commentators point to suggesting that Germans have abandoned the nation for a kind of cosmopolitanism. Thus, in November 2001, only 19 percent of Germans replied "very" and 42 percent "somewhat" to the question "Are you proud to be German?" Differences between east and west, male and female, were insignificant, and age mattered only slightly.[128] When compared with the United States, where 80 percent of those polled said they were "very proud" to be American, and Great Britain, where 52 percent answered similarly, the low numbers the Germans registered were conspicuous.[129] Moreover, for decades Germans had counted among those least willing Europeans to pick up arms: at the beginning of the new millennium, only 33 percent said they would fight for their country in the event of war.[130]

Yet these responses tell of a turn away from a form of nationalism that saw Germany as superior to other nations and defined dying for one's fatherland as an essential aspect of the social contract. Significantly, they do not imply a turn away from the nation as such. Telling in this regard was a different way of posing the question. When the Allensbach Institute merely asked whether Germans loved their country, nearly 80 percent answered in the affirmative, with only East Germans responding with lower levels of assent.[131] Moreover, despite the immense progress of the European Union in the 1990s, 76 percent of Germans, when forced to choose, said they felt German rather than European, while only 15 percent said "European," with the others undecided.[132] When they were asked whether they felt like Germans or citizens of the world, their answers fell in a nearly identical way.[133]

Do Germans, then, still live in the nationalist age? No, but they still live in the age of nationalism, and they continue to struggle with it. This is because nationalism, as in other countries, remains one way of conjuring the nation—but only one way. As citizens of a nation, Germans have instead by and large come to embrace what Dolf Sternberger imagined in 1947 as "a living not a deathly concept of fatherland."[134] This does not imply a turn away from the nation, or its troubled history. Rather, as Richard von Weizsäcker understood, it involves seeing German history as the source of a different kind of strength—and the compassion it can summon as new measure of the worth of a nation: the German nation.

THE REPUBLIC OF THE GERMANS AT THE BEGINNING OF THE TWENTY-SECOND CENTURY

ALMOST EVERY NIGHT IN THE SUMMER OF 2006, THE "FAN MILE," as the broad boulevard heading west from the Brandenburg Gate was called, filled with people from every conceivable nation. They proudly sported the jerseys of their teams, waved flags, sang songs, and some even danced together in the steady glow of the overhead lights. Germany was hosting the World Cup, and one night, July 8, seemed particularly magical.

The German team had just won a game against Portugal by a score of 3–1, allowing it to take third place overall. After the game, I proceeded with my friend Siegfried to the Kurfürstendamm, the storied West Berlin shopping street lined for that night with cheap stands selling black, red, and gold scarves and hats, and of course, small German flags. "Why don't you get one?" I asked Siegfried.

He demurred. I went ahead and bought him one anyway, as well as one for myself. We waved them around, a bit embarrassed.

I had already begun to think about writing *Germany: A Nation in Its Time* in the spring of 2005, when I was at the American Academy in Berlin, whose balcony looked out onto the same lake as did the Villa Wannsee. I assumed that the book would end in 1945—although not with the military defeat of Germany, as did so many of the classic works on

German history, but with the liberation of the camps. A brief epilogue was to be appended.

Yet on that night of July 8, I resolved to bring the story to the present, and to write a history of shifting understandings of the German nation from its first conception as a two-dimensional space until this moment, when Germans felt free to wave flags again, and many people, including myself, thought that this was actually a good thing. The radical nationalism that characterized Germany in the 1930s and 1940s—indeed, the toxic nationalism that had caused so much suffering—would not be the end of the story. Instead, it would form a crucial chapter within it.

II

In the summer of 2006, there appeared grounds for optimism about a country the American writer Thomas Wolfe once described, as would I, as "half my hearts' home."[1] The feeling commenced with the soccer team. Granted, I confess I had always rooted for the German team. As a boy, I remember watching the 1974 squad, captained by the elegant *libero* Franz Beckenbauer and led by its goal-scoring menace, Gerd Müller, "the Bomber," less elegant but no less effective. Thirty-two years later, the lineup appeared somewhat different. Coached by expatriate Jürgen Klinsmann, the 2006 team played fast-paced soccer and sported somewhat differently trimmed white jerseys. It also fielded three forwards born in foreign countries, Miroslav Klose and Lukas Podolski from Poland, and Gerald Asamoah, an Afro-German. Asamoah had moved from Ghana to Germany when he was twelve, and had become a German citizen in 2001.[2] As the team had been doing since October 1984 (on Beckenbauer's insistence), they also sang the national anthem.

The differences between 1974 and 2006 went far beyond soccer, however. Germany had, in the meantime, become an immigrant nation, and was roughly equal to the United States in terms of new immigrants as a percentage of the population. In 2000, it emphatically marked this status with a significant change in citizenship law. Since 1913, German citizenship had been based on the principle of *jus sanguinis*, the right of blood, rather than *jus soli*, the right of the soil. The older law implied that a person born in Germany was not necessarily a German citizen, since German is defined by heritage, with the result that neither the original guest workers, nor their children, or even their children's children, possessed German citizenship. The new citizenship law blends the two juridical traditions. It gives children born to foreign parents automatic German citizenship if one parent has been a legal resident of the Federal Republic for at least eight years and the child affirms German citizenship in some way before the age of twenty-three. Simply stated: just as anyone can move to the United States and become an American, so too any person from any corner of the world can now move to Germany, and their children, if born in Germany, will become Germans, if they wish.

Between the time the new citizenship law went into effect in 2000 and the 2006 World Cup, roughly a million immigrants had become German citizens. Immigrants constituted almost 9 percent of the population, and—perhaps the most telling statistic of all—a quarter of all new marriages were between Germans and people from other ethnic groups.[3]

There were, of course, warnings that this new inclusive, reflective nation, which I was witnessing, might not hold. At precisely the time of the World Cup tournament, German unemployment had soared past 10 percent. Two years earlier, a Muslim fundamentalist had murdered Theo van Gogh, the provocative Dutch filmmaker, bringing forth a wave of anti-Islamic sentiment in the Netherlands, one of the most tolerant nations in Europe. It could, I thought at the time, happen in Germany as well. Moreover, beneath the euphoria, there was considerable discontent, and this discontent was sometimes expressed in dubious terms. Countering the German soccer team's new, diverse image, the extreme right-wing National Democratic Party pursued a xenophobic campaign whose slogan was "White, it's more than just a jersey color. For a real national team."[4]

Nevertheless, I returned to my university in the United States that summer brimming with stories about the magic of Germany's hosting the World Cup.

Alas, in the years that followed, German nationalism did, in fact, become a more menacing force. The backsliding began with the financial crash of 2008, which slowed the global economy, crippled a string of financially strapped European countries, and forced the European Union, with Germany as its principal banker, to arrest the financial meltdown of Greece, and potentially a series of other nations as well.[5] Almost overnight, the debt policies of the European Union became the most important political issue for German voters, undermining widespread support for a united Europe. More important, Germans lost the sense that Europe constituted the inevitable next stage of a progressive, open future. Instead, bleak prognoses about the fate of the German nation suddenly darkened the horizon.

The most important of these prognoses was Thilo Sarrazin's *Deutschland schafft sich ab (Germany Self-Destructs)*. Published in the summer of 2010, this best-selling book put forth doomsday scenarios of the kind espoused in the late 1980s in Robert Hepp's *The Final Solution of the German Question*. Contrasting greater Muslim fertility and high levels of immigration with ethnic German demographic decline, Sarrazin calculated that by the beginning of the twenty-second century Germany would contain 35 million Muslims and only 20 million people belonging to what he called "the autochthone population."[6] Selling more than a million copies within the first months of its publication, the book's misinformed anti-Islamic prejudices and spurious calculations popularized ideas of impending German extinction and legitimized shrill xenophobia. The comparison drawn by commentators to the Prussian historian Heinrich von Treitschke's infamous "Our Prospects," the article that inaugurated the anti-Semitism of Imperial Germany in 1879, is disturbingly apt. Prominent thinkers of the newly ascendant nationalism immediately recognized Sarrazin's book as a "door-opener."[7]

Alongside these German political trends was the global rise of populist nationalism in the second decade of the twenty-first century. Reacting to the increased mobility of labor and capital, this new nationalism trades in a common currency of antielitism, antipluralism, and xenophobia.[8] Typically claiming to speak for the so-called real, authentic people, it has made significant inroads into the political landscapes of France, Great Britain, Holland, Italy, and, most recently, the United States, where it has deeply divided Americans and polarized political discourse.

Nevertheless, Germany had weathered the crash of 2008 better than most countries and seemed, perhaps more than any other nation at the time, relatively immune to populist nationalism. In the European elections of 2009, right-wing nationalist parties received a significant number of votes in such diverse countries as Italy, France, Great Britain, Austria, and Hungary, but not in Germany. In the German federal elections of the same year, even the newly created Pirate Party, which advocated for more internet freedoms, had more support than the extreme right. Finally, in Chancellor Angela Merkel, Germany had one of the most trusted leaders of the democratic world.

The deepening debt crisis had, however, begun to shift the political calculus, even in Germany. In April 2013, a group of scholars and economists founded a new political party, the Alternative for Germany (known by its acronym in German, AfD). Its policy proposals were initially economic. They included the dissolution of Europe as a currency zone, the reintroduction of the mark, and nationwide referendums to approve of the further transfer of state competencies to the EU. Although exploiting German frustration with the Greek bailout, the AfD did not, in the main, stoke antiforeigner resentment, and in the federal election of 2013, it narrowly missed the constitutionally mandated 5 percent hurdle necessary to clear in order to enter parliament. Soon, however, a fundamental divide became apparent, between the leadership, focused on finances, and the party's base, motivated by increasingly entrenched anger and frustration. In the two years after the election, this divide only widened, and by September 2015, new leadership ousted the economic-oriented founders and sought more demonstratively to play to the fears of its electoral base. The AfD now steered into unabashedly nationalist and xenophobic waters.

The establishment of Pegida (Patriotic Europeans Against the Islamicization of the Occident) in Dresden in October 2014 was yet another factor stoking xenophobic reactions. The movement played to the anxieties of ordinary people and expressed them in ways that caused an otherwise reticent Angela Merkel to warn, in her New Year's message of January 2015, that some leaders of the movement possess "prejudice, coldness, even hatred in their hearts."[9]

Then, as a result of the devastating civil war in Syria, the number of refugees flooding European borders swelled, and that September Chancellor Merkel arrived at a fateful decision, agreeing to allow unregistered asylum seekers entry into Germany.

In the larger context of German history, her decision to open Germany's borders was courageous. It counts among the remarkable moments of postwar German politics, along with President Theodor Heuss's confession, in Bergen-Belsen in 1952, that "we knew about these things"; the parliamentarian Ernst Benda's argument in 1965 for extending the statute of limitations for Nazi murderers who were about to be set free; and Chancellor Willy Brandt's falling to his knees in 1970 in front of the Warsaw Ghetto Memorial, a gesture that the German-Iranian author Navid Kermani recently characterized as the moment when a shamed nation found "its dignity again."[10]

As a result of Merkel's resolve, nearly half a million people poured into shelters of the Federal Republic in 2015, and nearly three-quarters of a million more the following year. "If we have to excuse ourselves for showing a friendly face in an emergency," a defiant Merkel insisted, "this is not my country."[11] In so many ways, however, Germany had become precisely *her* country. According to some estimates, nearly 10 percent of the adult population of Germany volunteered to help Syrian refugees, an outpouring of sympathy and activity that was historically unprecedented and matched in no other major nation.[12]

Yet the decision also had political costs. In the federal election of September 2017, migrants and foreigners became the most important issue, and the reconstituted, expressly xenophobic AfD received 11.5 percent of the national vote, and more than 20 percent of the vote in the eastern states, with the result that the AfD easily vaulted the 5 percent hurdle and now sat in the German parliament. Men, and in particular those aged thirty-five to fifty-nine, voted disproportionately for the AfD, especially in the east, where 27.6 percent of male voters supported this extreme nationalist party. Workers, traditionally a voting block for the left, also voted in significant numbers for the AfD, as did the unemployed, especially in the east, where they split their votes between the AfD and Die Linke, a left-wing populist party.[13] Since then, the AfD has extended its reach into state-level politics. In 2018, the AfD received more than 10 percent of the vote in the western states of Bavaria and Hesse.

The success of the populists has revealed a grim visage of prejudice and violence. German streets have become less safe for foreigners. Immigrants are regularly subject to taunting and aspersion. And public discourse now seems increasingly rife with prejudice toward outsiders.

Yet the story is not as one sided as it is often portrayed. While the new nationalists have created something like a significant subculture of anxiety, intolerance, and hate, they have not yet succeeded in reversing the fundamental attitudes of the majority of Germans.

Perhaps the most important result of a battery of closely constructed sociological analyses conducted in the past five years is that there is now a major gulf between the opinions and attitudes of those Germans who have distanced themselves from the AfD and those whose right-wing populist leanings have since brought them to embrace the new party. These analyses place latent enmity toward specific groups at fairly low levels for the vast non-AfD majority, and at alarmingly high levels for the AfD minority. Thus, in 2016, researchers placed anti-Semitism at less than 5 percent for the majority versus 15 percent for AfD sympathizers; racism at 5 percent for the first group and nearly 20 percent for the second; and anti-Muslim attitudes at just over 10 percent for most Germans versus nearly 45 percent for AfD supporters. The only category in which negative attitudes were broadly prevalent was toward asylum seekers, with 40 percent of the mainstream and nearly 75 percent of pro-AfD respondents showing markedly negative attitudes.[14] Even while the AfD has encouraged the expression of prejudices once kept under a bushel, chauvinism, such studies suggest, has not flourished in the wider population, with prejudice against asylum seekers an important exception.[15]

There are a number of reasons why this might be the case. More than in many other countries, Germans have long felt the fragility of their democracy, and they react with greater sensitivity than is evident elsewhere to signs of backsliding into the politics of an era that brought about a great deal of destruction and shame. The cumulative effect of many years of education, memorialization, and reflection, across a wide range of media, about the causes and consequences of National Socialist rule have surely had an important impact in this regard. Moreover, Germans are actually quite conscious of their country's role in a globalized economy and believe that tariff wars and decreased labor mobility bring its export-oriented manufacturers far more harm than good. This fundamental openness to globalization has even led Renate Köcher, the director of the Allensbach Institute, to claim that "Germany is different" from other western countries.[16] While a majority of Germans still think that Germany should accept fewer immigrants, this opinion does not seem to reflect a permanent rise in antiforeigner attitudes.

Unfortunately, credible polls also show that there remains a minority, likely larger than in the pre-AfD period, that harbors deep anti-immigrant and antiforeigner sentiment, and now feels emboldened to express it. More menacing still is that actual violence against immigrants and foreigners has remained at disturbingly high levels. According to the Amadeu Antonio Foundation, named after one of the first victims of xenophobic violence after German unification, there have been some two hundred nationalist-motivated murders of foreigners in the thirty years since 1990; this is roughly equivalent to the number of East Germans who were murdered in the preceding three decades trying to get past the Berlin Wall.[17] Other lists, including an official tally of the Federal Criminal Police Office, put the numbers lower, with the difficulty figuring out what counts as the motivation for the crime. Nevertheless, these murders, as well as roughly twenty-eight thousand cases of violent but nonfatal attacks on foreigners (according to official statistics), rose significantly during the early 1990s, receded in the first decade of the twenty-first century, and increased again, though not as markedly, during the migration crisis of 2016–2017.[18] Such disturbingly high levels of antiforeigner violence, it goes without saying, constitute a serious challenge to the basic self-conception of the Federal Republic as a country that has left nationalist violence behind it.

And yet, rejecting nationalism and leaving nationalist violence behind, while still embracing the nation, is actually what most Germans want. To many, this means, as it did during the World Cup of 2006, being a nation among other nations, as well as one bound into the complex sovereignties and mutual exchanges of the European Union. It means having a robust democracy capable of fending off threats, a humane social state, a diverse and open society, and a sustainable environment. It also means turning one's back on the nation conceived in terms of ethnic homogeneity—as indeed most Germans, to some extent, have. In 2001, more than 80 percent of Germans polled conceded that "different cultural groups enrich a society"—even though many still worried about social cohesion and some believed that too much cultural difference harmed national unity.[19] "Toward nationalism's end," as the great scholar of nationalism Hans Kohn understood, is not an easy road.[20] Nor is it a straight one.

III

Readers will recall that the philosopher Johann Gottlieb Fichte composed a fragment in 1807 entitled "The Republic of the Germans at the Beginning of the Twenty-Second Century." Inspired by the ideals of the French Revolution and by dismay at Prussia's defeat at the hands of Napoleon, Fichte imagined a for-Germans-only republic in which the first duty of each man was to sacrifice his life for the nation, just as each German woman was obligated to bring life forth. Animated by the ideals of liberty, fraternity, and equality for those who sacrificed for the nation, the Republic, once secure in its expanded borders, would renounce aggression and European countries would live in peace. Fichte's was an optimistic vision, even if we are likely not to share it.

By contrast, the new nationalists have only a declension narrative. They also have a vision of a "Republic of the Germans at the Beginning of the Twenty-second Century." It is to them a dystopia in which Muslims, not Germans, constitute the largest population, and Germany—its culture, its customs, its traditions, and even its language—dies a slow death. "According to current trends," writes Thilo Sarrazin, "Germany will have 35 million Germans in 100 years, 8 million in 200 years, and only 3 million in 300 years."[21] Such calculations blithely ignore the experiences of immigration societies, in which greater levels of welfare lead to lower levels of fertility, and ethnic and religious intermarriage, already significant in Germany, leads not to ethnic extinction but to a more inclusive understanding of what constitutes a nation.

Just as the new nationalists have a constricted image of Germany's future, they also have a distorted understanding of Germany's past. The distortions come in various versions.[22] Mainly, they represent a turn away from a form of historical thinking that foregrounds compassion for the victims of genocide. More than three decades after it was given, Richard von Weizsäcker's speech of May 8, 1985, remains the touchstone. It was, as we have seen, Germany's de Tocqueville moment. Yet Björn Höcke, a founder of the AfD in Thuringia, was hardly alone in denouncing it as being "against one's own people and not for one's own people."[23] There is also a still coarser form of disdain for the thought and work that has gone into understanding National Socialism. Alexander Gauland, a leading figure in the AfD, recently expressed it when he characterized the Nazi period as but "a bird turd in the 1000 years of German history."[24]

How is it that such a distorted understanding of the nation's past and such a bleak vision of its future speak to many Germans?

The answer is that, as it pertains to the nation's past, it does not. Among non-AfD Germans, the trivialization of National Socialism has virtually no traction. In serious polling studies, it barely gets a few percentage points (although for the AfD close to 10 percent). The same holds true of the worldviews that underpinned Nazism, like social Darwinism and manifest anti-Semitism; these ideologies attract very few Germans outside the AfD.[25] Even in polls that have been criticized for their skewed samples and overdramatization of antiforeigner sentiment, it appears that fewer than 10 percent of Germans agreed with such statements as "National Socialism also had its good sides" and "Were it not for the extermination of the Jews, Hitler would be seen today as one of the great statesmen."[26] Such utterances, it must be recalled, had significantly higher levels of assent in the carefully conducted polls of the early 1950s. Nor have the new nationalists succeeded in chipping away at the vast and damning evidence amassed by decades of historical work revealing the full dimensions of Nazi genocide. In these same problematic polls, only 10 percent of Germans assented to the statement that "the crimes of National Socialism are vastly exaggerated in the historiography."

It is, instead, the new nationalist's bleak vision of the future that persuades some people—the declension narrative was, after all, the secret to Sarrazin's success. Why should this be so?

One answer lies in the nation-state itself. As noted at the outset of this book, the nation-state retains a surprising relevance in people's lives. Despite all the forceful currents of globalization, some 97 percent of the people in the world will still die in the country of their birth. In an age where there is a growing chasm between rich and poor nations, the place of one's birth has remained the single most important determinant of one's prospects and well-being. Passports and visas, accordingly, are not just pieces of paper that allow people to cross borders. They are tickets to a better life. But from the vantage of the citizens of "host nations," the perceived devaluation of citizenship status—through fluid borders, double citizenship, and complicated sovereignties—calls forth anxiety, less about the immediate present, than about the distant future. This anxiety is not entirely groundless. In countries of significant demographic decline, an infusion of large numbers of migrants can certainly help the economy (this is especially true of Germany, whose skewed age pyramid reveals that by 2030 there will be almost twice as many people in Germany sixty years and older than under twenty).[27] But whether large-scale immigration helps the lower-middle and working classes within these host nations is, from a purely economic view, not clear. And whether it benefits their offspring remains an open question.[28]

The new nationalism appeals to both those who are disadvantaged by globalization and those who fear they might lose out. These groups see the nation-state as their protector, as indeed it appears to be in Germany's constitution, which describes the Federal Republic as a state defined by "a republican, democratic, and social rule of law."[29] They interpret that protection in ethnic or national terms and, for this reason, place more trust in politicians who assure them ethnic or national loyalty.[30] Such assurances, and whether they actually resonate, have a logic of their own. One might again echo Albert O. Hirschmann's triangulation of exit, voice, and loyalty, so prescient in 1989. In this model, well-educated elites will be perceived as seeking exit from rich countries animated by decline (which Germany's current anxiety about brain drain makes clear, as does popular mistrust of Brussels-centered Euro politicians). Voice is precisely what ordinary people fear they no longer have. And loyalty, whether ethnic or national, is what is left, and what the new nationalists promise them.

Historians may nevertheless point out that an ethnically and religiously homogeneous country, as the new nationalists wish it, is a conception of the nation with a short, destructive history. It was not part of the humanist understanding of Germany. It did not belong to the Prussia of Frederick the Great. And it belonged to only some of the initial formulations of German nationalism—Fichte's among them. Moreover, the conception of Germany as an ethnically homogeneous country gained widespread credence only with Heinrich von Treitschke and his ideological heirs in the Imperial period. Even then, there were many populations, as recent research has shown, who were indifferent to nationality, and even switched between nationalities. It is true that the early twentieth century spawned new conceptions of nationality, as social Darwinian and ethnic categories came to determine ideas of national community, and that the Nazis erected a spurious legal foundation for the ethnically and religiously homogeneous nation-state. But this was no utopia. Expulsions, nationality transfers, and killing sprees culminated in genocide in less than a decade after radical nationalists took over power in 1933. Thereafter, further expulsions—this time of Germans—did, in fact, create the very homogeneous nation-states that the nationalists of today dream about. Yet the iron bars of the "cage called fatherland," as Wolfgang Koeppen's character Keetenheuve called it in his fulminous 1953 novel, *The Hothouse*, had already begun to loosen in the late 1950s, and they continue to do so.[31] From a statistical standpoint, this brief age when Germans existed as a uniform homogeneous nation has passed. Today, it no longer exists. Nor does it constitute the reality of other western nations, even if nostalgia for it remains lodged in people's memories and consciousness. Moreover, to achieve this homogeneity again would involve literally tearing modern German society apart, much as anti-Semitism did in the 1930s. It will be recalled that this anti-Semitism, especially in the form of exceptional laws, brought about the radical reconstitution of the German nation. In our time, it would bring about the end of Germany as we know it.

IV

The future is, of course, not the proper domain of a historian. It is difficult enough to get the past and present right. One historian knew this very well. Writing a half century after Fichte sketched his vision in a fragment, Jacob Burckhardt, the renowned cultural historian, sought to situate his own present in historical context.[32] In his immensely popular lectures to the citizens of Basel in the 1860s and 1870s, Burckhardt told his audiences that the French Revolution was barely eighty years old, the "Wars of Liberation" not quite sixty, and that the period 1815 to 1848 may well have been nothing but an intermezzo in a great revolutionary drama. From his vantage, the French Revolution had brought equality before the law but also an immense centralization of the state, an intensification of its power, and the division of Europe into nations capable of genuine and dangerous emotions. According to Burckhardt, two issues—the national question and the social question—most affected the present, while a third, the "current unprecedented escalation of militarism," had become an essential characteristic of the era.[33]

We are now almost as far away from the collapse of National Socialism as Burckhardt was from the French Revolution. For him and his audience, the more recent collapse of 1848 was surely as alarming an event as the recrudescence of nationalist sentiment in the Federal Republic of Germany is to us. Thus, to use Burckhardt's logic, was "after nationalism" merely an "intermezzo"?

In the opinion of this author, the answer is no, but with the proviso that one should not confuse twenty-first-century patriotism, national identity, or a genuine love of one's country with the kind of toxic nationalism that defined Germany's nationalist age. In the 1990s, the conservative critic Karl Heinz Bohrer perspicaciously noted that there is no necessary connection between national identity on one side and the diminution, trivialization, and obliteration of the past on the other, and that a profound respect for German national traditions does not at all negate a genocidal past. On the contrary, it has often been a spur to that engagement. Moreover, a "living not a deathly concept of fatherland," to cite Dolf Sternberger again, is not only about the past. It is also about shaping Germany's present.[34] In this vein, it will be recalled that in the past two, and indeed almost three decades, a sense of the worth of the nation—even when expressed *ex negativo* as "this is not who we are"—has motivated Germans to demonstrate against outbreaks of antiforeigner violence. More recently, it has also spurred an enormous number of people to give aid during the refugee crisis. One of our most prescient observers of the European scene, Ivan Krastev, has even noted how remarkable Germany's response actually was, when compared with that of other nations, especially in eastern Europe.[35]

Of course, whether nationalism becomes, once again, the defining characteristic of the age, and not just one of many responses to politics, is a question that Germans will ultimately have to answer for themselves. But if our understanding of the past has any answers to give, it will contextualize the nation within a history that is far greater than its nationalism, and suggest that historical nationalism, especially in its modern, radical form, cannot make nations. On the contrary, it demeans, divides, and ultimately destroys them.

ACKNOWLEDGMENTS

I HAVE LOVED THE SUBJECT MATTER OF THIS BOOK, THE *longue durée* of modern German history, as the great historian Fernand Braudel once wrote he loved the seas. While researching it, I learned more about the past than in any course of study or in the writing of any other book. Starting with the sixteenth century, I worked on it chronologically, finding it difficult to leave historical epochs behind. Gradually, what began as an essay—"not a lesson for others but for me," as Montaigne defined the genre— grew into something more than an essay. And while it still retains some of the character of being "for me," it could not have been written without the help of many others. It gives me great pleasure to thank some of them.

In the world of making books, I have been helped by a fabulous group of professionals. Robert Weil, my gifted editor at Liveright/W. W. Norton, poured in his friendship, energy, and editorial sense into this project, while also slashing sentences and tightening prolix paragraphs. So too did his perceptive assistant, Gabriel Kachuck, who additionally coached a restless author through all sorts of hurdles in the process. I also want to thank Anna Oler for help with the maps for this book. (The maps themselves were made with ESRI base maps and software, while the georeferenced historical vector data is from Euratlas-Nüssli in Switzerland.) In the final rounds of editing, I was very fortunate to have a wonderful copy editor, Trent Duffy, whose sharp eye and painstaking attention to detail improved the manuscript significantly. My agent, Georges Borchardt, has helped at every step of the way, and I am honored to be counted among the authors he represents.

The project was first conceived more than a decade ago, during a stay at the American Academy of Berlin, when I was surrounded by an inspired group of fellow writers, artists, and scholars. Halfway through the writing, with my ideas still inchoate, a Guggenheim Fellowship generously funded it. I was very pleased to receive this prestigious fellowship. It was my third try at it, and the earlier attempts were, as the jury no doubt sensed, simply not ready. In the course of the work on this book, I also took a bit of time off to edit *The Oxford Handbook of Modern German History*. It was perhaps a foolish thing to do, but it allowed me to work with more than thirty German historians from at least five countries, and to think together about the shape of the field. My thanks to all the historians who contributed to that project—this book would not have been possible without that one, and their work on it.

Over the years, I have presented portions of the work to various audiences in North America and Europe. For invitations to share my ideas, I am grateful to a number of universities in Canada, including the University of Toronto, the Université de Montreal, York University in Toronto, and Carleton University in Ottawa; a number of universities and institutions in Germany, including the University of Freiburg, the Institute for Advanced Studies in Freiburg, and the University of Trier; a number in the United States, including Brandeis University, Cornell University, the University of Delaware, Christopher Newport University, Princeton University, Stanford University, the University of Connecticut, and Washington University in St. Louis. I also discussed some of my thoughts with faculty and students at the Universiteit van Amsterdam and the Université du Luxembourg. My thanks as well to a number of journals—including *Central European History*, *German History*, and *The Bulletin of the German Historical Institute* in Washington, D.C.—for allowing me to try out some of the ideas of this book in their pages.

At my home university, Vanderbilt, Martha Rivers Ingram generously endowed the chair in history that I am honored to hold, and I am happy to finally be able to present her with this work. At Vanderbilt, I have also been blessed with a wonderful community of scholars working in the field of central Europe; over the last few years they have read parts of this book and discussions with them have shaped the evolution of the work. Many thanks to Celia Applegate, Michael Bess, David Blackbourn, Bill Caferro, Emily Greble, Ari Joscowicz, Jim McFarland, David Price, and Frank Wcislo. Marshall Eakin, a historian of Latin America, invited me to present my work to his graduate class on nationalism, and the interest of his students helped me gauge the manuscript's progress. Thanks too to our graduate students and recent Ph.D.s in central European history. They think they come to graduate school to learn from professors, when really the reverse is just as true. For conversations about the work, my thanks especially to Pat Anthony, Jeremy Dewaal, Sonja Loomis, John Gillespie, Vladislav Lilic, Chris Mapes, Cassandra Painter, Trevor Thomas, and Brianne Wesolowski.

A special group of Vanderbilt history friends, whom I meet on late Friday afternoons, heard more than they wanted to about this book. They read, intervened when I was in despair, poked fun at me, and in the end shaped this work decisively. Cheers to Joel Harrington, Peter Lake, and Eddie Wright-Rios. Another special group of friends in Berlin—more precisely, within a small radius around Ludwigkirchplatz in Wilmersdorf—have also discussed the work, helped me appreciate its complexities, and encouraged me. My thanks especially to Elke Schmitter for the many inspiring conversations. I am also grateful to Jürgen Busche, Barbara Hahn, Kathrin Hoffmann-Curtius, Christian Jansen, Thomas Mergel, Barbara Wahlster, and Siegfried Weichlein (who actually makes a cameo in the book) for their support and criticism over the years.

At various points, friends and colleagues outside of Vanderbilt have also read chapters, and I am very grateful for their thoughts and support. My sincere appreciation to Jim Brophy, Steve Dowden, Jennifer Evans, Pieter Judson, Thomas Kühne, David Luebke, Deb Neill, Andrew Port, Till van Rahden, and Jim Retallack. The community of central European historians is not for the faint of heart. Criticism is freely given. But it is almost always given with good intention and a strong sense for getting things right. Some from this community will know that I shared drafts of my maps with my professional friends on Facebook. Thanks to all those who chimed in, supported, and corrected those maps. Thank you as well to Lindsey Fox and Jess Behrens for technical help on the digital side of my work, and to Cliff Anderson and Steven Wernke for giving me a sense of what one can accomplish in the digital humanities, even if, in books like this, one has to hide that work under a bushel. That kind of work involves a lot of gathering data, counting, and sometimes computing, and here I had help along the way from a number of students, including Steven Kornblum, Gabriel Zharov, and David Kessler.

One mark of good friends and colleagues is their ability to tell you when a work is not yet ready. At roughly the two-thirds mark of this book, two fellow historians and friends, James J. Sheehan and Steven Englund, read the entire manuscript as it then stood. Their close readings, sincere support, and gentle reservations forced me to step back and reshape the book, sharpening its arguments and bringing its parts more closely together. Close to the end, two younger readers, Robyn-Phalen Rayson and Alexandra Campana, also read it. Neither are historians. Robyn, a recent graduate of Kenyon College's storied writing program, and Alexandra, a recent Ph.D. in German literature from Vanderbilt who lives in Switzerland and is moving to a position in South Africa, brought a great deal of insight, critical questioning, precise and revealing queries, and helpful suggestions to the manuscript.

Finally, my greatest debt is the closest one. Meike Werner has supported this project when other people thought it was nuts; she has endured my all-too-often absences and my obsessive pursuits; and when others felt this book was falling apart, she believed it would come together. I could not have written it without her support and love. The book is dedicated to our son, Luca. He just turned sixteen. When he was little, he taught me a lot about what it means to see the world without fixed categories—in other words, with wonder. When he was five, he delighted a whole train of Berliners by exclaiming on the S-Bahn, "We are in the East, look, there are the trolleys!" In a city still riven with tension, there was no more innocent way to perceive the differences between the two Berlins than to note that the East still had trolleys, or *Strassenbahnen,* while the West did not. It is now the summer of 2019. In the last few weeks, he beat me in chess for the first time, outsprinted me on the bicycle, shared my admiration for Katherine Boo's *Behind the Beautiful Forevers*, and helped me make the maps for this book.

NOTES

INTRODUCTION

1   The historiography on German nationalism is vast. There are many places to enter this historiography, including the relevant sections of Hans-Ulrich Wehler, *Deutsche Gesellschaftsgeschichte*, 5 vols (Munich, 1987–2008); Otto Dann, *Nation und Nationalismus in Deutschland, 1770–1990*, 3rd ed. (Munich, 1996); and Dieter Langewiesche, *Nation, Nationalismus, und Nationalstaat in Deutschland und Europa* (Munich, 2000). For an English-language entry, see Christian Jansen, "The Formation of German Nationalism, 1740–1850," and Pieter M. Judson, "Nationalism in the Era of the Nation-State, 1870–1945," both in *The Oxford Handbook of Modern German History*, ed. Helmut Walser Smith (Oxford, 2011), 234–259 and 499–526.

2   Benedict Anderson, whose *Imagined Communities* remains the most influential book on the subject, contended that "nation-ness, as well as nationalism, are cultural artifacts of a particular kind"; he maintained that they were created "toward the end of the eighteenth century" and thus possessed an "objective modernity." See Benedict Anderson, *Imagined Communities: Reflections on the Origins and Spread of Nationalism* (London, 1983), 13–14. Likewise, Ernest Gellner, who saw nationalism as an early-nineteenth-century doctrine, famously asserted, "It is nationalism which engenders nations, not the other way around." Ernest Gellner, *Nations and Nationalism* (Oxford, 1983), 55. From these propositions, it follows that nations cannot predate the nationalists who invented them. For the argument that nationalism and nation ought to be separate, as nation is an older category, albeit differently than is here intended, see David A. Bell, *The Cult of Nation in France: Inventing Nationalism, 1680–1800* (Cambridge, Mass., 2001), 5–15. For the crucial role of the state in making nations, see John Breuilly, *Nationalism and the State* (Manchester, 1982).

3   Michael Howard, *The Invention of Peace. Reflections on War and International Order* (New Haven, 2001), 100.

4   The conflict catalogue was developed by Peter Brecke of Georgia State University. It can be accessed at: https://brecke.inta.gatech.edu/research/conflict/.

5   Christopher Clark, *Iron Kingdom: The Rise and Downfall of Prussia, 1600–1947* (Cambridge, Mass., 2006).

6   Consider Max Rosen's visualization of the conflict catalogue data: https://ourworldindata.org/wp-content/uploads/2013/08/Europe-only-ArmedConflictsInternational.png.

7   Erich Auerbach, *Mimesis: The Representation of Reality in Western Literature*, trans. Willard R. Trask (Princeton, N.J., 1953), 554.

8   Walter Benjamin, "Ursprung des deutschen Trauerspiels," in *Gesammelte Schriften*, ed. Rolf Tiedermann and Hermann Schweppenhäuser, vol. 1, part 1 (Frankfurt am Main, 1974), 409.

9   Konrad H. Jarausch, *After Hitler: Recivilizing Germans, 1945–1955*, trans. Brandon Hunzker (Oxford, 2006), 48.

10   Fernand Braudel, *Geschichte als Schlüssel zur Welt: Vorlesungen in deutscher Kriegsgefangenschaft*, ed. Peter Schöttler (Stuttgart, 2013), 22.

11   Immanuel Kant, "Beantwortung der Frage: Was ist Aufklärung?," in *Werkausgabe*, vol. 11, part 1, *Schriften zur Anthropologie, Geschichtsphilosophie, Politik und Pädagogik*, ed. Wilhelm Weischedel (Frankfurt am Main, 1968), 59.

12   Andreas Wimmer, *Waves of War: Nationalism, State Formation, and Ethnic Exclusion in the Modern World* (New York, 2012); Harm de Blij, *The Power of Place. Geography, Destiny, and Globalization's Rough Language* (Oxford, 2009), 136.

13   Johann Wolfgang Goethe, *Gedichte, 1756–1799*, ed. Karl Eibel, in Goethe, *Sämtliche Werke*, ed. Hendrik Birus et al. (Frankfurt am Main, 1987), 507.

CHAPTER 1. SEEING GERMANY FOR THE FIRST TIME (C. 1500)

1   Lucien Febvre, *The Problem of Unbelief in the Sixteenth Century: The Religion of Rabelais*, trans. Beatrice Gottlieb (Cambridge, Mass., 1982), 395.

2   P. D. A. Harvey, "Local and Regional Cartography in Medieval Europe," in *The History of Cartography*, vol. 1, *Cartography in Prehistoric, Ancient, and Medieval Europe and the Mediterranean*, ed. J. B. Harley and David Woodward (Chicago, 1987), 464–501.

3   Birgit Hahn-Woernle, *Die Ebstorfer Weltkarte* (Ebstorf, 1993), 8. See also *Die Ebstorfer Weltkarte: Kommentierte Neuausgabe*, ed. Hartmut Kugler, Sonja Glauch, and Antje Willing, 2 vols. (Berlin, 2007), 1:69.

4   Hahn-Woernle, *Die Ebstorfer Weltkarte*, 42–45.

5   For the argument that the *Germania* section of the map was based on itineraries, see Jürgen Wilke, *Die Ebstdorfer Weltkarte*, 2 vols. (Bielfeld, 2001), 1:22–28; for skepticism about that argument, see Kugler et al., eds., *Die Ebstorfer Weltkarte: Kommentierte Neuausgabe*, 2:58–59.

6   Wilke, *Die Ebstdorfer Weltkarte*, 2:24.

7   Ibid., 1:142–50.

8   On the Bruges itinerary, and on the importance of itineraries generally, see Catherine Delano-Smith, "Milieus of Mobility: Itineraries, Route Maps, and Road Maps," in *Cartographies of Travel and Navigation*, ed. James R. Akerman (Chicago, 2006), 16–68.

9   "Die Jerusalemfahrt des Heinrich von Zedlitz (1493)," ed. Reinhold Röhricht, in *Zeitschrift des Deutschen Palaestina-Vereins* 17 (1894): 100.

10   "Otto Heinrich, Pfalzgraf bei Rhein," in *Deutsche Pilgerreisen nach dem Heiligen Lande*, ed. Reinhold Röhricht and Heinrich Meisner (Berlin, 1880), 353–54.

11   Ibid.; J. H. Kohl, ed., *Pilgerfahrt des Landgrafen Wilhelm des Tapferen von Thüringen zum heiligen Lande im Jahre 1461* (Bremen, 1868), 76–77.

12   Kohl, ed., *Pilgerfahrt des Landgrafen Wilhelm des Tapferen*, 78. See also "Otto Heinrich, Pfalzgraf bei Rhein," 353–54.

13   Malcolm Henry Ikin Letts, and Eberhard von Groote, eds., *The Pilgrimage of Arnold von Harff, Knight* (London, 1946), 4.

14 Johannes Helmrath, "Enea Silvio Piccolomini (Pius II)—Ein Humanist als Vater des Europagedankens?," in *Europa und die Europäer: Quellen und Essays zur modernen europäischen Geschichte*, ed. Rüdiger Hohls, Iris Schröder, and Hannes Siegrist (Wiesbaden, 2005), 367-68.

15 Enea Silvio Piccolomini, *Deutschland: Der Brieftraktat an Martin Mayer*, ed. and trans. Adolf Schmidt (Cologne, 1962).

16 Ibid., 91, 92-93.

17 Ibid., 103; Klaus Voigt, *Italienische Berichte aus dem spätmittelalterlichen Deutschland* (Kiel, 1973), 90.

18 Piccolomini, *Deutschland*, 93, 94, 102.

19 Ibid., 107, 116.

20 Ibid., 122.

21 See the discussion about when Cusanus began to assemble these coordinates in Peter H. Meurer, *Corpus der älteren Germania-Karten: Ein annotierter Katalog der gedruckten Gesamtkarten des deutschen Raumes von den Anfängen bis um 1650* (Alphen aan den Rijn, 2001), 87.

22 Because no maps were appended to the copy found in Constantinople, scholars since have debated whether Ptolemy constructed maps conforming to his coordinates. See, on this subject, Joseph Fischer, S.J., *Ptolemäus als Kartograph* (Gotha, 1923), 113-29. On its reception, see Patrick Gautier Dalché, "The Reception of Ptolemy's Geography," in *The History of Cartography*, vol. 3, *Cartography in the European Renaissance*, part 1, ed. David Woodward (Chicago, 2007), 286, 298, 306-7.

23 Lloyd A. Brown, *The Story of Maps* (New York, 1949), 61.

24 J. H. Elliot, *The Old World and the New, 1492-1650* (Cambridge, 1970), 1.

25 The term comes from Juergen Schulz, "Jacopo de' Barbari's View of Venice: Map Making, City Views, and Moralized Geography Before the Year 1500," *Art Bulletin* 60, no. 3 (1978): 454.

26 Klaus A. Vogel, "European Expansion and Self-Definition," in *The Cambridge History of Science*, vol. 3, *Early Modern Science*, ed. Katharine Park and Lorraine Daston (New York, 2006), 818-39.

27 Carina L. Johnson, *Cultural Hierarchy in Sixteenth-Century Europe: The Ottomans and Mexicans* (New York, 2011), 37; on Mesoamerican city size, see Michael E. Smith, "City Size in Late Postclassical Mesoamerica," *Journal of Urban History* 31, no. 4 (2005): 403-34. Europeans could envision the Mexican city from a print, more fanciful than real, published in 1524: see Richard L. Kagan, *Urban Images of the Hispanic World, 1493-1793* (New Haven, 2000), 89.

28 Valentin Groebner, *Defaced. The Visual Culture of Violence in the Late Middle Ages*, trans. Pamela Selwyn (New York, 2004), 14-15.

29 Elizabeth L. Eisenstein, *The Printing Revolution in Early Modern Europe* (Cambridge, 1983), 10-11.

30 Ibid., 93.

31 William M. Ivins Jr., *Prints and Visual Communication* (Cambridge, Mass., 1953), 2.

32 Febvre, *The Problem of Unbelief in the Sixteenth Century*, 395.

33 Paul Münch, *Lebensformen in der frühen Neuzeit*, 2nd ed. (Berlin, 1998), 161.

34 David Woodward, "Cartography and the Renaissance: Continuity and Change," in Woodward, ed., *The History of Cartography*, vol. 3, part 1, 11.

35 Michel de Certeau, *The Practice of Everyday Life*, trans. Steven Rendall (Berkeley, Calif., 1984), 118-22.

36 Robert Karrow, "Centers of Map Publishing in Europe, 1472-1600," in Woodward, ed., *The History of Cartography*, vol. 3, part 1, 616.

37 The mapmaker Abraham Ortelius, cited in George Tolias, "Maps in Renaissance Libraries and Collections," in ibid., 642.

38 Walter Pohl, *Die Germanen*, 2nd ed. (Munich, 2004), ix.

39 Ingo Reiffenstein, "Bezeichnungen der deutschen Gesamtsprache," in *Sprachgeschichte: Ein Handbuch zur Geschichte der deutschen Sprache und ihrer Erforschung*, 2nd ed., ed. Werner Besch, Anne Betten, Oskar Reichmann and Stefan Sonderegger (Berlin, 2003), 3:2192–93.

40 Anon., "Annolied," in *Deutsche Dichtung des Mittelalters*, vol. 1, *Von den Anfängen bis zum Hohen Mittelalter*, ed. Michael Curschman and Ingeborg Glier (Frankfurt am Main, 1980), 95.

41 Ibid., 133.

42 Walter von der Vogelweide, "Ir sult sprechen willekomen," in *Deutsche Literatur im europäischen Mittelalter* (Munich, 1972), 1:701; Meurer, *Corpus der älteren Germania-Karten*, 7. See also Len Scales, *The Shaping of German Identity: Authority and Crisis, 1245–1414* (Cambridge, 2012), 452–55.

43 "The Golden Bull of the Emperor Charles IV of 1356," in Ernest F. Henderson, *Select Historical Documents of the Middle Ages* (London, 1905), 220–61 (the count is based on this translation). For the original Latin, see *Die Goldene Bulle Kaiser Karls IV vom Jahre 1356*, ed. Wolfgang D. Fritz (Weimar, 1972), 43–90.

44 Bernd Schönemann, "Volk, Nation," in *Geschichtliche Grundbegriffe*, ed. Otto Brunner, Werner Conze, and Reinhart Koselleck (Stuttgart, 1978), 7:285.

45 Jacob and Wilhelm Grimm, *Deutsches Wörterbuch* (Leipzig, 1860), vol. 2, col. 1052.

46 Marc Bloch, *Feudal Society*, trans. L. A. Manyon, 2 vols (Chicago, 1961), 1:145.

47 Benedict Anderson, *Imagined Communities: Reflections on the Origin and Spread of Nationalism*, 2nd ed. (London, 1991), 19.

48 Wolfgang Stürner, *Gebhardt Handbuch der deutschen Geschichte*, 10th ed., vol. 6, *13. Jahrhundert, 1198–1273* (Stuttgart, 2007), 61.

49 Jan de Vries, *European Urbanization, 1500–1800* (Cambridge, Mass., 1984), 29.

50 For cautious population estimates, see Peter Clark, ed., *The Oxford Handbook of Cities in World History* (Oxford, 2013), as well as the less guarded guesses in Luc-Normand Tellier, *Urban World History: An Economic and Geographical Perspective* (Montreal, 2009), 581–86. See also Fernand Braudel, *Civilization and Capitalism 15th–18th Century*, vol. 1, *The Structures of Everyday Life*, trans. Siân Reynolds (New York, 1979), 525–27.

51 Andrew Pettegree, *The Book in the Renaissance* (New Haven, 2010), 33, 36.

52 Niccolo Machiavelli, "Report on the Affairs of Germany," in *The Historical, Political and Diplomatic Works of Niccolo Machiavelli*, trans. Christian E. Detmold (Boston, 1882), 4:387.

53 Bodin cited in Gerald Strauss, *Nuremberg in the Sixteenth Century* (New York, 1966), 12.

54 "German Venice," in Wojciech Iwańczak, *Die Kartenmacher: Nürnberg als Zentrum der Kartographie im Zeitalter der Renaissance*, trans. Peter Oliver Loew (Darmstadt, 2009), 17.

55 Luther cited in Lewis W. Spitz, *Conrad Celtis: The German Arch-Humanist* (Cambridge, Mass., 1957), 35.

56 Iwańczak, *Die Kartenmacher*, 161.

57 Elisabeth Rücker, *Die Schedelsche Weltchronik: Das größte Buchunternehmen der Dürer-Zeit* (Munich, 1988), 8–10; Pettegree, *The Book in the Renaissance*, 41.

58 Stephan Füssel, introduction to *Weltchronik*, by Hartmann Schedel, ed. Stephan Füssel (Augsburg, 2004), 31–32. Pettegree, *The Book in the Renaissance*, 41–

42, 77–78, gives a printing number of 1500 Latin and 1000 German copies, but underscores that not all were sold. Remarkably, some 1200 copies have survived.

59   Rücker, *Die Schedelsche Weltchronik*, 37–38.

60   Richard M. Wunderli, *Peasant Fires: The Drummer of Niklashausen* (Bloomington, Ind., 1992).

61   Schedel, *Weltchronik*, folios cxlix, cci, ccliiii, cclvii.

62   Wolfgang Behringer, "Die großen Städtebücher und ihre Vorraussetzungen," in *Das Bild der Stadt in der Neuzeit, 1400–1800*, ed. Wolfgang Behringer and Bernd Roeck (Munich, 1999), 82–83; Elizabeth Ross, *Picturing Experience in the Early Printed Book: Breydenbach's Peregrinatio from Venice to Jerusalem* (Philadelphia, 2014), 2. For a list of realistic-seeming views based on empirical observation, see Rücker, *Die Schedelsche Weltchronik*, 130–31.

63   Stephanie Leitsch, *Mapping Ethnography in Early Modern Germany* (New York, 2010), 34.

64   Jessica Maier, "A 'True Likeness': The Renaissance City Portrait," *Renaissance Quarterly* 65 (2012): 717–18.

65   Ibid., 711–52.

66   Meurer, *Corpus der älteren Germania-Karten*, 110–11.

67   Cited in ibid., 109.

68   Richard Benz, ed., *Historia von D. Johann Fausten* (Stuttgart, 1964), 50.

69   Füssel, introduction to *Weltchronik*, 36–37; Stephan Füssel, afterword to *Historia von D. Johann Fausten* (Stuttgart, 1988), 336–37.

70   Fritz Schnelbögl, "Life and Work of the Nuremberg Cartographer Erhard Etzlaub," *Imago Mundi* 20 (1966): 11–18.

71   Johannes Cochlaeus, *Brevis Germaniae Descriptio*, ed. and trans. Karl Langosch (Darmstadt, 1976), 91.

72   *Schätze der Astronomie: Arabische und deutsche Instrumente aus dem Germanischen Nationalmuseum*, ed. Johannes Willers and Karin Holzamer (Nuremberg, 1983), 52–55.

73   Harvey, "Local and Regional Cartography in Medieval Europe," 464–501.

74   Cochlaeus, *Brevis Germaniae Descriptio*, 91.

75   Claudius Ptolemy, *The Geography*, ed. and trans. Edward Luther Stevenson (New York, 1991), 161.

76   A speculative line of reasoning suggests that Etzlaub's map reflected Islamic map-making traditions. See Dana Bennett Durand, *The Vienna-Klosterneuburg Map Corpus of the Fifteenth Century* (Leiden, 1952), 99–102, 266–71; J. B. Harley and David Woodward, *The History of Cartography*, vol. 2, part 1, *Cartography in Traditional Islamic and Asian Societies* (Chicago, 1992), 518.

77   Durand, *The Vienna-Klosterneuburg Map Corpus*, 266–67.

78   Grid analysis, which involves comparing points on old and modern maps, shows Etzlaub's relatively straight lines and right angles against the distended curves and varying angles of the Cusanus maps. See the comparison in Meurer, *Corpus der älteren Germania-Karten*, 223–24.

79   Herbert Krüger, "Des Nürnberger Meisters Erhard Etzlaub älteste Straßenkarte von Deutschland," in *Jahrbuch für fränkische Landesforschung* 18 (1958), 17–18.

80   Ibid.

81   Although preserved in the vaults of Germany's great libraries, the Etzlaub map remained unknown for centuries—until 1890, when a French researcher named Lucien Gallois reproduced it in a monograph titled *Les géographs allemands* (Paris, 1890).

82   Mark Greengrass, *Christendom Destroyed: Europe, 1517–1648* (New York, 2014),

234. The non-German parts of Etzlaub's itineraries were often less accurate: see Iwańczak, *Die Kartenmacher*, 190, for calculations for France and Italy.

83   Meurer, *Corpus der älteren Germania-Karten*, 148.

84   Ibid., 148-50.

85   August Wolkenhauer, "Eine Kaufmännische Itinerarrolle aus dem Anfange des 16. Jahrhunderts," *Hansische Geschichtsblätter* 14 (1908): 158; Iwańczak, *Die Kartenmacher*, 195.

86   Christopher B. Krebs, *A Most Dangerous Book: Tacitus' Germania from the Roman Empire to the Third Reich* (New York, 2011), 63-64.

87   Ibid., 81, 89.

88   On Tacitus's *Germania* in the context of Roman ethnography and stereotypes, see ibid., 44-49.

89   Allan A. Lund, "Versuch einer Gesamtinterpretation der 'Germania' des Tacitus," in *Aufstieg und Niedergang der römischen Welt*, series II, vol. 33, part 3, ed. Hildegard Temporini and Wolfgang Haase (Berlin, 1991), 1961-62.

90   Ibid., 91.

91   Gernot Michael Müller, *Die "Germania generalis," des Conrad Celtis: Studien mit Edition, Übersetzung und Kommentar* (Tübingen, 2001), 34; Todd Kontje, *German Literature Before and Beyond the Nation-State* (Ann Arbor, Mich., 2018), 51.

92   Müller, *Die "Germania generalis,"* 95, 123, 135.

93   See, for example, Caspar Hirschi, *Wettkampf der Nationen: Konstruktionen einer deutschen Ehrgemeinschaft an der Wende vom Mittelalter zur Neuzeit* (Göttingen, 2005), 117-19.

94   The model was Biondo Flavio, *Italy Illuminated*, vol. 1, ed. and trans. Jeffrey A. White (Cambridge, Mass., 2005).

95   Two recent analyses are Volker Reinhardt, introduction to Johannes Cochlaeus, "Kurze Beschreibung Germaniens," trans. Karl Langosch (Darmstadt, 2010), 9-26; and Gernot Michael Müller and J. Klaus Kipf, "Johannes Cochlaeus," in *Deutscher Humanismus, 1480-1520, Verfasserlexikon*, ed. Franz Jose Worstbrock, vol 1 (Berlin, 2006), part 2, 439-60.

96   Cochlaeus, *Brevis Germaniae Descriptio*, 61.

97   Ibid., 157, 159, 107, 99.

98   Ibid., 75. On this aspect of Cochlaeus, see Iwańczak, *Die Kartenmacher*, 21.

99   See the document entitled *Peroratio in Germaniam* appended to Cochlaeus, *Brevis Germaniae Descriptio*, 163.

100 Cochlaeus, *Brevis Germaniae Descriptio*, 8, 10.

101 Ibid., 119.

102 Ibid.

103 Ibid., 99.

104 Ibid., 161, 49.

105 Ibid., 133.

106 Ibid., 113.

107 Johann Wolfgang von Goethe, "Von deutscher Baukunst," in *Werke* (Hamburger edition), ed. Erich Trunz, vol. 12, *Schriften zur Kunst*, ed. Hans-Joachim Schrimpf (Munich, 1982), 12.

108 Harold Jantz, "Images of America in the German Renaissance," in *First Images of America: The Impact of the New World on the Old*, ed. Fredi Chiapelli (Berkeley, Calif., 1976), 96.

109 Jacob Wimpfeling, "Abriss der deutschen Geschichte," in *Der deutsche Renaissance-Humanismus*, ed. Winfried Trillitzsch (Leipzig, 1981), 401. On Wimpfeling, see Paul Joachimsen, *Geschichtsauffassung und Geschichtsschreibung*

in Deutschland unter dem Einfluss des Humanismus (Leipzig, 1910), 66–67. See also, and more recently, Hirschi, *Wettkampf der Nationen*, 253–301, which gives a darker view of the nation concept of early humanists.

110   The quotation follows the more literal translation in Jantz, "Images of America in the German Renaissance," 98. See especially Jantz's interpretation of this passage as an elaborate literary pun. For the whole text of the *Cosmographiae Introductio*, see Martin Waldseemüller, *Cosmographiae Introductio*, ed. and trans. Joseph Fischer and Franz von Wieser (Ann Arbor, Mich., 1966). On Matthias Ringmann as the author, see Franz Laubenberger, "The Naming of America," *Sixteenth Century Journal* 13, no. 4 (1982): 91–113; on the wider debate, see Christine Johnson, "Renaissance German Cosmographers and the Naming of America," *Past and Present* 191, no. 1 (2006): 3-43.

111   Hildegard Binder Johnson, "New Geographical Horizons," in Chiapelli, ed., *First Images of America*, 620.

112   Meurer, *Corpus der älteren Germania-Karten*, 155–60. Meurer deduces the 1511 date from contemporary descriptions of the map. The first extant surviving copy dates to 1520.

113   On the politics of editing the maps of Ptolemy, see Anthony Grafton, *Defenders of the Text: The Traditions of Scholarship in an Age of Science, 1450-1800* (Cambridge, Mass, 1994), 103–6.

114   Meurer, *Corpus der älteren Germania-Karten*, 160–61.

CHAPTER 2. "GERMANY . . . AS IF IN A MIRROR" (C. 1500–1580)

1   Michael Marius, *Martin Luther: The Christian Between God and Death* (Cambridge, Mass., 1999), 137–38. On the posting, see Erwin Iseroh, *The Theses Were Not Posted: Luther Between Reform and Reformation*, trans. Jared Wicks, S.J. (Boston, 1968).

2   Andrew Pettegree, *The Book in the Renaissance* (New Haven, 2010), 103–6.

3   Johann Huizinga, *Erasmus and the Age of Reformation*, trans. F. Hopman (London, 2001), 230–31.

4   Mark Greengrass, *Christendom Destroyed: Europe, 1517–1648* (New York, 2014), 241.

5   Erasmus to Albrecht of Brandenburg, epist. 1009, 15 August 1519, in *The Correspondence of Erasmus*, vol. 7, trans. R. A. B. Mynors, annotated Peter G. Bietenholz (Toronto, 1987), 61–64.

6   Marius, *Martin Luther*, 294.

7   Huizinga, *Erasmus and the Age of Reformation*, 104.

8   Johann Boemus, *Mores, Leges, et Ritus Omnium Gentium* (Lyon, 1541), 211, marginalia.

9   Margaret T. Hodgen, *Early Anthropology in the Sixteenth and Seventeenth Centuries* (Philadelphia, 1964), 22–23. On Boemus, see also Erich Schmidt, *Deutsche Volkskunde im Zeitalter des Humanismus und der Reformation* (Berlin, 1904); Hartmut Kugler, "Johannes Boemus," in *Deutscher Humanismus,1480–1520, Verfasserlexikon*, ed. Franz Jose Worstbrock, vol. 1 (Berlin, 2005), part 1, 210; and Klaus A. Vogel, "Cultural Variety in a Renaissance Perspective: Johannes Boemus on 'The Manners, Laws and Customs of All People' (1520)," in *Shifting Cultures: Interaction and Discourse in the Expansion of Europe*, ed. Henriette Bugge and Joan-Pau Rubiés (Münster, 1995), 17–34.

10   Boemus, *Mores, Leges, et Ritus Omnium Gentium*, 14.

11   Ibid., 197–98.

12   Ibid., 207.

13   Ibid., 211.

14   Ibid., 223.

15   Ibid., 227.

16   Richard Wunderli, *Peasant Fires: The Drummer of Niklashausen* (Indianapolis, 1992).

17   Thomas A. Brady Jr., *German Histories in the Age of Reformations, 1400–1650* (New York, 2009), 186.

18   Martin Luther, "Wider die räuberischen und mörderischen Rotten der Bauern," in *D. Martin Luthers Werke: Kritische Gesamtausgabe*, vol. 18 (Weimar, 1908), 357-61.

19   Lisa Jardine, *A New History of the Renaissance* (New York, 1996), 341; John L. Flood, "The Book in Reformation Germany," in *The Reformation and the Book*, ed. Jean-François Gilmont (Aldershot, Eng., 1998), 26, 68–69.

20   Sebastian Münster, cited in Matthew McLean, *The Cosmographia of Sebastian Münster* (Aldershot, Eng., 2007), 285.

21   Rhenanus cited in Peter Schaeffer, "The Emergence of the Concept 'Medieval' in Central European Humanism," *Sixteenth Century Journal* 7, no. 2 (1976): 21–30.

22   Paul Joachimsen, *Geschichtsauffassung und Geschichtsschreibung in Deutschland unter dem Einfluss des Humanismus* (Leipzig, 1910), 127.

23   Cited in John F. D'Amico, *Theory and Practice in Renaissance Textual Criticism: Beatus Rhenanus Between Conjecture and History* (Berkeley, Calif., 1988), 196. I have changed the syntax of this quotation slightly; otherwise, I follow D'Amico's reading. On Rhenanus, see also the fine biographical sketch by Ulrich Muhlack, "Beatus Rhenanus (1485–1547): Vom Humanismus zur Philologie," in *Humanismus im deutschen Südwesten* (Sigmaringen, 1993), 195–220. On the relationship between time and causality, see Reinhart Koselleck, *Vergangene Zukunft: Zur Semantik geschichtlicher Zeiten* (Frankfurt am Main, 1979), 17–37. On the importance of the "medieval," see Schaeffer, "The Emergence of the Concept 'Medieval,'" 21–30; François Hartog, *Regimes of Historicity. Presentism and Experiences of Time*, trans. Saskia Brown (New York, 2015), 12–13.

24   D'Amico, *Theory and Practice in Renaissance Textual Criticism*, 196.

25   Beatus Rhenanus, *Rerum Germanicarum Libri Tres*, ed. and trans. Felix Mundt (Tübingen, 2008), 31, and Mundt's excellent commentary, 542.

26   Joachimsen, *Geschichsauffassung und Geschichtsschreibung*, 142.

27   Ibid.

28   Erasmus to Reuchlin, epist. 713, 15 November 1517, in *The Correspondence of Erasmus*, vol. 5, trans. R. A. B. Mynors and D. F. S. Thompson, annotated Peter G. Bietenholz (Toronto, 1979), 203. This translation adds the word "modern," which is, however, not in the original Latin.

29   On the expulsions, see Michael Toch, "Die Verfolgungen des Spätmittelalters (1350–1550)," in *Germania Judaica*, vol. 3, part 3, ed. Arye Maimon, Mordechai Breuer and Yacov Guggenheim (Tübingen, 2003), 2298–327. On the arguments for expulsion, see also David Nirenberg, *Anti-Judaism: The Western Tradition* (New York, 2013), 246–68.

30   Hedwig Röckelein, "Die grabstein, so vil tauesent guldin wert sein: Vom Umgang der Christen mit Synagogen und jüdischen Friedhöfen im Mittelalter und am Beginn der Neuzeit," *Aschkenas: Zeitschrift für Geschichte und Kultur der Juden* 5, no. 1 (1995): 11–45.

31   Jerome Friedman, "Sebastian Münster, the Jewish Mission, and Protestant Anti-Semitism," *Archiv für Reformationsgeschichte* 70 (1979): 244–45; Jerome Fried-

man, *The Most Ancient Testimony: Sixteenth-Century Christian-Hebraica in the Age of Renaissance Nostalgia* (Athens, Ohio, 1983), 214–42.

32 Thomas Kaufmann, *Luthers "Judenschriften": Ein Beitrag zu ihrer historischen Kontextualisierung* (Tübingen, 2011), 172–74, notes all Luther's statements on Münster. On this topic, see especially Karl Heinz Burmeister, *Sebastian Münster: Versuch eines biographischen Gesamtbildes* (Basel, 1963), 96–97.

33 August Wolkenhauer, *Sebastian Münsters handschriftliches Kollegienbuch aus den Jahren 1515–1518 und seine Karten* (Berlin, 1909), 16–17, 37–38.

34 Ibid., 186. On Münster's cooperation with other humanists, see Jasper van Putten, *Networked Nation: Mapping German Cities in Sebastian Münster's Cosmographia* (Boston, 2018).

35 Cited in McLean, *The Cosmographia of Sebastian Münster*, 148.

36 Münster to Konrad Pellikan, 20 June 1549, in Karl Heinz Burmeister, ed., *Briefe Sebastian Münsters* (Frankfurt am Main, 1964), 147.

37 Ibid.

38 Karl Heinz Burmeister, *Sebastian Münster: Eine Bibliographie* (Wiesbaden, 1964), 141.

39 Burmeister, ed., *Briefe Sebastian Münsters,*135. By 1550, there were five printings but only three reworked editions.

40 A listing of translations appears in McLean, *The Cosmographia of Sebastian Münster*, 346–47. The size of the printings comes from Klaus A. Vogel, "Cosmography," in *The Cambridge History of Science*, vol. 3, *Early Modern Science*, ed. Katharine Park and Lorraine Daston (Cambridge, 2008), 489.

41 Pettegree, *The Book in the Renaissance*, 101–2.

42 On the reading public, see E. P. Goldschmidt, *Medieval Texts and Their First Appearance in Print* (London 1943), 14ff.; Flood, "The Book in Reformation Germany," 69, 85; Pettegree, *The Book in the Renaissance*, 196–97.

43 Bodin cited in Anthony Grafton, *New Worlds, Ancient Texts: The Power of Tradition and the Shock of Discovery* (Cambridge, Mass., 1995), 107.

44 Michel de Montaigne, "Travel Journal," in *The Complete Works*, trans. Donald M. Frame (New York, 2003), 1087.

45 Viktor Hantzsch, *Sebastian Münster: Leben, Werk, wissenschaftliche Bedeutung* (Leipzig, 1898), 64. McLean, *The Cosmographia of Sebastian Münster*, 193, calculates that the Latin edition of the *Cosmographia* of 1550 devotes 48 percent of its space to Germany.

46 On the range of Münster's collaborators, see van Putten, *Networked Nation*, esp. map, p. 52.

47 David Woodward, "The Woodcut Technique," in *Five Centuries of Map Printing*, ed. David Woodward (Chicago, 1975), 25–50.

48 Wolfgang Behringer, "Die großen Städtebücher und ihre Voraussetzungen," in *Das Bild der Stadt in der Neuzeit, 1400–1800*, ed. Wolfgang Behringer and Bernd Roeck (Munich, 1999), 92.

49 Ulman Weiß, "Erfurt," in Behringer and Roeck, eds., *Das Bild der Stadt in der Neuzeit*, 186–87.

50 Rolf Kießling and Peter Plaßmeyer, "Augsburg," in Behringer and Roeck, eds., *Das Bild der Stadt in der Neuzeit*, 134.

51 The description of Lindau as a "schwäbisches Venedig" is from the humanist Achilles Gasser, according to Burmeister, *Sebastian Münster: Versuch eines biographischen Gesamtbildes*, 145.

52 Wilhelm Heinrich Riehl, "Sebastian Münster und seine Kosmographie," in *Freie Vorträge* (Stuttgart, 1873), 145.

53   Walter S. Gibson, *Bruegel* (London, 1977), 146–75; on art and the discovery of the people, see also Stephanie Leitsch, "Burgkmair's Peoples of Africa and India (1508) and the Origins of Ethnography in Print," *The Art Bulletin* 91, no. 2 (2009): 134–59.

54   Sebastian Münster, *Cosmographia: Das ist; Die Beschreibung der gantzen Welt* (Basel, 1628), 882, 994, 837, 1092, 1164, 1314–15.

55   David Price, *Johannes Reuchlin and the Campaign to Destroy Jewish Books* (New York, 2011).

56   Grafton, *New Worlds, Ancient Texts*, 112–13.

57   On Münster's constricted wider reach, see Christine Johnson, *The German Discovery of the World: Renaissance Encounters with the Strange and Marvelous* (Charlottesville, Va., 2008).

58   Cited in Gerald Strauss, *Sixteenth Century Germany: Its Topography and Topographers* (Madison, Wisc., 1959), 112.

59   Cited in McLean, *The Cosmographia of Sebastian Münster*, 148.

60   Kepler cited in Svetlana Alpers, *The Art of Describing: Dutch Art in the Seventeenth Century* (Chicago, 1983), 34.

61   Document reprinted in Meurer, *Corpus der älteren Germania-Karten*, 330–33.

62   Bracciolini cited in Christopher B. Krebs, *A Most Dangerous Book: Tacitus's Germania from the Roman Empire to the Third Reich* (New York, 2011), 83.

63   Caspar Hirschi, *Wettkampf der Nationen: Konstruktionen einer deutschen Ehrgemeinschaft an der Wende vom Mittelalter zur Neuzeit* (Göttingen, 2005), 268–69. Hirschi extends this generation to 1530.

64   Winfried Schulze, "Die Entstehung des nationalen Vorurteils: Zur Kultur der Wahrnehmung fremder Nationen in der europäischen Frühen Neuzeit," *Geschichte in Wissenschaft und Unterricht* 46 (1995): 644.

65   Louis van Delft, *Literatur und Anthroplogie: Menschliche Natur und Charakterlehre* (Münster, 2005), 73.

66   For a study of an early-eighteenth-century stereotype grid, see Franz K. Stanzel, *Europäer: Ein imagologischer Essay*, 2nd ed. (Heidelberg, 1998).

67   Arno Borst, *Der Turmbau von Babel: Geschichte der Meinungen über Ursprung und Vielfalt der Völker*, 5 vol. (Stuttgart, 1957–1963), vol. 3, part 1, 1048–90.

68   Ibid., 1066–67; Werner Besch, *Die Rolle Luthers in der Deutschen Sprachgeschichte* (Heidelberg, 1999), 30.

69   *Das Büchlein, Hans Fabritius*, in Johannes Müller, *Quellenschriften und Geschichte des deutschsprachlichen Unterrichts bis zur Mitte des 16. Jahrhunderts* (Gotha, 1882), 53.

70   Borst, *Der Turmbau von Babel*, vol. 3, part 1, 1076.

71   John Rowe, "Sixteenth and Seventeenth Century Grammars," in *Studies in the History of Linguistics: Traditions and Paradigms*, ed. Dell Hymes (Bloomington, Ind., 1974), 364.

72   Ibid., 361.

73   Peter Burke, *Languages and Communities in Early Modern Europe* (Cambridge, 2004); Daniel Baggioni, *Langues et nations en Europe* (Paris, 1997).

74   Catherine Delano-Smith, "Signs on Printed Topographical Maps, ca. 1470–ca. 1640," in *The History of Cartography*, vol. 3, part 1, ed. David Woodward (Chicago, 2007), 565. There were however a few sixteenth-century maps of countries outside the Empire that showed religious division. They included Wolfgang Lazarus's map of Hungary, printed in 1528, and Bernard Wapnowski's map of Poland, printed in 1526. See also Wojciech Iwańczak, *Die Kartenmacher: Nürn-*

berg als Zentrum der Kartographie im Zeitalter der Renaissance, trans. Peter Oliver Loew (Darmstadt, 2009), 200–201.

75   McLean, *The Cosmographia of Sebatian Münster*, 285.

76   "I do not have a single [theology book] in my house, save for the Hebrew commentaries," Münster wrote Konrad Pellikan, his teacher, in an undated letter, in Burmeister, ed., *Briefe Sebastian Münsters*, 48; McLean, *The Cosmographia of Sebatian Münster*, 289.

77   McLean, *The Comographia of Sebastian Münster*, 289.

78   R. J. W. Evans, *The Making of the Habsburg Monarchy, 1550–1700* (Oxford, 1979), 3.

79   Arguing, however, for the different context, is Shimon Markish, *Erasmus and the Jews*, with an afterword by Arthur Cohen (Chicago, 1986).

80   *Index Librorum Prohibitorum*, 1559, Houghton Library, Harvard University, Cambridge, Mass.

81   The actual formulation was not coined until 1612. See Brady, *German Histories in the Age of the Reformations*, 231.

82   Ibid., 232.

83   Benjamin Kaplan, *Divided by Faith: Religious Conflict and the Practice of Toleration in Early Modern Europe* (Cambridge, Mass., 2010), 284.

84   Karl Heinz Burmeister, "Georg Joachim Rheticus as a Geographer and His Contribution to the First Map of Prussia," *Imago Mundi* 23 (1969): 73–76; Norman Thrower, *Maps and Civilization: Cartography in Culture and Society*, 2nd ed. (Chicago, 1999), 91.

85   Peter Meurer, "Cartography in the German Lands, 1450–1560," in Woodward, ed., *The History of Cartography*, vol. 3, part 2, 1225–28.

86   Ibid., 1223.

87   Partial copies of the copies survive in the Bavarian Land Survey Office. Robert W. Karrow Jr., *Mapmakers of the Sixteenth Century and Their Maps* (Winnetka, Ill., 1993), 65.

88   On Apian, see the essays in *Philipp Apian und die Kartographie der Renaissance*, ed. Hans Wolff (Weißenhorn, 1989).

89   Cited in Max Gasser, "Studien zu Philpp Apians Landesaufnahme," *Mitteilungen der Geographischen Gesellschaft in München*, 1 (1906): 23.

90   The views of smaller towns and hamlets are not precisely rendered, however, and even their geographical accuracy is at times unremarkable. See Fritz Bönisch, "The Geographical Accuracy of Sixteenth and Seventeenth Century Topographical Surveys," *Imago Mundi* 21 (1967): 63.

91   Lee Palmer Wandel, "Exile in the Reformation," in *Space and Self in Early Modern European Cultures,* ed. David Warren Sabean and Malina Stefanovska (Toronto, 2012), 200–18.

92   Ortelius was the mapmaker praising Mercator; see Peter H. Meurer, *Fontes Cartographici Orteliani: Das "Theatrum orbis terrarum" von Abraham Ortelius und seine Kartenquellen* (Weinheim, 1991), 194. For *"Lutherey,"* see Wandel, "Exile in the Reformation," 209.

93   Jesse Spohnholz, *The Tactics of Toleration: A Refugee Community in the Age of Religious Wars* (Newark, Del., 2010).

94   According to Mark Monmonier, *Rhumb Lines and Map Wars. A Social History of the Mercator Projection* (Chicago, 2004), 11, navigators did not even use his projection until the seventeenth century.

95   On the script, see Greengrass, *Christendom Destroyed*, 241.

96   Robert Karrow, "Centers of Map Publishing in Europe, 1472–1600," in Wood-
      ward, ed., *The History of Cartography*, vol. 3, part 1, 620.
97   Ibid., 621, 616.
98   The contributors are detailed in Meurer, *Fontes Cartographici Orteliani.*
99   Ibid., 98, 247, 145, 171.
100   Ibid., 189, 148.
101   On the religious dimension of Ortelius's mapmaking, see Pauline Moffitt Watts,
      "The European Religious Worldview and Its Influence on Mapping," in Wood-
      ward, ed. *The History of Cartography*, vol. 3, part 1, 392–93. On Ortelius and
      Familism, see Giorgio Mangani, "Abraham Ortelius and the Hermetic Meaning of
      the Cordiform Projection," *Imago Mundi* 50 (1998): 72. For skepticism concern-
      ing Ortelius's membership, see Jason Harris, "The Religious Position of Abraham
      Ortelius," in *The Low Countries as a Crossroads of Religious Beliefs*, ed. Arie-Jan
      Gelderblom and Jan L. de Jong (Leiden, 2004), 89–139.
102   Meurer, *Corpus der älteren Germania-Karten*, 302; Robert J. Karrow Jr., *Map-
      makers of the Sixteenth Century and Their Maps: Bio-bibliographies of the Car-
      tographers of Abraham Ortelius* (Chicago, 1992), 9. On the atlas's reception, see
      Cornelius Koeman, *The History of Abraham Ortelius and His Theatrum Orbis
      Terrarum* (New York, 1964), 36.
103   Cited in Koeman, *The History of Abraham Ortelius and His Theatrum Orbis Ter-
      rarum*, 36.
104   On this practice of display, see Walter S. Gibson, *"Mirror of the Earth": The
      World Landscape in Sixteenth-Century Flemish Painting* (Princeton, N.J., 1989),
      51; John Donne, "The Good-Morrow," in *The Norton Anthology of Poetry*, 3rd
      ed., ed. Alexander W. Allison et al. (New York, 1983), 205. On the price of the
      atlas, see Koeman, *The History of Abraham Ortelius and His Theatrum Orbis
      Terrarum, 39.*
105   Paul Binding, *Imagined Corners: Exploring the World's First Atlas* (London,
      2002), 205–6.
106   Mangani, "Abraham Ortelius and the Hermetic Meaning," 75; Denis Cosgrove,
      Apollo's Eye: A Cartographic Genealogy of the Earth in the Western Imagination
      (Baltimore, 2001), 133.
107   The color plates are now available in one beautifully produced volume: Georg
      Braun and Franz Hogenberg, *Cities of the World*, ed. Stephan Füssel (Cologne,
      2011).
108   Behringer, "Die großen Städtebücher und ihre Voraussetzungen," 92.
109   Lucia Nuti, "The Perspective Plan in the Sixteenth Century: The Invention of a
      Representational Language," *Art Bulletin* 76, no. 3 (1994): 106–7.

CHAPTER 3. THE TEARS OF STOICS (C. 1580–1700)

1   Johannes Burckhardt, *Der Dreißigjährige Krieg* (Frankfurt am Main, 1992), 236;
     Christian Pfister, *Bevölkerungsgeschichte und historische Demographie, 1500–
     1800*, 2nd ed. (Munich, 2007), 14.
2   For a comparison of various scholarly estimates, see Christoph Dipper, *Deutsche
     Geschichte, 1648–1789* (Frankfurt am Main, 1991), 44; John Theibault, "The
     Demography of the Thirty Years War Re-revisited: Günther Franz and His Crit-
     ics," *German History* 15 (1997): 1–21. For a recent compelling argument for tak-
     ing the dimensions of the catastrophe seriously, see the brilliant interpretation of
     the late Dieter Kittsteiner, *Die Stabilisierungsmoderne: Deutschland und Europa,*

1618-1715 (Munich, 2010). For deaths from battle and siege, see Peter H. Wilson, *The Thirty Years War: Europe's Tragedy* (Cambridge, Mass., 2009), 790. For a detailed analysis of one area, see John C. Theibault, *German Villages in Crisis: Rural Life in Hesse-Kassel and the Thirty Years' War, 1580-1720* (Atlantic Highlands, N.J., 1995).

3   For modern descriptions of the regional breakdown of destruction, see Pfister, *Bevölkerungsgeschichte und historische Demographie, 1500-1800*, 15; Wilson, *The Thirty Years War*, 786-95; Theibault, "The Demography of the Thirty Years War Re-revisited," 21.

4   Josef Ehmer, *Bevölkerungsgeschichte und historische Demographie, 1800-2000* (Munich, 2004), 13.

5   Ibid., 16. For a similar calculation, see Wilson, *The Thirty Years War*, 787, where he lists overall casualties for the Europe of the Second World War at 6 percent, at 5.5 percent for the First World War, and at 20 percent for the Thirty Years War (but only for the Holy Roman Empire).

6   Pfister, *Bevölkerungsgeschichte und historische Demographie, 1500-1800*, 18.

7   Wilhelm Abel, *Massenarmut und Hungerkrisen im vorindustriellen Europa* (Hamburg, 1974), 95.

8   On orphanages, see Joel Harrington, *The Unwanted Child: The Fate of Foundlings, Orphans, and Juvenile Criminals in Early Modern Germany* (Chicago, 2009).

9   Geoffrey Parker, *Europe in Crisis, 1598-1648* (Ithaca, 1979), 23-25; J. N. Biraben, *Les Hommes et la peste*, 2 vols. (Paris, 1975). For maps documenting the plague in these years, see Arthur E. Imhof, *Lost Worlds: How Our European Ancestors Coped with Everyday Life and Why Life Is So Hard Today*, trans. Thomas Robisheaux (Charlottesville, Va., 1996), 74-76.

10   Georg Schmidt, *Der Dreißigjährige Krieg*, 7th ed. (Munich, 2006), 15.

11   One used to think of this development as covering most of the German lands east of the Elbe. For a strongly revisionist view, see William H. Hagen, *Ordinary Prussians: Brandenburg Junkers and Villagers, 1500-1840* (Cambridge, 2002).

12   Maximillian Lanzinner, *Konfessionelles Zeitalter, 1555-1618*, vol 10 of *Gebhardt Handbuch der deutschen Geschichte* (Stuttgart, 2001), 243.

13   The emphasis on bad weather, bad harvests, and their attenuating circumstances, all induced by climactic change, is especially emphasized in Wolfgang Behringer, *Witches and Witch-Hunts: A Global History* (Cambridge, 2004), 88, 113-14, 129. The figures are from Lanzinner, *Konfessionelles Zeitalter*, 168-69.

14   Behringer, *Witches and Witch-Hunts*, 130.

15   Thomas A. Brady Jr., *German Histories in the Age of Reformations, 1400-1650* (New York, 2009), 339.

16   Ibid., 349, citing the poet Theobald Höck in 1601.

17   Cited in Bernd Roeck, *Als wollt die Welt schier brechen: Eine Stadt im Zeitalter des Dreißigjährigen Krieges* (Munich, 1991), 131; see also 26, 62.

18   Gerhard Oestreich, *Neostoicism and the Early Modern State*, trans. David McLintock (Cambridge, 1982), 8.

19   Ibid, 61.

20   Justus Lipsius, *De Constantia*, trans. Sir John Stradling (1595), ed. John Sellars (Exeter, Eng., 2006), 32.

21   Ibid., 37.

22   Ibid., 46.

23   Ibid., 48, 51.

24   See Reinhart Koselleck, *Begriffsgeschichten* (Frankfurt am Main, 2006), 218-39;

Christopher Clark, *Iron Kingdom: The Rise and Downfall of Prussia, 1600-1947* (Cambridge, Mass., 2006), 219-30.

25 The classic work on the Netherlands in this period remains Johann Huizinga, *Holländische Kultur im 17. Jahrhundert*, trans. Werner Kaegi (Munich, 2007), originally published in Holland in 1941.

26 Parker, *Europe in Crisis*, 37-38.

27 Cited in Michaela Schwegler, *Kleines Lexikon der Vorzeichen und Wunder* (Munich, 2004), 62. For a revealing account of religiosity in this period, see Sigrun Haude, "Religion während des Dreißigjährigen Krieges," in *Frömmigkeit— Theologie—Frömmigkeitstheologie*, ed. Berndt Hamm et al. (Leiden, 2005), 537-53.

28 Schmidt, *Der Dreißigjährige Krieg*, 96.

29 Moscherosch cited by Irmgard Weithase, *Die Darstellung von Krieg und Frieden in der deutschen Barockdichtung* (Weimar, 1953), 62n9.

30 Helmut Lahrkamp, *Dreißigjähriger Krieg—Westfälischer Frieden* (Münster, 1999), 159.

31 Geoffrey Parker, *The Thirty Years War*, 2nd ed. (London, 1997), 173. For details and the original calculations, see Jan Lindgren, "Frauenland und Soldatenleben: Perspektiven auf Schweden und den Dreißigjährigen Krieg," in *Zwischen Alltag und Katastrophe: Der Dreißigjährige Krieg aus der Nähe*, ed. Benigna Krusenstjern and Hans Medick, 2nd ed. (Göttingen, 2001), 135-58. The figures include the Northern Wars as well.

32 Schmidt, *Der Dreißigjährige Krieg*, 49.

33 C. V. Wedgwood, *The Thirty Years War* (New York, 2005), 201.

34 On Magdeburg as a media event, see Hans Medick, "Historisches Ereignis und zeitgenössische Erfahrung: Die Eroberung und Zerstörung Magdeburgs 1631," in Krusenstjern and Medick, eds., *Zwischen Alltag und Katastrophe*, 377-408.

35 For an indispensable guide to these narratives, see Benigna von Krusenstjern, *Selbstzeugnisse der Zeit des Dreißigjährigen Krieges: Beschreibendes Verzeichnis* (Berlin, 1997). For reflections on women in these documents, and in our conception of the Thirty Years War more generally, see Regina Schulte, "Das unerhörte Einordnen: Textschichten in Zeugnissen des Dreißigjährigen Krieges," in *Die verkehrte Welt des Krieges: Studien zu Geschlecht, Religion und Tod* (Frankfurt am Main, 1998), 59-94.

36 James Olney, *Memory and Narrative: The Weave of Life-Writing* (Chicago, 1998). For an introduction, and further literature, see the sophisticated treatment in Eva Kormann, *Ich, Welt und Gott: Autobiographik im 17. Jahrhundert* (Cologne, 2004); and the essays in *Mapping the "I": Research on Self-Narratives in Germany and Switzerland*, ed. Claudia Ulbrich, Kaspar von Greyerz, and Lorenz Heiligensetzer (Boston, 2015).

37 Gerd Zillhardt, *Der Dreißigjährige Krieg in zeitgenössischer Darstellung: Hans Heberles "Zeytregister" (1618-1672), Aufzeichnungen aus dem Ulmer Territorium; Ein Beitrag zu Geschichtsschreibung und Geschichtsverständnis der Unterschichten* (Ulm, 1971), 133.

38 Joseph A. Ruhl, ed., "Stausebacher Chronik des Kaspar Preis, 1637-1667," *Fuldaer Geschichtsblätter* 1 (1902): 123-24.

39 Ibid.

40 Zillhardt, *Der Dreißigjährige Krieg in zeitgenössischer Darstellung*, 133.

41 Jan Peters, ed., *Ein Söldnerleben im Dreißigjährigen Krieg* (Berlin, 1993), 142-43.

42 Ibid.

43 Lahrkamp, *Dreißigjähriger Krieg—Westfälischer Frieden*, 161.

44 Arnold Mengering, *Perversa Ultimi seculi militia: Oder Kriegs-Belial der Soldaten-Teufel*, 4th ed. (Leipzig, 1687), 440–41.
45 Ronald G. Asch, *The Thirty Years War* (London, 1997), 177.
46 Friedrich von Weech, ed., *Sebastian Bürsters Beschreibung des Schwedischen Krieges, 1630–1647* (Leipzig, 1875), 5.
47 Günther Bentele, *Protokolle einer Katastrophe: Zwei Bietigheimer Chroniken aus dem Dreißigjährigen Krieg* (Bietigheim-Bissingen, 1984), 198.
48 Ibid., 199.
49 E. F. Keller, *Die Drangsalen des Nassauischen Volkes* (Gotha, 1854), 281.
50 Ibid., 275.
51 Hans Jacob Christoffel von Grimmelshausen, "Verkehrte Welt: Satirische Schriften/Historische Romane/Legendenromane," in *Werke*, vol. 2, ed. Dieter Breuer (Frankfurt am Main, 1997).
52 J. C. von Grimmelshausen, *Satyrischer Pilgram*, ed. Wolfgang Bender (Tübingen, 1970), 160.
53 Hans Jacob Christoffel von Grimmelshausen, *Simplicissimus Teutsch*, in *Werke*, vol. 1, ed. Dieter Breuer (Frankfurt am Main, 1989), 29.
54 For this interpretation, see especially Eberhard Mannack, "Unvorgreifliche Gedanken über Möglichkeiten, unsere Kenntnisse von Barockautoren zu vertiefen: Demonstriert am Beispiel von J. C. von Grimmelshausen," in *Republica Guelpherbytana*, ed. August Buck and Martin Bircher (Amsterdam, 1987), 595–612. See also Volker Meid, *Die deutsche Literatur im Zeitalter des Barock* (Munich, 2009), 601.
55 One scholarly estimate places the total number of orations between 1550 and 1750 at 250,000. See Meid, *Die deutsche Literatur im Zeitalter des Barock*, 809.
56 Andreas Gryphius, "Grabschrift auf Anna Erhardine, die beste Mutter," in *Gesamtausgabe der deutschsprachigen Werke*, ed. Marian Szyrocki and Hugh Powell, vol. 1, *Sonette*, ed. Marian Szyrocki (Tübingen, 1963), 37 (hereafter cited as Gryphius, *Gesamtausgabe*, vol. 1). On Gryphius's early period, see Marian Szyrocki, *Der junge Gryphius* (Berlin, 1959).
57 Conrad Wiedemann, "Andreas Gryphius," in *Deutsche Dichter des 17. Jahrhunderts*, ed. Harald Steinhagen and Benno von Wiese (Berlin, 1984), 452.
58 The two books are in Gryphius, *Gesamtausgabe*, vol. 1, 1–26, 27–62.
59 On the uniqueness of Gryphius's tone, see Wiedemann, "Andreas Gryphius," 444–45, 450–52.
60 Marian Szyrocki, *Die deutsche Literatur des Barock* (Stuttgart, 1979), 56.
61 Cited in Wiedemann, "Andreas Gryphius," 452.
62 Martin Opitz, "*Trostgedichte in Widerwertigkeit des Krieges*," in *Gesammelte Werke: Kritische Ausgabe*, ed. Georg Schulz-Behrend, vol. 1 (Stuttgart, 1968), 210–11.
63 In the chronologically ordered anthology *Kennst du das Land? Deutschlandgedichte*, ed. Volker Meid (Stuttgart, 2012), 65, "Tears of the Fatherland" is the third poem, preceded only by Walther von der Vogelweide's Middle-High German "*Ir sult sprechen willekomen*" and an anonymous poem of the 1520s.
64 Gryphius, *Gesamtausgabe*, vol. 1, 48.
65 The translation is from George Schoolfield, "A Sonnet of Andreas Gryphius: Tears of the Fatherland, Anno 1636," *The German Quarterly* 25, no. 2 (1952): 110.
66 This interpretation follows Erich Truntz, *Weltbild und Dichtung im deutschen Barock* (Munich, 1992), 92–97. See also Theodor Verweyen, "Thränen des Vaterlandes/Anno 1636 von Gryphius—rhetorische Grundlagen, poetische Struk-

turen, Literarizität," in *Traditionen der Lyrik*, ed. Wolfgang Düsing (Tübingen, 1997), 31–46.

67   Verweyen, "Thränen des Vaterlandes," 41–42.

68   Wedgwood, *Thirty Years War*, 320.

69   Cited in Hermann Bingel, *Das Theatrum Europaeum: Ein Beitrag zur Publizistik des 17. und 18. Jahrhunderts* (Munich, 1909), 40.

70   Lucas Heinrich Wüthrich, *Matthaeus Merian d. Ä.* (Hamburg, 2007), 341, 351.

71   Ibid.

72   Ibid., 351.

73   Ibid., 354.

74   See the table in ibid., 354.

75   Lucas Heinrich Wüthrich, *Das druckgraphische Werk von Matthaeus Merian d. Ä.*, vol. 4, *Die Topographien* (Hamburg, 1996), 759–60.

76   Wüthrich, *Matthaeus Merian d. Ä.*, 161–84.

77   Ibid., 358.

78   Wilhelm Heinrich Riehl, "Sebastian Münster und seine Kosmographie," in *Freie Vorträge* (Stuttgart, 1873), 160.

79   The text of the treaty can be found at the Avalon Project of Yale University Law School.

80   H. G. Koenigsberger, *The Habsburgs and Europe* (Ithaca, N.Y., 1971), 263.

81   Samuel Pufendorf, *The Present State of Germany*, ed. Michael J. Seidler, trans. (in 1696) Edmund Bolun (Indianapolis, 2007), 176.

82   Ibid., 176–77. On the degree to which Pufendorf's insight still holds, see Peter Wilson, "Still a Monstrosity? Some Reflections on Early Modern Statehood," *The Historical Journal* 49, no. 2 (2006): 565–76.

83   The population figures are taken from Jan de Vries, *European Urbanization, 1500–1800* (Cambridge, 1984), 270–78.

84   Pufendorf, *The Present State of Germany*, 74.

85   Yair Mintzger, *The Defortification of the German City, 1689–1866* (New York, 2012), 86.

86   Ibid., 47, 49.

87   Cited in Christof Dipper, *Deutsche Geschichte, 1648–1789* (Frankfurt am Main, 1991), 46.

88   Johannes Burckhardt, *Vollendung und Neuorientierung des frühmodernen Reiches, 1648–1763* (Stuttgart, 2006), 98–115.

89   Dipper, *Deutsche Geschichte*, 55.

90   Paul Gerhardt, "Geh aus mein Herz," in *Sämtliche Deutsche Lieder*, ed. Reinhard Mawick (Leipzig, 2006), 101.

91   On this subject, see Hartmut Lehmann, "Frömmigkeitsgeschichtliche Aus-wirkungen der 'kleinen Eiszeit,'" in *Volksreligiosität in der modernen Sozialges-chichte,* ed. Wolfgang Schieder (Göttingen, 1986), 31–50. See also the essays in Matthias Asche and Anton Schindling, eds., *Das Strafgericht Gottes: Kriegser-fahrungen und Religion im Heiligen Römischen Reich Deutscher Nation im Zeit-alter des Dreißigjährigen Krieges* (Münster, 2001).

92   Gerhardt, "Geh aus, mein Herz," 110.

PART II. THE COPERNICAN TURN: PREFACE

1   Willem Janszoon Blaeu, "Introductio ad cosmographiam," *Theatrum Orbis Ter-rarum, sive, Atlas Novus* (Amsterdam, 1635), unpaginated introduction.

2 Peter van der Krogt, introduction to *Germania*, vol. 3 of Joan Blaeu, *Atlas Major of 1665*, facsimile (Hong Kong, 2006), 38–39.
3 Ibid., 41–42. Some $20,000 in today's prices.
4 Jorge Luis Borges, "On Exactitude in Science," in *Collected Fictions*, trans. Andrew Hurley (New York, 1998), 325.
5 Ibid.
6 Reinhart Koselleck, "Erfahrungsraum und 'Erwartungshorizont'—zwei historische Kategorien," in *Vergangene Zukunft: Zur Semantik geschichtlicher Zeiten* (Frankfurt am Main, 1979), 349–75.
7 Reinhart Koselleck, "Die Verzeitlichung der Utopie," in *Zeitschichten: Studien zur Historik* (Frankfurt am Main, 2000), 135.
8 Wilhelm Ludwig Wekhrlin, *Anselmus Rabiosus, Reise durch Oberdeutschland* (1772; repr., Leipzig, 1988), 89.
9 Johann Gottlieb Fichte, "Die Republik der Deutschen," in J. G. *Fichte Kritische Gesamtausgabe*, series II, vol. 9, *Nachgelassene Schriften*, ed. Reinhard Lauth and Hans Gliwitzky (Stuttgart, 1993), 387–89.
10 Johannes Cochlaeus, *Brevis Germaniae Descriptio*, ed. and trans. Karl Langosch (Darmstadt, 1976), 49.
11 James J. Sheehan, *German History, 1770–1866* (Oxford, 1989), 251.

CHAPTER 4. PARTITION AND PATRIOTISM (C. 1700–1770)

1 Friedrich Nicolai, *Gesammelte Werke*, vol 12, *Opera Minora*, "Ehrengedächtnis Herrn Ewald Christian von Kleist" (Hildesheim, 1994), 1–22.
2 Kleist to Gleim, 2 August 1758, in Ewald von Kleist, *Werke*, ed. August Sauer (Berlin, 1881–1882), vol. 2, *Briefe von Kleist*, 504. There is now a very fine modern edition of Kleist's "war novel," with a perceptive afterword: see Ewald Christian von Kleist, *Cissides und Paches in drey Gesängen*, ed. Martin Kagel (Hanover, 2006).
3 Anton Blok, *Honour and Violence* (Cambridge, 2001), 87–102.
4 Kleist, *Cissides und Paches*, 55.
5 Ibid.
6 On the centrality of glory to Frederick's calculations, Jürgen Luh, *Der Große: Friederich II, von Preußen* (Munich, 2011), 9–112.
7 Karl-Volker Neugebauer, ed., *Grundkurs deutsche Militärgeschichte* (Munich, 2006), 1:98.
8 Wenzel Anton Graf Kaunitz, memorandum dated 7 September 1778, in *Heiliges Römisches Reich, 1776–1806*, ed. Karl Otmar Freiherr von Aretin (Wiesbaden, 1967), 2:2.
9 Neugebauer, *Grundkurs deutsche Militärgeschichte*, 1:98.
10 Figure for Hesse-Kassel cited in Michael Hochedlinger, "The Habsburg Monarchy: From 'Military-Fiscal State' to Militarization," in *The Fiscal-Military State in Eighteenth-Century Europe*, ed. Christopher Storrs (Farnham, Eng., 2009), 65.
11 Michael Mann, *The Sources of Social Power* (Cambridge, 1993), 2:366–67; Hans-Ulrich Wehler, *Deutsche Gesellschaftsgeschichte* (Munich, 1987), 1:248.
12 Hans Rosenberg, *Bureaucracy, Aristocracy, and Autocracy: The Prussian Experience, 1660–1815* (Boston, 1966), 152.
13 Michael Hochedlinger, "Mars Ennobled: The Ascent of the Military and the Creation of a Military Nobility in Mid-Eighteenth-Century Austria," *German History* 17, no. 2 (1999): 150.

14   T. C. W. Blanning, *The Culture of Power and the Power of Culture: Old Regime Europe, 1660-1789* (Oxford, 2002), 206.

15   Johannes Kunisch, *Friedrich der Grosse: Der König und seine Zeit* (Munich, 2004), 155.

16   Otto Büsch, *Militärsystem und Sozialleben im alten Preußen, 1713-1807* (Berlin, 1962).

17   Hannah Schissler, "The Social and Political Power of the Prussian Junkers," in *Landownership and Power in Modern Europe*, ed. R. Gibson and M. Blinkhorn (London, 1991), 103. See also William Hagen, *Ordinary Prussians: Brandenburg Junkers and Villagers, 1500-1840* (Cambridge, 2002), which emphasizes the imperfect nature of that domination.

18   Klaus Latzel, " 'Schlachtbank' oder 'Feld der Ehre'? Der Beginn des Einstellungswandels gegenüber Krieg und Tod, 1756-1815," in *Der Krieg des kleinen Mannes: Eine Militärgeschichte von unten*, ed. Wolfram Wette (Munich, 1992), 77.

19   H. M. Scott, "The Fiscal-Military State and International Rivalry During the Long Eighteenth Century," in Storrs, ed., *The Fiscal-Military State in Eighteenth-Century Europe*, 43.

20   Latzel, " 'Schlachtbank' oder 'Feld der Ehre'?," 81.

21   Cited in Ulrich Bröckling, *Disziplin: Soziologie und Geschichte militärische Gehorsamsproduktion* (Munich, 1997), 73.

22   Christopher Clark, *Iron Kingdom: The Rise and Downfall of Prussia, 1600-1947* (Cambridge, Mass., 2006), 204. Jörg Muth, *Flucht aus dem militärischen Alltag: Ursachen und individuelle Ausprägung der Desertion in der Armee Friedrichs des Großen* (Freiburg im Breisgau, 2003), 88, points out that fixing the identity of the dead was itself often beside the point because cannon shots frequently tore bodies and limbs beyond the point of subsequent recognition.

23   Cited by Reinhart Koselleck, "Kriegerdenkmale als Identitätstiftungen der Überlebenden," in *Poetik und Hermeneutik*, vol. 8, *Identität,* ed. Odo Marquard and Karlheinz Stierle (Munich, 1979), 258.

24   Frederick the Great to Minister of State Finckenstein, in *Politische Korrespondenz des Friedrichs des Großen*, ed. Johann Gustav Droysen (Berlin, 1891), 18:481.

25   The territorial realignment is from Jacob Burckhardt, *Das Zeitalter Friedrichs des Großen*, ed. Ernst Ziegler, Bernd Klesman, and Philipp Müller (Munich, 2012), 14.

26   The comparisons are from Jan de Vries, *European Urbanization, 1500-1800* (Cambridge, 1984), 269-78.

27   On the reasons for their reticence, see Hans Delbrück, *History of the Art of War*, trans. Walter J. Renfroe (Westport, Conn., 1985), 4:355-58.

28   On the earlier genesis of the concept, see Robert von Friedeburg, "The Making of Patriots: Love of Fatherland and Negotiating Monarchy in Seventeenth-Century Germany," *Journal of Modern History* 77, no. 4 (2005): 881-916.

29   Wolfram Fischer et al., eds., *Handbuch der Europäischen Wirtschafts- und Sozialgeschichte*, vol. 4, *Europäische Wirtschafts- und Sozialgeschichte von der Mitte des 17. Jahrhunderts bis zur Mitte des 19. Jahrhunderts*, ed. Ilja Mieck (Stuttgart, 1993), 49-51.

30   Based on tabulations in ibid.

31   On Anhalt-Dessau, see Maiken Umbach, *Federalism and Enlightenment in Germany, 1740-1806* (London, 2000). An important exception is Schaumburg-Lippe, whose regent, Wilhelm von Schaumburg-Lippe, was a genuine "*Soldatenfanatiker*," as Jacob Burckhardt called him, and whose writings on military defense

were justly famous throughout Europe: see Burckhardt, *Das Zeitalter Friedrichs des Großen*, 98.

32 Willliam D. Godsey, *Nobles and Nation in Central Europe: Free Imperial Knights in the Age of Revolution, 1750–1850* (Cambridge, 2004), 8.

33 Wilhelm Franke, "Die Volkszahl deutscher Städte Ende des 18 und Anfang des 19. Jahrhunderts," *Zeitschrift des preußischen statistischen Landesamtes* (1922): 112–17.

34 See the passage and commentary by Albrecht Schöne on the famous scene in Faust "Frühe Fassung," in Johann Wolfgang Goethe, *Sämtliche Werke, Briefe, Tagebücher und Gespräche*, ed. Albrecht Schöne, vol. 7 (Frankfurt am Main, 1994), part 1, 487, part 2, 856.

35 Veit Ludwig von Seckendorff, *Teutscher Fürstenstaat* (Frankfurt am Main, 1656), 3.

36 Ibid., 49. Throughout the eighteenth century, works on border marking continued to cite Seckendorff; see, for example, Johannes Beck, *Tractatus de jure limitum, von Recht der Gränzen und Marksteine* (Nuremberg, 1729), 47–48.

37 Bernard W. Heise, "Visions of the World: Geography and Maps During the Baroque Age, 1550–1750" (Ph.D. diss., Cornell University, Ithaca, N.Y., 1998), 146–48, 264-65.

38 Bernard W. Heise, "From Tangible Sign to Deliberate Delineation: The Evolution of the Political Border in the Eighteenth and Early Nineteenth Centuries: The Example of Saxony," in *Menschen und Grenzen in der frühen Neuzeit*, ed. Wolfgang Schmale and Reinhard Stauber (Berlin, 1998), 179.

39 Wolfgang Schmale, "'Grenze,' in der deutschen und französischen Früheneuzeit," in *Menschen und Grenzen in der frühen Neuzeit*, 59; Ute Schneider, *Die Macht der Karten: Eine Geschichte der Kartographie vom Mittelalter bis heute* (Darmstadt, 2006), 11–23.

40 D. Anton Friderich Büsching, *Vorbereitung zur gründlichen und nützlichen Kenntniß der geographischen Beschaffenheit und Staatsverfassung der europäischen Reiche und Republiken, welche zugleich ein allgemeiner Abriss von Europa ist*, 3rd ed. (Hamburg, 1761), 11.

41 Heise, "From Tangible Sign to Deliberate Delineation," 172–73; Walter Ziegeler, "Die bayerisch-böhmische Grenze in der frühen Neuzeit," in Schmale and Stauber, eds., *Menschen und Grenzen in der frühen Neuzeit*, 124–25.

42 Michael Diefenbacher and Markus Heinz, eds., *"Auserlesene und allerneueste Landkarten": Der Verlag Homann in Nürnberg, 1702–1848* (Nuremberg, 2002), 122.

43 David Woodward, "The Manuscript, Engraved, and Typographical Traditions of Map Lettering," in *Art and Cartography: Six Historical Essays* (Chicago, 1987), 174–212.

44 Veit Ludwig von Seckendorff, *Teutscher Fürstenstaat*, ed. Andreas Simpson Biechlingen (Jena, 1720), quote from cover page. On the change, see Horst Kremer, *Der deutsche Kleinstaat des 17. Jahrhunderts im Spiegel von Seckendorffs "Teutschem Fürstenstaat,"* 2nd ed. (Darmstadt, 1974), 59.

45 See especially David Blackbourn, *The Conquest of Nature: Water, Landscape, and the Making of Modern Germany* (New York, 2006).

46 Joachim Whaley, *Germany and the Holy Roman Empire* (Oxford, 2012), 2:543.

47 The argument about harnessing and controlling the passions as a central strand of enlightened political economy is memorably made in Albert O. Hirschman, *The Passions and the Interests: Political Arguments for Capitalism Before its Triumph* (Princeton, N.J., 1977), 16.

48   Thomas Laqueur, *The Work of the Dead: A Cultural History of Mortal Remains* (Princeton, N.J., 2015), 391.

49   Justus Nipperdey, *Die Erfindung der Bevölkerungspolitik: Staat, politische Theorie und Population in der Frühen Neuzeit* (Göttingen, 2012), 140–41.

50   Ibid., 140–42.

51   Christian Pfister, *Bevölkerungsgeschichte und historische Demographie, 1500–1800* (Munich, 1994), 7. On the centrality of the new tabulations to the self-understanding of states, see Nipperdey, *Die Erfindung der Bevölkerungspolitik*; on the wider history of counting people, see Jane Caplan and John Torpey, eds., *Documenting Individual Identity: The Development of State Practices in the Modern World* (Princeton, N.J., 2001).

52   Gottfried Achenwall, *Staatsverfassung der heutigen vornehmsten europäischen Reiche und Völker im Grundrisse*, 5th ed. (Göttingen, 1768), 3. The word "statistic" did not get its current connotation of numbered description until the end of the eighteenth century, when the term replaced "political arithmetic": see Karl Pearson, *The History of Statistics in the 17th and 18th Centuries* (London, 1978), 8.

53   Achenwall, *Staatsverfassung*, 7.

54   August Friedrich Wilhelm Crome, *Über die Grösse und Bevölkerung der sämmtlichen europäischen Staaten* (Leipzig, 1785), 4 and unpaginated preface "sinnliche Vorstellung." On Crome, see Sybilla Nikolow, "A. F. W. Crome's Measurements of the 'Strength of the State': Statistical Representations in Central Europe, around 1800," *Journal of the History of Political Economy* 33 (1991): 33; Helmut Berding, "August Friedrich Wilhelm Crome: Politischer Gelehrter und Publizist in Gießen," in *Wege der Neuzeit: Festschrift für Heinz Schilling zum 65 Geburtstag*, ed. Stefan Ehrenpreis (Berlin, 2007), 553–73.

55   Thomas Abbt, "Vom Tode für das Vaterland," in *Aufklärung und Kriegserfahrung: Klassische Zeitzeugen zum Siebenjährigen Krieg*, ed. Johannes Kunisch (Frankfurt am Main, 1996), 610.

56   As was the case in England, the new patriotism also implied a critique of the ruling caste, the nobility, and suggested that their claim to social and political predominance rested not on birth but on commitment to the fatherland and blood sacrifice in the field. See Linda Colley, *Britons: Forging the Nation, 1707–1837* (New Haven, 1992), 153.

57   Moses Mendelssohn, *Rezensionsartikel in Briefe die neueste Literatur betreffend (1759–1765)*, in Mendelssohn, *Gesammelte Schriften*, vol. 5, part 1, ed. Eva J. Engel (Stuttgart, 1991).

58   Cited in Koppel Pinson, *Pietism as a Factor in the Rise of German Nationalism* (New York, 1968), 184.

59   Friedrich Karl von Moser, *Von dem Deutschen Nationalgeist* (1765), 5.

60   Ibid, 5–6.

61   Ibid, 35.

62   Ibid, 10, 56. On this aspect of Moser's pamphlet, see Rudolf Vierhaus, "Patriotismus," in *Deutschland im 18. Jahrhundert* (Göttingen, 1987), 105.

63   Wolfgang Burgdorf, *Reichskonstitution und Nation: Verfassungsreformprojekte für das Heilige Römische Reich Deutscher Nation im politischen Schrifttum von 1648 bis 1806* (Mainz, 1998), 191–94.

64   Ibid., 191n43.

65   Ibid., 194–95. For the argument that the Empire was the state of the German nation, see Georg Schmidt, *Geschichte des Alten Reiches: Staat und Nation in der Frühen Neuzeit, 1495–1806* (Munich, 1999), 347–54. For a critique, see Heinz

Schilling, "Reichs-Staat und frühneuzeitliche Nation der Deutschen oder teil-modernisiertes Reichssystem," *Historische Zeitschrift* 272 (2001): 377–95.

66 The opinion concerning the debate's popularity is from the contemporary author Johann Heinrich Eberhard. See Nicholas Vazsonyi, "Montesquieu, Friedrich Carl von Moser, and the 'National Spirit Debate' in Germany, 1765–1767," *German Studies Review* 22, no. 2 (May 1999): 236.

67 Thomas Abbt, "Letter One Hundred and Eighty," in *Briefe, die neueste Literatur betreffend* 11 (1761): 27–28.

68 Peter Wilson, *German Armies: War and German Politics, 1648–1806* (London, 1998), 268, 280–83; Barbara Stollberg-Rilinger, *Des Kaisers alte Kleider: Verfassungsgeschichte und Symbolsprache des Alten Reiches* (Munich, 2008), 227.

69 Clark, *Iron Kingdom*, 210.

70 Michael Hochedlinger, *Austria's Wars of Emergence: War, State, and Society in the Habsburg Monarchy, 1683–1797* (London, 2003), 92.

71 H. M. Scott, "The Decline of France and the Transformation of the European Power System, 1756–1792," in *The Transformation of European Politics, 1763–1848: Episode or Model in Modern History?*, ed. Peter Krüger and Paul W. Schroeder (Münster, 2002), 105–28.

72 The financial side is worked out and explained in P. G. M. Dickson, *Finance and Government under Maria Theresia, 1740–1780*, 2 vols. (Oxford, 1987).

73 Scott, "The Fiscal-Military State and International Rivalry," 39–40.

74 Tim Blanning, *The Pursuit of Glory: Europe, 1648–1815* (New York, 2007), 608; Peter H. Wilson, "Military Culture in the Reich, c. 1680–1806," in *Culture of Power in Europe During the Long Nineteenth Century*, ed. Hamish Scott and Brendan Simms (Cambridge, 2007), 43.

75 Justus Möser, *Sämtliche Werke: Historisch-kritische Ausgabe*, vol. 3, *Vermischte Schriften II* (Osnabrück, 1986), 248.

76 Justus Möser to Thomas Abbt, 26 June 1765, in Justus Möser, *Briefe*, ed. Ernst Beins and Werner Pleiter (Hanover, 1939), 190.

77 Möser, *Sämtliche Werke*, vol. 12, part 1, *Osnabrückische Geschichte*.

78 Ibid., 146.

79 Ibid., 161.

80 Cited in Jonathan B. Knudsen, *Justus Möser and the German Enlightenment* (Cambridge, 1986), 103.

81 This exchange is related in Friedrich Nicolai, "Ehrengedächtnis Herrn Thomas Abbt," in *Gesammelte Werke*, vol. 12, 12. See also Moses Mendelssohn to Thomas Abbt, 28 April 1762, in Thomas Abbt, *Vermischte Werke* (Frankfurt am Main, 1783), 2:96.

82 Justus Möser to Friedrich Nicolai, 11 February 1767, in Justus Möser, *Briefwechsel*, ed. William F. Sheldon and Horst-Rüdiger Jarck (Hanover, 1992), 419.

83 Ibid., 419–20.

84 Johann Gottfried Herder to Friedrich Nicolai, 19 February 1767, in Johann Gottfried Herder, *Briefe: Gesamtausgabe, 1763–1803*, ed. Karl-Heinz Hahn (Weimar, 1977), 1:71.

85 H. M. Scott, "Reform in the Habsburg Monarchy, 1740–1790," in *Enlightened Absolutism: Reform and Reformers in Later Eighteenth-Century Europe*, ed. H. M. Scott (Ann Arbor, Mich., 1990), 150.

86 Michael Hochedlinger, "The Habsburg Monarchy: From 'Military-Fiscal State' to 'Militarization,'" in Storrs, ed., *The Fiscal Military State in Eighteenth-Century Europe*, 55–56.

87 Derek Beales, *Joseph II: In the Shadow of Maria Theresa, 1741–1780* (1987; repr.,

Cambridge, 2008); Derek Beales, *Joseph II: Against the World, 1780–1790* (1987; repr., Cambridge, 2013).

88   Cited in Michael Hochedlinger and Anton Tantner, eds., *"Der größte Teil der Untertanen lebt elend und mühselig": Die Berichte des Hofkriegsrates zur sozialen und wirtschaftlichen Lage der Habsburgermonarchie, 1770–1771* (Vienna, 2005), xii.

89   Charles W. Ingrao, *The Hessian Mercenary State* (Cambridge, 1987), 132; Franz A. J. Szabo, *Kaunitz and Enlightened Absolutism, 1753–1780* (Cambridge, 1994), 282–83.

90   Anton Tantner, *Die Hausnummer: Eine Geschichte von Ordnung und Unordnung* (Marburg, 2007).

91   Hochedlinger and Tantner, eds., *"Der größte Teil der Untertanen lebt elend und mühselig,"* xli.

92   Hochedlinger, *Austria's Wars of Emergence*, 296.

93   Hochedlinger, "Mars Ennobled," 162, citing Franz von Rollin; Szabo, *Kaunitz and Enlightened Absolutism*, 275; Hochedlinger, "The Habsburg Monarchy," 91.

94   Cited in Stollberg-Rilinger, *Des Kaisers alte Kleider*, 237.

95   A complete map of Joseph's travels is in Beales, *Joseph II: In the Shadow of Maria Theresa*, 244–45.

96   James Vann, "Mapping under the Austrian Habsburgs," in *Monarchs, Ministers, and Maps*, ed. David Buisseret (Chicago, 1992), 163.

97   Cited in Hans-Jürgen Bömelburg, *Friedrich II zwischen Deutschland und Polen* (Stuttgart, 2011), 73.

98   Karl Otmar von Aretin, "Tausch, Teilung und Länderschacher als Folgen des Gleichgewichtssystems der europäischen Grossmächte," in *Polen und die Polnische Frage in der Geschichte der Hohenzollernmonarchie, 1701–1871*, ed. Klaus Zernack (Berlin, 1982), 53–68.

99   Cited in P. G. M. Dickson, *Finance and Government under Maria Theresia, 1740–1780* (Oxford, 1987), 2:149. On the scale of confrontations in late-eighteenth-century Europe, see Paul W. Schroeder, *The Transformation of European Politics, 1763–1848* (Oxford, 1994), 5.

100   Andrej Walicki, *The Enlightenment and the Birth of Modern Nationhood: Polish Political Thought from Noble Republicanism to Tadeusz Kościuszko* (Notre Dame, Ind., 1989), 39–40.

101   The Polish Constitution of May 3, 1791, in Dieter Gosewinkel and Johannes Masing, *Die Verfassungen in Europa* (Munich, 2006), 373–84, and Gosewinkel's and Masing's introductory comments, 21–22. Contemporary German opinions of the constitution are catalogued in H. Vahle, "Die polnische Verfassung vom 3. Mai im zeitgenössischen deutschen Urteil," *Jahrbücher für Geschichte Osteuropas* NF 19 (1971): 347–70.

102   Johann Georg von Lori and Karl Heinrich von Lang, *Chronologischer Auszug der Geschichte von Baiern*, vol. 1 (Munich, 1782), first page of unpaginated preface.

103   Ibid.

104   Cited in Wilhelm Haefs, *Aufklärung in Altbayern: Leben, Werk und Wirkung Lorenz Westenrieders* (Neuried, 1998), 120.

105   Lorenz von Westenrieder, *Briefe bairischer Denkungsart und Sitten* (Munich, 1778), 22.

106   Helfrich Bernhard Wenck, *Hessische Landesgeschichte*, vol. 1 (Darmstadt, 1783), 2nd page of unpaginated foreword.

107   Joist Grolle, *Landesgeschichte in der Zeit der deutschen Spätaufklärung: Ludwig Timotheus Spittler, 1752–1810* (Göttingen, 1963), 77–80, 85.

108 Schroeder, *The Transformation of European Politics*, 14.

109 Burgdorf, *Reichskonstitution und Nation*, 208 (citing Möser); Klopstock cited in Irmtraut Sahmland, *Christoph Martin Wieland und die deutsche Nation: Zwischen Patriotismus, Kosmopolitismus und Griechentum* (Tübingen, 1990), 73.

110 Johann Stephan Pütter, *An Historical Development of the Present Political Constitution of the German Empire*, trans. Josiah Dornford, 3 vols. (London, 1790), 3:226. On Pütter, see Christoph Link, "Johann Stephan Pütter," in *Staatsdenker in der frühen Neuzeit*, ed. Michael Stolleis (Munich, 1995), 310-31.

111 Schroeder, *The Transformation of European Politics*, 30.

CHAPTER 5. THE SURFACE AND THE INTERIOR (C. 1770-1790)

1 Peter H. Meurer, "Hintergründe und Analysen zu Tobias Mayers 'Kritischer Karte von Deutschland,'" *Geographica Helvetica* 12 (July 1995): 20-21.

2 Anton Friedrich Büsching, *A New System of Geography*, 6 vols (London, 1762), 4:3.

3 The official name of the German Surveying Office was Die deutsche Akademie der Weltbeschreibungs-Wissenschaft. See Eric G. Forbes, *Tobias Mayer (1723-1762), Pioneer of Enlightened Science in Germany* (Göttingen, 1980), 59-61; Michael Diefenbacher, Markus Heinz, and Ruth Bach-Damaskinos, eds., *"Auserlesene und allerneueste Landkarten": Der Verlag Homann in Nürnberg, 1702-1848* (Nuremberg, 2002), 40.

4 Forbes, *Tobias Mayer*, 63.

5 Meurer, "Hintergründe und Analysen," 19.

6 Johann Ernst Fabri, *Geographie für alle Stände* (Leipzig, 1786), 375.

7 On the history of the term "identity," see Lutz Niethammer, *Kollektive Identität: Heimliche Quellen einer unheimlichen Konjunktur* (Reinbek bei Hamburg, 2000).

8 John R. Hale, ed., *The Travel Journal of Antonio de Beatis Through Germany, Switzerland, the Low Countries, France and Italy, 1517-1518*, trans. John R. Hale and J. M. A. Lindon (London, 1979), 29, 50. On Ulm (before the spire's nineteenth-century completion), see Johann Georg Keyßler, *Neueste Reisen durch Deutschland, Böhmen, Ungarn, die Schweiz, Italien und Lothringen* (Hanover, 1751), 67.

9 Erasmus to Johannes Reuchlin, epist. 713, 15 November 1517, in *The Correspondence of Erasmus*, vol. 5, trans. R. A. B. Mynors and D. F. S. Thompson, annotated Peter G. Bietenholz (Toronto, 1979), 203.

10 Stephen Greenblatt, *Marvelous Possessions: The Wonder of the New World* (Chicago, 1991), 14.

11 This rough calculation is based on the extensive online biography at the Eutiner Landesbibliothek: http://www.lb-eutin.de. Not included in my calculation are works written by foreigners or works published posthumously.

12 Urs Bitterli, *Die "Wilden" und die "Zivilisierten": Grundzüge einer Geistes- und Kulturgeschichte der europäisch—überseeischen Begegnung* (Munich, 1991), 20-21.

13 Ibid.

14 Joyce E. Chaplin, *Round about the Earth: Circumnavigation from Magellan to Orbit* (New York, 2012), 106-38.

15 Fernand Braudel, *Civilization and Capitalism, 15th-18th Century*, vol. 3, *The Perspective of the World*, trans. Siân Reynolds (London, 1984), 316. Wolfgang Behringer, *Im Zeichen des Merkur: Reichspost und Kommunikationsrevolution in der Frühen Neuzeit* (Göttingen, 2003), calls the shift a revolution.

16   Behringer, *Im Zeichen des Merkur*, 664–65.

17   Ibid.

18   Ibid., 499–508; Diefenbacher, Heinz, and Bach-Damaskinos, eds., *"Auserlesene und allerneueste Landkarten,"* 108.

19   Behringer, *Im Zeichen des Merkur*, 661.

20   Johann Huizinga, *Herbst des Mittelalters: Studien über Lebens- und Geistesformen des 14. und 15. Jahrhunderts in Frankreich und in den Niederlanden*, trans. Kurt Köster (Stuttgart, 1975), 2–3.

21   Carlo Cippola, *Clocks and Culture* (London, 1967), 44.

22   On the history of timekeeping, see, in addition to ibid., David S. Landes, *Revolution in Time: Clocks and the Making of the Modern World* (Cambridge, Mass., 1983); and, for the impact of timekeeping on everyday life, see Paul Glennie and Nigel Thrift, *Shaping the Day: A History of Timekeeping in England and Wales, 1300–1800* (Oxford, 2009).

23   The army in question was that of Prince Leopold I of Anhalt Dessau. See Michael Maurer, "Alltagsleben," in *Handbuch der deutschen Bildungsgeschichte*, ed. Notker Hammerstein and Ulrich Herrmann (Munich, 2005), 2:36–37.

24   Cited in Craig Koslovsky, *Evening's Empire: A History of the Night in Early Modern Europe* (Cambridge, 2011), 135–36.

25   Zacharias Conrad von Uffenbach, *Merckwürdige Reisen durch Niedersachsen, Holland, und Engelland* (Ulm, 1753), 4–5. On the literature telling baroque travelers what to notice, see Justin Stagl, *Eine Geschichte des Reisens, 1550–1800* (Vienna, 2002). See also Bernard W. Heise, "Visions of the World: Geography and Maps During the Baroque Age, 1550–1750" (Ph.D. diss., Cornell University, Ithaca, N.Y., 1998), 98–120.

26   Ludwig Hirzel, ed., *Albrecht Hallers Tagebücher seiner Reisen nach Deutschland, Holland und England, 1723–1727* (Leipzig, 1883), 10–11.

27   Johann Georg Keyßler, *Neueste Reisen durch Deutschland, Böhmen, Ungarn, die Schweiz, Italien und Lothringen* (Hanover, 1751), 3. On Keyßler, see Winfried Siebers, *Johann Georg Keyßler und die Reisebeschreibung der Frühaufklärung* (Würzburg, 2009).

28   Lady Mary Wortley Montagu to Lady Mar, 16 January 1717 and 8 September 1716, in Mary Wortley Montagu, *The Turkish Embassy Letters*, ed. Malcom Jack (London, 1994), 42, 13.

29   Montagu to Lady Rich, 20 September 1716, and Montagu to Lady X, 1 October 1716, in ibid., 22, 28.

30   Charles-Louis de Montesquieu, *Meine Reisen in Deutschland, 1728–1729*, ed. Jürgen Overhoff, trans. Hans W. Schumacher (Stuttgart, 2014), 102.

31   Ibid., 109, 142.

32   James Boswell, *Boswell on the Grand Tour: Germany and Switzerland, 1764*, ed. Frederick A. Pottle (New York, 1928), 104, 125–27.

33   Ibid., 62, 126, 127.

34   Ibid., 44–45.

35   Ibid., 11.

36   Friedrich Nicolai, *Gesammelte Werke*, vol. 15, *Beschreibung einer Reise*, vol. 1, ed. Bernhard Fabian and Marie-Luise Spieckermann (Hildesheim, 1994), 87. (This huge multivolume work is hereafter cited as Nicolai, *GW*.)

37   Nicolai, *GW*, 15, *Beschreibung einer Reise*, 1:16, 21. On his gadgets and way of traveling, see especially Matthias Buschmeier, "Das rollende Büro: Nicolais Technik des statistischen Reiseberichts," in *Materialität und Reisen*, ed. Philip Bracher, Florian Hertweck, and Stefan Schröder (Münster, 2006), 125–52.

38 The route is reconstructed in Paul Raabe, "Friedrich Nicolais unbeschriebene Reise von der Schweiz nach Norddeutschland im Jahre 1781," in *Sehen und Beschreiben: Europäische Reisen im 18. und frühen 19. Jahrhundert*, ed. Wolfgang Griep (Eutin, 1991), 212.

39 Nicolai, *GW*, 15, *Beschreibung einer Reise*, 1:viii.

40 Nicolai, *GW*, 15, *Beschreibung einer Reise*, 1:viii. On the national idea behind Nicolai's travels, see Françoise Knopper, *Le Regard du voyageur en Allemagne du Sud et en Autriche dans les relations de voyageurs allemands* (Nancy, 1992), 84–88.

41 Nicolai, *GW*, 15, *Beschreibung einer Reise*, 1:110–11.

42 Nicolai, *GW*, 15, *Beschreibung einer Reise*, 2:490.

43 Johann Caspar Lavater, *Physiognomische Fragmente zur Beförderung der Menschenkenntnis und Menschenliebe* (Stuttgart, 1984), 21–22.

44 For Nicolai's own extended discussion of how to understand the physiognomy of people, see Nicolai, *GW*, 15, *Beschreibung einer Reise*, 1:130–34.

45 Nicolai, *GW*, 15, *Beschreibung einer Reise*, 1:161, 230.

46 Nicolai, *GW*, 15, *Beschreibung einer Reise*, 2:526.

47 Nicolai, *GW*, 17, *Beschreibung einer Reise*, 6:488.

48 Nicolai, *GW*, 18, *Beschreibung einer Reise*, 7:32, 101, 62.

49 Cited in David Bindman, *Ape to Apollo: Aesthetics and the Idea of Race in the 18th Century* (Ithaca, N.Y., 2002), 196.

50 Excerpt of translated text in Emmanuel Chukwudi Eze, ed., *Race and the Enlightenment. A Reader* (Malden, Mass., 1997), 86.

51 See Suzanne Marchand, *Down from Olympus: Archaeology and Philhellenism in Germany, 1750–1970* (Princeton, N.J., 1996).

52 See Sara Eigen and Mark Larrimore, eds., *The German Invention of Race* (Albany, N.Y., 2006); Carl Niekerk, "Man and Orangutan in Eighteenth-Century Thinking: Retracing the Early History of Dutch and German Anthropology," *Monatshefte* 96, no. 4 (2004): 477–502.

53 Cited in Bindman, *Ape to Apollo*, 95.

54 See the images in Edgar Peters Bowron, ed., *Bernardo Bellotto and the Capitals of Europe* (New Haven, 2001).

55 Nicolai, *GW*, 16, *Beschreibung einer Reise*, 3:211–13; Nicolai, *GW*, 16, *Beschreibung einer Reise*, 4:501.

56 Nicolai, *GW*, 16, *Beschreibung einer Reise*, 4:895.

57 Johann Kaspar Riesbeck, *Briefe eines reisenden Franzosen über Deutschland*, ed. Jochen Golz (Berlin, 1976), 88–89; Georg Forster, *Werke*, ed. Gerhard Steiner, vol. 2, *Kleine Schriften zur Naturgeschichte, Länder- und Völkerkunde* (Frankfurt am Main, 1969), 404–5.

58 Nicolai, *GW*, 15, *Beschreibung einer Reise*, 1:64; Nicolai, *GW*, *Beschreibung einer Reise*, 20:51.

59 Nicolai, *GW*, 20, *Beschreibung einer Reise*, 12:6.

60 Nicolai, *GW*, 16, *Beschreibung einer Reise*, vol. 3, 107–11; Nicolai, *GW*, 18, *Beschreibung einer Reise*, 7:28; Nicolai, *GW*, vol. 19, *Beschreibung einer Reise*, 9:6.

61 Nicolai, *GW*, 15, *Beschreibung einer Reise*, 1:43; Nicolai, *GW*, 17, *Beschreibung einer Reise*, 6:477. On Nicolai's sense of the beauty of the land, see Wolfgang Martens, "Ein Bürger auf Reisen," in *Friedrich Nicolai, 1733–1811*, ed. Bernhard Fabian (Berlin, 1983), 110.

62 Nicolai, *GW*, 20, *Beschreibung einer Reise*, 12:53.

63 Ibid. On St. Blaise, see Heinrich Klotz, *Geschichte der deutschen Kunst*, vol. 3, *Neuzeit und Moderne, 1750–2000* (Munich, 2000), 34.

64 Nicolai, *GW*, 20, *Beschreibung einer Reise*, 12:53.

65 Horst Möller, *Aufklärung in Preußen* (Berlin, 1974), 112.

66 Friedrich Schiller, *Gedichte*, ed. Georg Kurscheidt, vol. 1, in *Werke und Briefe*, ed. Otto Dann et al. (Frankfurt am Main, 1992), 600.

67 Johann Gottlieb Fichte, "Friedrich Nicolais Leben und sonderbare Meinungen," in Fichte, *Gesamtausgabe der bayerischen Akademie der Wissenschaften*, ed. Reinhard Lauth and Hans Gliwitzky, series I, vol. 7, *Werke 1800–1801* (Stuttgart, 1988), 410, 381, 420.

68 Nicolai, *GW*, 20, *Beschreibung einer Reise*, vol. 11, 121–22.

69 Johann Gottlieb Fichte, "Spottgedichte auf Nicolai, Kettner und Biester," in *Gesamtausgabe der bayerischen Akademie der Wissenschaften*, ed. Reinhard Lauth and Hans Gliwitzky, series II, vol. 6, *Nachgelassene Schriften, 1800–1803* (Stuttgart, 1983), 1–29.

70 Johann Gottfried Herder to Johann Georg Hamann, March 1769, in Johann Gottfried Herder, *Briefe: Gesamtausgabe, 1763–1803*, ed. Wilhelm Dobbeck and Günter Arnold (Weimar, 1977), 1:134.

71 Herder to Friedrich Nicolai, 30 November 1769, in ibid., 1:175. See also Otto Dann, "Herders Weg nach Deutschland," *Herder Jahrbuch* 2 (1994): 1–16.

72 Herder to Hamann, March 1769, in Herder, *Briefe*, 1:134. See also the discussion in Hans D. Irmscher, *Johann Gottfried Herder* (Stuttgart, 2001), 158–59.

73 Johann Gottfried Herder, "Vom Erkennen und Empfinden der menschlichen Seele," in *Werke*, vol. 4, *Schriften zu Philosophie, Literatur, Kunst, und Altertum, 1747–1787*, ed. Jürgen Brummack and Martin Bollacher (Frankfurt am Main, 1994), 347.

74 As the seventeenth-century theologian and historian of religion, Gottfried Arnold, put it. Cited in a still classic work by Koppel Pinson, *Pietism as a Factor in the Rise of German Nationalism* (New York, 1934), 41. See also Herder, "Vom Erkennen und Empfinden der menschlichen Seele," 348.

75 See commentary in Herder, *Werke*, vol. 3, *Volkslieder, Übertragungen, Dichtungen*, ed. Ulrich Gaier (Frankfurt am Main, 1990), 848–924.

76 Irmscher, *Johann Gottfried Herder*, 22. On the encounter, especially intriguing is Robert E. Norton, "Herder as Faust," in *Goethe's Faust and Cultural Memory: Comparatist Interfaces*, ed. Lorna Fitzsimmons (Bethlehem, Pa., 2012), 49–67. For Strasbourg in these years, see Franklin L. Ford, *Strasbourg in Transition, 1648–1789* (New York, 1958), 207–34.

77 Johann Wolfgang Goethe to Herder, c. October 1771, in Johann Wolfgang Goethe, *Sämtliche Werke: Briefe, Tagebücher und Gespräche*, vol. 28, *Von Frankfurt nach Weimar: Briefe, Tagebücher, Gespräche vom 23. Mai 1764 bis 30. Oktober 1775*, ed. Wilhelm Große (Frankfurt am Main, 1997), 246.

78 Richard van Dülmen, "Fest der Liebe: Heirat in der frühen Neuzeit," in *Armut, Liebe, Ehe: Studien zur historischen Kulturforschung* (Frankfurt am Main, 1988), 67.

79 Goethe, *Sämtliche Werke*, vol. 1, *Gedichte, 1756–1799*, ed. Karl Eibl (Frankfurt am Main, 1987), 283.

80 Goethe to Herder, September 1771, in Goethe, *Sämtliche Werke*, 28:239–40.

81 Ibid., 829.

82 Goethe, "Heidenröslein," in Goethe, *Sämtliche Werke*, 1:278.

83 Johann Gottfried Herder, "Auszug aus einem Briefwechsel über Ossian und die Lieder alter Völker," in "Von deutscher Art und Kunst," in Herder, *Werke*, vol. 2, *Schriften zur Ästhetik und Literatur, 1767–1781*, ed. Gunter E. Grimm (Frankfurt am Main, 1993), 493–94, 490.

84 Goethe, "Von deutscher Baukunst," in *Sämtliche Werke*, vol. 18, ed. Wilhelm Große (Frankfurt am Main, 1997), 113.

85 Ibid.

86 Ibid., 115.

87 Herder, "Auszug aus einem Briefwechsel," 2:480.

88 Elizabeth Blochmann, "Die deutsche Volksdichtungsbewegung in Sturm und Drang und Romantik," *Deutsche Vierteljahrsschrift für Literaturwissenschaft und Geistesgeschichte* 1, no. 3 (1923): 435.

89 Nicolai to Herder, 15 June 1771, in *Herder's Briefwechsel mit Nicolai*, ed. Otto Hoffmann (Berlin, 1887), 59-60. On this relationship, see Martin Sommerfeld, *Friedrich Nicolai und der Sturm und Drang: Ein Beitrag zur Geschichte der deutschen Aufklärung* (Halle, 1921).

90 Nicolai to Herder, 19 November 1771, in Hoffmann, ed., *Herder's Briefwechsel mit Nicolai*, 65.

91 Herder to Nicolai, 14 August 1773, in ibid., 102-3. On Nicolai as a publishing force, see Pamela E. Selwyn. *Everyday Life in the German Book Trade: Friedrich Nicolai as Bookseller and Publisher in the Age of Enlightenment, 1740-1810* (University Park, Pa., 2000).

92 Ute Schneider, *Friedrich Nicolais Allgemeine Deutsche Bibliothek als Integrationsmedium der Gelehrtenrepublik* (Wiesbaden, 1995).

93 Nicolai to Herder, 13 June 1774, in Hoffmann, ed., *Herder's Briefwechsel mit Nicolai*, 107. See also Walter D. Wetzels, "The Herder–Nicolai Controversy," in *Johann Gottfried Herder: Language, History, and the Enlightenment*, ed. Wulf Koepke (Columbia, S.C., 1990), 87-97.

94 Herder to Nicolai, 29 July 1774, in Hoffmann, ed., *Herder's Briefwechsel mit Nicolai*, 109.

95 Ibid.

96 Johann Wolfgang Goethe, "Götz von Berlichingen mit der eisernen Hand," in Goethe, *Dramen, 1765-1775*, in *Sämtliche Werke: Briefe, Tagebücher und Gespräche*, ed. Dieter Borchmeyer (Frankfurt am Main, 1985), 349.

97 Cited in Nicholas Boyle, *Goethe: The Poet and the Age*, vol. 1, *The Poetry of Desire* (Oxford, 1992), 187.

98 Gotthold Ephraim Lessing to Johann Joachim Eschenburg, 28 October 1774, in *Goethe im Urteil seiner Kritiker: Dokumente zur Wirkungsgeschichte Goethes in Deutschland*, ed. Karl Robert Mandelkow (Munich, 1975), 20-21.

99 Ibid.

100 Hans Schwerte, *Faust und das Faustische: Ein Kapitel deutscher Ideologie* (Stuttgart, 1962), 30-31. Hans Schwerte was the alias for Hans Ernst Schneider, a former SS officer.

101 Günther Jacoby, *Herder als Faust: Eine Untersuchung* (Leipzig, 1911).

102 Johann Wolfgang von Goethe, *Faust, Frühe Fassung*, in *Faust: Texte*, ed. Albrechte Schöne, vol. 1, *Texte* (Frankfurt am Main, 1999), 469, 472.

103 Ibid., 1:494.

104 Ibid., 1:521.

105 Cited in Boyle, *Goethe: The Poet and the Age,* 1:106.

106 Goethe, *Faust: Texte*, 1:534.

107 The prosody follows the commentary of Gerhard Sauder, in Goethe, *Sämtliche Werke* (Munich, 1987), vol. 1, part 2, 746.

108 Erich Auerbach, *Mimesis: The Representation of Reality in Western Literature*, trans. Willard R. Trask (Princeton, N.J., 1953), 444.

109 Rebekka Habermas, ed., *Das Frankfurter Gretchen: Der Prozeß gegen die Kinds-*

mörderin Susanna Margaretha Brandt (Munich, 1999), 16–17; Habermas's introduction, 7–42, works out the comparison. My own interpretation, given in more detail, is in Helmut Walser Smith, "The Confinement of Tragedy: Between Urfaust and Woyzeck," in *Tragedy in German Literature*, ed. Steven Dowden (New York, 2014), 21–39.

110   Stephen Broadberry and Kevin H. O'Rourke, eds., *The Cambridge Economic History of Modern Europe* (Cambridge, 2010), 1:19; Robert William Fogel, *The Escape from Hunger and Premature Death, 1700–2100* (Cambridge, 2004), 6.

111   Wolfgang Hardtwig, "Naturbeherrschung und aesthetische Landschaft: Zur Entstehung der ästhetischen Landschaft am Beispiel der 'Münchner Schule,' " in *Hochkultur des bürgerlichen Zeitalters* (Göttingen, 2005), 176, 186.

112   Johann Ernst Fabri, ed., *Neue Reisebeschreibungen in und über Deutschland*, 6 vols. (Halle, 1786–1791), preface to vol. 1.

113   Johann Christoph Friedrich GutsMuths, *Meine Reise im deutschen Vaterlande: Aus Thüringen ins Riesengebürge zu den Elbquellen und durch Böhmen ins Erzgebürge* (Breslau, 1799).

114   J. L. Ewald, *Fantasien auf einer Reise durch Gegenden des Friedens* (Hanover, 1799), esp. 372–94.

115   Johann Kaspar Riesbeck, *Briefe eines reisenden Franzosen über Deutschland* (East Berlin, 1976), 8.

116   Friedrich A. Köhler, *Eine Albreise im Jahre 1790*, ed. Eckart Frahm, Wolfgang Kaschuba, and Carola Lipp (Tübingen, 1979).

117   Wilhelm Heinrich Wackenroder, *Reisebriefe*, in *Sämtliche Werke und Briefe*, ed. Silvio Vietta and Richard Littlejohns (Heidelberg, 1991), 2:158.

118   Ibid., 2:175.

119   Ibid., 2:177.

120   Comment in ibid., 2:577.

121   Ibid., 2:203.

122   Ibid., 2:199; comment in ibid., 2:581.

123   Christoph Gottlieb von Murr, *Beschreibung der vornehmsten Merkwürdigkeiten in des H.R. Reichs freyen Stadt Nürnberg und auf der hohen Schule zu Altdorf* (Nuremberg, 1778). On the Romantic rediscovery of Nuremberg, see Stephen Brockmann, *Nuremberg. The Imaginary Capital* (Rochester, N.Y., 2006). 32–45.

124   Wackenroder, *Reisebriefe*, 2:187.

125   Ibid., 2:188.

126   Ibid.

127   Ibid, 2:222.

128   Ibid., 2:222–23.

129   Friedrich Schlegel, "Reise nach Frankreich," in *Europa: Eine Zeitschrift* (1803), 1:7–8.

130   Ibid., 8.

131   Ibid., 11.

132   Abbate de Bertola, *Mahlerische Rheinreise von Speyer bis Düsseldorf* (1796; repr., Heidelberg, 2004), 6. See also Ann Radcliffe, *A Journey Made in the Summer of 1794 Through Holland and the Western Frontier of Germany* (London, 1795).

133   Schlegel, "Reise nach Frankeich," 15.

134   *Novalis Schriften: Die Werke Friedrich von Hardenbergs*, vol. 2, *Das philosophische Werk*, ed. Richard Samuel, Hans-Joachim Mähl, and Gerhard Schulz (Stuttgart, 1965), 545.

CHAPTER 6. *DE L'ALLEMAGNE* (C. 1790-1815)

1   Madame (Anne Louise Germaine) de Staël, *De l'Allemagne*, ed. Jean de Pagne, 5 vols. (Paris, 1958), 1:29-30 (hereafter cited as *De l'Allemagne*).

2   Madame de Staël, *A Treatise on the Influence of the Passions upon the Happiness of Individuals and of Nations* (London, 1798), 316-20.

3   [Madame de Staël,] *Ten Years' Exile, or Memoirs of That Interesting Period of the Life of the Baroness de Staël-Holstein*, ch. 11.

4   The journal is reprinted in Simon Balayé, *Les Carnets de voyage de Madame de Staël* (Geneva, 1971), 29.

5   On Berlin, see Madame de Stäel to Johann Wolfgang Goethe, 7 April 1804, in Georges Solovieff, ed., *Madame de Stäel: Kein Herz das mehr geliebt hat* (Frankfurt am Main, 1971), 211 (hereafter cited as Staël: *Kein Herz*). On Weimar, see Balayé, *Les Carnets de voyage*, 64.

6   Staël to Jacques Necker, 2 February 1804, in Staël: *Kein Herz*, 191-92; Staël to Friedrich Schlegel, 4 November 1805, in ibid., 243.

7   Staël to Necker, 2 February 1804, in ibid., 191-92.

8   Her trips were mainly to the east, the part of Germany least under Napoleonic control and most capable of offering resistance. On Staël's eastern orientation in *De l'Allemagne*, see John Isbell, *The Birth of European Romanticism: Truth and Propaganda in Staël's "De l'Allemagne," 1810-1813* (Cambridge, 1994), 14.

9   Staël to Prince de Ligne, 26 September 1808, in *Staël: Kein Herz*, 278.

10   Simon Balayé, *Madame de Staël et le gouvernement impérial en 1810: Le Dossier de la suppression de "De l'Allemagne"* (Paris, 1974), 28.

11   Ibid., 28-29.

12   *De l'Allemagne*, 1:39.

13   Ibid., 1:55, 4:274.

14   Ibid., 4:273-74.

15   Ibid., 5:195.

16   Christopher Herold, *Madame de Staël: Herrin eines Jahrhunderts* (Munich, 1968), 391-92; *Staël: Kein Herz*, 304.

17   Staël to Camille Jordan, 1 November 1810, in *Staël: Kein Herz*, 311.

18   René Savary to Staël, 3 October 1810, in ibid., 304-5.

19   Balayé, *Madame de Staël et le gouvernement impérial en 1810*, 35.

20   Cited in Isbell, *The Birth of European Romanticism*, 156.

21   Jonathan Knudsen, *Justus Möser and the German Enlightenment* (Cambridge, 1986), 166-74.

22   Horst Möller, *Aufklärung in Preußen* (Berlin, 1974), 40-41; Pamela E. Selwyn, *Everyday Life in the German Book Trade: Friedrich Nicolai as Bookseller and Publisher in the Age of Enlightenment, 1740-1810* (University Park, Pa., 2000), 5-6.

23   Johann Gottfried von Herder, *Briefe zur Beförderung der Humanität*, ed. Hans Dietrich Irmscher, *Werke*, vol. 7 (Frankfurt am Main, 1991), 780-84.

24   Ibid., 789.

25   Claus Träger, ed., *Die Französische Revolution im Spiegel der deutschen Literatur* (Leipzig, 1975), 241.

26   Friedrich Gentz to Christian Garve, 5 December 1790, in ibid., 861.

27   Schlözer added, "As well as the constantly complaining and still calm Brit." See August Ludwig von Schlözer, "Aphorismen," 1793, excerpt in ibid., 945.

28   G. W. F. Hegel cited in James Sheehan, *German History, 1770-1866* (Oxford, 1989), 212; Friedrich Hölderlin to his brother, 21 August 1794, in Träger, ed., *Die Französische Revolution im Spiegel der deutschen Literatur*, 150.

29   Christoph Martin Wieland to Gerhard Anton von Halem, 30 November 1790, in Uta Motschmann, ed., *Wielands Briefwechsel* (Berlin, 1993), 10:425.

30   Christoph Martin Wieland, "Unparteiische Betrachtungen über die dermalige-Staatsrevolution in Frankreich," in *Die Französische Revolution: Berichte und Deutungen deutscher Schriftsteller und Historiker*, ed. Horst Günther, 4 vols. (Frankfurt am Main, 1985), 2:497, 516-17.

31   Christoph Martin Wieland, "Die französische Republik," in ibid., 2:518, 523.

32   Ibid., 2:573. The italicized emphases are Wieland's.

33   Christoph Martin Wieland, "Über deutschen Patriotismus," in ibid., 2:574.

34   Ibid., 2:576.

35   Ibid., 2:577, 580.

36   Abbé Sieyès, *Qu'est ce que le tiers état?*, ed. Roberto Zapperi (Geneva, 1970), 180-84. On this document, see William Sewell, *A Rhetoric of Bourgeois Revolution: The Abbé Sieyès and "What Is the Third Estate?"* (Durham, Eng., 1994). For its context in the pamphlet wars at the time of the convocation of the Estates General, see Lynn Hunt, "The 'National Assembly,'" in *The Political Culture of the Old Regime*, ed. Keith Michael Baker (Oxford, 1987), 413.

37   David A. Bell, *The Cult of the Nation in France: Inventing Nationalism, 1680-1800* (Cambridge, Mass., 2001), 3.

38   Document in Karl Otmar Freiherr von Aretin, *Heiliges Römisches Reich, 1776-1806: Reichsverfassung und Staatssouveränität*, vol. 2, *Ausgewählte Aktenstücke* (Wiesbaden, 1967), 249-55.

39   Karl Otmar Freiherr von Aretin, "Tausch, Teilung und Länderschacher als Folgen des Gleichgewichtssystems der europäischen Großmächte," in *Polen und die Polnische Frage in der Geschichte der Hohenzollernmonarchie, 1701-1871*, ed. Klaus Zernack (Berlin, 1982), 61.

40   Karl Roider, *Baron Thugut and Austria's Response to the French Revolution* (Princeton, N.J., 1987), 128.

41   Klaus Zernak, "Die Geschichte Preußens und das Problem der deutsch-polnischen Beziehungen," *Jahrbücher für Geschichte Osteuropas*, NF 31 (1983): 28-49.

42   A very detailed and insightful treatment is Georg Cavallar, *Pax Kantiana: Systematisch-historische Untersuchung des Entwurfs "Zum Ewigen Frieden" (1795) von Immanuel Kant* (Vienna, 1992).

43   Immanuel Kant, "Zum Ewigen Frieden," in *Werkausgabe*, ed. Wilhelm Weischedel, vol. 11, *Schriften zur Anthropologie, Geschichtsphilosophie, Politik und Pädagogik* (Frankfurt am Main, 1977), 196.

44   Ibid.

45   Ibid., 11:197-98.

46   Ibid., 11:207-8.

47   Ibid., 11:200.

48   Ute Planert, *Der Mythos vom Befreiungskrieg: Frankreichs Kriege und der deutsche Süden; Alltag—Wahrnehmung—Deutung, 1792-1841* (Paderborn, 2007), 113, shows that contemporaries considered it as a unified epoch.

49   Ibid., 184.

50   Anton Klebe, *Reise auf dem Rhein*, 1st ed. (Frankfurt am Main, 1801). The second edition, published when Bavaria belonged to the Rheinbund, was less critical.

51   Thomas Richter, "Textkonstitution als Interpretation: Schillers Gedichtentwurf 'Deutsche Größe' und seine Instrumentalisierung im Kaiserreich," in *Schrift—Text—Edition: Hans Walter Gabler zum 65. Geburtstag*, ed. Christiane Henkes et al. (Tübingen, 2003), 206-7. For a detailed interpretation, see Christian Grawe,

"Schillers Gedichtentwurf 'Deutsche Größe': Ein Nationalhymnos im höchsten Styl?," *Jahrbuch der deutschen Schillergesellschaft* 36 (1992): 167–96.

52 Friedrich Schiller, *Gedichte*, ed. Georg Kurscheidt, vol. 1, in *Werke und Briefe*, ed. Otto Dann et al. (Frankfurt am Main, 1992), 736.

53 See Georg Schmidt, "Friedrich Schillers 'Deutsche Größe' und der nationale Universalismus," in *Tradition und Umbruch: Geschichte zwischen Wissenschaft, Kultur und Politik*, ed. Werner Greiling and Hans-Werner Hahn (Rudolstadt, 2002), 20–26.

54 Schiller, *Gedichte*, 735–36.

55 Ibid., 736.

56 Ibid., 737.

57 On the fragment's completion in World War I, see Grawe, "Schillers Gedichtentwurf," 189–92; Richter, "Textkonstitution als Interpretation," 202n4.

58 Schiller, *Gedichte*, 739.

59 See especially Hans Ulrich Rudolf, ed., *Alte Klöster, Neue Herren: Die Säkularisation im deutschen Südwesten*, 3 vols. (Osfilden, 2003).

60 Peter Eitel, "Segnungen und Grausamkeiten des aufgeklärten Absolutismus: Die Reichstadt Ravensburg unter bayerischer und dann württembergischer Herrschaft," in ibid., vol. 2, part 2, 779–90, and Bernd Wunder, "80,000 Livres für eine Reichstadt! Die Mediatisierung der Reichstadt Schwäbisch Hall," in ibid., 791–806.

61 Yair Mintzger, *The Defortification of the German City, 1689–1866* (New York, 2012), 177–78.

62 As occurred, for example, with a map of the Peace of Tilsit. See Rudolf, ed., *Alte Klöster, Neue Herren: Die Säkularisation im deutschen Südwesten*, 1:144.

63 Johann Gottfried Seume to Carl August Böttiger, mid-December 1805, in Johann Gottfried Seume, *Briefe*, ed. Jörg Drews and Dirk Sangmeister (Frankfurt am Main, 2002), 522.

64 Ernst Moritz Arndt, *Reisen durch einen Theil Teutchlands, Ungarns, Italiens und Frankreichs in den Jahren 1798 und 1799*, 4 vols. (Leipzig, 1804), 3:197 (hereafter cited as Arndt, *Reisen*).

65 Ibid., 3:76.

66 On Arndt and the French Revolution, see Hans-Jürgen Lüsebrink, "Ein Nationalist aus französischer Inspiration: Ernst Moritz Arndt (1769–1860)," in *Frankreichfreunde: Mittler des französisch-deutschen Kulturtransfers (1750–1850)*, ed. Michel Espagne and Werner Greiling (Leipzig, 1997), 221–42.

67 Arndt, *Reisen*, 3:203.

68 Ibid., 3:204.

69 Michael Rowe, *From Reich to State: The Rhineland in the Revolutionary Age, 1780–1830* (New York, 2003), 51.

70 Arndt, *Reisen*, 4:327, 344, 369.

71 The historian is Jacques Godechot; see Timothy Blanning, *The French Revolution in Germany* (Oxford, 1983), 99.

72 William Doyle, *The Oxford History of the French Revolution* (Oxford, 1989), 352.

73 C. Kasper-Holtkotte, "Jud, gib dein Geld oder du bist des Todes: Die Banditengruppe des Schinderhannes und die Juden," *Aschkenas: Zeitschrift für Geschichte und Kultur der Juden* 1 (1993): 113–88.

74 Arndt, *Reisen*, 4:394.

75 Rowe, *From Reich to State*, 59.

76 Blanning, *The French Revolution in Germany*, 247, 219, 250.

77   Bernhard Struck and Claire Gantet, *Revolution, Krieg und Verflechtung, 1789 bis 1815* (Darmstadt, 2008), 25.

78   Ibid., 25–27.

79   Arndt, *Reisen*, 4:400.

80   Ernst Moritz Arndt, *Germanien und Europa* (Altona, 1803), 217.

81   Ibid., 216–17.

82   Ibid., 220.

83   Ibid.

84   See, for example, one of the few reviews, a piece in the *Allgemeine Literaturzeitung*, no. 297 (October 1803), 171–74.

85   Carl von Clausewitz, *On War*, ed. and trans. Michael Howard and Peter Paret (Princeton, N.J., 1976), 155. On Jena, see especially Peter Paret, *The Cognitive Challenge of War: Prussia, 1806* (Princeton, N.J., 2009).

86   Gustav Seibt, "Das Brandenburger Tor," in *Deutsche Erinnerungsorte*, ed. Etienne François and Hagen Schulze, 3 vols. (Munich, 2001), 2:67–85, esp. 69–73.

87   David A. Bell, *Napoleon* (New York, 2015), 73.

88   Estimates of the total French requisitions from rump Prussia in the two years after Jena suggest figures reaching sixteen times the Prussian government's annual revenue. See Mathew Levinger, *Enlightened Nationalism: The Transformation of Prussian Political Culture, 1806–1848* (Oxford, 2000), 44.

89   Cited in T. W. Blanning, "The French Revolution and the Modernization of Germany," *Central European History* 22 (1989): 109–29.

90   Ernst Moritz Arndt, "*Geist der Zeit*," in Arndt, *Ausgewählte Werke*, vol. 10 (Leipzig, 1908), 111. The passage counts as one of the earliest usages of the word "nationalism" ("*Nationalismus*") in German.

91   Karen Hagemann, "*Mannlicher Muth und Teutsche Ehre*": *Nation, Militär und Geschlecht zur Zeit der Antinapoleonischen Kriege Preußens* (Paderborn, 2002), 158–86.

92   Cited in Anthony J. LaVopa, *Fichte: The Self and the Calling of Philosophy, 1762–1799* (Cambridge, 2001), 110.

93   Johann Gottlieb Fichte, *Die Grundzüge des Gegenwärtigen Zeitalters*, 4th ed. (Hamburg, 1978), 14–15, 21.

94   Reinhart Koselleck, "'Erfahrungsraum' und 'Erwartungshorizont': Zwei historische Kategorien," in *Vergangene Zukunft: Zur Semantik geschichtlicher Zeiten* (Frankfurt am Main, 1979), 349–75.

95   Johann Gottlieb Fichte, "Der Patriotismus und sein Gegentheil," in *J. G. Fichte Kritische Gesamtausgabe*, series II, vol. 9, *Nachgelassene Schriften*, ed. Reinhard Lauth and Hans Gliwitzky (Stuttgart, 1993), 403. On Prussian patriotism, see Christopher Clark, *Iron Kingdom: The Rise and Downfall of Prussia, 1600–1947* (Cambridge, Mass., 2006), 350–58, 378–85, and, especially for the use of "nation" to mean Germany or Prussia or both, 386–87.

96   Fichte, "Der Patriotismus und sein Gegentheil," 445.

97   Johann Gottlieb Fichte, "Die Republik der Deutschen, zu Anfang des zwei und zwanzigsten Jahrhunderts, unter ihrem fünften Reichsvogte," in Lauth and Gliwitzky, eds., *Nachgelassene Schriften*, 9:388–89.

98   Ibid., 9:387–89.

99   Ibid., 9:387.

100   Ibid., 9:387, 389.

101   Ibid., 9:416.

102   Ibid., 9:419.

103   Ibid., 9:423.

104   Ibid., 9:392.

105   For an entry into this literature, see Karen Hagemann and Jean Quataert, eds., *Gendering Modern German History* (Ann Arbor, Mich., 2007). For an extended analysis of Fichte, see Isabel V. Hull, *Sexuality, State, and Civil Society in Germany, 1700-1815* (Ithaca, N.Y., 1996), 314-23.

106   Fichte, "Die Republik der Deutschen," 9:384, 394.

107   Ibid., 9:393.

108   Johann Gottlieb Fichte, "Deliberation über politische Objekte," in *J. G. Fichte Kritische Gesamtausgabe*, series II, vol. 10, *Nachgelassene Schriften 1806-1807*, ed. Hans Gliwitzky and Reinhard Lauth (Stuttgart, 1994), 298. The quotations are from Johann Gottlieb Fichte, *Reden an die deutsche Nation*, in Fichte, *Werke 1808-1812*, ed. Reinhard Lauth et al., in J. G. Fichte, *Gesamtausgabe*, series I, vol. 10 (Stuttgart, 2005), 106, 112. For the broader context of the *Addresses*, see Jörg Echternkamp, *Der Aufstieg des deutschen Nationalismus, 1740-1840* (Frankfurt am Main, 1998), 216-75; Levinger, *Enlightened Nationalism*, 97-126; and, still classic, Aira Kemiläinen, *Auffassungen über die Sendung des deutschen Volkes um die Wende des 18. und 19. Jahrhunderts* (Helsinki, 1956).

109   Carl von Clausewitz, *Historische Briefe über die großen Kriegsereignisse im Oktober 1806*, ed. Joachim Niemeyer (Bonn, 1977), 72.

110   Carl von Clausewitz, *Politische Schriften und Briefe*, ed. Hans Rothfels (Munich, 1922), 20.

111   Ibid., 29-34.

112   Cited in Clark, *Iron Kingdom*, 326.

113   Cited in Michael Stolleis, *Geschichte des öffentlichen Rechts in Deutschland* (Munich, 1992), 2:61.

114   Josef Leo Koerner, *Caspar David Friedrich and the Subject of Landscape* (London, 1990), 10-11.

115   On Kleist as a soldier-poet, the fundamental work remains Wolf Kittler, *Die Geburt des Partisanen aus dem Geist der Poesie: Heinrich von Kleist und die Strategie der Befreiungskriege* (Freiburg im Breisgau, 1987). For a fine biographical treatment, see Gerhard Schulz, *Kleist* (Munich, 2007).

116   On religion and ideas of nationhood in the early nineteenth century, see Wolfgang Altgeld, *Katholizismus, Protestantismus, Judentum: Über religiös begründete Gegensätze und nationalreligiöse Ideen in der Geschichte des deutschen Nationalismus* (Mainz, 1992).

117   Heinrich von Kleist, "Die Hermannsschlacht," in *Sämtliche Werke und Briefe*, ed. Helmut Sembder (Munich, 1984), 1:628.

118   Stefan Nienhaus, *Geschichte der deutschen Tischgesellschaft* (Tübingen, 2003), 351-73, 14-24.

119   Helmut Walser Smith, *The Continuities of German History: Nation, Religion, and Race Across the Long Nineteenth Century* (New York, 2008), 101-2.

120   Gustav Seibt, *Goethe und Napoleon: Eine historische Begegnung* (Munich, 2008), 55, and, on Goethe's *Dichtung und Wahrheit*, 172, 179.

121   Jean Paul, *Friedenspredigt an Deutschland* (Heidelberg, 1808), 7.

122   Hagemann, *"Mannlicher Muth und Teutsche Ehre,"* 115.

123   Ernst Moritz Arndt, "Letztes Wort an die Deutschen," in *Ausgewählte Werke* 10:118-89.

124   Cited in Hagemann, *"Mannlicher Muth und Teutsche Ehre,"* 192.

125   Jakob Walter, *The Diary of a Napoleonic Foot Soldier*, ed. Marc Raeff (New York, 1991), 81.

126   Cited in Clark, *Iron Kingdom*, 359.

127 The appeal published in *Schlesische Privilegierte Zeitung*, no. 34, March 13, 1813.

128 Hagemann, *"Mannlicher Muth und Teutsche Ehre,"* 132.

129 Emil Peschel, ed., *Theodor Körners Tagebuch und Kriegslieder aus dem Jahre 1813* (Freiburg im Breisgau, 1893), 95-96.

130 Carl Schmitt, *Theorie des Partisanen*, 6th ed. (Berlin, 2006), 39.

131 Hagemann, *"Mannlicher Muth und Teutsche Ehre,"* 139.

132 Ibid., 384-85.

133 Estimated by Peter Brandt, *Deutschland an der Schwelle zur Moderne: Deutschland um 1800* (Bonn, 1999), 101.

134 Ibid.

135 Thomas Abbt, "Vom Tode für das Vaterland," in *Aufklärung und Kriegserfahrung: Klassische Zeitzeugen zum Siebenjährigen Krieg*, ed. Johannes Kunisch (Frankfurt am Main, 1996), 595.

136 Cited in Anne-Charlott Trepp, *Sanfte Männlichkeit und selbständige Weiblichkeit: Frauen und Männer im Hamburger Bürgertum zwischen 1770 und 1840* (Göttingen, 1996), 275.

137 On women's organizations, see Dirk Alexander Reder, *Frauenbewegung und Nation: Patriotische Frauenvereine in Deutschland im frühen 19. Jahrhundert, 1813-1830* (Cologne, 1998), 489-503. On the topic of women and national sacrifice in the nineteenth century, see especially Jean H. Quataert, *Staging Philanthropy: Patriotic Women and the National Imagination in Dynastic Germany, 1813-1916* (Ann Arbor, Mich., 2001).

138 Rahel Levin to Karl Gustav von Brinckmann, cited in Heidi Thomann Tewarson, *Rahel Varnhagen* (Reinbek, 1988), 92-93.

139 Levin to Karl August Varnhagen von Ense, in Barbara Hahn, ed., *Rahel: Ein Buch des Andenkens für ihre Freunde*, 6 vols. (Göttingen, 2011), 3:24.

140 Levin to Sophie von Grotthuß, 2 March 1814, in ibid., 3:81.

141 Levin to Marcus Theodor, 16 August 1813, in Renata Buzzo Màrgari Barovero, ed., *Rahel Levin Varnhagen, Familienbriefe* (Munich, 2009), 319; Levin to Theodor, 19 November 1813, in ibid., 348.

142 Levin to Karl August Varnhagen, 4 October 1813, in Hahn, ed., *Rahel: Ein Buch des Andenkens*, 3:12; Levin to Ludwig Robert, early May 1814, in ibid., 3:118.

143 Levin to Theodor, 16 August 1813, in Barovero, ed., *Rahel Levin Varnhagen, Familienbriefe*, 320 and (commentary) 1166.

144 Levin to Varnhagen, 4 October 1813, in Hahn, ed., *Rahel: Ein Buch des Andenkens*, 3:12.

145 Prince de Metternich, *Mémoires, documents et écrits divers*, 8 vols. (Paris, 1880), 1:151.

146 Ibid.

147 Ibid., 1:152.

148 Levin to Ludwig Robert, early May 1814, in *Rahel Levin Varnhagen, Briefwechsel mit Ludwig Robert*, ed. Consolina Vigliero (Munich, 2001), 123.

149 Ibid.

150 *De l'Allemagne*, 188, 147.

151 On her famous Faust chapter, see John C. Isbell, "The First French Faust: *De l'Allemagne*'s Faust Chapter, 1810/1814," *French Studies* 45, no. 4 (1991): 417-34. See also Isbell, *The Birth of European Romanticism*, 93.

152 *De l'Allemagne*, 733.

153 Ibid., 729.

154 Levin to Varnhagen, 23 May 1814, in Hahn, ed., *Rahel: Ein Buch des Andenkens*, 3:125-28.

PART III. THE AGE OF NATIONALISM: PREFACE

1   Heinrich Heine to Julius Campe, 20 February 1844, cited in Gerhard Höhn, *Heine-Handbuch: Zeit, Person, Werk*, 2nd ed. (Stuttgart, 1997), 115. On the genre, see Friedrich Sengle, *Biedermeierzeit: Deutsche Literatur im Spannungs-feld zwischen Restauration und Revolution, 1815-1848*, vol. 2, *Die Formenwelt, 1815-1848* (Stuttgart, 1971), 241.

2   Heinrich Heine, *Säkularausgabe, Werke, Briefwechsel, Lebenszeugnisse*, ed. Klassik Stiftung Weimar and Centre National de la Recherche Scientifique, vol. 2, *Gedichte 1827-1844 und Versepen* (Berlin, 1979), 359-63, stanza 298 (hereafter cited as HH, *Säkularausgabe*).

3   Ibid., 304.

4   Ibid., 310.

5   Ibid., 317, 318.

6   Ibid., 347.

7   The counts are 667 and 308, respectively, according to searches in http://hhp .uni-trier.de/Projekte/HHP, using the Düsseldorf edition of Heine's works, and "Goethes Werke im WWW," based on the Weimar edition of Goethe's work, and searching only the literary work.

8   HH, *Säkularausgabe*, 2:347.

9   Heine to Jacques-Julien Dubochet, 29 August 1848, in HH, *Säkularausgabe*, 22:289.

10   Immanuel Kant, "Beantwortung der Frage: Was ist Aufklärung?," *Berlinische Monatsschrift* 4 (1784): 481-94.

11   Tara Zahra, "Imagined Noncommunities: National Indifference as a Category of Analysis," *Slavic Review* 69, no. 1 (Spring 2010): 93-119.

12   Wolfgang Menzel, *Die deutsche Literatur*, 2 vols. (Stuttgart, 1828), 1:1.

13   The conflict catalogue can be accessed at https://brecke.inta.gatech.edu/research/ conflict/.

14   This is the argument of Siegfried Weichlein, *Nation und Region: Integrationsproz-esse im Bismarckreich* (Düsseldorf, 2004).

CHAPTER 7. DEVELOPING NATION (C. 1815-1850)

1   Hannah Arendt, "Friedrich von Gentz: On the 100th Anniversary of His Death, June 9, 1932," in *Reflections on Literature and Culture* (Palo Alto, Calif., 2007), 31.

2   Friedrich von Gentz, *The Origin and Principles of the American Revolution Com-pared with the Origin and Principles of the French Revolution*, trans. John Quincy Adams, ed. Peter Koslowski (Indianapolis, 2010), esp. 53, 63, 67.

3   Friedrich von Gentz, *Fragmente aus der neuesten Geschichte des politischen Gleich-gewichts in Europa*, in *Staatsschriften und Briefe*, ed. Hans von Eckart (Munich, 1921), 1:106-7, 111, 112.

4   Ibid., 1:132-33, 139.

5   Friedrich Gentz to Rahel Varnhagen, 1803, in Rahel Varnhagen, *Briefwechsel*, vol. 3, *Rahel und ihre Freunde*, ed. Friedhelm Kemp (Munich, 1979), 122.

6   See especially Barbara Hahn, *Antworten Sie mir: Rahel Levin Varnhagens Brief-wechsel* (Frankfurt am Main, 1990), 77-99.

7   Ibid., 79-80.

8   Paul W. Schroeder, *The Transformation of European Politics, 1763-1848* (Oxford, 1994), 539.

9 For a precise listing of the territorial changes, see Ernst Rudolf Huber, *Deutsche Verfassungsgeschichte seit 1789*, vol. 1, 2nd ed., *Reform und Restauration, 1789 bis 1830* (Stuttgart, 1960), 577.

10 Rahel Levin to Markus Theodor Robert, 15 January 1815, in Barbara Hahn, ed., *Rahel: Ein Buch des Andenkens für ihre Freunde*, 6 vols. (Göttingen, 2011), 3:181–82; Levin to Markus Theodor Robert, 13 June 1814, in ibid., 3:135.

11 Cited in Golo Mann, *Secretary of Europe: The Life of Friedrich Gentz, Enemy of Napoleon*, trans. William H. Woglom (New Haven, 1946), 216.

12 Adam Zamoyski, *Rites of Peace: The Fall of Napoleon and the Congress of Vienna* (New York, 2007), 407; Christopher Clark, *Iron Kingdom: The Rise and Downfall of Prussia, 1600–1947* (Cambridge, Mass., 2006), 389.

13 Inge Schlieper, "Die Diskussion um die territoriale Neuordnung des Rheinlandes, 1813–1815" (Ph.D. diss. University of Cologne, 1971), 18–19.

14 Mann, *Secretary of Europe*, 216.

15 Daniel-Erasmus Kahn, *Die deutschen Staatsgrenzen: Rechtshistorische Grundlagen und offene Rechtsfragen* (Tübingen, 2004), 124–25, 141–60.

16 Ibid., 372.

17 *British Envoys to Germany, 1816–1866*, vol. 2, *1830–1847*, ed. Markus Mösslang, Sabine Freitag, and Peter Wende (Cambridge, 2002), 107n234.

18 Jordan Branch, *The Cartographic State: Maps, Territory, and the Origins of Sovereignty* (Cambridge, 2014), 135–38.

19 Dieter Gosewinkel and Johannes Masing, eds., *Die Verfassungen in Europa, 1789–1949* (Munich, 2006), 740.

20 Huber, *Deutsche Verfassungsgeschichte*, 1:610–11; Heinrich August Winkler, *Geschichte des Westens* (Munich, 2009), 1:458.

21 Jürgen Osterhammel, *Die Verwandlung der Welt: Eine Geschichte des 19. Jahrhunderts* (Munich, 2009), 1134.

22 Steven M. Press, "False Fire: The Wartburg Book-Burning of 1817," *Central European History* 42, no. 4 (2009): 621–46.

23 Friedrich Gentz, "Über das Wartburgfest," in *Staatsschriften und Briefe* (Munich, 1921), 2:32, 34, 42, 47–48.

24 The term comes from Steven Press's article "False Fire."

25 George S. Williamson, "What Killed August von Kotzebue? The Temptations of Virtue and the Political Theology of German Nationalism, 1789–1819," *Journal of Modern History* 72, no. 4 (2000): 890–943.

26 "Karlsbader Beschlüsse: Untersuchungsgesetz, 20 September 1819," in Huber, *Deutsche Verfassungsgeschichte*, 1:746–47.

27 Dieter Düding, *Organisierter gesellschaftlicher Nationalismus in Deutschland (1808–1847): Bedeutung und Funktion der Turner- und Sängervereine für die deutsche Nationalbewegung* (Munich, 1984), 67.

28 Cited in Peter Paret, *Clausewitz and the State: The Man, His Theories, and His Times*, 2nd ed. (Princeton, N.J., 1985), 281.

29 Ludwig Robert to Rahel Levin, 28 August 1819, in Rahel Levin Varnhagen, *Briefwechsel mit Ludwig Robert*, ed. Consolina Vigliero (Munich, 2001), 240–42.

30 Levin to Robert, 29 August 1819, in ibid., 243–44.

31 Hermann Glaser, *Kleinstadt-Ideologie: Zwischen Furschenglück und Sphärenflug* (Freiburg im Breisgau, 1969), cited in Mack Walker, *German Hometowns: Community, State and General Estate, 1648–1871* (Ithaca, N.Y., 1971), 324.

32 On the origins of the term "Biedermeier," see Friedrich Sengle, *Biedermeierzeit: Deutsche Literatur im Spannungsfeld zwischen Restauration und Revolution,*

1815–1848 (Stuttgart, 1971), vol. 1, *Allgemeine Voraussetzungen, Richtungen, Darstellungsmittel*, 121, 77–100.

33   Ibid., 1:111–12.

34   Ibid., 1:268. For the numbers, see Hans-Ulrich Wehler, *Gesellschaftsgeschichte*, vol. 2, *Von der Reformära bis zur industriellen und politischen "Deutschen Doppelrevolution," 1815–1845/49* (Munich, 1987), 524; *Handbuch der deutschen Bildungsgeschichte*, vol. 3, *1800–1870: Von der Neuordnung Deutschlands bis zur Gründung des Deutschen Reiches*, ed. Karl-Ernst Jeismann and Peter Lundgreen (Munich, 1987), 382.

35   Wolfgang Menzel, *Die deutsche Literatur* (Stuttgart, 1828), 3–4; for the exact formulation, see Wolfgang Menzel, "Dichtkunst," in *Literaturblatt auf das Jahr 1828* (Stuttgart, 1828), 66.

36   Menzel, *Die deutsche Literatur*, 3–4.

37   *Handbuch der deutschen Bildungsgeschichte*, 3:383; Wehler, *Gesellschaftsgeschichte*, 2:522–23.

38   James Brophy, *Popular Culture and the Public Sphere in the Rhineland* (New York, 2007), 24.

39   Wehler, *Gesellschaftsgeschichte*, 2:522.

40   Brophy, *Popular Culture*, 1–2.

41   Theodore S. Hamerow, *The Birth of a New Europe: State and Society in the Nineteenth Century* (Chapel Hill, N.C., 1989), 152.

42   See especially the essays in Hans Erich Bödeker, ed., *Alphabetisierung und Literalisierung in Deutschland in der Frühen Neuzeit* (Tübingen, 1999). For Austria, see the statistics, drawn from a later date, in Norbert Bachleitner, Franz M. Eybl, and Ernst Fischer, *Geschichte des Buchhandels in Österreich* (Wiesbaden, 2000), 235.

43   Hartmut Titze, *Die Politisierung der Erziehung: Untersuchungen über die soziale und politische Funktion der Erziehung von der Aufklärung bis zum Hochkapitalismus* (Frankfurt am Main, 1973), 82.

44   Kenneth Barkin, "Social Control and the Volksschule in Vormärz Prussia," *Central European History* 16, no. 1 (1983): 41.

45   Frank-Michael Kuhlemann, *Modernisierung und Disziplinierung: Sozialgeschichte des preußichen Volksschulwesens, 1794–1872* (Göttingen, 1992), 107–8; Peter Lundgreen, *Sozialgeschichte der deutschen Schule im Überblick* (Götttingen, 1981), 81–87.

46   Cited in Thomas Nipperdey, "Volksschule und Revolution im Vormärz: Eine Fallstudie zur Modernisierung II," in *Gesellschaft, Kultur, Theorie* (Göttingen, 1976), 206.

47   Wehler, *Gesellschaftsgeschichte*, 2:380.

48   Otto Weitzel, *Entwicklung der Staatsausgaben in Deutschland* (Erlangen, 1967), 236, table 1a.

49   Wehler, *Gesellschaftsgeschichte*, 2:383.

50   Michael Mann, *Sources of Social Power*, vol. 2, *The Rise of Classes and Nation-States, 1760–1914* (Cambridge, 1993), 366.

51   Ute Frevert, *Die Kasernierte Nation: Militärdienst und Zivilgesellschaft in Deutschland* (Munich, 2001), 71–95; Wehler, *Gesellschaftsgeschichte*, 2:384.

52   Charles Tilly, *Coercion, Capital, and European States: AD 990–1992*, rev. ed. (London, 1992), 230.

53   James M. Brophy, "Violence Between Civilians and State Authorities in the Prussian Rhineland, 1830–1848," *Central European History* 22, no. 1 (2004): 1–35.

54   Alf Ludtke, *Police and State in Prussia, 1815–1850*, trans. Peter Burgess (New York, 1989), 137–38.

55 Mann, *Sources of Social Power*, 2:373.

56 Ibid., 2:376-77.

57 Herbert Grundmann, *Monumenta Germaniae Historica, 1819-1969* (Munich, 1969), 2.

58 Georg Kunz, *Verortete Geschichte: Regionales Geschichtsbewußtsein in den deutschen historischen Vereinen des 19. Jahrhunderts* (Göttingen, 2000); Susan A. Crane, *Collecting and Historical Consciousness in Early Nineteenth-Century Germany* (Ithaca, N.Y., 2000).

59 On Schinkel's "liberation cathedral," see Barry Bergdoll, *Karl Friedrich Schinkel: An Architecture for Prussia* (New York, 1994), 40-41. On the Cologne Cathedral, see Michael James Lewis, "August Reichensperger (1808-1895) and the Gothic Revival" (Ph.D. diss., University of Pennsylvania, Philadelphia, 1989), 52-53.

60 Uwe Heckmann, *Die Sammlung Boisserée: Konzeption und Rezeptionsgeschichte einer romantischen Kunstsammlung zwischen 1804 und 1827* (Munich, 2003).

61 Gustav Friedrich Waagen, *Kunstwerke und Künstler in Deutschland*, 2 vols. (Leipzig, 1843-1845), 1:319, 117.

62 *The Complete First Edition of the Original Folk and Fairy Tales of the Brothers Grimm*, trans. Jack Zipes (Princeton, N.J., 2014), 3.

63 See, for this argument, John Toews, *Becoming Historical: Cultural Reformation and Public Memory in Early Nineteenth-Century Berlin* (Cambridge, 2004), 323-29; Gerhard Schulz, *Die deutsche Literatur zwischen Französischer Revolution und Restauration* (Munich, 1989), 2:267-68.

64 The best short introduction remains Heinz Rölleke, *Die Märchen der Brüder Grimm*, 4th ed. (Stuttgart, 2004).

65 Michael Schmitt, *Die Illustrierten Rhein-Beschreibungen* (Cologne, 1996), xvii. On Lang, see Jörg Ulrich Fechner, *Erfahrene und erfundene Landschaft: Aurelio de' Giorgi Bertolas Deutschlandbild und die Begründung der Rheinromantik* (Opladen, 1974), 124-29.

66 Charles Rosen, *The Romantic Generation* (Cambridge, 1995), 116-236, esp. 160; W. G. Fearnside, ed., *Tombleson's "Views of the Rhine"* (London, 1932), 176-77.

67 Karl Simrock, *Das malerische und romantische Rheinland* (Leipzig, 1838), 7-8.

68 Karl Geib, *Malerische Wanderungen am Rhein von Constanz bis Cöln* (Karlsruhe, 1838).

69 Karl Baedeker, *Rheinreise von Basel bis Düsseldorf*, 6th ed. (Koblenz, 1849), ii-iii.

70 Ibid., vii.

71 Cited in Horst Johannes Tümmers, *Der Rhein: Ein europäischer Fluß und seine Geschichte* (Munich, 1994), 212.

72 Richard W. Gassen and Bernhard Holeczek, eds., *Mythos Rhein: Ein Fluß in Kitsch und Kommerz* (Ludwigshafen, 1985).

73 Simon Schama, *Landscape and Memory* (New York, 1996), 411-513; Byron cited in Andrew Beattie, *The Alps: A Cultural History* (Oxford, 2006), 127; Marjorie Hope Nicolson, *Mountain Gloom and Mountain Glory: The Development of the Aesthetics of the Sublime* (Ithaca, N.Y., 1959).

74 Jon Mathieu, *History of the Alps, 1500-1900*, trans. Matthew Vester (Morgantown, W.Va., 2009), 83-113.

75 Otto Uhlig, *Die Schwabenkinder aus Tirol und Vorarlberg* (Innsbruck, 1978).

76 Joseph Leo Koerner, *Caspar David Friedrich and the Subject of Landscape* (London, 1990), 119; Adam Müller, "Etwas über Landschaftsmalerei," in *Kritische/ ästhetische und philosophische Schriften* (Newied, 1967), 2:188-89. See also Wolfgang Ullrich, *Die Geschichte der Unschärfe* (Berlin, 2002), 9.

77 Jost Hermand, "Die touristische Erschließung und Nationalisierung des Harzes im 18. Jahrhundert," in *Reise und soziale Realität am Ende des 18. Jahrhunderts*, ed. Wolfgang Griep and Hans-Wolf Jäger (Heidelberg, 1963), 176.

78 Friedrich Dennert, *Geschichte des Brockens und der Brockenreisen* (Braunschweig, 1954), 17.

79 Johann Wolfgang Goethe to Charlotte von Stein, 10 and 11 December 1777, in Johann Wolfgang Goethe, *Briefe* (Hamburger Ausgabe), ed. Karl Robert Mandelkow, 4th ed. (Munich, 1988), 1:246–47; Goethe to Johann Heinrich Merck, 5 August 1777, in ibid., 1:253.

80 On this day, Heinrich Heine climbed the mountain. For the list of the others, see HH, *Säkularausgabe*, vol. 5, *Reisebilder I, 1824–1828, Kommentar*, ed. Sikander Singh and Christa Stöcker (Berlin, 2009), 154–55.

81 C. E. Nehse, ed., *Brocken-Stammbuch* (Sondershausen, 1850).

82 HH, *Säkularausgabe*, 5:40.

83 On Heine's Biedermeier side, see Sengle, *Biedermeierzeit*, 1:111.

84 HH, *Säkularauraausgabe*, 5:40

85 Ibid.; Sengle, *Biedermeierzeit*, 2:259.

86 On the eighteenth-century background, see Michael Williams, "Forests," in *The Earth as Transformed by Human Action: Global and Regional Changes in the Biosphere in the Past 300 Years*, ed. B. L. Turner II et al. (Cambridge, 1990), 181. More generally, see H. C. Darby, "The Clearing of the Woodland in Europe," in *Man's Role in Changing the Face of the Earth*, ed. William L. Thomas (Chicago, 1956), 183–216.

87 Michael Williams, *Deforesting the Earth: From Prehistory to Global Crisis* (Chicago, 2003), 160–67. Williams, "Forests," 181, assumes that circa 1800 peninsular and insular Europe was about 10 percent covered, France and the lands of Austria and Germany about 25 percent, and eastern Europe between one- and two-thirds.

88 Reinhold Reith, *Umweltgeschichte der frühen Neuzeit* (Munich, 2011), 103–13.

89 James C. Scott, *Seeing like a State: How Certain Schemes to Improve the Human Condition Have Failed* (New Haven, 1998), 18–19; Henry E. Lowood, "The Calculating Forester: Quantification, Cameral Science, and the Emergence of Scientific Forestry Management in Germany," in *The Quantifying Spirit in the Eighteenth Century*, ed. Tore Frangsmyer et al. (Berkeley, Calif., 1990), 329, 318.

90 Elias Canetti, *Masse und Macht* (Hamburg, 1960), 202.

91 George Eliot, "Three Months in Weimar" in *Works*, vol. 20, *Essays and Leaves from a Notebook* (Boston, 1900), 191.

92 Charles Sealsfield, *Austria as It Is: or Sketches of Continental Courts*, in *Sämtliche Werke*, ed. Karl J. R. Arndt (Hildesheim, 1972), 144.

93 Ibid., 85.

94 Frederik Ohles, *Germany's Rude Awakening: Censorship in the Land of the Brothers Grimm* (Kent, Ohio, 1992), 52–53, 169.

95 Charles Tilly, Louise Tilly, and Richard Tilly, *The Rebellious Century, 1830–1930* (Cambridge, Mass., 1975), 218. On Austria, see Pieter M. Judson, *The Habsburg Empire: A New History* (Cambridge, Mass., 2016), 134.

96 Heinrich Volkmann, "Protesträger und Protestformen in den Unruhen 1830–1832," in *Sozialer Protest: Studien zu traditioneller Resistenz und kollektiver Gewalt in Deutschland vom Vormärz bis zur Reichsgründung*, ed. Heinrich Volkmann and Jürgen Bergmann (Opladen, 1984), 56–75.

97   Ernst Rolf Huber, *Deutsche Verfassungsgeschichte seit 1789*, vol. 2, *Der Kampf um Einheit und Freiheit, 1830 bis 1850* (Stuttgart, 1960), 175–77.

98   Ibid.

99   According to Frank Thomas Hoefer, *Pressepolitik und Polizeistaat Metternichs* (Munich, 1983), 26, there were 40,000 Germans in Switzerland before 1848, 13,000 in Belgium in 1846, and 170,000 in France (including 62,000 in Paris) in 1847.

100   David Blackbourn, *The Long Nineteenth Century: A History of Germany, 1780–1918* (London, 1997), 194. On German Paris, see especially Mareike König, ed., *Deutsche Handwerker, Arbeiter und Dienstmädchen in Paris: Eine vergessene Migration im 19. Jahrhundert* (Munich, 2003).

101   Peter J. Katzenstein, *Disjoined Partners: Austria and Germany since 1815* (Berkeley, Calif., 1976), 57.

102   "Denkschrift über die gegenwärtigen Zustände der Zensur in Österreich," in Eduard von Bauernfeld, *Gesammelte Aufsätze*, ed. Stefan Hock (Vienna, 1905), 1–27. On censorship, see James M. Brophy, "Grautöne: Verleger und Zensurregime in Mitteleuropa 1800–1850," *Historische Zeitschrift* 301, no. 2 (2015): 297–346.

103   Katzenstein, *Disjoined Partners*, 39.

104   Thomas Cartwright to Viscount Palmerston, 20 April 1833, in Mösslang, Freitag, and Wende, eds., *British Envoys to Germany*, 2:49.

105   Georg Büchner, "Der Hessische Landbote," in Büchner, *Sämtliche Werke, Briefe und Dokumente*, 2 vols., ed. Henri Poschmann, vol. 2, *Schriften, Briefe, Dokumente* (Frankfurt am Main, 1999), 54, 55, 61. See also, for context, James M. Brophy, "Der Hessische Landbote and the Landscape of Radical Print, 1830–1834," in *"Friede den Hütten, Krieg den Palästen": Der Hessische Landbote in interdisziplinärer Perspektive*, ed. Markus May, Udo Roth, and Gideon Stiening (Heidelberg, 2016), 67–94.

106   Büchner, "Der Hessische Landbote," 2:66.

107   For an explicit comparison of the prison scenes in the two dramatic fragments, see Helmut Walser Smith, "The Confinement of Tragedy: Between *Urfaust* and *Woyzeck*," in *Tragedy and the Tragic in German Literature, Art, and Thought*, ed. Stephen D. Dowden and Thomas P. Quinn (Rochester, N.Y., 2015), 21–39.

108   George Steiner, *The Death of Tragedy* (New York, 1961), 274.

109   Aristotle, "Poetics," ch. 15, in *The Basic Works of Aristotle*, ed. Richard McKeon (New York, 2001), 1470.

110   Hans Jürgen Teuteberg and Günter Wiegelmann, *Nahrungsgewohnheiten in der Industrialisierung des 19. Jahrhunderts*, 2nd ed. (Münster, 2005), 165–77.

111   Wilhelm Abel, *Massenarmut und Hungerkrisen im vorindustriellen Europa* (Hamburg, 1974), 369–70, 376.

112   Stephen Broadberry, Rainer Fremdling, and Peter Solar, "Industry," in *The Cambridge Economic History of Modern Europe*, ed. Stephen Broadberry and Kevin H. O'Rourke (Cambridge, 2010), 1:172.

113   "GDP per Person," available at http://www.gapminder.org/data/.

114   Robert C. Allen, "The Great Divergence in European Wages and Prices from the Middle Ages to the First World War," *Explorations in Economic History* 38 (2001): 416; Carole Shammas, "Standard of Living, Consumption, and Political Economy over the Past 500 Years," in *The Oxford Handbook of the History of Consumption*, ed. Frank Trentman (Oxford, 2012), 218–19.

115   Etienne van de Walle, "Historical Demography," in *Handbook of Population*, ed. Dudley L. Poston and Michael Micklin (New York, 2005), 591–92; Loftur Guttormsson, "Parent-Child Relations" in *Family Life in the Long Nineteenth Cen-*

tury, ed. David I. Kertzer and Mario Barbagli (New Haven, 2002), 254–55; Şevket Pamuk and Jan Luiten van Zanden, "Standards of Living," in *The Cambridge Economic History of Modern Europe*, 227.

116   "Infant Mortality Rate (per 1,000 Live Births)," available at http://www .gapminder.org/data/.

117   Pamuk and van Zanden, "Standards of Living," 227.

118   Roderick Floud, Robert W. Fogel, Bernard Harris, and Sok Chul Hong, *The Changing Body: Health, Nutrition, and Human Development in the Western World since 1700* (Cambridge, 2011), 230; Jörg Baten and John E. Murray, "Heights of Men and Women in 19th-Century Bavaria: Economic, Nutritional, and Disease Influences," *Explorations in Economic History* 37 (2000): 364; Sophia Twarog, "Heights and Living Standards in Germany, 1850–1939: The Case of Württemberg," in *Health and Welfare During Industrialization*, ed. Richard H. Steckel and Roderick Floud (Chicago, 1997), 297.

119   John Komlos, "Stature and Nutrition in the Habsburg Monarchy: The Standard of Living and Economic Development in the Eighteenth Century," *American Historical Review* 90 (1985): 1155; Gregory Clark, *A Farewell to Alms: A Brief Economic History of the World* (Princeton, N.J., 2007), 55–57.

120   W. O. Henderson, *Friedrich List: Economist and Visionary, 1789–1846* (London, 1983), 20–28. On List, see the succinct analysis in Roman Szporluk, *Communism and Nationalism: Karl Marx versus Friedrich List* (Oxford, 1993).

121   James M. Brophy, "The End of the Economic Old Order: The Great Transition, 1750–1860," in *The Oxford Handbook of Modern German History*, ed. Helmut Walser Smith (Oxford, 2011), 188–89.

122   Friedrich List, *Le Système naturel d'économie politique*, in *Schriften, Reden, Briefe*, ed. Erwin V. Beckerath et al., vol. 4 (Berlin, 1927), 326, 327.

123   Friedrich List, *Das nationale System der politischen Ökonomie*, in ibid., vol. 6 (Berlin, 1930), 156.

124   List, *Le Système naturel d'économie politique*, in ibid., 4:182, 183.

125   Friedrich List, *Das deutsche National-Transport-System in volks- und staatswirtschaftlicher Beziehung* (Altona, 1838), 6.

126   Friedrich List, "Ein sächsisches Eisenbahnsystem," in Beckerath et al., eds., *Schriften, Reden, Briefe*, vol. 3 (Berlin, 1929), 165; List, "Die Eisenbahn von Mannheim nach Basel, " in ibid., 3:239; List, "Deutschlands Eisenbahnsystem in militärischer Beziehung," in ibid., 3:260–69.

127   Gertrude Himmelfarb, *The Idea of Poverty: England in the Early Industrial Age* (New York, 1984), 3.

128   There is no one place to consider all of these thinkers. The best place to start, however, is the broad background sketched out in Jonathan Sperber, *Karl Marx: A Nineteenth-Century Life* (New York, 2013).

129   Johann Fr. Geist and Klaus Kürvers, eds., *Das Berliner Mietshaus*, vol. 1, *1740–1862* (Munich, 1980), esp. 242–74.

130   Bettina von Arnim, *Werke*, vol. 3, *Politische Schriften*, ed. Wolfgang Bunzel et al. (Frankfurt am Main, 1991), 331–68.

131   Ibid., 3:411.

132   Ibid., 3:331.

133   Ibid., 3:514.

134   Ibid., 3:528.

135   Convincingly argued in Christina von Hodenberg, *Aufstand der Weber: Die Revolte von 1844 und ihr Aufstieg zum Mythos* (Bonn, 1997).

136   HH, *Säkularausgabe*, vol. 2, *Gedichte 1827–1844 und Versepen*, 137.

137 Some 80 percent of the riots in 1847 in the territory of what would become Imperial Germany occurred in this belt (unfortunately, we do not know the corresponding figures for the Habsburg lands). They peaked early in April and May 1847 and then returned again between March and May 1848. See Manfred Gailus, *Straße und Brot: Sozialer Protest in den deutschen Staaten unter besonderer Berücksichtigung Preußens, 1847–1849* (Göttingen, 1990), 214, 78.

138 On anti-Semitic riots, see especially Manfred Gailus, "Anti-Jewish Emotion and Violence in the 1848 Crisis of German Society," in *Exclusionary Violence: Antisemitic Riots in Modern German History*, ed. Christhard Hoffmann, Werner Bergmann, and Helmut Walser Smith (Ann Arbor, Mich., 2002), 43–66.

139 As put by the radical democrat Maximilian Reinganum during the Pre-Parliament. See *Verhandlungen des Deutschen Parlaments*, 2nd ed. (Frankfurt am Main, 1848), 21.

140 "Dangerous experiment" comes from Earl of Westmoreland to Viscount Palmerston, 6 April 1848, in *British Envoys to Germany, 1816–1866*, vol. 3, *1848–1850*, ed. Markus Mösslang, Torsten Riotte, and Hagen Schulze (Cambridge, 2006), 117. On nineteenth-century suffrage regimes, see Wolfgang Reinhard, *Geschichte der Staatsgewalt: Eine vergleichende Verfassungsgeschichte Europas von den Anfängen bis zur Gegenwart* (Munich, 2002), 432–33.

141 Thomas Nipperdey, *Deutsche Geschichte 1800–1866* (Munich, 1983), 609.

142 Dieter Gosewinkel and Johannes Masing, eds., *Die Verfassungen in Europa, 1789–1949* (Munich, 2006), 775.

143 Georg Herwegh, "Das Reden nimmt kein End," in *Deutsche Londoner Zeitung: Blätter für Politik, Literatur und Kunst,* 7 July 1848 (no. 170), 680.

144 Nipperdey, *Deutsche Geschichte, 1800–1866,* 599.

145 On the turn in German nationalist sentiment, see Judson, *The Habsburg Empire*, 208–9.

146 For casualties at Custoza, see Otto Berndt, *Die Zahl im Kriege: Statistische Daten aus der neueren Kriegsgeschichte in graphischer Darstellung* (Vienna, 1897), 60.

147 Wolfgang Häusler, "Wien," in *1848: Revolution in Deutschland*, ed. Christoph Dipper and Ulrich Speck (Frankfurt am Main, 1998), 107.

148 Wolfgang Häusler, *Von der Massenarmut zur Arbeiterbewegung: Demokratie und soziale Frage in der Wiener Revolution von 1848* (Vienna, 1979), 395–96.

149 Summaries of these proposals are in Paul Wentzke, *Kritische Bibliographie der Flugschriften zur deutschen Verfassungsfrage, 1848–1851* (Halle, 1911).

150 *Stenographischer Bericht über die Verhandlungen der deutschen constituirenden Nationalversammlung zu Frankfurt am Main* (Leipzig, 1848), 2:1127.

151 Ibid., 2:1143.

152 Ibid., 2:1144.

153 Ibid., 2:1145.

154 Judson, *The Habsburg Empire*, 212–14.

155 See Heinrich Best, "Strukturen parlamentarischer Repräsentation in den Revolutionen von 1848," in *Europa in den Revolutionen von 1848: Revolution und Reform*, ed. Dieter Dowe et al. (Bonn, 1998), 662–64; Heinrich Best, *Die Männer von Bildung und Besitz: Struktur und Handeln parlamentarischer Führungsgruppen in Deutschland und Frankreich 1848/49* (Düsseldorf, 1990), 439–45.

156 Mapped out in Best, "Strukturen parlamentarischer Repräsentation in den Revolutionen von 1848," 662–64.

157 Cited in Wolfram Siemann, *Die deutsche Revolution von 1848/49* (Frankfurt am Main, 1985), 203.

158 A stirring account is in Friedrich Engels to Jenny Marx, 25 July 1849, in *MEGA (Marx-Engels Gesamtausgabe)*, sect. 3, vol. 3, *Briefwechsel, Januar 1849 bis Dezember 1850* (Berlin, 1981), 30.

159 Wolfgang von Hippel, *Revolutionen im deutschen Südwesten* (Stuttgart, 1998).

160 István Deák, *The Lawful Revolution. Louis Kossuth and the Hungarians, 1848-1849* (New York, 1979), 329.

161 Gaston Bodart, ed., *Militär-historisches Kriegs-Lexikon, 1618-1905* (Vienna, 1908), 502-12.

162 Von Hippel, *Revolutionen im deutschen Südwesten*, 381, estimates nearly 700 dead and 2800 wounded, most on the revolutionary side.

163 Judson, *The Habsburg Empire*, 216, estimates that the "bloody Italian and Hungarian wars had cost the lives of over 100,000 Austrians."

164 Ernst Pawel, *The Poet Dying: Heinrich Heine's Last Years in Paris* (New York, 1995).

165 Heinrich Heine to Alfred Meissner, 14 April 1848, in HH, *Säkularausgabe*, vol. 22, *Briefe, 1842-1849*, 270-71.

166 Heine to Jacques-Julien Dubochet, 29 August 1848, in ibid., 22:289.

167 HH, *Säkularausgabe*, vol. 3, *Gedichte*, 101-2.

CHAPTER 8. NATION SHAPES (C. 1850-1870)

1 George Eliot to Charles Bray, 12 November 1854, in *The Letters of George Eliot*, ed. Gordon S. Haight (New Haven, 1954), 185; for her views on Franz Liszt, see Eliot to Bray, 16 August 1854, in ibid., 171.

2 George Eliot, "Recollections of Berlin, 1854-1855," in *The Journals of George Eliot*, ed. Margaret Harris and Judith Johnston (Cambridge, 1998), 258.

3 George Eliot, "Heinrich Heine," in *Essays and Leaves from a Notebook* (Boston, 1908), 75.

4 Ibid., 76.

5 Ibid., 114, 116, 118.

6 George Eliot, *Adam Bede*, ed. Carol A. Martin (Oxford, 2001), 166.

7 George Eliot, "Recollections of Our Journey from Munich to Dresden," in *The Journals of George Eliot*, 319, 324, 325.

8 George Eliot, "Natural History of German Life: Riehl," in *Essays and Leaves from a Notebook*, 196.

9 Ibid., 199, 202.

10 Ibid.

11 For prominent positive evaluations, see Wolf Lepenies, *Die drei Kulturen* (Hamburg, 1988), 239-43; Celia Applegate, "The Mediated Nation: Regions, Readers, and the German Past," in *Saxony in German History*, ed. James Retallack (Ann Arbor, Mich., 2000), 33-50, esp. 38-43. The best in-depth study is Jasper von Altenbockum, *Wilhelm Heinrich Riehl, 1823-1897: Sozialwissenschaft zwischen Kulturgeschichte und Ethnographie* (Cologne, 1994); for a biographical account shedding warmth as well as light, see Viktor Geramb, *Wilhelm Heinrich Riehl* (Salzburg, 1954).

12 Wilhelm Heinrich Riehl, *Nassauische Chronik des Jahres 1848*, ed. Winfried Schüler and Guntram Müller-Schellenberg (Idstein, 1979), 11-12, 31.

13 Peter Steinbach, "Introduction," to Wilhelm Heinrich Riehl, *Die bürgerliche Gesellschaft* (Frankfurt am Main, 1976), 12.

14 Ibid., 11-13. The statistics come from Jürgen Kocka, *Arbeitsverhältnisse und*

Arbeiterexistenzen: Grundlagen der Klassenbildung im 19. Jahrhundert (Bonn, 1990), 52, 77.

15 Mack Walker, *German Hometowns: Community, State, and General Estate, 1648–1871* (Ithaca, N.Y., 1971), 1–2, 7.

16 Walker defined hometowns in statistically idiosyncratic terms, placing their lower limit at 750 people and their upper at 10,000, perhaps 15,000; on this basis, he calculated that Germany, including German-speaking Austria, and all of Prussia, had roughly 4000 hometowns with a population of some seven million people in 1800. Ibid., 21–22, 31–32.

17 For partial listings of Riehl's hikes, see Geramb, *Wilhelm Heinrich Riehl*, 69, 73, 135–36. On the enthusiasm for walking, see Gudrun M. König, *Eine Kulturgeschichte des Spazierganges: Spuren einer bürgerlichen Praktik, 1780–1850* (Vienna, 1996).

18 Wilhelm Heinrich Riehl, *Land und Leute* (Stuttgart, 1883), 225.

19 Georg Kunz, *Verortete Geschichte: Regionales Bewußtsein in den deutschen Historischen Vereinen des 19. Jahrhunderts* (Göttingen, 2000), 59, counts more than sixty local and regional historical societies in Germany in the 1850s.

20 On Riehl's method, see Wilhelm Heinrich Riehl, *Wanderbuch*, 2nd ed. (Stuttgart, 1869), 6, 10, 13, 17, 28–30; on the "landscape eye," see Wilhelm Heinrich Riehl, "Das landschaftliche Auge," in *Culturstudien aus drei Jahrhunderten*, 2nd ed. (Stuttgart, 1959), 57–79.

21 Riehl, *Land und Leute*, 4–5; on Sebastian Münster, see Wilhelm Heinrich Riehl, "Sebastian Münster und seine Kosmographie," in Riehl, *Freie Vorträge: Erste Sammlung* (Stuttgart, 1873), 159.

22 On these works in home libraries, see Riehl, "Sebastian Münster," 160.

23 Wilhelm Heinrich Riehl, "Der hommanische Atlas," in *Culturstudien*, 11, 14–15.

24 Riehl, *Land und Leute*, 52; Riehl, "Das landschaftliche Auge," 64–65.

25 Riehl, *Land und Leute*, 135–36.

26 Ibid., 294–302.

27 Travel times for 1840 are calculated from *Allgemeines Post- und Reisebuch von Deutschland und dessen angrenzenden Ländern* (Frankfurt am Main, 1819).

28 Riehl, *Land und Leute*, 95.

29 Riehl, *Wanderbuch*, 35–36. See also Wolfgang Schivelbusch, *Geschichte der Eisenbahnreise: Zur Industrialisierung von Raum und Zeit im 19. Jahrhundert* (Frankfurt am Main, 1977), 34, 39.

30 Raymond Williams, *The Country and the City* (New York, 1973), 120.

31 Walter D. Kamphoener, Wolfgang Helbich, and Ulrike Sommer, eds., *News from the Land of Freedom* (Ithaca, N.Y., 1991), 16–17.

32 Karen Schniedewind, "Fremde in der alten Welt: Die transatlantische Rückwanderung," in *Deutsche im Ausland—Fremde in Deutschland. Migration in Geschichte und Gegenwart*, ed. Klaus J. Bade, 3rd ed. (Munich, 1993), 180.

33 Robert H. Wiebe, *Who We Are: A History of Popular Nationalism* (Princeton, N.J., 2002), 29; H. Glenn Penny, *Kindred by Choice: Germans and American Indians since 1800* (Chapel Hill, N.C., 2013), 54.

34 Riehl, *Die bürgerliche Gesellschaft*, 80, 149, 257.

35 Ibid., 149, 257.

36 Wilhelm Heinrich Riehl, *Die Familie* (Stuttgart, 1882).

37 Ibid., 34.

38 Erich Auerbach, *Mimesis: The Representation of Reality in Western Literature*, trans. Willard R. Trask (Princeton, N.J., 1953), 453.

39 Ibid., 518, 443.

40   Classic works remain Klaus Tenfelde, *Sozialgeschichte der Bergarbeiterschaft an der Ruhr im 19. Jahrhundert* (Bonn, 1977); and Jürgen Kocka, *Arbeitsverhältnisse und Arbeiterexistenzen: Grundlagen der Klassenbildung im 19. Jahrhundert* (Bonn, 1990).

41   The claim made here is only for the period 1850 to 1870; in the 1840s and the 1870s, this was a very different matter. On the history of urban ethnography in the nineteenth century, see Andrew Lees, *Cities Perceived: Urban Society in European and American Thought, 1820–1940* (New York, 1985), 22–90, focusing on Wilhelm Heinrich Riehl for this period; and Rolf Linder, *Walks on the Wild Side: Eine Geschichte der Stadtforschung* (Frankfurt am Main, 2004).

42   See the entries in Carl Jantke and Dietrich Hilger, eds., *Die Eigentumslosen: Der deutsche Pauperismus und die Emanzipationskrise in Darstellungen und Deutungen der zeitgenössischen Literatur* (Munich, 1965).

43   Riehl, *Land und Leute*, 278–394.

44   In this chapter, my observations on German literature are constricted to works published between 1850 and 1870.

45   Wilhelm Raabe, *Die Chronik der Sperlingsgasse*, ed. Hans-Werner Peter (Frankfurt am Main, 1979), 14.

46   On this topic, see Franco Moretti's inspired *Atlas of the European Novel, 1800–1900* (London, 1998), 75–140.

47   Wolfram Fischer, Jochen Krengel, and Jutta Wietog, eds., *Sozialgeschichtliches Arbeitsbuch I: Materialien zur Statistik des Deutschen Bundes, 1815–1870* (Munich, 1982), 37.

48   Schivelbusch, *Geschichte der Eisenbahnreise*, 154–59; Michael Fried, *Menzel's Realism: Art and Embodiment in Nineteenth-Century Berlin* (New Haven, 2002), 70.

49   Ernst Engel, "Die Productions- und Consumtionsverhältnisse des Königreichs Sachsen," *Zeitschrift des statistischen Bureaus des Königlich Sächsischen Ministeriums des Inneren* 8–9 (1857): 28–29.

50   Cited in Fried, *Menzel's Realism*, 10.

51   Claude Keisch and Marie Ursula Riemann-Reyher, eds., *Adolph Menzel, 1815–1905: Between Romanticism and Expressionism* (New Haven, 1996), 274–75.

52   For the painting, see ibid., 175–76. On being "immediate without being momentary" as an esssential characteristic of realist painting, see Linda Nochlin, *Realism* (Harmondsworth, Eng., 1971), 162. In German, the term "empathetic seeing," as applied to viewing art, is *"Einfühlung"*: see Rovert Vischer, *Über das optische Formgefühl: Ein Beitrag zur Ästhetik* (Tübingen, 1872).

53   Ludwig von Rochau, *Grundsätze der Realpolitik*, ed. Hans-Ulrich Wehler (Frankfurt am Main, 1972), 100.

54   Abigail Green, *Fatherlands: State-Building and Nationhood in Nineteenth-Century Germany* (Oxford, 2011), 151.

55   Ibid., 62.

56   Siegfried Weichlein, *Nation und Region: Integrationsprozesse im Bismarckreich* (Düsseldorf, 2004), 70–104.

57   Michael Wolffsohn and Thomas Brechenmacher, *Die Deutschen und ihre Vornamen: 200 Jahre Politik und öffentliche Meinung* (Munich, 1999), 131–35.

58   Jason D. Hansen, *Mapping the Germans: Statistical Science, Cartography, and the Visualization of the German Nation, 1848–1914* (Oxford, 2015), 23.

59   Thomas W. Laqueur, *The Work of the Dead: A Cultural History of Mortal Remains* (Princeton, N.J., 2015), 392–93.

60   Arthur A. Robinson, *Early Thematic Mapping in the History of Cartography* (Chicago, 1982), 114.

61   Richard Böckh, *Der Deutschen Volkszahl und Sprachgebiet in den europäischen Staaten: Eine statistische Untersuchung* (Berlin, 1869), 36. On Böckh, see Hansen, *Mapping the Germans*, 30-31.

62   Tara Zahra, "Imagined Noncommunities: National Indifference as a Category of Analysis," *Slavic Review* 69, no. 1 (Spring 2010): 93-119.

63   On Czoernig, see Morgan Labbé, "La Carte ethnographique de l'empire autrichien: La Multinationalité dans l'ordre des choses," *Mondes du cartes: Histoire de la cartographie* 180 (2004): 71-84.

64   Michael Mann, *The Sources of Social Power*, vol. 2, *The Rise of Classes and Nation-States, 1760-1914* (Cambridge, 1993), 363.

65   Oscar Jászi, *The Dissolution of the Habsburg Monarchy* (Chicago, 1929), 102.

66   Mann, *The Sources of Social Power*, 2:373, 393, 803-5, 808-9.

67   Cited in Gordon Craig, *The Politics of the Prussian Army, 1640-1945* (Oxford, 1955), 164.

68   Cited in Jonathan Steinberg, *Bismarck: A Life* (Oxford, 2011), 180-81.

69   Ibid.

70   Michael Geyer, *Deutsche Rüstungspolitik, 1860-1980* (Frankfurt am Main, 1984), 25-44.

71   Roger Chickering, Dennis Showalter, and Hans van den Ven, eds., *The Cambridge History of War* (Cambridge, 2012), 4:16.

72   Hans Rosenberg, *Die nationalpolitische Publizistik Deutschlands*, 2 vols. (Munich, 1935), 1:52.

73   Anon., *Der Kampf gegen den Bonapartismus jetzt und vor fünfzig Jahren*, excerpted in Rosenberg, *Die nationalpolitische Publizistik Deutschlands*, 52.

74   The locus classicus of this argument remains John Breuilly, *Nationalism and the State* (Manchester, 1982).

75   Otto Hausner, *Vergleichende Statistik von Europa*, 2 vols. (Lemberg, 1865).

76   The indispensable guide to this conflict is Geoffrey Wawro, *The Austro-Prussian War: Austria's War with Prussia and Italy in 1866* (Cambridge, 1996).

77   Adolph Menzel to Karl Eduard Eitner, 25 April 1867, in Adolph Menzel, *Briefe*, ed. Claude Keisch and Marie Ursula Riemann-Reyher (Berlin, 2019), 2:626.

78   Ibid., 2:627.

79   Frank Becker, *Bilder von Krieg und Nation: Die Einigungskriege in der bürgerlichen Öffentlichkeit Deutschlands, 1864-1913* (Munich, 2001), 135.

80   George G. Windell, *The Catholics and German Unity, 1866-1871* (Minneapolis, 1954).

81   James Q. Whitman, *The Verdict of Battle: The Law of Victory and the Making of Modern War* (Cambridge, Mass., 2012), 229.

82   On the settlement, see Pieter M. Judson, *The Habsburg Empire: A New History* (Cambridge, Mass., 2016), 249-64.

83   Heinrich von Srbik, "Der Geheimvertrag Österreichs und Frankreichs vom 12 Juni 1866," *Historisches Jahrbuch* 57 (1937): 454-507.

84   For a history of the countries that lost out in the process of consolidation, see Norman Davies, *Vanished Kingdoms: The Rise and Fall of States and Nations* (New York, 2011).

85   Charles Tilly, *Coercion, Capital, and European States, AD 990-1992* (Malden, Mass., 1990), 42-43.

86   Heinrich von Treitschke to Emma von Bodman, 12 December 1866, in Hein-

rich von Treitschke, *Briefe*, ed. Max Cornicelius, vol. 3, part 1 (Leipzig, 1897), 122. On this process, see Charles Maier, "Leviathan 2.0," in *A World Connecting, 1870–1945*, ed. Emily S. Rosenberg (Cambridge, Mass., 2012).

87   Hausner, *Vergleichende Statistik von Europa*, 1:10–18. Following Hausner, I define medium-sized states as having an area between 500 and 4000 square miles; Baden, Württemberg, and Saxony fell just below this threshold.

88   Ibid.

89   Jonathan F. Wagner, *Germany's 19th Century Cassandra: The Liberal Federalist Georg Gottfried Gervinus* (New York, 1995), 161.

90   On this topic, see John Merriman, *Massacre: The Life and Death of the Paris Commune* (New York, 2014).

91   Windell, *The Catholics and German Unity*, 249–50.

92   Ibid., 250–51

93   Ibid., 200–261.

94   On Windthorst, see Margaret Lavinia Anderson, *Windthorst: A Political Biography* (Oxford, 1981).

95   G. G. Gervinus, "Denkschrift zum Frieden an das preußische Königshaus," in *Hinterlassene Schriften*, ed. Victoria Gervinus (Vienna, 1872), 10.

96   Ibid., 22, 24.

97   Ibid., 21.

98   Ibid., 27; Wagner, *Germany's 19th Century Cassandra*, 172.

99   Dieter Gosewinkel and Johannes Masing, eds., *Die Verfassungen von Europa, 1789–1949* (Munich, 2006), 784.

100   Theodor Schieder, *Deutschland als Nationalstaat* (Cologne, 1961), 86.

101   Gosewinkel and Masing, eds., *Die Verfassungen von Europa*, 783–805.

CHAPTER 9. OBJECTIVE NATION (C. 1870–1914)

1   Theodor Fontane, *Wanderungen durch die Mark Brandenburg*, 5 vols. (Munich, 1960), 1:7. On Fontane's fascination with Scotland, see Gordon A. Craig, *Theodor Fontane: Literature and History in the Bismarck Reich* (New York, 1999), 23–47.

2   Fontane, *Wanderungen durch die Mark Brandenburg*, 1:97–117 (on Schinkel), 1:34 (on Knesebeck), and 3:97–117 (on Wust).

3   Michael Billig, *Banal Nationalism* (London, 1995), 8–9.

4   On the banal sense of nationhood, see ibid; on "national activists," Pieter M. Judson, *Guardians of the Nation: Activists on the Language Frontiers of Imperial Austria* (Cambridge, Mass., 2006).

5   Pioneers in this line of research include Leora Auslander, *Taste and Power: Furnishing Modern France* (Berkeley, Calif., 1996); Eva Geloi, *Monarchy, Myth, and Material Culture in Germany, 1750–1950* (Cambridge, 2001); as well as the essays in Etienne François and Hagen Schulze, eds., *Deutsche Erinnerungsorte*, 3 vols. (Munich, 2001). Although it is aimed at a wider audience, Neil MacGregor, *Germany: Memories of a Nation* (London, 2014) is full of surprising connections.

6   For a comparative context, see Eric Hobsbawm, "Mass-Producing Traditions: Europe, 1870–1914," in *The Invention of Tradition*, ed. Eric Hobsbawm and Terence Ranger (Cambridge, 1983), 263–308. On the national anthem and national tree, see Jeffrey K. Wilson, *The German Forest: Nature, Identity, and the Contestation of a National Symbol, 1871–1914* (Toronto, 2012), 17, 179. On Sedan Day (the national holiday that did emerge), see Jakob Vogel, "2 September 1870: Der Tag von Sedan," in *Erinnerungstage: Wendepunkte der Geschichte von der Antike bis zur Gegenwart*, ed. Etienne François and Uwe Puschner (Munich, 2010), 201–18;

and from the vantage of Württemberg, see Alon Confino, *The Nation as a Local Metaphor: Württemberg, Imperial Germany, and National Memory, 1871–1918* (Chapel Hill, N.C., 1997), 27–96. On the creation of symbols in the new nation-state, see Rudy Koshar, *From Monuments to Traces: Artifacts of German Memory, 1870–1990* (Berkeley, Calif., 2000), 27.

7   Hobsbawm, "Mass-Producing Traditions," 276.

8   This whole line of reasoning is indebted to Siegfried Weichlein, *Nation und Region: Integrationsprozesse im Bismarckreich* (Düsseldorf, 2004).

9   Cited in ibid., 136.

10   Ibid., 98–99, 75–77; Ralf Roth, *Das Jahrhundert der Eisenbahn* (Ostfildern, 2005), 131–33, 243.

11   Judson, *Guardians of the Nation.*

12   Jane Caplan, "'This or That Particular Person': Protocols of Identification in Nineteenth-Century Europe," in *Documenting Individual Identity: The Development of State Practices in the Modern World*, ed. Jane Caplan and John Torpey (Princeton, N.J., 2001), 49–66; Andreas Fahrmeier, "Governments and Forgers: Passports in Nineteenth-Century Europe," in ibid., 218–34, esp. 219–20.

13   John Torpey, *The Invention of the Passport: Surveillance, Citizenship and the State* (Cambridge, 2000), 9.

14   Leo Lucassen, "A Many-Headed Monster: The Evolution of the Passport System in the Netherlands and Germany in the Long Nineteenth Century," in Caplan and Torpey, eds., *Documenting Individual Identity*, 247.

15   Torpey, *The Invention of the Passport*, 111–16; John Torpey, "The Great War and the Birth of the Modern Passport System," in Caplan and Torpey, eds., *Documenting Individual Identity*, 256–70.

16   Bernhard Struck, *Nicht West, Nicht Ost: Frankreich und Polen in der Wahrnehmung deutscher Reisender zwischen 1750 und 1850* (Göttingen, 2006).

17   Alfred Dove, cited in Heinrich von Treitschke, *Briefe*, ed. Max Cornicelius, vol. 3, part 2 (Leipzig, 1913), 348n. The scholarship on Treitschke is voluminous. See the sharp treatment of George Iggers, "Heinrich von Treitschke," in *Deutsche Historiker*, ed. Hans-Ulrich Wehler (Göttingen, 1973), 174–324; the fullest biography remains Andreas Dorpalen, *Heinrich von Treitschke* (New Haven, 1957).

18   Treitschke to Emma von Treitschke, 15 September 1876, in Treitschke, *Briefe*, 3:438; Treitschke to Emma von Treitschke, 1 September 1874, in ibid., 3:402–3; Treitschke to Emma von Treitschke, 20 August 1880, in ibid., 3:523; Treitschke to Emma von Treitschke, 24 October 1879, in ibid., 3:514; Treitschke to Emma von Treitschke, 8 April 1886, in ibid., 3:590; Treitschke to Emma von Treitschke, 19 September 1876, in ibid., 3:438.

19   Treitschke to Emma von Treitschke, 25 August 1874, in ibid., 3:401–2.

20   Treitschke to Emma von Treitschke, 19 September 1871, in ibid., 3:335.

21   Ibid.

22   Ibid.

23   Brian Porter, *When Nationalism Began to Hate: Imagining Modern Politics in Nineteenth-Century Poland* (Oxford, 2002).

24   Heinrich von Treitschke, "Unsere Aussichten," *Preußische Jahrbücher* 44, no. 5 (1879): 559–76; Uffa Jensen, *Gebildete Doppelgänger: Bürgerliche Juden und Protestanten im 19. Jahrhundert* (Göttingen, 2005), 197–268.

25   On Treitschke's trip to the Memel, see Isaac Rülf, "Auch eine Kleinigkeit in Sachen Treitschke et Compe," in *Der Berliner Antisemitismusstreit, 1879–1881: Kommentierte Quellenedition*, ed. Karsten Krieger, 2 vols. (Munich, 2004) 1:416–18.

26   Heinrich von Treitschke, "Unsere Aussichten," in ibid., 1:11.

27 Ibid., 1:12, 15.
28 "Manifest der Berliner Notabeln gegen den Antisemitismus von 12.11.1880," in ibid., 2:552.
29 Theodor Mommsen, "Auch ein Wort über unser Judenthum," in ibid., 2:698, 700.
30 Ibid., 2:700.
31 On the scholarship of German nationalism in this period, see Pieter M. Judson, "Nationalism in the Era of the Nation State, 1870-1945," in *The Oxford Handbook of Modern German History*, ed. Helmut Walser Smith (Oxford, 2011), 499-526. See also the more extended reflections on the state of the debate in James Retallack, *The German Right, 1860-1920: Political Limits of the Authoritarian Imagination* (Toronto, 2006).
32 Hans-Ernst Mittig, "Über Denkmalkritik," in *Denkmäler im 19. Jahrhundert*, ed. Hans-Ernst Mittig and Volker Plagemann (Munich, 1972), 284; Richard Mutter, "Die Denkmalseuche," in *Aufsätze über bildende Kunst*, 2 vols. (Berlin, 1914), 2:59-68.
33 Fritz Abshoff, *Deutschlands Ruhm und Stolz: Unsere hervorragendsten vaterländischen Denkmäler in Wort und Bild* (Berlin, 1904).
34 For Kaiser Wilhelm monuments, see Otto Kuntzemüller, *Die Denkmäler Kaiser Wilhelm des Großen in Abbildungen mit erläuterndem Text* (Bremen, 1902); for Bismarck monuments, see Günter Kloss and Sieglinde Seele, *Bismarck-Türme und Bismarck-Säulen: Eine Bestandsaufnahme* (Petersberg, 1997).
35 Geloi, *Monarchy, Myth, and Material Culture in Germany*, 186-214.
36 Ibid., 157-85.
37 Ibid., 274; Otto May, *Deutsch sein heißt treu sein: Ansichtskarten als Spiegel von Mentalität und Untertanenerziehung in der Wilhelminischen Ära, 1888-1918* (Hildesheim, 1998), 60.
38 Mrs. Alfred Sidgwick, *Home Life in Germany* (London, 1908), 97.
39 Prussia counted some 60 percent of all monuments (a figure roughly commensurate with the percentage of the Prussian population in the German Empire): see Robert Gerwarth, *The Bismarck Myth: Weimar Germany and the Legacy of the Iron Chancellor* (Oxford, 2005), 18-24.
40 Konrad Breitenborn, *Bismarck: Kult und Kitsch um den Reichsgründer* (Leipzig, 1990), 7.
41 May, *Deutsch sein heißt treu sein*, 149.
42 Ibid.
43 In 1901, Fritz Abshoff photographed nearly 250 of them so that, if only a fraction of the whole, his images allow us to get a sense of the relative weight of motifs. See Fritz Abshoff, *Deutschlands Ruhm und Stolz* (Berlin, 1901).
44 For more detail, see Helmut Walser Smith, "Monuments, Kitsch, and the Sense of Nation in Imperial Germany," *Central European History* 49, no. 3-4 (2016): 322-40.
45 Cited in Klaus Sauer and German Werth, *Lorbeer und Palme: Patriotismus in deutschen Festspielen* (Munich, 1971), 138.
46 R. Ron Heiligenstein, *Regimental Beer Steins* (Milwaukee, 1997), 49-52.
47 Ibid.
48 W. E. B. Du Bois, "Commencement Speech delivered at Fisk University, June 1888" in W. E. B. Dubois Papers (MS 312), Special Collections and University Archives, University of Massachusetts Amherst Libraries (hereafter cited as Du Bois Papers).
49 W. E. B. Du Bois to the John F. Slater Fund, 28 October 1892, in Du Bois

Papers. The draft of this letter contains more information than the final version, which is printed in W. E. B. Du Bois, *The Correspondence of W. E. B. Du Bois,* ed. Herbert Aptheker, 3 vols. (Amherst, Mass. 1973–1978), 1:20–21. See also W. E. B. Du Bois, *Dusk of Dawn: An Essay Toward an Autobiography of a Race Concept* (Oxford, 2007), 23.

50   W. E. B. Du Bois, "Early Germanic Institutions as Mentioned by Tacitus," October 20, 1890, in Du Bois Papers; W. E. B. Du Bois, "Origin and Methods of the German Railway System," March 16, 1889, in ibid.

51   W. E. B. Du Bois, "Commencement Speech Delivered at Fisk University, June 1888," in ibid.

52   W. E. B. Du Bois, *The Autobiography* (New York, 1968), 164–65.

53   Ibid., 103.

54   Ibid.

55   Ibid.

56   Georg Brandes, *Berlin als deutsche Reichshauptstadt: Erinnerungen aus den Jahren 1877–1883*, trans. Peter Urban-Halle, ed. Erik M. Christensen and Hans-Dietrich Loock (Berlin, 1989), 344.

57   Kris Manjapra, *Age of Entanglement: German and Indian Intellectuals Across Empire* (Cambridge, 2014), 47.

58   Robert C. Williams, *Russian Emigrés in Germany, 1881–1941* (Ithaca, N.Y., 1972), 1–53.

59   Anja Werner, *The Transatlantic World of Higher Education: Americans at German Universities, 1776–1914* (New York, 2013).

60   W. E. B. Du Bois, "A Spring Wandering," 1893, in Du Bois Papers.

61   Ibid.; W. E. B. Du Bois, "Quarter Centennial Celebration of my Life [fragment]," c. 1893, in Du Bois Papers; W. E. B. Du Bois to himself, 23 February 1894, in ibid.

62   Du Bois, "A Spring Wandering." This incident is also recounted in David Levering Lewis, *W. E. B. Du Bois, 1868–1919: Biography of a Race* (New York, 1994), 138–39.

63   Du Bois, *The Autobiography*, 106.

64   Ibid.

65   Ibid.

66   W. E. B. Du Bois, "Some Impressions of Europe, ca. July 1894," in Du Bois Papers.

67   W. E. B. Du Bois, "The Present Condition in German Politics (1893)," *Central European History* 31, no. 3 (1998): 175.

68   Kenneth Barkin, "W. E. B. Du Bois' Love Affair with Imperial Germany," *German Studies Review* 28, no. 2 (2005): 287.

69   Koshar, *From Monuments to Traces*, 25.

70   Wolfgang König, *Wilhelm II und die Moderne* (Paderborn, 2007), 197.

71   The critic was Maximilian Harden—see Martin Kohlrauch, "Der Mann mit dem Adlerhelm: Wilhelm II—Medienstar um 1900," in *Das Jahrhundert der Bilder*, ed. Gerhard Paul, 2 vols. (Göttingen, 2009), 1:73–74.

72   John Phillip Short, *Magic Lantern Empire: Colonialism and Society in Germany* (Ithaca, N.Y., 2012), 38.

73   Ibid.

74   David Ciarlo, *Advertising Empire: Race and Visual Culture in Imperial Germany* (Cambridge, 2011), 76–81.

75   Ibid., 3.

76   Rebecca Ayako Bennette, *Fighting for the Soul of Germany: The Catholic Struggle for Inclusion after Unification* (Cambridge, Mass., 2012).

77 Wolfgang Hardtwig, "Nationsbildung und politische Mentalität: Denkmal und Fest im Kaiserreich," in *Geschichtskultur und Wissenschaft*, ed. Wolfgang Hardtwig (Munich, 1990), 283.

78 Vogel, "2. September 1870," 213.

79 Bennette, *Fighting for the Soul of Germany*, 11-112; Ingo Löppenberg, *"Wider Raubstaat, Grosskapital und Pickelhaube": Die katholische Militarismuskritik und Militärpolitik des Zentrums 1860 bis 1914* (Frankfurt am Main, 2009).

80 Vernon L. Lidtke, *The Alternative Culture: Socialist Labor in Imperial Germany* (New York, 1985), 77.

81 Ibid., 102-35.

82 Ibid.,186-87.

83 Franz Mehring, "Der erste Aasgeier," in *Zur Kriegsgeschichte und Militärfrage*, vol. 5, *Gesammelte Schriften* (Berlin, 1967), 280-83.

84 Dieter Groh, *Negative Integration und revolutionärer Attentismus: Die deutsche Sozialdemokratie am Vorabend des Ersten Weltkrieges* (Frankfurt am Main, 1973); Nicholas Stargardt, *The German Idea of Militarism: Radical and Socialist Critics, 1866-1914* (Cambridge, 1994).

85 Roger Chickering, "'Casting Their Gaze More Broadly': Women's Patriotic Activism in Imperial Germany," *Past and Present* 118, no. 1 (1998): 181.

86 Ibid.

87 The words are Otto von Bismarck's, cited in Nancy R. Reagin, *Sweeping the German Nation: Domesticity and National Identity in Germany, 1870-1945* (New York, 2007), 1. On the crisis in gendered conceptions of patriotism that ensued, see Jean H. Quataert, *Staging Philanthropy: Patriotic Women and the National Imagination in Dynastic Germany, 1813-1916* (Ann Arbor, Mich., 2001), 257-68.

88 For the government's role in supporting preservation efforts, see especially Winfried Speitkamp, *Die Verwaltung der Geschichte: Denkmalpflege und Staat in Deutschland, 1871-1933* (Göttingen, 1996); for the public sphere, see Rudy Koshar, *Germany's Transient Pasts: Preservation and National Memory in the Twentieth Century* (Chapel Hill, N.C., 1998).

89 The source for these calculations is Willy Hoppe and Gerhard Lüdtke, eds., *Die deutschen Kommissionen und Vereine für Geschichte und Altertumskunde* (Berlin, 1940).

90 Based on the list in Hoppe and Lüdtke, eds., *Die deutschen Kommissionen*, the pace of new organizations was spread out remarkably evenly until 1933.

91 On the contemporary understanding of the term "monument," see Koshar, *Germany's Transient Pasts*, 14.

92 Peter Betthausen, *Georg Dehio: Ein deutscher Kunsthistoriker* (Berlin, 2004), 258-59.

93 Georg Dehio, *Handbuch der deutschen Kunstdenkmäler: Mitteldeutschland* (Berlin, 1905), 307.

94 Betthausen, *Georg Dehio*, 261-62.

95 Wilson, *The German Forest*, 32-33.

96 David Blackbourn, *The Conquest of Nature: Water, Landscape, and the Making of Modern Germany* (New York, 2006), 77-120.

97 Thomas Lekan, "A 'Noble Prospect': Tourism, Heimat, and Conservation on the Rhine, 1880-1914," *Journal of Modern History* 81, no. 4 (2009): 826-27.

98 Wilson, *The German Forest*, 19, 23.

99 Thomas Lekan, *Imagining the Nation in Nature: Landscape Preservation and German Identity, 1885-1945* (London, 2004), 6; Wilson, *The German Forest*, 31.

100   Rolf Selbmann, *Dichterdenkmäler in Deutschland: Literaturgeschichte in Erz und Stein* (Stuttgart, 1988), 25-26.

101   Rainer Noltenius, *Dichterfeiern in Deutschland: Rezeptionsgeschichte als Sozialgeschichte am Beispiel der Schiller- und Freiligrath-Feiern* (Munich, 1984); Hartmut Lehmann, "Das Lutherjubiläum 1883," in *Protestantische Weltsichten* (Göttingen, 1998), 105-29.

102   Reimer Lacher, "Die Denkmalsstatue der Anna Louisa Karsch von J. C. Stubenitzky aus dem Landschaftspark Spiegelsberge bei Halberstadt," in *Frauen im 18. Jahrhundert: Entdeckungen zu Lebensbildern in Museen und Archiven in Sachsen-Anhalt*, ed. Thomas Weiss, Katrin Dziekan, and Ingo Pfeifer (Halle, 2009), 71-83.

103   Maria Zimmermann, "Denkmäler für Henrich Heine in Deutschland: Ein Spiegel seiner Rezeptionsgeschichte," *Mitteldeutsches Jahrbuch für Kultur und Geschichte* 3 (1996): 181.

104   The quotation is from a member of the city council—see Dietrich Schubert, "Der Kampf um das erste Heine-Denkmal. Düsseldorf 1887-1893, Mainz 1893-1894, New York 1899," *Wallraf-Richartz-Jahrbuch: Westdeutsches Jahrbuch für Kunstgeschichte* 51 (1990): 251.

105   "Heine Monument Unveiled," *New York Times*, 9 July 1899.

106   Zimmermann, "Denkmäler für Heinrich Heine in Deutschland."

107   For an introduction to recent literature on 1913, see Gangolf Hübinger, "Das Jahr 1913 in Geschichte und Gegenwart," *Internationales Archiv für Sozialgeschichte der deutschen Literatur* 38, no. 1 (2013), 172-90; and Meike G. Werner, "Warum 1913?," *Internationales Archiv für Sozialgeschichte der deutschen Literatur* 38, no. 2 (2013): 443-51.

108   Christoph Asendorf, "Widersprüchliche Optionen: Stationen der Künste 1913," *Internationales Archiv für Sozialgeschichte der deutschen Literatur* 38, no. 1 (2013): 194; Koshar, *From Monuments to Traces*, 34, 44.

109   On the increasingly secular cast of national monuments and festivals after 1900, see Hardtwig, "Nationsbildung und politische Mentalität"; and for the monument commemorating the Leipzig Battle of Nations, see Stefan Ludwig-Hoffmann, "Sakraler Monumentalismus um 1900: Das Leipziger Völkerschlachtdenkmal," in *Der Politische Totenkult: Kriegerdenkmäler in der Moderne*, ed. Reinhart Koselleck and Michael Jeismann (Munich, 1994), 272.

110   See the complaint of Graf Lerchenfeld to von Hertling in Ernst Deuerlein, ed., *Briefwechsel Hertling-Lerchenfeld 1912-1917: Dienstliche Privatkorrespondenz zwischen dem bayerischen Ministerpräsidenten Georg Graf von Hertling und dem bayerischen Gesandten in Berlin Hugo Graf von und zu Lerchenfeld* (Boppard am Rhein, 1973), 20.

111   *Vossische Zeitung* (Berlin), 17 October 1913.

112   Hans-Ernst Mittig, "Über Denkmalkritik," in *Denkmäler im 19. Jahrhundert*, ed. Hans-Ernst Mittig and Volker Plagemann (Munich, 1972), 283-89; Hardtwig, "Nationsbildung und politische Mentalität," 289; Koshar, *From Monuments to Traces*, 48.

113   Helmut Walser Smith, *The Continuities of German History: Nation, Religion, and Race Across the Long Nineteenth Century* (New York, 2008), 199-200.

114   Quotation from Michael Geyer, *Deutsche Rüstungspolitik, 1860-1980* (Frankfurt am Main: Suhrkamp, 1984), 89; see also Daniel Frymann (pseud.), *Wenn ich der Kaiser wär . . . : Politische Wahrheiten und Notwendigkeiten* (Leipzig, 1912). On Heinrich Class, see the penetrating analyses in Roger Chickering, *"We Men Who Feel Most German": A Cultural Study of the Pan-German League, 1886-1914*

(Boston, 1984), 286-87; and Geoff Eley, *Reshaping the German Right: Radical Nationalism and Political Change after Bismarck* (New Haven, 1980), 320-21, 147-205. On Class in the Weimar Republic and the Third Reich, see Rainer Hering, *Konstruierte Nation: Der Alldeutsche Verband, 1890 bis 1939* (Hamburg, 2003), 355-65.

115   For a terse analysis of the difference between Class and Treitschke, see Stefan Breuer, *Grundpositionen der deutschen Rechten* (Tübingen, 1999), 40.

116   Ibid., 124.

117   Smith, *The Continuities of German History*, 208.

118   Georg Brandes, "Deutsche Vaterländerei," in *Der Wahrheitshass: Über Deutschland und Europa, 1880-1925* (Berlin, 2007).

119   Brandes, "Deutsche Vaterländerei," 112.

120   Ibid., 110.

PART IV. THE NATIONALIST AGE: PREFACE

1   The lecture first appeared in print as Ernst H. Kantorowicz, "Pro Patria Mori in Medieval Political Thought," *The American Historical Review*, 56, 3, (April 1951), 472-92; I've quoted from the version in Ernst H. Kantorowicz, *Selected Studies* (New York, 1965), 314.

2   Ibid., 324.

3   Ibid.

4   Mannheim quoted in Peter Gay, *Weimar Culture: The Outsider as Insider* (New York, 1968), xiv.

5   Kantorowicz, "Pro Patria Mori in Medieval Political Thought," 324.

6   Ulrich Bielefeld, *Nation und Gesellschaft: Selbstthematisierung in Deutschland und Frankreich* (Hamburg, 2003), 14.

7   Reinhart Koselleck, "Deutschland: Eine verspätete Nation?," in *Zeitschichten: Studien zur Historik* (Frankfurt am Main, 2000), 367.

8   Robert Gerwarth, *The Vanquished: Why the First World War Failed to End, 1917-1923* (London, 2016).

9   Max Weber, "Politik als Beruf," in *Max Weber Gesamtausgabe*, vol. 17, *Wissenschaft als Beruf 1917/1919: Politik als Beruf 1919*, ed. Wolfgang J. Mommsen, Wolfgang Schluchter, and Birgitt Morgenbrod (Tübingen, 1992), 36.

10   Sebastian Haffner, *Defying Hitler: A Memoir*, trans. Oliver Pretzel (New York, 2002), 67-68.

11   Otto Weitzel, *Die Entwicklung der Staatsausgaben in Deutschland* (Nuremberg, 1967), 236.

12   Ibid., appendix, table 31. The bar graph on page 296 is based on this table.

13   On the pre-World War I arms race, see David G. Hermann, *The Arming of Europe and the Making of the First World War* (Princeton, N.J., 1996).

14   Weitzel, *Die Entwicklung der Staatsausgaben in Deutschland*, 236ff.

15   George Kennan, *The Decline of Bismarck's European Order: Franco-Russian Relations, 1875-1890* (Princeton, N.J., 1979), 3.

16   This story is powerfully told in Adam Tooze, *The Wages of Destruction: The Making and Breaking of the Nazi Economy* (New York, 2006), 639-40.

17   Dieter Langewiesche, *Der gewaltsame Lehrer: Europas Kriege in der Moderne* (Munich, 2019).

18   These comparisons are based on Peter Brecke's conflict catalogue, 1400-2000. The data and a description of it can be accessed at http://www.cgeh.nl/data#conflict.

19   Stéphane Audoin-Rouzeau and Annette Becker, *1914-1918: Understanding the Great War,* trans. Catherine Temerson (New York, 2002), 22.

20   Monthly figures are in Rüdiger Overmans, *Deutsche militärische Verluste im Zweiten Weltkrieg* (Munich, 1999), 239.

21   On the numbers of deaths in the great battles of World War I, see Jay Winter, "Demography," in *A Companion to World War I,* ed. John Horne (Oxford, 2010), 253.

22   Benjamin Ziemann, "Soldaten," in *Enzyklopädie Erster Weltkrieg,* ed. Gerhard Hirschfeld, Gerd Krumeich, and Irina Renz, 2nd ed. (Paderborn, 2014), 156; Richard Bessel, *Germany after the First World War* (Oxford 1993), 8.

23   Overmans, *Deutsche militärische Verluste im Zweiten Weltkrieg,* 232-35.

24   Winter, "Demography," 252; Bessel, *Germany after the First World War,* 10.

25   Cited in Eva Dempewolf, *Blut und Tinte: Eine Interpretation der verschiedenen Fassungen von Ernst Jüngers Kriegstagebüchern vor dem politischen Hintergrund der Jahre 1920 bis 1980* (Würzburg, 1992), 95.

26   Ziemann, "Soldaten," 157; Audoin-Rouzeau and Becker, *1914-1918,* 39.

27   Richard Bessel, "Death and Survival in the Second World War," in *The Cambridge History of the Second World War,* ed. Evan Mawdsley, vol. 3, *Total War: Economy, Society and Culture,* ed. Michael Geyer and Adam Tooze, 259; Michael Geyer and Adam Tooze, "Introduction to Part II," in ibid., 3:249.

28   Wolfgang Hardtwig, "Volksgemeinschaft im Übergang: Von der Demokratie zum rassistischen Führerstaat," in *Gemeinschaftsdenken in Europa: Das Gesellschaftskonzept "Volksheim" im Vergleich, 1900-1938,* ed. Detlef Lehnert (Cologne, 2013), 248.

29   This point is made in Mark Roseman, "Racial Discourse, Nazi Violence, and the Limits of the Racial State Model," in *Beyond the Racial State: Rethinking Nazi Germany,* ed. Devin O. Pendas, Mark Roseman, and Richard F. Wetzell (Cambridge, 2017), 41.

30   Andreas Wirsching, "Hitler's Authenticity: A Functionalist Interpretation," *Contemporary History Yearbook* 3 (2018): 23-57, Helmut Walser Smith, "When Was Adolf Hitler?," ibid., 59-70.

31   Reinhart Koselleck, "Sprachwandel und Ereignisgeschichte," in *Begriffsgeschichten: Studien zur Semantik und Pragmatik der politischen und sozialen Sprache* (Frankfurt am Main, 2006), 35.

32   Of the older studies, the best are Chickering, *"We Men Who Feel Most German": A Cultural Study of the Pan-German Leauge, 1866-1914* (Boston, 1984), and Geoff Eley, *Reshaping the German Right: Radical Nationalism and Political Change after Bismarck* (New Haven, 1980); of the newer, James Retallack, *The German Right, 1860-1920: Political Limits of the Authoritarian Imagination* (Toronto, 2006), and Peter Walkenhorst, *Nation—Volk—Rasse: Radikaler Nationalismus im Deutschen Kaiserreich, 1890-1914* (Göttingen, 2010).

33   Gerhard L. Weinberg ed., *Hitler's Second Book: The Unpublished Sequel to Mein Kampf* (New York, 2003), 105. On this topic generally, see Alan E. Steinweis, "Eastern Europe and the Notion of the 'Frontier' in Germany to 1945," *Yearbook of European Studies* 13 (1999): 56-90.

34   *Hitler's Second Book,* 152.

35   Giorgio Agamben, *Homo Sacer: Sovereign Power and Bare Life,* trans. Daniel Heller-Roazen (Palo Alto, Calif., 1998), 8.

36   Max Weber, *Wirtschaft und Gesellschaft: Grundriss der verstehenden Soziologie,* ed. Johannes Winckelmann, 5th ed. (Tübingen, 1972), 28.

37   Christian Gerlach, *The Extermination of the European Jews* (Cambridge, 2016), 65.

38   *Die "Ereignismeldungen UdSSR" 1941: Dokumente der Einsatzgruppen in der Sowjetunion*, ed. Klaus-Michael Mallmann et al. (Darmstadt, 2011), 8, gives the number 535,000 for the *Einsatzgruppen* "until the spring of 1942."

39   Yehuda Bauer, "Re-Rethinking the Holocaust," in *The Jews: "A Contrary People"* (Zurich, 2014), 216. Bauer then qualified this statement with "No Hitler, no Holocaust either."

40   Timothy Snyder, *Bloodlands: Europe Between Hitler and Stalin* (New York, 2010), viii.

41   Comment to Adolf Hitler in *Mein Kampf: Eine Kritische Editon*, ed. Christian Hartmann et al. (Munich, 2016), 2:996n12.

42   "The 25 Point Program" in *Der Aufstieg der NSDAP 1919–1933 in Augenzeugenberichten* (Düsseldorf, 1968), 108–12.

43   Hartmann et al., eds., *Mein Kampf: Eine Kritische Editon*, 1:777.

44   On the imperialist roots of thinking that certain classes of people may be killable, see Hannah Arendt, *The Origins of Totalitarianism* (New York, 1951), 185–86.

45   Primo Levi, *The Drowned and the Saved*, trans. Raymond Rosenthal (New York, 1988), 37.

CHAPTER 10. SACRIFICE FOR (C. 1914–1933)

1   Rainer Maria Rilke, *Die Aufzeichnungen des Malte Laurids Brigge*, in *Werke*, vol. 6, ed. Rilke Archiv (Frankfurt am Main, 1987), 714.

2   *Deutscher Reichsanzeiger und Königlicher Preußischer Staatsanzeiger* (Berlin), August 3, 1914 (evening edition), 4.

3   Wolfgang Schivelbusch, *The Culture of Defeat: On National Trauma, Mourning, and Recovery* (New York, 2004), 222.

4   Jeffrey Verhey, *The Spirit of 1914: Militarism, Myth, and Mobilization in Germany* (Cambridge, 2006), 94–96.

5   This book does not address the role of Imperial Germany in the outbreak of World War I. Readers interested in this problem may turn with profit to Chris Clark, *Sleepwalkers: How Europe Went to War in 1914* (New York, 2012), which emphasizes the concatenation of Europe-wide events, and Geoffrey Wawro, *A Mad Catastrophe: The Outbreak of World War I and the Collapse of the Habsburg Empire* (New York, 2014), which stresses the larger role of the Central Powers. On nationalism as less cause than consequence of the war, see Michael Mann, *The Sources of Social Power*, vol. 3, *Global Empires and Revolution, 1890–1945* (Cambridge, 2012), 139, 159.

6   Verhey, *The Spirit of 1914*, 97.

7   Ibid., 100.

8   Stéphane Audoin-Rouzeau and Annette Becker, *1914–1918: Understanding the Great War*, trans. Catherine Temerson (New York, 2002), 98.

9   Cited in Thomas W. Laqueur, *The Work of the Dead: A Cultural History of Mortal Remains* (Princeton, N.J., 2015), 453.

10   Verhey, *The Spirit of 1914*, 98.

11   For an extended reflection, see Svenja Goltermann, *Opfer: Die Wahrnehmung von Krieg und Gewalt in der Moderne* (Munich, 2018).

12   On these lists, see Robert Weldon Whalen, *Bitter Wounds: German Victims of the Great War, 1914–1939* (Ithaca, N.Y., 1984), 38–39; Roger Chickering, *The Great War and Urban Life in Germany: Freiburg, 1914–1918* (Cambridge, 2007), 320.

13   Benjamin Ziemann, "Soldaten," in *Enzyklopädie Erster Weltkrieg*, ed. Gerhard Hirschfeld, Gerd Krumeich, and Irina Renz, 2nd ed. (Paderborn, 2014), 156.

14   Alexander Watson, *Enduring the Great War: Combat, Morale and Collapse in the German and British Armies, 1914–1918* (Cambridge, 2008), 51–52.

15   The term "second acceptance" is in Audoin-Rouzeau and Becker, *1914–1918*, 100. On "stoic resolve," see Chickering, *The Great War and Urban Life in Germany*, 323, 412.

16   Max Weber, "Zwischenbetrachtung: Stufen und Richtungen der religiösen Weltablehnung," *Archiv für Sozialwissenschaft und Sozialpolitik* 41 (1916): 398, cited in *German Soldiers in the Great War: Letters and Eyewitness Accounts*, ed. Bernd Ulrich and Benjamin Ziemann, trans. Christine Brocks (South Yorkshire, Eng., 1910), 42. See also Schivelbusch, *Culture of Defeat*, 206.

17   Cited in Whalen, *Bitter Wounds*, 79.

18   Two remarkable exceptions are *Ulrich Bräker, Sämtliche Schriften*, 5 vols., ed. Andreas Bürgi et al. (Munich, 1998–2010); and Jakob Walter, *The Diary of a Napoleonic Foot Soldier*, ed. Marc Raeff (New York, 1991).

19   Bernd Ulrich, *Die Augenzeugen: Deutsche Feldpostbriefe in Kriegs- und Nachkriegszeit 1914–1933* (Essen, 1997), 40. Roughly one-quarter of the mails sent consisted of postcards. See Christine Brocks, *Die bunte Welt des Krieges: Bildpostkarten aus den Ersten Weltkrieg, 1914–1918* (Essen, 2008), 29.

20   Cited in Ulrich, *Die Augenzeugen*, 30.

21   Margarete Ackermann and Marie Nock to Mother Superior in Lichtenrade, in *Vom Augusterlebnis zur Novemberrevolution: Briefe aus dem Weltkrieg, 1914–1918*, ed. Jens Ebert (Göttingen, 2014), 113. See also Vejas Gabriel Liulevicius, *War Land on the Eastern Front: Culture, National Identity and German Occupation in World War I* (Cambridge, 2000), 153.

22   Aribert Reimann, "Die heile Welt im Stahlgewitter: Deutsche und englische Feldpost aus dem Ersten Weltkrieg," in *Kriegserfahrungen: Studien zur Sozial- und Mentalitätsgeschichte des Ersten Weltkriegs*, ed. Gerhard Hirschfeld (Essen, 1997), 129–45.

23   See, for example, Junior Officer Albert Peetz to the father of Friedrich Grüneberg, 23 May 1915, in Ebert, ed., *Vom Augusterlebnis zur Novemberrevolution*, 90.

24   Hugo Frick to his family in Ellwangen, 29 September 1916, and Hugo Frick to his mother, 17 February 1917, in *Die Deutschen an der Somme, 1914–1918: Krieg, Besatzung, Verbrannte Erde*, ed. Gerhard Hirschfeld, Gerd Krumeich, and Irina Renz (Essen, 2006), 146, 151.

25   Cited in Ulrich and Ziemann, eds., *German Soldiers in the Great War*, 115.

26   Hedwig Lauth to her husband, 2 February 1917, in Museumsstiftung Post und Telekommunikation, available at http://www.museumsstiftung.de/briefsammlung/feldpost-erster-weltkrieg/brief.html?action=detail&what=letter&id=2028.

27   Roger Chickering, *Imperial Germany and the Great War, 1914–1918* (Cambridge, 1998), 142.

28   Chickering, *The Great War and Urban Life in Germany*, 319–20.

29   Lauth to her husband, 2 February 1917.

30   Wilhelm Kaisen to Helene Kaisen, 7 November 1918, in Ebert, ed., *Vom Augusterlebnis zur Novemberrevolution*, 302.

31   Chickering, *The Great War and Urban Life in Germany*, 329. Even the Socialists evoked "fatherland" in a third of their announcements.

32   Käthe Kollwitz, *Die Tagebücher, 1908–1943* (Berlin, 1989), 158, entry of 27 August 1914. On Kollwitz's reaction to the outbreak of the war and her struggles

during it, the decisive work is now Yvonne Schymura, *Käthe Kollwitz, 1867–2000: Biographie und Rezeptionsgeschichte einer deutschen Künstlerin* (Essen, 2014), 145–60.

33   Kollwitz, *Die Tagebücher*, 177, 1 December 1914.

34   Ibid.

35   Schymura, *Käthe Kollwitz*, 167.

36   Kollwitz, *Die Tagebücher*, 193, late July 1915.

37   Regina Schulte, "Käthe Kollwitz's Sacrifice," trans. Pamela Selwyn, *History Workshop Journal* 41 (1996): 197–204, 209.

38   Kollwitz, *Die Tagebücher*, 270, 27 August 1916.

39   Ibid., 279, 11 October 1916.

40   Ibid., 323, 18 July 1917.

41   On Beckmann, see Annegret Jürgens-Kirchhoff, ed., *Schreckensbilder: Krieg und Kunst im 20. Jahrhundert* (Berlin, 1993), 151–68. On Marc, see Franz Marc, *Briefe, Aufzeichnungen und Aphorismen*, ed. Paul Cassirer (Berlin, 1920), 1:8, entry of 12 December 1914; and Franz Marc, *Briefe aus dem Feld 1914–1916* (Munich, 2014), 21 (letter of 12 September 1914) and 72 (letter of 6 April 1915).

42   Jürgens-Kirchhoff, ed., *Schreckensbilder*, 246.

43   The story of German women artists is told in Claudia Siebrecht, *The Aesthetics of Loss: German Women's Art of the First World War* (Oxford, 2013).

44   Ibid., 149.

45   Nicolas Beaupré, *Écrits de guerre, 1914–1918* (Paris, 2006), 50.

46   Ibid., 41–42.

47   Cited in Siebrecht, *The Aesthetics of Loss*, 138.

48   Ricarda Huch to Marie Baum, 9 August 1914, in Peter Walther, ed., *Endzeit Europa: Ein kollektives Tagebuch deutschsprachiger Schriftsteller, Künstler und Gelehrter im Ersten Weltkrieg* (Göttingen, 2008), 43.

49   Thea Sternheim, *Tagebücher, 1903–1971*, vol. 1 (Göttingen, 2002), 219, entry of 18 August 1914.

50   Theodor Lessing, *Geschichte als Sinngebung des Sinnlosen* (Munich, 1919).

51   See Burcu Dogramaci and Friederike Weimar, eds., *Sie Starben Jung! Künstler und Dichter, Ideen und Ideale vor dem Ersten Weltkrieg* (Berlin, 2014).

52   August Stramm, "Sturmangriff," in *Das Werk*, ed. René Radrizzani (Wiesbaden, 1963), 73.

53   August Stramm to his wife, 6 October 1914, in *Alles ist Gedicht: Briefe, Gedichte, Bilder, Dokumente*, ed. Jeremy D. Adler (Zurich, 1990), 22; August Stramm, "Fünfundzwanzig Briefe an seine Frau," in Jeremy D. Adler and J. J. White, eds., *August Stamm: Kritische Essays und unveröffentliches Quellenmaterial aus dem Nachlass des Dichters* (Berlin, 1979), letter no. 12, 5 May 1915, 138.

54   Max Weber, *Max Weber Gesamtausgabe*, part 1, vol. 15, *Zur Politik im Weltkrieg: Schriften und Reden, 1914–1918,* part I, vol. 15, ed. Wolfgang J. Mommsen and Gangolf Hübinger (Tübingen, 1984), 95–98, 661 (hereafter cited as I/15).

55   Heinrich Class, *Denkschrift betreffend die national-wirtschafts-und sozialpolitischen Ziele des deutschen Volkes im gegenwärtigen Kriege* (Berlin, 1914), 58.

56   Ibid., 24–27, 32–33.

57   For greater detail, see Helmut Walser Smith, *The Continuities of Modern German History: Nation, Religion, and Race Across the Long Nineteenth Century* (New York, 2008), 208.

58   Class, *Denkschrift*, 45.

59   Ibid., 45–50. See also Heinz Hagenlücke, *Deutsche Vaterlandspartei: Die nationale Rechte am Ende des Kaiserreichs* (Düsseldorf, 1997), 53–57; Fritz Fischer,

Griff nach der Weltmacht: Die Kriegszielpolitik des kaiserlichen Deutschland 1914/18 (Düsseldorf, 1961), mentions the expulsions almost as an afterthought, on 112–14.

60   Alexander Watson, *Ring of Steel: Germany and Austria-Hungary in World War I* (New York, 2014), 392.

61   The German left-liberal Friedrich von Payer cited in Isabel V. Hull, *Absolute Destruction: Military Culture and the Practices of War in Imperial Germany* (Ithaca, N.Y., 2005), 243.

62   Cited in ibid., 119.

63   On the geopolitical importance of Brest-Litovsk, see especially John Darwin, *After Tamerlane: The Global History of Empire since 1405* (New York, 2008), 378–79.

64   Ibid., 378.

65   Liulevicius, *War Land on the Eastern Front*, 210–11.

66   Ibid., 212–13; Richard Bessel, *Germany after the First World War* (Oxford, 1993), 45.

67   Bessel, *Germany after the First World War*, 47. On the remarkable increase in German soldiers reporting sick, see the graph reproduced in Niall Ferguson, *The War of the World: History's Age of Hatred* (London, 2006), 146.

68   Kollwitz, *Die Tagebücher*, 360, 20 March 1918.

69   Ibid.

70   Ibid., 374, 1 October 1918.

71   *Vorwärts*, 30 October 1918, in ibid., 840.

72   Ibid.

73   Michael Geyer, "Insurrectionary Warfare: The German Debate about a Levée en Masse in October 1918," *Journal of Modern History* 73 (2001): 504, 488.

74   For recent research on the German Revolution, see *Germany 1916–23: A Revolution in Context*, ed. Klaus Weinhauer, Anthony McElligot, and Kirsten Heinsohn (Bielefeld, 2015), especially 7–36.

75   Ibid.; also see now Mark Jones's revisionist work, *Founding Weimar: Violence and the German Revolution of 1918–1919* (Cambridge, 2016).

76   Rosa Luxemburg to Clara Zetkin, December 1918, in *The Letters of Rosa Luxemburg*, ed. Georg Adler et al., trans. George Schriver (London, 2013), 489.

77   Bessel, *Germany after the First World War*, 74–79.

78   Luxemburg to Zetkin, 11 January 1919, in Adler et al., eds., *The Letters of Rosa Luxemburg*, 798, as well as the editor's note on the same page.

79   The Weimar Constitution in *Die Verfassungen von Europa, 1789–1949*, ed. Dieter Gosewinkel and Johannes Masing (Munich, 2006), 806, 809, 812. On Hugo Preuss's original formulation, see Michael Wildt, *Volksgemeinschaft als Selbstermächtigung: Gewalt gegen Juden in der deutschen Provinz, 1919 bis 1939* (Hamburg, 2007), 43.

80   Helmuth Plessner, *Die Verspätete Nation: Über die Verführbarkeit bürgerlichen Geistes* (Stuttgart, 1959); Andreas Wimmer, *Nationalism, State Formation, and Ethnic Exclusion in the Modern World* (New York, 2003), 2. Wimmers counts Imperial Germany as a nation-state in 1871.

81   Richard J. Evans, *The Coming of the Third Reich* (New York, 2004), 83.

82   Ibid., 80; Evans writes that President Friedrich Ebert employed such decrees 136 times. On the proximity of democracy and dictatorship in the Weimar Republic, see especially Thomas Mergel, "Dictatorship and Democracy, 1918–1939," in *The Oxford Handbook of Modern German History*, ed. Helmut Walser Smith (Oxford, 2011), 423–52.

83 On ethnographic mapping at Versailles, see Janson D. Hansen, *Mapping the Germans: Statistical Science, Cartography, and the Visualization of the German Nation, 1848-1914* (Oxford, 2015), 150-61.

84 Michael Mann, *The Dark Side of Democracy: Explaining Ethnic Cleansing* (Cambridge, 2005), 212-39.

85 See Jones, *Founding Weimar.*

86 Jay Winter, "Demography," in *A Companion to World War I*, ed. John Horne (Oxford, 2010), 256.

87 Emil Gumbel, *Vier Jahre politischer Mord* (Berlin, 1922), 81.

88 Gerald D. Feldman, *The Great Disorder: Politics, Economics, and Society in the German Inflation, 1914-1924* (New York, 1997), 4-5.

89 Kollwitz, *Die Tagebücher*, 428, 25 June 1919.

90 Alexandra von dem Knesebeck, *Käthe Kollwitz: Werkverzeichnis der Graphik* (Bern, 2002), 2:512-39.

91 Kollwitz, *Die Tagebücher*, 564-65, 11 January 1924; Schymura, *Käthe Kollwitz*, 247-48.

92 Ulrich Linse, "'Saatfrüchte sollen nicht vermahlen warden!' Zur Resymbolisierung des Soldatentodes," in *Kriegserlebnis: Der Erste Weltrkrieg in der literarischen Gestaltung und symbolischen Deutung der Nationen* (Göttingen, 1980), 266-67. Nevertheless, as Jay Winter argues, traditional war memorials continued to hold, deep into the 1960s: see Jay Winter, *Sites of Memory, Sites of Mourning: The Great War in European Cultural History* (Cambridge, 1995), 115-16, 223.

93 Chickering, *The Great War and Urban Life in Germany*, 320.

94 Bessel, *Germany after the First World War*, 225. Just over 30 percent of the soldiers were married. Given that nearly two million German soldiers fell in the war, the number of widows must have been around 600,000.

95 Siebrecht, *The Aesthetics of Loss*, 142.

96 Silke Fehlemann, "'Stille Trauer': Deutsche Soldatenmütter in der Zwischenkriegszeit," *Historical Social Research* 34 (2009): 331-42.

97 Ibid.; Siebrecht, *The Aesthetics of Loss*, 12; Chickering, *The Great War and Urban Life in Germany*, 323.

98 Fehlemann, "'Stille Trauer,'" 331-42; Bessel, *Germany after the First World War*, 225.

99 Statistical document reprinted in Richard Wall and Jay Winter, eds., *The Upheaval of War: Family, Work, and Welfare in Europe, 1914-1918* (Cambridge, 1988), 27.

100 Oliver Janz, *Der grosse Krieg* (Frankfurt am Main, 2013), 353.

101 Audoin-Rouzeau and Becker, *1914-1918*, 214.

102 Deborah Cohen, *The War Come Home: Disabled Veterans in Britain and Germany, 1914-1939* (Berkeley, Calif., 2001), 193.

103 Heather Perry, *Recycling the Disabled: Army, Medicine, and Modernity in WWI Germany* (Manchester, 2014).

104 Whalen, *Bitter Wounds*, 55-60.

105 Ibid.

106 Joseph Roth, "Lebende Kriegsdenkmäler," in *Berliner Saisonbericht: Unbekannte Reportagen und journalistische Arbeiten, 1920-39*, ed. Klaus Westerman (Cologne, 1984), 85-90.

107 Cohen, *The War Come Home*, 4, 7, 194.

108 Ibid., 5.

109 Ibid., 63.

110 For a description of the Kaufmann method, see Wolfgang U. Eckart, *Medizin und Krieg: Deutschland, 1914–1924* (Paderborn, 2014), 149–50.

111 Paul Lerner, *Hysterical Men: War, Psychiatry, and the Politics of Trauma, 1890–1930* (Ithaca, N.Y., 2003), 226–28.

112 Ibid., 243.

113 On the long-term repercussions of this hardening, see Michael Geyer, "The Place of the Second World War in German Memory and History," trans. Michael Latham, *New German Critique* 71 (1997): 13–19.

114 See Philipp Rauh, "Psychisch-kranke Veteranen des Ersten Weltkrieges als Opfer der nationalsozialistischen Krankenmorde," in *Krieg und Psychiatrie, 1914–1950*, ed. Babette Quinkert, Philipp Rauh, and Ulrike Winkler (Göttingen, 2010); Stephanie Neuner, *Politik und Psychiatrie: Die Staatliche Versorgung psychisch Kriegsbeschädigter in Deutschland, 1920–1939* (Göttingen, 2011), 321.

115 Andrew Donson, *Youth in the Fatherless Land: War Pedagogy, Nationalism, and Authority in Germany, 1914–1918* (Cambridge, 2010).

116 Karin Hausen, "Mütter, Söhne und der Markt der Symbole und Waren: Der deutsche Muttertag, 1923–1933," in *Emotionen und Materielle Interessen: Sozialanthropologische und historische Beiträge zur Familienforschung* (Göttingen, 1984), 515–16.

117 Detlev J. K. Peukert, *Die Weimarer Republik* (Frankfurt am Main, 1987), 27–30.

118 Detlev J. K. Peukert, *Jugend zwischen Krieg und Krise: Lebenswelten von Arbeiterjungen in der Weimarer Republik* (Cologne, 1987), 31–35.

119 Anton Kaes, *Shell Shock Cinema: Weimar Culture and the Wounds of War* (Princeton, N.J., 2009).

120 Cited in Eva Dempenwolf, *Blut und Tinte: Eine Interpretation der verschiedenen Fassungen von Ernst Jüngers Kriegstagebüchern vor dem politischen Hintergrund der Jahre 1920 bis 1980* (Cologne, 1992), 129.

121 Cited in ibid., 133.

122 Cited in ibid., 131.

123 Cited in ibid., 130.

124 Kollwitz, *Die Tagebücher*, 669, 14 August 1932.

CHAPTER 11. SACRIFICE OF (C. 1933–1941)

1 This story comes from Thomas Weber, *Hitler's First War: Adolf Hitler, the Men of the List Regiment, and the First World War* (Oxford, 2010); quotation on 345.

2 Thomas Weber, *Becoming Hitler: The Making of a Nazi* (New York, 2017), 45.

3 Andreas Wirsching, "Hitler's Authenticity: A Functionalist Interpretation," *Contemporary History Yearbook* 3 (2018), 40.

4 Adolf Hitler, *Sämtliche Aufzeichnungen, 1905-1924*, ed. Eberhard Jäckel and Axel Kuhn (Stuttgart, 1980), 88.

5 Ibid., 89–90.

6 Ibid.

7 Ibid.

8 Ibid.

9 Ibid.

10 Adolf Hitler, *Mein Kampf: Eine Kritische Edition*, ed. Christian Hartmann et al. (Munich, 2016), 1:737.

11 Ibid., 1:741.

12 Ibid., 1:67–68.

13 Wirsching, "Hitler's Authenticity," 116. See also Albrecht Koschorke, *On Hit-*

ler's Mein Kampf: The Poetics of National Socialism, tr. Erik Butler (Cambridge, Mass., 2017).

14 Nancy Bermeo, *Ordinary People in Extraordinary Times: The Citizenry and the Breakdown of Democracy* (Princeton, N.J., 2003), 21.

15 Michael Mann, *Fascists* (Cambridge, 2004), 60.

16 Bermeo, *Ordinary People*, 23, table 2.1.

17 Mann, *Fascists*, 139.

18 On this subject, the standard work remains Jürgen W. Falter, *Hitlers Wähler* (Munich, 1991).

19 Nikolaus Wachsmann, *KL: A History of the Nazi Concentration Camps* (New York, 2015), 31.

20 Ibid., 36.

21 Victor Klemperer, *Ich will Zeugnis ablegen bis zum letzten: Tagebücher, 1933–1941*, ed. Walter Nowojski (Berlin, 1995), 1:20.

22 Marion A. Kaplan, *Between Dignity and Despair: Jewish Life in Nazi Germany* (New York, 1999), 24.

23 Otto Dov Kulka and Eberhard Jäckel, eds., *The Jews in the Secret Nazi Reports on Popular Opinion in Germany, 1933–1945*, trans. William Templer (New Haven, 2010). Document numbers in later notes citing this source refer to the German-language originals reproduced in the CD-Rom collection that accompanies the volume.

24 These cases are detailed in Joseph Walk, *Das Sonderrecht für die Juden im NS-Staat* (Heidelberg, 1981).

25 Ibid., 23.

26 Kaplan, *Between Dignity and Despair*, 22.

27 Kulka and Jäckel, eds., *The Jews in the Secret Nazi Reports*, doc. 207: Ansbach, 9 August 1934, Regierungspräsident Ober- und Mittelfranken, Bericht für Juli.

28 Kaplan, *Between Dignity and Despair*, 23.

29 Cited in Kulka and Jäckel, eds., *The Jews in the Secret Nazi Reports*, 671.

30 Kulka and Jäckel, eds., *The Jews in the Secret Nazi Reports*, doc. 106.

31 Ibid., doc. 116; doc. 124, p. 128.

32 Virginia Woolf, "On the Rhine with Mitzi," in *Travels in the Reich*, 74–75.

33 Kulka and Jäckel, eds., *The Jews in the Secret Nazi Reports*, docs. 100, 122, 120.

34 Joachim Prinz, "Das Leben ohne Nachbarn," in *Die Verfolgung und Ermordung der europäischen Juden durch das nationalsozialistische Deutschland, 1933–1945*, vol. 1, *Deutsches Reich, 1933–1937*, ed. Wolf Gruner (Munich, 2008), 521–23, doc. 210.

35 Michael Wildt, *Volksgemeinschaft als Selbstermächtigung: Gewalt gegen Juden in der deutschen Provinz, 1919 bis 1939* (Hamburg, 2007), 176–218. Wildt's remains the best book on the subject. For my disagreement on an interpretive point (whether local branches of the Nazi Party or the people were the active agents), see Helmut Walser Smith, "A National Socialist People?," *Yad Vashem Studies* 36, no. 2 (2008): 189–202. Very few of the reports collected in the CD-ROM of *The Jews in the Secret Nazi Reports* refer to spontaneous anti-Semitism or that the push came from nonaffiliated segments of the population.

36 *Reichsgesetzblatt*, 1935, Part 1; Reichsbürgergesetz, 15 September 1939.

37 The Nuremberg Laws also prohibited Jews from employing female German nationals under forty-five years of age.

38 James Q. Whitman, *Hitler's American Model: The United States and the Making of Nazi Race Law* (New Haven, 2017).

39   Ernst Fraenkel, *The Dual State: A Contribution to the Theory of Dictatorship* (New York, 1941), 140–41.

40   Benedict Anderson, *Imagined Communities: Reflections on the Origin and Spread of Nationalism* (London, 1982), 136.

41   Penetrating on this phenomenon is John Connelly, "The Uses of Volksgemein-schaft: Letters to the NSDAP Kreisleitung Eisenach, 1939–1940," *Journal of Modern History* 68, no. 4 (1996): 899–930.

42   Albert Camus, "Into the Bottomless Pit," in *Travels in the Reich, 1933–1945: Foreign Authors Report from Germany*, ed. Oliver Lubrich, trans. Kenneth Northcott, Sonia Wichmann, and Dean Krouk (Chicago, 2010), 134.

43   Thomas Wolfe, "I Have a Thing to Tell You," in ibid., 130.

44   The visit is detailed in David Levering Lewis, *W. E. B. Du Bois: The Fight for Equality and the American Century, 1919–1963* (New York, 2000), 405.

45   Ibid., 401.

46   W. E. B. Du Bois, "Search for Democracy in Germany" [fragment], c. 1936, in W. E. B. Du Bois Papers (MS 312), Special Collections and University Archives, University of Massachusetts Amherst Libraries.

47   Ibid.

48   Ibid.

49   Ibid.

50   W. E. B. Du Bois, "What of the Color-Line," in Lubrich, ed., *Travels in the Reich*, 142.

51   Ibid., 143.

52   Ibid., 147.

53   Ibid., 150.

54   Kurt Grübler, *Journey Through the Night: Jacob Littner's Holocaust Memoir* (New York, 2000).

55   Wolf-Arno-Kropat, *Reichskristallnacht: Der Judenpogrom vom 7. bis 10. November 1938* (Wiesbaden, 1997), 43–47.

56   Raphael Gross, *Novemberpogrom 1938* (Munich, 2013), 45, gives the number 1406—though the number is likely too high.

57   Some historians suggest that the mayhem can be traced to historical Christian rites of violence. See Alon Confino, *A World Without Jews: The Nazi Imagination from Persecution to Genocide* (New Haven, 2014); for reservations about the religious dimension of the interpretation, see Helmut Walser Smith, "Culture as Consensus in Nazi Germany," *Journal of Genocide Research* 18 (2016): 6–11.

58   Gross, *Novemberpogrom 1938*, 67; on 45, Gross gives the number of Jews who died in the November pogrom and the subsequent internment of Jewish men at 1300 to 1500.

59   Testimony of Marga Randall, "Kristallnacht in a Small German Town," available at http://www.yadvashem.org/yv/en/exhibitions/kristallnacht/video.asp.

60   Anon, n.d., doc 046-EA-0450 [B.241], Wiener Library, http://wienerlibrarycollections.co.uk/novemberpogrom/testimonies-and-reports/b1-b50/b.421; anon, n.d., Doc 046-EA-0450 [B.240], Wiener Library, http://wienerlibrarycollections.co.uk/novemberpogrom/testimonies-and-reports/b1-b50/b.240.

61   http://wienerlibrarycollections.co.uk/novemberpogrom/testimonies-and-reports/b1-b50/b.16 and b19. On Dinslaken, see Anne Prior, "*Wo die Juden geblieben sind, ist (. . .) nicht bekannt": Novemberpogrom in Dinslaken 1938 und die Deportation Dinslakener Juden, 1941–1944* (Essen, 2010), 22–33.

62   Alan Steinweis, *Kristallnacht 1938* (Cambridge, 2009), 83.

63   Anon., n.d. [B.104], Wiener Library, http://wienerlibrarycollections.co.uk/novemberpogrom/testimonies-and-reports/b1-b50/b.104.

64   Anon., 14 November 1938 [B.31], Wiener Library, http://wienerlibrarycollections.co.uk/novemberpogrom/testimonies-and-reports/b1-b50/b.31.

65   Margarette Dörr, *"Wer die Zeit nicht miterlebt hat . . .": Frauenerfahrungen im Zweiten Weltkrieg und in den Jahren danach* (Frankfurt am Main, 1998), vol. 3, *Das Verhältnis zum Nationalsozialismus und zum Krieg*, 300; available at http://www.alemannia-judaica.de/freudental_synagoge.htm.

66   It also seems the case that in letters and diaries, non-Jewish women rarely remarked on the pogrom, and the weekly "women's page" of the *Völkische Beobachter*, the official Nazi newspaper, barely mentioned the rampage. See Dorr, "Wer die Zeit", 3:191, 300–301.

67   Ibid., 3:197.

68   On the extent of destruction—nearly a billion marks in property was damaged—see Kulka and Jäckel, eds., *The Jews in the Secret Nazi Reports*, 340–43, doc. 356.

69   Ibid.; 362, doc. 371; 371, doc. 385.

70   Ibid., 362, doc. 371; Kurt Krimmel, n.d. [B.148], Wiener Library, http://wienerlibrarycollections.co.uk/novemberpogrom/testimonies-and-reports/b1-b50/b.148.

71   Kulka and Jäckel, eds., *The Jews in the Secret Nazi Reports*, 362, doc. 371.

72   Anon., 14 November 1938 [B.31], Wiener Library.

73   Cohn was one of roughly 100,000 German-Jewish men who served in World War I, some 80,000 of whom saw active combat. See Tim Grady, *The German-Jewish Soldiers of the First World War in History and Memory* (Liverpool, 2011), 35; Peter Hayes, *Why? Explaining the Holocaust* (New York, 2017), 53.

74   Willy Cohn, *Kein Recht, Nirgends: Tagebuch vom Untergang des Breslauer Judentums, 1933–1941*, ed. Norbert Conrads, 2 vols. (Cologne, 2006), 1:219, entry of 28 April 1935.

75   Ibid., 2:541, 12 November 1938.

76   *Jewish Responses to Persecution*, 5 vols., ed. Jürgen Matthäus and Mark Roseman, vol. 1, *1933–1938* (Lanham, Md., 2010), 353, 196.

77   Gross, *Novemberpogrom 1938*, 57, puts the number of Jewish men arrested at 30,756.

78   Ibid., 64.

79   Wachsmann, *KL*, 181.

80   "Note on the Situation of Jews in Germany," 20 December 1938 [B.204], Wiener Library, http://wienerlibrarycollections.co.uk/novemberpogrom/testimonies-and-reports/b1-b50/b.204.

81   Wachsmann, *KL*, 186.

82   Elisabeth Freund, memoir, in *Jüdisches Leben in Deutschland: Selbstzeugnisse zur Sozialgeschichte, 1918–1945*, vol. 3, ed. Monika Richarz (Stuttgart, 1982), 380.

83   Debórah Dwork and Robert Jan van Pelt, *Flight from the Reich: Refugee Jews, 1933–1946* (New York, 2009).

84   See the remarkable reconstruction of the lives of these passengers in Sarah A. Oglive and Scott Miller, *Refuge Denied: The St. Louis Passengers and the Holocaust* (Madison, Wisc., 2006), x.

85   Ibid., 58.

86   Wachsmann, *KL*, 151. Dieter Pohl also offers the figure of 10,000 people killed by the Nazis before September 1939. See Dieter Pohl, "Historiography and Nazi Killing Sites," in *Killing Sites: Research and Remembrance*, ed. International Holocaust Remembrance Alliance (Berlin, 2015), 32.

87   Nicholas Wachsmann, *Hitler's Prisons: Legal Terror in Nazi Germany* (New Haven, 2004), 145–46; Burkhard Jellonek and Rüdiger Lautmann, eds., *Nationalsozialistischer Terror gegen Homosexuelle: Verdrängt und ungesühnt* (Paderborn, 2002).

88   Wachsmann, *KL*, 150–51.

89   Henry Friedlander, *The Origins of Nazi Genocide: From Euthanasia to the Final Solution* (Chapel Hill, N.C., 1995).

90   Christian Gerlach, *The Extermination of the European Jews* (Cambridge, 2016), 8–9. For the concept, see Christian Gerlach, *Extremely Violent Societies: Mass Violence in the Twentieth Century World* (Cambridge, 2010).

91   Peter J. Gay, *Freud, Jews and Other Germans. Master and Victims in Modernist Culture* (Oxford, 1978), xiii.

92   Cohn, *Kein Recht, Nirgends*, 2:679, 28 August 1939.

93   Ibid., 2:703, 7 October 1939.

94   Ibid., 2:732, 21 December 1939.

95   Ibid., 2:713, 5 November 1939.

96   Cited in Jürgen Matthäus, Jochen Böhler, and Klaus-Michael Mallmann, eds., *War, Pacification, and Mass Murder, 1939: The Einsatzgruppen in Poland* (Lanham, Md., 2014), 7.

97   Alexander Rossino, *Hitler Strikes Poland: Blitzkrieg, Ideology, and Atrocity* (Lawrence, Kans., 2003), 10.

98   Catherine Epstein, *Model Nazi: Arthur Greiser and the Occupation of Poland* (Oxford, 2010).

99   Ibid., 234–35.

100   Ibid., 199.

101   Claude Lanzmann, *Shoah: An Oral History of the Holocaust; The Complete Text of the Film* (New York, 1985), 81. The figures come from Epstein, *Model Nazi*, 175.

102   Epstein, *Model Nazi*, 177, 166.

103   Ibid., 160

104   Ibid., 192

105   Rossino, *Hitler Strikes Poland*, 142, 144–52, 161–62.

106   Ibid., 186.

107   Ibid.

108   Matthäus, Böhler, and Mallmann, eds., *War, Pacification, and Mass Murder*, 83, citing Richard Evans, that self-defense units accounted for one half of 65,000 Poles killed.

109   Ibid., 62.

110   Christian Jansen and Arno Weckbecker, *Der "Volksdeutsche Selbstschutz" in Polen 1933/1940* (Munich, 1992), 212–29.

111   Geoffrey P. Megargee, ed., *The United States Holocaust Memorial Museum Encyclopedia of Camps and Ghettos, 1933–1945*, vol. 2, *Ghettos in German-Occupied Eastern Europe*, ed. Martin Dean, part A, 409 (hereafter cited as USHMM, *Ghettos*).

112   Ibid., part A, 440; ibid., part A, 26.

113   Ibid., part A, 428.

114   Dan Michman, *The Emergence of Jewish Ghettos During the Holocaust* (New York, 2011), 36–37; Kulka and Jäckel, eds., *The Jews in The Secret Nazi Reports*, CD-ROM, search term "Ghetto."

115   A full copy of Heydrich's circular can be found in Klaus-Peter Friedrich and Andrea Löw, eds., *Die Verfolgung und Ermordung der europäischen Juden*, vol. 4, *Polen: September 1939—Juli 1941* (Munich, 2011), 88–92.

116   Raul Hilberg, Stanislaw Staron, and Josef Kermisz, eds., *The Warsaw Diary of*

Adam Czerniakow (New York, 1979), 300. For a remarkable reconstruction, see Barbara Engelking and Jacek Leociak, *The Warsaw Ghetto: A Guide to a Perished City*, trans. Emma Harris (New Haven, 2009).

117   Dan Michman, "The Jewish Ghettos under the Nazis," preface to *The Yad Vashem Encyclopedia of the Ghettos During the Holocaust*, 2 vols. (New York, 2010), 1:xxv-xxvii.

118   See Regina Mühlhäuser, *Eroberungen: Sexuelle Gewalttaten und intime Beziehungen deutscher Soldaten in der Sowjetunion, 1941-1945* (Hamburg, 2010).

119   Timothy Snyder, *Bloodlands: Europe Between Hitler and Stalin* (New York, 2010), 126.

120   Hartmann et al., eds., *Mein Kampf: Eine Kritische Edition*, 2:1657.

121   Snyder, *Bloodlands*, 165.

CHAPTER 12. DEATH SPACES (1941-1945)

1   Susanne Heim et al., eds., *Die Verfolgung und Ermordung der europäischen Juden durch das nationalsozialistische Deutschland, 1933-1945* (hereafter cited as *VEJ*), vol. 7, *Sowjetunion mit annektierten Gebieten I*, ed. Bert Hoppe and Hildrun Glass (Munich, 2011), doc. 2, "Hitler erläutert am 30. März vor der Wehrmachtsführung die Zielsetzung des Krieges gegen die Sowjetunion."

2   "Wirtschaftliche Richtlinien für die Wirtschaftsorganisation Ost," 23 May 1941, reproduced, in part, in Hamburg Institut für Sozialgeschichte, ed., *Verbrechen der Wehrmacht: Dimensionen des Vernichtungskrieges, 1941-1944; Ausstellungskatalog* (Hamburg, 2002), 64-65 (hereafter cited as *VdW*); Alex J. Kay, " 'The Purpose of the Russian Campaign Is the Decimation of the Slavic Population by Thirty Million': The Radicalization of German Food Policy in Early 1941," in *Nazi Policy on the Eastern Front, 1941: Total War, Genocide, and Radicalization*, ed. Alex J. Kay, Jeff Rutherford, and David Stahel (Rochester, N.Y., 2012), 107-11.

3   *VdW*, 64-65.

4   Ibid.; Lizzie Collingham, "The Human Fuel: Food as Global Commodity and Local Scarcity," in *The Cambridge History of the Second World War*, ed. Evan Mawdsley, vol. 3, *Total War: Economy, Society and Culture*, ed. Michael Geyer and Adam Tooze (Cambridge, 2015), 149-73.

5   Cited in Michael Wildt, *Generation der Unbedingten: Das Führungskorps des Reichssicherheitshauptamtes* (Hamburg, 2002), 536.

6   Cited in ibid., 536, 559. On the *Einsatzgruppen*, see Waitman Wade Beorn, *The Holocaust in Eastern Europe* (London, 2018), 128-33.

7   On this issue, see Peter Longerich, *Politik der Vernichtung: Eine Gesamtdarstellung der nationalsozialistischen Judenverfolgung* (Munich, 1998), 310-20.

8   Ibid., 320.

9   *VEJ*, 7:185-86. The meeting was recorded by Martin Bormann, doc. 28, 16 July 1941, in ibid., 7:183-87.

10   Ibid., 7:183-84.

11   Ibid., 7:186.

12   Ibid.

13   Ibid., 7:183-84.

14   Ibid., 7:184.

15   Christian Streit, *Keine Kameraden: Die Wehrmacht und die sowjetischen Kriegsgefangenen, 1941-1945* (Stuttgart, 1978), 152-53.

16   Rolf Keller, *Sowjetische Kriegsgefangene im Deutschen Reich, 1941/42: Behandlung und Arbeitseinsatz zwischen Vernichtungspolitik und kriegswirtschaftlichen*

Erfordernissen (Göttingen, 2011), 320–23, has recalculated Streit's estimates and suggested modest corrections.

17 Streit, *Keine Kameraden.*

18 Vera Hilbich, *Der "Friedhof der Namenlosen"* in *Oerbke: Lokale Erinnerung und Auseinandersetzungen nach Kriegsende* (Göttingen, 2017).

19 Streit, *Keine Kameraden*, 134.

20 Cited in ibid., 135. On Lamsdorf, see Bernard Linek, "Lamsdorf: Können Täter Opfer werden?," in *Deutsch-Polnische Erinnerungsorte*, vol. 2, ed. Hans Henning Hahn and Robert Traba (Paderborn, 2014), 365–66.

21 Streit, *Keine Kameraden*, 135.

22 Ibid., 366n157.

23 On Minsk, see *VdW*, 228–29.

24 "Bericht des Kriegsgefangenen-Bezirkskommandanten J über den Transport in offenen Waggons," 22 November 1941, partially reprinted in ibid., 221.

25 Cited in Peter Fritzsche, *An Iron Wind: Europe under Hitler* (New York, 2016), 139–40.

26 Cited in Streit, *Keine Kameraden*, 169.

27 Willy Peter Reese, *A Stranger to Myself: The Inhumanity of War, Russia, 1941–1944*, trans. Michael Hoffmann (New York, 2003), 23.

28 Helmuth James von Moltke to Freya von Moltke, 26 August 1941, in Helmuth James von Moltke, *Briefe an Freya, 1939–1945*, ed. Beate Ruhm von Oppen (Munich, 1991), 278.

29 Ibid.

30 Timothy Snyder, *Bloodlands: Europe Between Hitler and Stalin* (New York, 2010); and, more recently, the east European chapters in Götz Aly, *Europa gegen die Juden, 1880–1945* (Frankfurt am Main, 2017).

31 Cited in Dieter Pohl, *Nationalsozialistische Judenverfolgung in Ostgalizien, 1941–1944* (Munich, 1996), 58–59.

32 Klaus-Michael Mallmann et al., eds., *Die "Ereignismeldungen UdSSR," 1941: Dokumente der Einsatzgruppen in der Sowjetunion* (Darmstadt, 2011), 103.

33 Ibid., 76, 130.

34 Ibid., 83, 132, 208, 264.

35 A recent attempt to bring them together, Jeffrey S. Kopstein and Jason Wittenberg, *Intimate Violence: Anti-Jewish Pogroms on the Eve of the Holocaust* (Ithaca, N.Y., 2018), 2, 44, counts 219 localities in which pogroms occurred in 1941 in the area occupied by the Soviet Union in 1939, then by Nazi Germany in 1941; the authors define as a pogrom "a collective attack on one or more Jewish civilians that is geographically limited in scope."

36 Ibid. argues that weak state control opened up possibilities. On the other hand, Alexander Rossino, "Polish 'Neighbors' and German Invaders: Contextualizing Anti-Jewish Violence in the Białystok District During the Opening Weeks of Operation Barbarossa," *Polin: Studies in Polish Jewry* 16 (2003): 431–52, emphasizes the role of German presence.

37 Jan Gross, *Neighbors: The Destruction of the Jewish Community in Jedwabne, Poland* (Princeton, N.J., 2001); Joanna B. Michlic and Antony Polonsky, eds., *The Neighbors Respond: The Controversy over the Jedwabne Massacre in Poland* (Princeton, N.J., 2003).

38 Wendy Lower, "Pogroms, Mob Violence and Genocide in Western Ukraine, Summer 1941: Varied Histories, Explanations and Comparisons," *Journal of Genocide Research* 13, no. 3 (2011): 217–46.

39 On the centrality of collusion, see Pohl, *Nationalsozialistische Judenverfolgung*

in Ostgalizien, 55–56; Lower, "Pogroms, Mob Violence and Genocide in Western Ukraine," 222.

40   A copy can be accessed at: https://encyclopedia.ushmm.org/content/en/film/ pogrom-in-lvov.

41   Christoph Dieckmann, *Deutsche Besatzungspolitik in Litauen, 1941–1944,* 2nd ed., 2 vols. (Göttingen, 2016), 1:360.

42   Ibid., 2:1512.

43   On the radicalization of the unit's killing practices, see Wolfram Wette, *Karl Jäger: Mörder der litauischen Juden* (Frankfurt am Main, 2011), 50.

44   Umberto Eco in an interview with Spiegel-online, 11 November 2009.

45   For a facsimile of the original, see Wette, *Karl Jäger,* 237–45.

46   Ibid.

47   Ibid. For a compelling analysis using tools of digital humanities, see Waitman Wade Beorn with Anne Kelly Knowles, "Killing on the Ground and in the Mind: The Spatialities of Genocide in the East," in *Geographies of the Holocaust,* ed. Anne Kelly Knowles, Tim Cole, and Alberto Giordano (Bloomington, Ind., 2014), 88–118.

48   Yaffa Eliach, *There Once Was a World: A 900-Year Chronicle of the Shtetl of Eishyshok* (Boston, 1998), 593–95.

49   The contrast with the four months after the invasion of Poland on September 1, 1939, is instructive: in that case, there were several mass murders with victim tolls over 1000, a few over 5000, and two over 10,000, with the larger massacres typically stretched out over a period of months.

50   The following discussion is largely based on data and narratives compiled in the killing site catalogue of Yad Vashem: http://www.yadvashem.org/research/ research-projects/killing-sites/killing-sites-catalog. This catalogue, which necessarily remains incomplete, covers the area of the former Soviet Union. It may be supplemented by evidence, likewise incomplete, from https://yahadmap .org/#map.

51   As becomes clear in illuminating local studies—see, for instance, Jeffrey Burds, *Holocaust in Rovno: The Massacre at Sosenki Forest, November 1941* (New York, 2013); Elisabeth Freundlich, *Die Ermordung einer Stadt namens Stanislau: NS Vernichtungspolitik in Polen, 1939–1945,* 2nd ed. (Vienna, 2016).

52   David Shneer, *Through Soviet Eyes: Photography, War, and the Holocaust* (New Brunswick, N.J., 2011), 149.

53   Patrick Desbois, *In Broad Daylight: The Secret Procedures Behind the Holocaust by Bullets,* trans. Hillary Reyl and Calvert Barksdale (New York, 2018), 15–23; Saul Friedländer, *The Years of Extermination: Nazi Germany and the Jews, 1939–1945* (New York, 2007), 2, 234.

54   Pohl, *Nationalsozialistische Judenverfolgung in Ostgalizien,* 37.

55   Ibid., 39.

56   Patrick Desbois, *The Holocaust by Bullets. A Priest's Journey to Uncover the Truth Behind the Murder of 1.5 Million Jews* (New York, 2008), 81–98, draws attention to the many people requisitioned, often by coercion, in the killings.

57   Ibid., 84.

58   Dieter Pohl, "Historiography and Nazi Killing Sites," in *Killing Sites: Research and Remembrance,* ed. International Holocaust Remembrance Alliance (Berlin, 2015), 42.

59   Desbois, *The Holocaust by Bullets,* 58.

60   Cited in Freundlich, *Die Ermordung einer Stadt namens Stanislau,* 167.

| NOTES TO PAGES 379-384

61 Calel Perechodnik, *Am I A Murderer? Testament of a Jewish Ghetto Policeman*, trans. Frank Fox (Boulder, Colo., 1996), 90.

62 Ibid.; Fritzsche, *An Iron Wind*, 184.

63 Walter Manoschek, *Militärische Besatzungspolitik und Judenvernichtung in Serbien, 1941/42* (Munich, 1993), 91-96. Between January and March 1942, the women and children were killed in gas vans.

64 From the "Jäger Report," in Wette, *Karl Jäger*, 241.

65 Wette, *Karl Jäger*, 126.

66 The story of this transport is told in Stadtarchiv München, ed., *"Verzogen, unbekannt wohin": Die erste Deportation von Münchner Juden im November 1941* (Zurich, 2000).

67 From the "Jäger Report," in Wette, *Karl Jäger*, 241. For a documentation of all the transports from the Reich, see Alfred Gottwaldt and Diana Schulle, *Die "Judendeportationen" aus dem Deutschen Reich, 1941-1945* (Wiesbaden, 2005).

68 Office of the United States Chief of Counsel for Prosecution of Axis Criminality, *Nazi Conspiracy and Aggression* (Washington, D.C., 1946), 7:978-95.

69 The Höppner memorandum can be found in Peter Longerich, ed., *Die Ermordung der europäischen Juden* (Munich, 1989), 74-75; for a translation, see *Documents of Destruction: Germany and Jewry, 1933-1945*, ed. Raul Hilberg (Chicago, 1971), 87-88.

70 Ibid.

71 Ibid.

72 Patrick Montague, *Chełmno and the Holocaust: The History of Hitler's First Death Camp* (Chapel Hill, N.C., 2012), 39.

73 Catherine Epstein, *Model Nazi: Arthur Greiser and the Occupation of Western Poland* (Oxford, 2010), 185; Montague, *Chełmno and the Holocaust*, 35, surmises the date was closer to July.

74 Epstein, *Model Nazi*, 185-91.

75 Peter Witte et al., eds., *Der Dienstkalender Heinrich Himmlers, 1941/42* (Hamburg, 1999), 183; Wolfgang Curilla, *Die deutsche Ordnungspolizei und der Holocaust im Baltikum und in Weissrussland, 1941-1944* (Paderborn, 2006), 532.

76 Witte et al., eds., *Der Dienstkalender Heinrich Himmlers*, 195n14, 196.

77 Annotation in Katrin Himmler and Michael Wildt, *Himmler privat: Briefe eines Massenmörders* (Munich, 2014), 254.

78 Mark Roseman, *The Villa, the Lake, the Meeting: The Wannsee Conference and the "Final Solution"* (Harmondsworth, Eng., 2002), 75-77.

79 The earlier order referred to is in Hermann Göring to Reinhard Heydrich, 31 July 1941. A translation appears in Hilberg, ed., *Documents of Destruction*, 233 (doc. 106).

80 Ibid.

81 Ibid. For an analysis, see Roseman, *The Villa, the Lake, the Meeting*.

82 Christopher Browning with Jürgen Matthäus, *The Origins of the Final Solution: The Evolution of Nazi Jewish Policy, September 1939-March 1942* (Lincoln, Neb. 2004), 315-16. Peter Hayes, *Why? Explaining the Holocaust* (New York, 2017), 117, notes that "this letter was the surest sign that the Nazi state already was looking for a comprehensive method to apply continent-wide, and Heydrich's task was to find it."

83 Cited in Ulrich Herbert, "Arbeit und Vernichtung: Ökonomisches Interesse und Primat der 'Weltanschauung' im Nationalsozialismus," in *Europa und der "Reichseinsatz": Ausländische Zivilarbeiter, Kriegsgefangene und KZ-Häftlinge in Deutschland, 1938-1945*, ed. Ulrich Herbert (Essen, 1991), 405.

84 Ulrich Herbert, *Fremdarbeiter: Politik und Praxis des "Ausländer-Einsatzes" in der Kriegswirtschaft des Dritten Reiches* (Bonn, 1999), 142.

85 Witte et al., eds., *Der Dienstkalender Heinrich Himmlers*, 262; Jürgen Matthäus and Frank Bajohr, eds., *The Political Diary of Alfred Rosenberg and the Onset of the Holocaust* (Lanham, Md., 2015), 388.

86 On Rosenberg, see *The Political Diary of Alfred Rosenberg*, 385; on Frank, see Witte et al., eds., *Der Dienstkalender Heinrich Himmlers*, 277n99; on Himmler's claim, see Witte et al., eds., *Der Dienstkalender Heinrich Himmlers*, 274.

87 Roseman, *The Villa, the Lake, the Meeting*, 57.

88 The most concentrated argument is in Christian Gerlach, "Die Wannsee-Konferenz, das Schicksal der deutschen Juden und Hitlers politische Grund-satzentscheidung alle Juden Europas zu ermordern," in *Krieg, Ernährung, Völkermord: Forschungen zur Deutschen Vernichtungspolitik im Zweiten Weltkrieg* (Hamburg, 1998), 85-166.

89 Friedländer, *The Years of Extermination*, 281.

90 An excerpt is reproduced in Browning with Matthäus, *The Origins of the Final Solution*, 407-8. The German original can be found at https://www.ns-archiv.de/personen/frank/16-12-1941.php.

91 Browning with Matthäus, *The Origins of the Final Solution*, 407-8.

92 Ibid., 408.

93 Ibid., 409.

94 Ibid.

95 Ibid.

96 Witte et al., eds., *Der Dienstkalender Heinrich Himmlers*, 290n48.

97 Ibid., 294.

98 John Barber and Andrei Dzeniskevich, *Life and Death in Besieged Leningrad, 1941-44* (New York, 2005).

99 The Wannsee Protocol is printed and translated in Hilberg, ed., *Documents of Destruction*, 89-99. A facsimile of the original (hereafter cited as the Wannsee Protocol) can be downloaded from the homepage of the Haus-der-Wannsee-Konferenz—Gedenk- und Bildungstätte: https://www.ghwk.de/fileadmin/user_upload/pdf-wannsee/dokumente/protokoll-januar1942_barrierefrei.pdf.

100 Ibid.

101 Ibid. Even the "remnant" of Jews who survived slavelike work would be "treated accordingly," the protocol states. By January 1942, "treated," or "specially treated," had already become a widely understood euphemism for killing.

102 Ibid. Emphasis in original.

103 Despite the existence of a protocol, written by Eichmann, revised by Heydrich, we know very little of what was actually said at the meeting. The protocol merely summed up the results in the form of general guidelines. See Longerich, *Politik der Vernichtung*, 469; Roseman, *The Villa, the Lake, the Meeting*, 103.

104 Roseman, *The Villa, the Lake, the Meeting*, 84, 87.

105 Ibid., 76-77.

106 Christopher Browning, "Introduction," in USHMM, *Ghettos*, xxxiv.

107 Zygmunt Klukowski, *Diary from the Years of Occupation, 1933-44* (Urbana, Ill., 1993), 224.

108 Fritzsche, *An Iron Wind*, 176-79.

109 Desbois, *In Broad Daylight*, 24-46.

110 Jan Grabowski, *Hunt for the Jews: Betrayal and Murder in German-Occupied Poland* (Bloomington, Ind., 2013), 172. Calculating that during Operation Rein-hard the Nazis killed one of five Jews in the local community and not in the gas

chambers, Stephan Lehnstaedt, *Der Kern des Holocaust: Belzec, Sobibor, Treblinka und die Aktion Reinhardt* (Munich, 2017), 85, 67, provides grounds for thinking that the number is higher still.

111 Evgeny Finkel, *Ordinary Jews: Choice and Survival During the Holocaust* (Princeton, N.J., 2017), 212–13.

112 Klukowski, *Diary from the Years of Occupation,* 219.

113 Lehnstaedt, *Der Kern des Holocaust,* 25.

114 Grabowski, *Hunt for the Jews,* 61.

115 The pioneering essay is Raul Hilberg, "German Railroads/Jewish Souls," *Society* 35, no. 2 (1998): 162–74. On this topic, see also Simone Gigliotti, *The Train Journey: Transit, Captivity, and Witnessing in the Holocaust* (New York, 2009).

116 Manuscript, RG-60.5045, Raul Hilberg, transcript, p. 35, United States Holocaust Memorial Museum.

117 Klukowski, *Diary from the Years of Occupation,* 191.

118 In the village of Baczki, for example. See *The Yad Vashem Encyclopedia of the Ghettos During the Holocaust,* 2 vols. (New York, 2010), 1:12. On the comparative numbers of trains, see Hayes, *Why? Explaining the Holocaust,* 135, 328–29.

119 Yitzhak Arad, *Belzec, Sobibór, Treblinka: The Operation Reinhard Death Camps* (Bloomington, Ind., 1987), 64. Here Jewish and Polish testimony diverges, Jewish survivors typically writing that they paid for water, Poles emphasizing that the water was given freely.

120 Klukowski, *Diary from the Years of Occupation,* 191.

121 Nikolaus Wachsmann, *KL: A History of the Nazi Concentration Camps* (New York, 2015), 294–95.

122 Sara Berger, *Experten der Vernichtung: Das T-4 Reinhardt-Netzwerk in den Lagern Belzec, Sobibór und Treblinka* (Hamburg, 2013), 31.

123 Arad, *Belzec, Sobibór, Treblinka,* 121.

124 Wachsmann, *KL,* 40.

125 Graphic descriptions can be found in the testimonies of Franz Suchomehl, a Treblinka guard, and Abraham Bomba, a survivor, in Claude Lanzmann's movie *Shoah* (1985); transcripts in Lanzmann, *Shoah: An Oral History of the Holocaust; The Complete Text of the Film* (New York, 1985), 52–57, 61–63, 105–11, 118–20, 146–47 (for Suchomehl); 43–49, 111–17 (for Bomba).

126 Hayes, *Why? Explaining the Holocaust,* 127.

127 Lehnstaedt, *Der Kern des Holocaust,* 81; Arad, *Belzec, Sobibór, Treblinka,* 94.

128 Arad, *Belzec, Sobibór, Treblinka,* 177. See also Rachel Auerbach, "In the Fields of Treblinka," in *The Death Camp Treblinka,* ed. Alexander Donat (New York, 1979), 65; and Jan Tomasz Gross with Irena Grudzinska Gross, *Golden Harvest: Events at the Periphery of the Holocaust* (Oxford, 2012).

129 Auerbach, "In the Fields of Treblinka," 71, 70, 67.

130 This was also true for Auschwitz and the Jews of Silesia. See Wachsmann, *KL,* 300.

131 There were isolated exceptions to this pattern, some within Poland, some from farther away, and one extermination camp, which began receiving trainloads of victims from western Europe in the summer of 1942, was not meant to be a regional death camp at all.

132 Fritzsche, *An Iron Wind,* 169.

133 Vasily Grossman, "The Hell of Treblinka," in *The Road,* ed. Robert Chandler, trans. Robert Chandler, Elizabeth Chandler, and Olga Mukovnikova (New York, 2010), 117, 162.

134 Beate Klarsfeld and Serge Klarsfeld, *Erinnerungen,* trans. Anna Schade, Andrea

Stephani, and Helmut Reuter (Munich, 2015), 51. On the transport's arrival in Auschwitz, see Danuta Czech, *The Auschwitz Chronicle, 1939–1945* (New York, 1990), 517. On the route, see the deportation database at Yad Vashem: https:// deportation.yadvashem.org.

135   For the story of their survival, see Klarsfeld and Klarsfeld, *Erinnerungen*, 52–59.

136   Serge Klarsfeld, *Le Mémorial de la déportation des Juifs de France* (Paris, 1978).

137   Serge Klarsfeld, *French Children of the Holocaust: A Memorial*, trans. Glorianne Depondt and Howard M. Epstein (New York, 1996), 3.

138   Ibid., xi.

139   Walter Manoschek, ed. *"Es gibt nur eines für das Judentum: Vernichtung": Das Judenbild in deutschen Soldatenbriefen, 1939–1944* (Hamburg, 1995). On the relationship of Wehrmacht crimes and fears of Jewish revenge, see Sven Oliver Müller, *Deutsche Soldaten und ihre Feinde* (Frankfurt am Main, 2007), 194–246, and Thomas Kühne, *Belonging and Genocide: Hitler's Community, 1918–1945* (New Haven, 2010), 131–35.

140   Cited in Hannes Heer et al., eds., *Wie Geschichte gemacht wird: Zur Konstruktion von Erinnerungen an Wehrmacht und Zweiten Weltkrieg* (Vienna, 2003), 54.

141   On this topic, see especially Nicholas Stargardt, *The German War: A Nation Under Arms, 1939–1945* (New York, 2015), 233–67.

142   Reinhart Koselleck, "Glühende Lava, zur Erinnerung geronnen," *Frankfurter Allgemeine Zeitung*, 6 May 1995.

143   Sönke Neitzel and Harald Welzer, *Soldaten: Protokolle vom Kämpfen, Töten und Sterben* (Frankfurt am Main, 2011), 148.

144   Regina Mühlhäuser, *Eroberungen: Sexuelle Gewalttaten und intime Beziehungen deutscher Soldaten in der Sowjetunion, 1941–1945* (Hamburg, 2010).

145   Neitzel and Welzer, *Soldaten*, 197.

146   See especially Bernward Dörner, "Justiz und Judenmord: Zur Unterdrückung von Äußerungen über den Genozid an den europäischen Juden durch die deutsche Justiz," *Jahrbuch für Antisemitismusforschung* 4 (1995), 226–53.

147   Cited in Frank Bajohr and Dieter Pohl, *Der Holocaust als offenes Geheimnis: Die Deutschen, die NS-Führung und die Alliierten* (Munich, 2006), 62.

148   Friedrich Kellner, *"Vernebelt, verdunkelt sind alle Hirne": Tagebücher, 1939–1945* (Göttingen, 2011), 1:311, entry of 16 September 1942.

149   The case of Kurt Dürkelfäden, as well as those of many others, appears in Thomas Kühne, *Belonging and Genocide: Hitler's Community, 1918–1945* (New Haven, 2010), 158.

150   The two positions are discussed in Eric A. Johnson and Karl-Heinz Reuband, *What We Knew: Terror, Mass Murder, and Everyday Life in Nazi Germany* (Cambridge, Mass., 2005).

151   Koselleck, "Glühende Lava, zur Erinnerung geronnen."

152   Lehnstaedt, *Der Kern des Holocaust*, 48; Desbois, *In Broad Daylight*, 104.

153   Hayes, *Why? Explaining the Holocaust*, 306.

154   Christopher R. Browning, *Ordinary Men: Reserve Police Battalion 101 and the Final Solution in Poland* (New York, 1992), 10.

155   Hayes, *Why? Explaining the Holocaust*, 310.

156   Wendy Lowry, *Hitler's Furies* (New York, 2013) 6–7, 21.

157   Lehnstaedt, *Der Kern des Holocaust*, 76.

158   Ibid., 131; Nicholas Lane, "Tourism in Nazi-Occupied Poland: Baedeker's Generalgouvernement," *Journal of East European Jewish Affairs* 27, no. 1 (1997): 45–56.

159   Wachsmann, *KL*, 464.

160 Roland Barthes, *Camera Lucinda: Reflections on Photography*, trans. Richard Howard (New York, 1980), 43–47.
161 These are now mapped out at http://www.deutschland-ein-denkmal.de.
162 Wachsmann, *KL*, 485.
163 Ibid., 343.
164 Paul Celan, "Todesfuge," in *Werke: Historisch-Kritische Ausgabe*, series 1, vol. 2, part 1, ed. Andreas Lohr et al. (Frankfurt am Main, 2003), 65–66.
165 On the registration of Soviet POWs, see Keller, *Sowjetische Kriegsgefangene im Deutschen Reich*, 266–71.
166 Thomas W. Laqueur, *The Work of the Dead: A Cultural History of Mortal Remains* (Princeton, N.J., 2015), 432–33.
167 Arad, *Belzec, Sobibór, Treblinka*, 125.
168 Based on the entries in USHMM, *Ghettos*.
169 See International Holocaust Remembrance Alliance, ed. *Killing Sites*, 27. In this publication, a killing site is defined for medium and large communities as involving 20 or more victims, and for small communities as over 10 victims. The number "of at least 1000" is based on my own counting of the sites listed and described in https://www.yadvashem.org/research/research-projects/killing-sites/killing-sites-catalog.html. Another such effort—by Father Patrick Desbois and the team at Yahud et Unum (Faith and Unity)—has identified more than 1500 sites where bodies are buried.
170 https://www.yahadmap.org/#map/. The counting is my own. Of 1578 sites (January 2019), Yahad et Unum lists 667 as having memorials, 362 without memorials, and 549 without information. The historian Dieter Pohl estimates that in Poland, the former Soviet Union, and the former Yugoslavia, the numbers are likely to be between 5000 and 10,000 killing sites: see Pohl, "Historiography and Nazi Killing Sites," 37.
171 Paul Celan, "Espenbaum," in *Werke*, series 1, vol. 2, part 1, 79.
172 Jacob Littner, *Mein Weg durch die Nacht*, ed. Roland Ulrich and Reinhard Zachau (Berlin, 2002).
173 Cited in Barbara Engelking, *Such a Beautiful Sunny Day: Jews Seeking Refuge in the Polish Countryside, 1942–1945*, trans. Jerzy Michalowicz (Jerusalem, 2016), 94.
174 Abraham Sutzkever, "Stalks," in *Art from the Ashes: A Holocaust Anthology*, ed. Lawrence L. Langer (New York, 1995), 572; Nelly Sachs, "O die Schornsteine," in *Sämtliche Gedichte*, ed. Nikola Herweg and Melanie Reinhold (Frankfurt am Main, 2009).
175 Edith P., Holocaust Testimony (HVT-107). Fortunoff Video Archive for Holocaust Testimonies, Yale University Library, New Haven.
176 Ibid.
177 Ibid.

PART V. AFTER NATIONALISM: PREFACE

1 Julius Posener, *In Deutschland, 1945 bis 1946*, 2nd ed. (Berlin, 2001), 24–25.
2 Ibid. 25.
3 Sergej Mironenko, Lutz Niethammer, and Alexander von Plato, eds., *Sowjetische Speziallager in Deutschland 1945 bis 1950* (Berlin, 1998). See also Hanno Müller, ed., *Recht oder Rache: Buchenwald, 1945–1950* (Frankfurt am Main, 1991), 112.
4 Willy Brandt, *Verbrecher und andere Deutsche: Ein Bericht aus Deutschland, 1946* (Bonn, 2007), 124.

5   Cited in Amos Elon, *Journey Through a Haunted Land: The New Germany*, trans. Michael Roloff (New York, 1967), 127.

6   Harold Marcuse, *Legacies of Dachau: The Uses and Abuses of a Concentration Camp, 1933-2001* (New York, 2001), illustration 74.

CHAPTER 13. A LIVING CONCEPT OF FATHERLAND (C. 1945-1950)

1   Rüdiger Overmans, *Deutsche militärische Verluste im Zweiten Weltkrieg* (Munich, 1999), 239.

2   Ibid., 239, 265

3   Richard Bessel, *Germany 1945: From War to Peace* (New York, 2009), 1-9.

4   Hans Erich Nossack, *The End: Hamburg, 1943*, trans. Joel Agee (Chicago, 2004), 33, 41, 29, 31.

5   Leonard O. Mosely, *Report from Germany* (London, 1945), 71.

6   Julius Posener, *In Deutschland, 1945 bis 1946*, 2nd ed. (Berlin, 2001), 8.

7   Stephen Spender, *European Witness* (New York, 1946), 16.

8   Isaac Deutscher, *Reportagen aus Nachkriegsdeutschland*, trans. Harry Maor and Erich Steiner (Hamburg, 1980), 64-65.

9   Alfred Döblin, *Schicksalsreise: Bericht und Bekenntnis* (Munich, 1993), 316.

10   Jan M. Piskorski, *Vertreibung und deutsch-polnische Geschichte: Eine Streitschrift*, trans. Andreas Warnecke, 2nd ed. (Berlin, 2007), 26-27.

11   Eagle Glassheim, "National Mythologies and Ethnic Cleansing: The Expulsion of Czechoslovak Germans in 1945," *Central European History* 33 (2000): 463-86.

12   R. M. Douglas, *Orderly and Humane: The Expulsion of the Germans after the Second World War* (New Haven, 2012), 131-37.

13   Ibid.

14   Rüdiger Overmans, "Personelle Verluste der deutschen Bevölkerung durch Flucht und Vertreibung," *Dzieje Najnowsze* 26, no. 2 (1994): 50-65; Andreas Kossert, *Kalte Heimat: Die Geschichte der deutschen Vertriebenen nach 1945* (Berlin, 2008), 41.

15   Fenner Brockway, *German Diary* (London, 1946), 50. Bessel, *Germany 1945*, 352, cites the case of Trier, where the rate of newborns dying was as high as a third.

16   Christopher Klessmann, *Die doppelte Staatsgründung: Deutsche Geschichte, 1945-1955*, 5th ed. (Göttingen, 1991), 1:51.

17   Readers should consult Miriam Gebhardt, *Als die Soldaten kamen: Die Vergewaltigung deutscher Frauen am Ende des Zweiten Weltkrieges* (Munich, 2015), who argues, forcefully but not altogether convincingly, that the attention paid to the rapes committed by the Red Army is in large measure a result of distortions created by the Cold War and lingering prejudice against the east.

18   Cited in Norman Naimark, *The Russians in Germany: A History of the Soviet Zone of Occupation, 1945-1949* (Cambridge, Mass., 1995), 73.

19   Kossert, *Kalte Heimat*, 40, but without further, geographically specific, evidence.

20   Ibid., 328.

21   Naimark, *The Russians in Germany*, 84.

22   Ibid., 92.

23   Cited in Atina Grossmann, "The Question of Silence: The Rape of German Women by Occupation Soldiers," *October* 72 (1993): 53.

24   Anthony Beever, introduction to Anonyma, *A Woman in Berlin*, trans. Philipp Boehm (New York, 2005), xv.

25   Gebhardt, *Als die Soldaten kamen*, 33, 38.

26   Naimark, *The Russians in Germany*, 122-23.
27   Jennifer V. Evans, *Life among the Ruins: Cityscape and Sexuality in Cold War Berlin* (New York, 2011), 35-36.
28   Anonyma, *A Woman in Berlin*, 43.
29   Daniel Blatman, *The Death Marches: The Final Phase of Nazi Genocide*, trans. Chaya Galai (Cambridge, Mass., 2013), 404.
30   Cited in Nikolaus Wachsmann, *KL: A History of the Nazi Concentration Camps* (New York, 2015), 591.
31   Ibid., 592; see also 771n291.
32   Ibid., 588.
33   Cited in Margarete Myers Feinstein, *Holocaust Survivors in Postwar Germany, 1945-1957* (New York, 2010), 34; the quotation is from from USC Shoah Foundation Visual History Archive (hereafter cited as VHA), IC 18706, seg. 66, interview date 19 August 1996.
34   Cited in Feinstein, *Holocaust Survivors in Postwar Germany*, 35; quoted from VHA, IC 32285, seg. 15, interview date 24 August 1997.
35   Jan Gross, *Fear: Anti-Semitism in Poland after Auschwitz* (New York, 2006), 35.
36   Cited in Frank Stern, "The Historic Triangle: Occupiers, Germans and Jews in Postwar Germany," in *West Germany under Construction: Politics, Society, and Culture in the Adenauer Era*, ed. Robert G. Moeller (Ann Arbor, Mich., 1997), 209.
37   Feinstein, *Holocaust Survivors in Postwar Germany*, 38.
38   Dagmar Barnouw, *Germany 1945: Views of War and Violence* (Bloomington, Ind., 1996), 7; Susan Sontag, *On Photography* (New York, 1973), 6.
39   Elisabeth Noelle and Erich Peter Neumann, eds., *Jahrbuch der öffentlichen Meinung, 1947-1955*, 2nd ed. (Allensbach, 1956), 62.
40   Wachsmann, *KL*, 614; Ulrike Weckel, *Beschämende Bilder: Deutsche Reaktionen auf alliierte Dokumentarfilme über befreite Konzentrationslager* (Stuttgart, 2012).
41   U.S. War Information Department, *Death Mills*, 1945: quotation at 18:17.
42   Brewster S. Chamberlin, "Todesmühlen: Ein früher Versuch zur Massen-'Umerziehung' im besetzten Deutschland, 1945-1946," *Vierteljahrshefte für Zeitgeschichte* 29 (1981): 431.
43   Ibid., 434.
44   Dorothea Zeemann, *Jungfrau und Reptil: Leben zwischen 1945 und 1972* (Frankfurt am Main, 1982), 13.
45   Ibid., 23.
46   Ibid.
47   Bessel, *Germany 1945*, 6
48   Elisabeth Noelle and Erich Peter Neumann, eds., *Jahrbuch der öffentlichen Meinung, 1958-1964* (Allensbach, 1965), 230.
49   Spender, *European Witness*, 44.
50   Carl Zuckmayer, *Geheimreport* (Göttingen, 2002), 12-13.
51   Theodor Adorno, "What Does Coming to Terms with the Past Mean," in *Bitburg in Moral Perspective*, ed. Geoffrey Hartmann (Bloomington, Ind., 1986), 124. The preponderance of new historiography has, for nearly two decades now, argued against this position. See Robert Moeller, *War Stories: The Search for a Usable Past in the Federal Republic of Germany* (Berkeley, Calif., 2001), 16.
52   Evans, *Life among the Ruins*, 8.
53   "Dokumente zu den Geisteskranken-Morden," *Die Wandlung* 2, no. 2 (1947): 160-75, and no. 2/3 (1947), 251-67.
54   Elisabeth Langgässer, *Der Torso* (Hamburg, 1947).

55 Cited in Peter Demetz, *After the Fires: Recent Writing in the Germanies, Austria, and Switzerland* (New York, 1986), 9.

56 Helmut Peitsch, *Deutschlands Gedächtnis an seine dunkelste Zeit: Zur Funktion der Autobiographik in den Westzonen Deutschlands und den Westsektoren von Berlin, 1945 bis 1949* (Berlin, 1990), 55–60.

57 Ruth Andreas-Fischer, *Der Schattenmann: Tagebuchaufzeichnungen, 1938-1948*, 3rd ed. (Frankfurt am Main, 2001), 569. For a discussion of rape in this memoir, see Helke Sander and Barbara Johr, ed., *Befreier und Befreite: Krieg, Vergewaltigung, Kinder* (Munich, 1992), 18.

58 On Mann and the bombing of German cities, see Volker Hage, *Zeugen der Zerstörung: Die Literaten und der Luftkrieg* (Frankfurt am Main, 2002), 21.

59 Holm Kirsten and Wulf Kirsten, eds., *Stimmen aus Buchenwald: Ein Lesebuch* (Göttingen, 2002), 311.

60 Nikolaus Wachsmann, "Introduction," in Eugen Kogon, *Theory and Practice of Hell: The German Concentration Camps and the System Behind Them* (New York, 2006), xiv.

61 Ibid.

62 Albrecht Haushofer, *Moabiter Sonette* (Berlin, 1945), 26.

63 H. G. Adler, *Theresienstadt, 1941-1945: Das Antlitz einer Zwangsgemeinschaft* (Tübingen, 1955).

64 H. G. Adler, "Nach der Befreiung—ein Wort an die Mitwelt," in *Nach der Befreiung: Ausgewählte Essays zur Geschichte und Soziologie*, ed. Peter Filkins (Konstanz, 2013), 43–47.

65 Max Frisch, *Tagebuch, 1946-1949* (Frankfurt am Main, 1985), 128.

66 Dolf Sternberger, "Begriff des Vaterlandes," *Die Wandlung* 2, no. 6 (1947): 511; Dolf Sternberger, "Toleranz als Leidenschaft für die Wahrheit," *Die Wandlung* 2, no. 3 (1947): 249.

CHAPTER 14. THE PRESENCE OF COMPASSION (C. 1950–2000)

1 Rainer Geißler, *Die Sozialstruktur Deutschlands: Zur gesellschaftlichen Entwicklung mit einer Bilanz zur Vereinigung*, 5th ed. (Wiesbaden, 2008), 234.

2 Walter G. Hoffmann, *Das Wachstum der deutschen Wirtschaft seit der Mitte des 19. Jahrhunderts* (Berlin, 1965), 151.

3 Richard Maetz, ed., *Zahlenspiegel der Deutschen Reichspost, 1871 bis 1945*, 2nd ed. (Bonn, 1957); *Statistische Ergebnisse der Deutschen Bundespost, Rechnungsjahr 1958 und 1963* (Bonn, 1964).

4 Elisabeth Noelle and Erich Peter Neumann, eds., *Jahrbuch der öffentlichen Meinung, 1947-1955*, 2nd ed. (Allensbach, 1956), 48, 98.

5 Ibid., 49.

6 *Das Dritte Reich: Eine Studie über Nachwirkungen des Nationalsozialismus* (Allensbach, 1949).

7 On this topic, see Sonja G. Ostrow, "A Public in Process. The Frankfurt School, the Allensbach Institute, and the Pursuit of 'Public Opinion' in 1950s West Germany" (Ph.D. diss., Vanderbilt University, Nashville, 2017).

8 *Das Dritte Reich: Eine Studie über Nachwirkungen des Nationalsozialismus* 22, table 3.

9 Ibid., 14.

10 Ibid., 16.

11 Ibid., 135.

12 Ibid.

13 Ibid.

14 In a survey conducted in 1947, the U.S. Office of Military Government for Germany characterized more than 60 percent of the German population as racists, anti-Semites, or intense anti-Semites (a follow-up poll in 1949 yielded only slightly better results). Anna J. Merrit and Richard J. Merrit, *Public Opinion in Germany: The OMGUS Surveys, 1945–1949* (Urbana, Ill., 1970), 146–48, 239–40.

15 *Jahrbuch der öffentlichen Meinung, 1947–1955*, 131.

16 Merrit and Merrit, *Public Opinion in Germany*, 146–48, 239–40.

17 Elisabeth Noelle and Erich Peter Neumann, eds., *Jahrbuch der öffentlichen Meinung, 1958–1964* (Allensbach, 1965), 214.

18 Carlo Levi, *Ich kam mit ein wenig Angst: Reisebilder aus Deutschland*, trans. Elisabeth Schweiger (Frankfurt am Main, 1984), 13.

19 *Jahrbuch der öffentlichen Meinung, 1947–1955*, 126; *Jahrbuch der öffentlichen Meinung, 1958–1964*.

20 Ute Frevert, *Die Kasernierte Nation* (Munich, 2001), 336.

21 Ibid., 338.

22 Harold Marcuse, *Legacies of Dachau: The Uses and Abuses of a Concentration Camp, 1933–2001* (New York, 2001), 200, citing a government memorandum of February 1960.

23 Frances Goodrich and Albert Hackett, *The Diary of Anne Frank* (New York, 1958), 101.

24 Knut Hickethier, *Geschichte des deutschen Fernsehens* (Stuttgart, 1998), 201.

25 *Jahrbuch der öffentlichen Meinung, 1958–1964*, 106.

26 Golo Mann, *Deutsche Geschichte des Neunzehnten und Zwanzigsten Jahrhunderts* (Frankfurt am Main, 1959), 929.

27 Amos Elon, *Journey Through a Haunted Land: The New Germany*, trans. Michael Roloff (New York, 1967), 41–42.

28 Cornelia Brink, "Ein Buch von Totem: Gerhard Schoenberners Fotodokumentation der Judenverfolgung," in *50 Klassiker der Zeitgeschichte*, ed. Jürgen Danyel, Jan-Holger Kirsch, and Martin Sabrow (Göttingen, 2007), 62.

29 Knut Hickethier, "Nur Histotainment? Das Dritte Reich im bundesdeutschen Fernsehen," in *Der Nationalsozialismus, die zweite Geschichte: Überwindung, Deutung, Erinnerung*, ed. Peter Reichel, Harald Schmid, and Peter Steinbach (Munich, 2009), 302–3. Resnais's film had been the subject of considerable controversy after the German government tried, in the previous year, to prevent its showing at the Cannes Film Festival.

30 *Jahrbuch der öffentlichen Meinung, 1958–1964*, 122.

31 Cited in Edgar Lersch, "Vom 'SS-Staat' zu 'Auschwitz': Zwei Fernseh-Dokumentationen zur Vernichtung der europäischen Juden vor und nach 'Holocaust,'" Zeitgeschichte-online, March 2004, 6–7; https://zeitgeschichte-online.de/thema/vom-ss-staat-zu-auschwitz.

32 *Jahrbuch der öffentlichen Meinung, 1958–1964*, 229.

33 Hermann Langbein, *Im Namen des deutschen Volkes: Zwischenbilanz der Prozesse wegen nationalsozialistischer Verbrechen* (Vienna, 1963), 149–97.

34 Ulrich Herbert, *Geschichte Deutschlands im 20 Jahrhundert* (Munich, 2014), 853.

35 Cited in ibid., 776.

36 *Jahrbuch der öffentlichen Meinung, 1958–1964*, 219.

37 Ibid., 225.

38 Ibid., 227.

39 Press conference with Walter Ulbricht, 15 June 1961, Deutsches Rundfunkarchiv OBC18907: TC 10:30:25–10:32:27.

40   This is nearly 10 percent more than had been the case in the mid-1950s; see Elisabeth Noelle and Erich Peter Neumann, eds., *Jahrbuch der öffentlichen Meinung, 1968–1973* (Allensbach, 1974), 510–11.

41   Ibid., 506.

42   Elisabeth Noelle and Erich Peter Neumann, eds. *Jahrbuch der öffentlichen Meinung, 1965–1967* (Allensbach, 1967), 401.

43   Karl-Heinz Janßen, "Was ist Deutschland? Ein Begriff im Wandel der Generationen," *Die Zeit*, 25 February 1972, 8.

44   *Jahrbuch der öffentlichen Meinung, 1968–1973*, 525.

45   On these maps, see Mathew D. Mingus, *Remapping Modern Germany after National Socialism, 1945–1961* (Syracuse, N.Y., 2017), 68–85.

46   Elisabeth Noelle and Erich Peter Neumann, eds., *The Germans: Public Opinion Polls, 1947–1966* (Allensbach, 1967), 390, 202.

47   Cited in "Der Endkampf," *Der Spiegel* 15 (1961), 14.

48   Michael Howard, *The Invention of Peace: Reflections on War and International Order* (New Haven, 2000), 1, the phrase, coined in 1887, is originally from Sir Henry Maine.

49   Real GDP per capita calculated from GDP per capita in current prices in Peter Flora, *State, Economy, and Society in Western Europe, 1815–1975: The Growth of Industrial Societies and Capitalist Economies*, 2 vols. (Frankfurt am Main, 1983), 2:350.

50   James J. Sheehan, *Where Have All the Soldiers Gone? The Transformation of Modern Europe* (Boston, 2008), 176.

51   Bernhard Fleckenstein, "50 Jahre Bundeswehr: Der 50. Jahrestag der Bundeswehr ist Anlass für eine Rückschau auf die Geschichte der Streitkräfte von ihren Anfängen bis in die Gegenwart," *Aus Politik und Zeitgeschichte* 21 (2005): 6–7.

52   Harold James, *A German Identity, 1770–1990* (New York, 1989), 188.

53   *Jahrbuch der öffentlichen Meinung, 1958–1964*, 177–78.

54   *Jahrbuch der öffentlichen Meinung, 1968–1973*, 219.

55   Michael Wolffsohn and Thomas Brechenmacher, *Die Deutschen und ihre Vornamen: 200 Jahre Politik und öffentliche Meinung* (Munich, 1999), 265.

56   Ibid., 25–26, 266, 294, 341, 387–88.

57   Christina von Hodenberg, *Das andere Achtundsechzig: Gesellschaftsgeschichte einer Revolte* (Munich, 2018), 77–78.

58   Ibid., 75.

59   Ibid., 65.

60   This involvement can be traced in Beate Klarsfeld and Serge Klarsfeld, *Erinnerungen* (Munich, 2015).

61   Herbert, *Geschichte Deutschlands im 20. Jahrhundert*, 853.

62   Explored with considerable polemic in Hans Kundani, *Utopia or Auschwitz: Germany's 1968 Generation and the Holocaust* (New York, 2009).

63   Alexander and Margarete Mitscherlich, *Die Unfähigkeit zu Trauern: Grundlagen Kollektiven Verhaltens*, 20th ed. (Munich, 1988), 40.

64   Ibid., 34–36.

65   See http://www.denkmalprojekt.org/.

66   Stephan Scholz, *Vertriebenendenkmäler: Topographie einer deutschen Erinnerungslandschaft* (Paderborn, 2015), 41–42.

67   As it does, for example, in the Hessian town of Bald Wildungen. For extensive lists of expellee monuments with their various dedications, see https://de.wikipedia.org/wiki/Kategorie:Liste_(Vertriebenendenkmale).

68   Elon, *Journey Through a Haunted Land*, 191.

69 In September 1964, 27 percent said they would return "if your homeland belonged to Germany tomorrow," and 33 percent said they might. See Noelle and Neumann, eds., *The Germans*, 483.

70 Marion Dönhoff, *Namen die keiner mehr nennt* (Cologne, 1962).

71 My count of Berlin memorials, based on Stefanie Endlich et al., eds., *Gedenkstätten für die Opfer des Nationalsozialismus: Eine Dokumentation* (Bonn, 1998), 2:27-227.

72 Cited in James Young, *The Texture of Memory: Holocaust Memorials and Meaning* (New Haven, 1994), 51.

73 See Rudy Koshar, *From Monuments to Traces: Artifacts of German Memory, 1870-1990* (Berkeley, Calif., 2000), 182-84.

74 Endlich et al., eds., *Gedenkstätten*, 2:213.

75 Ibid., 2:22, 43.

76 Young, *The Texture of Memory*, 53-54.

77 The squares were Rathenauplatz, named for the Weimar foreign minister in 1957, and Rudolf Mosse Platz, named in 1959 at the site of the family's once prominent publishing house. Three of the streets—the Karl-Marx-Straße in Neukölln; the Fraenkel Promenade (named for the medical researcher) in Kreuzberg; and the (Ottilie) Pohlstraße in the Tiergarten—were already named in 1947; thereafter, until 1966, only the Einstein Promenade in 1955, the Gollansczstraße (named for a prominent, pro-German Anglo-Jewish publicist) in the same year, and the Leo-Baeck-Straße in 1961.

78 Deniz Göktürk, David Gramling, and Anton Kaes, eds., *Germany in Transit: Nation and Migration, 1955-2005* (Berkeley, Calif., 2007), 9.

79 Max Frisch, "Überfremdung," in *Gesammelte Werke in zeitlicher Folge* (Frankfurt am Main, 1976), 10:374.

80 Jennifer A. Miller, *Turkish Guest Workers in Germany: Hidden Lives and Contested Borders, 1960s to 1980s* (Toronto, 2018), 81.

81 Özdamar cited in ibid., 83.

82 The challenges the workers faced are catalogued in Günter Wallraff, *Ganz unten: Beschreibung des Schicksals von illegal eingeschleusten Arbeitern* (Cologne, 1985).

83 Elisabeth Noelle-Neumann, ed., *Allensbacher Jahrbuch der Demoskopie, 1976* (Vienna, 1976), 152.

84 Wallraff, *Ganz unten*, 12. Emphasis in original.

85 Ibid.

86 Michael Meng, *Shattered Spaces: Encountering Jewish Ruins in Postwar Germany and Poland* (Cambridge, Mass., 2011), 110.

87 Ulrike Puvogel et al., eds., *Gedenkstätten für die Opfer des Nationalsozialismus: Eine Dokumentation*, vol. 1, 2nd ed. (Bonn, 1995).

88 Klaus-Dieter Alicke, *Lexikon der jüdischen Gemeinden im deutschen Sprachraum* (Gütersloh, 2008), 1:1191.

89 Ibid.

90 Calculated from material in ibid. On East German preservation efforts, see Jan Palmowski, *Inventing a Socialist Nation: Heimat and the Politics of Everyday Life in the GDR, 1945-1990* (New York, 2009).

91 Alicke, *Lexikon der jüdischen Gemeinden*, 1:1115.

92 Peter Reichel, *Erfundene Erinnerung: Weltkrieg und Judenmord in Film und Theater* (Frankfurt am Main, 2007), 253. The 60 percent figure comes from Elisabeth Noelle-Neumann and Edgar Piel, eds., *Allensbacher Jahrbuch der Demoskopie, 1978-1983* (Munich, 1983), 552.

93 Susanne Brandt, "Wenig Anschauung? Die Ausstrahlung des Film 'Holocaust' im

westdeutschen Fernsehen (1978/79)," in *Erinnerungskulturen: Deutschland, Italien und Japan seit 1945*, ed. Christoph Cornelißen (Frankfurt am Main, 2003), 258.

94   *Holocaust*, directed by Marvin Chomsky, screenplay by Gerald Green, 1978, episode 4.

95   Ibid.

96   Elie Wiesel, "Trivializing the Holocaust: Semi-Fact and Semi-Fiction," *New York Times*, 16 April 1978.

97   Carl Schmitt, *Ex Captivitate Salus*, 2nd ed. (Cologne, 2002), 27.

98   Richard von Weizsäcker, "Der 8. Mai 1945—40 Jahre danach," in *Von Deutschland aus: Reden des Bundespräsidenten* (Munich, 1987), 13–14, 15.

99   Ibid., 16–17.

100   Ibid., 17, 18.

101   Gunter Hofmann, "Das lästige Leitbild," *Die Zeit*, 5 December 1986.

102   Göktürk, Gramling, and Kaes, eds., *Germany in Transit*, 248.

103   Ibid.

104   Elisabeth Noelle-Neumann und Edgar Piel, eds., *Allensbacher Jahrbuch der Demoskopie*, 1978–1983 (Munich, 1983), 175, 177.

105   Ibid., 177.

106   Ibid.

107   "Nimm deine Prämie und hau ab," *Der Spiegel*, 8 August 1983.

108   Facsimile available at https://www.apabiz.de/archiv/material/Profile/Heidelberger%20Kreis.htm.

109   Robert Hepp, *Die Endlösung der deutschen Frage: Grundlinien einer politischen Demographie der Bundesrepublik Deutschland* (Tübingen, 1988), 11.

110   "Amateure am Werk: Ronald Reagans Berlin; Initiative vom Juni vorigen Jahres erweist sich als Flop; mit womöglich schädlichen Folgen," *Der Spiegel*, 18 January 1988, 34–37.

111   Gary Bruce, *The Firm: The Inside Story of the Stasi* (Oxford, 2010), 2, 10–14. The historian Helmut Müller-Enbergs offers the number of a quarter million East Germans serving as full-time Stasi workers, with 600,000 informers during the forty years of the regime, in ibid., 10.

112   Mary Sarotte, *The Collapse: The Accidental Opening of the Berlin Wall* (New York, 2014), 10–11.

113   Pertti Ahonen, *Death at the Berlin Wall* (Oxford, 2011). Images and information on each of these deaths are available at http://www.chronik-der-mauer.de/todesopfer/.

114   Jeremy Adelman, *Worldly Philosopher: The Odyssey of Albert O. Hirschman* (Princeton, N.J., 2013), 16–17.

115   Albert O. Hirschman, *Exit, Voice, and Loyalty: Responses to Decline in Firms, Organizations, and States* (Cambridge, Mass., 1970).

116   Albert O. Hirschman, "Voice and the Fate of the GDR: An Essay in Conceptual History," *World Politics* 45 (1993): 186.

117   Ibid., 195–96.

118   A concise recounting in David F. Patton, "Annus Mirabilis: 1989 and German Unification," in *The Oxford Handbook of Modern German History*, ed. Helmut Walser Smith (Oxford, 2011), 753–74.

119   Jürgen Habermas, "Der DM-Nationalismus, " *Die Zeit*, 30 March 1990.

120   Ulrike Thoms, "Sehnsucht nach dem guten Leben: Italienische Küche in Deutschland, " in *Essen und Trinken in der Moderne*, ed. Ruth-E. Mohrmann (Waxmann, 2006), 48.

121 Elisabeth Noelle-Neumann and Renate Köcher, eds., *Allensbacher Jahrbuch der Demoskopie, 1993–1997* (Munich, 1997), 496–97.

122 Herbert, *Deutsche Geschichte im 20. Jahrhundert*, 1173–77, figures on 1177.

123 Göktürk, Gramling, and Kaes, eds., *Germany in Transit*, 505.

124 Helke Sander and Barbara Johr, eds., *Befreier und Befreite: Krieg, Vergewaltigungen, Kinder* (Munich, 1992). See also the discussion of the film in *Berlin 1945: War and Rape; "Liberators Take Liberties,"* a special issue of the journal *October* 72 (Spring 1995).

125 Landeszentrale für politische Bildung Baden-Württemberg, ed., *Gedenkstätten in Baden-Württemberg*, 5th ed. (Stuttgart, 2012). The first decade of the twenty-first century saw the establishment of twenty new memorial sites. For Hamburg, see Detlef Garbe and Kerstin Klingel, *Gedenkstätten in Hamburg: Ein Wegweiser zu Stätten der Erinnerung an die Jahre 1933 bis 1945* (Hamburg, 2008).

126 Ulrike Puvogel, introduction to *Gedenkstätten für die Opfer des Nationalsozialismus: Eine Dokumentation*, vol. 2, ed. Stefanie Endlich et al. (Bonn, 1998), 24 (citing the writer Regina Scheer).

127 Ibid., 2:16, 19.

128 Ibid., 19.

129 Elisabeth Noelle-Neumann and Renate Köcher, eds., *Allensbacher Jahrbuch der Demoskopie, 1998–2002* (Munich, 2002), 526.

130 Ibid., 530, compared with 44 percent for France and 60 percent for Great Britain.

131 Ibid., 528. The institute posed the question as "All in all, do you love your country—Germany?" In East Germany, 80 percent said yes in 1993 compared with 66 percent in 2001.

132 Ibid., 538. Among young people, the corresponding percentages were 65 percent and 20 percent.

133 Ibid., 539.

134 Dolf Sternberger, "Begriff des Vaterlandes," *Die Wandlung* 2, no. 6 (1947): 511; Dolf Sternberger, "Toleranz als Leidenschaft für die Wahrheit," *Die Wandlung* 2, no. 3 (1947): 249.

EPILOGUE: THE REPUBLIC OF THE GERMANS AT THE BEGINNING OF THE TWENTY-SECOND CENTURY

1 Thomas Wolfe, "I Have a Thing to Tell You," in *Travels in the Reich: Foreign Authors Report from Germany*, ed. Oliver Lubrich, trans. Kenneth Northcott, Sonia Wichmann, and Dean Krouk (Chicago, 2010), 130.

2 William A. Barbieri Jr. "Toward a Multicultural Society?," in *The Oxford Handbook of Modern German History* (Oxford, 2011), ed. Helmut Walser Smith, 795–96.

3 Deniz Göktürk, David Gramling, and Anton Kaes, eds., *Germany in Transit: Nation and Migration, 1955–2005* (Berkeley, Calif., 2007), 511.

4 Ibid., 796.

5 A forceful guide is now Adam Tooze, *Crashed: How a Decade of Financial Crises Changed the World* (New York, 2018).

6 Thilo Sarrazin, *Deutschland schafft sich ab* (Berlin, 2010).

7 Volker Weiß, *Die autoritäre Revolte: Die neue Rechte und der Untergang des Abendlandes* (Stuttgart, 2017), 10.

8 Jan-Werner Müller, *What Is Populism?* (Princeton, N.J., 2016), 2–4.

9 *Süddeusche Zeitung*, 31 December 2015; https://www.sueddeutsche.de/politik/

neujahrsansprache-der-kanzlerin-merkel-verurteilt-kaelte-und-hass-bei-pegida-1
.2287216.

10   Navid Kermani, in "Feierstunde des Deutschen Bundestages aus Anlass des
65. Jahrestages des Inkrafttretens des Grundgesetzes für die Bundesrepublik Deutschland Berlin," 23 May 2014, 68; https://www.btg-bestellservice.de/
pdf/20099850.pdf.

11   *Süddeutsche Zeitung*, 17 September 2015; https://www.sueddeutsche.de/politik/
merkel-zur-fluechtlingsdebatte-der-gefuehlsausbruch-der-kanzlerin-1.2650051.

12   Ivan Krastev, *After Europe* (Philadelphia, 2017), 45.

13   *Aus Fehlern Lernen: Eine Analyse der Bundestagswahl 2017*; available at https://
www.spd.de/fileadmin/Dokumente/Sonstiges/Evaluierung_SPD__BTW2017
.pdf.

14   Cited in Wilhelm Heitmeyer, *Autoritäre Versuchungen* (Frankfurt am Main,
2018), 223. See also Thomas Petersen, "Wie antisemitisch ist Deutschland?,"
Frankfurter Allgemeine Zeitung, 20 June 2018.

15   Heitmeyer, *Autoritäre Versuchungen*, 223.

16   Renate Köcher, "Deutschland ist Anders," *Frankfurter Allgemeine Zeitung*, 22
December 2016; https://www.ifd-allensbach.de/uploads/tx_reportsndocs/FAZ_
Dezember_2016.pdf.

17   https://www.amadeu-antonio-stiftung.de/todesopfer-rechter-gewalt/.

18   Bundeszentrale für politische Bildung, "Straf- und Gewalttaten von rechts: Was
sagen die offiziellen Statistiken?," 13 November 2018; http://www.bpb.de/politik/
extremismus/rechtsextremismus/264178/pmk-statistiken.

19   Heitmeyer, *Autoritäre Versuchungen*, 172.

20   See Adi Gordon, *Toward Nationalism's End: An Intellectual Biography of Hans
Kohn* (Waltham, Mass., 2017).

21   Sarrazin, *Deutschland schafft sich ab*.

22   Weiß, *Die autoritäre Revolte*, 149–51.

23   Cited in Heitmeyer, *Autoritäre Versuchungen*, 269.

24   There are various versions of the quotation. For the AfD version, see https://www
.afdbundestag.de/wortlaut-der-umstrittenen-passage-der-rede-von-alexander
-gauland/.

25   Heitmeyer, *Autoritäre Versuchungen*, 242.

26   Oliver Decker et al., "Die Leipziger Autoritarismus-Studie 2018," in Oliver
Decker and Elmar Brähler, *Flucht ins Autoritäre: Rechtsextreme Dynamiken in
der Mitte der Gesellschaft* (Leipzig, 2018), 65–116.

27   Bundeszentrale für politische Bildung, "Bevölkerungsentwicklung und
Altersstruktur," 27 December 2015; https://www.bpb.de/nachschlagen/zahlen
-und-fakten/soziale-situation-in-deutschland/61541/altersstruktur.

28   Paul Collier, *Exodus: How Migration Is Changing Our World* (Oxford, 2013),
111–34.

29   Dieter Gosewinkel and Johannes Masing, eds., *Die Verfassungen in Europa*
(Munich, 2006), 841.

30   Krastev, *After Europe*, 91.

31   Readers of the novel will recall that for the protagonist, a former political refugee
from Nazi Germany, there was no second exile. There was only the steel-girded
bridge across the Rhine, and only the "leap from the bridge made him free." Wolfgang Koeppen, *The Hothouse*, trans. Michael Hoffmann (New York, 2001), 216.
On the loosening of the iron bars, see Michael Mann, *The Sources of Social Power*,
vol. 2, *The Rise of Classes and Nation States, 1760–1914* (Cambridge, 1993), 482.

32   Jacob Burckhardt, *Geschichte des Revolutionszeitalters*, ed. Wolfgang Hardtwig et

al., in Jacob Burckhardt, *Werke: Kritische Gesamtausgabe*, ed. Jacob-Burckhardt-Stiftung, vol. 28 (Munich, 2009), 11.

33   Ibid., 28:14–15, 17, 350.

34   An astute analysis of Bohrer's positions can be found in Jan-Werner Müller, *Another Country: German Intellectuals, Unification and National Identity* (New Haven, 200), 177–98 and especially 192–94.

35   Krastev, *After Europe*, 45.

ILLUSTRATION CREDITS

━

411   INTERFOTO/Alamy Stock Photo.
414   Bpk Bildagentur/anonymous photographer/Alamy Stock Photo.
448   MARKA/Alamy Stock Photo.
450   dpa picture alliance/Alamy Stock Photo.

INDEX

ABOUT THE AUTHOR

Helmut Walser Smith is the Martha Rivers Ingram Professor of History at Vanderbilt University, and the author and editor of numerous works on German history, including, most recently, *The Oxford Book of Modern German History*. With W. W. Norton, he published the acclaimed *The Butcher's Tale: Murder and Anti-Semitism in a German Town* in 2002. He lives with his wife, Meike, and his son, Luca, in Nashville, Tennessee.